Sacred Games

Sacred Games

A History of Christian Worship

Bernhard Lang

Yale University Press
New Haven and London

Set in Ehrhardt by Best-set Typesetter Ltd., Hong Kong
Printed in Great Britain by the Bath Press

Library of Congress Catalog Card Number 97–60406

ISBN 0–300–06932 4

A catalogue record for this book is available from the British Library.

2 4 6 8 10 9 7 5 3 1

For
Alain Boureau, Michel Meslin, Gérard Fussman
friends who invited me to teach in Paris, 1991–4

Contents

The Fifth Game: Sacrament

The Sixth Game: Spiritual Ecstasy

Epilogue: Divine Meekness, Divine Majesty

Preface

What, then, is our right course? We should pass our lives in the playing of games—certain games, that is, sacrifice, song, and dance—with the result of ability to gain heaven's grace. . . . All of us, men and women alike, must fall in with our role and spend life in making our play as perfect as possible.[1]

Plato

Such is the wonderful fact that the liturgy demonstrates: it unites art and reality in a supernatural childhood before God. . . . [Worship] has one thing in common with the play of the child and the life of art—it has no purpose, but is full of profound meaning. It is not work, but play. To be at play, or to fashion a work of art in God's sight—not to create, but to exist—such is the essence of the liturgy. From this is derived its sublime mingling of profound earnestness and divine joyfulness.[2]

Romano Guardini

When I visited the Vatican's Sistine Chapel in order to see how Michelangelo's huge and rightly famous frescoes looked after their recent restoration, I was struck by the central scene depicted on the ceiling. The bearded Creator, clad in a robe, floats in the air, stretching his arm in a forceful and elegant gesture toward Adam, the naked man, who, newly created, is depicted as just awaking to life. Adam himself stretches his arm toward God, looking at him as if in a dreamlike state. Their eyes meet, and the two hands almost touch. God and the human being are shown as primordially and eternally related. Ever since its completion in 1512, the fresco has never failed to impress those who have seen it, and it ranks as one of the finest works ever produced by an artist. In the hall below the ceiling decorated by Michelangelo, the Catholic Mass has been celebrated regularly ever since, and the scene reminds thoughtful participants and visitors of the fact that the sacred ceremonies here enacted reflect the same structure. Christian worship, too, represents the mutual gaze of the human and the divine eye. All believers would agree that when they worship in church, they turn to the divine arm that waits for them. "Draw near to God, and he will draw near to you," says the New Testament (Jas. 4:8). In the liturgy, the divine and the human hands meet and almost touch.

When contemporary—Catholic, Protestant, Orthodox, or Pentecostal—

Christians worship, they engage in a variety of ritual acts whose diversity and complexity may at first puzzle the observer. They seem to have little of the grand simplicity of Michelangelo's painting. People sing, pray, are spoken to, make music or listen to it, share a rudimentary meal, and occasionally even cry and dance. At times, the meal seems to form the central focus; at other times, attention falls on the preacher addressing the congregation, but often enough several ritual acts follow one after another so that the focus shifts as the celebration unfolds and fills an hour or two or even most of Sunday morning. A closer look reveals that worship includes a limited number of major components that are repeated and form the backbone of whatever else may happen. One can easily discern three acts, for they are quite visible: people speak to God, asking favors from him—which is called praying; an individual, generally the leader, addresses the congregation in speech—which is called preaching; some bread and wine (or grape juice) are consumed and often shared among those present—which is termed the Eucharist or the Lord's Supper. But there are other central acts which, although having less visibility for the first-time observer, rank as crucial in much of Christian worship.

The refined typology of ritual acts used in the present study includes six elementary forms, and we will designate them as praise, prayer, sermon, sacrifice, sacrament, and spiritual ecstasy. In the spirit not only of Plato, the ancient pagan philosopher, but also of Romano Guardini (1885–1968), the great Catholic teacher of liturgical spirituality, we may call them the six sacred games played out in Christian worship. Here is a brief description of each of these:

Praise (I), sung or spoken, regularly stands at the beginning of Christian worship. It consists in saying good things about God and thanking him for favors received. In the book of Psalms, the Jews had a collection of songs they termed "praises." Christians adopted this ritual idiom with much enthusiasm. Petitionary prayer (II) serves to bring the community's needs to the attention of God. Common to most religions, it came to constitute an essential form of regular worship in Christianity. While praise and prayer are rather common patterns of ritual behavior in the history of religions, this cannot be said of the sermon (III). Christians inherited this ritual idiom from Judaism, as they did the sacred scriptures on which preaching is often based. Instruction and exhortation are common aims of the speech made by a priest or pastor. By sacrifice (IV) we designate a spiritual act in which something is given or dedicated to God. Christians understand their sacrificial activity as a spiritual, "unbloody" form of what other ancient religions practiced by slaughtering an animal which served as a gift for the god thus honored. The sacrament (V) regularly celebrated by most Christian congregations is a ritual meal. It has its roots in a common ancient ritual pattern, that of magic. As they did with sacrifice, Christians adapted the ancient ritual idiom of magic to their own purposes. Ecstasy (VI), while peripheral during long periods of earlier Christian history, has become a prominent feature of charismatic worship in the twentieth century. It figured in certain ancient cults like that of the Greek god Dionysos, whom women venerated with wild, enthusiastic dances. Christians have adopted this ritual idiom, understanding their trances and ecstasies as the visible effects of the divine Spirit's invisible presence in the community.

The present book argues that the essential meaning of Christian worship is embodied in the six patterns of praise, prayer, preaching, sacrifice, sacrament, and spiritual ecstasy, all of which have their roots in ancient, pre-Christian ritual life. Accordingly, the book is divided into six interpretive essays that explain the theological meaning of each of these "sacred games," explore its ancient and biblical roots, and follow its course through history with special emphasis on historic and contemporary forms.

With the exception of preaching, which, like the use of sacred books, originated relatively late in the history of religions, these patterns are rather old and practiced by many religions in all parts of the world. Sacrifice and ecstatic rituals seem to belong to the most archaic, prehistorical religious acts that can be discerned. Adopting traditional patterns, Christianity participates in a universal ritual language. But just as there is no universal language, as people speak specific languages, so the ritual idiom exists only in specific, historical, local forms. That is why our account will only rarely be concerned with religious ritual in general. Instead, we will study the way in which Christians express themselves in a ritual idiom, some of whose elements can be found among and are understood by many non-Christians as well. In ritual, as in other areas of culture, Christians participate in the shared heritage of humankind.

Writing a history of worship is fraught with difficulties. For the early period, especially for the first century CE, sources are both scarce and hard to understand. The reader should be alerted to the fact that the study of early Christianity is currently in an exciting period of discovery and revision. There are few comprehensive and compelling interpretations that are adopted by a majority of experts. At the center of the controversies is of course the figure of Jesus. Morton Smith (d. 1991), Bruce Chilton, and Margaret Barker—scholars and friends who acted as my mentors and advisors in matters relating to the New Testament—agree that in the past, scholars underrated the ritual dimension of Jesus' ministry. In dialogue with them, I have tried to sketch the ritual world of Jesus and his earliest followers in new ways (and sometimes in ways with which my advisors may not fully agree). So I venture the suggestion that the most sacred words pronounced in Christian worship—"This is my body, This is my blood"—echo words the ancient priests spoke when offering animal sacrifices at the temple of Jerusalem. I also suggest that the Our Father (whose words are also known as the Lord's Prayer), seen in its first-century Jewish context, makes more sense when attributed to John the Baptist and seen as only later adopted by Jesus or his early followers. I am, of course, aware that such interpretations involve a certain amount of conjecture and risk rejection by some readers. Yet, the present state of research—quite apart from personal honesty—has forced me to propose certain reconstructions that I would, of course, be willing to modify if convincing arguments obliged me to do so. Here nothing is to be gained by personal pride and stubbornness. Perhaps it may be helpful for the reader to know that when beginning research for *Sacred Games*, I tended to share Morton Smith's view of Jesus the Magician, but came to realize that for all his expert knowledge of the subject, Smith had a far too negative view of ancient magic and its varieties. As I dug ever more deeply into the history of "thaumaturgy" and "theurgy," I came to appreciate its spiritual qualities.

In a subject as vast and as difficult as the history of Christian worship, the historian is constantly looking for interpretive keys. Two friends—Colleen McDannell and Michel Meslin—encouraged me to look at popular culture as an important key. As some of the illustrations used in *Sacred Games* demonstrate, their advice was not in vain. A conversation with Mary Douglas helped me to come to grips with some of the issues involved in understanding charismatic worship and its transformations. Much interpretive help came from a quite unexpected source: from ancient Neoplatonic literature. In the third century CE, under the leadership of Plotinus, Plato's philosophy enjoyed a renaissance that was to continue throughout late antiquity. This school of thought had much in common with Christianity: it believed in one God (the "One"), in the necessity of ritual, and in the saving contact with deities that were distinct from the ineffable One and stood closer to humanity. Like Judaism and Christianity, it also had its sacred books—the writings of Plato and, in its later phase, also the *Chaldean Oracles*. In fact, major early Christian theologians—Origen, Augustine, Pseudo-Dionysius—can at the same time be considered major representatives of the Neoplatonic school of thought. The affinity of Neoplatonism and Christianity justifies the use of this philosophy for understanding certain aspects of worship. What Augustine says about sacrifice corresponds closely to what the fourth-century pagan philosopher Sallustius wrote in his treatise *Concerning the Gods and the Universe*. Neoplatonists practiced a kind of sacred magic they called theurgy, an art that arguably corresponds to the Christian sacraments and has the same aim, namely, to unite the believer with the god who becomes present at the moment of worship. The ancient Neoplatonists described the soul's progressive assimilation to the divine as a process that involves the three stages of purification, illumination, and final union. Christians have often used this three-stage model for describing the ascetic and mystical path to perfection. I use the Neoplatonic model several times. In the analysis of the various types of Christian preaching, for instance, I borrow the idea of the three stages, arguing that moral exhortation purifies, instructional preaching illuminates, and the preaching of faith aims at union with the Lord. When in late antiquity the religious elite of the Roman Empire rethought religion and ritual, the choice was not between Mithraism and Christianity (as Ernest Renan suggested in the nineteenth century) but between pagan Neoplatonism and Neoplatonic Christianity. For this reason, a historical and structural study of worship can learn much from the ancient Neoplatonic thinkers.

Among contemporary Christians one can find a great variety of attitudes toward worship, ranging from enthusiasm and eager participation to boredom and total neglect. In America and the "Third World," Pentecostal worship attracts people in rapidly increasing numbers. Especially in Europe, by contrast, non-attendance at church has become a major problem discussed by ministers, church councils, and bishops. As a historian I am not particularly concerned about the popularity or unpopularity of the subject of my study. Those who consider centuries are not easily upset by recent developments. The significance of worship does not depend on the number of those who go to church on Sunday mornings. The historian of religion has to tell a fascinating, long story about human interaction with the divine reality that challenges as much as Michelangelo's art: it is too intriguing, too alarming, too puzzling, and too beautiful to be passed over in silence.

A project of almost encyclopedic dimensions like the present one starts with ideas but then needs the special help of many librarians and scholars around the world. I am glad to report that this help was available. In Germany, it came from Annelene Fenger, Edeltrud Büchler, Anke Schüttfort, Rolf Pöhler, Gia Toussaint, Matthias Romann, Friedrich Möbius, Denise Sokolowski, Paderborn's Center for Cultural Studies, and the Venerable Canonesses of St. Michael's Convent in Paderborn. In Austria, from Peter Dinzelbacher. In Switzerland, from Christoph Uehlinger. In the Netherlands, from Paul Post and Kees D. Grijs. In England, from Gabriele vom Bruck and Colin Buchanan. In France, from Ilona Jacobi, Françoise Smyth-Florentin, and the Sorbonne's Bibliothèque de l'Histoire des Religions. In Italy, from Sofia Cavalletti. In the US, from Jane Williams-Hogan (my project advisor), Kira Williams-Gartner (my English editor), Alden Thompson, Jacob Milgrom, Carroll Odhner, Karen Jo Torjesen, Paul Jerome Croce, Robert Shore (my copy-editor), and the Holy Spirit Research Center of Oral Roberts University in Tulsa, Oklahoma. To all of them, I am very much indebted.

Introduction: Six Sacred Games

In order to enable the pressed reader to follow the book's argument without too much effort, we offer a brief summary.

Christian worship, as studied in the present essay, can be seen as meaningful human action oriented toward the divine, celebrated communally and in public, and unfolding in the six patterns (here called "sacred games") of praise, prayer, preaching a sermon, sacrifice, sacrament (or magic), and spiritual ecstasy.

Although theologians sometimes refer to *praise* as the aim of all worship, it also forms a distinct pattern of ritual expression. In the biblical Psalms, three elementary forms of praise can be distinguished: (1) songs of thanksgiving, in which an individual publicly recounts how the Lord has helped him (or her) in a situation of distress; (2) hymns of glorification, in which God's acts on behalf of his people are recounted; the events narrated form a comprehensive sacred story; and (3) anthems of adoration, in which angelic beings or people extoll God's greatness, majesty, and power without reference to specific acts he has done or continues to do on their behalf. The Jewish (Old Testament) book of Psalms has become a book of the church, and its three forms of praise have been developed in the long history of Christian worship. The anthem of adoration can be found in the Gloria and the Sanctus of the Catholic Mass, two texts often set to music, notably by Haydn and Mozart. The singing of hymns of glorification has been institutionalized in monasteries and convents where monks, friars, and nuns spend much time in the communal recitation of Psalms and New Testament hymns like the Magnificat, thereby reminding themselves that their existence rests on a sacred story. In modern times, the songs of thanksgiving, though also found in the poetry of congregational hymnals, have developed an important prose equivalent. Individuals often give praise to the Lord by speaking to the congregation about their own experience of divine help and guidance. The giving of lay testimonies can be traced back to its Puritan and free-church beginnings in the seventeenth century. We have delineated its renewal, under Methodist inspiration, among nineteenth-century evangelists, Adventists, Christian Scientists, Mormons, and other groups. As a democratic institution not dominated by clerical supervision, the giving of lay testimony corresponds to an ideal of universal participation in and contribution to worship. It seems to function as a typically modern variety of praise, in tune with notions of individual religious experience.

Public *petitionary prayer*, said or sung by or on behalf of the entire religious community, has two historical roots: one in the practice of regular sacrifice for the common well-being and the other in the prayer meetings held in times of crisis. When Judaism joined the two institutions to create public prayer at the synagogue, it brought one main petition before God: the wish that the Jewish state might be restored. In the Our Father, which we tentatively attribute to John the Baptist, the petition for the restoration of God's kingdom (i.e., the Jewish commonwealth) survives into Christianity. When the Jesus move-ment—or presumably Jesus himself—adopted the Our Father as the Lord's Prayer, its meaning was shifted from national to more private, individual, or small-group concerns, in accordance with Jesus' focus on liberating individuals from demonic assaults. But it is not only Jesuanic prayer that reflects exorcistic and therefore magical concerns: these concerns survive in the practice of "praying in the name of Jesus," that is of joining Jesus' miracle-working name to all prayers. Christians have consistently addressed their supplications to God, but they never fail to add that they do so "through Jesus Christ." Jesus is at the same time intercessor with God for his devotees and the power that resides in his name.

From its biblical beginnings, Christians have struggled with the promise of prayer and asked whether God would actually answer. The New Testament, the liturgical tradition, and theology all deal with the problem in a different way. A careful reading of the biblical evidence suggests that only the Our Father is promised unconditional efficacy. Other prayer is never promised success. Rather, this depends upon faith and on God's will. In preferring rather general petitions, the liturgy on the whole avoids confronting the issue. Another liturgical strategy consists in giving liturgical answers to prayers: sins are forgiven through the word of the pastor, or words of blessing assure the congregation of divine benevolence. When discussing the promise of prayer, theologians generally consider the problem of determinism and providence and they call for restraint; one should not expect miracles to happen, for God mostly works calmly and imperceptibly rather than by way of dramatic inter-vention. However, many theologians, especially in twentieth-century America, have radically changed their perspective. Rather than looking at prayer from the point of view of God's providence, they prefer to discuss the human experience of it. Some authors have developed William James's observation that prayer, whatever else it may accomplish, inspires courage, releases energy, and generally promotes an optimistic attitude.

The intellectual ritual in which the spoken word dominates consists of readings from sacred scripture and preaching a *sermon*. In the New Testament, Luke gives us a glimpse of how early Christian believers and perhaps even Jesus himself disrupted traditional synagogue worship by introducing a new and powerful message incompatible with what people usually heard. As the Church developed its liturgy of the word through two millennia, three great patterns of preaching emerged: didactic, moral, and affective, each focusing on a different aspect of transmitting Christian values. Some preachers like Origen in the third and Karl Barth in the twentieth century saw themselves primarily as teachers who explained and expounded the biblical text in order to promote saving knowledge and thus contribute to the salvation of their audience. Other occupants of the pulpit, especially Catholics, preferred moral exhortation, for there can be no eternal salvation apart from bringing one's life in line with moral standards taught in or implied by the Bible. Ever since Gregory the Great (ca. 600 CE), preachers have considered themselves doctors whose advice functions as medicine that heals moral, social, and spiritual ills. In twentieth-century America, Harry Emerson Fosdick practiced and promoted the thera-peutic approach to preaching in a radical manner. His individual counseling supported his pulpit ministry in a way reminiscent of Catholic confession. For a third group of theologians, the individual act of faith decides about salvation. Therefore the sermon's chief aim must be to lead everyone in the audience to that act. In the days of the Reformation, Martin Luther's affective preaching remained unrivaled. More recent affective preachers include a wide variety of revivalists and evangelists like Jonathan Edwards and John Wesley in the eighteenth and Billy Graham in the twentieth century who have wanted to "convert" the lukewarm to ardent Christian commitment.

In addition to discussing the three aims of preaching, we also deal with one aspect of audience reaction—sleeping, whose story begins in the New Testa-ment and culminates in the satirical art of William Hogarth.

The notion of *sacrifice*, deeply rooted in the history of religions and ingrained in the cultural heritage of Christians, structured the practice and understanding of their worship. It meant to present and hand over a gift to the deity, and oneself together with that gift. I argue, with Bruce Chilton and Hartmut Gese, that the Lord's Supper *originally* belonged to this category, and not only in the later speculation of theologians. After having failed to reform the animal sacrifices that were sponsored by the laity and conducted by priests at the Jerusalem Temple, Jesus practiced a substitute sacrifice in which bread and wine represented the animal's body and blood and were presented to the deity. The words "This is my body" and "This is my blood" accompanied the gesture of presentation, as they presumably accompanied the presentation of slaughtered animals at the Jewish Temple. I follow a wide, though not unani-mous, consensus among biblical scholars that the gospel reports on the Last Supper, held by Jesus the day before his crucifixion, must be considered neither a Passover celebration nor even a historical event. Like Jesus, early Christianity opted out of the Jewish sacrificial system, a process no doubt facilitated by sacrificial interpretations of Jesus' death (as the final sacrifice that needs no complement or repetition) and the decline of Jewish Temple activities after the Roman destruction of the Temple in 70 CE. However, Christians continued to apply sacrificial terminology to their eucharistic celebrations in which they presented to God many of the good gifts brought forth by the good creation (e.g., Irenaeus of Lyons). The present study concentrates on the two classic theological models of the sacrificial perspective on the Eucharist. The first, represented by Cyprian of Carthage, Augustine of Hippo, and Jean-Jacques Olier of Paris, understands the Eucharist as a unique possibility for the faithful to join Christ in his self-abandonment to the Father. While at least some contemporary theologians recommend this view as a valid perspective on the central Christian ritual, the second model seems to have more critics than supporters in the twentieth century. In its medieval form, best represented by the scholastic theologian Gabriel Biel of Tübingen, this model emphasizes not sacrificial giving but sacrificial receiving. At Mass, when being reminded of Christ's sacrifice on the cross, the Father bestows grace on priest and people, drawing from the inexhaustible spiritual treasure acquired by the Lord.

While originally a sacrificial gesture, the Lord's Supper soon became a *sacrament*. This happened when it came into the orbit of magical thought and practice whose relevance scholars like Morton Smith have rediscovered. Although this may sound strange and perhaps even blasphemous to twentieth-century Christians, magic was foreign neither to Jesus nor to his early followers. In the world of Jesus, magical rites not only served the selfish purposes of their practitioners, but also formed the center of communally celebrated mystery cults. The gospels themselves make the Last Supper the central act of a mystery religion and give it a magical meaning. Just as in the days of Moses the Passover blood served as a powerful protection, so did the sacramental meal of Jesus in the days of the great tribulation. While the magical meaning of bread and wine remains more implicit in the synoptic accounts of the Last Supper, the meal's magical character cannot be mistaken in Paul and the fourth Gospel. Used in Christian worship, bread and wine came to function as carriers of supernatural power. If we compare Christian eucharistic rites with ancient theurgy as practiced by Neoplatonic philosophers like Iamblichus and Proclus, it seems quite in tune with the educated mentality of late antiquity. In the relevant chapters, special care has been taken to sketch the classic sacramental views of the orthodox churches (Pseudo-Dionysius, Nicholas Kabasilas), of Catholicism (Thomas Aquinas), and the Reformation (Luther, Calvin). In the twentieth century, two conflicting trends can be discerned. While "minimalists" come close to denying any sacramental effect or property of the celebration (Paul Althaus, Karl Rahner, Matthew Fox), others renew the ancient magical view in their attempt to complement their esoteric world view with a heightened sacramentalism comparable to that of ancient mystery religions (Teilhard de Chardin and, especially, Rudolf Steiner).

Interestingly, we find the twentieth century's most famous Jesuits—Rahner and Teilhard—in two different camps of sacramental thought, inverting national stereotypes. As a mystic, Teilhard is uncommitted to the Cartesian rationalism of France, and Rahner the rationalist remains uninvolved with German mysticism.

In the Christian community that Paul founded at Corinth, Greece, we find enthusiasts whose *ecstatic ritual* parallels at least some features of Dionysian cults: movement, noise, participation of women, excitement, and the almost tangible presence of Christ who "possesses" the congregation. The magical food of bread and wine serves as a carrier of the divine Spirit which the faithful identify with Christ. Christ's rulership, exercised through "possessed" men and women, manifests itself in special gifts of which the speaking in tongues (glossolalia) and uttering divine messages are the most prominent. Although later ecclesiastical development has promoted more calm and ordered modes of worship, the ecstatic pattern appears again and again on the fringes of mainstream churches. In the early 1900s, ecstatic Christianity suddenly emerged as a contagious movement whose worship can be studied in the writings of Frank Bartleman, an early Pentecostal leader. In addition to its biblical roots, we also study some of the African connections of Christian trance and ecstasy. Having inherited ecstatic cults from their African ancestors, African Americans have been particularly receptive to, and made important contributions to, the charismatic mode of worship.

A comparison of the modern, twentieth-century Pentecostal and charismatic worship with its biblical precedent yields an interesting result. The Corinthian ecstatic ritual was eventually replaced by different forms, especially by intellectual worship, consisting of scriptural reading. Pentecostalism, by contrast, found ways of conserving its original enthusiastic inspiration. Rather than replacing ecstasy, Pentecostal churches came to routinize its enthusiastic worship. Rhythmic instrumental music, communal singing (often animated by soloists and choirs), and a preacher's exhortation create an emotionally charged atmosphere that allows ecstatic experiences like speaking in tongues and proclaiming revealed messages to occur. Although this routinized ecstasy may have lost some of its original spontaneity, it never lacks fervor. The Pentecostal experience still attracts large crowds to worship and encourages committed Christians to participate in prophetic groups, whose members may eventually speak up in public worship.

As I wrote the chapters just summarized, I came to realize that two fundamental attitudes govern behavior in Christian worship. According to one view, God appears as the distant, majestic Father who must be approached with solemnity, ceremonial, and awe. Others, by contrast, think of God as a benign, understanding, friendly spirit with whom people can establish a close relationship. The Epilogue studies these attitudes from the four angles of comparative religion, history, psychology, and art. It is not unfitting that the book should end with a discussion of art. Throughout our study, visual sources—from manuscript illumination to woodcut, from oil painting to photo, from cartoon to holy card—have helped to elucidate the sacred games of Christian worship.

The First Game: Praise
Thanking God by Proclaiming His Mighty Acts in Song and Testimony

O come, let us sing to the Lord; let us make a joyful noise to the rock of our salvation! Let us come into his presence with thanksgiving; let us make a joyful noise to him with songs of praise! For the Lord is a great God.

Psalm 95:1–3 (NRSV)

Those who do not praise God here on earth will remain without the power of speech in eternity.[1]

John Ruusbroec (1293–1381)

This is my story, this is my song, praising my Savior all the day long.[2]

Fanny C. Crosby, "Blessed Assurance" (hymn, 1873)

1. On Praise

To praise the gods or God means to say something good of them, and most religions address their deities with words of praise and thanksgiving, for this is the primary way of approaching kindly spirits upon whose benevolence human well-being depends. Praise is so common a feature of ancient ritual that we can speak of it as an elementary form of ritual expression.

We used the phrase "praise and thanksgiving." Since we are here dealing with an elementary pattern characteristic of *ancient* religion as the soil out of which Christian worship grew, we cannot distinguish between praise and thanksgiving. Unlike modern languages, ancient Hebrew and Greek (and some other ancient languages) do not distinguish between the two. Claus Westermann explains:

> The fact that there is no word for "to thank" in Hebrew has never been properly evaluated. The ignoring of this fact can be explained only in that we live so unquestioningly in the rhythm between the poles of thanks and request, of "please!" and "thank you!", and the thought does not occur to anyone that these concepts are *not* common to all humankind, have *not* always been present as a matter of course, do *not* belong to the presuppositions of human intercourse nor to those of the contact of God and man. We are compelled to imagine a world in which petition plays a thoroughly essential and noteworthy role, but where the antithesis of petition is not primarily thanks but praise. And this praise is a stronger, more lively, broader concept which includes our "thanksgiving" in it. Thanking is here included entirely within praise.

Not having developed an independent concept of "thanking," the biblical languages have no separate, special word to say "thank you." If an ancient Hebrew- or Greek-speaking individual wanted to thank someone for a favor received, he or she would say something like "I praise you." Accordingly, translators have a hard time deciding how to render certain words. "*I shall praise you* for ever for what you have done," the Revised English Bible has an ancient Hebrew poet sing; the translator of the New Revised Standard Version decided to use a different verb: "*I will thank you* forever, because of what you have done" (Ps. 52:9). Occasionally, the translator cannot avoid juxtaposing both terms, for instance when the psalmist invites the pilgrims to enter God's

Temple: "Enter his gates with thanksgiving, his courts with praise" (Ps. 100:4).[3]

The Cultic Setting of Praise

In the first book of Homer's *Iliad* we hear of a thanksgiving sacrifice presided over by Chryses, whose daughter had been captured by the enemy but who was freed and returned. After a long ceremony which included prayer, the slaying of animals, and a joyous meal, the feasting community broke into loud praise of Apollo: "All the day long they gave to lauding the god with singing, chanting glad paeans of praise, and the god took pleasure in their voices." In Aeschylus' *Suppliant Maidens*, the Chorus asks Zeus to grant the city of Argos that "minstrels may sing hymns of praise at the altars; and from pure lips let there proceed the chant that attends the harp." Although Plato expressed his dislike of the performance of praise, his description provides graphic detail:

A magistrate offers a public sacrifice, and there come in not one but many choruses, who take up a position a little way from the altar, and from time to time pour forth all sorts of horrible blasphemies on the sacred rites, exciting the souls of the audience with words and rhythms and melodies most sorrowful to hear; and he who at the moment when the city is offering sacrifice makes the citizens weep most, carries away the palm of victory.

Praise has its precise place at the altar, the place where people approach God or the gods with sacrifice. A typical ancient Greek form of praise, the "paean," was performed by a choir under the direction of a leader to the accompaniment of the cithara. The choir not only sang, but also danced in a stately step. Sometimes the entire community of attending worshippers took up the refrain "*iê paian*" (Hail, Paian!), presumably an echo of the paean's origin in the cult of a deity named Paian. Aelius Aristides (117–80 CE), who spent much time in the sanatorium-like sanctuary of Asclepius in Pergamum, composed paeans in praise of Apollo, Asclepius, Hekate, Pan, Athena, and other deities. During the years he stayed in Pergamum (ca. 144–7), he and his wealthy friends maintained a chorus of boys who sang Aristides' lyrics in public performances. In the paeans that survive in literature or have been found in inscriptions, we can discern their three standard parts: after a summons addressing the worshippers there followed an account of the mythical story of the deity, which constituted the longest part and formed the actual praise; by way of conclusion, the paean prayed for the welfare of the worshippers and the state. Interestingly enough, the earliest musical notations on record in history are for Greek paeans, found inscribed on stones and dating from second-century CE Delphi.[4]

Ancient ritual can be either public or private, that is involving an entire community or just a few individuals or perhaps a family or clan. Accordingly, we can speak of private and public praise offered to the deity. While ancient sources tell us very little about the forms and circumstances of private praise, we can get a fairly detailed picture about praise in public worship. One ancient book has made public praise one of its favorite subjects: the biblical book of Chronicles. No other ancient source reveals as much about the ritual setting of praise as does this one book. Written around 400 BCE, it sketches the history of Israel as the story of a community whose life is geared toward and culminates in the worship of Yahweh in the Temple of Jerusalem. Accordingly, public religious ceremonies and nationally celebrated festivals punctuate the course of history and provide a literary framework for other events.[5]

According to the book of Chronicles, temple worship had four important founders and patrons: the Judaean kings David, Solomon, Hezekiah, and Josiah. David, by bringing the "ark of the covenant," an ancient ritual object, to Jerusalem, gave Israel its central ritual focus; Solomon built and dedicated the Temple, and Hezekiah and Josiah reformed the ritual. Among these four, David is the most important, for he created an orchestra of harps, lyres, trumpets, and cymbals, as well as a choir that had to perform within daily sacrificial worship. He established a pool of four thousand Levites as potential musicians and singers and determined that they should praise Yahweh during the presentation of the daily burnt offerings. The profession of singer was to be handed on within the appointed families and managed by an organized guild. A "Levite" was the member of a family that traditionally performed certain ritual functions which were different from those done by "priests." King Hezekiah in a way completed the organization begun by David, for he ordered the choir to sing psalms composed by David and the choir-master Asaph, presumably from a newly edited collection that enabled the choir to rely on a number of set texts. From the modern historian's perspective, all of this is of course very speculative. What the Chronicler describes are in fact not historical origins; what he presents as history is presumably just an idealized picture of ritual organization at the time of his own writing. The supposed revivals of Davidic liturgical institutions at the time of Hezekiah and Josiah seem to reveal more about the ritual revival the Chronicler saw or promoted in his own time than about the already distant days of the monarchy. Nevertheless, King Hezekiah may well have ordered the collection of songs into one book, which we can perhaps take to be the first edition of the book of Psalms.[6]

The book of Chronicles defines the exact location of praise within the Temple ritual, gives the full text of a song of praise, and indicates how its author—and perhaps the singers themselves—understood its meaning.

At the Jerusalem Temple, public ritual consisted essentially in the immolation and complete burning of one lamb in the morning and one lamb in the evening. Now the Temple choir's singing was not an activity that accompanied the entire proceedings involved with the offering. The choir neither accompanied the slaughtering nor the dashing of the animal's blood at the foot of the altar. Singing had its precise location: it accompanied the final stage of the sacrifice, the burning of the corpse on the altar. When the priests placed the corpse onto the burning pyre, the choir began to sing, and when the lamb was turned to ashes, the choir stopped singing. Singing and burning also happened in close proximity to each other, for the choir stood in front of the altar as the burnt offering was presented upon it. The burning and the singing seem to have qualified each other as two complementary ritual acts.

Occasionally the Chronicler, when writing about the singers, refers to them as being appointed to "render thanks to Yahweh, for his steadfast love endures forever" (1 Chr. 16:41; see 2 Chr. 5:13; 20:21). This expression echoes a refrain apparently characteristic of what the choir sang, for it not only appears in the canonical book of Psalms, but also in the one song whose text the Chronicler inserted in his work. Here are some lines of this long hymn:

> O give thanks to Yahweh, call on his name,
> make known his deeds among the peoples.
> Sing of him, sing his praises,
> tell of all his wonderful works! . . .
> When they [our ancestors] were few in number,
> of little account, and strangers in the land,
> wandering from nation to nation,
> from one kingdom to another people,
> he allowed no one to oppress them;
> he rebuked kings on their account,
> saying, "Do not touch my anointed ones;
> do my prophets no harm."
> Sing of Yahweh, all the earth!
> Tell of his salvation from day to day! . . .
> for great is Yahweh, and greatly to be praised;
> he is to be revered above all the gods! . . .
> O give thanks to Yahweh, for he is good;
> for his steadfast love endures forever!

Here the singers praise Yahweh by telling how he has in the past protected his chosen people, the Israelites, against their enemies. (As we shall see in the next section, the account of divine help in ages past is the very stuff of praise.)[7]

One can see that the hymn has no direct relationship to the sacrifice the priests offer during the singing. The singers do not ask Yahweh to accept the sacrifice or to bless the sacrificers in answer to the gift they are offering. Far from being simply a part of the sacrifice, it serves as its complement. We cannot understand it apart from the belief that as the flames consume the burnt offering, the deity is present. Or, more precisely, the sacrificial presentation at the altar invites and as it were produces the presence of Yahweh. In the ritual

echoed in the book of Chronicles, the response to Yahweh's presence is fourfold: (1) the singers sing a song of praise; (2) to the singing of praise they join
a petition, asking Yahweh to rescue and gather his people from among the
nations; (3) then the people respond to the choir by shouting Amen and words
of praise, presumably by repeating the last words of the hymn: "Truly he is
good, truly his steadfast love endures forever" or simply by crying "hallelujah";
(4) finally, as a concluding rite, people prostrate themselves before the deity.
With prostration, the celebration ends.[8]

The highly formal, well-defined cultic setting of the hymn requires artful,
carefully chosen words and phrases. Rather than chanting a prose text, the
priests sing a poem of high artistic quality. At all times people have known, as
Thomas Hobbes has it, "that prayers and thanksgiving be made in words and
phrases not sudden, nor light, nor plebeian, but beautiful and well composed;
for else we do not God as much honor as we can." It is reasonable, to do so "in
verse, and with music, both of voice and instruments."[9]

In sketching how praise was joined to sacrifice, we have insisted on its
original cultic setting. However, praise could also be an independent ritual act
and serve as a substitute for animal sacrifice or, more generally, as an act that
responds to God's presence.

The Primacy of Praise

After having dealt with praise as an elementary form of ancient worship, we
may ask how it related to other forms of verbal expression in the cult. What we
find is evidence for a wide appreciation of praise; indeed, we can speak of its
primacy over other forms of prayer.

In the ancient world, some pagans privileged praise over petitionary prayer.
One of them, the philosopher Epictetus (ca. 60–140 CE), has no doubts about
the matter: "If we had understanding, ought we to do anything else both jointly
and severally than to sing hymns and bless the deity, and tell of his benefits?"
The Greek philosopher gives an example:

> Ought we not when we are digging and plowing and eating to sing this hymn to
> God: "Great is God who gives us such implements with which we shall cultivate
> the earth. Great is God who has given us hands, the power of swallowing, a
> stomach, imperceptible growth, and the power of breathing while we sleep."
> This is what we ought to sing on every occasion.

Epictetus' discourse ends on a note of invitation: "I am a rational creature, and
I ought to praise God: this is my work. I do it, nor will I desert this post, so long
as I am allowed to keep it; and I exhort you to join in this same song." Far from
being just a sectarian concern, praise could develop in this favorable cultural
climate.[10]

Epictetus' insistence on the primacy of praise has an unexpected echo in Voltaire's *Philosophical Dictionary*. In his entry on "God" the eighteenth-century philosopher ridicules the word-mongering of theological speculation to which the healthy yet considered praise of a heathen householder provides a refreshing contrast. Asked what he tells his god in the presence of his wife, his sons and daughters, his kindred and servants, Voltaire's Dondindac is quick to give an answer that seems to echo Epictetus: "I thank him for the good things I enjoy, and even for the evils with which he tries me; but I take great care not to ask him for anything. He knows better than we do what we need, and in any case, I'd be afraid to ask him for fine weather when my neighbor might be asking for rain." For Voltaire's generation, praise as practiced by Dondindac is the rational alternative to the production of ever new scholastic distinctions.[11]

In the earliest sources that tell us about Christian worship, the evidence for the importance of praise is overwhelming. However, praise did not have its later precedence over petition right from the start. Early Christian prayer actually mingles petition with praise. The gospels that include the Our Father seem to reflect Jesus' own preference for petitionary prayer. The Our Father asks for daily bread and forgiveness of sins. According to Jesus, a humble prayer of petition ("God, be merciful to me, a sinner") is to be preferred to one of thanksgiving ("God, I thank you that I am not like other people: thieves, rogues, adulterers," Luke 18:11ff.). The Pharisee thanks, the tax-collector asks. Thanksgiving all too easily degenerates into boasting and self-glorification. Jesus not only recommended petition; he also promised divine response: "Ask, and it will be given you" (Matt. 7:7). Can one be more confident about petitionary prayer? Yet, the Jesuanic emphasis on petitionary prayer did not establish itself as the dominant approach. Within the New Testament itself we can detect a shift from petition to praise. Paul's emphasis on thanksgiving cannot be missed by any reader of his letters. "I give thanks to my God always for you," he writes to the Christian community of Corinth, "because of the grace of God that has been given you in Christ Jesus" (1 Cor. 1:4). Most of Paul's letters begin on a similar note. Colossians, generally believed to be a pseudo-Pauline letter, echoes and develops the apostle's exhortation to praise: "Dedicate yourselves to thankfulness! . . . Sing gratefully to God from your hearts in psalms, hymns, and inspired songs!" (Col. 3:15–16). Petitionary prayer would always form an important element of Christian worship; yet thanksgiving and praise came to dominate. The passage from the letter to the Colossians, just referred to, merits being quoted in full. Its words seem to echo the structure of worship:

praise	Dedicate yourselves to thankfulness!
exhortation	Let the gospel of Christ dwell among you in all its richness; teach and instruct one another with all the wisdom it gives you.

hymns of praise	Sing gratefully to God from your hearts in psalms, hymns, and inspired songs.
sacramental action (Eucharist)	Let every word and action, everything you do, be in the name of the Lord Jesus, and
praise	give thanks through him to God the Father. (Col. 3:15–17)

Here thanksgiving and praise not only form the first and the concluding part of the service, but dominate the entire meeting! We can understand why Origen, basing himself on what he has found "scattered in the scriptures," gives the following instruction:

> Each person should organize his prayer according to these topics. This is what they are: In the beginning and the preface of the prayer something having the force of *praise* should be said of God through Christ, who is praised with Him, and by the Holy Spirit, who is hymned with Him. After this each person should place general *thanksgivings*, bringing forward for thanksgiving the benefits given many people and those he has himself received from God. After thanksgiving it seems to me that he ought to blame himself bitterly before God for his own sins and then ask, first, for healing that he may be delivered from the habit that brings him to sin, and, second, for *forgiveness* of the sins that have been committed. And after confession, the fourth topic that seems to me must be added is the *request* for great and heavenly things, both private and general, and concerning his household and his dearest. And, finally, the prayer should be concluded with a *doxology* [formula of praise] of God through Christ in the Holy Spirit.[12]

Among the five parts of Origen's "complete" prayer—praise, thanksgiving, confession, requests, doxology—three are dedicated to praise and thanksgiving!

We must not think that the precedence of praise reflects a distinctive Christian view. In the Talmud, Jewish tradition recommends the same attitude: "Let people always declare the praise of God [first] and afterwards present their petition."[13]

Early Christian writers did not spend much time reflecting on the primacy of praise. It sufficed to state that petitionary prayer was inferior to praise. Nor did the sixteenth-century reformers belabor the point. "The first requirement of a good prayer is that it give thanks to God and recall in the heart and in words the benefits you have received from God." Thus Martin Luther. "Let this be the first rule of right prayer," wrote John Calvin, "that we abandon all thought of our own glory, that we cast off all notion of our own worth, that we put away all our self-assurance, in our abjection and our humility giving glory to the Lord." More recent Protestant authors, like Albrecht Ritschl (1822–89) in the nineteenth, and Peter Brunner (1900–81) in the twentieth century, developed the theme further. For them, to pray means to put God and his glory first. "Within the general notion of prayer," explains Ritschl, "petition and thanksgiving are far from being equal." The idea of an equal status for the two would promote the erroneous assumption that even the most egoistic petition could be a legitimate act of veneration. We have to thank God not only *after* our prayers have been answered. "On the contrary: prayer as a whole and in all circumstances must focus on thanksgiving, praise, acknowledgment, and adoration." The misleading term of prayer, with makes us think first of petition, often prevents people from developing a proper understanding. In communal, corporate worship, praise and thanksgiving take clear precedence over petition and intercession. The worshipping community looks to God. In view of God's overwhelming glory and majesty, the congregation's own petty wishes vanish, and *must* vanish, into the background.[14]

Giving Calvin's and Ritschl's thought the shortest and most powerful expression, Peter Brunner defines "adoration of the Creator in submission, veneration, thanksgiving and praise" as the most original form or "*Urgestalt*" of worship. Praise implies the acknowledgment of God's lordship and our dependence, and these two provide the very foundation of liturgy.[15]

A natural, healthy expression of religion needs little support from learned theory. Throughout the centuries, Christians have engaged more in the practice of praise than in debates about its meaning and essence. That God should be praised has appeared obvious and has never been questioned. Unlike sacrament or sacrifice, it has never been the subject of major controversies or magisterial definitions. While authors rarely fail to emphasize the importance of praising God, they have written little about its essence, its theory, or its particular theological dimensions. There has been little incentive to work out sophisticated theologies dealing with the subject. People grew into worship and thus no one had to be persuaded. Why theorize about a meaningful, self-evident religious practice? But, the general reluctance to theorize about praise notwithstanding, *implicit* theologies do exist. What we find in sermons, devotional writers, theological manuals, and of course in the Bible and in Christian liturgy, forms a repertoire of ideas that is often invoked though rarely developed into full-fledged theories. This repertoire consists of three elementary philosophies of praise, inherited from the Old Testament book of Psalms and embodied in three basic forms: adoration, celebratory recital, and thanksgiving.

2. The Elementary Forms of Praise in the Book of Psalms

The Bible insists that God is more worthy of praise than human beings. Rarely, if ever, would biblical authors praise a man or a woman for a heroic deed, and seldom is a hero given a special reward. Of Moses it is once said that "he was unequaled" (Deut. 34:11), and a certain Othniel gets the daughter of the judge Caleb for having conquered a town. These passages remain as isolated and rare as the praise of the human body—the male one as well as that of a youthful woman—in the Song of Solomon. In the second century BCE, however, under the influence of Greek culture, Jewish authors began to be more open to celebrating heroic deeds and to composing poems in praise of biblical figures. Beautiful Judith is extolled for enticing Holophernes with her charms and killing this enemy of the Jews. The Hasmonean leaders Judas and Simon are celebrated for having liberated their people from foreign rule. And Sirach, in a long poem, dazzles his readers with a triumphal procession of all the noteworthy men of Israel's history. Although in early Judaism people could be praised, we can still detect a definite restraint. When Judith is to be praised, then the God of Israel must be named first: "O daughter, you are blessed by the Most High God above all other women on earth; and blessed be the Lord God, who created the heavens and the earth, who has guided you to cut off the head of the leader of our enemies" (Jud. 13:18). Or, shorter, in the Magnificat: "From now on, all generations will call me blessed, for the Mighty One has done great things for me" (Luke 1:48–49). Thus the old rule still holds: God is to be praised more than human beings, and human individuals are praised only in relation to divine deeds.[16]

While the praise of the gods or of God pervades all ancient documents of religion, praise is particularly characteristic of one biblical book—the Psalms. A careful reading of this book will reveal to us what it meant in ancient ritual to praise a deity. When Christians began to split off from Judaism, they took with them the psalms and the psalmists' practice of praise.

The book of Psalms is in many ways a mysterious writing. Neither the date of its compilation, nor the date of the 150 poems collected in this book, nor the use of song in Israel's ritual life can be determined with certainty. Although many of Israel's psalms are traditionally attributed to King David, scholars agree that very few if any of the 150 songs reflect the time of tenth-century BCE Israel. Some of the psalms seem to reflect moods and conditions that can be traced back to the second millennium BCE, i.e., to pre-Israelite days. Others clearly echo the early Judaism of the fourth or third centuries BCE, the period in which the Psalms may have been collected into one scroll.

Despite our ignorance concerning their origins, the Psalms themselves reveal much about Israel's religious life and thought. Far from being a figure of philosophical abstraction, Israel's God, Yahweh, was close and active, always ready to intervene on behalf of his faithful. People felt his active presence in nature, in their national history as well as in their personal lives. Worship, for Israelites, culminated in praise. And praise was expressed in many ways: in thanksgiving for divine favors received, in extolling the mighty acts God has done for his people, and in adoring Yahweh's majesty. If we are to enter Israel's world of praise, we must study its three elementary forms: the song of thanksgiving, the hymn of glorification, and the anthem of adoration.

The Song of Thanksgiving

The first and most elementary form of praise is the individual thanksgiving for divine favors and benefits received. In Psalm 30, we hear the voice of a man (or a woman) who was in trouble. In his distress, he called upon Yahweh, crying for help. And that help was granted. In joy and gratitude he goes to the Temple to give thanks to the Lord, accompanied by friends. His thanksgiving culminates in a joyous song—this very psalm—in which he recounts his story and celebrates Yahweh's saving act.

Scholars believe that psalms of thanksgiving were generally part of a larger ritual complex. They belonged to the celebration of a sacrifice of thanksgiving. Such a sacrifice, performed in the presence of a celebrating congregation, involved the slaughtering of at least one goat or sheep, the burning of some of its entrails, and the dashing of the victim's blood against the altar. At some point of the ritual, the psalm of thanksgiving was performed, either by the lay sponsor of the ritual or perhaps by a singer hired for the occasion. The meat of the victim was cooked and immediately consumed by the celebrating community. To participate in the celebration meant not only to listen to a singer, but also to join in the praises. Naturally, people would also be invited to partake of the sacrificial meal.

Psalm 30 can serve as an example of a song of thanksgiving. This song is instructive from its very first line in which the singer states the reason for which the individual praises Yahweh: "I will extol you, O Lord, for you have drawn me up, and did not let my foes rejoice over me." In this first line of the song, the psalmist says, in summary fashion, all he wants to say: I praise Yahweh, and I do so for a very definite reason: that reason is divine intervention on my behalf. The statement of the reason for praise is identical with praise itself. In what follows, the singer elaborates on his story. He had felt in harmony with God, thinking that Yahweh had established him "as a strong mountain." However, one day Yahweh began to hide his face, so that "I was dismayed." In distress, he called upon Yahweh, praying to him:

> To you, O Yahweh, I cried,
> and to Yahweh I made supplication:
> "What profit is there in my death,
> if I go down to the Pit?
> Will the dust praise you?
> Will it tell of your faithfulness?
> Hear, O Yahweh, and be gracious to me!
> O Yahweh, be my helper!"

The outcome of the story is quickly told: "O Yahweh, my God, I cried to you for help, and you have healed me. O Yahweh, you brought up my soul from Sheol, restored my life from among those gone down to the Pit." Yahweh, in fact, rescued the poor man or woman from a terrible illness or some other crisis that had put him in the fear of descending to the Nether World (Sheol). Now, he can go to the Temple and sing the Lord's praises:

> You have turned my mourning into dancing;
> you have taken off my sackcloth
> and clothed me with joy,
> so that I may praise you and not be silent.
> O Yahweh, my God, I will give thanks to you forever.

The reference to sackcloth must not be understood as a mere figure of speech. Most likely, our poor man reacted to his trouble not only by praying to his God, but also by wearing a rough, uncouth garment to indicate to others, including his God, that he was mourning his fate. The reference to dancing, too, implies not only the mood for joyous movement. At a thanksgiving ritual, Israelites would both sing and dance.

In one section of his song, the singer invites his celebrating community to join him in his praises, for praise and dance are never lonely matters. Just as a sacrifice and the ensuing meal involves participating guests, so the singing always involves a group of people who join in the thanksgiving of the one who delivers a psalm:

> Sing praises to Yahweh, O you his faithful ones,
> and give thanks to his holy name.
> For his anger is but for a moment;
> his favor is for a lifetime.
> Weeping we may linger for the night,
> but joy comes with the morning.

Again, we can see that the singer's call to praise is accompanied by a reason ("for"). And we can also see that the reason given constitutes the praise. In the example quoted, the distressed person who had been helped understands the lesson: God's anger is but for a moment. By proclaiming this fact publicly, in delivering the song, he praises Yahweh.

Psalm 30 includes all the elements characteristic of prayers of thanksgiving: the recounting of the singer's story of distress, the cry for divine intervention, and the event of divine help; the presentation of this story as the expression and reason for praise; and the invitation to others to join the singer in his praise and rejoicing. Yahweh, then, is praised by the very act of recounting a story. Just as someone would praise a human person by referring to his or her deeds, so an Israelite extolls God by showing how he has affected a human life. In thanksgiving, the Israelite gives a testimony of divine help.

The Hymn of Glorification

While songs of thanksgiving relate to God's intervention on behalf of individuals, hymns of glorification extoll Yahweh's glorious deeds in creation or in the sacred story of Israel's past. One example is Psalm 117, notable for its brevity:

> Praise Yahweh (*hallelujah*), all you nations!
> Extoll him, all you peoples!
> For great is his steadfast love toward us,
> and the faithfulness of Yahweh endures forever!
> Praise Yahweh (*hallelujah*)!

As in the song of thanksgiving, the hymn of glorification never fails to state a reason for praise. Yahweh is to be praised "*for* great is his steadfast love toward us." Also, as in the song of thanksgiving, merely stating the reasons constitutes the praise. The people are exhorted to glorify God by singing: "Great is his steadfast love toward us, and the faithfulness of Yahweh endures forever." In shorthand fashion, the expressions "steadfast love" (or "solidarity") and "faithfulness" sum up what God has done and how he acts. Of course, the psalmists can be more specific and spell out Yahweh's deeds in detail by recounting God's intervention on behalf of Israel; or they focus on the more general theme of God's benevolence toward all his creation.

Psalm 105, for instance, recounts Israel's or, more precisely, Yahweh's sacred story. Beginning with "the covenant that he made with Abraham," the psalmist sings of Joseph's slavery and advancement to royal stewardship, the magic battle against Pharaoh fought by Moses, Israel's flight out of Egypt, and the conquest of "the lands of the nations." In another passage, the singer moves from creation to the redemptive acts in history: "O give thanks to Yahweh . . . who by understanding made the heavens . . . who spread out the earth on the waters . . . who made the great lights . . . who struck Egypt through their firstborn . . . and brought Israel out from among them" (Ps. 136:1.5–11). The acts recorded in celebratory recital form the basis of Israel's sacred story as recounted in the narrative parts of the Old Testament, especially in the Pentateuch and the book of Joshua. While the prose account develops the hallowed themes with much detail and narrative flourish, biblical poetry simply lists them, presupposing their being generally known by those who sing or listen. God is glorified in the very act of telling a story about what God has done—and does—for his people. In an oracle published through Second Isaiah, God himself explains the meaning of the saving deeds he does in terms of praise: "I give water in the wilderness, rivers in the desert, to give drink to my chosen people, the people whom I formed for myself so that they might declare my praise" (Isa. 43:20–21). Only in glorification can God's acts find their aim, their end and fulfillment.

Another group of psalms shifts the focus from Israel to creation and humanity in general, for God not only guides his chosen people through history but also cares for the entire world. The psalmists make an effort to tell how God supplies food for animals and humans. "He covers the heavens with clouds, prepares rain for the earth, makes grass grow on the hills. He gives to the animals their food, and to the young ravens when they cry," reads one passage (Ps. 147:8–9). "You cause the grass to grow for the cattle, and plants for people to use, to bring forth food from the earth, and wine to gladden the human heart, oil to make the face shine, and bread to strengthen the human heart," reads another one (Ps. 104:14–15). God, who sees everything, acts as a savior of the downtrodden and as a judge of the wicked. "Yahweh upholds all who are falling, and raises up all who are bowed down. . . . Yahweh watches over all who love him, but all the wicked he will destroy" (Ps. 145:14.20). Just as Yahweh's acts in Israel's history have to be recounted so that God is thereby glorified, so also must his regular acts in creation be told and extolled. And again, it is only in glorification that God's wondrous works find their aim, their end and fulfillment.

To praise God means to recount his deeds and virtues in the context of sacred celebrations. One setting is described in the book of Chronicles. In the days of King David, the "ark of the covenant" (a symbol of Yahweh's presence) was brought to Jerusalem in solemn procession, "with shouting, to the sound of the horn, trumpets, and cymbals," with "loud music on harps and lyres," with "leaping and dancing" (1 Chr. 15:28–29). If we add the clapping of hands and the waving of ivy-wreathed wands, leafy branches and fronds of palm, we get a complete picture of shouting, the use of musical instruments, of movement and dancing. Celebrating, in biblical times, was a joyous and noisy matter. After the ark has been installed in the sanctuary on Mount Zion, the mighty acts of Yahweh are commemorated in a magnificent hymn whose text corresponds to Psalm 105. So important to the community was the ark's transfer to

Jerusalem that, as some have suggested, it may have been commemorated in an annual festive recitation of the psalm. Other occasions for recounting Yahweh's deeds included the great national feast of Passover. Celebrated each spring, it commemorated Yahweh's initiative in guiding his people out of Egypt. The celebration of Yahweh's mighty acts held a central place in Israel's ritual life.[17]

A regular feature of the hymns of glorification is the summons to praise. Psalm 117, for instance, begins and ends with an invitation to join the singer or the choir. In the jubilant shout of *hallelujah*, the summons to glorify and the object of their praise come together in one single word: "Praise Yahweh!" In Psalm 117, the group invited to join in the praising extends beyond those who are present and can actually listen to the singer: "Praise Yahweh, all you nations!" Thus not only Israelites, but pagans also are called on, as in the words of Luther: "the psalmist makes one people of gentiles and Jews . . . without any Law and Moses, simply through glorification and praise." Addressing a group that cannot possibly be present seems to reflect a convention of ancient Israelite rhetoric. The prophets frequently addressed their oracles to the Israelite nation as a whole while actually speaking to just a few people. In saying "Hear this word, O house of Israel!" (Amos 5:1), the address names the *intended* audience rather than the actual one. Singers and prophets address all for whom a message is intended and valid.[18]

Perhaps we can go one step further and speak of the "evangelistic," missionary character of praise. The psalmist's invitation aims not only at other people's *momentary* joining in the praises of Yahweh, but at their having a permanent relationship with the Creator. "The praise of God is the most prominent and extended formulation of the *universal* and *conversionary* dimension of the Old Testament," explains Patrick Miller. "One might even speak of a missionary aim if that did not risk distorting the material by suggesting a program of proselytizing to bring individuals into the visible community of Israel." How close the invitation to praise comes to missionary activity can be seen in the New Testament, when Paul uses the psalmist's words as a scriptural support for his missionary activity among the Gentiles. However, the difference between a proselytizing attitude and the summons to praise never gets lost, for the hymn of glorification looks not so much at the human community of Israel as it does toward God, seeking to promote his glory by acknowledging his good deeds.[19]

The Anthem of Adoration

Our reading of the Psalms has insisted on the pragmatic, down-to-earth motivation of praise. We have defined praise as thanksgiving for, acknowledgment of, and response to some divine act. People who praise have a continuing interest in God as their protector, their helper, their divine patron and benefactor. Yet we must not neglect another side of praise: its disinterested, nonpragmatic dimension, revealed in the act of *adoration*. This kind of praise was heard by the eighth-century BCE prophet Isaiah. Transported in a vision into Yahweh's throne chamber, he heard the seraphs, God's throne attendants. Flying around the throne, they were singing in unison: "Holy, holy, holy is Yahweh of hosts; the whole earth is full of his glory" (Isa. 6:3). This seems to be the entire song the prophet heard. Unlike human psalmody, their liturgy consists just of this one powerful acclamation.[20]

In Psalm 29 there is also an acclamation the heavenly court shouts in homage of a God who displays his power in thunder, storm, and earthquake. They acclaim God's majesty:

Ascribe to Yahweh, O heavenly beings,
ascribe to Yahweh glory and strength.
Ascribe to Yahweh the glory of his name;
worship him in holy splendor. . . .
And in his [heavenly] temple all cry,
"Glory."

In both Psalm 29 and Isaiah's vision the words of praise are not uttered by human beings on earth, but by heavenly beings who prostrate themselves in a celestial sanctuary or throne chamber. To this divine world human beings have no regular access; only in exceptional cases the likes of a prophet, a shaman or a seer may be admitted for a short moment.

The anthems of adoration are quite different from earthly, self-interested praise. Reasons for praising are completely omitted or replaced by a simple reference to God as the Creator. General, unspecific praise does not evoke a world in which the poor are helped by divine intervention, but one in which a happy, organic world of splendor, harmony, and well-being is celebrated as founded and sustained by God. The ideal world rings with angelic voices: "Holy, holy, holy is Yahweh of hosts; the whole earth is full of his glory." Heaven functions as the center of this ideal universe, and from that center, "glory" and "well-being" (*shalom*) radiate on to earth. Like a mirror earth reflects the divine—hence Isaiah's reference to the earth being full of glory and the psalmist's concluding statement about Yahweh's giving of "strength" and *shalom* to his people (Ps. 29:11).[21]

Who sang the anthems of adoration in Old Testament times? And on what occasions? Ancient Jewish manuscripts, found in Qumran near the Dead Sea and published in 1985, can provide at least a partial answer. By joining together numerous fragments, the American scholar Carol Newsom reconstructed a cycle of anthems she terms "Songs of the Sabbath Sacrifice." They appear to have been used in a liturgy of praise performed by priestly members of the sectarian community of Qumran. That community rejected the Jerusalem Temple whose priesthood they considered illegitimate and corrupt. Not participating in the sacrificial life of the Temple, they found consolation in a higher form of worship: they imitated and joined the angels in their worship of the Creator. That worship is of course nonsacrificial. It consists of anthems of adoration sung both in heaven (by the angelic powers) and on earth (by the priests). One of the fragments uses a prophetic vision—that of Ezekiel—to describe the setting of angelic adoration: "The cherubim prostrate themselves before Him and bless. As they rise, a whispered divine voice is heard, and there is a roar of praise." Like everyone who sings Psalm 29 or acclaims God with Isaiah's three cries of "holy," the sectarian priests join in the celestial roar of praise.[22]

The Qumran sectarians did not invent the liturgical setting of adoration. Most biblical accounts of adoration actually include references to its home in the realm of ritual. The heavenly beings of Psalm 29 acclaim Yahweh as he manifests his presence not only in nature but also in his heavenly temple. Equally, Isaiah saw God in his celestial throne chamber, which is also called a temple: "I saw Yahweh sitting on a throne, high and lofty; and the hem of his robe filled the temple" (Isa. 6:1). The prophet lay prostrate in front of the throne; not daring to look up, he only saw the hem of the heavenly king's robe. Here we are dealing with the idea and experience of a cultic theophany, a manifestation of the divine presence in the place of worship. Adoration serves as the ritual response to cultic theophany. Pragmatic praise, on the other hand, responds to extra-cultic, real-life manifestations of God in national history or the life of individuals. Claus Westermann rightly speaks of two basic ways in which Israel experienced the divine: in epiphanies, Yahweh came to rescue people in need of succor, and he did so wherever help was needed; in theophanies, he manifested his presence in sacred places. Adoration is the appropriate response to God's theophanic presence.[23]

The difference between praising the more abstract qualities of God—his holiness, goodness, rulership, or fatherhood—and the more pragmatic reference to divine acts of help and deliverance has not escaped the notice of those who study the forms of religious language. John Chrysostom, the fourth-century bishop, explained to his Christian flock the difference between disinterested and interested praise by using two different terms: hymns and psalms. Disinterested, hymnic praise—the one we have termed adoration—is eternal, free from all human dimensions, and sung by the heavenly powers. "Psalms," on the other hand (our songs of thanksgiving and hymns of glorification), remain earth-bound and saturated with human experience. In the eighteenth century, Jonathan Edwards suggested a similar distinction. "The grace of God," he explains, "may appear lovely in two ways; either as *bonum utile*, a profitable good to me, that which greatly serves my interest, and so suits my self-love; or as *bonum formosum*, a beautiful good in itself, and part of the moral and spiritual excellency of the divine nature." While "the true saints" praise the transcendent *bonum formosum*, most Christians appreciate God's goodness shown to them in this life. As long as people live—and suffer—on earth, the psalmists' self-interested praise will often determine the tune of prayer.[24]

The Worlds of Praise

Paying close attention to the various forms of praise in the Psalms, we can recognize the spiritual milieu and mental world in which they originated. The *song of thanksgiving* evidently belongs to the personal piety of people who in distress call upon God (or a god) and after deliverance sing his praises. Here the individual speaks in a tone of trust and confidence to "my God" and extols his God as "my shepherd" or "my refuge and my fortress, my God, in whom I trust" (Ps. 30:2; 23:1; 91:2). The *hymn of glorification* can hardly have originated in the same milieu. Poets and priests related to Israel's national religion and to the cult of the state must have compiled the songs that celebrate Yahweh's sacred story, a story of creation, election, and liberation from the Egyptian slavery. Here God is presented as king, judge, warrior, creator, and helper: i.e., as a powerful and majestic figure. The dominant note is that of Yahweh's kingship; see Psalm 145:1 "I will extol you, my God and King!" Or Psalm 98:6: "Make a joyful noise before Yahweh, the king!"

What we have termed the *anthem of adoration* again reflects a different setting. It seems to be of prophetic origin or inspiration. Prophets like Isaiah and shamanlike figures would in their trances ascend to heaven and hear the sound of angels. They would bring the angelic voices down to earth and communicate them to others, overwhelming their audience with heavenly, nonhuman beauty. Eduard Norden, in his treatise on ancient forms of prayer, demonstrated that the abstract form of praise did not form part of the religious rhetoric of the ancient Greeks and Romans; these came to adopt abstract praise of the gods only when coming under the influence of eastern religions. Norden traced the "adoration" style of prayer back to the ancient Egyptians, Babylonians, and Jews, attributing it to the talent of these peoples for lofty mystical notions and abstract thought.[25]

For the modern, analytical mind, these three categories of praise seem distinct if not disparate. In the Bible, however, they are related very closely and naturally. As we have explained, some ancient languages lack words that correspond to our "thanking." To thank and to praise are not recognized as two different acts; they are one. When in present-day Israel people thank someone by saying *todah*, they use the biblical term for "praise." Thus language itself points to an underlying unity of praise and thanksgiving. But we have more than mere linguistic evidence for defining the unity of Israel's praise.

From what we know about the history of Israel's religion, we can also show how our three types of praise came to be closely associated. Underneath the official, monotheistic religion of the Old Testament, historians have detected an older, polytheistic layer. That layer reflects common Near Eastern mythology and ritual practice. If the theory that Israel's pre-canonical religion was polytheistic is correct, we can see how the three forms of praise were addressed to three different deities. Personal thanksgiving would be addressed to the "personal god," seen as someone's special protecting spirit. This god (or goddess) would be called upon in situations of need and distress, and the devotee would rejoice in his or her divine patron. The god whose mighty acts are celebrated would, of course, be a different deity. Here we must think of Israel's national or state god whose worship is not individual and personal but rather communal, attached to institutions of tribe, monarchy, state, and temple. Nonpragmatic, pure praise addressed yet another god or category of gods, distinct from both the national and the personal deity. The more abstract forms of hymnic praise originally addressed a majestic creator God ruling from his heavenly abode. In the case of Psalm 29, we may think of a deity presiding over nature, weather, rain, and storm.

The present canonical text of the Bible no longer distinguishes these three categories of gods. Monotheistic faith boldly identifies them, creating the One out of the Many by incorporating the Creator and the personal deity into the national god. Thus Jewish orthodoxy directs all praise and thanksgiving to the One. Although some traces of the earlier polytheism remain, the leaders of the emerging monotheistic faith have done much to suppress and eradicate the old pre-orthodox religion. In giving the biblical text its present monotheistic cast, they completed a process that can be traced back at least to Hosea in the eighth century BCE, a prophet whose insistence on the exclusive worship of Israel's national god helped to inaugurate that school of thought and practice scholars have termed the "Yahweh-alone movement." This movement forged the idea of the one God of Israel and prepared its development into monotheism. While the Psalms permit an occasional glimpse of pre-canonical Israelite polytheism, those who use this text in their worship no longer think of its prehistory. They sing the praises of the one and only God, creator of the world, protector of the individual, and savior of Israel.

The Old Testament book of Psalms, of which we have studied just small sections, includes petitionary prayers as well as songs of praise. In the early part of the Psalms, petition and complaint, though interspersed with some praise, would seem to be more frequent and more characteristic. Toward the end of the collection, however, praise clearly dominates. Those who gave the Psalter its Hebrew title of *tehillim* ("praises") even understood the totality of Israel's prayer, including the many songs of lamentation and the didactic, meditative ones, as one single symphony of praise to God. The title of *tehillim* tells the reader that what follows is praise; like a clef placed at the beginning of musical notation, it determines the entire performance, giving it its particular key and tune. "All the way through the book of Psalms," comments James Stewart,

> even in its most sorrow-laden passages, you feel that you are walking on a volcano of praise, liable to burst out at any moment into a great flame of

gratitude to God. And as the book draws to its close, the flame leaps clear from the smoke: here you have praise, and nothing but praise.

For the biblical people, worship culminated in praise. With the book of Psalms, the early Christians inherited a book of praise. Although many of the early Christians did not understand the Hebrew of this book, they used the ancient call to praise, *hallelujah* ("Praise Yahweh!"), which for them has become a shout of jubilation (Rev. 19:3.4.6). Christians used the Psalms in Greek translation, produced their own Latin versions, and adopted the book for much use in public worship and private devotion. For them, the Psalms became one of the main texts of praise.[26]

Appreciated and sung by two religions, Judaism and Christianity, the Psalms form a "sacred bridge" (Eric Werner) over the chasm that came to separate them. Christians not only use the Psalms as well as other Old Testament poetry as their own liturgical texts, they also understand them as a school of worship. It is not surprising, therefore, that Christian conceptions of praise should echo and develop the attitudes and philosophies embodied in the Psalms. But Christians not only echo the Psalms' philosophy of praise; they also use the Psalter in their liturgy. Although the early history of this use is obscure, we can tentatively discern three phases in the liturgical use of the Psalms: (1) In ancient Israel, many psalms originated in liturgical settings; (2) in the first century CE, neither Jews nor Christians seem to have made extensive use of psalms in temple, synagogue, and church worship; for both groups, the book of Psalms served rather as a resource for the pious meditation of individuals; (3) later, both Christians and Jews gradually rediscovered the psalms and introduced them into their regular worship; Christians perhaps as early as the late second century CE, Jews after 500 CE.[27]

3. The Practice of Praise in Christianity

From ancient Judaism in general and the book of Psalms in particular, Christianity inherited what we may term the grammar of praise. God is praised when his mighty acts in history are recounted, when personal testimony is given of his dealings with individuals, and when the congregation in its most solemn liturgies joins the angelic choirs in their hymnic adoration. We may speak of celebratory recital, testimony giving, and hymnic adoration as the three elementary forms of Christian praise. Through the centuries, Christians have developed these forms into a rich and sophisticated culture. Monasteries gave celebratory recital a firm institutional basis, Protestant lay people discovered the value of personal testimony, and musicians contributed some of their most famous compositions to hymnic adoration as sung in the Catholic Mass. In this chapter, we will join the canonesses of St. Michael's Convent, listen to evangelical Christians as they give testimony to their congregations, and go to Mass with Mozart.

Reciting God's Mighty Acts in St. Michael's Convent

Like its Old Testament equivalent and model, Christian praise often refers to and indeed lists the mighty acts of God that form the Bible's sacred narrative. The last event the Old Testament includes in the standard story is Yahweh's giving of the promised land to his people. Christians have added to this story. One New Testament passage defines the Christian vocation as a calling to praise God by telling what he did for them. Believers are summoned to "proclaim the mighty acts of him who called you out of darkness into his marvelous light," that is the light of Christ (1 Pet. 2:9). Spiritual authors often echo this biblical passage. For them, worship consists in "the public proclamation of the *mirabilia Dei* [God's wondrous acts]," "the joyful proclamation of his saving deeds" in praise and thanksgiving. "In its liturgy the Church's concern is to proclaim and extoll God's mighty acts in Jesus Christ." Or again, liturgy "reminds us of the powerful deeds of God in Christ. And being reminded we remember, and remembering we celebrate."[28]

What are these mighty saving acts extolled in Christian worship? Explicit and sometimes even elaborate rehearsals of God's acts can be found in some set

texts composed for use in communion worship. One such text, taken from the
Roman Mass, can serve as an example:

> Father, we acknowledge your greatness: all your actions show your wisdom and
> love. You formed man in your own likeness and set him over the whole world to
> serve you, his creator, and to rule over all creatures. Even when he disobeyed
> you and lost your friendship, you did not abandon him to the power of death,
> but helped all men to seek and find you. Again and again you offered a covenant
> to man, and through the prophets taught him to hope for salvation. Father, you
> so loved the world that in the fullness of time you sent your only Son to be our
> Savior.

Starting with creation, God's covenants (with Abraham and Moses), and
prophetic proclamation, this summary of the sacred story culminates in
God's sending of his son. And, as in the Old Testament, the very recital is
praise: acknowledgment of, and thanksgiving for, God's constant efforts to
redeem fallen humanity. The example quoted serves as the introduction to the
celebration of the Eucharist, and scholars have traced back this "narrative"
form to the beginnings of Christian worship. It can be found, for instance, in
the *Didache*, a second-century manual of church order, where it serves as
a prayer to be said after communion. Aptly enough, the Eucharist received
its traditional name from this very type of prayer, for "Eucharist" means
"thanksgiving."[29]

Similar recitals take the form of professions of faith and are spoken by
the whole congregation. "I believe in God, the Father almighty, creator of
heaven and earth. I believe in Jesus Christ, his only Son, our Lord. He was
conceived by the power of the Holy Spirit and born of the Virgin Mary.
He suffered under Pontius Pilate, was crucified, died, and was buried.
He descended to the dead. On the third day he rose again." Far from being
simply statements of belief or miniature catechisms, such texts are actually
understood as praise. Peter Brunner has well expressed their meaning and
mood: "God has intervened, God has acted upon us. We profess and testify to
what he has done with us and for us. The creed is a public acknowledgment and
praise of God's saving act, of the work of Christ, of the Holy Spirit's new
creation. The joy of the saved is its general tenor. It celebrates and rejoices in
salvation."[30]

The references to God's saving acts are often very brief, only reminders of
the divine plan in history. But the underlying pattern makes possible almost
any degree of amplification. The recital of God's acts may be as long as or even
more elaborate than the ten printed pages used in the liturgy proposed by the
fourth-century *Apostolic Constitutions*. In fact, it can structure the whole cycle
of celebrations known as the liturgical year or the church year. It starts with a
period of four weeks called Advent, commemorating the expectation of the

1a. Reciting the Divine Office (1). Several times a day, Catholic nuns, monks, and friars assemble to recite prayers, sing psalms, and listen to spiritual reading. They spend close to two hours each day celebrating the Divine Office or the Liturgy of the Hours. Before recent liturgical reforms, the time spent in the choir stalls could be up to six hours. St. Michaelskloster, Paderborn, Germany, 1995.

Messiah and the ministry of John the Baptist as the forerunner of Jesus. This first phase ends with Christmas, the celebration of Christ's birth. After the lapse of several weeks, a new period begins with a penitential season that prepares for Holy Week. The first day of Holy Week is a Sunday dedicated to Christ's triumphal entrance into Jerusalem (Palm Sunday). Holy Week moves on to the day of the institution of the Lord's Supper on Maundy Thursday and the commemoration of Christ's crucifixion (Good Friday). Finally, it culminates in Easter, the day of Christ's resurrection. In the aftermath of Easter, two Sundays celebrate Christ's ascension to heaven and his sending of the Holy Spirit (Pentecost), respectively. When the Benedictine abbot Prosper Guéranger (1805–75), one of the fathers of the liturgical revival in the Catholic church, wrote about praise as one of the major dimensions of worship, he defined it in terms of the cycle of feasts celebrated in honor of Christ and the saints, which culminate in Easter. For him, the entire liturgical year is born out of an enthusiastic spirit of praise and joy.[31]

While liturgies may not always include actual recitals of the sacred story, that story is always implied, presupposed, and present. God's mighty acts function as the general frame of worship, as the context in which all prayer and praise is firmly set. To borrow terms from linguistics and the study of literature: the Bible's sacred story serves as the foundational "intertext" or "deep structure" of *most* forms of liturgy. However, there is one form of institutionalized prayer that is dominated by or in fact exclusively dedicated to celebratory recital: the

1b. Reciting the Divine Office (2). The German Augustinian canonesses shown here are reciting Evening Prayer (Vespers) which they conclude by saying the Our Father with open and extended hands, an ancient gesture of prayer which they have recently readopted. St. Michaelskloster, Paderborn, Germany, 1995.

Divine Office. In order to introduce the Divine Office, we will look at how the nuns of one specific Catholic convent celebrate it.

On a normal weekday, the Augustinian canonesses of St. Michael's Convent in Paderborn, Germany, meet five times in the choir of their church to celebrate the Office (ills. 1a and 1b). The schedule is as follows:

6.00–6.20 Morning Prayer ("Lauds")
6.50–7.00 Daytime Prayer ("Terce")
15.00–15.25 Office of Readings
18.05–18.30 Evening Prayer ("Vespers")
20.15–20.30 Night Prayer ("Compline")

Between Lauds and Terce, Mass is celebrated. The Catholic nuns spend about an hour and forty minutes every day in the choir, reading scripture and reciting or singing psalms and prayers.

A bell announces prayer time. One by one or in small groups, the nuns enter the chapel in silence. They wear their traditional long black habits, their hair hidden under a simply draped white veil that also covers the throat. A gong invites them to stand up in the choir stalls, arranged in two rows facing each other. A prayer is proposed. One person reads to the others from a lectern. Later, they all—some twenty women—sing or speak in unison. Then a psalm may be presented in Gregorian chant, whereby two choruses alternate, each contributing just one single line. Time and again, the nuns bow their heads as they chant (in German) "Glory to the Father, and to the Son, and to the Holy Spirit; as it was in the beginning, is now, and will be forever. Amen." Then everything seems to be repeated with only slight variation. Eventually, the end of Vespers has arrived. The nuns leave the choir quickly, bowing their heads to a statue of the Virgin and genuflecting to the altar.

To the uninformed visitor, the nuns' liturgy seems like an endless, unstructured sequence of readings, prayers, singing, and chanting. Only upon close study of the nuns' choir books does the Office reveal its careful arrangement, its simple yet profound logic, its implied theology. Almost every word said, read, and sung is taken from a biblical text. Three major elements can be discerned: *biblical readings*, mostly in prose and always read by one person appointed for the task of reader; *psalms*, either chanted or sung in alternate fashion by two choruses; and *canticles*, biblical songs not taken from the Psalms. These key ingredients make up the bulk of what is said, sung, and recited. In them, we can also recognize the underlying theology and logic of the Office.

The biblical readings are generally very short exhortations—two or three biblical verses. In the Office of Readings, however, one longer passage is read, normally about one chapter. It is here that the nuns get a sense of the sacred story as it moves from the Old to the New Testament, from Creation to the Last Judgment, from promise to fulfillment, from Adam and Abraham to Jesus and Paul. The reading celebrates the sacred story in its many details. Key passages are never omitted, and often entire biblical books are read within a few days. Thus the New Testament as a whole is read each year, partly at Mass and partly in the liturgy of the hours. From the Old Testament a selection has been made of those parts "that are of greater importance for the understanding of the history of salvation." As the relevant liturgical legislation explains, the readings are arranged "so as to follow the history of salvation: God reveals himself in the history of his people as he leads and enlightens them in progressive stages." So the readings provide a firm grounding of the entire liturgy in the sacred story, some part of which is recounted every day. Whenever the nuns listen to short extracts from the Bible, these serve as reminders of the larger biblical context and its sacred story.[32]

Although the nuns have their Office of Readings in the afternoon, the liturgical books place it before Morning Prayer. Irrespective of the placement of the Readings, the Word of God has precedence and what follows is a joyful celebration and acclamation of his Word. The ideal sequence of first readings and then hymnic praise reveals the hours' true character of responses to the acts of God recounted in the sacred narrative of the Bible.

The nuns sing or chant twelve psalms (or sections of psalms) each day, and these are selected so that the entire book of Psalms will be read in one month. Only one psalm is used regularly as the first prayer on the nuns' lips each day:

Come let us sing to the Lord
and shout with joy to the Rock who saves us.
Let us approach him with praise and thanksgiving
and sing joyful songs to the Lord.
The Lord is God, the mighty God,
the great king over all the gods.
He holds in his hands the depth of the earth
and the highest mountains as well.
He made the sea; it belongs to him,
the dry land, too, for it was formed by his hands.
Come, then, let us bow down and worship,
bending the knee before the Lord, our maker. (Ps. 95, 1–6)

This psalm, like many others, creates an exalted, joyful atmosphere of praise. In the continuation of Psalm 95, which we have not quoted, reference is made to an episode of the biblical story: to the Israelites' rebellion against God in the wilderness. In this way, a link to the Office of Readings with its panorama of the sacred story is established. The main task of psalmody, however, is to provide an endless variation of praise. Even texts whose wording does not convey a sense of praise and thanksgiving are drawn into the orbit of praise by the so-called doxology appended to each of the psalms recited: "Glory to the Father, and to the Son, and to the Holy Spirit; as it was in the beginning, is now, and will be forever. Amen." While this acclamation punctuates the entire celebration of the Office, an equally characteristic one is used only occasionally: "We celebrate your mighty works with songs of praise."[33]

The third element, the canticle, is always present in the Office. The two canticles the nuns single out as most important are two biblical poems sung every day: the Benedictus at the Morning Prayer and the Magnificat at the Evening Prayer (Luke 1:68–75; 1:46–55). On ordinary days of the week, the nuns of St. Michael's Convent chant rather than sing the psalms. However, they would always sing the two canticles which they consider the culmination of their praise. These canticles praise God for his new initiative of redemption:

Blessed be the Lord, the God of Israel;
he has come to his people and set them free.
He has raised up for us a mighty savior,
born of the house of his servant David. . . .
This was the oath he swore to our father Abraham:
to set us free from the hands of our enemies,
free to worship him without fear,
holy and righteous in his sight
all the days of our life.
Benedictus (Luke 1:68–75)

Whereas the Benedictus praises God for just one deed: the sending of "a mighty savior," the Magnificat extols the Lord with an entire list of divine acts:

> My soul proclaims the greatness of the Lord,
> my spirit rejoices in God my Savior,
> for he has looked with favor on his lowly servant. . . .
> He has mercy on those who fear him
> in every generation.
> He has shown the strength of his arm,
> he has scattered the proud in their conceit.
> He has cast down the mighty from their thrones,
> and has lifted up the lowly.
> He has filled the hungry with good things,
> and the rich he has sent away empty.
> He has come to the help of his servant Israel
> for he has remembered his promise of mercy,
> the promise he made to our fathers,
> to Abraham and his children for ever.
> Magnificat (Luke 1:46–55)

Both poems invoke the relevant Old Testament announcement: "this was the oath he swore to our father Abraham"; "he has remembered his promise of mercy, the promise he made to our fathers, to Abraham and his children for ever." With the coming of the Savior, the sacred story has reached its climax.

Careful readers of the gospel of Luke have often commented on the discrepancy between the idyllic context in which the songs are presented and their actual wording. In the gospel the Magnificat and the Benedictus are attributed to Mary celebrating the upcoming birth of Jesus and to Zechariah celebrating the birth of his son John the Baptist. However, the words seem to be celebrating not the birth of future leaders but rather accomplished military victories. They are reminiscent more of the violent nationalism of the Jewish revolt than of the meekness of Christ. Stimulated by this discrepancy, scholarship has invested much energy in elucidating the background and provenance of these poems. Historically, they seem to antedate Christianity by almost two centuries and what they celebrate is a military event rather than the birth of a hero. They form "a kind of Jewish Marseillaise." The Savior celebrated may have been one of the leaders of the successful Jewish revolt (ca. 166–141 BCE) against Seleucid domination in Palestine: presumably Simon, who achieved independence for his people and created a new Jewish state. The two poems survived in nationalist circles, and even after Palestine fell into the hands of the Romans (63 BCE), they were not forgotten. In John the Baptist's circle, they seem to have been used as songs that, by celebrating victory over the now dominant Roman Empire, would promote and hasten its downfall. The followers of John the

Baptist edited the Benedictus to celebrate John as the immediate precursor of Israel's political liberation. Some manuscripts have actually conserved the gospel's original attribution of the Magnificat to John's mother Elizabeth (rather than to Mary, mother of Jesus).[34]

Some of the nuns may be vaguely aware of the historical background of the Magnificat and the Benedictus, for one of their authorities on biblical exegesis, Father Josef Ernst, has actually written on the subject. Yet, for them, the two canticles celebrate the spiritual event of the coming first of John the Baptist and then Christ. They blend psalmody with the telling of the sacred story. There is no element of petition; as pure praise, the hymns celebrate the sending of Jesus and John the Baptist (Benedictus) and the election of Mary (Magnificat) as mighty, central, and saving acts of God. Like all prayer, the Benedictus and the Magnificat must be understood as "a glorification of God that wells up from the joyful proclamation of his saving deeds: The almighty has done great things for me! Holy is his name! (Luke 1:49)."[35]

The nuns not only take their task of celebrating the Office very seriously. They also study and discuss its meaning, its theology, and spirituality, often through books they have in their library or notes taken during retreats. When asked by me how she understood the Office, one of the younger sisters, Sister Angelika of St. Michael's, disappeared into her study. After a few minutes, she returned with her notes. The various canonical hours, according to these notes, commemorate certain events of the "history of salvation." Lauds celebrates the resurrection of Christ, because the rising sun can be considered an apt symbol of this event. Moreover, Christ actually rose from the dead in the early hours of the morning. At Vespers, one might think of the Lord's Supper celebrated in the evening. The nuns are also reminded of the convent's own morning Mass: thus the day has a kind of eucharistic frame. Finally, Compline, or evening prayer, commemorates the hour of Christ's nocturnal retreat to the Mount of Olives where he prayed fervently in anticipation of his imminent death.

While these ideas may inspire the nuns' reflection and meditation, they have little grounding in the actual texts they sing or recite. The nuns of Paderborn have of course not invented the daily commemoration of events from the sacred story and their association with the canonical hours; they simply subscribe to a tradition that reflects the monastic imagination of both antiquity and the Middle Ages. The *Golden Legend*, compiled in the thirteenth century by James of Voragine, gives one version of what was already a venerable tradition. A church is consecrated, wrote Archbishop James,

in order that God's praises may be sung within it. This is done in the seven canonical hours [of medieval monastic practice], namely Matins, Prime, Terce, Sext, Nones, Vespers, and Compline. For although God is to be praised at every hour of the day, yet, because our weakness could not suffice thereto, it was ordained that we should praise him especially at those hours, for as much as they are more privileged than the others. For at midnight, when Matins are sung, Christ was born, taken captive, and mocked by the Jews. And in that hour he harrowed Hell. . . . Moreover, he rose from the dead before dawn, and appeared at the first hour of the day; and it is said that he will come to the Judgment in the middle of the night. . . . Hence we praise God at midnight [in the Office of Matins] in order to thank him for his birth, for his capture, and for his setting free the fathers [from Hell], and to await his coming watchfully. And the [psalms of] morning praise [Lauds] are added [to Matins], because it was in the morning that God drowned the Egyptians in the sea, created the world, and rose from the dead. Hence we sing [psalms of] praise at that hour, in order not to be submerged with the Egyptians in the sea of this world, and to thank God for our creation and for his Resurrection.

The *Golden Legend* finds for each of the canonical hours a multiplicity of biblical events. Monks and nuns cannot help but be constantly reminded of the sacred story for whose events they praise the Lord. How deeply the medieval symbolism has penetrated the Christian mind can be seen in the Protestant theologian Dietrich Bonhoeffer. When in the 1930s he devised patterns of common prayer for Protestant groups, he echoed the monastic way of thought. "In the dawn of Easter morning, Christ rose in victory from the grave. . . . The early morning belongs to the Church of the risen Christ. At the break of light she remembers the morning on which death and sin lay prostrate in defeat and new life and salvation were given to humankind." Bonhoeffer, not unlike the monks and nuns of all times, defines communal morning prayer as thanksgiving for the new life that appeared with Christ's resurrection.[36]

Before the 1960s (i.e., before the liturgical reform initiated by the Second Vatican Council), spiritual writers and monastic books of rules would distinguish between two groups of the faithful. On the one hand, there are the faithful who are married, live worldly lives, and engage themselves in some business, trade, or profession. On the other hand, there are those who remain celibate, dedicate their entire lives to God alone and, perhaps, to some cause such as educating children, nursing the sick, or helping the poor. Those who belong to the second and much smaller group are bound by canon law to recite the Office. They perform the liturgy of the hours on behalf of and as delegated representatives of the Church. The old book of rules used by the nuns of St. Michael's states quite succinctly that the nuns "have to pray in humility, reverence, and devotion on behalf of the entire Church who has appointed the religious to sing in her name the praises of God, to thank Him, and to deal with Him concerning the various matters relevant to the kingdom of God and eternity." Through their dedication to the liturgy, monastic communities are like living prayer wheels that spin on vicariously for the world that goes about its profane business, taking little notice of its duty to praise the Lord. Did not the Lord once ask Sister Gertrude of Helfta (d. 1302) to pray the psalm "Praise the Lord, all you nations" (Ps. 117) 365 times to compensate for the negligence of others? Monastic praise, as a nineteenth-century spiritual director once remarked, also compensates for those worldly voices that never cease, day and night, to insult and blaspheme God or Christ.[37]

Francis de Sales, a bishop and saint of the seventeenth century, devised a colorful way of referring to the task of the religious. He compared them to birds chirping in a cage and thus delighting and entertaining their master. "The souls, that have locked themselves into the monasteries, act like those little birds: they entertain their master through the melody of their song." At least in sermons preached to nuns the singing of the Divine Office can be termed an entertainment of God. The image of the cage conveys the idea of the ecclesiastical division of labor: while the worldly people go about their mundane business, nuns are set apart for the work of praise.[38]

More recent spiritual writers, and indeed the nuns of St. Michael's Convent, no longer support the idea that religious specialists are set apart to pray. They insist, with a recent reform document, that "the Church's praise is not to be considered either by origin or by nature the exclusive possession of clerics and monks but belongs to the whole Christian community." Nuns, therefore, should not feel obliged to offer praise in seclusion; rather, they should feel "the responsibility of initiating and directing the prayer of the community." In practical terms, this means that worship in the choir ought to be open to all who wish to attend. Ideally, the entire local community of Christians should participate by saying at least their morning and evening prayers together with the nuns.[39]

The *Constitution* of the Augustinian Canonesses, in its revised 1986 version, includes a passage that invites "people who do not belong to our monastic community . . . to participate actively in our liturgy of the hours." Occasionally, the nuns of St. Michael's make an effort to invite others to join their prayer, and their posters can be seen in churches and even in the theology division of the local university. However, very few respond to the invitation. There may be an occasional visitor at Vespers (like the present writer) who enjoys the nuns' beautiful singing and recitations. But usually, the nuns chant or sing their psalms and hymns by themselves. They are regularly joined only by one middle-aged lady, a former teacher at the convent's high school for girls. The general lack of interest does not discourage the nuns. Some of the older members of the community remember a book by a French spiritual director which points out the cosmic meaning of their prayer. In heaven, the Church Triumphant never ceases to pray. In Purgatory, the Suffering Church also prays incessantly. On earth, the Church Militant is represented by those who sing the Office in order to complete the universal praise. Seen with worldly eyes, the twenty-seven nuns and their one novice may seem to represent a lost cause. It is the universal, cosmic dimension of their praise that gives them courage and infuses their song with purpose and significance. As they recite the Divine Office, they feel caught up into a bigger whole—the truly universal Church.[40]

The nuns, educated women several of whom teach at the convent's girls' high school, are aware of the long history of their liturgy of the hours. Most of them have experienced the most recent phase of that history when, in the aftermath of the Second Vatican Council, the Office came to be celebrated in the vernacular rather than in Latin. The Latin language itself indicates the venerable antiquity of the Office.

As often is the case in the history of worship, we know little about the beginnings of particular customs and institutions. The origins of communal praise remain obscure. Early third-century Christian leaders considered congregational Morning Prayer the ideal. The *Apostolic Tradition*, a third-century book of ecclesiastical rules, urges the faithful to go to church every morning. The text implies, however, that some Christians thought themselves too busy to attend. The most characteristic feature of the early morning meeting was the combination of communal praise with instruction by a teacher. Although people were exhorted to go to church, both morning prayer and learning could be done at home in the form of private devotions and personal reading. A hundred years after the *Apostolic Tradition*'s compilation, in 313 CE, Bishop Eusebius tells us of much more elaborate daily prayer meetings. "It is surely no small sign of God's power," wrote the famous church historian and advisor to Emperor Constantine, "that throughout the whole world in the churches of God at the rising of the sun and at the evening hours, hymns, praises, and truly divine delights are offered to God. God's delights are indeed the hymns sent up everywhere in his Church at the times of morning and evening." In episcopal churches like the one of Caesarea in Palestine, where Eusebius held the office of bishop, some of the faithful met both in the early morning and in the late afternoon. They would sing hymns and psalms in honor of God, and they would have such celebrations *every day*. By Eusebius' time, Christians met not just once, as stated in the *Apostolic Tradition*, but twice: morning and evening.[41]

Many early Christians developed great enthusiasm for services of praise. Around 400, John Chrysostom refers to a wealthy landowner and country squire who built his own chapel on his estate and is borne to morning and evening prayer on his litter: "How pleasant to go forth and enter the house of God and know that one built it oneself; to fling himself on his back in his litter, and after the bodily benefit of this pleasant airing, be present at the evening and morning hymns!" However, going to church not only belonged to the pleasures of country life; it could also provide a sacred rhythm to urban existence. In the report of a Spanish noblewoman who visited the city of Jerusalem in the 380s, we read of no fewer than five daily celebrations of singing. In Jerusalem, the faithful met before daybreak and began to praise the Lord; at daybreak, they entered the church to sing the morning hymns. They met again at noon, at three o'clock, and at four. Priests and the bishop were present, and through priestly prayers and episcopal blessings the various services received an official, liturgical character. Although Jerusalem, as a center of pilgrimage and favorite place of monks and nuns, may have been exceptional, its five prayer meetings indicate the general trend of liturgical development. Corporate prayer became more frequent, and in places like Jerusalem it began to structure the day of the bishop, his clergy, monks, and some of the lay people who lived close to the church.[42]

Can we account for the progressive multiplication of daily prayer meetings—which meant, at least for people engaged in some kind of work or business, a frequent and not necessarily welcome interruption? Apparently, fourth-century Christians were responding to the scriptural injunction to "pray without ceasing," which, for them, did not sound as impractical as it does for us (1 Thess. 5:17). Ceaseless prayer could of course be performed individually and in private. However, the faithful preferred institutionalized and structured communal prayer as a procedure that enabled them to comply more easily with St. Paul's injunction.[43]

Later, the system of daily prayer meetings was given the name of Divine Office or, more recently, the Liturgy of the Hours. The various hours at which people met received their own names. The prayer before daybreak would be called the Vigil, the first service at daylight Matins or Lauds, the late-afternoon celebration Vespers or Evensong, and so on. Some of these names are still used.

The Liturgy of the Hours, as celebrated in major churches and cathedrals, has a complex history with alternating periods of decline and revival. Both decline and reinvigoration largely depend on the way Christians organize their lives. Whenever they practice intense forms of communal existence, there is a chance that communal praise will have a resurgence of popularity. In one milieu this prerequisite has always existed and therefore the Liturgy of the Hours has always flourished without interruption: in monasticism. St. Benedict's classic *Rule* for monks, compiled around 530 CE, makes the monk's participation in a daily round of praise compulsory. Benedictine monks—and many nuns, monks, and friars whose rules echo the mind of Benedict—normally meet eight times a day in a special section of their church, aptly called a "choir," in order to sing or recite the Divine Office. Benedict himself established detailed and precise rules for this liturgy, which he termed the *opus Dei* or *opus divinum*, "the work of God." He also determined that "nothing is to be set before the work of God" (*nihil operi Dei praeponatur*). This "work" takes between four and five hours every day; the rest of the monk's time is divided between individual devotional reading and manual work. In order to ensure the primacy of praise, the day was begun as well as concluded with the singing of psalms. All recitation and singing was of course done in Latin, the official language of the church.[44]

At the center of the Divine Office as celebrated by the Benedictine monks stand the psalms. In the early period, an individual singer sang a psalm while the community listened to it as the word of God. Those present might have added the same single verse or an exclamation like *hallelujah* in response to each verse; but they still listened. The heart of the early monastic Office was silent meditation. The psalms provided the "food" for prayer. The monks listened to the words of the psalm, engaged in interior reflection on its meaning, and prayed for the grace necessary to grow spiritually. The Divine Office was thus part of an ascetical exercise, directed toward individual sanctification. Only gradually did the monks discover the psalms' own intrinsic meaning, which is often that of praise, and then the division between an individual singer and the listening community was abandoned. *All* the faithful sing, not merely one soloist. The congregation is divided into two choirs, and these alternately sing a verse to each other.[45]

While earlier only the soloist stood while the other monks sat and listened, now all stand and sing. The prayers that had come to be attached to each psalm are now omitted. They have been replaced by a Trinitarian doxology, a word of praise: "Glory to the Father, and to the Son, and to the Holy Spirit; as it was in the beginning, is now, and will be forever. Amen." Now the psalms themselves are considered prayers of praise, and this view is made explicit in the doxology. The new addition concludes and summarizes the essential and invariable content of each psalm. It says, as it were: if you do not understand the words, here is the meaning—*Glory to the Father*, etc. Or, if the actual wording of a psalm has little to do with praise, the doxology supplies the missing words of homage.

Doxologies such as the one used to conclude the psalms belong to the oldest and most common Christian language of praise. The *Didache* (a second-century book of ecclesiastical discipline) and many New Testament manuscripts (beginning in the fifth century CE) add a doxology to the Lord's Prayer; with but few variations, it reads: "For the kingdom, the power, and the glory are yours, now and forever." This addition no doubt reflects liturgical usage. Early scribes were steeped in the liturgy and transcribed the text as they knew it from church. Similar concluding sentences also developed along with the formation of patterned liturgies. In the third century, according to Origen, each proper prayer ended with "praise of God through Christ in the Holy Spirit."[46]

For all its brevity, the Trinitarian doxology is pregnant with meaning. In addition to serving as a prayer conclusion, at one point it also served as a significant dogmatic statement in a doctrinal controversy. Between the fourth and the sixth centuries, the formulaic prayer conclusion became a source of discord. Some Christians preferred a form close to the one we find in Origen, because they took it to imply a subordination of Christ to the Father. Others insisted on placing the Son and the Holy Spirit on a level with the Father, emphasizing their equality and eternity. Thus they added the following words to their prayers: "Glory to the Father, and to the Son, and to the Holy Spirit;

as it was in the beginning, is now, and will be forever." The Son and the Spirit, like the Father, have always existed, will continue to exist, and they all share the same glory. In their original Greek and Latin forms, variations of this text date from the third century. They found their way into vernacular psalmody and hymnody and are used to this day by many Christian groups. The formula attests to the victory of a particular version of Trinitarian belief. Punctuating psalmody and being attached to many prayers like a seal, doxologies serve as a constant reminder of praise. Without such a seal, prayers would be incomplete, and without the omnipresent reminder being woven into its texture, traditional liturgy would lose much of its dense aura of adoration.[47]

The introduction and constant use of the doxology, then, indicates a new understanding of the meaning of psalmody. The worshipping community no longer felt that psalms should merely be listened to. Instead, they are considered to be hymns of praise that should be—and actually are—sung by the entire community. While participants continued to pay attention to *how* God is praised in each psalm, we also hear of monks who simply tried to keep their mind absorbed in God. They recited the words without attending to their meaning. In this practice, praise itself, with its quality of bringing us near to God, was more important than the precise meaning of its words.[48]

By the ninth or tenth century, the trend toward making the Divine Office a pure liturgy of praise was complete. It was not only liturgical sensibilities cultivated in monasteries that had contributed to this development; it also had to do with the new social profile of Western monasticism. As monasteries became wealthy, they increasingly attracted young men of noble families. Since manual labor was now taken care of by lay servants, the priest monks, unaccustomed to such labor on account of their feudal background, needed a more spiritual occupation. According to one commentator on St. Benedict's *Rule*, spiritual reading or the chanting of psalms may legitimately take the place of labor. Thus the monastery became a place of reading, silent study, and meditation, but also of the chanting of psalms. As a matter of fact, liturgy came to be considered the monastery's main task. "The proper and distinctive work of the Benedictine," explains an abbot, "his portion, his mission, is the liturgy. He makes his profession in order to be one in the Church—the society of divine praise—who glorifies God according to the forms instituted by herself." The monastery sees itself as a palace or court with God as the divine ruler at its center. The Liturgy of the Hours serves as "the daily service and formal homage rendered to the divine majesty." That liturgy forms "the crown of the whole structure of the monastic edifice." The singing of the Psalms in praise of God became the *raison d'être* of the monk.[49]

Monks not only adhered to St. Benedict's *Rule*, which required that "nothing be set before the Work of God." Occasionally, they exceeded this standard, reciting not just the 37 psalms prescribed by the *Rule*, but another 101 or 138 psalms in addition. Or they maintained a *laus perennis*, a perpetual praise with groups of monks taking their shift in the choir and reciting some 450 psalms around the clock, that is three times the entire book of Psalms each day! When visiting the monastery of Cluny, France, in 1063, Peter Damian observed that "the Offices succeeded each other with such rapidity, that even in the long days of summer there remains only half an hour in which the brethren can talk in the cloister." Although these excesses occurred only during brief periods in some medieval monasteries, they show that monks and nuns prolonged rather than shortened the time they spent in glorifying the Lord.[50]

Irrespective of how much time medieval monks devoted to communal prayer, communities admitted to the choir only healthy, strong persons. Although this ideal of physical fitness may echo notions inherited from the lifestyle of the nobility, it can be explained in terms of the lengthy Office, which demanded considerable stamina. As a measure of mercy, the main choir was barred to those who could not stand through the long ceremony. The arthritic, the lame, the old, the weak, and those stricken by some infirmity or having to lean on crutches were not admitted. These physically handicapped monks had their own, smaller choir—separated from, but close to, the main one. Praying and meditating in silence, they listened to the others as they sang the Psalms. Physical strength, once spent in manual labor, went into liturgical activity.[51]

The excessive psalmody practiced in some medieval monasteries has long since disappeared. The weak and the old have returned to the main choir. The official Catholic Liturgy of the Hours, as revised under Pope Paul VI and introduced in the 1970s, prescribes nuns, monks, and clerics to recite no more than twelve psalms a day, and the whole Psalter is distributed over a month. Reducing the number of psalms is not indicative of their devaluation. Owing to their venerable antiquity, traditional status, lyrical beauty, and musical quality, they are still held in high esteem. With their joyous atmosphere of praise, they provide an ideal setting for the reading of the sacred story of salvation. In fact, they belong to this story as responses to God's mighty acts.

Praise in Prose, or From Puritan Relation to Evangelical Testimony-Giving

As we have seen, the celebratory recital of God's mighty acts, apart from being the specialty of monks and nuns, forms part of all Christian worship. Occasionally, the recital is supplemented by congregational thanksgiving for events that concern the life of the worshipping community in a more immediate sense. God not only acted in biblical times; he still acts today. The Book of Common Prayer, the Anglican Church's traditional book of worship, includes a special section of prayers in which the community thanks God "For Rain; For fair Weather; For Plenty [a plentiful harvest]; For Peace and Deliverance from our Enemies; For Restoring Publick Peace at Home; For Deliverance from the Plague, or other common Sickness." While we may smile at the English habit of placing thanks for rain before that for fair weather, the list reveals to us the existential issues of sixteenth-century communities that had to live in a world marked not only by an overcast sky, but also by war, famine, and mortal sickness. This special section was inserted in the Book of Common Prayer in 1562, at the request of the Puritans; the Puritans thereby asserted their strong sense of being "Israelites": a people to whom God speaks through rain and drought, war and peace, sickness and recovery. Twentieth-century theological sensibilities add one more item (at least) to the list of events for which a congregation can express its thankfulness: someone's completed life. The Anglican memorial service celebrated after someone's death is sometimes designed as "a Service of Thanksgiving for the life and work of N." When the memorial service for Miss Rachel Pearse, headmistress of a girls' school, was held at St. Martin-in-the-Fields, her colleagues and former pupils thanked God for her as a divine gift made to them.[52]

While churches continue to practice thanksgiving for events that concern all or most of their members, individualism has also left its mark on worship. Alongside the more traditional theologies of communal praise, a new kind has emerged and increasingly gained acceptance. Individual thanksgiving, in the form of giving personal testimony to God's activity, has become a regular feature of worship especially in charismatic and free-Protestant churches. During ordinary services ministers sometimes call Christian lay persons to speak up and give "testimony." Individuals are asked to tell the congregation what the Lord has done with them and for them. They might hesitate, then eventually pluck up courage and speak about being drawn out of a sinful or meaningless life. Young and old people, men and women, and even children will tell how they found faith in Christ and how Jesus transformed their lives, bringing them from nominal church membership to true belief and sincere commitment. At other times they might explain how their prayers have been answered, how the Lord has helped them in unexpected and unforeseeable ways, or how their lives have been affected by God in the past week or month. They also tell about the dreams and revelations they have received from the Lord. Like their Puritan or Methodist ancestors, members of contemporary charismatic communities delight in sharing their experiences.

Testimonies can be as short as a few sentences, forming just one element of a service of worship. But they can also be long and become the center around which the service is organized. This was the case when, in an English church in 1912, a woman told her story. She related how she had had a bad swelling in her breast. After giving many circumstantial details of names, dates, and places, her testimony culminated in a triumphal "I'm healed. The Lord has healed me and blessed me. . . . Glory to Jesus." Deeply moved, the congregation joined the healed woman in her thanksgiving. In the report printed in a church magazine, the writer does not fail to mention the congregational applause: "You won't be surprised to hear that we sang the Hallelujah Hymn Chorus *twice over*, with all our hearts saying, Praise Him! Praise Him!" Without a congregational response, the act of thanksgiving would be incomplete, because praise must engender further praise.[53]

While the individual thanksgiving is a decidedly modern phenomenon, its deep historical roots can be traced back to the Bible. We have seen how in Old Testament times individuals celebrated and sang about the help they received from Yahweh. In the New Testament, we find immediate and spontaneous praise as the regular response to Jesus' acts of healing: "Woman, you are set free from your ailment." When Jesus had laid his hands on her, "immediately she stood up straight and began praising God" (Luke 13:13; cf. 18:43). Others then join in that thanksgiving: "The whole multitude began to praise God joyfully with a loud voice for all the deeds of power they had seen" (Luke 19:37). Witnesses to divine intervention, the curious onlookers and passers-by suddenly find themselves united to form a choir that sings in acknowledgment of the deeds of power they have seen with their own eyes. Interestingly, one gospel passage shows how Jesus himself can be included in this praise. One man, realizing that Christ had healed him from leprosy, turned back, "praising God with a loud voice. He prostrated himself at Jesus' feet and thanked him" (Luke 17:15–16). Christian thanksgiving, like its Old Testament equivalents, is rooted in the experience of some powerful event. Closely tied to such events, which at least for the believers are obvious and tangible, it is pragmatic and looks forward to further experience. Pragmatic praise assumes that God's help is not confined to ages past; it reaches down to our own generation and will continue. Some Christians feel that in their own lives, first in their conversion, and then often thereafter, they have been helped, protected, or commissioned by the Lord. They would make the biblical Magnificat (the prayer with which the Virgin Mary praised God) their own song: "My soul magnifies the Lord, and my spirit rejoices in God my Savior . . . for the Mighty One has done great things for me" (Luke 1:47.49).

Throughout history, Christian individuals have never failed to thank God for answering prayers, for his intervention in their lives, and for his guidance, which they have seen as real and tangible. Some Christians celebrate their thanksgiving in public. In the early church, this was quite common, and from Augustine we can get an idea of its ritual. After someone had experienced a miraculous cure or deliverance, he would urge him or her "to publish an account of it that it might be read to the people." In the *City of God*, Augustine recalls the cure of Paulus and Palladia from a "hideous shaking in all their limbs," an event that took place near the relics of St. Stephen, which were displayed in a chapel of the bishop's church in Hippo, North Africa. Augustine had the story written down immediately, and a few days later, he held a special service for them. He made brother and sister stand on the steps of the platform from which he used to preach, presenting them to "the whole congregation, men and women alike" while he read out their story. As we might expect, it ends on a note of thanksgiving. For Augustine, the public reading and presentation completed the joyful shouting of "Thanks to God! Praised be God" with which people had responded on the Easter Sunday the miracle had happened. Augustine's account shows us the shift from a spontaneous expression of joy and praise to a public, more ordered ritual of thanksgiving.[54]

The public expression of thanksgiving for God's activity in individual Christian lives, though rarely documented, did continue in later history. An interesting account of public thanksgiving comes from present-day Indonesia. Among Indonesian Presbyterians a family that has been through a crisis issues invitations at church and also invites non-Christian relatives and neighbors. At worship the father or mother says a prayer of thanks, a passage from the Bible is read and explained, and a hymn sung. Eventually, the guests share a meal to which all contribute, the family serving rice and tea. Or, after a member's return from hospital, the community organizes a thanksgiving meeting (*ucapan syukur*) in the returnee's home. In Indonesia, as in the Old Testament, thanksgiving is considered a public act.[55]

Often, however, Christians have preferred more private settings for their worship. There they address their thanksgiving to a patron saint whom they trust as a powerful intercessor with God. Rather than invite others, they go to a church or chapel and light a candle, place flowers in front of a statue of the Virgin Mary, or put a coin into a collection-box placed at the feet of St. Anthony. They might also visit pilgrimage shrines dedicated to St. Patrick. Sometimes, they sponsor the painting of a picture to be placed in a church or chapel. Most of the traditional European pilgrimage shrines have impressive collections of ex-votos: garments, models of healed legs, feet, fingers, and other limbs, crutches of grateful devotees, cured of deformities or disease. Catholic votive gifts, like their ancient Greek models, are symbols (condensed stories) of supernatural help and healing, easily understood by the faithful, even the illiterate to whom they are displayed. They serve as miniature monuments, dedicated to the glory of Christ, God, or a saint. While most ex-votos carry no written message, others are inscribed with short and simple texts like "Merci mère" or "Thank you." Occasionally longer texts publish the saving act of God done at the intercession of a saint. To this day, American newspapers frequently carry advertisements in gratitude to St. Jude. Thus divine intervention is made public and the power of a saint celebrated.

Just as it opposed the cult of the saints, the Reformation also fought against and abolished the popular custom of giving votive offerings for divine blessings. Protestants prefer communal forms of worship to the private dealings of individuals with patron saints. But the idea survived that divine help should be acknowledged and made public. Among independent Protestant denominations with a strong belief in the priesthood of all believers, individual thanksgiving took on new institutionalized forms. This is especially evident among the early Puritans, the early Moravians, and Methodists, as well as groups belonging to the Pentecostal and charismatic movements.

Testimony-giving began in New England, in the 1630s, among the Puritan congregations that split from the established Church. In these congregations, new members were not only scrutinized regarding their beliefs, they were also expected to give evidence about their spiritual life: their struggle with sin, their calling by God, and their gradual conversion to true faith in God. At first, applicants seeking to join a congregation were heard and scrutinized by the elders. However, other members became interested in listening to the stories of faith, and so the admission procedure became a formal event in the presence of the entire congregation. Had not Timothy, in biblical days, also "professed a good profession *before many witnesses*" (1 Tim. 6:12)? At the conclusion of the afternoon service on Sunday, people could listen to the stories of male and female applicants—with men delivering their speech in person and women having it read out for them and expressing their assent. The congregation could ask questions and eventually voted on the rejection or admission. The 1648 "Platform of Church Discipline," drawn up by leading Puritan divines, explained the practice and recommended it to all congregations.[56]

At least some of those questioned enjoyed the opportunity to speak, and their "relations" bordered on preaching. But of course, more popular than talking was listening, which Cotton Mather, in 1702, praised as a "useful curiosity." Mather (1663–1728), an eminent Puritan divine and early historian of American Christianity, defended the practice against the accusation of being a measure of "tyranny" and "cruelty." He saw no reason to depart from the "Platform of Church Discipline," among whose authors he lists his grandfather, Richard Mather. "Nothing is more for the honor of God," he insisted, "or for the comfort of his people, than to hear good Christians thus making that invitation: Come and hear, all ye that fear God, and I will declare what he hath done for my soul [Ps. 66:16]." While Cotton Mather refers only to the public admission procedure of fifteen minutes, we hear of more informal settings called "experience meetings," where people exchanged their stories. Early sources report such meetings in New England during the 1630s and in England in the 1650s. Listening to "relations" of God's dealings with individuals—in their conversions as well as in their daily lives—thus became a popular sacred entertainment. Puritan divines recorded people's stories in their notebooks and some made their edifying collections available in print. The Puritans created a new mode of publishing the mighty acts God worked in the hearts of the faithful. And at the same time, they created new opportunities for individuals to extoll their Savior. One John Collins, in the 1650s, ended his relation on a note of thanksgiving, like most of those speaking about their own lives did in similar words: "I do therefore with all all thanks bless his name."[57]

The Puritan "relation" did not survive the seventeenth century. In 1679, the (Puritan) Reforming Synod of America, while requiring applicants to give "a personal and public profession of their faith and repentance," no longer insisted on "a relation of the work of God's Spirit upon their hearts." A generation later, divines like Jonathan Edwards (1703–58) came to think of it as lacking a basis in scripture: "There is no footstep in the Scripture of any such way of the apostles, or primitive ministers and Christians requiring any such relation."[58]

In the eighteenth century, Moravians and Methodists created their own equivalent of the Puritan experience meetings. The idea seems to go back to Count Zinzendorf, one of the esteemed founding fathers of German pietism. In 1727, Count Zinzendorf made the Agape or love-feast a regular event in his Moravian community at Herrnhut (near Dresden, Germany), claiming that he was simply restoring early Christian practice. The new service involved a common meal, with token food and drink. Its main features, however, were prayer, praise, and fellowship, with the emphasis on personal testimony and thanksgiving. John Wesley had attended such meetings when he met Moravians in America and Germany in 1737–38. As the Methodist movement began to develop its own forms of communal and liturgical life, Wesley adopted the love-feast as a sacred fellowship. "We had a happy love-feast at the chapel [in London]," he noted in his diary on March 1, 1761. "Many of our brethren spoke plainly and artlessly what God had done for their souls. I think none were offended; but many were strengthened and comforted." Giving instruction on how to conduct the feast, Wesley declared: "The very design of a love-feast is free and familiar conversation, in which every man, yea, and woman, has liberty to speak whatever may be to the glory of God."[59]

"I think none were offended." What to some may have seemed strange, soon developed into a widely followed practice among Methodists. Love-feasts, according to an early report, "commence with praise and prayer. In a few minutes a little bread and water is distributed, and a collection is made for the poor. The great portion of the time allowed, which is generally about two hours, is occupied by such as feel disposed, in relating their own personal experience of the saving grace of God." On such occasions, testimonies from more than twenty individuals might be heard. Praise culminated in, and was nourished by, testimonies that celebrated the goodness of God. Love-feasts were very popular with early Methodists, who described them as "generally very agreeable, edifying, and refreshing seasons."[60]

During the nineteenth century, the giving of testimonies became increasingly unpopular among Moravians and Methodists. Although Methodist love-feasts continued to be held in some communities until the 1960s, they were no longer considered an important form of worship. With the Moravians, they ceased to be occasions for speaking about one's fellowship with God. As the early enthusiasm waned, many felt uneasy about sharing their most intimate feelings. Religion, for them, belonged to the privacy of their heart. People began to forget, in the words of a twentieth-century Methodist, that a testimony "celebrates the graciousness of God, and not the fruits of personal striving and achievement."[61]

While the giving of personal, autobiographical accounts declined in Europe, it gained some popularity at "revivals" and in the ordinary Sunday services of American Baptists, Adventists, Christian Scientists, and Mormons. When in 1825 the revivalist Charles Finney made lay testimony a regular feature of his ministry, he happened to work in a Methodist environment. In the case of the "camp" or "tent" revivals, the Methodist connection can also be discerned, for Methodists participated in them with much enthusiasm. A typical American camp meeting of the early nineteenth century invited hundreds of people to spend a few days with an assorted group of ministers and lay helpers. These meetings were held somewhere out in the country, where people would stay in tents and pass the day in singing and listening to preachers. Preaching was designed to reinvigorate faith or to produce conversions to true belief in Christ. Lay "exhorters" and the testimonies of new converts supported the ministerial activity. A report, written by a Methodist minister in 1824, describes a love-feast held at a Tennessee camp. Many of the two hundred persons admitted to the feast "testified the great things that God had done for them," while floods of tears burst from the eyes of those attending. At the "First National Camp-Meeting of American Methodists," held in Vineland, New Jersey, in 1867, lay testimony was given in abundance and was included in the published report of the event.[62]

Testimony-giving also became a common feature of some free-Protestant churches, where it developed as a variety of lay preaching which can be traced back to the 1600s. As ministers became increasingly well educated and trained in the Bible, lay preaching seemed more and more inadequate. So ministers like the Baptist Jacob Knapp began in the mid-nineteenth century to limit lay speaking to "tell[ing] what God had done for their souls." This attitude reso-nated especially with women who, as some authors assure us, love to tell their story. Among the first to promote or introduce the giving of testimony in regular worship were three women whose informal meetings provided the opportunity to experiment with new, modern forms: Phoebe Palmer (1807–74), a Methodist revivalist; Ellen White (1827–1915), a former Methodist who became an early leader and prophet of the Adventist church; and Mary Baker Eddy (1821–1910), the founder of Christian Science. As early as the 1830s, Mrs. Palmer presided at a ladies' meeting, held every Tuesday afternoon in her home in New York. This meeting was later opened to men, and became a well-known institution, a mixture of social event, service of worship, and inquiry meeting, spiced with reports on spiritual experiences. There can be little doubt that Mrs. Palmer had knowledge of the Methodist love-feast and its ritual of narrative praise. In her ladies' meeting, an honorable Methodist institution came back to life. The same can be said of the corresponding institution in the Seventh-day Adventist church. Ellen White, before assuming leadership in her own group, not only belonged to a Methodist church but had also stood up in one of this church's "class meetings" and testified about her experience of the love of Christ. Later, she introduced the giving of testimonies to Adventism. In 1851 Mrs. White insisted that Sabbath meetings should be "interesting," with the faithful contributing "short, pointed testimonies and prayers." Since in heaven the angels cry their "holy, holy, holy" day and night, why should we be afraid of telling the same story over and over again? She explained that

> All have not the same experience in their religious life. But those of diverse experiences come together and with simplicity and humbleness of mind talk out their experience. All who are pursuing the onward Christian course should have, and will have, an experience that is living, that is new and interesting. A living experience is made up of daily trials, conflicts, and temptations, strong efforts and victories, and great peace and joy gained through Jesus. A simple relation of such experiences gives light, strength, and knowledge that will aid others in their advancement in the divine life. The worship of God should be both interesting and instructive to those who have any love for divine and heavenly things.

While Ellen White could refer to the testimony as "instruction," stressing its didactic side, she could also comment on testimonies being "full of joy and praise to God." Hence the Adventist tradition of the "praise service."[63]

Mary Baker Eddy gave clear instructions about the matter. Because her church is based on spiritual healing, reports of success were (and still are) important for attracting prospective members and strengthening the faith of the converted. In the 1890s, Eddy established a weekly "experience or testimonial meeting" at which people would testify about their healing. "More than a mere rehearsal of blessings," she explains, public testimony "scales the pinnacle of praise and illustrates the demonstration of Christ, 'who healeth all thy diseases' (Ps. 103:3)." To this day, Christian Scientists have their testimony meetings on Wednesday evenings.[64]

By the end of the nineteenth century, testimony-giving had achieved a definite form and style and could be imitated by other groups. With twentieth-century charismatic Christians, Christian Scientists, Adventists, Mormons, and many independent Protestant churches, it has become a regular feature of worship. As we have seen, it took its inspiration from the Methodist love-feasts, which in turn were inspired by Moravian practice. In creating or adopting this new form of public thanksgiving, the promoters never thought of themselves as innovators, for the practice of the individual's public praise of God has recognizable biblical roots.

Despite their great variety of style and content, testimonies can generally be defined as autobiographical stories that include a religious interpretation. Without that interpretation, the story would not be a testimony and therefore, in the eyes of the congregation, not worth telling. The religious coloring, however, is not imposed upon an event as a debatable opinion coming from the outside. Perceiving the world in a religious way, those who give a testimony inhabit a Christian universe. If a crisis is overcome, it is the Lord who has helped. If a bad dream has shown evil powers entering a house like swarming insects, this is taken to be evidence of Satan's last assault before the Lord's return. What to the outsider may appear as mere rhetoric is in fact deeply ingrained in the minds of the faithful, who cannot suppress the automatic functioning of a perceptional set nourished or "conditioned" by the biblical story as well as by other testimonies they have heard. In their minds, all the stories they have ever heard or read, biblical and nonbiblical, blend to create a universe in which God and evil powers are constantly at work.[65]

Although individual thanksgiving has biblical roots, its particular emphasis is decidedly "modern." It relies on an empirical, experiential view of religion, a conception of personal faith, and a do-it-yourself attitude combined with a democratic sense of worship. Faith, for many Christians, does not mean simply believing what the church believes and teaches. Rather, it means having a personal relationship with God, who is to be trusted as a caring father. In the eyes of many Puritans and Methodists, the relationship with the Father has its basis in an individually concluded and publicly ratified covenant. This covenant obliges the human partner to be faithful to the Lord, while God provides fatherly care, protection, guidance, and even miracles. Many modern Christians refuse to leave preaching to trained specialists and to rely on a spiritual elite for religious experience. Unlike the recital form of praise, the giving of a testimony does not presuppose liturgical expertise and specialized biblical learning; nor does it rely on choirs, orchestras, and set texts. Every believer, every lay person can, and perhaps should, give a testimony. Since no special training, preparation, or ordination are required, one can speak of it as a function of the "priesthood of all the faithful," exercised in free, informal, non-clericalized worship. The Reformation idea of general priesthood blends with the concept of equality in a democratic world and leads to what Catherine Albanese has termed "the glorification of the common people." We can also invoke the modern, democratic ideal of balancing and tempering the expertise of specialists with the lay person's wisdom and practical sense. In worship, as in the work of parliaments, "expertocracy" must be avoided. Far from being a one-man show conducted by a trained minister, worship is seen as a communal matter to which all are welcome to contribute. In New Testament times Paul wrote, "When you come together, each one has a hymn, a lesson, a revelation, a tongue, or an interpretation" (1 Cor. 14:26). Modern, democratic forms of praise restore the forgotten Pauline ideal.[66]

Hymnic Adoration, or At Mass with Mozart

While pragmatic praise given in the form of testimony or sacred recital belongs to earth and reflects God's intervention on behalf of an individual or the chosen people, adoration is the pure praise typical of heaven. Human beings have no regular access to the divine world; in exceptional cases the likes of a seer may be admitted for a short moment. Such admission was granted to John of Patmos, who reports on what he heard and saw in the book of Revelation. He saw and heard the seraphim, angelic attendants to the divine throne, singing unceasingly "Holy, holy, holy, the Lord God the Almighty" in homage to their Lord (Rev. 4:8; cf. Isa. 6:3).

According to John's report, another group of throne attendants, twenty-four men called the elders, respond to the threefold calls of "holy" by prostrating themselves and then divesting themselves of their priestly crowns. Standing before God, human persons must humble themselves. And as they prostrate themselves, the elders chant: "You are worthy, our Lord and God, to receive glory and honor and power, for you created all things and by your will they existed and were created" (Rev. 4:11). Prostration is the appropriate gesture and praise the appropriate word said or sung in the presence of God. While the expression of praise is motivated by creation ("for you created all things"), any reference to specific acts on behalf of human beings is absent. We are in heaven, not on earth!

The idea—and prophetic experience—of the hymnic affirmation of God's sovereignty in heaven has made a tremendous impact. In texts and hymns designed for regular use at church, in theological reflection, and not least, in music, it shaped, and continues to shape, Christian liturgy.

The most typical hymn of adoration is, of course, the threefold acclamation of "holy" in which Christians join the seraphim in their praise of God. Presumably introduced during the third or fourth century, this hymn, known in Latin as the Sanctus, has become part of most Christian liturgies and is often sung with much power and expression. Liturgies find ever new words to give this simple acclamation an appropriate, majestic setting. In the Catholic Mass, it may be given the following introduction:

> Father in heaven, it is right that we should give you thanks and glory: you are the one God, living and true. Through all eternity you live in unapproachable light. Source of life and goodness, you have created all things, to fill you creatures with every blessing and lead all men to the joyful vision of your light. Countless hosts of angels stand before you to do your will; they look upon your splendor and praise you, night and day. United with them, and in the name of every creature under heaven, we too praise your glory as we sing: Holy, holy, holy Lord, God of power and might, heaven and earth are full of your glory. Hosanna in the highest. Blessed is he who comes in the name of the Lord. Hosanna in the highest. (*Roman Missal* of Paul VI)

While the hymn culminates in the threefold acclamation of "holy" addressed to God, it does not end there. The concluding words turn the attention to Christ, who is also praised, in this case not with the angelic song but with the words shouted by the crowd as he entered Jerusalem. The Hebrew word "hosanna" literally asks Christ to have mercy and deliver from evil, but here it has assumed, as Augustine explains, the meaning of "glory."[67]

Besides the Sanctus, the *Gloria in excelsis*, a Latin text first attested in the fifth century, ranks as another classic hymn of adoration. The *Book of Common Worship* (1993, Presbyterian) uses the following English version:

> Glory to God in the highest,
> and peace to God's people on earth.
> Lord God, heavenly King,
> almighty God and Father,
> we worship you, we give you thanks,
> we praise you for your glory.
> *Lord Jesus Christ, only Son of the Father.*
> *Lord God, Lamb of God,*
> *you take away the sin of the world;*
> *have mercy on us;*
> *you are seated at the right hand of the Father:*
> *receive our prayer.*
> For you alone are the Holy One,
> you alone are the Most High,
> Jesus Christ,
> with the Holy Spirit,
> in the glory of God the Father.

In Christian worship, hymns of adoration are used in the context of celebrating the mighty acts of God. The biblical story of God's sending of his Son to earth is dominant. Firmly set in this context, the hymns supplement the ever-present biblical story. However, this story not only frames the hymns; it also forms part of them, so that a clear distinction between recital and adoration seems difficult. The Gloria, for instance, starts as an "adoration" of God, whose heavenly glory, in the manner of Isaiah's seraphic hymn, radiates down to earth. After a few lines, however, it abandons the adoration by referring to facts of the sacred story and addresses a petition to Christ (printed in italics). In other words: the Gloria, like many hymns, does not represent a pure example of the "adoration" form of praise. If liturgical hymns like the Gloria cannot be identified as belonging to the adoration type of praise, this does not mean that they do not *include* adoration. While a twentieth-century reader would most likely analyze the entire hymn as a meaningful textual unit, this "holistic" approach was not always used in the past. Composers who set the Gloria to music often divided the text into what musicologists term "movements" and "sub-movements," treating each one as a separate unit, giving every unit independent musical articulation. We can compare this "fragmentation" approach with that of some readers of the Bible who, instead of reading an entire letter of St. Paul in continuous fashion, treat it as a collection of wise sayings that can be appreciated individually. Using their method of fragmentation, composers treated the beginning and the end of the Gloria as a hymn of adoration.

The Sanctus and the Gloria do not exhaust the repertoire of hymnic praise. Through the centuries, Christian hymn writers have vied with one another in creating ever new hymns of adoration, of which Charles Wesley's "Lo! God is here, let us adore" is but one example found in contemporary hymnals:

> Lo! God is here! him day and night
> The united choirs of angels sing;
> To him, enthroned above all height,
> Heaven's host their noblest praises bring.
> Disdain not, Lord, our meaner song,
> Who praise thee with a stammering tongue.[68]

While mainly a matter of liturgical practice, hymnic adoration has also received theological comment and justification. The explanations which John Chrysostom gave in the fourth century and which Sicard of Cremona gave in the twelfth have often been repeated. According to John Chrysostom, it is legitimate for the faithful to join the angels in singing the Sanctus, because "Christ has removed the separating wall [between heaven and earth] . . . and made one realm of the two." In the Sanctus, explains Sicard of Cremona, "human beings and angels unite in singing the praises of the King. Since it represents the angelic praise, it is to be sung with loud and beautiful voice." Sicard and his twelfth-century contemporaries were well-acquainted with the courtly acclamation of kings. They understood that the Sanctus was the celestial version of the mundane *laudes regiae* of their own day. Hymnic adoration, in joining the faithful and the angels to form a unified choir, obliterates the difference between material and spiritual creatures, between heaven and earth. Theologians were so enthusiastic about the idea that they spoke of praise as our only occupation in life everlasting. In the uncompromising words of Augustine: "When after this period of toil we come to that time of rest, our only business will be the praise of God. Our activity there will be hallelujah. . . . There, our fare will be the [singing of] hallelujah, our drink will be hallelujah, our rest hallelujah, all our joy hallelujah, that is to say the praise of God." In their liturgical praise, the faithful anticipate, or prepare for, this eternal hallelujah. The liturgy is open, as it were, to the transcendent, eternal realm, making Christians members of a different and higher world. Nonparticipation in worship, by contrast, brings to mind eternal damnation. "Those who do not praise God here on earth will remain without the power of speech in eternity," warns the medieval mystic John Ruusbroec.[69]

While twentieth-century liturgies continue to use ancient hymns, critics express their difficulties with the notion of adoration. For them, adoration is not a concept they can easily understand, let alone appreciate. It seems to belong to a feudal, monarchical, or, at any rate, pre-modern culture. Can contemporaries imagine God to be a monarch surrounded by angels that pay him homage? "Can you imagine anything more appallingly idiotic than the Christian idea of heaven? What kind of deity is it that would be capable of creating angels and men to sing his praises day and night to all eternity?" asked philosopher Alfred N. Whitehead (1861–1947). This god is clearly portrayed after "the figure of an Oriental despot, with his inane and barbaric vanity." The true God, according to Whitehead, cannot and should not be praised. The angels, traditionally the chief agents of adoration, have become as problematic as the despotic God criticized by Whitehead. Our modern universe, as analyzed by scientists and experienced by urban populations, is free from angels and demons. How should we conceive of adoration, if angels are nothing but poetic figures of speech? How can we join beings that we believe may not exist?[70]

Theologians have felt challenged to respond to the religious doubts characteristic of the twentieth-century Christian mind. They agree that traditional interpretations of adoration as an angelic activity, although based upon the Bible, fall short of demonstrating the legitimacy of glorification. Modern men and women seem to be estranged from the very idea of adoring God. If traditional notions of praise are no longer understandable or no longer in tune with the general cultural mood, theologians try new approaches. As often, help comes from philosophy, theology's time-honored handmaid. The promise of philosophy is that here we have an intellectual discipline that allows for speaking about God while at the same time moving beyond the childish anthropomorphic notions implied in the traditional view. Only if God is appreciated as "the ground of being," the "ultimate concern," or the "highest value" can we discover the true essence of praise.

Praise, according to twentieth-century theological and spiritual writers, expresses the acknowledgment of the value of something or someone valuable and worthy. Now if God is the most worthy being we can conceive of and admire, then he is also the most praiseworthy being. This conclusion has been supported by Rudolf Otto (1896–1937), who would otherwise insist on the irrational quality of the divine that manifests itself in numinous feelings of awe and fascination. In general, Otto would agree with the medieval Byzantine liturgist Nicholas Kabasilas that "when we approach God, we immediately recognize the inaccessibility and force and grandeur of his glory, and are filled with wonder and awe and similar feelings that lead automatically to the expression of praise." Yet Otto defines praise as an eminently rational act. The Gloria's liturgical shout of "*Tu solus sanctus*" (you alone are holy), according to Rudolf Otto, must be seen as

> a paean of praise, which, so far from being merely a faltering confession of the divine supremacy, recognizes and extols a value, precious beyond all conceiving. The object of such praise is not simply absolute might, making its claims and compelling their fulfillment, but a might that has at the same time the supremest right to make the highest claim to service, and receives praise because it is in an absolute sense worthy to be praised. "You are worthy to receive praise and honor and power". (Rev. 4:11)

To glorify God therefore is the logical consequence of our understanding of who he is.[71]

This somewhat abstract reasoning has been given a higher profile by C.S. Lewis (1898–1963). He refers to our natural tendency to praise: lovers praise their beloved, readers their favorite poet, walkers praise the countryside, players extoll their favorite game, students the teacher they prefer to others, and so on. And, more importantly, Lewis reminds us of our frustration if we cannot share our appreciation of something. "It is frustrating," he reports, "to have discovered a new author and not to be able to tell anyone how good he is; to come suddenly, at the turn of the road, upon some mountain valley of unexpected grandeur and then to have to keep silent because the people with you care for it no more than for a tin can in the ditch." Praise, according to Lewis, not merely expresses, but actually completes the enjoyment.[72]

Christians praise God, according to Lewis, in very much the same way lovers love their partner. To see what praising really means, explains Lewis, "we must suppose ourselves to be in perfect love with God—drunk with, drowned in, dissolved by, that delight which, far from remaining pent up within ourselves as incommunicable, hence hardly tolerable, bliss, flows out from us incessantly again in effortless and perfect expression, our joy no more separable from the praise in which it liberates and utters itself than the brightness a mirror receives is separable from the brightness it sheds." It is not only C.S. Lewis who prefers intimate and even erotic vocabulary when speaking of praise. The same language can be found in a recent Catholic document that refers to communal prayer as "the voice of the bride [the church] addressing her bridegroom." Lewis, despite his mystical psychology and elegant rhetoric in explaining praise, is of course aware that things are not always so simple. The glorification of God rarely flows as effortlessly as would be characteristic of the highest state of mystical love. Praise, seen with the eyes of everyday life, often seems more like a duty and a chore.[73]

The God who is to be praised stands above his deeds in history. Contemporary theologians assert God's absolute transcendence. True, Christians celebrate God's saving acts, and they praise God himself as the author of these mighty deeds. Yet, God cannot be reduced to his deeds, as if his deeds were all that can be known and said of him. In a very important way God transcends his intervention in history. *Deus semper maior*: he transcends what people normally say of him. God wants, explains Edmund Schlink, that "not only his deed, but he himself is praised . . . as the one who he is in his everlasting glory, holiness, power, and wisdom." Christians celebrate God's holiness not because God loves them and sent his son. They praise him, because he is praiseworthy in himself. "He would be totally worthy of it even if he had chosen to condemn the whole human race for our sin and rebellion, without any hope of salvation."[74]

In the act of adoration, people not only bypass God's mighty acts or their personal experience of his providence; they also look beyond the small worshiping group with its narrow and perhaps sectarian concerns. True liturgy, according to Cardinal Ratzinger, never takes the human congregation or group as its focus and measure; rather, it can be recognized by its cosmic and universal orientation. In praising God himself, then, people step as it were outside the history of salvation and the confines of social groups in order to enter the realm of the absolute, the realm of heaven.[75]

Whereas theological thought may help clarify the essence of hymnic adoration, it may not convince its critics. These are presumably only silenced when exposed to the most powerful advocate of praise—music. When, in the early Middle Ages, instruments lost their former pagan associations and began to be introduced into Christian liturgy, they were first used for the Sanctus. Instrumental music, before being used in worship, served for the acclamation and praise of the emperor, the pope, and the bishops. The Christian emperors, like their pagan predecessors, were acclaimed with a great deal of noise and sometimes with ordered shouts and solemn music from the organ whenever they appeared in public. Music gradually became part of the ceremonial proceedings of the imperial court at Constantinople. It soon made its appearance at the papal court in Rome as well as at the Frankish court of Aachen. Musical homage and entertainment could be heard and enjoyed at receptions for guests. During the eighth or ninth century, instruments were introduced into the liturgy, so that music did not remain a privilege of worldly and ecclesiastical courts. Benedictine monasteries seem to have been the first to introduce organs in tenth-century northwestern Europe, as can be seen from an elaborate poem that deals with the dedication in 993 of the enlarged Benedictine abbey-church of Winchester, England. By 1300, all major churches in Western Europe owned an organ and had musicians practiced in playing it. However, it still took some time before musical instruments came to accompany and support a choir. Initially, the organ and altar bells were mainly used to produce the joyful noise that acclaimed God at the Sanctus, the threefold seraphic "holy" at Mass.[76]

The musical elaboration of the Sanctus did not, of course, stay at the level of acclamatory noise. As more sophisticated musical settings for the Mass developed, composers tried to give their best to the Sanctus as well as to the other hymns. The most festive creations of liturgical music are the compositions for choir, solo singers, and orchestra performed at the Catholic High Mass of feast days, created in the Baroque atmosphere of conspicuous liturgical celebration. Whether they preferred the sound of thunder or slow, solemn melodies, composers and musicians alike felt challenged to make the angelic music audible to their pious and enraptured audience.

Compositions for the Mass reached their highest complexity and quality in the work of Haydn (1732–1809), Mozart (1756–91), and Beethoven (1770–1827). The many Masses of Haydn and Mozart and the two relevant compositions of Beethoven rank not only among their best and most widely appreciated works. They also belong to the acme of Western musical expression.

Although the classical composers paid close attention to the text of the Mass, they sought a musically unified understanding of the liturgy. They found this understanding in making the *entire* Mass, beginning with the acclamatory Kyrie at the opening, into a celebration of victory and triumph. The "adoration" movements of the Gloria set the basic mood the composers sought to express and celebrate. In order to produce the special note of victorious festivity required for the *missa solemnis*, or High Mass, Mozart often relied on the use of trumpets, trombones, and drums, instruments already traditional in the cathedral of Salzburg and used, especially, for the Sanctus. "In every Mass, the Sanctus forms the most festive moment," explains a music historian. Writing on Mozart, he adds: "The nonexpressive 'C,' which in most Masses serves as the basic key, lifts this part up into the realm of the impersonal and transtemporal. The divine majesty is being adored with utter simplicity and monumentality. In many cases, trumpets, drums, and strains of the violin accompaniment underscore the solemn manner of adoration." Mozart clearly distinguishes between the slow and majestic angelic voices of the Sanctus and the fast movement of explosive joy in the human voices of the piece immediately following, the Hosanna. He lends his musical genius to both worlds. Moving from adoration to the *allegro* of jubilant praise, he contrasts and unites heaven and earth. Music can make the words meaningless and blend all the texts into one movement, transforming the entire liturgy into a single humble gesture of respect and adoration.[77]

The classical Mass compositions were typically written for the cathedral of Salzburg (Mozart in the 1770s) or for patron-saint's celebrations in Eisenstadt, the residence of the music-loving Hungarian prince Esterházy (Haydn 1796–1802 and Beethoven 1807). While a bishop or priest, accompanied by a cortège of attendants, would say Mass at the high altar, a choir of about twenty singers and soloists, and an orchestra of some fifteen persons (violins, violoncello,

double bass, organ, trumpets, bassoons, horns, and of course the drum) performed the composition, usually from a balcony in the rear of the church.
Products of late Baroque culture, the symphonic Masses reflect archiepiscopal
and princely taste in tune with the exuberance, pomp, and playfulness of
contemporary church architecture.[78]

In those days, symphonic Masses had their adversaries who opted for simpler liturgical settings. Inspired by Enlightenment ideas about education, the
Austrian emperor Joseph II promoted a vernacular liturgy with congregational
singing. The liturgy, in his opinion, was for inculcating morality rather than for
the elite's conspicuous consumption. A first imperial order of 1754 prohibited
the use of trumpets and drums in all church music, and in 1782 a second one
restricted, if not prohibited, orchestral Masses altogether. During an entire
decade, composers no longer produced pieces for the liturgy. Only after the
emperor's death in 1790 did the restrictions lose their initial impact. Orchestras and choirs began to return to the churches. Within and without the
Austro-Hungarian empire, printing houses published the music. Some of the
Mass compositions were rather popular. "I have heard this Mass often, rather
well performed, in a Catholic church," wrote a critic on Haydn's "Kettledrum
Mass" (*Paukenmesse*); the article appeared in 1803 in the *Allgemeine
musikalische Zeitung* of Leipzig.[79]

In Austria and elsewhere, liturgical splendor continued to be attacked by
writers who wanted worship to be a matter of the heart, and the funds to be
spent on helping the poor. Catholic apologists disagreed. Magnificent worship,
for them, was not only for promoting piety among the faithful. If the beauty
and sumptuousness of vestments, illumination, music, and pomp surpassed
that of court and theater, it would give a proper idea of who the true Lord of
the world is. The apologists would have endorsed historian James White's
remark that the Baroque imagination aimed at "adorning the throne room of
God with sound," just as it did with splendid visual decoration. They insisted
that paying musical respect to God was entirely in keeping with the general
culture; for them, it was simply a matter of correct behavior. So long as the
gentlemen critics of Baroque musical culture paid respect to their ladies by
spending thousands of guilders to adorn them, their insistence on plain worship seemed hardly credible. "As long as people take the greatest magnificence
to be the expression of the highest respect . . . so long you must permit that the
Catholic Church makes legitimate use of the greatest magnificence in its liturgy, thereby indicating its greatest respect for God." Written in 1791, these
lines echo a common sentiment of music lovers whose taste survived Enlightenment ideas of a didactic liturgy, the French Revolution, and indeed the
declining *anciens régimes* of the European princely courts.[80]

Of course, the sentiment expressed in defense of musical splendor did not
originate in the late eighteenth century, nor is it limited to Catholics. In
seventeenth-century Germany, Lutherans were involved in a similar contro-

2. The Choir in Church and in Heaven. This seventeenth-century engraving shows organ and musicians in the gallery of a church (bottom), the sacred ark of the Old Testament whose procession is accompanied by musicians (middle), and a scene from the book of Revelation in which saints and angels praise the Lamb of God (top). Only expert musicians are qualified to join the angelic choir, which never ceases to sing the praises of God. Art is here enlisted to promote Protestant sacred music and to devalue simple congregational singing. German engraving, 1665.

versy about music. In 1661, a Lutheran pastor active in Rostock published a treatise that aimed at encouraging congregational singing. In his *Wächterstimme* (The Watchman's Voice), Theophilus Großgebauer (1627–61) attacked the Baroque splendor of Protestant worship in which "organists, cantors, town pipers, and musicians—for the most part unspiritual people—have control. . . . They play, sing, bow, and ring according to their pleasure." The organist "sits, plays, and shows his art; in order that the art of one person be shown, the whole congregation of Jesus Christ is supposed to sit and hear the sound of pipes. This makes the congregation drowsy and lazy: some sleep, some gossip." By admitting the virtuoso into the service, the church foregoes the opportunity to have the congregation "well instructed by the spiritual songs" sung by the entire community. We can easily see that Großgebauer was a kind of rationalist intent on instructing the congregation as well as an early pietist intent on creating a warm devotional atmosphere.[81]

Großgebauer's argument provoked another Lutheran to respond and defend the aristocratic, Baroque point of view. For Hector Mithobius's *Psalmodia Christiana* (1665), church music must not have any didactic aims; its addressee is God, not the congregation. The hierarchic universe of Mithobius culminates in an enthroned heavenly deity to whom angels and saints perpetually sing praises. As in the time of the Old Testament kings, God expects to be glorified in the manner appropriate to his supreme majesty. Using the analogy of an earthly monarch honored with the most splendid music possible, Mithobius argues that God likewise must be praised with all resources available. "So one should many thousand times more apply all skill, wit, sense, reason, and understanding to the music of the king of kings." For the Lutheran author, this argument entails the implementation of all varieties of musical form at the highest level of professional skill. The frontispiece of Mithobius's book (ill. 2) displays this perspective vividly: the musicians on the church balcony are not too distant from the angels in heaven and from David in the middle; but the congregation below seems far removed and insignificant. God's court music can be performed only by well-trained specialists! In this, Baroque Lutheranism agreed with Baroque Catholicism.[82]

The Baroque controversy over the competing claims of professional and congregational music as the most appropriate form was never resolved. In eighteenth-century England, the advocates of congregational singing came from the ranks of those who, like the hymn-writer Isaac Watts (1674–1748), stood outside or who, like the Wesley brothers, were on the fringes of the Church of England which still had reservations, if not about the simple singing of metrical psalms, then at least about the use of nonscriptural hymns and the catchy melodies of the Methodists. Both sides continued to have their advocates in Victorian England, and so they have in our own day—both in England and elsewhere. Although most contemporary church leaders promote congregational singing, traditionalists still insist that real liturgical beauty can be achieved only when a highly trained choir or orchestra performs expertly crafted music. "Real praise," so they secretly believe, does not come from the pews. However, despite such controversies, both sides agree that hymnic adoration belongs to Christian worship and should be supported by music.[83]

4. Conclusion: Praise and Preference

Christian praise is very rich: it draws on the long experience of Israel's psalmody and from the sacred story of both Testaments. In Christian praise and thanksgiving, angelic and human voices mingle, individual, contemporary experience blends with sacred stories, and Abraham and Christ appear in a complex, structured harmony. In this harmony, we can distinguish three different philosophies of praise, and they appeal to different types of participants in worship.

Pragmatic thanksgiving, with its emphasis on personal and individual experience, appeals to people with a pragmatic cast of mind. They inhabit a world peopled with enemies (some natural, some supernatural) and live a life often troubled by misery, conflict and affliction, but they hope and, indeed, expect that God will act on their behalf. They may be skeptical, but typically they are rather religious, having a sense of God's direct involvement in their everyday lives. The rival system, wherein God has removed himself from active interference in a clockwork universe, remains alien to the pious mind. In prayer and praise, believers reflect their own experience and find ever new traces of God's hidden dealings with them. Worship supports, nurtures, and satisfies personal piety. It increases trust in a benign and kindly God who cares about the widow's mite and each individual hair on the head of a believer.

Celebratory recital, on the other hand, will be preferred by those who think of religion as a matter of a great tradition, the sacred story of which must be learned and appropriated as one's own. Although God may not act visibly in their own personal lives, the echo of his steps can be heard in the history of peoples and empires, especially in the sacred history as told in the biblical record. Those trained in biblical literature and lore will feel at home when Abraham's calling, the liberation from Egypt, the giving of the land, or the resurrection of Christ are celebrated. They find pleasure in a liturgy that features, in prose, poetry, and song, the narrative of salvation. That narrative implies "a confession of faith: it declares our belief that we ourselves are included in the scope of God's redeeming action and have been touched by it." God's action comes first and must be recalled first; only after does there follow its effect on men and women. Or, more radically, what counts is God's sacred story and nothing else: our own stories are of less importance, if not entirely negligible and irrelevant. In praising God, "we lay aside ourselves and all our interests and glorify the Lord for his own sake, for his power and his glory." Christians have to wean themselves from self-aggrandizement and self-glorification, because glory belongs to God alone. Those who insist on praising God primarily for what he has done in their own lives appear as self-centered, as too much involved with themselves and their own petty lives. In personal praise, one critic argues, "there is a cutting loose from an objective revelation of God in history, a surrender to subjective feelings of the moment, a lapse into an existentialism overlaid with Christian terminology."[84]

Compared to the individual thanksgiving with its intense emotional involvement, the recital form of praise stays completely objective and independent of our feeling. "The singing of the Christian congregation must assume that certain facts of the history of salvation simply exist and are valid, irrespective of our manifold individual biographies," asserts a German author. And an American scholar concurs: "Even when the worshiper is low in spirit, he is bidden to raise up his head and contemplate the 'mighty works of God' done 'out there,' whether or not he feels at that moment like entering upon a celebration of God." Since God acts without asking us, in his absolute sovereignty doing "over our heads" what he wants to do, our relationship to his mighty acts may remain unknown to us. God's dealing with us, through Christ, remains hidden to us, asserted the reformed theologian Karl Barth; only after death, in the beyond, will the veil be removed. Thus our praise must respond to God's sending of his son, rather than to our subjective awareness or emotional state. Barth seems to imply that personal, individual thanksgiving will be possible only hereafter.[85]

The "objectivity" of God's acts, extolled in celebratory recital, does not seem to be appreciated by all Christians. As we have seen, many prefer what we have termed pragmatic thanksgiving: a form of praise saturated with personal experience. Eugen Drewermann, a controversial Catholic psychotherapist, has argued against the communal praying of the Liturgy of the Hours in monasteries and convents. Here, he feels, people mechanically recite dead words whose meaning escapes them, and thus experience prayer as alienating, depersonalizing. Real prayer, he claims, must allow them to use the immediacy of their own language and refer to their own life. Perhaps one can invoke here an observation made by the English sociolinguist Basil Bernstein. According to his research, one can be more precise than just saying, as everyone does, that the way people speak reflects their social class. Class-bound language shows a definite pattern. The lower classes and the aristocratic upper class prefer a highly stylized, ritualized, repetitive language, often made up of ready-made phrases and set expressions whose meaning is more implicit than explicit. One has to be an insider to understand. The middle class, by contrast, delights in finding ever new nuances of expression, desiring to achieve a maximum of flexibility and individuality. Understanding is not bound to insider-status; instead, people make an effort to communicate with everyone. If we apply this insight to Drewermann's critique of formalized prayer rituals, we can perhaps recognize the rebellion of a middle-class intellectual who in religion, as in all other spheres of life, strives for flexibility, individuality, and spontaneity at the expense of the rigid forms prescribed by tradition. In the jargon of sociolinguistics, one could say that he prefers the more varied and sentimental "elaborated code" over the traditional and stiff "restricted" one and has reservations about all formal, set texts.[86]

The preference for either songs of thanksgiving (the ones Drewermann would favor) or hymns of glorification can be discerned in religious hymnody. Writing on nineteenth- and twentieth-century hymnals, Lionel Adey has aptly distinguished between learned or liturgical and popular or devotional hymns. The learned tradition of hymnody focuses on the objective events of what he calls the Christian myth: the nativity, life and death of Christ, and the coming of the Spirit. By contrast, the popular tradition prefers to sing of the singers' burdens and weariness, of their love for the Savior, of divine guidance in everyday life. Of the two kinds, the one is "liable to become intemperate and egocentric, the other formal and restrained to the point of coldness. Inevitably the former [the popular tradition] characterized popular worship, out of doors or in the Methodist chapel, the latter [the learned tradition] genteel worship in cathedral, or college, or simpler services in the squire-dominated village church." While the two traditions converged in late nineteenth-century Britain and America, they have diverged again. In our day the rift has widened between mainstream and Pentecostal churches.[87]

A third group—people with a more liberal personality and a romantic interest in nature, art, and aestheticism—will no doubt appreciate the awe and fascination with the divine expressed in the pure, heavenly praise that remains untinged, unsoiled by earthly concerns. They resemble the royal devotees of the ancient Egyptian deity Aton who (at least in the vision of Sigmund Freud), absorbed in the beauty of their poetry of praise, turn away from worldly matters and hardly even realize that the Egyptian empire is beginning to dissolve. If their life is not perfect and may, in fact, be rather miserable, they are nevertheless attracted to the world of hymnic praise: an organic universe of harmony, full of God's glory. They can understand and feel attracted to a liturgy that, like the Sanctus, transcends the distance between heaven and earth. Worship, for them, must take place in an ideal, culturally sophisticated atmosphere, saturated by the sound of sacred anthems, the swell of the organ, and, perhaps, the sweet smell of incense. In this atmosphere, the faithful are lifted above the chaos of the world. In the words of Reinhard Raffalt, a Catholic organ virtuoso: "The chaotic turbulence of our world can only be prevented from swallowing us up, I think, by the new creation of a beauty whose only aim it is to glorify God." Some Christians escape into the realm of divine beauty and are saved by praise.[88]

While Christian liturgies are often rich enough to accommodate all of these orientations and tastes, the three philosophies of praise are sometimes developed into distinct liturgical patterns. A presentation of sacred music is likely to correspond to the "angelic" pattern. Services based on scriptural readings or the singing of psalms may give prominence to the sacred story. And some Christian denominations have special services that feature the giving of personal testimonies. Frequently, however, the forms of worship lose the exclusivity of one dominant pattern. One contemporary song outlines God's acts in creating the world, in the incarnation, life, death, and resurrection of Jesus, but intersperses the stanzas with a refrain of pure praise:

> Lord, I praise You because of who You are
> not just for all the mighty deeds You have done.
> Lord, I worship You because of who You are,
> You're all the reason that I need to voice my praise.

Overlapping, mixing, and blending into ever new configurations, real worship often belies our clean academic distinctions. The varieties of praise belong together, forming a single, overwhelming symphony.[89]

The symphony of praise addresses God, often right at the beginning of a service of worship. Thus far, we have not dealt with one further aspect of addressing God, which is nonetheless never absent from Christian worship: the practice of petitionary prayer. This will be the subject of the next chapter.

The Second Game: Prayer
Asking for God's Help

Very truly, I tell you, if you ask anything of the Father in my name, he will give it to you.

Jesus (John 16:23, NRSV)

While all are silent, the priest begins with the appointed service, and before anything else he offers prayer to God, because before all other things that are indispensable to the fear of God, he has necessarily to begin with prayer.[1]

Theodore of Mopsuestia, ca. 380/90

In the Mass a Christian shall keep in mind the shortcomings or excesses he feels, and pour out all these freely before God with weeping and groaning, as woefully as he can, as to his faithful Father.[2]

Martin Luther, 1520

Try prayer power.[3]
Norman Vincent Peale, 1952

1. On Petitionary Prayer

In most religions, people talk to the invisible gods, asking them for favors or for help. Since gods are more powerful than human creatures and since they have control over history and nature, even control over the entire universe, they can rightly be expected to intervene in the course of things. In the ancient world, prayer was considered a normal, almost everyday activity, engaged in with a sense of trust and great expectation. Although gods may sometimes have their reasons for not complying with human wishes, prayer often simply "worked." Since Christians, as they developed their forms of worship, followed ancient patterns, we have to ask first how the ancients prayed. More specifically, we have to answer the three questions: Who is praying? What are the gods asked for? How does God help? Quotations from ancient prayer texts, Jewish and pagan, will help us to answer these questions and to understand the use of prayer in worship and everyday life.

Who Is Praying?

> [no. 1] "The Lord struck the child . . . and it became very ill. David therefore pleaded with God for the child. David fasted, and went in and lay all night on the ground." (2 Sam. 12:15–16)
>
> [no. 2] "O Lord God and King, God of Abraham, spare your people; for the eyes of our foes are upon us to annihilate us." (Esther. LXX 4:17)

King David, so the Old Testament story goes, had an illegitimate child by a woman living in a neighboring harem. And, worse, he had her husband killed in order to be able to receive the mother into his own harem. After the child, a boy, was born, he became very ill; but David loved the boy and hoped that he would survive. So David fasted, put on sackcloth, slept on the floor, and pleaded with God for the life of his child. By accompanying his prayer with customary gestures of humiliation, he hoped to appeal to God's mercy. However, since David had sinned, God did not answer his prayer, and the boy died. Example no. 1 depicts an individual, spontaneous act of prayer that invites God to heal the sick child. No. 2, by contrast, is spoken in a very different situation. The book of Esther, a short novel dating from the fourth or third century BCE, tells us the story of a royal Persian edict which gave the order "to destroy, to kill, and to annihilate all Jews, young and old, women and children, in one day." When Mordecai, an influential Jewish leader, heard of this, he tore his clothes (as was the custom) and with a loud cry informed his co-religionists living in the same city. All Jews responded with fasting and weeping. Mordecai gathered the Jews in Susa to "hold a fast," i.e., for a special prayer meeting. In the case of a crisis, this Jewish community held a public assembly and addressed God in prayer, asking for his help. Typically, people underscored public prayer with fasting, donning sackcloth, rolling in ashes, weeping, and abstaining from the use of ointment, for they assumed that God would be more inclined to answer prayers that were accompanied by these special customs of self-humiliation. "To hold a fast" became synonymous with "to hold a public assembly for prayer." Communal prayer was typically held in the Temple of Jerusalem or, if this was not possible, people prayed in the direction of the Temple (just as Muslims orient their devotions toward Mecca). An ancient instruction concerning prayer, possibly dating from the sixth century BCE, indicates the occasions on which prayer meetings are to be held (1 Kings 8:33–53): when an enemy besieges a Jewish city; when people go out to battle against their enemy; when there is no rain; when there is a famine in the land or a catastrophe caused by plague, blight, mildew, locusts, or caterpillars; after a military defeat; when Yahweh has punished the people by allowing their enemies to bring them into exile in a foreign country.

As we can see from examples 1 and 2, petitionary prayer is linked to a situation of crisis: a catastrophe or an imminent danger. The state of divine blessing is the normal one, and under normal circumstances, one does not have to pray. However, as soon as untoward events disturb the normal, good situation, prayer and repentance provide for restoration. A crisis must be responded to by some ritual action, and communal, public prayer is deemed an adequate—and efficient—response. When God has answered the prayer and thus restored the initial situation (for example by making the Persian king revoke his inimical decree), then prayer is no longer needed. Linked to a crisis, prayer has a specific reason and ends when the crisis is over.

Example no. 1 gives prayer a private setting; no. 2 is a public prayer. The praying is done by the suffering individual or by the afflicted group.

What Is God Asked For?

The prayer situations of nos. 1 and 2 are essentially identical: in an acute moment of distress God is asked to intervene quickly. Prayer uttered in a situation of acute crisis is presumably the most common form; in the ancient world, however, not all prayers asked for or expected *immediate* divine help. The following example shows another possibility:

[no. 3] "Restore our judges as of old, and our leaders as in the days of yore." (Eighteen Benedictions—Palestinian version)[4]

This is a line from one of the oldest Jewish prayers, still in use today in the synagogue. Unlike nos. 1 and 2, the prayer is not occasioned by an acute crisis, but by the Jews' long-term dissatisfaction with their national fate. After the kingdom of Judah had been destroyed by the Babylonians in 586 BCE, memorial services of penitence and lamentation were held, and in these the appeal for national restoration was voiced: "Slaves rule over us; there is no one to liberate us out of their hand. . . . Restore us to yourself, O Lord, that we may be restored; renew our days as of old" (Lam. 5:8.21). "Set Israel free, O God, from all her misfortunes!" (Ps. 25:22). Since the Jews have never recovered completely from the blow received from the Babylonians and, until the twentieth century, have rarely enjoyed much political freedom, the synagogue has never ceased to pray for the restoration of the Jewish state. While prayers 1 and 2 ask for immediate deliverance in life-threatening situations, prayer 3 asks in a time of diminished life for liberation from general misery to be granted one day in the future. Both deliverance and liberation involve the dramatic intervention of God. Not all prayers ask for such dramatic divine action. God may be asked to act in other ways, as can be seen in the following example:

[no. 4] "Never may the wanton lord of war, insatiate of battle cry, destroy by fire this Pelasgian land. . . . And may Zeus cause the earth to render its tribute of fruit by the produce of every season; may their grazing cattle in the fields have abundant increase." (Aeschylus, *The Suppliant Maidens*[5])

In Aeschylus' play *The Suppliant Maidens* (ca. 490 BCE), the chorus of women prays to Zeus, asking him to protect the city of Argos. While the prayer occurs in a piece of fiction, we know from other ancient sources that, in the Greek-speaking world, people actually assembled for common prayer, asking a god to protect and bless their city. An inscription dated 196 BCE, found in Magnesia-on-Maeander, refers to an annual fair of the city whose celebration involved the presence of priest and priestess, nine boys and nine girls, military officers, stewards, the secretary of the city council, as well as an officer called "the public sacrificer." When a bull was offered to Zeus, they prayed "for the safety of the city and the land, the women and children and all inhabitants of the city and the land, for peace and wealth and bearing of grain and all other fruits and possessions." In a similar vein, the Athenians had a civic prayer which included the line: "Rain, rain, O dear Zeus, upon the corn-land of the Athenians and their meads." Public supplication took place at a temple, had a well-defined ritual frame, involved the co-operation of priests, and was always accompanied by animal sacrifices. (Private prayer, by contrast, never involved the presence of clergy.) Jews had customs very similar to those of the Greeks: supplication for the community had to be made in public, that is at the Jerusalem Temple or in the synagogue. An ancient Jewish prayer, still in use today, reads: "Bless this year for us, O Lord, our God, and may its harvest be abundant. . . . Provide dew and rain for the earth, and satiate your world from your storehouse of goodness, and bestow a blessing upon the work of our hands."[6]

[no. 5] "Have mercy on me, O God, . . . blot out my transgressions. Wash me thoroughly from my iniquity and cleanse me from my sin. . . . You desire truth in the inward being, therefore teach me wisdom in my secret heart." (Ps. 51:1–2.6)

While prayer no. 4 and its equivalents ask for tangible, material blessings to be bestowed on the community, prayer no. 5 requests only spiritual benefits: purity and wisdom. Modern commentators generally agree that this psalm must have originated in a cultic setting in which someone asked for divine forgiveness, and in which the ritual cleansing was done by a priest who took a brush made of the hairy leaves of marjoram (hyssop) and sprinkled water or blood on the penitent, so that the request was immediately answered. The text gives no clue as to the occasion on which this ritual was performed. One may think of the royal enthronement, which seems to have included the new king's request for wisdom. Or one may think of an annual penitential rite in which the king took on himself the sins of the community and was purified on behalf of the community. Or, to offer just one more interpretation, one may think of a ritual of penance, conducted by a healer in the home of a sick individual as the first step toward healing. While the precise ritual setting of the psalm cannot be reconstructed with any degree of certainty, it is clear enough that the praying person here asks for the establishment of a very special relationship with God, a relationship for which he or she has to be prepared by purification. The purified person is as it were brought closer to God and made more like him. God can bestow the gift of wisdom—which is the intellectual power to rule—only on someone who has been duly prepared by purification. That the request for wisdom is not unheard of in the ancient world can be shown with reference to another prayer, spoken by King Solomon: "Give your servant an understanding mind to govern your people, able to discern between good and evil" (1 Kings 3:9). A similar text, dating from ca. 300 BCE, comes from the Greek philosopher Cleanthes: "Bountiful Zeus, . . . rescue humankind from its grievous misunderstanding. Scatter this from our soul, and give us the power of judgment."[7]

One ancient Jewish group, the community of Qumran, whose library was rediscovered after the Second World War, laid great emphasis on prayer for spiritual goods. In a renewal ceremony, presumably held annually, the members confess their sins collectively, saying: "We have strayed. We have disobeyed. We and our fathers before us have sinned and done wickedly, etc.," upon which the priests speak a blessing: "May He bless you with all good and preserve you from all evil! May He enlighten your heart with life-giving wisdom and grant you eternal knowledge!" Once the sin is publicly acknowledged and removed, divine wisdom can be given as a spiritual benefit. The

Qumran *Hodayot* (Book of Hymns) echoes the same line of thought: "I know that no one is righteous except through you, and therefore I implore you by the spirit which you have given me, to perfect your favors to your servant for ever, purifying me by your Holy Spirit, and drawing me near to you by your grace." A close scrutiny of the Dead Sea Scrolls leads to the surprising conclusion that the members of the community did not practice any other kind of petitionary prayer. According to them, God has fixed the fate of his elect from the beginning and carries out his plan; all events are foreordained and cannot be altered. There is no use asking God to change his plan. However, those who are chosen by God may ask him to deepen the wisdom that he has freely bestowed.[8]

In the ancient world, some philosophers went beyond the requests of purification and illumination by adding a third, more daring petition. Neoplatonic philosophers defined union with the divine as the ultimate aim to which theurgical prayer should lead us. In the fifth century CE, the pagan philosopher Proclus described the various stages of increasing closeness to the gods. According to him, the praying person would climb a spiritual ladder toward the gods. The highest stage has been reached when prayer leads someone into lasting contact with the divine world and makes him or her participate in the divine light. Although Proclus does not discourage the more elementary and often more pressing prayer for outward goods like rain, health, or deliverance from danger, he certainly thought of theurgical prayer as the highest form, befitting the philosopher. (Later, in the Middle Ages, Christian mystics adopted Proclus' view of the theurgical ascent to God or to Christ.)[9]

A comparison of the various requests—plea for deliverance or liberation, request for blessing, and petition for spiritual benefits—reveals striking differences. The first relates to the distinction between blessing, liberation, deliverance, and spiritual goods. The Jews of Persia ask for *immediate* deliverance or rescue in a situation of acute crisis. By contrast, despite their use of emphatic language, the petitions for a continuing state of divine blessing, for divine forgiveness, and for the liberation from foreign domination, followed by the restoration of the Jewish state, lack a sense of immediacy and urgency. Prayers of deliverance and liberation ask for specific, often miraculous and datable events that are understood as acts of God, whereas requests for blessing relate to the natural processes of God's guidance or nurturing creation. Due to its undramatic, quiet, continuous character, God's blessing activity often remains unnoticed and goes without acknowledgment. The second difference is one of regularity and irregularity. People expressed their request for blessing, liberation, and spiritual goods repeatedly and regularly (such as yearly, or more often), not just in times of crisis, and we sense that they considered their "liturgical prayer," as specialists call it, a permanent duty of the community and its ritual officiants. Finally, the third difference is that between the different types of language used. While requests for deliverance invent their words spontaneously, the prayer for blessing, liberation, or purification tends to adopt more or less fixed forms, so that the prayer tends to become a list of standard petitions, focusing on general well-being or spiritual goods rather than on specific, urgent needs.[10]

Prayer practiced irrespective of the community's well-being or distress may be an institution of great antiquity, linked to the emergence of collective ritual acts for the promotion of the fertility of animals and fields. In Old Testament times, regular and perhaps annual prayer for the king's well-being may have existed. For early times, however, there is no evidence for more frequent—weekly or even daily—communal prayer, either among the Israelites or the ancient pagan religions. In fact, among the ancient Mediterranean religions, only the Jews seem to have developed frequent public prayer. Within Judaism, early promoters of regular communal prayer seem to have been small, radical, first-century CE groups like the Essenes whose shared life, reminiscent of monasticism, facilitated their regular prayer in morning and evening services. Joseph Heinemann, historian of Jewish worship, emphasized the rabbinical contribution to the development of regular prayer as an elementary form of communal ritual by calling it "an authentic and original Jewish creation." In other ancient religions, he explains, "regular worship-through-prayer was unheard of, save as a subsidiary element of other ritual and cultic forms, or as a device to be resorted to only in extraordinary circumstances. Fixed prayer, in and of itself constituting the entirety of the divine service, was a startling innovation in the ancient world, which both Christianity and Islam inherited from Judaism." While Jewish liturgical prayer can be traced back to the emergence of the synagogue before the time of Christ, its importance grew after the First and Second destructions of the Jerusalem Temple in 70 and 135 CE respectively. Serving as a substitute for archaic animal sacrifices, prayer became a leading ritual in Judaism as well as an important model for Christian worship.[11]

How Does God Help?

In antiquity (as today), men and women expected their prayers to be answered by God. We will briefly explore how, in the mind of the ancients, God manifests himself when helping, granting favors, or bestowing benefits. Our first example comes from the Psalms:

> [no. 6] "O Lord my God, I cried to you for help, and you have healed me." (Ps. 30:2)

In a song of praise, the psalmist acknowledges the help received from God: through divine intervention, he has recovered from illness and has been restored to full health. While the words of Psalm 30 do not indicate how God healed the singer, we may assume that God's intervention was nondramatic.

The psalmist recovered, and now gives thanks to the Lord. The believer knows that God often grants blessings or special favors in ways that only he himself knows. God sustains and heals his creation in many ways, known only to himself and to some of the believers. We may call this kind of divine intervention a "small" miracle or a "small" thaumaturgical event (from Greek *thauma*, "startling event" or "miracle"). The following example, by contrast, explicitly refers to a "big" and dramatic miraculous intervention:

[no. 7] "When the Egyptians treated us harshly and afflicted us, by imposing hard labor on us, we cried to the Lord, the god of our ancestors. The Lord heard our voice and saw our affliction, our toil, and our oppression. The Lord brought us out of Egypt with a mighty hand and an outstretched arm, with a terrifying display of power, with signs and wonders." (Deut. 26:6–8)

Part of a ritual recitation of the dealings of Yahweh with his people, this text refers to God's "signs and wonders," i.e., to the miracles of the Exodus legend. God turned the life-giving waters of the Nile to blood, sent plagues to both livestock and people, and eventually opened the sea of reeds for his people, so that they could escape, while the pursuing army drowned in the closing waters. When asking God for liberation from foreign domination, Jesus Sirach prays for miracles: "Give new signs, and work other wonders. . . . Crush the heads of hostile rulers" (Sir. 36:6.12). Presumably, the ancients did not expect such impressive miracles to happen very frequently. They were more likely to believe that God works calmly and imperceptibly. A more common miracle, acknowledged by both ancient Jews and pagans, was the vision or dream in which a god or goddess appears, speaking to the supplicant and responding to the human request. The legend of King Solomon reports on one incident of this kind:

[no. 8] " 'Give your servant an understanding mind to govern your people, able to discern between good and evil; for who can govern this your great people?' It pleased the Lord that Solomon had asked this. God said to him . . . 'I now do according to your word. Indeed I give you a wise and discerning mind.' . . . Then Solomon awoke, it had been a dream." (1 Kings 3:9–12.15)

Solomon's request for wisdom was not only granted; God himself appeared to him in a dream and told him of his approval. Commentators have often felt that King Solomon actually expected to have such a dream, for he did not have it in Jerusalem, but in Gibeon, presumably in a temple known for divine dream apparitions. In some ancient temples people slept in the hope of being visited by the god worshipped there; the sacred sleep has been given the name of "incubation." In the 140s CE the Greek orator Aelius Aristides spent two years as an "incubant" in the Asclepius temple at Pergamum, Asia Minor, where the god appeared to him in his dreams and instructed him how to cure his asthma. Ancient priests and ritual specialists actually knew how to guide people to have visions and sacred dreams, and their art came to be known as "theurgy" or divine operation. Using this word, we may speak of divine response to prayer as either theurgical (no. 8) or miraculous (or thaumaturgical), and distinguish between the "small" (no. 6) and the "big" miracle (no. 7).[12]

It was in this world of thaumaturgical and theurgical expectations that Christian prayer originated. As we shall see, Christians not only shared the expectations of ancient Jews and pagans; they also brought the same requests before God.

2. The Our Father: The Story of a Political Prayer

In twentieth-century worship, the Our Father, also called the Lord's Prayer, is undoubtedly the most well-known and widely used single text. Whether Christians meet for prayer, or to listen to a sermon, or to celebrate the Eucharist, they always recite the Our Father as part of the liturgy. The constant use of the Our Father has made most Christians familiar with its words; generally, they know it by heart from childhood. English-speaking Catholics use the following words, a traditional rendering of the Greek text included in the gospel of Matthew:

Our Father, who art in heaven,
hallowed be thy name,
thy kingdom come;
thy will be done on earth
as it is in heaven.
Give us this day our daily bread;
and forgive us our trespasses
as we forgive those who trespass against us;
and lead us not into temptation,
but deliver us from evil.   (Matt. 6:9–13)

This version can be found in the English edition, published in 1974, of the Roman Missal of Paul VI. In the same year, an international commission of liturgical experts suggested the following, philologically perhaps more accurate, and somewhat less archaic rendering:

Our Father in heaven,
hallowed be your name,
your kingdom come,
your will be done,
on earth as in heaven.
Give us today our daily bread.
Forgive us our sins as we forgive those
who sin against us.
Save us from the time of trial
and deliver us from evil.[13]

Some Protestant and Anglican liturgical books include this text as an alternative to a more archaic version that resembles the Catholic text. However, neither more traditional nor more contemporary English renderings make the Our Father an easy text. When asked about its precise meaning, contemporary Christians are unlikely to give very precise explanations. In fact, only one petition seems immediately understandable: "Give us today our daily bread." Everyone agrees that the frequency of use of the Our Father is far from being matched by the frequency of its comprehension. On reflection, most are ready to call it a difficult text, an assemblage of religious expressions that convey no precise meaning. The Our Father does not represent the words of prayer that suggest themselves to twentieth-century congregations who want to bring their petitions before God.

Our investigation starts with a look at the prayer's original and quite surprising meanings in first-century CE Judaism and the early Jesus movement. These will include political and therapeutic meanings unknown to and unsuspected by twentieth-century church-goers. We will also show that after the biblical period, the prayer soon ceased to be understood in its entirety.

First Suggestion: The Our Father is a Jewish prayer for regular use; it asks for national liberation

The Our Father must be seen in the context of first-century Jewish prayer. At least two prayers still in use today seem to reflect not only concerns but the actual wording of prayers already in use in the first-century CE synagogue. These are the Abounding Love and the Eighteen Benedictions. The Abounding Love reads as follows:

> With abounding love hast thou loved us, Lord our God, great and exceeding mercy hast thou bestowed upon us. Our Father, our King, for our fathers' sake, who trusted in thee, and whom thou didst teach laws of life, be gracious unto us and teach us. . . . Unite our hearts to love and fear thy name, so that we be never put to shame. Because we have trusted in thy holy, great, and revered name, we shall rejoice and be glad in thy salvation. O bring us in peace from the four corners of the earth, and make us go upright to our land; for thou art a God who works salvation. Thou hast chosen us from all peoples and tongues, and hast brought us near unto thy great name for ever in faithfulness, that we might in love give thanks unto thee and proclaim thy unity. Blessed art thou, O Lord, who hast chosen thy people Israel in love.[14]

This somewhat wordy and repetitive prayer reflects the important concerns of the class of scholars and "doctors of law" who were associated with the House of Assembly (Synagogue) and the House of Study. In these two institutions devoted to study, worship, and education, people prayed that they might be able to learn and heed the commandments. However, synagogue prayer, like prayer sung at the Temple, also asks for the re-establishment of the Jewish state or, in the word of the Abounding Love, for the end of the Diaspora and the return of all Jews to their country (which of course involves the restoration of the state).[15]

The Eighteen Benedictions are known in several versions; it is also believed that not all eighteen (or, according to some versions, nineteen) parts of the prayer date from the first century. However, there can be no doubt that the central thrust has always been to ask of God the restoration of Israel as a state. An old version of the eleventh benediction reads as follows: "Restore our judges as of old, and our leaders as in the days of yore. And reign over us—thou alone. Blessed art thou, O Lord, lover of justice."[16]

While the main emphasis of the Abounding Love is on learning and scriptural scholarship, the Eighteen Benedictions focus on political concerns. Hope for the restoration of the Jewish state was apparently entertained primarily by the priestly aristocracy. They hoped not only for the restoration, but also that they would be the ruling class of the new commonwealth. The chief enemies of early rabbinical Judaism were the pagan rulers, that is the Romans. As soon as their empire perishes, the kingdom of God can be established. This is what they ask God to make happen.

Of course, nothing happens—or at least very little. Here we find the paradox of Jewish prayer: people address the Lord "who answers prayer" (Ps. 65:2 and fifteenth benediction), while knowing that God will not immediately respond. The book of Daniel permits a glimpse into the heart whose logic we have difficulty understanding: when threatened with death by command of the king of Babel, the persecuted Jews insist that even if the Lord does not deliver them, they will still remain faithful to him. People accepted that their prayer for personal and national liberation might remain unanswered. Although they continued to pray, Jews were ready to accept the will of God.[17]

While the Eighteen Benedictions give much space to the restoration of Israel (about half of the benedictions are about this central concern), some more everyday matters are also included: prayer for knowledge of God's Law, forgiveness of sins, the granting of sufficient rain and an abundant harvest. Political concerns are mixed with religious ones and with those of interest to the peasant. Palestinian Jews, we must remember, remained a peasant people for a long time.

The oldest prayer reflecting the concerns usually expressed in synagogue worship was not transmitted in Judaism but in Christianity: the Our Father. It cannot be stressed enough that we have here a purely Jewish prayer; although it is attributed to Jesus and transmitted in writings of the early Church, there is nothing specifically Christian about it. Practically all its words have parallels in standard synagogue prayers: the address "Father" in the Abounding Love; the petition for the coming of the kingdom in both the Abounding Love and the Eighteen Benedictions; the petition for forgiveness again in the Eighteen Benedictions, and so on. Seen in the context of first-century synagogue prayer, the Our Father appears to be a prayer for regular use in public worship, asking God for the deliverance of Israel from its enemies and the restoration of the Jewish state, called the "kingdom of God."

Second Suggestion: The Our Father originated with John the Baptist and was linked to baptism

We do not know for sure when and with whom the Our Father originated. Composed of what seem to be stock phrases of ancient Jewish prayer language, it has few links with the distinctive Jesus tradition. In fact, the context in which the Our Father was transmitted and the way early Christians used it point away from Jesus and to John the Baptist. Luke presents the prayer as the equivalent of a prayer taught to his disciples by John the Baptist. This idea, that the Our Father was equivalent to John's prayer, may imply that the two prayers are actually identical: Jesus presumably taught the same prayer as John. Since Jesus seems to have been active in the Baptist's movement prior to pursuing his own, independent career, presumably as his chief disciple, it is quite natural that he should teach this prayer. Just as Christians adopted the rite of purification, i.e., baptism, from John's movement, so they adopted the text of a prayer used in the Baptist's community.[18]

The Baptist movement saw John as a new prophet Elijah who was expected "to restore all things" (Mark 9:12); this somewhat cryptic phrase refers to the restoration of an independent Jewish state (Sir. 48:10). In anticipation of such an event, the movement already sang a song of victory, celebrating God as the one who brings down the powerful—the Romans and the Herodians—from their thrones and lifts up the lowly, i.e., the Jewish people. As Paul Winter and others have pointed out, the Magnificat—originally sung by Elizabeth, John's mother—makes more sense when we attribute it to the circle of the Baptist. It is precisely this political expectation that provides the key to understanding both John's baptism and the Our Father.[19]

John "baptized," i.e., he assembled people and invited them to be immersed in water for a special religious purpose. John's baptism is a ritual cleansing or, more precisely, an inner, spiritual purification made visible in an outer, physical washing. In ancient Judaism, ideas and practices were regularly derived from or justified with reference to the sacred scriptures that were not only studied by specialists but also publicly read (and translated into the vernacular) in the synagogue. Baptism also has a scriptural basis. John seems to have derived the idea from an Old Testament passage found in the book of Ezekiel. The prophet Ezekiel was active among the exiles from Judah in Babylonia in the early sixth century BCE, and he proclaimed to them Yahweh's announcement of salvation:

I shall hallow my great name [says Yahweh], which you have profaned among those [foreign] nations. When they see that I reveal my holiness through you [Israel], they will know that I am Yahweh, says the God Yahweh. . . . I shall sprinkle pure water over you, and you will be purified from everything that defiles you. . . . I shall put my spirit within you and make you conform to my statutes. (Ezek. 36:23–27)

For the sake of his reputation—his holy name—Yahweh will redeem his people. He will restore them to their home country, Palestine. When this happens, pagans will no longer ridicule the God of Israel who appears to them a weak, second-rate deity, unable to protect his second-rate people. In the eyes of the prophet, the Judaeans deserved to be exiled to Babylonia: God punished them, for they had defiled themselves with sins of idolatry and unfaithfulness. Yahweh has the prophet announce his intervention, and that intervention involves a cleansing of the Judaeans. The prophet speaks of the divine cleansing in ritual terms as a lustration, a cleansing done with water.

The idea that God's name or reputation is closely linked to that of Israel is not peculiar to Ezekiel, but can be found in other biblical traditions (for instance in the book of Joshua: when the Canaanites prevail over the Israelites and cause their name to disappear, then God's great name is also affected). Equally the idea of ritual cleansing was not peculiar to Ezekiel; others also refer to it, most notably Deutero-Zechariah who predicted: "In that day [of redemption] there shall be a fountain opened to the house of David and to the inhabitants of Jerusalem, for purification and sprinkling" (Zech. 13:1).[20]

While in Ezekiel and Zechariah the divine cleansing done with water must be seen as a metaphor for God's invisible action, corresponding to the giving of a "new heart" or attitude (Ezek. 36:26), John the Baptist took it literally, as did the second-century Rabbi Akiba who quoted the Ezekiel passage in approval of Jews cleansing themselves in the *miqveh*, the synagogue's ritual immersion pool. In John's rite of baptism, God is seen as the one who sprinkles pure water over his people to purify them from their defilement. Another explanation might be that John "pre-imitates" the divine action: his baptism "of repentance" invites God to act himself and purify those whom John has prepared.[21]

It seems that John considered himself a precursor—not of Jesus, as the later Christian tradition has it, but as a precursor of God himself who would complete the work begun by his prophet John. "One who is more powerful than I is coming," John proclaimed, and the mightier one is of course a king who with divine help will restore Israel as an independent state, indeed as God's own kingdom (Luke 3:16); hence the announcement: "Repent, for the kingdom of Heaven is at hand!" (Matt. 3:2). Thus John's baptism marks the first phase in the drama of redemption in which Yahweh vindicates the holiness and reputation of his name by re-establishing the political independence and glory of his people. For John, Yahweh's sanctifying of his own name implies the sanctification of Israel; this connection had already been made explicit by Ezekiel.[22]

John's baptism must have involved the invocation of God's own name; he baptized, we assume, "in the name of God." By doing so, he marked his followers with a spiritual sign so that they would be recognized as members of the true Israel when that kingdom was re-established. The coming of the kingdom was to be preceded by God's powerful intervention, which would destroy pagan empires (or just that of the Romans) and also destroy unworthy Jews. "Repent, for the kingdom of heaven is at hand! You brood of vipers! Who warned you to flee from the wrath to come? Even now the axe is laid to the root of the trees; every tree that does not bear good fruit is cut down and thrown into the fire" (Matt. 3:2.7.10). In war and upheaval, the spiritual sign of baptism will serve as a sign of protection: the baptized will be recognized and spared when God's angels come and destroy the Roman Empire. The idea of a protective sign can also be found in Ezekiel, the book on which the idea of baptism is based.[23]

We suggest that the meaning of the Our Father matches with the central concerns of John the Baptist.

The gospels give two versions of the Our Father: a shorter one (Luke) and a longer one (Matthew). While the version in Luke is presumably older and reflects John the Baptist's theology in a clearer way than the longer text, both traditions lend themselves to a reading in the context of John's theology. Set in this context the prayer has a natural and obvious meaning. For the sake of convenience, we insert here an English translation of the two versions and then comment briefly on the Baptist background of the petitions. The commentary will use a variety of paraphrases and translations of the biblical text in order to bring out its meaning as accurately as possible.

The Two Versions of the Our Father

Luke 11:2–4
Father,
hallowed be your name.
Your kingdom come.
[Some manuscripts add: Your holy
    spirit come upon us and
    cleanse us.]
Give us each day our daily bread.
And forgive us our sins, for we
    ourselves forgive all who
    have done us wrong.
And do not bring us to the
    time of trial.

Matthew 6:9–13
Our Father in heaven,
hallowed be your name.
Your kingdom come.
Your will be done, on earth
    as it is in heaven.

Give us this day our daily bread.
And forgive us the wrong we have
    done, as we have forgiven those
    who have done us wrong.
And do not lead us to the time of
    trial, but rescue us from evil.

(I) *Our Father . . . hallowed be your name*. The first three petitions of the Our Father are distinguished by their making God's name, his kingdom, and his will the subject of actions whose actor remains implicit. As all commentators agree, the implication is that God himself is asked to hallow his name, to bring his rule, and to do his will. Therefore the authors of *Praying Together: Agreed Liturgical Texts* are justified when they paraphrase the first petition by saying, "Father, show yourself to be the Holy One!" A more detailed, explanatory paraphrase might run as follows: Restore the holiness of your name by restoring the reputation of those who, through (John's) baptism, bear your divine name! In this context we can understand why the petition "your kingdom come" is in some biblical manuscripts followed by the request, "may your holy Spirit come upon us and cleanse us" (Luke 11:2, manuscripts). This second petition simply explains the first one: God restores his kingdom by sending his cleansing spirit. While Ezekiel, on whom the Baptist generally relied, refers to the sending of God's spirit and to the cleansing from iniquities, he does not link the two ideas explicitly; however, an Isaianic oracle may have suggested the idea: "Yahweh . . . will cleanse the blood of Jerusalem from her midst by a spirit of judgment and a spirit of burning" (Isa. 4:4).[24]

Why is God addressed as Father? Ancient Jewish prayer language includes several possible ways of addressing the deity, one of them being Father, others being God, Yahweh, Lord, and King. Father seems to be the preferred address in particularly urgent supplications, when the praying group's or individual's life is at stake. The priest Eleazar uses it when the enraged King Ptolemy's elephant brigade advances against the Alexandrian Jews; Jesus uses it in the garden of Gethsemane in face of his forthcoming arrest. In situations of extreme distress, God is addressed with a kinship term. In a society in which kinship implies solidarity, we can understand why this should be the case: in times of need, people would also ask the help of their kinsfolk. In Hebrew, one can associate Father with Redeemer, a term denoting a kinsman whose task it is to help. A prayer for Israel's national liberation actually calls God both Father and Redeemer and refers to the Jews as a people called by the divine name: "You, O Yahweh, are our father; our Redeemer from of old is your name. . . . We have long been like those not called by your name" (Isa. 63:16.19). Traditional prayer language allows the deity to be addressed as Father in an urgent plea; the address aims at giving the plea for national liberation a new note of urgency.[25]

(II) *Your kingdom come*. "Bring in your kingdom" runs the correct paraphrase in *Praying Together*. We might suggest a more detailed version: Restore the independent Jewish kingdom! The new Jewish commonwealth already announced by Ezekiel will be the kingdom of God. "You shall be my people and I shall be your God" (Ezek. 36:28). God's royal rule will be exercised by his human representative, a Davidic king. The expression "kingdom of God" has so often been misunderstood that it is necessary to refer to and refute meanings that have been read into the Our Father. Misconstruing the original sense, Christians have often thought of God's kingdom as a universal empire, which will be established after the end of human history as we know it, a commonwealth directly and miraculously ruled by God or Christ, a kingdom not of this world. This is clearly not what John the Baptist and his circle were expecting and praying for. For them, the kingdom of God was a rather small, this-worldly state in Palestine, ruled by an ordinary human person. The second petition echoes the eminently political character of John's preaching and expectations.[26]

The brief—to us, all too brief—second petition reveals a fundamental characteristic of the Our Father, namely, its elliptical, condensed form. Its meaning is not spelled out in plain, accessible language; rather, it is encoded in short formulaic phrases. Despite all that commentators have said about the intimacy of a prayer directed to the heavenly Father, the Our Father lacks immediacy. The formulaic, "restricted" code, as we may call it, was of course not the only one the ancient Jews used in their prayers. They also knew the more wordy, direct, and informal "elaborated" code. The difference can easily be seen when we juxtapose certain petitions of the Our Father with a prayer found in the book of Jesus Sirach:

Our Father	*Sirach*
Our Father—your kingdom come.	Have mercy upon us, O God of all, and put all the nations in fear of you. Lift up your hand against foreign nations and let them see your might. Destroy the adversary and wipe out the enemy. . . . Gather all the tribes of Jacob, and give them their inheritance, as in the beginning (Sir. 36:1–3.9.13.16).
Hallowed be your name.	Have mercy, O Lord, on the people called by your name (Sir. 36:17).

Prayers in the elaborated code are wordy and informal; they also aim at graphic clarity which contributes to an immediate understanding. By contrast, the condensed, restricted code is terse and enigmatic. We sense that the Our Father is not a naïve prayer, born out of a momentary mood; its short phrases betray its origin in learned circles associated with John the Baptist. It is a short text whose words are pregnant with meaning. "When you are praying, do not heap up empty phrases as the Gentiles do; for they think that they will be heard because of their many words" (Matt. 6:7). This word of Jesus reflects common sapiential teaching. "Let your words be few" [in praying], teaches Ecclesiastes, referring to God's heavenly majesty (Eccl. 5:1 [Eng. 5:2]). Jesus Sirach, in a similar injunction, gives the advice to use economical, nonrepetitive speech when praying, comparable to the formal speech used when one speaks in an assembly. Matthew places Jesus' exhortation right next to the Our Father, knowing, it seems, that the Our Father is in the concise, formal style, made up of pregnant rather than "empty" phrases. The Matthean injunction not to "heap up empty phrases" may reflect the pride of those Jews who cultivated the art of writing short prayers in the "restricted" style.[27]

(III) *Your will be done*. "Establish your will" is the paraphrase proposed by *Praying Together*. A more detailed version might be: Cause us to do your will, which is the only law of your kingdom! In the restored divine kingdom, the faithful will of course do God's will, as Ezekiel clearly indicated: "I will put my spirit within you, and cause you to walk in my statutes and be careful to observe my ordinances" (Ezek. 36:27; cf. 37:24). The Jewish historian Josephus called John "a good man, who had exhorted the Jews to lead righteous lives, to practice justice toward their fellows and piety toward God." The insistence on God's will may reflect the Baptist's focus on legal and moral preaching and his opposition to King Herod Antipas's divorce (which eventually cost him his life). The third petition may be an echo of an ancient synagogue prayer, the Abounding Love: "Our Father, . . . put it into our hearts to understand and to discern, to mark, learn, and teach, to heed, to do, and to fulfill in love all the words of instruction in thy Torah."[28]

(IV) *Give us today our daily bread*. Give us abundant harvests! If we stay with our Ezekielian reading of the Our Father, we can refer to the prophet's announcement of miraculously rich harvests: "I will summon the grain [says Yahweh] and make it abundant and lay no famine upon you. I will make the fruit of the tree and the increase of the field abundant, that you may never again suffer the disgrace of famine" (Ezek. 36:29–30). The land will indeed become "like the garden of Eden" (v. 35). The petition's reference to daily bread echoes a tradition not found in Ezekiel, but in the Pentateuch. According to the story of Israel's wanderings in the desert, God fed his people with daily portions of manna, called the "bread from heaven" (Exod. 16:4). As in the Old Testament, the heavenly bread is identified as real bread, not as something merely spiritual.

The Magnificat, which we venture to attribute to the Baptist tradition, gives us another glimpse of what the fourth petition has in mind: "He has filled the hungry with good things, and sent the rich away empty" (Luke 1:53). There will be a rich harvest for the hungry.

(V) *Forgive us our sins (trespasses, debts), as we forgive those who sin against us*. Forgive us our sins of idolatry and apostasy, as we forgive our enemies who have defeated us and continue to oppress us! The meaning of the fifth petition remains obscure as long as the precise nature of the sin to be forgiven is not determined. In keeping with our contention that the Our Father is a "national" prayer, the sin to be forgiven can only be a national sin or rather an accumulation of national sins. The sins to be forgiven can only be those that led to punishment with the destruction of the monarchy and the Babylonian exile. As soon as God forgives, he will also restore the exiles to their home country. Interestingly enough, the Old Testament includes a prayer that spells out in detail the meaning the Our Father expresses in an abridged form: "When your people Israel, having sinned against you, are defeated before an enemy but turn to you, confess your name, pray and plead with you in this house [the Temple of Jerusalem], then hear in heaven, forgive the sin of your people Israel, and bring them again to the land that you gave to their ancestors" (1 Kings 8:33–34). In a similar vein, Daniel, after enumerating the sins that led to exile, asks God for collective forgiveness: "O Lord, hear; O Lord, forgive; O Lord, listen and act and do not delay! For your own sake, O my God, because your city and your people bear your name!" (Dan. 9:19). Daniel's prayer shares with the Our Father the petition for forgiveness and the reference to the divine name; both are stock items belonging to early Jewish political prayer.

A condition for God's forgiving seems to be that the faithful also forgive their oppressors, i.e., the Babylonians, Greeks, Romans, and so on. If this is the correct understanding, it has an important implication: John's message is essentially pacifist. Although he expects an independent Jewish kingdom to emerge shortly, he does not encourage hostile, let alone military, action against the Romans. A confirmation of this idea is the tradition that even tax collectors, as collaborators with the imperial authorities, found nothing contradictory about being baptized and belonging to John's movement. Later, Jesus echoed the Baptist's pacifist attitude when he advised against retaliation: "You have heard that it was said, An eye for an eye and a tooth for a tooth. But I say to you, Do not resist an evildoer. But if anyone strikes you on the right cheek, turn the other also" (Matt. 5:38–39).[29]

When in the sixth century BCE God had summoned Israel's mighty neighbors to punish his people by destroying their state, he established enmity and hatred between them. When God forgives his people and restores their independence, the enmity between Israel and its pagan neighbors must also end. The seventh petition—"deliver us from evil"—seems to envisage universal political peace and harmony. That such an ecumenical, generous vision existed can be shown from an oracle pronounced in a mood of reconciliation: "In that day shall Israel be the third [power] with Egypt and with Assyria, a blessing in the midst of the earth; for Yahweh of hosts has blessed her, saying: Blessed be Egypt my people, and Assyria the work of my hands, and Israel my inheritance" (Isa. 19:24–25). This vision of a community of empires that all belong to the encompassing kingdom of God involves the renunciation of vengeance in an act of forgiveness. Israel must renounce the wish "to execute vengeance upon the nations, and chastisement upon the peoples; to bind their kings with chains, and their nobles with fetters of iron" (Ps. 149:7–8). The phrase "as we forgive those who sin against us" involves an important political program.

The new forgiving attitude vis-à-vis the traditional enemies of Israel seems to prelude if not to "pre-imitate" divine forgiveness, just as John's baptism presumably pre-imitates God's purificatory action. The Greek wording of the petition suggests that the human initiative must come first: "Forgive us the wrong we have done, as we [already] have forgiven those who have wronged us" (Revised English Bible). Once Israel has forgiven her enemies, God "must" also forgive her—and restore her to her pristine glory! One ancient source about John the Baptist includes a hint at the proper meaning of forgiveness. John's baptism, reports Josephus, "would be acceptable if they used it, not for putting away of certain sins, but for the purification of the body, the soul having previously been cleansed by righteousness." First comes the symbolic purificatory ritual, and then comes God's forgiving of the national sins (the "putting away of certain sins"), which latter act becomes visible in the re-establishment of the Jewish state. John does not claim the power to forgive sins; he only prepares people, making them worthy for this divine, national act.[30]

(VI) *Save us from the time of trial.* The traditional rendering, "lead us not into temptation," has been abandoned by recent scholarship. The New Revised Standard Version of the Bible (1989) translates: "Do not bring us to the time of trial." A similar understanding can be found in the Revised English Bible (1989): "Do not put us to the test." The book of Ezekiel does not seem to provide a clue to the understanding of this petition. So we must look elsewhere, and the most obvious relevant tradition can be found in the Pentateuch. God repeatedly "tests" the faithfulness and loyalty of his people by submitting them to hardship and challenge. Apparently, such a test has three characteristics: the entire people is involved; there is great distress; and people are tempted to commit acts of disloyalty, such as returning to Egypt and worshiping other gods. While the hardship Israel experienced in the desert is a mere legend, every Jew knew of the Babylonian Exile as such a test: the entire people was involved; they suffered losses and many were deported to Babylonia; many Jews were tempted to forsake loyalty to Yahweh and to turn to other gods. Viewed in this light, the petition can only mean: Do not bring us to another time of trial, for we have passed through enough national trials.[31]

(VII) *Deliver us from evil.* Deliver us from all our misfortunes! The final petition echoes a phrase known from a prayer text dating from the second century BCE which sums up what God is expected to do: "You rescue Israel from every evil," i.e., from foreign domination (2 Macc. 1:25). In the form of a petition, similar phrases are frequently appended to Jewish prayers: "Set Israel free, O God, from all her misfortunes!" (Ps. 25:22). These misfortunes are of course political ones, and so the last petition of the Our Father is for liberation from foreign domination. Similar requests are appended to other psalms: "Save your people, and bless your inheritance; and tend them, and carry them for ever" (Ps. 28:9). "O Yahweh, God of hosts, restore us; cause your face to shine, and we shall be saved" (Ps. 80:[19]20). And again: "O that deliverance for Israel would come from Zion, when God restores the fortunes of his people" (Ps. 53:6). Since the Our Father, as recorded in the gospel of

Luke, does not have the seventh petition, it may well be an early addition that reflects the style of standard Jewish prayer.

If we are justified in attributing the prayer to John the Baptist and his circle, we may consider the meaning of fasting as practiced by John's disciples. According to Luke, they "frequently fast and pray" (Luke 5:33). Fasting and praying belong together and form one public ritual response to a situation of crisis caused by nature (like drought) or people (like pagan oppression and persecution). It may well be that John and his disciples promoted that ritual response to the absence of God's kingdom. Like baptizing, both praying the Our Father and fasting aimed at speeding up the coming of a great reversal in the history of Jewish political existence. Even if John did not frequently hold public prayer assemblies, he would no doubt have considered private fasting as part of a communal ritual, ideally to be practiced by all Jews. Widely practiced individual devotion would constitute a collective act and bring the same result one expected from assemblies: delivery from oppression and the coming of the kingdom.[32]

Baptism and praying also belong together and form an established ritual sequence: baptism cleanses and thus prepares the individual for participation in the kingdom, and then the newly baptized person joins—or may join—the group in its prayer for the coming of the kingdom. But who is this group? Here a hint given by Origen seems to be relevant. John, he reports, seems to have taught his prayer "secretly," and "not to all who came to be baptized, but to those who became his disciples in addition to being baptized." In other words: there was a wider circle of the merely baptized and a narrower, "esoteric" circle of the actual disciples. These disciples, it seems, practiced the full ritual sequence of fasting, being baptized, and praying for the coming of the kingdom. The "esoteric" quality of the Our Father can still be felt by us in the twentieth century. As a prayer with a rather complex scriptural and ideological background it betrays its origins with the learned and highly motivated religious elite. It is a prayer not for the masses, but for the few.[33]

As we can see from a second-century source, the *Didache*, the ritual sequence of baptism and recitation of the Our Father was also practiced in the early Christian community. This practice seems to predate the second century; in the first century, the New Testament seems to presuppose it. According to Paul, the newly baptized address God for the first time in the Aramaic idiom as Abba, "Father" (Gal. 4:6; Rom. 8:15). This invocation appears to represent the first word of the Our Father, for psalms and prayers (as well as other ancient Jewish texts, e.g., biblical books) were often referred to not by a formal "title," but simply by their first word. Another echo of the Our Father can be detected in the account of Jesus' baptism by John. After having been ritually cleansed by washing, Jesus prays and hears God's voice calling him his "beloved son" (Luke 3:22). If we can take Jesus' baptism as reflecting the pattern of baptism as practiced in Luke's community, then we can conclude that the ritual changes the candidate's status from stranger to son. As a son, he may address God as the Father. Now if the first two Christian generations—those of Paul and Luke—knew the sequence of baptism and reciting the Our Father, then we may be justified in attributing this sequence to John. In other words: the central ritual practiced in the Baptist's community—baptism followed by the recitation of a special prayer—has been preserved in Christianity. Jesus himself, during the time he baptized and proclaimed the closeness of God's kingdom, may have used both the ritual and the text recited in conjunction with it.[34]

Summing up our argument, we can say that the Our Father was originally used as a prayer in ritual assemblies in which John the Baptist announced the re-establishment of the Jewish state (termed God's kingdom) and contributed to its coming by baptizing its citizens. At the center of the promise was, of course, a renewed Jewish state. According to John the Baptist, both the ritual cleansing with water and a newly devised prayer—the Our Father—would serve as a promising invitation of divine intervention and could indeed help inaugurate the new era of divine blessings. In brief paraphrase: "Our Father in heaven, fulfill for your people Israel all you have promised through your prophets!"

Third Suggestion: The Our Father was given unconditional promise of being answered by God

In the gospel of Luke, the text of the Our Father is immediately followed by a statement on the promise of prayer. The general thrust of the teaching is: persistent prayer will be successful, and besides persistence there are no other conditions necessary for success. One passage is particularly illuminating:

> Is there anyone among you who, if your son asks for a fish, will give a snake instead of a fish? Or if he asks for an egg, will give a scorpion? If you then, who are evil, know how to give good gifts to your children, how much more will the heavenly Father give the Holy Spirit to those who ask him! (Luke 11:11–13)

In Matthew's version, the wording of the passage is slightly different, and the conclusion states, "how much more will your Father in heaven give good things to those who ask him" (Matt. 7:11).

We can recognize three links between the Our Father and the teaching on the promise of prayer: the very term of address, Father; the reference to (daily) food; and, somewhat less obviously, the reference to the Holy Spirit. According to certain ancient manuscripts, the version in Luke of the Lord's Prayer includes this petition: "May your holy Spirit come upon us and cleanse us" (Luke 11:2, manuscripts). So we can conclude with some confidence that the saying forms part of the same teaching on prayer to which the Our Father belongs. What believers pray for is listed in the Our Father, and this prayer will certainly be answered. It will be answered as surely as a father responds to his child's requests. Like the text of the Our Father, this additional teaching on the efficacy of praying may ultimately go back not to Jesus but to John the Baptist.[35]

Apparently, John the Baptist (or Jesus) here relies on natural evidence: that fathers grant their children's wishes is a universally acknowledged fact, known to and experienced by everyone. We may call this a "wisdom" kind of argument, for it is based on general knowledge. However, the reference to the Father-child relationship may have overtones that are easily missed by those who are not biblical experts. Behind the sapiential argument there seems to lurk another, scripturalist one, and in what follows we venture to reconstruct how the scripturalists may have supported the promise that the Our Father will unfailingly be answered by God. Apparently, the "wisdom" argument given in the gospels was meant for the general audience of early Christian preaching, while the scripturalist argument had its home in the more esoteric circles of religious specialists.

Those of John the Baptist (or Jesus') followers who were well-versed in the ancient scriptures must have discerned an additional, quite subtle message in the parable of the asking child. If the Our Father is indeed the prayer of God's sons and daughters, experts cannot but think of an Old Testament promise given to the Israelite king as the privileged son of Yahweh: "You are my Son; today I have begotten you. Ask of me, and I will give you . . ." (Ps. 2:7–8). For all its humility, the child's prayer to the divine Father echoes the request made, in ancient times, by the newly enthroned monarch to Yahweh; equally, despite its different setting, the assurance that prayers will be answered echoes the divine promise made to the king. We may see here a "democratic" reading of the psalm: the privilege of having one's prayers answered is no longer confined to the king on the day of his accession to the throne; instead, it belongs to everyone and is always valid. Interestingly, one of the "childlike" requests ancient Israelite kings made to God was for the gift of wisdom, and the model king to receive wisdom was Solomon. "And God said: 'Ask what I should give you.' And Solomon said, '. . . I am only a little child. . . . Give your servant therefore an understanding mind'" (1 Kings 3:5.6.9). In the days of Christ, the book of Wisdom echoed the ancient legend about Solomon's wisdom: "When I was born . . . I was nursed with care. . . . I prayed, and understanding was given me; I called on God, and the spirit of wisdom came to me" (Wisd. 7:3.4.7). Wisdom was associated if not identified with the Holy Spirit. Here we can discover why the Luke version of Jesus' saying implies that prayer in the first place requests the Spirit.

The assurance that prayer will be heard was not confined to royal ritual and legend. Some of the prophets, too, had oracles promising that Israel's prayer would be answered. One prophetic oracle uttered by (or attributed to) Ezekiel not only promises Israel an increase in its population, which had been so drastically diminished during the war with the Babylonians; it also states that Israel is authorized to pray for it: "Thus says the Lord Yahweh: I will also let the house of Israel ask me to do this for them: to increase their population like a flock [of sheep]" (Ezek. 36:37). Or again: "When you call upon me and come and pray to me, I will hear you. . . . I will restore your fortunes and gather you from all the nations and all the places where I have driven you" (Jer. 29:12.14). The request for an increase in the Jewish population and a renewal of the (Davidic) empire is therefore legitimate and prayer can appeal to God's promise. While some public prayers such as the Eighteen Benedictions make certain scriptural connections explicit, these links may remain unspoken (but understood by scriptural scholars). "Your kingdom come": uttered in first-century Jewish worship, perhaps by John the Baptist or one of his followers, this request may actually ask for the increase in the population and the restoration of the Jewish empire. For first-century Jewish scriptural experts, the expression "Kingdom of God" has a precise political meaning which can be discovered through biblical texts such as the ones quoted above.

From our discussion we conclude that the promise of success attached to the Our Father views the praying community—Israel—as a child, presumably a royal child whose request God will certainly grant. This confident promise seems to reflect the teaching of John the Baptist and not that of Jesus. The unconditional promise makes sense in the teaching of someone who, like John the Baptist, thinks in the first place of the petitions made in the Our Father, which we have explained as a political prayer for the restoration of Israel as an independent state. John and his circle have no doubt that God will soon grant what this prayer requests.

Fourth Suggestion: The Our Father took on a different meaning in the Jesus movement

Striking differences distinguish Jesus the Healer from John the Baptist. John had not performed miracles, but Jesus did. We have no means of telling whether Jesus had the role of exorcist within the Baptist movement or whether he developed his exorcistic skills only after the death of his master, John. What we know is that he came to develop a new theological vision which was no longer dependent on John's teaching but on his own exorcistic experience. For Jesus and most of his followers, the term "God's kingdom" came to assume a different meaning. For John the Baptist, God's kingdom comes with the destruction of the Roman Empire and other important political upheavals that were expected to lead to the restoration of the Jewish state in Palestine. For Jesus, who (presumably after the Baptist's death) decided to pursue a mission different from that of John, the kingdom came in a different, more "private" way. While John the Baptist apparently expected a restored, "healed" nation as the kingdom of God, Jesus was more interested in the social and physical healing of individuals. Reconciliation with God remained paramount in his message, but the national focus receded into the background or vanished altogether. God's kingdom arrives when the sick are healed through exorcism. Jesus' interest centered on spiritual healing and exorcizing evil spirits. He proclaimed that "the kingdom of God is among you," i.e., it is visible whenever made present in the act of healing (Luke 11:20;17:20–21). He sent out his disciples, telling them: "Heal those who are sick and say: the kingdom of God has come upon you" (Luke 10:9). Of course, the magician cannot always make the kingdom visible; nonetheless, it is a present reality. While John longed for the arrival of dramatic political changes that would affect the entire Jewish population, Jesus believed in a God whose rule can be seen in individually experienced acts. The beginning of the book of Acts has preserved an echo of the debate whether after Jesus' death the "kingdom will be restored to Israel" or whether his disciples will be empowered by his (magic) *dynamis* in order to continue his work; of course, the latter is the case (Acts 1:6–8). Magical acts represent God's rule: this is the central teaching about the kingdom, and presumably part of what the early community saw as "the mystery of the kingdom." It is these different notions of God's kingdom in particular that allow us to speak of two quite distinct meanings of the prayer: while John prays for the coming of the Jewish kingdom as a political reality, Jesus prays for the kingdom as an exorcistic event. We can thus distinguish between a Johannine political prayer and a Jesuanic exorcistic one.[36]

A look at Jesus' "inaugural sermon" as presented in the gospel of Luke may help us to summarize the distinction between the message of John and the message of Jesus. The biblical reading on which the sermon is based refers to the prophet's task of proclaiming "release to the captives and recovery of sight to the blind, to let the oppressed go free" (Luke 4:18). John would no doubt have preached about the release of the captives and the liberation of the oppressed in a new, politically independent kingdom of God. Jesus, as presented by Luke, concentrates on the individual. His model is the prophet Elijah, bearer of the divine spirit, who helped a poor widow and restored the health of a foreigner.

As we know, the Baptist's prayer became attributed to Jesus, and the latter may have encouraged its use at least in the early period of his ministry, when he still worked in the Baptist movement and preached within its theological tradition. Short and laconic as the prayer was, it could be given a new meaning, a meaning more compatible with his own exorcistic and moral, nonpolitical concerns. The new meaning was of course not entirely new, for the Our Father had originated in a predominantly magical milieu, one dominated by the magic rite of baptism. With Jesus, the magical dimension intensified, and we may postulate a specifically magical understanding of several of the petitions.

(I) *Our Father in heaven: Hallowed be your name* (i.e., hallow your name). While first-century Jews were quite familiar with addressing God as their father in prayer language, it seems that one group had a special preference for the address: the miracle-working pietists of Galilee. They thought of themselves as "sons" who could address God as their "father." According to an anecdote reported in the Mishnah, Honi the Circle Drawer considered himself "a son of the family" of God; as a family member, he could ask all kinds of favors from his heavenly father, including the sending of rain. However, Honi did not simply utter words of prayer: he uttered his words while standing in a magical circle which he had drawn. The intimate father-son relationship was not only characteristic of the mentality of the Galilean magicians, but also of Jesus, who was one of them.[37]

Jesus, of course, did not claim sonship exclusively for himself. His followers and associates were also sons and daughters of the heavenly father. Some of Jesus' followers actually left their families in order to join Jesus and share his homelessness as well as his "family," the metaphorical household headed by God, the Father. As a healer, Jesus may well have understood that suffering individuals could be permanently cured from their demonic possession (or, in modern parlance, from psychological troubles) only by being taken out of the pathogenic milieu in which they lived. His new community of brothers and sisters who venerated the one Father provided them with a substitute family and home. When addressing God as the "Father," they reassured themselves of their new emotional and social situation.[38]

The reference to God's "name" has strong magical connotations. The exorcist and miracle worker invokes God's name as the name of the authority under which he acts, and when the action—e.g., of healing—succeeds, everyone attributes the success to God's name and praises it. By acting through the healer, God hallows or glorifies his own name. In a magical context, "hallowing" means glorifying: "making the divine name famous, demonstrating its power by miracles."[39]

There is another possibility, however. It may well be that Jesus and his early followers still remembered the first petition's original baptismal link. Jesus may have continued to view baptism as a ritual that inaugurated or helped inaugurate the sanctification of the divine name. But he presumably gave the idea a more individualistic focus: the emphasis is on individual sanctification and healing rather than on that of the nation or a holy remnant. One could easily have invoked the example of Naaman, whom the prophet Elisha healed of a skin disease by having him dip himself seven times in the Jordan river.[40]

Cyprian of Carthage, one of the earliest Christians to write a commentary on the Our Father, has detected the baptismal meaning of the petition, "Hallowed be your name." When we pray for the hallowing or sanctification of God's name, he explained, we have to remember that it is God himself who sanctifies, and that he has sanctified the faithful in baptism. You Christians, Paul had said, are washed and made acceptable to God and "sanctified in the name of our Lord Jesus Christ and by the Spirit of God" (1 Cor. 6:11). Bearers of the divine name, Christians must be kept in this status of sanctity by God's continual intervention. "We beseech of Him," Cyprian explains, "that His Name may be hallowed of us. . . . We ask and entreat, that we who were sanctified in baptism may continue in that which we have begun to be. And this we daily pray for, for we have need of daily sanctification, that we who daily fall away may wash our sins by continual sanctification." Cyprian seems to be saying that the holiness of the faithful and that of God are associated, and with divine help, the faithful can daily renew their baptismal state of purity and freedom from the stains of sin. By helping the faithful, God keeps his own name clean. While Cyprian's argument is brief and somewhat cryptic, one can understand it by considering the baptismal rite itself which sanctified the catechumen in the name of God. By helping baptized Christians to preserve their holiness or renew it, God promotes the holiness of his own name! "Not that we wish for God that He may be hallowed by our prayers, but that we beseech of Him that His Name may be hallowed in us." Cyprian has here preserved or rediscovered what we consider one of the keys to the original meaning of the Our Father.[41]

(II) *Your kingdom come* [i.e., exercise your royal rule]. While John the Baptist and his contemporaries thought of God's kingdom as a political reality brought about by the renewal of a Jewish state, Jesus sees God's rule realized in the present. His parables make clear that he redefines John's apocalyptic vision, replacing it by a magical concept. The magical kingdom looks to the present rather than to the future and imagines how one could live here and now within an already or always available divine dominion. One enters that kingdom by being healed from possession or other forms of demonic affliction. Since the magical, spiritual kingdom is present and provides healing and life under divine protection here and now, hope for a future political kingdom recedes into the background. God's dominion can be visible and tangible. Its force shines forth, especially in the brief moments of divine intervention in healings and manifestations of magical power. Among the early authors, only Luke has preserved the distinctive magical dimension of the divine kingdom. "If it is by the finger of God that I cast out the demons, then the kingdom of God has come to you," Luke explains (Luke 11:20). God rules where demons, confronted with the exorcist's word and gesture, leave the body of a sick and suffering person. So by praying for the kingdom's coming one actually prays for divine assistance in the fight against demonic powers. Interestingly enough, an Old Testament psalm already sees God's intervention on behalf of an individual oppressed by hostile forces (including demonic powers) as an act of God's royal rulership. Psalm 22 exemplifies the ancient mentality: as soon as the personal God (who acts as an equivalent to the guardian angel of Christian lore) leaves his protégé, hostile forces take over. When he resumes his rulership, the demons flee and can no longer do any harm. Jesus the Magician places the suffering individual under God's protection and so brings God's kingdom to him or her. God's kingdom can be defined as the demon-free area brought about by Jesus the Healer.[42]

(III) *Your will be done* (i.e., do your will) *on earth as it is in heaven.* This petition can be seen as synonymous with the preceding one, "exercise your royal rule." However, the early Jesus tradition may have understood it as a formula of submission to God's will. Jesus himself is reported to have prayed, "Father, if you are willing, remove this cup from me; yet, not my will but yours be done" (Luke 22:42). When God includes the earth in his heavenly rule, then demons and suffering have to disappear; however, it may be God's will to tolerate the powers of evil for some time. If this interpretation is correct, then we can paraphrase the two petitions as follows: "Exercise your royal rule; yet, not my will but yours be done."

(IV) *Give us today our daily bread.* Here we will try to speculate about a quite mundane meaning of the petition as understood by Jesus and his immediate disciples. As persons without regular income, they relied on the irregular donations and hospitality of friends and wealthy sponsors. It is through them that God provides for daily bread. Morton Smith comments: " 'Give us today the food to carry us over to the next' brings us down to the earth, to the real life of a vagrant performer—actor, magician, holy man or whatever—dependent from day to day on the contributions of the audience he would find in the next country town." Here our distinction between a plea for deliverance and a request for blessing can be helpful: John the Baptist's urgent request for the daily manna belongs to the plea for immediate deliverance, for it implies the end of the Roman oppression and the advent of God's kingdom; when Jesus asks for daily bread, he simply asks for God's motherly care and blessings to continue—though there may be a slight note of urgency, for if Smith is correct, daily bread for the itinerant man of God did not come by itself. It had to be begged for every time.[43]

(V) *Forgive us our sins as we forgive those who sin against us.* Divine and human forgiveness seem to have figured prominently in the preaching of Jesus. John, by contrast, while attacking the unjust behavior of individuals, seems to have taken little interest in forgiving individually committed sins; his interest was in the national sin of apostasy. Unlike John the Baptist, Jesus emphasized the former, the divine forgiveness of individually committed sins. The practice of forgiveness among individuals helps to "heal" human lives and relationships in the same way exorcism heals diseases.[44]

(VI) *Save us from the time of trial (or, temptation).* The time of trial or temptation (Greek, *peirasmós*) can be seen as a time of special demonic assaults that assail the individual and jeopardize his (or her) exorcistic mission. We must remember that in the earliest Christian community, *every* believer was supposed to be able to work wonders and perform miraculous healings. However, it was clear that there are special trials connected with the career of an exorcist, trials prefigured in the life of Jesus. A demonic being called "the tempter" (*ho peirázôn*) had asked Jesus to acknowledge him as his lord and spirit-helper and to perform special miracles with his assistance, such as to change stones into bread (Matt. 4:1–11). Jesus of course resisted the temptation to replace his "white magic," in which God worked, by "black magic," related to Satanic powers. God himself must save exorcists in such situations of spiritual crisis that accompany their careers: this is what the Our Father prays for.[45]

(VII) *Deliver us from evil (or, the Evil One).* Again, the prayer is here no longer for Israel but again for individual delivery from misfortune, from sickness, or demonic powers. According to a traditional interpretation of the seventh petition, found for instance in the work of the church fathers Origen, Tertullian, and Cyprian, the "evil" is actually the Evil One: Satan or the devil. This understanding also seems to be echoed by the Odes of Solomon, an early-Christian hymn book dating from around 100 CE: "because of your name let me be saved from the Evil One." Both the New Revised Standard Version of the Bible (1989) and the Revised English Bible (1989) adopt this reading by rendering the petition as "rescue us from the evil one" and "save us from the evil one." If this interpretation is accepted, we could point to the dualism of God's divine rule and the rule of the Evil One. With God's help, the exorcist delivers people from the Evil One.[46]

In conclusion to this brief commentary it is necessary to emphasize the tentative nature of our understanding of the Our Father. The prayer's brevity and coded language remains a challenge to scholarship. In the case of the "baptist" reading, we can stay relatively close to the literal meaning of the words, but given our limited knowledge of the Baptist movement, we must admit that our interpretation is experimental. When attempting to describe the prayer as it was understood in the Jesus movement, we must admit to being unable to move beyond conjecture. We feel, however, that our interpretation is plausible and can account for more features than other ones that have been suggested.

Fifth Suggestion: The Our Father belongs to traditional,
not to utopian religion

While details of interpretation remain uncertain, the general religious background of the Our Father is clear enough. Both readings, the "baptist" and the "Jesuanic" one, reveal the same mentality, rooted in the same traditional Mediterranean religion. The best way to characterize this religion is to compare it with another form which Jonathan Smith has called the "utopian" type. According to traditional religion, in some mythic past, God or the gods had set the world in order, and it was in essence immutable. However, it has always been a troubled world. Traditional religion sees human life, society, and state as essentially fragile. By means of flood and drought, famine and plague, defeat in war, oppression of the poor, and so on, demonic forces threaten and impair it. Various combat myths explain how a divine warrior keeps the forces of chaos at bay and enables the world to survive. Of course, that battle never ends, for after each defeat, the forces of evil somehow renew their strength. At a practical level, this means that society's integrity has to be maintained and restored through acts of conscious labor, performed either by humans or by God, or by a co-operative effort of both. Frequently, traditional religion prefers the "thaumaturgical" response to evil. This "miracle-working" response focuses on the individual's concern for relief from current, specific problems by special dispensations. The request for supernatural help is personal and local, and its operation magical. Salvation is immediate, but has no general application beyond the given case and others like it. It takes the form of healing, assuagement of grief, restoration after loss, reassurance, the foresight and avoidance of calamity, and sometimes also the promise of continuing life after death. It is a "religion of sanctification," geared toward the reparation of things that are out of place: rectification, cleansing, and healing restore the ideal state of things, producing healthy social, political and individual human bodies in a specific place, i.e., in the holy land of Palestine.[47]

Jonathan Smith contrasts the traditional religion, which he also calls a religion of "place" (he terms it "locative"), to a "utopian" form of religion. For utopian religion, the world is far from immutable. It moves, through incessant conflict, toward a final, conflictless state—cosmos without chaos. The essential myth tells of a time when, in a prodigious battle, the supreme god will utterly defeat the forces of chaos and their human allies and eliminate them forever, and so bring an absolutely good world into being. As the Greek term "utopian" suggests, place is no longer an issue. Rather than being interested in restoration, cleansing, and healing, one waits for a universal cataclysm out of which a new universal order will emerge—an order which will then prevail forever in heaven or on earth, or in both realms at the same time.

In the Bible, there is evidence for both types of religion. John the Baptist and Jesus seem to represent the traditional type, for their project is the healing of Palestinian society either by re-establishing a Jewish state or by healing individuals. Paul and the book of Revelation, by contrast, are no longer interested in a local project of repairing an impaired social and political system. Paul focuses on separation from the world and on being in heaven with Christ. The book of Revelation describes the final universal battle between God and the powers of darkness in detail and looks forward to God's final victory. The book of Revelation culminates in a depiction of the final, conflictless state in which all the saints rejoice in their Lord in the New Jerusalem.

With its emphasis on political liberation (John the Baptist) or exorcistic healing (Jesus), the Our Father reflects the "traditional" religion's concerns of sanctification. In later Christianity, of course, it could be given a "utopian" meaning. Set in the context of the expectation that God would destroy the powers of evil once and for all, "Your kingdom come" and "Deliver us from the Evil One" could be taken to look forward to the establishment of God's everlasting, universal rulership. The expectation of the end of all evil, shared by Paul and the book of Revelation, has certainly influenced the way many early Christians understood the Our Father; yet, it seems that Jesus himself never gave his message such a utopian frame. Even though he may have hoped to cure Jewish society as a whole, he never went beyond hoping for the immediate, though temporary, triumph over the forces of evil. He remained a local healer.

Sixth Suggestion: In post-biblical times, Christians used the entire prayer, but stressed only certain petitions

There can be no doubt that from the early days Christian congregations used the Our Father. However, there was a great variation in its importance to different groups. The fact that of the four gospels only two—Matthew and Luke—give the text and that they differ in the precise wording, is quite telling. Some communities either never heard of the Our Father or discontinued its use; others had their own version which they either conserved or adapted to new tastes. Unfortunately, the early sources tell us nothing about the use of the Our Father in congregational worship. In fact, whether it was used congregationally at all is not stated unambiguously before the mid-third century CE, when Cyprian provides the evidence. If we take a closer look at the liturgical sources, we discover a rather puzzling fact: the Our Father was no longer a prayer in which all the words carried a precise meaning. Instead, certain phrases were highlighted by the liturgical context; while the others remained present, their meaning was as it were "screened out."[48]

The basic idea of using the Our Father selectively by emphasizing one phrase can be illustrated from Saint Benedict's monastic *Rule* (ca. 550 CE). The Benedictine monks' daily round of communal prayer includes the recitation of the Our Father. The relevant passage merits full quotation:

> The Offices of Lauds and Vespers [morning and evening prayer] shall never be allowed to end without the superior finally reciting, in the hearing of all, the whole of the Lord's Prayer. The purpose of this is the removal of those thorns of scandal, or mutual offense, which are wont to arise in communities. For, being warned by the covenant which they make in that prayer, when they say, *Forgive us as we forgive*, the brethren will cleanse their souls of such faults.[49]

Although the complete text of the Our Father is recited, the intention focuses on *one single* petition: "Forgive us as we forgive." However, the petitions that are not emphasized in a specific situation are not omitted, for the liturgy never tampers with the text of the Our Father. This text is never recited in an incomplete, abridged form, but always retains its full wording. Like most of the ancients, especially the Romans, the church has come to believe in the value and efficacy of fixed ritual formulae. Most liturgical uses of the Our Father resort to the same approach as St. Benedict's *Rule* and stress one or two petitions while neglecting the rest. The most common emphases are on forgiveness, daily bread, and deliverance from evil. Occasionally, we also find an emphasis on calling God "Father."[50]

When it is used as a communion prayer, the Our Father highlights the petition for daily bread and for forgiveness. An early historical source illustrating this liturgical custom dates from ca. 400 CE and comes from Augustine. He indicates that the Our Father was spoken by the entire community between the eucharistic consecration and the people's communion. In one of his sermons, Augustine (or pseudo-Augustine, for the attribution is not clear) explains that communicants need God's forgiveness; otherwise, they would not be worthy to receive communion. The official introduction printed in the Missal of Paul VI (1970) repeats this traditional view by saying that the Our Father "is a petition both for daily food, which for Christians means also the eucharistic bread, and for forgiveness from sin, so that what is holy may be given to those who are holy [i.e., communion to the faithful]."[51]

A second emphasis is on the final petition, deliverance. After the consecration of sacramental bread and wine, the Catholic priest and the congregation pray together as follows:

Priest:	Let us pray with confidence to the Father in the words our Savior gave us.
Congregation:	Our Father, who art in heaven . . . but deliver us from evil.
Priest:	Deliver us, Lord, from every evil, and grant us peace in our day. In your mercy keep us free from sin and protect us from all anxiety as we wait in joyful hope for the coming of our Savior, Jesus Christ.
Congregation:	For the kingdom, the power and the glory are yours, now and forever. (Missal of Paul VI, 1970)

As we can see, the priest takes up and develops the last petition ("deliver us from evil") and thus "begs in the name of the community deliverance from the power of evil."[52]

The Selective Use of the Our Father in the Catholic Mass

What is said:	*What is meant*:
Our Father, who art in heaven,	Our Father, who art in heaven,
hallowed be thy name,	
thy kingdom come;	
thy will be done on earth	
as it is in heaven.	

Give us this day our daily bread;	Give us this day our daily bread;
and forgive us our trespasses	and forgive us our trespasses
as we forgive those who trespass against us;	as we forgive those who trespass against us;
and lead us not into temptation,	and
but deliver us from evil.	deliver us from evil.

Another idea highlighted in post-biblical uses of the Our Father is the idea of calling God "Father." In the late fourth century in Augustine's episcopal city, Hippo, baptismal candidates received their main instruction during the forty days before Easter Sunday. The instruction culminated in the explanation of two texts they had to learn by heart: the apostolic creed and the Our Father, for the one embodies the teaching of the Apostles and the other that of Christ. In the Easter Night, the catechumens received their baptism and in the following Mass, which they attended with the entire community, they recited the Our Father for the first time. The Our Father could not be spoken by just anyone; one had to be authorized to call God one's "Father": by being a baptized member of the community. According to another fourth-century source, the *Apostolic Constitutions*, the newly baptized Christians say it as they emerge from the baptismal font, i.e., immediately after baptism. Here, the prayer does not belong to the Eucharist but forms part of the baptismal rite. In fact, one can say that baptism culminates in the congregational recitation of the Our Father. Through baptism, the candidate has become a "child of God" and may legitimately address him as "Father."[53]

In our century, Rudolf Otto (1869–1937), Protestant theologian and promoter of liturgical renewal, advocated a use of the Our Father that would also highlight its first words. He made sure that the liturgy he devised for his congregation that met in St. Jost, a small Gothic chapel near Marburg (ill. 3), did not end abruptly with the sermon. After the sermon came an elaborate part he termed "veneration." In this concluding part of the service, the Our Father was carefully staged. The minister called attention to God's presence by saying: "The Lord is in his holy temple; let all the earth keep silence before him!" After a period of general silence during which the congregation knelt, a bell was rung three times. Then everyone stood up for the congregational recitation of the Our Father. What Otto felt he lacked in St. Jost's chapel was a visible focus for the recitation. In his book on liturgical renewal he included a drawing of what such a focus could be: a kind of Gothic rose window, placed in the apse above the altar and inscribed *Vater unser* (ill. 4). Otto seems to have felt that the crucifix, which normally provides a ritual focus on or near the altar, was not appropriate for the liturgical act he had in mind. A crucifix represents the Son rather than the Father, and the latter should therefore have his own symbol.[54]

Using the prayer to call God "Father" or to ask God for forgiveness and

3. Rudolf Otto's Chapel. This fourteenth-century Gothic chapel in Marburg, Germany, seats fewer than a hundred people. Rudolf Otto in the 1920s conducted his experiments with "silent worship" here. The Lutheran author of *The Idea of the Holy* (1917) wanted to restore a sense of the "numinous" to Protestant worship. In sacred silence people should experience the divine presence and respond to it with adoration. Chapel of St. Jost, Marburg, Germany.

4. A Place for Prayer. For Rudolf Otto, Protestant worship should culminate in a period of silent adoration, followed by the recitation of the Lord's Prayer. In 1925 he had an artist sketch the ideal architectural setting for his liturgy. The window inscribed *Vater Unser* ("Our Father") represents the numinous presence of the deity and provides a visible focus for the praying congregation. He lacked such a focus in his own chapel of St. Jost. Rudolf Otto's ideal sanctuary. Artist's rendering, 1925.

communion is using it selectively. However, Christian worship can go as far as using it without any real meaning. When Catholics pray the "Rosary," they recite the Our Father fifteen times; within this prayer, the Our Father has no precise meaning at all; at most, it may be called a form of greeting God. As a sacred text, its recitation creates an atmosphere charged with the sacred. The same can be said of Protestant uses. Typical Protestant services of worship insert its recitation after more or less elaborate prayers for specific causes. When the congregation has brought its petitions before God, these are somehow "summarized" in the Our Father. It is used not as an independent series of petitions, but as a kind of sacramental device that ensures that the petitions said earlier get a better chance of being answered by God. Its recitation also creates a sacred atmosphere that impresses, if not the entire congregation, then at least some of its members, satisfying their thirst for a numinous experience. Friedrich Heiler (1892–1967), a German Catholic who became a Lutheran and a respected advocate of liturgical renewal, reported about the awe he felt when he first attended a Protestant service of worship. It was the minister's recitation of the Our Father which he experienced as the most sacred moment. As the minister spoke the text, the bells of the Bavarian church rang, presumably in imitation of the ringing of Catholic bells at the moment of eucharistic consecration. This somehow made up for the sacred drama lacking in sermon-centered Protestantism.[55]

With our tentative reading of the Our Father as a first-century prayer that reflects concerns of John the Baptist and later those of Jesus, we are very far away from the meanings that later liturgical practice has found in this most widely used Christian prayer text. The more the Our Father becomes separated from its original historical and ritual setting, the less understandable it becomes. Those who design liturgies tend to highlight certain of its apparently meaningful parts, or they forget about any meaning and make use only of its sacred sound and traditional authority. Only for those who dig deeply into the history of Christian and even pre-Christian worship do its words begin to transmit their concealed, "encoded" message, which is, ultimately, a message not for humans but for God.

As a prayer to be used in congregational worship, the Our Father has lost much of its original meaning. However, it has acquired a new and unprecedented status as a condensed statement of Christian doctrine. The church fathers considered the prayer a summary of the gospel teaching or, in the words of Cyprian, "a compendium of heavenly doctrine" (*caelestis doctrinae compendium*). The compendium form ensures "that the memory of the students might not be burdened in the celestial learning, but might quickly learn what is necessary to a simple faith." The Our Father was understood to embody the message of the New Testament in the same way the Ten Commandments of Moses represent the Old Testament: a short text, easy to memorize, ascribed to the major teacher, and serving as a condensation of the key ideas represented by a large body of texts and traditions. The two form, as it were, miniature bibles. Accordingly, all the elementary textbooks of Christian instruction ("catechisms") explain both the Ten Commandments and the Our Father and by doing so they establish a common Judeo-Christian world view. The sacred words have become an object of study and learned discourse. However, as books aimed at edification and rudimentary instruction, catechisms tell us little if anything about the original meaning of the Our Father as a congregational prayer. While the words of the Our Father are still used in worship, their meaning—or imagined meaning—has emigrated to doctrine.[56]

3. Christian Prayer: Origins, Forms, and Promises

The right words used when addressing God may come to some Christians quite naturally, but generally one has to learn how to pray properly. Prayer has a form and a history. Public prayer relies on biblical precedents as well as models included in liturgies and authorized books of worship. The present chapter studies the origins of Christian prayer in the New Testament period, illustrates the forms of regular liturgical prayer, and surveys past and present ideas about the hopes and expectations entertained by those who bring their supplications to the Lord.

Thaumaturgy and Theurgy: The Original Settings of Christian Prayer

Unlike the Our Father, whose origin we have sought in the circle around John the Baptist, Christian prayer originated with Jesus. The gospels include two paradigmatic scenes in which Jesus is shown as praying or relying on prayer. The first one is a scene of miraculous ("thaumaturgical") healing. Here we meet Jesus as a healer and exorcist, surrounded by disciples who share their master's magical powers. Nevertheless, they sometimes fail. Certain disciples were reported not to have been able to heal an epileptic boy, so that Jesus himself had to do the job. In private, the unsuccessful disciples asked their master to tell them the reason of their failure. He answered that it was "because of your little faith. For truly I tell you, if you have faith the size of a mustard seed, you will say to this mountain, 'Move from here to there,' and it will move; and nothing will be impossible for you" (Matt. 17:20). "To have faith" here does not mean "to accept the Christian message" (as elsewhere in the Bible) but "to trust in God's miracle-working power." According to another tradition, Jesus did not refer to insufficiency of faith but to inadequate prayer: "This kind [of demon] can come out only through prayer" (Mark 9:29). The second paradigmatic scene shows us Jesus on the Mount of Olives, shortly before he was arrested by Roman soldiers. Luke portrays him as praying for deliverance: "Father, if you are willing, remove this cup [of suffering and death] from me; yet, not my will but yours be done." God does not grant the request; instead, he sends an angel to give him strength (Luke 22:42–43). This second scene is quite unlike the first one. Here Jesus does not pray for someone else, but for himself. The answer he receives shows that what we have here is not a thaumaturgical context, but one in which a being from heaven appears to comfort the praying individual. Jesus may have heard the angel saying something like, "Do not fear, greatly beloved, you are safe. Be strong and courageous" (Dan. 10:19, presumably the Old Testament model of the scene). Using the terminology of the ancients, we will refer to this type of quest for the visionary presence of a heavenly being as "theurgical" prayer. (More on theurgy and thaumaturgy can be found in the introduction to part V of the present study; see below, pp. 287–8.)

Both kinds of prayer—the thaumaturgical kind for healing and the theurgical type in answer to which God sends an angel—have had an enormous impact upon the way the early Christians understood and practiced their ritual. In the case of thaumaturgical prayer we can actually see how it developed into a regular ritual. The relevant instruction on healing prayer is in the letter of James:

> Are any among you sick? They should call the elders of the church and have them pray over them, anointing them with oil in the name of the Lord. The prayer of faith will save the sick, and the Lord will raise them up; and anyone who has committed sins will be forgiven. Therefore confess your sins to one another and pray for one another so that you may be healed. The prayer of the righteous is powerful and effective. [The Old Testament prophet] Elijah was a human being like us, and he prayed fervently that it might not rain, and for three years and six months it did not rain on the earth. Then he prayed again, and the heaven gave rain and the earth yielded its harvest. (Jas. 5:14–18)

The elders of the church act as healers. Their healing ritual involves a rite of purification from sin (usually placed at the beginning) and a prayer or spell which accompanies the anointing of the sick person "in the name of the Lord." A close reading of the passage in James suggests that here an older, pre-Christian ritual has been adapted to church use by the addition of the "name of the Lord." Originally, it was not Christ's name that was thought to do the healing, but the invocation of an Old Testament precedent according to which the prophet Elijah could make rain fall. The use of oil also points to a pre-Christian basis of the ritual. Jewish lore believed in the healing properties of the "oil of life" gained from a tree in Paradise; while after expulsion from Paradise people had no access to this oil, it is now again made available. Characteristically, the success of the "sacramental" cure is not taken for granted. The actual healing is not promised unconditionally. As in the paradigmatic passage discussed earlier, it is only "the prayer *of faith*" that will be successful, i.e., the prayer based on trust in God's miracle-working power.[57]

The success of thaumaturgical prayer depends not only on faith, but also on the reference to "the name of Jesus." Magical Judaism and its Christian heirs believed in the power of certain names associated with the divine or with

personalities of the past credited with supernatural potency. Some contemporaries of Jesus used the magical power connected with the name of King
Solomon. According to legend, demons had obeyed that great king; and they
would obey the magician who uses Solomon's spells, his ring, and his name.
Josephus tells us of one Eleazar, whose successful exorcism he himself witnessed. After the evil spirit had left his victim, Eleazar "adjured the demon
never to come back to him, speaking Solomon's name and reciting the incantations which he had composed." Jewish tradition tells a story of an early second-
century healer, Jacob of the village of Sama in Galilee, treating a snake-bitten
rabbi "in the name of Jesus ben Pantera"; while it is not clear whether Jesus
(here given his Talmudic name) forms part of the original tradition, the reference demonstrates the importance of invoking a powerful name. Many first-
century Jews believed in the protective virtue of "baptism," a cleansing ritual
that involved ablutions and apparently a reference to the name of John the
Baptist. Others relied on the virtue of the names Simon, Menander, and
Carpocrates of Alexandria, i.e., names of famous magicians living in the first
and second centuries. Christians, of course, performed their exorcisms not in
the name of Solomon, but in the name of Jesus, and their baptism as well as
their anointing of the sick was done in the same name, that of Jesus. For them,
it was only natural to assimilate prayer to the art of magic and hence join the
name of Jesus to it. The name ensured efficacy. Even non-Christians acknowledged the power assumed to reside in Jesus' name. If we can trust the gospel of
Mark, even during the lifetime of the master exorcists expelled demons "in the
name of Jesus" (Mark 9:38). Christians, apparently, were not against the use of
Jesus' name in non-Christian exorcism; in fact, they understood it as a half-
allegiance to their group. In late antiquity, Greek-speaking exorcists relied on
the invocation of multiple divine names, and they sometimes included the
name of Jesus on their list, joining it to names like "God of Abraham" and "Iao
Sabaoth."[58]

In patristic times, theologians such as Origen still knew and defended the
magical use of the name of Jesus. Born and raised in Egypt and bearing the
name of the pagan god Horus, Origen (i.e., Horigenes, "born of Horus") lived
in a world saturated with magical lore. When confronted with skeptical questions on the subject, Origen simply replied that "by the name of Jesus, with the
recital of the histories about him" miracles have often been produced. And
when being told that it makes little difference if one calls the supreme deity by
the names used among the Greeks or by those used among Indians or Egyptians, he replies as any expert magician of his day would reply:

> Now if by a special study we could show the nature of powerful names . . . and
> if we could establish that so-called magic is not, as the followers of Epicurus and
> Aristotle think, utterly incoherent, but as the experts in these things prove, is a
> consistent system, which has principles known to very few; then we would say

that the names Sabaoth, Adonaï, and all the other names that have been handed down by the Hebrews with great reverence, are not concerned with ordinary created things, but with a certain mysterious divine science, that is related to the creator of the universe.

In other words, the use of names like those of the Old Testament God or of Jesus belongs to the world of magic; although very few understand its theory, that theory can be justified.[59]

Theurgical prayer, like the thaumaturgical kind, was not practiced by everyone, but only by qualified or gifted individuals. Particularly revealing is the scene in which the priest Zechariah, officiating at the altar of incense inside the actual Temple building, was visited by an angel. It may well be that theurgical prayer originated with priests at the Jerusalem Temple and that angels and other beings of the divine world were expected to manifest themselves primarily in the sanctuary. This is still the case with Paul who, when praying in the Temple, has a vision of the Lord who tells him to leave Jerusalem and to go and preach to the gentiles. But as the scene of Jesus on the Mount of Olives demonstrates, theurgical prayer was no longer bound to its original setting. Others, not just priests, could perform theurgical prayer and experience its overwhelming result, namely, to come into contact with the divine world. Occasionally, this contact left visible traces, for those in theurgical contact with God may radiate light, especially from their faces, as has been reported for Moses and Jesus. In a theurgical situation, the praying individual receives God's answer, which does not necessarily imply the granting of the wish for visible "thaumaturgical" benefits. Paul prayed to be delivered from the power of a demon who attacked him as he stood in a vision before Christ's heavenly throne. The answer he received from the Lord, who spoke to him in the vision, was negative. The thorn will stay, this is God's will, and there is no appealing against it. So Paul's prayer was not answered. Like Jesus, he was well aware of the condition basic to all individual supplication for deliverance: whether God will grant the request or not depends on his will. There is no general expectation that individual prayer for deliverance will be answered.[60]

We have already become acquainted with two characteristics of theurgical prayer: it seems to be practiced by specially gifted individuals, and although the divine world manifests itself in response to the supplication, the actual granting of the request depends upon God's will. Theurgical prayer "opens up a doorway between earth and heaven, but once that door is opened only God himself knows what may pass back through it from heaven to earth." The establishment or activation of a special relationship with God is more important than getting a request granted. A further characteristic of theurgical prayer has to do with its use in a communal context: it can actually be practiced in a group. The gospels present Jesus as a master theurgist initiating others into having an experience of the other world. Thus, he went up on a mountain to pray in the company of Peter, John, and James, and together they had a vision of Moses and the prophet Elijah. In another, more subdued scene, Jesus' theurgical prayer leads his disciples to a special experience that made them acknowledge their master as the Messiah. In such situations, the small group of individuals having a theurgical experience is dependent on the intercessory prayer and guidance of a master, i.e., Jesus. Having experience and being on special, unique terms with the divine Father, Jesus can help others to have contact with the divine world and its manifestations. After the death of Jesus, his followers still believed in Jesus' intercessory powers. A good example of this belief can be found in the Acts of the Apostles. Luke tells how the apostles Peter and John were arrested by Jewish authorities and held in custody for having healed a lame man. Eventually, the two were restored to freedom but urged to stop preaching in the name of Jesus. It was not healing as such that was their crime, but doing so in the name of Jesus. The Jerusalem Christians responded to this incident with a fervent prayer addressed to God:[61]

> Sovereign Lord, who made the heaven and the earth, the sea, and everything in them, it is you who said by the Holy Spirit through our ancestor David, your servant: "Why did the Gentiles rage, and the peoples imagine vain things? The kings of the earth took their stand, and the rulers have gathered together against the Lord and against his Messiah." For in this city, in fact, both Herod and Pontius Pilate, with the Gentiles and the peoples of Israel, gathered together against your holy servant Jesus, whom you anointed, to do whatever your hand and your plan had predestined to take place. And now, Lord, look at their threats, and grant to your servants to speak your word with all boldness, while you stretch out your hand to heal, and signs and wonders are performed through the name of your holy servant Jesus. (Acts 4:24–30)

Christian prayer, like its Jewish equivalent, is addressed to God, creator of heaven and earth. We may compare the first of the Eighteen Benedictions which addresses "God Most High, creator of heaven and earth," or the elaborate predication of Mordecai's prayer found in the Septuagint Bible: "O Lord, Lord, you rule as King over all things, for the universe is in your power and there is no one who can oppose you when it is your will to save Israel, for you have made heaven and earth and every wonderful thing under heaven" (Est.LXX C1–3). The Christian text adds a reference to the name of Jesus. "The name of your holy servant Jesus": this phrase explains in whose name the apostles perform their healing miracles or, in our terminology, their thaumaturgical rituals. However, the reference to Jesus seems to have another, theurgical implication: Jesus' name is invoked as the name of the intercessor and mediator with God, as the Lord "standing at the right hand of God" in heaven (Acts 7:55). Given the unfailing intercession of such a powerful mediator, God cannot but respond to the request, and so the divine world manifests itself: "When they had prayed, the place in which they were gathered together was shaken; and they were filled with the Holy Spirit and spoke the word of God with boldness" (Acts 4:31). What we have here is of course a prayer tied to a specific incident and therefore not a regularly repeated text. After God has answered the community's request by granting courage to Peter and John in their work, there is no reason to come back to it.

By the end of the first century, Christians had a well-established repertoire of set phrases and themes used in regular communal prayer. The earliest example is a rather long text found in First Clement, a letter included in modern collections of the apostolic fathers. Some ancient manuscripts such as the fifth-century Codex Alexandrinus counted it as part of the New Testament. Written by the Christian community of Rome around 96 CE, the letter was sent to Corinth, where the church was riven by conflict. At the end, the author uses hymnic language and in mid-sentence decides to address God himself. Characteristically, the prayer of Clement ends with praise of God; this praise is offered "through Jesus Christ" and thus sealed not only with the traditional Jewish "Amen," but also with the name of Jesus: "You, who alone are able to do these and even greater things for us, we praise through the high priest and guardian of our souls, Jesus Christ, through whom be the glory and the majesty to you both now and for all generations and for ever and ever. Amen." The communal prayer we quoted from the Acts of the Apostles ends in a similar way: those who pray expect God to work wonders "through the name of your holy servant Jesus." We can see that what counts is the Christian "sealing" of the prayer with Jesus' name, not the precise way in which this name was joined to the end of a prayer. The letter to the Colossians, dated about the end of the first century, includes an exhortation that seals the entire service of worship—its sacramental actions as well as its words—with the name of Jesus: "Let every word and action, everything you do, be in the name of the Lord Jesus, and give thanks through him to God the Father" (Col. 3:17).[62]

When the early Christians prayed to God (as they usually did) rather than to Jesus, they nevertheless thought of Jesus as a second deity. For them, as for many first-century Jews, belief in two deities rather than one was quite common. It was clear to everyone that one God, the heavenly Father and Creator, held the supreme power over heaven and earth. However, the Creator had also delegated some of his power to a second, subordinated being. One could invoke the book of Daniel or the book of Wisdom in support of such a view. According to a vision of Daniel, the Creator, called "the Ancient in Years," delegated some of his power to a mighty angel: "Sovereignty and glory and kingly power were given to him [i.e., the angel], so that all peoples and nations should serve him; his sovereignty was to be everlasting" (Dan. 7:14). The book of Wisdom presents the second deity as Sophia, i.e., in female form.

Christians saw Jesus as an incarnation or earthly form of Daniel's angel and the book of Wisdom's Sophia. In their prayers, they called upon either God or the second deity; typically, they addressed God and concluded with a reference to the second deity.[63]

The early Christians thought of Jesus as an intercessor. In their view he functions in very much the same way a Semitic "personal god" functioned for an individual. The personal deity of an ancient Mesopotamian or Hebrew was typically a lesser divinity, but one with access to the throne of one of the great and more powerful gods. The personal deity acted as an intercessor for his or her devotee. Christ, of course, "is at the right hand of God, interceding for us" (Rom. 8:34). When, in the gospel of John, Thomas prostrates himself before Christ, acknowledging him as "my Lord and my God", he uses the exact phrase with which a Semite would refer to his personal deity, "my god" (John 20:28). So we can see behind the seemingly innocent formula, "through Jesus (Christ)," a complex religious world with a long history. In classic Judaism, with its uncompromising monotheism, the individual's personal deity has been identified with the one and only God. Christianity, however, still reflects older and more complex notions of the divine world. Traces of these can even be found in the Hebrew Bible: for example in the Psalms where Yahweh is described as the greatest and as it were the president of the gods whose existence is not denied. Jesus, as a divine being who presents our prayers to the Father, belongs to just such a complex divine world, peopled with beings that cannot be reduced to simple angelic spirits in the service of the one God. Whenever early Christians prayed "through Jesus," they evoked and indeed recreated an ancient Semitic world other Jews had long since abandoned.[64]

As a personal deity, Jesus could also be called upon independently of the Father. In this case, he served as a kind of "familiar spirit." An early tradition about Jesus illustrates the notion of the familiar spirit quite well. Some of Jesus' contemporaries accused him of having a powerful demon as his familiar spirit, arguing that "He has Beelzebul, and by the ruler of the demons he casts out demons" (Mark 3:22). According to the New Testament, Jesus always acted in his own name, and never appealed to a spirit helper. Christians, however, adopted the spirit of Jesus as their familiar and tutelary spirit whose name they could invoke independently of God. For this reason, they were called "those who invoke the name of Jesus." Stephen, the first martyr to die for the Christian cause, is reported to have cried to Jesus as he died: "Lord Jesus, receive my spirit" (Acts 7:59). Stephen invoked Jesus as his personal deity. Yet he is also reported to have seen "the heaven open and the Son of Man standing at the right hand of God" (v. 56). The personal deity, in the Christian universe, always stands in close relationship to the Father. As Bultmann suggests, we may assume that prayer directed to Christ typically happened "outside of formal, liturgical worship . . . in the personal lives of individuals." There seem to be exceptions, though. When all the members of the congregation venerate

Jesus as their personal God, why should they not also address their prayers to him? However, petitionary prayer was more often and more typically directed to the Father "in the name of Jesus" or "through Jesus Christ."[65]

These two distinct notions—that of Jesus as an intercessor with God and that of the power residing in his name—readily merge in the early Christian mentality. A phrase like "through Jesus Christ" is added to a prayer both as a formula of efficacy and a formula of mediation. People even pray to Jesus "in the name of Jesus": when addressing a prayer explicitly to Jesus, the faithful would not omit the reference to Jesus' powerful "name" (John 14:14). However people may conceptualize the way in which prayer "works," ultimately it is Jesus' name, a name "above every name" (Phil. 2:10), that invests the supplication with special power. Traditional scholarship has erected a clear-cut boundary between what is considered despicable "magic" (which relies on the efficacy of Jesus' name) and honorable "religion" (which hopes for Christ's intercession with God). Although such distinctions reflect ancient polemical language, in reality magic and religion overlapped to the point where they were indistinguishable.

Before we end this discussion of prayer in the New Testament, we have to consider a subject already referred to: the promise of prayer; for no one prays without the hope of being answered by God. We found that Christians are relatively realistic about what to expect. In the thaumaturgical setting, the efficacy of prayer or exorcism depends upon the strength of one's faith; so if the miracle does not happen, the explanation is found in lack of faith. In the case of theurgical prayer, one is sure that an angel will manifest himself or that divine revelation will be given; but one is aware that the granting of the actual request depends upon the inscrutable divine will. Whenever the New Testament refers to the efficacy of prayer, one of the two conditions is involved. The most obvious example is in the story about Jesus cursing a fig tree. Accompanied by his disciples, Jesus approached a fig tree in order to eat some of its fruit. As the tree had no fruit, the frustrated master cursed it, and "at once" it withered. (In Mark's version, the disciples discovered the fact that the tree had withered only the day after Jesus had pronounced his curse.) To this story, the gospel report attaches the following teaching, given by Jesus himself: "Truly I tell you, if you have faith and do not doubt, not only will you do what has been done to the fig tree, but even if you say to this mountain 'Be lifted up and thrown into the sea,' it will be done. Whatever you ask for in prayer with faith, you will receive" (Matt. 21:21–22). In other words: as long as magicians believe in their powers, they can accomplish whatever they want; but if their thaumaturgy fails, it is owing to lack of faith.

In the gospel of John, we find the following promise, made by Jesus himself: "Very truly, I tell you, the one who believes in me will also do the works that I do and, in fact, will do greater works than these, because I am going to the Father. I will do whatever you ask in my name, so that the Father may be glorified in the Son. If in my name you ask me for anything, I will do it" (John 14:12–14). Christ says that he himself will answer prayers, for he and the Father are one. While the promise seems to be very inclusive indeed, the context suggests a rather limited application in a theurgical situation. The "works" Christ's disciples will do are ritual acts in which the Father is seen in visionary experience; this seems to be the implication of the demand "Lord, show us the Father, and we will be satisfied" (John 14:8), to which Christ's promise is the answer. In John, the promise of successful prayer is given not to all believers, but only to a narrow circle of Jesus' followers, and it relates not to all petitions they might bring before the Lord, but only to the petition of having a successful visionary experience of the Father or Christ or both, for both are one. When the gospel of John repeats Christ's promise elsewhere, we have to accept it in the same context: his departure from the world. After his death, his disciples can no longer rely on Jesus as the master theurgist; they have to perform the ritual themselves. "Very truly, I tell you, if you ask anything of the Father in my name, he will give it to you. Until now you have not asked for anything in my name. Ask and you will receive, so that your joy may be complete" (John 16:23–24). The disciples' joy will be complete when they see their Lord in a heavenly vision.

Thus far we have passed over one saying of Jesus which seems to be particularly relevant to a theology of corporate prayer. It seems to promise unconditional success: "Truly I tell you, if two of you agree on earth about anything you ask, it will be done for you by my Father in heaven. For where two or three are gathered in my name, I am there among them" (Matt. 18:19–20). This looks like an instruction for a prayer séance in which two or three invoke the name of Jesus in order to have a particular wish fulfilled. However, a recent commentator has followed the same interpretive strategy we have adopted, namely to pay careful attention to the context in which prayer is promised an answer. Duncan Derrett points out that the context establishes a quite different meaning for the scene here envisaged. Apparently, the reference is not to two or three believers who pray for a miracle, but to trustees or elders who meet to decide about controversies in the name of the Lord. The saying of Jesus deals with offenses, not prayer! The "two or three" are arbitrators, one from each of the opponents in the dispute and the third from the church if the two cannot resolve the dispute. Unofficial dispute settlers and peacemakers "perform a divine function. The Christian, submitting to Christian discipline, has faith that the arbitrators whom he has partly chosen for himself, supplemented perhaps by one chosen by the Church, will act as colleagues of Christ himself, and therefore he will believe that their solution is his will." We follow Derrett in assuming that the "legal" interpretation of Matt. 18:19—"if two of you agree on earth about anything you ask, it will be done for you"—corresponds to its original meaning. The passage should not be read as a general and unconditional promise of success accorded to corporate prayer.[66]

The Form and Promise of Liturgical Prayer

In the post-biblical period, as Christian worship became more and more institutionalized and settled into fixed forms, its prayer increasingly lost its original
thaumaturgical and theurgical settings. It became "liturgical," i.e., part of a
regularly celebrated ritual in which neither healing miracles nor manifestations
of angels were expected to occur. Despite this change in the atmosphere in
which people worshiped, liturgical prayer still shares essential characteristics of
the earlier form. It continues to refer to the name of Jesus, it still addresses
the Father, it conserves a preference for using biblical language, and it ends
with "Amen."

The *reference to Jesus Christ* remains the distinguishing mark of liturgical
prayer. Whatever Christians pray for, they approach the Father "through our
Lord Jesus Christ" and pray "in the name of Jesus." Specifically magical
connotations have disappeared from theological commentaries. Christ is seen
as mediator and intercessor. Some authors give little meaning to the formulaic
conclusion; according to Schleiermacher, for instance, it denotes simply
that Christians pray in the spirit of Jesus, i.e., for the advancement of the
kingdom of God.[67]

Origen, when giving advice to those who are "scrupulous about prayer,"
insisted that petitions be *addressed "only to the God and Father of all,"* not to
Christ. In a fine piece of rhetoric, he imagines Christ saying: "Why do you pray
to me? You should pray only to the Father, to whom I pray myself. This is what
you learn from the Holy Scriptures." Contrary to what Origen's advice might
lead us to expect, early Christian prayer often followed St. Stephen who, before
his death as a martyr, prayed to Jesus. Modern researchers have discussed
several examples of early prayers and praises first addressed to Christ and later
re-addressed to God, the most frequently quoted example being the Sanctus.
From the days of Origen, theologians preferred to pray to the Father. In the
West, the synod of Hippo Regius (393 CE) declared: "No one shall name the
Father for the Son or the Son for the Father in prayers; and when one assists
at the altar the oration shall be directed always to the Father." Origen and
his followers decided that Christian prayer should be theocentric, not
Christocentric.[68]

Typically, Christians have sought to address God in an appropriate way,
which for them meant to heap up epithets or references to divine deeds. Such
introductions of course have their models in the Old Testament, e.g., in King
Hezekiah's prayer: "O Yahweh, God of Israel, who are enthroned above the
cherubim, you are God, you alone, of all the kingdoms of the earth; you have
made heaven and earth. Incline your ear" (2 Kgs. 19:15). Among the sixteenth-
century reformers, Luther's friend Philipp Melanchthon (1497–1560) gave
much thought to prayer. Both his little manual compiled for the ordained
clergy of Wittenberg and his larger *Basic Topics of Theology* included

substantial chapters on praying, complete with model texts. A proper prayer, he explains, must begin with an invocation and predication of God and a reference to Jesus, our mediator. Melanchthon insisted that Christian prayer should be recognizable as such; it should be different from that of pagans, Jews, and Turks, who also address God as the creator of heaven and earth. All of Melanchthon's prayers start with rather elaborate introductions. He wanted, of course, to Christianize the prologue to prayer. The model introduction he gives in *Basic Topics of Theology* reads as follows: "O almighty, eternal and living God, eternal Father of our Lord Jesus Christ, who hast revealed thyself in thy abounding goodness and who hast said of your Son, our Lord Jesus Christ: Hear him. Maker and preserver of all things, together with thy coeternal Son, our Lord Jesus Christ, and the Holy Spirit, poured out unto the Apostles, O God of wisdom, goodness, mercy, justice, and strength!" The threefold reference to Jesus ensures the Christian character of the prayer that follows. Melanchthon, who mistrusts very general forms of addressing God (like "Our Father, who art in heaven"), recommends using his well-thought-out introduction also when reciting the Our Father.[69]

In actual liturgical usage, the "predication" attached to the divine addressee of the petition may be very short: "Almighty and merciful Father" (*Book of Common Worship*, 1946). It can be much more elaborate, as the following examples demonstrate:

"Almighty and everlasting God, who dost govern all things in heaven and earth" (*Book of Common Prayer*)
". . . who hast caused all holy Scriptures to be written for our learning" (*Book of Common Prayer*)
". . . creator of all, you ordered the earth to bring forth life and crowned its goodness by creating the family of man. In history's moment when all was ready, you sent your Son to dwell in time, obedient to the laws of life in our world" (*Roman Missal* of Paul VI).

These predications serve to motivate the request put before God or, more importantly, "to adumbrate the very answer of God to the cry of our souls." They also weave the petitions into the complex fabric of the biblical story which is continually recalled. The petitions grow as it were out of scripture itself.[70]

Prayers with elaborate predications of God have an archaic flavor. They are a continuation of ancient prayer language. Apparently, the ancient Jews preferred to predicate the deity on the basis of qualities, while the Greeks exclusively referred to the deeds of a deity. Two examples demonstrate the pattern:

"Thou, [Heracles,] unconquered one, thou with thy hand art slayer of the cloud-born creatures of double shape, Hylaeus and Pholus, the monsters of Crete, and the huge lion beneath Nemea's rock. Before thee the Stygian lakes trembled;

before thee trembled the warder of Hell, as he lay on half-gnawn bones in his bloody cave . . . [petitions follow]." (Virgil)

"Incline your ear, O Lord, and answer me. . . . For you, O Lord, are good and forgiving, abounding in steadfast love to all who call on you." (Ps. 86:1.5)

While the first predication lists the deeds of the demi-god Heracles, the second one refers to the compassionate character of the Jewish god; the first one reflects the distinctively Greek style (imitated by the Roman author, Virgil), the second one the Semitic tradition. In Christianity, the two styles often get mixed together, but one can still discern them and trace their ancestry.[71]

Throughout its long history, liturgical prayer has preferred *biblical language*. "Cause Thy Church to increase more and more, and that every knee may bow before Thee, and every tongue confess that Jesus Christ is Lord." Many prayers, like this one found in the Presbyterian *Book of Common Worship* (1946), make ample use of scriptural language. Instead of saying that God may grant that all the world should acknowledge the rulership of God and Christ, the same idea is formulated biblically, using an expression found in one of the Pauline letters—"that every knee may bow before Thee" (Phil. 2:10–11). Although prayers composed toward the end of the twentieth century are perhaps less rich in biblical allusions and the use of scriptural language, the ideal is still maintained. A good prayer must echo the Bible. An unexpected witness of the appreciation of biblical prayer language is Joseph Addison (1672–1719), the famous English essayist. In one of his many contributions to the magazine *The Spectator*, he extolled the Hebrew idiom and commented on the ease with which its poetry translated into English. For him, a prayer phrased in elegant English but not couched in scriptural language is "cold and dead." The relevant passage, published on June 14, 1712, merits being quoted in full:

There is a certain coldness and indifference in the phrases of our European languages, when they are compared with the oriental forms of speech; and it happens very luckily, that the Hebrew idioms run into the English tongue with a particular grace and beauty. Our language has received innumerable elegancies and improvements from that infusion of Hebraisms, which are derived to it out of the poetical passages in Holy Writ. They give a force and energy to our expressions, warm and animate our language, and convey our thoughts in more ardent and intense phrases than any that are to be met with in our own tongue. There is something so pathetic in this kind of diction, that it often sends the mind in a flame, and makes our hearts burn within us [Luke 24:32]. How cold and dead does a prayer appear that is composed in the most elegant and polite forms of speech, which are natural to our tongue, when it is not heightened by that solemnity of phrase, which may be drawn from the sacred writings.

In the early eighteenth century, very few Englishmen appreciated the language of the King James Bible. Prepared at the proposal of King James I and introduced in 1611, it became the standard translation used by all English-speaking Protestants. However, early critics often scorned its clumsy language, and they did so for several generations. Addison ranks among the first to discover its beauty.[72]

Outside the English-speaking world, experts used and recommended biblical language with equal enthusiasm. German Protestants appreciated the language of Luther's Bible for its simplicity and graphic clarity. When Friedrich Seiler (1733–1807) established guidelines for the composition of liturgical prayer, he urged pastors to rely on the Bible. It is "the biblical expression of religious truth" that gives to prayers the necessary "unction and higher dignity." Luther's vocabulary and phrases assumed the canonical status of sacred words.[73]

Twentieth-century prayer has lost much of the earlier richness of biblical allusion. People no longer feel at home in the scriptures. To them, biblical expressions often "sound like pious jargon" or even "slightly humorous" and must therefore be avoided. They also feel increasingly uneasy about the obsolete language of the King James Bible. Theologians like the Presbyterian Henry Sloane Coffin (1877–1954) lament the "widespread biblical illiteracy among even churchgoers." Unable to rely on biblical learning among the congregation, the pastor must refrain from using "allusions or phrases which are not plain in themselves." Nevertheless, theological authors as well as liturgical guidelines still insist on the use of scriptural language. Henry Coffin, while being aware of the problems of Hebraisms, recommends a prayer language that is in tune with that of the King James Bible of 1611. Like Addison, he feels that there are more than historical reasons for using the archaic idiom; for "happily a vast amount of the biblical thought and speech expresses current moods aptly and felicitously, and touches the spirit of men with overtones which other language lacks." In 1979, the (American Catholic) Bishops' Committee on Liturgy expressed the same sentiment. Even in the twentieth century, traditional biblical language seems indispensable if not attractive.[74]

Prayers end with Amen. Before being used in worship, Amen—"truly, yes"—served as a term of emphatic affirmation in the context of legal disputes and military command, and may be a word the Hebrews borrowed from the Egyptians. Like the reference to Jesus Christ, God as the addressee, and the biblical language used, the Amen has never disappeared as an element of Christian prayer. The text we quoted from the late first-century CE letter of Clement, though written in the Greek vernacular, ends with the Hebrew word "Amen." This term, still placed at the end of prayers today, is familiar to all Christians. Greek-speaking Christians like Clement inherited it from the Greek-speaking synagogue. Like Palestinian Jews who said their prayers in Hebrew and Aramaic, the Diaspora synagogues ended their prayers with the same traditional term. Both the term and its use at the end of prayers are biblical. A scene in the book of Nehemiah helps us to understand its original meaning and use in worship. As the leader of public worship, Ezra says a prayer, to which the congregation give their assent by raising their hands and shouting in unison "Amen, Amen" (Neh. 8:6). The Hebrew term can be translated as "truly" and serves to express assent. By saying Amen, the congregation makes the leader's prayer its own. We could say that the community puts its—oral not written—signature under the prayer after it has been pronounced. Just as it is the leader's place to pray on behalf of the community, so it is the congregation's place to conclude the prayer by responding with Amen. Incidentally, neither in the ancient synagogue nor in the early church did people pronounce set prayers in unison; the exception to this rule was, and still is, the Our Father. In order to involve people in public prayer, they were invited to respond by shouting Amen. The church father Jerome mentioned one time that the Amen in the Roman basilicas reverberated like a heavenly thunder. Jerome also knew that the less simple people understand a foreign-sounding word, the more they are impressed with it.[75]

Amen is a Hebrew word. Why did Christians of all nations and languages adopt it into their ritual language? First of all, because the church descended from the synagogue and continued its practice of communal prayer. When an individual stood up in Paul's community in Corinth to pray, those present responded by saying Amen. As late as the fourth century, long after the separation of church and synagogue, some Christians considered the Jews the true masters of the art of prayer and adopted their texts, complete with petitions and Amens, adapting them only slightly by adding an occasional reference to the name of Christ. When in the second century the church father Justin explained Christian worship to pagans (and presumably new converts), he also had to explain the meaning of Amen: once the worship leader "has finished the prayers and the thanksgiving, the whole congregation present assents, saying Amen. Amen in the Hebrew language means, *So be it.*" This is all Justin wrote; no further explanations, no apologies for using a Hebrew term; no reference to the fact that the book of Revelation uses Amen as a name of Christ. Justin, like many early Christians, was enchanted by the Hebrew term and its sacred sound. Two centuries after Justin, Augustine explains that terms like Amen and hallelujah are generally left untranslated on account of the "more sacred authority" attached to their original form. The "sacred authority" to which Augustine refers may sound rather innocent to our ears. For the ancients, sacred authority implied magical force, for in ritual, as one ancient source explains, the Eastern peoples "do not so much use [empty] 'words' but 'sounds' which are powerful." Amen, for them, is a powerful word, a term that adds to the efficacy of prayers and chases demons. It helps to channel the divine forces and scares away the devil, for, as a sixth-century Christian amulet has it, the evil spirits are "fearful of the Amen and the Hallelujah and the gospel of the Lord." In Christianity, as in Judaism, prayers traditionally end with Amen, and this has not changed through centuries of liturgical reform and experimentation. Even the French and Italian Catholics, who sometimes use *ainsi soit-il* and *così sia* as a vernacular equivalent, have never abandoned the Amen in their official liturgies.[76]

When Christians meet to present their request to God, they expect *divine response*. After the Amen, it is God's turn to act. How he is expected to react depends of course upon the request itself. The manifold petitions brought before God in Christian public prayer can be classified in three categories: congregations pray for deliverance, i.e., for dramatic divine intervention on their own behalf or on behalf of others; for purely spiritual goods such as illumination by the Holy Spirit or the forgiveness of sins, i.e., the restoration of a positive relationship between God and humans; and for the granting of divine favor, i.e., for peace, prosperity, well-being, protection, and continuing health. The three categories of petition correspond to three distinct divine activities: God delivers, he grants spiritual goods, he blesses. Illumination and forgiveness have to do with an interpersonal relationship. Deliverance concentrates on specific, often miraculous, and datable events that are understood as acts of God, whereas blessing deals with the natural processes of God's guidance and nurturing of his creation.

Of the three kinds of requests, the first one—redemption or deliverance—requires the most immediately visible and, as it were, tangible divine response. If a congregation prays in a situation of real and pressing need, for instance for rain in a time of drought, then God's response is expected to occur from the clouds: nothing but real rain will be identified as God's answer. In this case, prayer transcends the sanctuary in which it may be pronounced on Sunday morning. The petition for immediate deliverance or help is for straightforward miracles. The most common request in this group is for individual healing from suffering and illness, and such prayer has accompanied the entire Christian history. A notable example of a healing service involved the English and French monarchs. On special days, generally Good Friday, the king or queen would touch epileptics or people suffering from scrofula, a skin disease called "the King's Evil." A typical prayer said by the officiating chaplain runs as follows: "God give a Blessing to this Work; And grant that *these* Sick *Persons* on whom the Queen lays Her Hands, may recover, through Jesus Christ our Lord." The ceremony was still being practiced in England in 1807, and in France in 1825, but thereafter fell out of use. However, the practice of healing through prayer never ceased, and the twentieth century actually saw a massive revival of it, especially in American free churches and in the Church of England. Where special services for the sick are held, pastors invoke the epistle of James which recommends anointing the sick and affirms that "the prayer of the righteous is powerful and effective" (Jas. 5:16). All reports on contemporary healing liturgies give more or less spectacular results. We hear of a cancer that disappeared the day before a patient was going to have surgery. However, we are also told that most healings happen as the outcome of "gradual, persistent, soaking prayer."[77]

Of course, not all Christians, let alone theologians, believe in the miraculous power of prayer. Luther, for all his belief in the promises made by Christ, remained skeptical about regular miracles brought about by prayer. Commenting on the letter of James and ritual anointing, he denied its sacramental status and healing efficacy. "Christ did not make anointing with oil a sacrament, nor do St. James's words apply to the present day. For in those days there was a ritual that had the effect of miraculously healing the sick as requested in the earnest prayer of faith." *In those days*, in the early years of the church—but not today! In a similar vein, John Calvin explained that in the days of James, the church had the gift of healing; but as a "temporary gift" or ministry exercised by the apostles, it "quickly perished, partly on account of human ungratefulness." According to Luther and Calvin, the role of the magician is no longer available for the post-apostolic pastor. The more a congregation's petitions are specific and God's response accessible to verification, the more cautious some theologians become, while others are confident and celebrate God's miraculous power.[78]

Requests for purely spiritual goods are often made in worship. The most common ones are for the spiritual cleansing of the congregation, for spiritual illumination, and for the redemption of the dead. Spiritual cleansing, generally termed "forgiveness of sins," is often prayed for at the beginning of a service of worship, and God's granting of the request may actually be confirmed by the priest or minister. The request "Have mercy on us, O God. . . . In your great compassion, cleanse us from our sin," may be answered by the Presbyterian pastor: "I declare to you in the name of Jesus Christ, you are forgiven" (*Book of Common Worship*, 1993). The pastor here acts as God's representative. Through the words of the priest or pastor, God forgives here and now, at the very moment of worship. Forgiveness "happens," as it were, during the liturgy; no reality outside of worship (like rain or deliverance from illness) corresponds to God's answer. Since here the divine response to prayer forms part of the liturgy itself, the act of forgiving is exclusively liturgical. Often, the scriptural reading during worship is preceded by a prayer for illumination in which the Lord is asked that through the inner working of the Holy Spirit, the congregation might hear the reading and preaching with true understanding. One example is: "God our helper, by your Holy Spirit, open our minds, that as the Scriptures are read and your Word is proclaimed, we may be led into your truth" (*Book of Common Worship*, 1993). Catholics regularly ask God to grant a particular spiritual good to their departed ones: that they be admitted into heavenly glory. Protestants either reject or take a nuanced view of the practice of praying for the dead. Since in the beyond, punishment or reward will be based on deeds done in this life, and on nothing else, prayer for the departed is simply useless and a waste of time. In the sixteenth century, Calvin termed it "a perverse mode of prayer" (*perversus orandi mos*). Luther did not go as far as the reformer of Geneva. He suggested the following prayer: "Dear God, if the departed souls be in a state that they may yet be helped, then I pray that you would be gracious." To which he added: "When you have thus prayed once or twice, then let it be sufficient and commend them unto God." Following their master, Lutherans generally exclude intercession for the dead from public prayer; they leave it to the individual to approach God as he or she wishes. The congregation cannot "test" the efficacy of prayer for spiritual goods, so that trust in their being granted remains a matter of belief.[79]

With the third group of petitions—for general assistance—we move back into the realm of empirical reality. Here are some examples: "Almighty and everlasting God, . . . mercifully hear the supplications of thy people, and grant us peace all the days of our life" (*Book of Common Prayer*, Second Sunday after Epiphany). "All-powerful God, increase our strength of will for doing good that Christ may find an eager welcome at his coming and call us to his side in the kingdom of heaven" (*Roman Missal* of Paul VI, First Sunday of Advent). Where the venerable Book of Common Prayer with its echoes of medieval tradition is still in use, people also pray in the so-called litany: "That it may please thee to preserve [alive] all that travel by land or by water, all women labouring of child, all sick persons, all young children; and to shew thy pity upon all prisoners and captives." The tenor of such supplications and intercessions (as they are called) remains vague and general, so that the congregation will have no way of finding out whether God actually grants the request. God is here seen as a power working quietly behind the scenes. Reminded by the congregation, he may direct his attention to those praying for themselves or being prayed for.[80]

God's response to the general request for protection and well-being clearly transcends the situation of worship, for health, peace, prosperity, etc., are tangible realities of everyday life. However, Christian worship also includes a liturgical response to this request. Generally placed at the end of the service, the pastor or priest pronounces an authoritative declaration of divine favor, called a "blessing." Accompanied by a solemn gesture designating the cross, the Catholic priest ends Mass by saying, "May almighty God bless you—the Father, and the Son, and the Holy Spirit," to which the congregation responds "Amen." Both Catholics and Protestants often use more elaborate forms such as the "priestly benediction," found in the Old Testament and employed in antiquity at the Jerusalem Temple (and still used in the synagogue today):

May the Lord bless you and keep you.
May his face shine upon you,
and be gracious to you.
May he look upon you with kindness,
and give you his peace. (Num. 6:24–26)

May almighty God bless you,
the Father, and the Son, and the Holy Spirit.[81]

5. The Sun God Blesses the Entire Creation. Some people work, while others raise their hands in adoration of Aton, the sun god of ancient Egypt, who blesses all creation by sending his rays of light. The words of blessing which the ancient Israelite priest spoke over the congregation referred to God's shining face, for the biblical God, though not represented by an image, could be thought of as a sunlike being. The biblical priest's blessing is still used in Christian worship: "May the Lord bless you and keep you. May his face shine upon you, and be gracious to you. May he look upon you with kindness and give you his peace" (Num. 6:24–26). Limestone relief, Amarna period, Egypt, fourteenth century BCE.

"May his face shine upon you, may he look upon you": these words seem to reflect the archaic idea that the sun is a manifestation of Israel's God. The ancient Israelites had a great taste for light breaking through the clouds and for the rainbow which they thought of as a manifestation of the divine majesty. The presence of the sun and its beneficial light served as a powerful assurance of divine presence and blessing. In ancient Egypt, we find similar notions in the art of the Amarna period (fourteenth century BCE), when King Akhenaten has the sun disk depicted as the supreme deity whose rays are given hands that touch the earth in tender gestures of love (ill. 5). Thus the priest, when pronouncing the benediction, seems to say: May God's presence be visible to you as the sun is visible! Or, in the jargon of religious studies: May you live in an everlasting hierophany![82]

Central to the priestly benediction are the assurance of God's protection ("may the Lord . . . keep you," Hebrew *shamar* "to protect"), his favor or kindness (Hebrew *hanan* "to be kind"), and his peace (Hebrew *shalom*). The three terms used here culminate in *shalom*, a word denoting wholeness, abundance, health, well-being, peace, and victory, and thus summing up all one can expect from continuous divine protection and assistance. By granting his *shalom*, God maintains a good relationship with his devotees and sustains them with all they need. The biblical passage from which the priestly benediction is taken includes an explanation: by using these words, the priests shall put God's name on the congregation and God himself will bless them. The priests act as an instrument of God; by establishing a kind of magical link between the divine name (Yahweh, rendered as the Lord) and the people, they prepare the way for God's own action. The Catholic form in which we have given the benediction has only one reference to the divine name; the Hebrew text has "May Yahweh bless you . . . , may Yahweh's face shine . . . , may Yahweh look upon you." Here we get a glimpse of the magical power ascribed by the ancient Israelites to the divine name, Yahweh: pronounced three times, the divine name protects. Even after ancient Jewish practice had substituted the divine name by terms such as "the Lord," the name Yahweh continued to be used in the benediction the priests pronounced twice daily at the Temple. As long as there was a Jerusalem Temple (until 70 or 135 CE), it functioned as the place God had chosen as the dwelling place of his divine name; it was at the Temple that this name was to make *shalom* available to Jews. The Christian benediction makes up for the suppression of the Hebrew divine name by adding its own version of God's full name: the Father, the Son, and the Holy Spirit. The three divine persons of the Christian deity still echo the magical belief in the efficacy of the threefold repetition of the "correct" divine name.[83]

The blessing provides a service of worship with a good ending: the manifold request for divine favor, brought before God in supplication and intercession, seems to get its final answer. A service of worship appears to be incomplete if God does not in some way or other immediately respond to the requests brought before him. But once the service is ended, questions remain, for it is in "real life" that people hope to see the effect of divine blessing. To these questions theologians of all times have tried to respond, and we will now look at the answers some of them offer.

Does Prayer Work? Two Answers

In the situation of prayer, two agents interact with each other: human beings ask for help or benefits, and God listens and perhaps grants the request. Theologians and philosophers have spent much energy on explaining what happens when Christians bring their requests before God in a more sophisticated way. They emphasize the inequality of the two interacting partners: the all-powerful, all-knowing, transcendent God on the one side, and the limited, weak human being who nevertheless has some experiential knowledge of the Creator. Some thinkers place much emphasis on the majesty and superiority of God, while others proceed in their analysis from the human experience of God. From the theocentric and the anthropocentric emphases two quite different theories of prayer flow.

Theocentric thinkers believe in a powerful God who rules over his creation. God, and not the creature, determines what happens. Once this or a similar description is granted, prayer becomes a paradox. For if people pray and their prayer is answered, this in no way implies that God changes his plans. God would have ended the dry season anyway by sending rain, with or without people's asking for it. So why bother to pray? The most radical and perhaps the most consistent theocentric approach leaves everything with God and declares prayer a naïve, foolish, and absurd attempt to influence God. So prayer should be given up, and men and women should accept their fate in stoic resignation. This was the position of Enlightenment philosophers like Voltaire in France and Immanuel Kant in Germany. We will briefly look at how three theocentric theologians—Thomas Aquinas, Friedrich Schleiermacher, and Norman Pittenger—try to avoid the conclusion that prayer is superfluous.[84]

Thomas Aquinas (1226–74), like all medieval scholastic theologians, had inherited a strong view of God's foreordainment from patristic authors, especially Augustine. God knows and has predetermined everything that happens in nature and in human history. It cannot be changed. When considering prayer, Aquinas felt confronted with a paradox. On the one hand, scripture implies that God answers prayers. On the other, God clearly determines all events independently, according to his own will. The two assertions, "God determines all events according to his own will" and "God answers human prayers, i.e., he allows human wishes to determine the course of events," seem contradictory. In his *Questions on Truth* (*Quaestiones disputatae de veritate*), Aquinas develops his answer by studying a scriptural passage. According to the book of Genesis, Isaac prayed to God to make his wife Rebekah pregnant with a son, "and God heard him and granted it to Rebekah that she should conceive" (Gen. 25:21). Aquinas insists that here God in no way changed his plans. Quite the contrary is true, for God must be presumed to have known about and indeed foreordained Rebekah's upcoming pregnancy all along. However, God wanted Isaac to co-operate in the realization of his plan; his prayer thus has the status of a contributory cause. Isaac's prayer, to be sure, does not challenge God to work a miracle. Instead, it motivates God simply to set a natural process in motion. God here acts through the chain of natural causality. Aquinas argues that while the created world is somehow independent of divine intervention, it is never completely so. For this idea, he relied on the *Liber de causis* (Book of Causes), an anonymous tenth-century compilation of philosophical statements which summarized the philosophy of Proclus, a Neoplatonic thinker of the fifth century CE. This book not only supplied the Aristotelian distinction between the First Cause (i.e., God) and secondary causes, but at the same time transcended it. On the one hand, the book asserts, in the manner of Aristotle, that "the First Cause governs all things without intermingling with them"; on the other hand, it states that "the First Cause does not cease illuminating its effect." In Neoplatonic thought, the First Cause is so much stronger than the created causes that its presence can always be felt in them; created causes never achieve complete independence. The Neoplatonic emphasis on the universe's utter dependence on the First Cause enabled Aquinas to introduce his idea of subtle intervention.[85]

While Thomas Aquinas's metaphysical system enabled theologians to pray and at the same time to assert predestination, it has its flaws. Aquinas never raised the question of whether God ultimately determines the wishes and desires that Christian believers express in their supplications. Norman Pittenger (b. 1905) is certainly right when he calls Aquinas a "double man": one half of him being a devout Christian, nourished on biblical images and in "deep communion with God who was for him living and active and affected by prayer; and the other half being a philosophical theologian whose theoretical description of God contradicted what in his heart of hearts he both believed and practiced."[86]

The Reformed German theologian Friedrich Schleiermacher (1768–1834) struggled with two problems. The first one was the impossibility of influencing God, a problem already considered by Aquinas. He calls God "the Unchangeable in whose mind no new thought or purpose can arise since the day when he said, *all is very good*," that is, the day of creation. "What was then decreed, will take place; we must not lose sight of the indisputable certainty of this thought." It is "our primary and fundamental presupposition that there can be no relation of interaction between creature and Creator; and a theory of prayer which starts with ideas like those just indicated we can only describe . . . as a lapse into magic." In view of the lack of interaction between creature and Creator and of God's pre-established plan, petitionary prayer does not make sense. The second problem is the contradiction between the scriptural promise that all prayers will be answered and the fact that even Christ's own prayer to be spared crucifixion was not heard. If Christ's prayer was not answered, how can we hope that God will respond to our requests?[87]

Schleiermacher concludes that true Christian prayer must not express wishes but humility before God's will. Not the optimism of the scriptural promises but the submissive attitude of Christ must be the dominant note. True, we may be allowed to bring our wishes before God in an attitude of childlike trust, but we must check them by adding that we are ready to accept his will. Thus the model prayer is that of Jesus, spoken in the garden of Gethsemane before his suffering: "My Father, if it is possible, let this cup [of suffering and death] pass from me; yet not what I want but what you want" (Matt. 26:39). If submission is to be the keynote, Christians should actually renounce petitionary prayer altogether. "I will say to you frankly that it seems to me a mark of greater and more genuine piety when this entreating kind of prayer is only seldom used by us, and we do not allow our thoughts to be long occupied with it." Petitionary prayer may be allowed in personal devotion, but it should be absent from public worship. If prayer does not have "the effect of moderating the wish that is expressed, of replacing the eager desire with quiet submission, the anxious expectation with devout calmness; then it was no true prayer, and gives sure proof that we are not yet at all capable of this real kind of prayer."[88]

Schleiermacher's recommendation of resignation, moderation, quiet submission, and devout calmness gives his theology an unmistakable note of stoicism. For him, Christ himself spoke to God as a Stoic philosopher would. The ancient Stoic philosophers and their numerous disciples through the centuries, from Cicero and Seneca to Spinoza, believed in a divinely decreed fate in the face of which one should remain calm and even serene. Stoics believe in tranquility. Schleiermacher seems to have assimilated Christ to Socrates, the great model of the Stoics: Socrates, condemned to death by the city of Athens, drank his poison, unmoved by those who wept. The idea of comparing the two persons was not new and actually goes back to the patristic period; in the eighteenth century, it gained renewed currency. In America, for instance, Benjamin Franklin (1706–90) recommended Jesus and Socrates for their sense of humility. Heir to a long tradition, Schleiermacher presents Jesus and, by implication, the pagan philosopher as models of behavior.[89]

If we are to submit in a stoic attitude to God's unchangeable and often inscrutable will, what about the scriptural promises that assure us of God's answer to our prayers? Schleiermacher simply ignores them. He ignores them in the same spirit in which he plays down the significance of miracles recounted in the gospels. When Jesus prayed in the garden of Gethsemane, no miracle happened, and so Christian believers have no right to expect that God will do for them what he denied his son. Before God, Christians share Christ's position; to believe God would grant them more and better privileges is simply absurd.[90]

The most recent attempt to sketch a theocentric view of prayer comes from "process theology," of which Norman Pittenger is a major representative. Process theology places God at the center of its thought, but refuses to believe in a God who has decided in advance about all the details of human history on the very day of creation. Like creation itself which reflects his character, God is in movement. For these ideas, process theology is indebted to the philosophy of Alfred North Whitehead (1861–1947). According to Whitehead, God is involved with, and in a way identical with, the creative process of nature and history, and we as humans participate in this process, both actively and passively. We are affected by this process and can also contribute to it. Prayer, according to Pittenger, helps the individual as well as the community to surrender to and become part of the cosmic process of Love (Love being just another word for God). Prayer serves first of all as "the intentional opening of human lives to . . . cosmic Love." Once someone is open to this Love, he or she becomes part of the process. "One who has been caught up into the divine Love becomes, through his praying, a participant in the ongoing movement of that love in the world; he becomes a lover." And once someone has become part of the movement of love, he or she can draw others into it and contribute to it—and do so through the spiritual technique of prayer. "When we intercede," writes Pittenger, "we bring others within the ambit of our own willed relationship to God; we also add . . . our bit of goodwill to the cosmic thrust for good in the world." Spiritually united in Love, Christians can serve as "fellow-workers with God" (2 Cor. 6:1). Mythically speaking, God no longer operates in isolation, for those in union with him sustain the cosmic process. Therefore, corporate prayer "is a good idea," not because there are more fists beating on the heavenly door, but because "there are more wills to be aligned with the divine will." Corporate prayer somehow promotes the cosmic process.[91]

Granted that human prayer sustains the cosmic process, does it actually change things? Robert Cooper, who recommends process thought as "a philosophy of prayer in which prayer actually does change things," adds a note of caution. He admits that "like God, the person who prays . . . does not control what happens except only in a very few instances in a lifetime and in those instances to a very limited extent." The God of process theology is not almighty, and therefore cannot change much! John Polkinghorne, scientist and process theologian, invokes the hiddenness of divine action. God does act, but his action "will be contained within the cloudy unpredictabilities of what is going on. It may be discernible by the eye of faith but it will not be exhibitable by experiment. It will more readily have the character of benign coincidence than of a naked act of power." Reluctant to reject prayer in the way Voltaire and Kant had done, process thinkers compromise. For them, it seems, the cosmic process can do as well without prayer. They join Thomas Aquinas and Schleiermacher in advocating an enlightened doctrine of restraint.[92]

The *anthropocentric* approach to prayer does not proceed from considering the power of God; instead, it considers the beneficial effects people feel when praying. However God may respond to the petitions brought before him, he frequently grants a kind of spiritual refreshment to those who approach him in prayer. We will illustrate this with reference to traditional Catholic spirituality (Ignatius of Loyola, Pascal) and several twentieth-century American authors (William James, Norman Vincent Peale, Paul Tillich, and others).

Ever since its early days, Christian spirituality has known the refreshing effect prayer may have for the soul. They heard or read that Jesus, before his passion, was "given strength" by an angel (Luke 22:43). Angelic consolation provided him with the courage to endure suffering and death. In addition to, or as an alternative to, answering requests, God sends "consolation" and "sweetness," filling the human heart with delight, which often results in melting moods or sudden tears of joy. In addition to the sense of being strengthened, the early monks emphasize the sense of, the overwhelming feeling of joy. John Cassian, who in the early fifth century introduced monasticism in southern Gaul, reported of his monastic teachers that they often shed tears when thinking of their sins, but then "at the coming of the Lord" (*visitante*

Domino) felt revived by unspeakable joy, so that their souls burst into loud shouts of exultation. Religious autobiographies, lives of the saints, and books of spiritual direction have often described similar effects of prayer to which divine response comes from an angel or from the Lord himself. According to his medieval biographer, Francis of Assisi frequently wept when praying and then "was filled with no little consolation," or even "with excessive joy." Some medieval women's monasteries chronicled such events for devotional purposes and so have left us accounts of nuns who at Mass or during communal prayer burst into tears or showed other signs of mystical transport. In the eighteenth century, the English devotional writer William Law, a Protestant, referred to the consolatory force of prayer in similar words: "If we are to pray often, 'tis that we may be often happy in such secret joys as only prayer can give, in such communications of the divine presence as will fill our minds with all the happiness that beings not in Heaven are capable of." While these quotations focus on joy, others refer to a wider range of feelings: Ignatius of Loyola, for instance, mentions "courage and strength, consolations, tears, inspirations, and peace," and Bishop Bossuet speaks of "a real pleasure that strengthens the human heart" (*véritable plaisir qui fortifie le cœur de l'homme*). Earlier, in the late Middle Ages, Thomas à Kempis had specified: "Divine comfort gives us the strength to bear up under adversity" (*Datur autem consolatio ut homo fortior sit ad sustinendum adversa*). Devotional exercises, then, are sometimes accompanied by sentiments of love, joy, and peace that are so strong that they overwhelm the praying persons, bringing them to tears of emotion. One could speak here of a regressive, self-indulgent, sentimental, lachrymose, passive spirituality, associated with traditional notions of female piety. Occasionally, however, a more masculine, self-assured spirituality comes into view. When asking the question "Why has God instituted prayer?" the seventeenth-century apologist Blaise Pascal did not refer to the quasi-feminine intimacy with "the God of Abraham," so dear to him, but immediately answered in the masculine mode: "To impart to his creatures the dignity of causality." Prayer is effective and powerful; with prayer, the believer confronts life and conquers the world. In our terminology we could say: the theurgical form of prayer gives way to the thaumaturgical.[93]

Toward the end of the nineteenth century, people increasingly report on their experience in these muscular terms. Far from being a source merely of consolation, prayer is felt to be a source of courage, energy, and determination. In *The Varieties of Religious Experience* (1902), the Harvard philosopher William James considered the beneficial effect of prayer an established fact. The documents James discussed in the Gifford lectures—letters, diaries, and personal testimonies collected in England and America—clearly show that speaking to God makes people happier and more able to cope with life. When someone keeps in touch with the world's creator, "fear and egotism fall away; and in the equanimity that follows, one finds in the hours, as they succeed each other, a series of purely benignant opportunities. It is as if all doors were opened." Prayer "exerts an influence, raises our center of personal energy, and produces regenerative effects unattainable in other ways." Thus, "at all stages of the prayerful life we find the persuasion that in the process of communion [with God] energy from on high flows in to meet demand, and becomes operative within the phenomenal world." This energy has healing properties. "If any medical fact can be considered to stand firm," observes James, it is that "prayers may contribute to recovery, and should be encouraged as a therapeutic measure." The practical defense calls for a theoretical justification, and James supplies it, albeit in rather vague terms. While he is reluctant to call the source of this transcendent power "God," as Christians would do, he does accept the notion of something that is greater than the human being. He defines the source as "something ideal, which in one sense is part of ourselves and in another sense is not ourselves," the unconscious mind that somehow stretches beyond the individual and is in communion with "a larger power which is friendly." Those who heard James's lectures or read his book got the impression that the philosopher's firm belief in the power of prayer was not matched by an equally firm belief in God. The effects of prayer were somehow more real and more certain than the existence of God. But whatever its metaphysical implications, prayer was possible even at the threshold of the twentieth century.[94]

While in public William James seemed to encourage prayer, he had privately given it up. When one of his fellow-researchers sent him a questionnaire, his answer to "do you pray, and if so, why?" is straightforward: "I can't possibly pray—it feels foolish & artificial." But at the same time he admitted to having a certain "susceptibility to ideals" and "a certain amount of 'other worldly' fancy." What counted for him was to realize the ways in which our ideal selves connect with higher powers, often through the medium of traditional religion and prayer, and thus supply us with energies beyond the abilities of our conscious selves.[95]

James's anthropocentric approach to prayer has become paradigmatic for many twentieth-century thinkers. One of them is Norman Vincent Peale (1898–1993). Sold in over five million copies and still in print today, his book *The Power of Positive Thinking* (1952) ranks as one of the most popular devotional books of the twentieth century. "The Bible of American autohypnotism," as it has been called, teaches how a peaceful mind and a confident view of life can work as self-fulfilling prophecies. Peale encourages people to believe in themselves and their own potential and thus overcome anxieties and the feeling of inadequacy. At the same time, he leaves no doubt about his deep commitment to traditional Christian notions. "Positive thinking" includes and even culminates in prayer. The praying person, according to Peale, can tap hidden sources of psychological as well as divine energy. "You can receive guidance in problems if prayer is allowed to permeate your subconscious, the seat of the forces which determines whether you take right or wrong actions." Peale recommends speaking to God as one of the most efficient spiritual techniques. In the stories he tells about the success of "prayer power," Peale refers mainly to businessmen; to avoid a "sissy" image of religion and to make sure that no one would misunderstand him, his stories involve about nineteen men but only two women. Prayer is good for success-oriented men! The author, a Methodist who later became pastor of the (Reformed) Marble Collegiate Church in New York City, considers himself a popular psychologist and a teacher of practical Christianity. His contemporaries would look for his publications in the self-help section of their bookstore and find his articles in the *Reader's Digest*. While Peale rarely cared to quote his sources, it is clear that much of his writing is indebted to the "new thought" school, a movement that originated toward the end of the nineteenth century, promoted spiritual healing, and believed that good thought creates good reality, either immediately or through the all-powerful subconscious mind. Peale also relied on the books of Florence Shinn (d. 1940), a relatively obscure New York-based theosophical author who wrote and privately published *The Secret Door to Success* (1940). Reading "new thought" books and the work of Shinn, Peale became an adept of a philosophy that he took to represent the practical side of Christianity. Of course, Peale was neither the only nor the first author to adapt "new thought" to more mainstream Christian persuasions; he was preceded by Essek William Kenyon's *Sign Posts on the Road to Success* (1938) and followed by Kenneth Hagin's *Four Steps to Answered Prayer* (1980), whose claims about prayer making "all things possible" even surpass the promises made by Peale.[96]

The Power of Positive Thinking shares the fate of all of "new thought" books: intellectuals feel ambivalent about it. William James, who wrote fifty years before Peale, acknowledged new thought as the "only decidedly original contribution" Americans had made to the philosophy of life; but for all his admiration of its practical results, he disliked the "verbiage" of much of its mass-produced literature and described it as "so moonstruck with optimism and so vaguely expressed that an academically trained intellect finds it almost impossible to read." Today, no one would hesitate to class *The Power of Positive Thinking* with this "moonstruck" literature the promises of which overstep the limits set by a realistic attitude. Peale's books were—and are still—widely read, and President Richard Nixon admired the author; but new-thought religion never gained intellectual respectability in theological circles. Ironically for Peale, whose target audience was male rather than female, middle-class American women found his stories, his promises, his intuitive reasoning, and his magazine *Guideposts* more attractive than men.[97]

But moonstruck or not, popular new-thought theology regularly refers to astonishing effects its prayer technique seems to have on the life of its followers. Prayer, as William James acknowledged, promotes health, and may actually lead to miraculous healing. How is this possible? The explanation usually given refers to the psychosomatic nature of many diseases. Since health involves both body and soul, so sickness also affects both. In fact, it has been argued that very many diseases, including cancer, may be caused by psychological factors, such as anxiety, stress, or grief. While the medical profession generally concentrates on physical symptoms, healing through prayer may deal effectively with the psychological side. The most elaborate theory of "faith healing" has been suggested by Felicitas Goodman, an American anthropologist specializing in "altered states of consciousness." Religious ceremonies, she argues, may not only affect the participants' mood, but may also affect them quite deeply, bringing them into a state of trance. In a state of trance, someone's normal consciousness is reduced and replaced by ecstasy, frenzy, and exhaustion. Now, trance is of course a temporary state, and people return to their normal state after some time. However, they may be profoundly changed, and even become new beings, enjoying new psychological and physical forces. This process of transformation may even involve the healing of physical ailments. But why does "trance therapy" work?

At this point, Goodman refers to current research on the "multiple personality" syndrome known to specialists as a psychological disease. Patients of this type do not exhibit just one personality, but several, which they experience as inhabiting them. Someone may have a criminal personality responsible for acts of crime and another, "normal" personality, which may not be aware of the other side. Such people, when in conflict with the law, need treatment for insanity rather than punishment for crimes they have committed. In the 1950s, a book entitled *The Three Faces of Eve*, written by the psychologists Corbett Thigpen and Hervey Cleckley, brought the multiple personality syndrome to the attention of a wide public. It describes a young woman who showed evidence of having three distinct personalities: the sedate, timid Eve White; the frivolous, irresponsible and bright Eve Black; and the mature, thoughtful Jane. Now the most startling fact about the young woman was the medical conditions that correlated with her various personalities. Eve Black's skin, for instance, was allergic to nylon stockings; but as soon as Eve White's personality emerged, the allergy disappeared. Consequently, if the personality of Eve Black could have been permanently suppressed, the allergy would have been cured. From *The Three Faces of Eve* and similar documents, Goodman constructs an explanatory model for healing through trances and through prayer. Diseases seem to be dependent on an inner disposition, presumably located in the human brain. If, through whatever technique—psychotherapy, trance, prayer—someone's "brain map" and therefore his or her personality center can be permanently changed, then one can remove diseases associated with the old, problematic "brain map." A similar correlation between illness and mental states has been demonstrated by specialists: certain allergic reactions are not produced by unconscious human persons. Patients allergic to horse serum can be treated with this substance without risk when they are unconscious.

Researchers have also pointed out that more often than people think it is not the medicine that heals, but rather the brain: the healing process is often tricked into motion by a placebo. Whatever scientific value Goodman's theory may have, in the last analysis, it is a straightforward affirmation of popular new-thought religion: prayer works and belongs (in Peale's words) to the "scientific procedure for successful living."[98]

Academic theologians did of course react to the new-thought theory of prayer. Some of them, like Ann and Barry Ulanov and John Yungblut, replaced it by the depth-psychology of Carl Gustav Jung. Jungian analysts define God as an aspect of the inner self, the inner person, but they also insist that he must not be confused with the conscious ego personality with which we identify in everyday life. God must be thought of as a sort of alter ego or divine friend who speaks his sacred word to us as we reflect or confront our unconscious mind. According to Jungian psychologist-theologians, there can be no personal growth toward wholeness, spiritual health, and maturity without prayer. Prayer, according to Yungblut, "may be the best means I have of getting myself together in psychological wholeness and health, and growing toward the realization of my best potential." The way Jungians describe this path is reminiscent of the lower stages of the traditional mystical ascent that leads from purgation to illumination.[99]

Ann and Barry Ulanov have written an entire book on "purgative prayer" as an unsurpassed spiritual technique to help the individual to cope with reality. For them, prayer is "primary speech," the soul's preferred way of dealing with its own fantasies and wishes. A praying person brings before God all his or her wounds and desires; meditation "is the place where we sort out our desires and where we are ourselves sorted out by the desires we choose to follow." The self-critical act of "sorting out" orders and cleanses the mind, helping people to "disidentify" with certain wishes they might have. With some practice, one can be quite successful and arrive at a calm review of one's own inner life. We may have a sexual fantasy, but we are not carried away by it. We may feel again a painful childhood experience, but we are not lost to it. We may carry in ourselves a strong urge to achieve an end—"to make the biggest sale, to write the perfect book, to make the house spotless once and for all"—but we are not swept away in the strong currents of ambition. "This is hard, painful work, necessary work, rewarding work." Purgation "energizes" one's psychological life. "The graces that come in answer to prayer come . . . in the form of new energies, freshly stimulated memories, openings in the self and the world, agreeable changes in what we thought was our disagreeably fixed nature." In other words: purgation and illumination enable men and women to grow to more happiness.[100]

As regards God, Jungian psychology remains as vague as the philosophy of William James. John Yungblut and the Ulanovs cannot escape the ambivalence built into Jung's work. Their master's psychology does not decide about the reality of God; for, according to Jung, scientists must limit themselves to exploring the ways in which God's image exists in the human mind, symbolizing the totality of the unconscious human self. As soon as an individual successfully confronts that totality, it releases an energy—termed *libido* or love by psychologists—which can help us to face both ourselves and life. Two opposing interpretations of purgation and illumination are possible, a nonreligious one and a religious one. Viewed from the nonreligious perspective of naturalism, prayer serves as an instrument of psychological self-care, and one wonders whether "God's merciful presence" must be invoked at all. The praying person acts, but God does not seem to be actively involved in the process. Although the Ulanovs maintain traditional religious language, their analysis of prayer as "primary speech" comes close to a humanistic, innerworldly reinterpretation. From their analysis, God seems to emerge as an inner aspect of the human soul rather than as a personal agent who responds to creaturely needs. The second, religious interpretation takes a very different view of what happens in prayer. Instead of waking up the soul's dormant energy, prayer gains access to what one may call an inner avenue to the transcendent, supernatural source through which God sends new and hitherto unavailable energy. In this view, the unconscious mind is not like an untapped inner battery but like an electric outlet fed from outside the house. While not feeling it necessary to explain exactly how prayer works, Jungian theologians insist that it does produce visible effects, at least within the individual.[101]

The last representative of the anthropocentric approach whose work we will consider is Paul Tillich (1886–1965). In 1952, the same year Peale published *The Power of Positive Thinking*, Tillich wrote a sophisticated little book entitled *The Courage to Be*. Though perhaps not widely known outside theological circles, it ranks as the author's boldest interpretation of Christianity. The Christian message, for America's leading philosophical theologian, conveys if not optimism, then at least the courage to face life in the midst of anxieties and fears, especially in face of the threat of an utterly meaningless existence. Tillich rarely referred to prayer. He seems to have admitted that he did not pray in the usual sense of the term. Nevertheless, *The Courage to Be* allows us to discern what he thought about it. For him, prayer can be an instrument for finding the answer to what he sees as the central form of estrangement in the twentieth century: the threat of an empty existence. Prayer, or perhaps meditation, culminates in a mystical union to which we are led by the existential threat of meaninglessness and the paradoxes of traditional prayer. Those who think about it "are aware of the paradoxical character of every prayer, of speaking to somebody to whom you cannot speak because he is not 'somebody,' of asking somebody of whom you cannot ask anything because he gives or gives not before you ask, of saying 'thou' to somebody who is nearer to the I than the I is to itself." Each of these paradoxes of prayer, when carefully analyzed, "drives the religious consciousness toward a God above the God of theism." While the

"God above God" cannot be prayed to in the ordinary sense of the term (and, as we suppose, Tillich never prayed), there can be a kind of life-giving, courage-inspiring mystical union with him. Tillich even envisaged a church that renounces its historical focus on orthodox teaching by transforming itself into a therapeutic agency that helps people to discover mystical courage: "the courage to be."[102]

But how to acquire that "courage"? Tillich presumably thought of it in terms of lonely contemplation. German idealist philosophers like Friedrich Wilhelm Schelling (1775–1854) and David Friedrich Strauß (1808–74), whose work Tillich admired, had written about "receiving the power of being directly by contemplation." Strauss depicted human life as being structured according to a rhythm in which periods of work and times of contemplation alternate. During the latter, we touch the ground of being with all our wishes and needs. Contemplation is the means whereby "we plunge ourselves—with all the restlessness and heat which is in us from the realm of work, with all our needs and wishes—into the refreshing depth of the one ground of all being."[103]

Summing up the discussion, we can again say that two approaches dominate the theological and philosophical debates about the effects of prayer. Does God grant what he is asked for in prayer? Yes, answer those who take an anthropocentric approach, an approach that relies on the evidence of consolation or empowerment derived from praying. No, or rarely, is the response we hear most often from those thinkers who emphasize God's superiority and transcendence. While theocentric theologians sometimes make concessions to allow for the practice of petitionary prayer and even, like Thomas Aquinas, try to work out a metaphysical system with a niche for prayer, they tend to discourage its practice. The limiting cases are God without prayer (Kant) and prayer without belief in God (of which the "natural" explanation of Goodman is an example). Today, most Christian intellectuals side either with Schleiermacher who advised against petitionary prayer, or with William James, who acknowledged its value.

4. Conclusion: The Two Kinds of Prayer Used in Christian Worship

From the very beginning of their history Christians have consistently used two kinds of prayer in their worship: the Our Father and "other prayers." The Our Father must be considered a genre consisting of one single specimen, while the other type, which we may call, for lack of better terminology, Christian prayer, allows for infinite multiplication. After having studied the Our Father and Christian prayer, we can compare the two, highlight their differences as well as the features they share, and thus define the nature of petitionary prayer.

The first observation relates to their historical origins. The Our Father is a Jewish, not a Christian text, and it certainly existed prior to the formation of a Christian community that distinguished itself from its Jewish parent religion. Neither Jesus (whom tradition calls the prayer's author) nor John the Baptist (whom the present study assumes to be the author) can be called a Christian. In fact, there is nothing in the Our Father which would make the text unusable in the orthodox synagogue of the first or the twentieth century. Christian prayer shares with the Our Father the addressee, God, and the "Amen" as the traditional word of conclusion. Only rarely is Christian prayer addressed to Christ. However, Christian prayer regularly includes a reference to Jesus Christ whose name serves as a "seal" or label which identifies the words uttered as Christian in origin and nature. The Our Father does not include a reference to Jesus Christ.

Second, the Our Father, an ancient Jewish text still used in its ancient form, is more difficult to understand than a Christian prayer. Christian prayers have rarely become set texts meant to remain unaltered and so are periodically updated to be in tune with contemporary mentalities and tastes. We have argued that the original meaning of the Our Father (which we defined as a political prayer for national deliverance) has actually been lost in Christianity, and presumably this happened at a very early date. Normally, a Christian prayer used in worship should be immediately understandable to the churchgoer. Though people are generally familiar with the words of the Our Father, their meaning eludes them or remains vague. As people listen to or join in saying this traditional text, it is only by degrees that words take on meaning.

The third observation has to do with magic, and here we have again to refer to the name of Jesus as Christian prayer's "seal" or "trade mark." Without this name, prayer is not identified as Christian prayer and thus it is neither acceptable to God nor has it a fair chance of being answered. As we have seen in our discussion of the origins of Christian prayer, it is the name of Jesus that makes prayer "effective." We have also seen that belief in the special efficacy of a name derives ultimately from a magical world view and its magic rituals. To many twentieth-century Christians, the term "magic," used to describe prayer, has a strange ring, for it seems to suggest notions of primitive sorcery and superstition. For Kant, traditional prayer was a good example of superstition. But, although modern theology may prefer not to refer to magic at all or to speak of Jesus as an intercessor bringing human prayers before the divine Father, even in the twentieth century, Christian prayer has preserved at least traces of its magical origins. The Our Father is here the exception to the rule, for it does not use the name of Jesus. The mere attribution of the Our Father to Jesus sufficed to qualify it as an effective text (just as other efficient prayers were attributed to famous "authors" like patriarch Jacob or King Solomon). Apart from the baptismal and therefore magical link we detected in the original meaning of the Our Father, this text lacks any immediately recognizable magical element.[104]

Another feature of the two kinds of prayer is scripturalism, and this brings us to a fourth observation. Christian prayer texts, we explained, are based on certain rules. According to one rule, every prayer must include a reference to the name of Jesus. A second rule links prayer with biblical texts and contexts, so that one can speak about the ever-present "scripturalism" of prayer. As we have seen, some traditional public prayers are "saturated" with more or less recognizable references to the Bible and, especially in the past, a good prayer had to use scriptural language. While scripturalism in prayer sounds old-fashioned to many contemporaries, its significance must be emphasized. In both Judaism and Christianity, public prayer cannot be understood without its scripturalist character.

Scripturalism is based on the existence of canonical, i.e., classical and authoritative texts. Between the late seventh and the second century BCE, Judaism developed into a "book religion," a religion based on authoritative texts. After that time, religious discourse, whether theological or edifying, tended to become strongly dependent on scriptural language and interpretation. Rather than relying on spontaneous language (if this is at all possible), religious leaders couched their discussions, their writings, their legislation, their sermons, and of course also their prayers in traditional scriptural language. Scripture serves as the basic frame of reference for all utterances. Without a good or even excellent knowledge of scripture, one simply cannot grasp the nuances implied in what someone has said in a sermon or expressed in a prayer. As a scholar well-versed in the Hebrew Bible, Jesus Sirach (second century BCE) "seeks out the hidden meanings" of scripture and composes prayers that "petition the Most High" (Sir. 39:3.5). Scripturalism presupposes biblical learning and therefore a class of people like Jesus Sirach: men schooled in scripture. While we do not know whether John the Baptist or Jesus can be classified as scriptural specialists, we know that all movements within early Judaism and Christianity had their scriptural specialists. If the leaders were themselves not experts, they often relied on the advice of scriptural specialists in their movement. For example, Paul, and the compilers of the gospels were not only literate people with a certain amount of general education; they had also mastered scripture and this served as the basis of much of their theology. Scripturalists read all events in the light of the ancient Jewish scriptures and insist on the strict application of that law's moral and legal implications, arguing that "it is easier for heaven and earth to pass away, than for one stroke of a letter in the [Jewish] law to be dropped" (Luke 16:17). The circle of John the Baptist shared the scripturalist attitude; the verse just quoted from Luke seems to reflect a basic idea of that circle.[105]

As we have seen, the Our Father is a thoroughly scripturalist prayer. Christian prayer often also echoes the scripturalist attitude, but in many cases its scripturalism remains ornamental and stylistic. Christian prayers can be composed without reference to scripture.

When we turn to the promises and expectations connected with the two types of prayer, a fifth observation can be made. Here again, the Our Father and Christian prayer differ. The Our Father is given an unconditional promise of being answered by God, while Christian prayer is hedged with conditions. The efficacy of Christian prayer depends upon the praying person's "faith" and upon God's will. If faith fails or God has determined that someone's request should not be granted, then prayer is offered in vain. But since Christians do not generally believe that God has fixed the course of history or the course of someone's life in advance, or that his will is unchangeable, they continue praying in the hope of being heard and answered. Interestingly, all theologizing on the expectations the praying community may legitimately have relates to Christian prayer, not to the Our Father.

The sixth and final observation has to do with the liturgical setting of prayer. The world of the liturgy has a tendency to close itself off from life and thus to form a sacred world which is complete in itself and closed in on itself. The outside world with its conflicts is not allowed into the cathedral. In this closed world, petitions are addressed to God and immediately answered liturgically. The two kinds of prayer are drawn into the process of what we may term "liturgy in love with itself" or liturgical narcissism. In this process, prayer for divine blessing and spiritual goods like forgiveness and illumination is privileged over the request for dramatic divine intervention. The history of the concept of "forgiveness" provides a good example for the spiritualizing trend characteristic of liturgical narcissism. Forgiveness or divine pardon is a concept whose precise meaning eludes those unfamiliar with religious practice. But even the faithful pay little attention to its meaning and history. Yet, only its history can reveal its rather unexpected original meaning. In Old Testament times, God's mercy and will to forgive were appealed to in situations of crisis, for instance in the Babylonian Exile, which was understood as a divine punishment for sin. To forgive, in its original biblical context, often implies the termination of punishment; that is, in practical terms, the end of the situation of exile. To ask for divine pardon meant to ask for a concrete, empirically verifiable action by God. In other words: if God indeed forgives, then something has to happen. Pardoned Israel may return home to Palestine. In Christian liturgical practice, the remission of sins has lost its practical implications: it is a spiritual cleansing that enables the renewal of one's moral effort. The pardoned sinner, while still living in the same place, shifts his spiritual home in that he returns to God.

While the forgiveness is spiritualized and thus loses its originally tangible nature, other vocabulary may lose all meaning whatsoever. As we have seen, the Our Father is often used "selectively" in the liturgy, so that the entire text is said or sung, but only certain petitions are actually meant (such as "give us this day our daily bread" and "forgive us our debts" when the Our Father is used as a Communion prayer). The Our Father here survives only with residual meaning.

In prayer, Christians address God. Although God is expected to react in manifold ways, he is also expected to speak to the congregation through his ministers and preachers. This will be the subject of the next chapter.

The Third Game: Sermon
God's Word in Biblical Reading and Preaching

They opened the book of the Law to inquire into those matters about which the Gentiles consulted the likenesses of their gods.

1 Maccabees 3:48 (NRSV)

Blessed is the one who reads aloud the words of the prophecy, and blessed are those who hear.

Revelation 1:3 (NRSV)

The Christian church speaks: catholic and protestant, orthodox and liberal, decent and not-so-decent. This great, wondrous song of praise is a fact. "It preaches" in the world, as certainly and as perceptibly as it rains.[1]

Karl Barth, 1927

1.   On Intellectual Ritual

Roman tradition celebrates Numa Pompilus, the successor to Romulus, as the founder of Roman religion and its sacred rites. Numa taught these rules to the priests and told them to transmit them orally. According to legend, he also wrote books that explained the rites and the duties of the priests. But since King Numa did not believe in the value of books, he had them put in a chest to be buried next to himself. Four hundred years later, in a time of heavy rains, a violent torrent washed away the earth so that the chest was uncovered. Upon inspection of the books, a praetor made oath to the Senate that their contents were not fit to be made public. So they were burned.[2]

Biblical tradition celebrates Moses as the founder of ancient Israelite religion. Moses, like Numa, wrote a sacred book. Legend tells that before his death, Moses entrusted it to the priests. Apparently, the book remained unread for a long time. Many hundreds of years later, when the priest Hilkiah discovered it in the Temple of Jerusalem, it was immediately brought to the attention of the king. The ensuing religious reform began with the public reading of all the words of the book of Moses.[3]

While these two legendary accounts may not be accurate in their detail, they do reflect two historical attitudes to sacred books. The Romans had no use for texts in a religion in which custom and oral tradition shaped the ritual procedures. In Israel, by contrast, books became increasingly important. They not only shaped ritual procedure, but also became part of the ritual itself. Reading from a sacred text, delivering a sermon, or a combination of these two (so that the sermon becomes an explanation or an afterthought to the recitation of scripture) is peculiar to only a few religions such as Buddhism and Judaism. Of course, every religion has its traditional stories and often also specialists who tell them on ceremonial occasions. In most religions, these stories belong to oral lore: they are learned from listening to a story-teller and they are again passed on orally to whoever wants to listen to them. A different situation obtains where the oral lore is put down in writing and eventually assumes canonical authority within a "textual community," that is a group of people "whose social activities are centered around texts," interpreters of texts, and interpretations of texts. If a holy scripture becomes the central focus of a tradition, we are justified in calling it a "book religion." In the ancient Mediterranean and Middle Eastern world, only the Jews compiled sacred scriptures and instituted a ritual that features their recitation, translation, explanation, and homiletic elaboration. "All the other legislators seem to have neglected this," remarked the ancient Jewish historian Josephus. It was within ancient Judaism that Christianity emerged as a separate textual community.[4]

Ancient Judaism as a Textual Community

Throughout the Persian empire of the fifth century BCE, ethnic groups formed local communities which were united by historical memories (generally of a state that had been overthrown by one of the great political powers), a common language, and religious and cultural practices. One of these groups was the Jews. Both in the Diaspora and in Palestine, they enjoyed recognition by the Persian state and generally led the peaceful life of small artisans and peasants. Among the Jewish leaders were men of letters who compiled and studied Hebrew books, cultivated religious and legal learning, offered their advice to others, and enjoyed the status of sages. By imposing their standards, these men gave Jewish groups a certain measure of cultural, religious, and legal uniformity. They also wished to extend their influence to groups and areas in which none of the sages lived. One of these men was Ezra, the first Jew referred to in the Bible as a *sofer*, i.e., a "scribe" or scriptural scholar. This great-grandson of the priest Hilkiah traveled from the Persian Diaspora to Jerusalem to carry out the mission he had chosen for himself: the restoration of "pure" Jewish life. Armed with the "book of the Law," most likely a version of the book of Deuteronomy (but possibly the entire Pentateuch), Ezra set out to establish law and order.[5]

Within a few days of his arrival in Jerusalem (ca. 458 BCE), Ezra had established his charismatic rule. He spoke and admonished in a way that made his audience burst into tears on more than one occasion; he assembled people out of doors despite heavy rain; and he had people celebrate holy days hitherto unknown or neglected. In Jerusalem, this was unprecedented. Ezra could do whatever he wished—even dissolve more than a hundred marriages with non-Jewish women, having the names of the guilty men carefully recorded. One of the most conspicuous of his activities was a public reading from the book of the Law. He had a wooden platform built on a square outside one of the city gates, a place that could accommodate a large crowd. The platform served as a pulpit for the first "liturgy of the word" on record in history. Ezra's own report, which survives in the Bible, reads as follows:

> Ezra opened the scroll so that all the people might see it (for he was standing higher up than any of the people); and, as he opened it, all the people rose. Ezra blessed Yahweh, the great God, and all the people, their hands raised high, answered, "Amen, amen." Then they bowed down and prostrated themselves before Yahweh, their faces to the ground. . . . Ezra read plainly from the book of

the Law of God, interpreting [?] it so that all could understand what was read. Then . . . Ezra the priest-scribe . . . said to all the people: "This day is holy to Yahweh your God. Do not be sad, and do not weep"—for all the people were weeping as they heard the words of the Law. (Neh. 8:2–9)

The reading lasted "from early morning until midday," i.e., for four or five hours, and people listened with excitement, "for they understood the words that had been expounded to them" (Neh. 8:12). Eventually, Ezra dismissed everyone, but only to reassemble them on the next day for another reading. He did so for a whole week, until the entire book was finished.

Ezra, it seems, did not invent the "liturgy of the word" celebrated in Jerusalem. He presumably imported this kind of worship—the public reading, the blessing, the congregational "Amen"—from the Diaspora, where it must have been practiced for some time. People wept, we may infer, because they recognized the worship they had known before their emigration from Babylonia to Jerusalem. Unfortunately, Ezra's memoirs give no information about the frequency of such events, but it makes sense to assume that they were more frequent than is prescribed in Deuteronomy, i.e., every seventh year (Deut. 31:9–13). Although Deuteronomy does not provide any clue to how the public reading of the Law was performed, it indicates how the idea emerged. Every seventh year, according to utopian legislation, Israel should neither sow nor reap, but live from its reserves. In this sabbatical year the annual thanksgiving service should be replaced by a public reading from scripture. If the thanksgiving service of a sabbatical year is dedicated to studying God's Law, can we infer that some people already dedicated every seventh day—the Sabbath—to a public reading of the Law? Historians of Jewish worship would very much like to have more information about the early history of what became the traditional Jewish Sabbath service.

Returning to Ezra's report, we may note one particular feature of his liturgy of the word: the "interpretation" of the Law. The Hebrew term is ambiguous and may refer to translation, explanation, or simply to clear articulation in reading. Most likely, Ezra did not preach in the way that became customary in the later synagogue. He had to deal with another, more elementary problem. The people belonging to the exilic community of Jerusalem spoke Aramaic, a language they had adopted in Babylonia. Many of them were no longer fluent in Hebrew, which was the language of the Law and also the language spoken by the Jews of Palestine. Ezra, it seems, translated the Hebrew text into the Aramaic vernacular of the exilic community. The concluding statement that the audience was pleased "for they understood the words" echoes both the interpreter's pride and the people's joy in listening to Aramaic spoken in public. The Aramaic vernacular was therefore received as an acceptable liturgical language.[6]

Like modern preachers, Ezra and other leaders would rarely have read and translated the Law without adding a word of exhortation and encouragement. According to Claus Westermann, certain patterns of early preaching can actually be reconstructed. "Hear, O Israel" seems to have been the way preachers like Ezra addressed their audience. Generally, the preacher reminded his congregation of the great deeds that Yahweh has done for his people: liberating their fathers from the yoke of Egypt, driving out nations greater than Israel to give them the beautiful land, a land flowing with milk and honey. Toward the end of his sermon, he urged people to acknowledge Yahweh's greatness: "So acknowledge today and take to heart that Yahweh is God in heaven above and on earth beneath; there is no other" (Deut. 4:39). While the preacher could end his exhortation here, he could also continue and speak about the necessity of keeping Yahweh's Law. "Keep his statutes and his commandments; so all will be well with you and with your children after you, and you will enjoy long life in the land that Yahweh your God is giving you for all time" (Deut. 4:40). Taking the goodwill of their hearers for granted, the early preachers mixed legal, moral, and spiritual instruction. They admonished, made promises, and rarely refrained from repeating what their audience already knew.[7]

Whether accompanied by a sermon or not, Ezra's public reading served to inculcate the Law. On the day after the public reading, the notables met "to study the words of the Law" under Ezra (Neh. 8:13). He persuaded them that they should celebrate the Feast of Tabernacles. Later, Ezra and a commission of leaders examined the issue of mixed marriages (Ezra 10). Legal matters figured prominently in Ezra's mission. In this context the Law had a double function. It served not only as a repository of Jewish tradition which should be taught to everyone, but also as an officially recognized legal code. To read that Law in public, and to explain its meaning, amounted to an act of state. By listening to the Law and responding to it with an assenting "Amen," people renewed their allegiance to it. The word-centered liturgy, with whatever frequency it was celebrated, taught the provisions of law and inculcated fidelity to God's holy tradition.

Who "invented" the public reading of the book of Law? Naturally scholars have asked this question and have tried to trace the history of public gatherings and readings. Is it possible that a widespread custom of public readings in monarchical Israel served as Ezra's model? If we look for antecedents there, we have to rely on inference and imagination. At religious festivals, scribes may have entertained the largely illiterate population with readings from their books of stories. Later scribes used these textual materials when they compiled the Bible. While the "Israelite" hypothesis is tempting, it cannot be substantiated from the sources. According to another theory, Ezra's reading of the book of Law has its background in Persian imperial policy; the Persians, so it is maintained, not only recognized the Jewish book of Law, but actually commissioned its compilation and urged its proclamation. However, this theory also rests on fragile evidence. According to a third theory, which we may term the "juridical" one, the reading of the Law has its roots in the ancient Near Eastern legal practice of periodically reminding people of their duties. A fourteenth-century BCE cuneiform document concerning slaves and domestics of the palace ends with the instruction: "This document shall be read to them every third year or every fourth year, lest it be forgotten." Treaty texts between an overlord and a dependent ruler had to be read to the latter "three times yearly" (thirteenth century BCE). But not only palace slaves and dependent kings, but also entire populations had to be reminded of their obligations. As we know, the Assyrian emperor relied on an intricate system of vassal treaties to control his semi-independent subjects among whom we find the Judaeans. Public gatherings of local noblemen, at which readings of treaties were held and loyalty was sworn, were held at regular intervals. Toward the end of the seventh century, the Assyrian Empire collapsed (612 BCE); but by this time, the Assyrian practice may already have left its mark on Judah and may have inspired the holding of public readings as a tool for religious propaganda. Scholars have been successful in tracing the influence of Assyrian loyalty propaganda in Deuteronomy, a book that reuses Assyrian-inspired vocabulary not for political, but for religious propaganda. Ezra may stand in the double tradition of the Assyrian imperial propaganda and the Deuteronomic movement.[8]

Unfortunately, not only the beginnings, but also the further story of public reading in the synagogue remain obscure. Writing during one of the first four decades of the first century CE, Philo of Alexandria (ca. 30 BCE–45 CE) refers to synagogue worship as a regular feature of Jewish life. To a pagan audience he presents the Jews as a philosophical people and the synagogue as a school of sacred philosophy. "So each seventh day there stand wide open in every city thousands of schools." His description looks like an idealized picture of what happens in a major Alexandrian synagogue on Sabbath:

> He [Moses] required them to assemble in the same place on these seventh days, and sitting together in a respectful and orderly manner hear the laws read so that none should be ignorant of them. And indeed they do always assemble and sit together, most of them in silence except when it is the practice to add something to signify approval of what is read. But some priest who is present or one of the elders reads the holy laws to them and expounds them point by point till about late afternoon.

Most likely, the regular Sabbath service with scriptural reading and explanation originated with "radical" groups like the Essene movement, known for its interest in learning. Intellectuals like Philo promoted it. Later, after the destruction of the Jerusalem Temple by the Romans in 70 CE, sabbatical worship at the synagogue became more and more prominent and was practiced, ideally, everywhere and by everyone. At the end of the first century CE, Josephus and Luke agreed that "in every city, for generations past, Moses has had those who proclaim him, for he has been read aloud every Sabbath in the synagogues."[9]

Jewish "book religion" or, more precisely, the creation of Judaism as a textual community must be seen as a creative response to the destruction of the ancient Israelite monarchy by Babylonian imperialism. Widely dispersed throughout the Middle East (Palestine, Babylonia, and Egypt) and eventually also throughout the Mediterranean world, Jewish culture was threatened with loss of identity and eventual disappearance. To counter this threat, intellectuals began to collect and edit books, thus creating a library which eventually became the Hebrew Bible. Those with an antiquarian interest were often also members of an old and ever more influential religious movement that promoted the exclusive worship of one deity, the Israelite national god Yahweh. Within this movement, book learning and regular book-centered rituals came to be established, serving as Judaism's permanent and collective memory. In the education-minded climate of the Hellenistic era, the Jewish zeal for their holy books and for sacred learning intensified. Intellectual leaders and wealthy benefactors began to found synagogues, to establish schools, and to promote public education. Thus Judaism, even before the time of Christ, had developed into a textual community, having a religion of the book, of learning, and of book-centered rituals. The destruction of the Jerusalem Temple by the Romans in 70 CE meant the end of sacrificial ritual, which had by this time already become less important if not obsolete. Just as at an earlier stage of development, the study of oracular texts had replaced the living prophetic utterance, so the study of ritual texts had begun to supersede the performance of the rituals themselves. In the words of an ancient Jewish sage: "One who studies the [biblical] text on the burnt offering is as though he actually brings a burnt-offering."[10]

The fact that both Christianity and Islam adopted the idea of the sacred book from Judaism makes the early history of the Jewish textual community into one of the fundamental stories of the world's cultural memory. In the words of Sigfried Morenz: "As a type, the book religion is Judaism's gift to the world, in its comprehensive, multiplex, and deep impact comparable to the most significant gifts of a people to humanity. Just as in the case of the Phoenician alphabet or classical Greek art, we can witness how a world-transforming power originated in a small area at a very particular historical moment."[11]

Christianity's Textually Oriented Ritual

Without its sacred library, Judaism would not have been able to survive in an often hostile environment. The book proved to be an eminently cohesive force within the community. However, the book invited ever new interpretations and therefore could also be a divisive factor that contributed to the emergence of dissenting textual communities. The most important dissenting group to emerge within early Judaism was Christianity, and, like its parent religion, it never ceased to be a textual community, centered around sacred literature and its interpretation. Accordingly, "intellectual" or "textually oriented" rituals figure prominently in its worship.

One of the earliest Christians who has left us a description of such a ritual is Justin Martyr (ca. 100–65 CE). Born in Palestine and presumably of Roman or Greek descent, he studied philosophy and lived for some time in Ephesus in Asia Minor. It was there that he encountered Christianity and as a convert embraced this new philosophy. Like other itinerant pagan and Christian teachers, Justin found his way to Rome where he carried on a long teaching ministry during the reign of Antoninus Pius (138–61), to whom he addressed his *First Apology* in about 153–55. This book includes the following description of worship:

> On the day called Sunday [*tou hêliou hêmera*] there is a meeting in one place of those who live in cities or the country, and the memoirs of the apostles or the writings of the prophets are read as long as time permits. When the reader has finished, the president in a discourse urges and invites [us] to the imitation of these noble things. Then we stand up together and offer prayers.[12]

For Justin, Christian worship is a class of philosophy. He states that Christian worship involves not merely instruction, but book-based instruction. The Christian teachers' activities were very similar to those of their contemporary pagan philosophers: they taught on the basis of ancient texts. In a philosophical school, teaching involved the reading of texts, formal lectures, and informal discussions. The texts read and studied would be the writings of the masters of the school to which the teacher adhered—that of the Stoics or the followers of Plato. In Athens, for instance, the philosopher Taurus (ca. 100–65, an exact contemporary of Justin) read Plato's *Symposium* with his students. The method followed by Justin and Origen was similar to that of the Roman schools where boys could acquire a familiarity with classical literature and the finer points of correct and elegant style. That method featured the *praelectio*, the reading of a text with explanatory commentary. The fact that the reading was done by an attendant rather than by the master, also echoed the ancient school: the attendant was presumably a younger person whom the master trained in the profession. An outsider present at Justin's meeting who was used to the readings, let us say, from Chrysippus or Plato, and familiar with the moral exhortation of a Stoic teacher, would certainly have recognized the pattern. To him or her, the Christian service would have appeared to be a class in moral philosophy.[13]

Even the weekly meeting of Justin's community, on Sunday night, would not have astonished outsiders. A class of philosophy must have a certain regularity, after all. In the city of Rhodes, a noted first-century CE grammarian named Diogenes refused to lecture on any day but the Sabbath. The historian

Suetonius, who tells us of Diogenes, does not explain why the philosopher preferred this particular day; but most likely he did so because Jewish influence had begun to make the Sabbath a day of intellectual activities—both inside and outside the synagogue.[14]

Before his death as a martyr in ca. 165 CE, Justin lived in Rome, most likely as the head of a small Christian community which had formed itself around him. We must beware of defining early Roman Christianity as being a comprehensive organization with a hierarchy made up of a bishop and a group of presbyters. In the second century, Roman Christians still formed a number of independent "school communities" that met in private homes to listen to and worship with a Christian teacher. Justin had set himself up in a rented dwelling and offered to teach those who would see him, just as Paul had done a hundred years earlier in the same city (Acts 28:30). Justin's students and friends formed a group that met, for worship and instruction, in their leader's home. If Christianity is presented as a philosophy, worship can be considered as part of the proceedings—indeed the regular teaching—of a school of philosophy.[15]

In Justin's report we find all the elements characteristic of the "textual community": sacred literature (the gospels and prophetic books) and a group of people "whose social activities center around texts or, more precisely, a literate interpreter of them." We also find what Brian Stock has termed "an intellectualism inseparable from the study of texts." In the textual community, religion becomes increasingly intellectual, and its essence can be defined as "saving knowledge." Jesus himself prized listening and learning over other activities, calling it "the one thing needful." He praised his friend Mary who sat at his feet and listened, while her sister Martha was distracted by household tasks. In the early second century, a pseudo-Pauline letter refers to "God our savior, who desires everyone to be saved and to come to the knowledge of the truth," a statement that all but identifies salvation with knowledge (1 Tim. 2:3–4). In the Middle Ages, the Council of Basel (1438) insisted that episcopal churches should have a theologian-preacher "who through his teaching and preaching must bring the fruit of salvation." In the sixteenth century, the Anglican divine Richard Hooker (1553–1600) expressed a common sentiment when he stated that "the way for all men to be saved is by the knowledge of that truth which the word [of God] hath taught. . . . It saveth because it maketh 'wise unto salvation' (2 Tim. 3:15). Wherefore the ignorant it saveth not."[16]

If one's salvation depends on knowledge, then it depends on listening more than on anything else. While the educated should study and preach, others should acquire at least some knowledge through faithfully and regularly listening to the divine word as read and explained in synagogue or church. On ritual occasions, even regular ones, specialists bring one of the sacred books before the congregation, read passages from holy scripture, translate their archaic or obsolete language, and explain the sacred story or God's precepts and teachings to the laity. Reading and preaching can develop into a community's main ritual activity. The intellectually oriented ritualist rejects ecstasy and frowns upon magic and sacrifice. He often calls them secondary or, worse, despicable superstitions, unworthy of an educated person, to be repudiated, just as an angry Moses had rejected the people's ecstatic dance around the golden calf. Religion is increasingly defined in terms of belief: as the true teaching about God and salvation, a doctrine to be taught and learned, a creed to be believed, a book to be studied. Religion consists mainly in reading about, in listening to sermons about, and in discussions about—religion. These activities have to be repeated again and again so that saving knowledge will not be forgotten and spiritual fervor will not fade (which seems to be a real possibility and hence a threat). Christian leaders recognize, at least implicitly, an "entropic" tendency of faith to slide away. Often lacking practical value, religious knowledge tends to take no more than thin roots in the minds of the masses. Since the human mind is normally preoccupied with other, more mundane matters, religious leaders must remind the faithful of the holy book and the sacred doctrine. Since salvation builds on knowledge, oral instruction must be first on the list of clerical duties. Contrary to Paul's dictum that the kingdom of God does not depend on talk but on power, it in fact does rely on speech. As Gregory the Great, an early theorist of Christian preaching, observed: Suppress preaching, and "the hearts of those in whom eternal hope germinates will quickly dry up."[17]

While it is true that during the first millennium priests were not always eager to warm up the hearts of their communities, preaching remained a major ritual expression of Christianity. With the advent of Protestantism, preaching intensified, and Protestant and Catholic pulpits often vied with one another. In the words of Karl Barth: "The Christian church speaks: catholic and protestant, orthodox and liberal, decent and not-so-decent. This great, wondrous song of praise is a fact. 'It preaches' in the world, as certainly and as perceptibly as it rains." Even post-Christian thought—in antiquity and modern times—does not seem to be able to think of a society without some form of intellectual ritual. When the Roman emperor Julian the Apostate (r. 361–63 CE) attempted, but ultimately failed, to reinvigorate and reform pagan religion in an increasingly Christian world, he did so by creating what modern scholars have termed a "pagan church." His reforming project included an imitation of Christian worship. In his *Oration against Julian*, the church father Gregory of Nazianzus tells us the relevant facts. Julian had not only attended Christian worship, but in his youth had actively participated as a "reader" (*hypanagnôstês*), i.e., as someone reading the scriptural lesson to the congregation. When Julian became emperor, he became very critical of Christianity, but was convinced of the relevance of studying literature and performing intellectual rituals. So he promoted public readings from pagan books, accompanied by explanatory discourse. While Gregory only briefly refers to this particular part of Julian's reforming project, it was certainly clear to him that it reflected a Christian model. Paganism lacked public readings and explanatory sermons, but Julian found this Christian pattern of worship useful for the religious propaganda that he envisaged. In 1794, when the Revolution swept France, many churches were rededicated to be Temples of Reason. In the South, near Nîmes, the *citoyens* of Pont-Cèze decided that in the Temple, people should meet every tenth day (the new Sunday) and listen to a *"lecture et explication simple des lois"* (reading and simple explanation of the laws). Those who wanted to destroy Christianity wished to be the legitimate heirs of its intellectual ritual. In the nineteenth century, Ralph Waldo Emerson, the ex-pastor and writer, had a similar idea. "Two inestimable advantages Christianity has given us," he declared in his *Divinity School Address* of 1838: "first the Sabbath, the jubilee of the whole world. . . . And secondly, the institution of preaching." What he had in mind was not traditional preaching as practiced in the churches, but the free teaching of learned philosophers like himself who were committed not to scripture and tradition, but to truth and creative insight. Post-Christian society seems to have little use for the contents of traditional preaching; yet it retains the Sunday as a day of intellectual occupation.[18]

But in order to get a fuller understanding of Christian preaching, we have to consider its early history as it is reflected in the New Testament.

2. From Luke to Luther: The Beginnings and Aims of Christian Preaching

The public reading of biblical texts, followed by a minister's or priest's oral explanation, is a regular feature of Christian worship. Although preaching may be more prominent in some churches than in others, it is never absent from the liturgical repertoire. There has never been a Christian church that did not have some equivalent of preaching, and preachers of all times have shared an essential aim in their work: to contribute to their audience's salvation. "So, my brothers and sisters, after the God of truth [has spoken to you in the scriptural lesson], I am reading you an exhortation to heed what was there written, so that you may save yourselves." The Second Letter of Clement, dating from the second century and often called the oldest extant Christian sermon, states the purpose of preaching in unambiguous terms. Christianity promises its believers and practitioners "eternal salvation," that is, everlasting life after death in a place near God, more commonly called heaven. In the nineteenth century, Charles Spurgeon repeated and restated the view of Clement in his *Lectures to My Students*:

> God has sent us to preach in order that through the gospel of Jesus Christ the sons of men may be reconciled to Him. Here and there a preacher of righteousness, like Noah, may labor on and bring none beyond his own family circle into the ark of salvation; and another, like Jeremiah, may weep in vain over an impenitent nation; but, for the most part, the work of preaching is intended to save the hearers.

Salvation is not the automatic reward for membership in a Christian church or community. Christians are not "saved" without some sort of human contribution to the process (often debated and endlessly qualified in theological speculation); rather, they generally have to work out their salvation quite consciously in a complex and lifelong struggle. The intellectual dimension of worship—reading from the scriptures and preaching—is designed to help with that struggle.[19]

Despite their unanimity about their aim, preachers have not always agreed about the way leading to salvation. Some have emphasized knowledge: those who have enough knowledge and understanding of the Christian message as it is embodied in scripture and as it is taught in preaching will attain everlasting life. Others, while not neglecting the intellectual aspect, have emphasized the leading of a faultless life as the foremost prerequisite for salvation. Such a view privileges the inculcation of morality as the preacher's essential task. A third group of theologians and preachers appreciate the contribution of both morality and biblical knowledge to the process of salvation; yet, they define faith as that on which salvation hinges. Accordingly, their preaching aims at provoking a response of faith.

The following chapters will look at the origins of word-centered Christian worship as it is documented in the New Testament, and then explore the three classical aims of preaching by studying the work of eminent preachers and theologians from major eras of ecclesiastical history: from the early church (Origen), the Middle Ages (Gregory the Great and Humbert of Romans), and the time of the Reformation (Martin Luther).

Beginnings: Luke, the First Christian Historian

When Christianity emerged in the first century, word-centered worship held a prominent place in Judaism, its parent religion. Judaism had a sacred book or, more precisely, a collection of sacred scrolls, and people gathered around these scrolls in the community's meeting house, the synagogue. Inscriptions attest one third-century BCE synagogue in Egypt, and the institution may not antedate this period. By the first century CE, the synagogue had been imported from the Diaspora into Palestine, and even Jerusalem boasted numerous meeting houses. A particularly elaborate Greek inscription that dates from the first century CE celebrates the donor of a Jerusalem synagogue that served (like all synagogues) "for the reading of the Law and for the study of the precepts." We must not think of the synagogue as a sacred building, specifically designed for worship. Nor should we think that a great number of first-century Jewish communities were committed to regular synagogue worship in which the pious met every Sabbath and had some pages from the scriptures read to them. Instead, the synagogue must be thought of as a meeting house used for both secular and religious purposes, a place where Jewish books were available for study and prayer, where meetings were held, news exchanged, travelers accommodated, and even where community members could be punished. People with a special interest in understanding the traditional scriptures seem to have had informal meetings in which they discussed novel interpretations of sacred literature (which, as we know, could lead to heated debates). Sometimes, scholars established their own meeting house which they called the House of Study; there, they kept their books and met for instruction and scholarly exchange, but also for prayer and preaching. Some zealous Jews promoted the idea of regular synagogue worship in the form of reciting prayers and having public readings from the scriptures. If the community was lucky, a scholar or a story-teller versed in traditional religious lore would explain the text and offer edifying reflections. But we should have no illusions that there was regular worship with practically the entire community in attendance. Not every community actually had a synagogue![20]

During the second half of the first century, as tensions grew between "traditional Jews" and "Christian Jews," the latter left the established synagogues. When they set up their own Christian synagogues, these groups continued and no doubt intensified their liturgical tradition, possibly because they wanted to demonstrate that they were the "better Jews" and had a superior understanding of scripture. They still read from the Hebrew Bible (or perhaps from a Greek translation), discussed it, and listened to expository preaching. At an early stage, they also introduced Christian texts that were used along with the older sacred literature. Toward the end of the first century, biographies of Jesus were compiled, perhaps commissioned for use at worship. Timothy, to whom Luke dedicates his gospel, may well have been the patron and sponsor of a Christian synagogue, presumably somewhere in Greece. Perhaps Timothy understood the special needs of his community and so decided to commission a biography of Jesus (the gospel of Luke), supplemented by an account of the beginnings of the church (the Acts of the Apostles).

Unfortunately, the beginnings of word-centered Christian worship are not documented, and the outline indicated remains conjectural. The letters of St. Paul, which form the earliest extant sources for Christian history, never mention the practice of the synagogue type of worship in the new movement. The rest of the New Testament includes either no evidence at all or, if read with care, produces only some scattered and indirect references. Yet, by exploiting these references and by setting them in the context of their sources, we can gain much insight into the development and meaning of word-centered worship. Our account relies on the earliest Christian historian, Luke.

Toward the end of the first century CE, when Luke wrote his history of Christian origins (the gospel of Luke, Acts of the Apostles), the synagogue had outgrown its uncertain beginnings, which we traced back to the days of Ezra in the fifth century BCE. "In every city, for generations past, Moses has had those who proclaim him, for he has been read aloud every Sabbath in the synagogues," writes Luke (Acts 15:21). He also tells of a wealthy Roman officer who had sponsored the building of a synagogue in Galilee—a good example of ancient philanthropy (Luke 7:5). Jewish communities had developed their own religious architecture, consisting, most likely, of a simple hall and a shrine for storing the sacred scrolls.

Like all ancient historians, Luke invented scenes and speeches to enliven his presentation. He pictures Jesus as a devout Jew who went to synagogue every Sabbath morning and who would sometimes be invited to serve as a reader and to address the congregation from the preaching chair:

When he came to Nazareth, where he had been brought up, he went to the synagogue on the Sabbath day, as was his custom. He stood up to read, and the scroll of the prophet Isaiah was given to him. He unrolled the scroll and found the place where it was written:

"The spirit of the Lord is upon me, because he has anointed me to bring good news to the poor. He has sent me to proclaim release to the captives and recovery of sight to the blind, and let the oppressed go free, to proclaim the year of the Lord's favor."

And he rolled up the scroll, gave it back to the attendant, and sat down [on the preaching chair]. The eyes of all in the synagogue were fixed on him. Then he began to say to them, "Today this scripture has been fulfilled in your hearing." All spoke well of him and were amazed at the gracious words that came from his mouth. (Luke 4:16–22a)

For Luke, Jesus epitomized the successful charismatic preacher whom the audience liked and who won entire congregations over to his special message. Far from simply explaining and inculcating the Law (as earlier, in the days of Ezra), the Jesus depicted by Luke reads a passage of a prophetic book and applies the prophecy to his own work of magic healing and proclaiming the goodness of God. Historically, Jesus most likely had little interest in the synagogue and stayed away from its affairs. Contemporary research paints a picture of the historical Jesus that resembles an itinerant philosopher and street-teacher more than a respected member of a synagogue who would be invited to speak to the congregation. However, Luke presumably lacked all direct information about the details of his Lord's life. Luke's text reflects not the historical preaching of Jesus but rather the way in which prophetic texts were understood and preached in Christian synagogues of the late first century. The passage echoes the enthusiasm with which early Christian preachers celebrated the miracles of their Lord and, of course, their own deeds of healing.[21]

While the Jesus of history, unlike the Lord of the legends, seems to have had few connections with the synagogue, his followers became quite involved. When they preached, they often created uproar and controversy. Either Luke himself or an early editor of his gospel added a sequel to the "ideal scene" (quoted above) in which Jesus' preaching was favorably received. This sequel tells a different story. In what amounted to a second sermon, "Jesus" criticized his audience for not appreciating his ministry, for "no prophet is accepted in the prophet's hometown." The audience quickly responded with rage. They got up and drove him out of town, threatening to hurl him off a cliff (Luke 4:22b–30). The opposition to and anger about Jesus' preaching reflect an experience no doubt quite common in the early Christian community. Guardians of traditional Jewish orthodoxy fought against the new movement, driving more than one preacher near the cliff and threatening his life. Luke reports how a certain Saul ("also known as Paul," Acts 13:9) in his pre-Christian days had persecuted the church, punished its members, and tried to destroy the community of believers. Christian preachers, and eventually all Christians, had to leave the synagogue. When the inevitable rupture came, missionaries took their followers away from it to establish a new community.[22]

Luke, in the Acts of the Apostles, describes a scene of Christian preaching in a Diaspora synagogue in a city in Asia Minor. "On the Sabbath day," he reports, Paul and his companions

> went to the synagogue and sat down. After the reading of the Law and the Prophets, the officials of the synagogue sent them a message, saying, "Brothers, if you have any word of consolation for the people, give it." So Paul stood up and with a gesture began to speak. (Acts 13:14–16)

Luke's account of apostolic preaching in the Diaspora synagogue closely parallels his report of Jesus' sermon. In both cases a traveling person is invited to speak to the congregation. And in both cases the audience has a mixed response: initially, people react favorably, urging Paul to speak again; but eventually, "they contradicted what was spoken by Paul" and drove him and his companions out of the region (13:45.50). The sequence of invitation, preaching, and controversy structures both accounts.

Both Jesus and Paul deliver two sermons or, more precisely, one sermon in two parts. The audience accepts and hails the first one, while the second one creates controversy and leads to the threatening and expulsion of the preacher. Jesus delivers his two sermons, it seems, on the same occasion. In the book of Acts, where Luke is apparently less bound by tradition, he has Paul preach on two successive Sabbaths. The audience acclaims his first sermon; his second one, by contrast, meets much opposition. The mixed reaction, from initial enthusiasm to eventual rejection, mirrors the historical development. Christianity started as a movement within the synagogue; eventually, as opposition grew, Christians had to separate from their original home. Or, more precisely, the preachers were forced to leave, and they then founded new communities outside traditional Judaism. The preacher's role in leaving the synagogue—and in establishing the new community—comes into sharp focus. Many of the early Christians did not like to be excluded. Luke's Jesus has words of consolation for them. "Blessed are you," he proclaimed, "when people hate you, and when they exclude you, and defame you on account of the Son of Man. Rejoice in that day [of exclusion] and leap for joy, for surely your reward is great in heaven!" (Luke 6:22–23). Christ promised them reward in heaven; on earth, they had little to expect and much to regret. To leave a community that enjoyed the recognition of the Roman authorities and certain privileges like exemption from military duty must have been a very difficult choice in a society in which people depended on the ethnic and religious group they belonged to.[23]

Synagogue sermons were designed to explain biblical texts and at the same time to address the situation of the listening community. Unlike "Jesus," the Paul in Luke starts his sermon with a reference to the Law. However, he follows traditional exegetical technique in combining Law and Prophecy, and in commenting on the two scriptural lessons read to the congregation. Soon he is commenting on the "words of the prophets that are read every Sabbath" (Acts 13:27). Thus the two preachers in Luke, "Jesus" and Paul, agree in their emphasis on the prophetic message. This echoes the liturgical practice of taking two scriptural readings from two different bodies of biblical literature; it also reflects a Christian preference. Christian preaching, like the original words of Jesus, continues the prophetic ministry that announces God's salvation to the contemporary generation. While the Old Testament Law lost much of its importance in early Christianity, the prophetic writings retained their importance. Preaching, for early Christians, was quite different from Ezra's inculcation of the Law. It emphasized prophecy and the visible fulfillment of ancient promises.

Luke's work, then, provides some insight into the earliest forms of Christian preaching. Worship, for Christians, included the reading of biblical texts and commenting on them. A gifted speaker would point out how the prophetic message had become true in the work of Christ. In Christ, God had begun to comfort, to help, and to save his people. A good preacher had to be well versed in the Jewish scriptures and to know the expository techniques. Above all, however, he had to make a convincing statement about the consolation God has begun to offer to his people in the message, the magical work, and the resurrection of Jesus. In synagogues that included few (if any) adherents of the new faith, Christian preachers relied chiefly on prophetic literature to promote their specific exegesis and point of view.[24]

The work of Luke not only provides insight into controversial preaching within the pre-Christian synagogue; it also gives us an occasional glimpse of how Christians organized their own meetings and devised their own ritual. Luke takes the existence of such meetings for granted; apparently, they were so much part of his world that he does not feel the need to tell us about their beginnings. But in his description of Paul's visit to the community of Troas (a port town in Asia Minor, south of the Hellespont), Luke supplies some information on the proceedings of a Christian meeting. The community met in the private home of a member, located on the third floor of a building we may identify as a tenement house. It was Sunday night, most likely the usual time when Christians assembled. The ritual involved a long public address (by Paul), followed by the "breaking of the bread," the Eucharist (Acts 20:7–12). Luke does not tell us what Paul talked about; apparently, the talk was informal and very long—so long, in fact, that a young man sank into sleep and fell out of the window in which he sat. He dropped to the ground three floors below and was recovered dead. Luckily, the apostle managed to animate the unfortunate man's body and restored him to life (Acts 20:9–12). Troas is a place close to ancient Troy, the famous city of the Trojan War. Both the plot of the story and the style in which it is told seem to echo the fate of a minor character in Homer's *Odyssey*. A certain young man named Elpenor, who had become dizzy from drinking, fell asleep on the roof of a house and, awaking, forgot to use the ladder. He fell headlong from the roof and died. To the same degree that the ancient readers must have relished the biblical author's play on the Homeric theme, they must also have smiled at the theme of sleeping in church, a phenomenon that was not unfamiliar to them. After the incident, Paul continued to talk until dawn. Other texts in Luke may help us to define the kind of preaching done when the Christians of Troas and other cities assembled. Paul no doubt spoke about the "teaching of the apostles" whose exposition characterized worship from its very beginning (Acts 4:42). If he made specific reference to scripture, one would expect that "beginning with Moses and all the prophets, he interpreted to them all the things concerning [the Christ]." Preaching helps all those who are "foolish and slow to believe all that the prophets have declared" (Luke 24:27.25).[25]

A careful reading of the work of Luke produces much information about the meaning and early development of Christian preaching. We can discern two types of meeting in which Christians preached: in the synagogues to which they belonged, and in private homes. In the synagogues, followers of "the Way" (this is how Luke refers to the church in Acts 9:1) often stirred up controversies which ended with Christians separating themselves from the Jewish community. When they met in private homes, Christians were among themselves. Preaching always has a relationship to the Jewish scriptures, especially to the prophets. These scriptures are interpreted in a new key: the Christian key. According to this key, what the prophets wrote is an announcement of things to come, and now, ever since the ministry of Jesus Christ, they have begun to happen. This can be known and should be "believed." Some are "foolish and slow to believe [Greek, *pisteuein*]," but a good preacher will convince them (Luke 24:25). "Believing" is here not an existential commitment (as in much of modern theology), but knowledge of facts and assent to a teaching that bears rational demonstration and argument. In other words, the preacher transmits and explains Christian knowledge in a persuasive way. Acts as a whole can be seen as an extended sermon: what the preacher normally does in brief is carried out by Luke in the form of a systematic presentation. Whereas the preacher usually comments on just one or two points, the books tell the whole story. In the preface to his work, Luke explains his project of "writing an orderly account for you, most excellent Theophilus, so that you may know the truth concerning the things about which you have been instructed" (Luke 1:3–4). The key words are "to know" and "to instruct," and these terms accurately describe the purpose of preaching. In the third century, Origen of Alexandria's preaching pursued the same aims, but in a much more systematic way.

Instruction in Saving Knowledge: Origen

In liturgical development, the third century marks a new phase. Now Christians no longer assembled just on Sundays as Luke's report from the late first century seems to imply. They actually assembled—at least ideally—every day for a scripture-based liturgy. The church experienced an immense growth. Many pagans joined Christianity, churches were built, persecutions became rarer. The third century's most famous theologian, Origen (185–255), has left us a substantial body of sermons. These not only give us a glimpse of their liturgical setting; they also permit us to meet Origen the preacher.

The most conspicuous feature of the church of Caesarea in Palestine—the city where Origen lived, wrote books, and preached—was its daily worship. Christians met every morning in church. A reader stood up to read two or three chapters from an Old Testament book, and then Origen would sit down in a preaching chair and talk for almost an hour. The idea was to read and preach through the entire Old Testament in three years. All Christians, including the catechumens preparing for baptism, were expected to follow the daily lectures. Sunday worship interrupted the cycle by replacing the ritual of instruction with a eucharistic service (which of course also included preaching; three readings and three sermons, it seems). For the daily assemblies, the Old Testament was preferred to the New, for the catechumens attended, and they had not yet been introduced to the gospels. Scriptural reading and preaching figured also in the two week-day eucharistic services, held on Wednesdays and Fridays. Caesarea had a very intense liturgical life, dominated by preaching. The church was a school of Christian philosophy.[26]

In fact, the term "school" aptly describes the daily assembly. Origen had worked as a schoolmaster before converting to the new faith, and in this assembly he used the standard methods with which ancient teachers read and explained texts in the classroom. In a secular school, classes met every morning; an attendant read a text to the class, and then the master, sitting in his chair, explained the vocabulary, variant readings, the style, the content, and often added a moralizing commentary. According to Origen, a good grammarian "explains philosophically the poems, adding to each that which is profitable for the young." Ancient instruction in grammar has a moral aim; the grammarian "searches the annals of the past for heroic examples of human perfection." Classical scholarship has pointed out that the very genre of the simple scriptural homily with its lack of rhetorical flourish has its roots in the ancient classroom where the *grammaticus* expounded the text. This is exactly what Origen did, and his preoccupation with explaining words and his occasional discussion of variant readings alone would suffice to betray him as a teacher. Significantly, the Greek language of Origen's day did not have a special term for designating the liturgical preacher; *didaskalos* refers to both the secular, pagan schoolmaster and the Christian preacher.[27]

The ancients themselves saw the similarities between their book ritual and the teaching at secular schools. There was little difference between the learning of the Bible in church and the school in which pupils had classical literature explained to them, such as the work of Homer and the speeches of Demosthenes. Origen, in one of his morning homilies, complains of the inattentiveness and lack of interest of the congregation: some leave right after the reading, others leave even before the reading ends; others stay, but hide somewhere in the back of the church in order to chat. Thus people show little interest in the study of God's law. Parents, by contrast, when sending their sons to secular schools, spare no expense to ensure the progress in grammar and rhetoric. Origen wants people to understand that attending a service of worship also means going to school![28]

Despite these similarities, one characteristic difference between church and school cannot be overlooked. Most people in the preacher's audience were illiterate, and the preacher would never even think of turning worship into a writing class. The preacher's presentation, although indebted to methods of classroom instruction, remained strangely indifferent toward his audience's "general education." If we look at the synagogue in Origen's time, we meet a very different situation. Judaism promoted an intense climate of education, and the idea was to train all the male members of the community in the elementary skills of reading and writing. The textbook used in this training was of course the Hebrew Bible. So when Jews listened to their preachers on Sabbath morning, they knew the text much better than their Christian neighbors—or at least had better access to it. By the time of Origen, Jews could already look back at a long tradition of religious schools.

Unlike Jewish culture, Christians showed little interest in education. Or rather, education, for them, remained an activity closely related to paganism. For Christians, to go to school meant to study pagan literature. Even in the fourth century (and later), when the Roman Empire had become Christian, hardly anyone seems to have considered the establishment of Christian schools in which biblical literature would serve as the text for study. We know of epic versions of the Pentateuch, and attempts to produce gospels in dialogue form in order to bring biblical literature into line with literary types used at school. These fourth-century attempts were not inspired by an enthusiasm to reform existing pagan curricula. Rather, they were failed responses to the (also failed) attempt of Emperor Julian ("the Apostate," r. 361–63 CE) to accredit only pagan teachers. Julian, the pagan romantic, hated the idea of "Galilean" schoolmasters teaching and, at the same time, ridiculing the crude polytheistic mythology of authors like Homer and Hesiod. For him, these teachers lacked the attitude required for serious education. They should leave the teaching profession and do their job in the church; there they could "expound Matthew and Luke."[29]

As Julian's pagan revival proved to be short-lived, the idea of creating separate Christian schools also vanished. In late antiquity, the school system retained its conservative pagan curriculum. Christianity, it seems, had little interest in inserting itself completely into classical culture, let alone merging with it. Its leaders never thought of reforming pagan culture. Citizens of a different, heavenly world, they cared little about mundane institutions controlled by pagan traditions. As a consequence, the church's intellectual ritual transmitted the doctrine of salvation rather than practical skills and cultural knowledge. Despite its reliance on holy scriptures and its development of a highly educated literary elite, Christianity remained an oral religion. This situation began to change only when the Roman Empire, its cultural world, and institutions began to dissolve in the fifth and sixth centuries. In fifth-century Marseilles, Marius Victor seems to have had some success with his Genesis rewritten as an epic in Latin hexameters. However, in Marius's attempt we can still see the traditional preference for poetry. The values of the old school system still prevailed. In the sixth century, a Greek traveler coming back from Syria reported that he saw, in the city of Nisibis, a Jewish school "where professors, employed by the state, teach well-structured courses on Holy Scripture in the way secular subjects like grammar and rhetoric are taught in our schools." Two eminent scholars and book-lovers, Cassiodorus and Pope Agapetus, planned the founding of a Christian academy in Rome in 535/36, but their project never went beyond the establishment of a library. Not only were the times too troubled for reinvigorating academic life; the pope's problematic finances would simply not permit it. Christians living in the former Roman empire did not imitate either the pagan schools or the Jewish academy of Nisibis. They continued to leave the task of education to the declining pagan institutions. Only in the Middle Ages, when monastic schools emerged, did things change. In early medieval times, we also hear about an educator in Constantinople who used the Greek translation of the Psalms as a textbook for a course in elementary grammar. Now as teachers began to adopt the Bible as a text, or even as a primer, a genuinely Christian culture could develop. Although the monastery schools used and copied texts of Cicero, Seneca, and other pagan authors, these no longer defined and dominated the canon of cultural knowledge.[30]

Origen's preaching, although indebted to methods of the pagan educational system, did not simply replicate that system. The church appeared as an imperfect school. Confined to oral instruction, it did not wish to transmit the practical skills of writing and reading. Neglecting such profane matters, Origen's interest lay exclusively with religious, saving knowledge. As a teacher skilled in the methods of textual criticism and grammar, he had great respect for the textual side of the Bible. The text, however, was only the garment, the outer side of something more valuable, which was concealed below the surface of the mere word, like a treasure in an earthen vessel. Often, the "surface" of the text made little sense and actually contradicted all that seemed sensible or even decent. One must look "behind" the text, discover its hidden meaning, its spiritual rather than material sense. By applying special exegetical techniques, especially allegory (literally, "different meaning"), one can crack the code and gain access to immense spiritual power. The text appears like the cloak of Jesus or its fringe; when touched in the right manner (as was done by that anonymous woman of the gospel), it would release its healing power.[31]

The experience of the healing power flowing from the text is only the beginning of a long and complex process of redemption. As the Christian believer penetrates into the mysteries of divine knowledge, he or she progresses through the stages of purification and illumination in order to ascend, finally, to the knowledge of God. The first stage, that of purification, restores the image of God in the human soul, which, once it gains health and strength, will be capable of exercise in the knowledge of things divine. The next stage, that of progress in learning, is attained by exposure to the Old Testament. Here the soul finds a training ground for developing practical intelligence and orientation in the created world. However, in the Old Testament, the soul also gets in touch with the heavenly realm of the intelligible, hidden and shadowed in the literal sense of the scriptural text.

The final stage in Origen's view of the process of salvation is the knowledge of God. It begins with a knowledge of Christ's humanity and proceeds to an understanding of the divinity, finally attaining an unmediated, pure vision of God himself.

In Origen's theological system, the human soul needs two guides in this process. The first guide is of course the preacher who makes the teaching of scripture accessible to the congregation. The second and more important guide is Christ. As the divine word or *logos*, he mediates the knowledge of God through his self-disclosure in the scriptures. When listening to the biblical text as read and preached in church, Christians are somehow taught by Christ himself.

In practical terms, Origen considered his preaching as putting the audience in contact with the scriptural truth that "purifies us and banishes in us all thoughts which obsess us with business and purchases." By "applying the written text to the healing of souls," the preacher initiates and promotes the process of salvation that will, hopefully, lead to everyone's attainment of the perfect vision and knowledge of God. On the one hand, Origen's preaching aims at salvation itself—what more could he promise? On the other hand, he views his job realistically enough to know that his audience will often stay at the beginning of understanding. So he hopes for gradual progress and spiritual development—which will continue, after death, in the beyond.[32]

Musing on a biblical place name, the "City of Letters," Origen decides that it must be a designation for heaven, seen as a place of everlasting learning. What Christians must do in this world is to start studying for eventual admission to the higher place of learning. "If you devote yourself to the Law of God," he explains, and meditate on it day and night, if the book of the Law never departs from your hand, as it is said to Joshua (Josh. 1:8), if you remember our Savior's command to "search the scriptures" (John 5:39)—if you devote yourself to such studies and thereby acquire the knowledge of the divine law through reading and listening, then the "City of Letters" (Josh. 15:15) will be your portion.

Without scriptural knowledge, according to Origen, no Christian can enter heaven, the "City of Letters."[33]

Origen knows, of course, that Bible study does not always produce immediate results. Sometimes we do not even get initial insight into the meaning of scripture. Even then, however, listening to the reading of scripture is profitable. Just as the pagans believe in the healing force of their magic incantations and charms, so Christians should believe in the efficacy of the sacred words of the Bible. If we listen to scripture, the angels that surround us feel called upon to help us. Those powers that are in charge of us will chase away evil spirits and help our souls to advance even though our knowledge may make no visible progress. The scriptural text can serve as that form of prayer of which Paul says that "my spirit prays but my mind stays barren" (1 Cor. 14:14). Thus Origen, believing in the secret power of God's word, has a promise even for those who do not get much out of listening to the scriptural lesson and the preacher's commentary.[34]

By the time of Origen, the liturgy of the word had developed fully as an institution. In Origen's Caesarea, it had become a most important element of worship and often served as liturgy itself. While daily preaching does not seem to have been very common in ancient Christianity, it did have a firm place during the forty days preceding Easter and during the Easter week. Preaching was widespread, frequent, and done with enthusiasm. We can also discern the underlying theology. Although Origen did not leave us any systematic account of his view of what happens in the church's liturgy of the word, we can discern notions that are as precise as they are sophisticated. These notions amount to a full program of spiritual guidance and schooling. Just as, in the Middle Ages, Beatrice would guide Dante through the heavens in order to leave him at the place of divine light, so the preacher would guide each member of the congregation.[35]

Moral Medicine: Gregory the Great and Humbert of Romans

In the history of preaching, Gregory (ca. 540–606) and Humbert (ca. 1200–77) are remembered as the authors of influential treatises in which they explained the nature and meaning of preaching. After Gregory was elected bishop of Rome in 590, the noble Italian monk compiled the *Book of Pastoral Rule* (590/91) in which he described his vision of ideal episcopal leadership. He defined preaching as the bishop's single most important task. In the early Middle Ages, preaching was the bishop's rather than the priest's responsibility. More than six centuries later, when the Frenchman Humbert took up the subject, the situation had changed radically. Now friars and priests, and not only bishops, did much of the preaching, and the friars were of course more numerous and often better trained than the priests. Humbert served as the Master General of the Dominican Order, and after his retirement from this position he wrote a huge book entitled *On the Formation of Preachers* (after 1263). It shows close affinity with the work of Gregory and occasionally quotes it as an authority. However, Humbert did more than just paraphrase the *Book of Pastoral Rule*. He developed and adapted his source to suit the specific tasks of his community, whose official name was *ordo praedicatorum*, the order of preachers.[36]

Gregory built his theory of preaching on the distinction between Christian doctrine and moral exhortation. While the first is the same for all Christians, for men and women, for the educated and the uneducated, for the nobleman and the peasant, such is not the case with exhortation. "One and the same exhortation is not suited to all," he explains, "because they are not compassed by the same quality of character."[37]

Gregory goes on to list the differences between the individuals, and he does so in a fairly sophisticated (though not systematic) manner. Obviously, the preacher must speak differently to men and women, subjects and superiors, slaves and masters, the educated and the uneducated, the married and the celibate. But it is not sex, class, and social standing alone that determine someone's character. People may be joyful or sad, healthy or sick, meek or choleric, humble or haughty, slothful or hasty, living in peace or sowing discord. And they may have all sorts of more or less habitual sins; some are addicted to thieving or to gluttony or impatience.[38]

In their manuals, both Gregory and Humbert compile material that can be used in preaching effectively to the various groups, callings, and characters, reminding them of their specific duties and their peculiar temptations to sin. Humbert's book includes one hundred sermon sketches for all classes of listeners (for women, for lay brothers belonging to the Dominican Order, etc.), one hundred for all kinds of circumstances (tournaments of the noble, general chapters of religious orders, weddings, funerals, fairs), thirty-three for liturgical seasons, and twenty-five for saints' feast days, especially for the Virgin Mary, Mary Magdalene, and Doctors of the Church. Reading this material, we meet a variety of interesting characters and situations: the careless Benedictine monk who neglects his duties to provide hospitality and give alms; the nobleman who spends extravagantly on tournaments and ruins his family; the Spartan lifestyle of the eremitic orders; city life that concentrates both the population and sin; the urban wealthy who rarely go to church and refuse their obligations to their feudal lords; the drunkard and the glutton at wedding feasts where people also indulge in excessive singing, games, and worse forms of levity. Preaching, for Humbert, calls on its audience to change their lives, and turn away from the sins and vanities rampant in the culture of his day, especially in the urban culture of France.

However, Humbert does not take an entirely negative view of society. He consistently tries to point out something positive, some value that may be hidden to the eye of the world-renouncing friar. Even a tournament, although an occasion for many sins, has its beneficent side—it may prepare for fighting against the Saracens, for defending the rights of the church or any other legitimate rights, especially those of the nation. When speaking to women, for example, the preacher must dissuade them from fortune-telling and witchcraft, from shamelessness in dressing, from being talkative, and from wandering about instead of staying at home. But the preacher must not leave it at that. A good psychologist, Humbert knows that a female audience will never like a preacher who has nothing to offer but a list of possible sins. Humbert provides a theological sketch about the nobility of women. Unlike men, they were not created "in this dingy world" but in Paradise; our Lord's body was not taken from a man but from a woman; and after this life, the community of the saints will be ruled not by a man but by a woman—Mary, who will be their queen. "All of this," he concludes, "ought to encourage women to love the God who gave them all this, and to pursue for love of him all that is good in a woman. It should also deter them from all that is evil."[39]

Humbert's *Formation of Preachers* follows Gregory in providing hundreds of thematic sketches out of which a good preacher could construct his sermons. Both abstained from writing model sermons, for a good preacher was expected to present his message on the basis of a closely and often allegorically interpreted biblical text. The ethical preaching envisaged by medieval theorists must be based upon and saturated with scripture. Humbert quotes Gregory: the preacher "must take all his points from scripture, so that he can trace everything he says back to the fundamental authority of scripture and build on that the whole structure of his discourse." A friar would create his presentation out of at least two books: scripture and the preacher's manual. His training would enable him to take bits and pieces from the manual, assemble it around a scriptural text, and of course adapt it to the specific needs of his audience.[40]

While composing a sermon, in medieval theory, ranked as sophisticated intellectual work, the actual delivery was something practical. To describe the effect a preacher is supposed to have on his audience, Gregory the Great resorted to the medical metaphor he had inherited from Augustine and Ambrose and which had particularly fascinated his namesake Gregory, bishop of Nazianzus (d. 390), on whose work he relied for his *Book of Pastoral Rule*. Ultimately, the assimilation of the preacher to the doctor derives from ancient popular philosophy. Like the Stoic or Cynic philosopher, the preacher is a doctor who dispenses medicine in order to cure the souls of those in his audience. Preaching provides the medicine that alleviates moral ailments and heals the wounds of sin. In using medical metaphors, Gregory was not merely repeating traditional language; he identified with that language. A permanent invalid, he was fascinated with physical ailments and their treatment. Medical terms and allusions are scattered throughout his writings, culled from traditional sources and no doubt also from the physician in permanent attendance on him. Gregory the Great displayed a touching and deeply felt concern for the ill-health of his friends and episcopal colleagues. Occasionally, he would play the experienced physician and send a warm cloak or prescribe a special diet. Considering the preacher a kind of doctor, then, made sense to someone who liked playing the medical practitioner in the literal sense.[41]

Humbert echoes Gregory's medical metaphor by stating that preachers are doctors. Did not the Lord himself say, "it is not the healthy who need a doctor, but the sick" (Matt. 9:12)? "When there is a lack of preaching," he adds, "epidemics of disease rage unchecked." Indeed, "the company of preachers is the health of the world." The sermon, of course, serves as a universal, powerful medicine.[42]

In the days of Gregory, the local bishop was the one who restored the people's spiritual health. By the time of Humbert, the situation had changed. It was no longer the bishop who was the most prominent preacher, but the priest, the friar, or the monk. Unlike the bishop, these enjoyed little or no feudal, patriarchal authority. They served as advisors and, above all, as confessors. In the days of Gregory, the confession of sins to a priest had not emerged as a regular sacrament. Confession, then, had been a public act for public sinners who had to be reconciled with the community. By the thirteenth century, however, it had become a regular means of spiritual guidance, and the Lateran Council of 1215 had made annual confession a duty of all the faithful. So the confessional, in addition to the pulpit, became a working place for the friars.

"Sometimes there are a lot of people who are moved by a sermon and come eagerly to the preacher to make their confessions." Ethical preaching, for Humbert, ideally moved the individual listener to repentance and to make a good confession in which the Lord himself, speaking through the priest, provides forgiveness, reconciles the penitent with God, and restores his life of grace. Humbert exhorts his fellow Dominicans not to prefer certain groups of penitents like the educated and wealthy. He also tells them not to misuse this sacrament for begging or forming close, unlawful relationships with young women. The healing words of preaching and of the sacramental absolution must not be soiled through the creation of impure bonds. Sometimes, Dominicans share the vices of worldly people and, accordingly, must be warned of the dangers entailed in the ministry of preaching and hearing confession.[43]

Medieval preachers like Gregory and Humbert, then, defined their task as that of healing society's moral injuries. The process of healing, like all salvation, begins with preaching.

The Preaching of Saving Faith: Martin Luther

For the sixteenth-century reformers the only adequate response to the preaching of the gospel was faith, i.e., an existential commitment to God and Christ. For Martin Luther (1483–1546), this idea had practical consequences. When he started to establish new patterns of worship in the 1520s, his services culminated in preaching, for "the chief and greatest aim of any Service consists in preaching and teaching God's word." Luther also created the most important tool for preaching: a version of the Bible in the German vernacular. In 1522, he published his immediately successful German New Testament, and by 1534, the entire Bible was available. Before delivering their sermons, ministers favoring the Reformation approach would always read a scriptural passage in the vernacular (rather than in Latin), so that everyone could understand. Luther knew, however, that many ministers were not talented at speaking in public or had simply never received an adequate training. Luther's idea was to have a good Postil, i.e., a book of printed sermons on the traditional lessons prescribed for each Sunday of the year. A Postil, he thought, would also prevent misuse of the pulpit for sectarian concerns. If every minister produces his own sermons, "the final result will be that everyone preaches his own whims and instead of the gospel and its exposition we shall again have sermons on blue ducks." So Luther himself supplied several books of sermons that could be read to the congregation. Eventually he combined them into the *Church Postil* (1522/28, with later revised editions), and they proved to be very successful. The reformer himself hailed the *Church Postil* as his best book, and its use made Luther *the* authoritative preacher, at least in Electoral Saxony where he received the support of his prince.[44]

Although Luther never bothered to write systematically on the task and theory of preaching, his scattered remarks provide a clear picture of his thoughts about the subject. Preaching for him had three aims, and each of the three builds on the others: to teach Christian knowledge, to produce a radical response of saving faith, and to instruct in the Christian way of life.

The first aim is to teach Christian knowledge. The common people have little education, and they live "as if they were pigs and irrational beasts" (*WA* 30/1:361). One cannot leave them in ignorance; they must be taught. Luther separated catechetical preaching from preaching connected with normal Sunday services. He wanted congregations to go through intensive instruction four times a year. For two weeks, the congregation would meet four times a week (at two o'clock in the afternoon) and have "the elements and fundamentals of Christian knowledge and life" explained to them (*WA* 27:444). These "elements" can be found in the Christian creed, the ten commandments, the Lord's Prayer, and the sacraments (baptism and the Lord's Supper). Luther wanted entire families to be present at these lectures, including adults, children, and servants. After he had preached catechetical sermons several times in Wittenberg, Luther condensed them in two catechisms, a larger one for pastors and a small one for popular use (published in 1529). Like his published sermons, he envisioned that they could serve as models for those who lacked theological training or were looking for a convenient textbook. But although preaching on the catechism transmits the elements of Christian doctrine, all preaching must have a didactic side to it. In particular, by listening daily to the preacher, people will "become proficient, skillful, and well versed in the Bible" (*WA* 12:36). Luther's interest in education is well known, as is his contribution to the establishment of public schools. He urged princes and magistrates to care for the education of all.[45]

The second and central aim of preaching is to make Christian knowledge existential for the individual. Luther did not see knowledge as merely an intellectual pursuit; like his humanist contemporaries he understood knowledge to be "a total experience involving the feelings, penetrating the heart, shaping the will, and stimulating the whole person to some active response." This total experience is called, in Latin, *fides*, i.e., faith. Luther agrees with the ancient rhetorical tradition, so dear to his humanist friends, that it is through effective speaking that human beings are moved to faith.[46]

Luther distinguishes between "historical faith," i.e., mere knowledge of the biblical story of Christ's birth, life, and death, and "true faith." True faith comes when an individual realizes that in sending Christ God has acted on his or her behalf and has given a unique gift, especially the remission of sins. "This means," explains Luther, "that when you see or hear of Christ doing or suffering something, you do not doubt that Christ himself, with his deeds and suffering, belongs to you. On this you may depend as surely as if you had done it yourself; indeed as if you were Christ himself" (*WA* 10/I, 1:11). The preacher must move from an elementary presentation of biblical facts to a deeper interpretation. "It is not enough nor is it Christian, to preach the works, life and words of Christ as historical facts, as if the knowledge of these would suffice for the conduct of life. . . . Rather ought Christ to be preached to the end that faith in him may be established, that he may not only be Christ, but be Christ for you and for me, and that what is said of him and what his name denotes [Jesus = Savior] may be effectual in us. Such faith is produced and preserved in us by preaching why Christ came, what he brought and bestowed, what benefit it is to us to accept him" (*WA* 7:58–59). For Luther, the existential aim of preaching claims priority over the other aims. In his recorded Table Talk, he said, "the first aim [of preaching] is to fell [the hearers'] consciousness to the ground" (*primo est deicienda conscientia*). A sermon must aim at conquering the conscience, the heart, the very center of everyone in the audience.[47]

A good example of existential preaching is the sermon Luther gave on the afternoon of Christmas Day, 1530. He began by asserting that the message of

6a. The Attentive Audience of Lutheran Preaching (1). The sixteenth-century reformers made the Sunday service culminate in the sermon. This woodcut illustrates the explanation of the biblical commandment, "You shall sanctify the holy day," in an early edition of Martin Luther's *Large Catechism*. In the background, a wood-gatherer is profaning the Sabbath. Although the congregation listens attentively to the preacher, the dog is allowed to sleep and the little child to play and to look around. Woodcut, workshop of Lucas Cranach the Elder, 1529.

6b. The Attentive Audience of Lutheran Preaching (2). Lucas Cranach the Elder's painting for the city church of Wittenberg shows Luther himself in the pulpit. Cranach departs from the woodcut (ill. 6a) by omitting the dog and by making even the child and the baby look up to the crucifix and the preacher. Luther had been the preacher in this church from 1514 to his death in 1546. It has been suggested that the woman and boy in front are Luther's wife Kathy and their son, Hans. Altar predella by Lucas Cranach the Elder, 1531 or 1547.

strove for a graphic, appealing presentation, using proverbs and the language of common folk. Despite his efforts, though, Luther's popular appeal remained limited. Serious preaching was a thankless task.[48]

For understanding the contrast between the ideal and the reality of early Lutheran preaching, a woodcut (ill. 6a) inserted into Luther's *Large Catechism*

7. The Sleeping Audience of Lutheran Preaching. Some members of the congregation of Johannes Sprenger, Lutheran pastor in sixteenth-century Soest, Germany, seem to be sleeping. While the painting certainly reflects reality, the artist may also be alluding to the gospel parable that compares preaching with sowing: not all seeds produce plants and fruit. German memorial painting, 1580s.

of 1529 provides a convenient starting point. Illustrating the third command-ment of the Decalogue (which tells people to keep the Lord's day holy), it depicts a congregation listening attentively to the preacher's words. In the background, a wood gatherer profanes the Sabbath. At church, people have to listen. Only the child is allowed to play and the dog to sleep. Later, the woodcut served as the model for a painting that depicted Luther as the preacher of the city church of Wittenberg. Lucas Cranach transferred the scene from outdoors to the interior of the church, retained the preacher's gesture, omitted the little dog, and added the crucifix (which originally had formed part of the woodcut: see the breach in the wall). He also made the congregation look even more attentive than in his model. Now even the little boy (not to mention the baby) seems to fix his eyes on the crucifix, or the preacher, or both. The first generation of Lutherans, whether depicted as being more idyllic as in the catechism, or more formal as in Cranach's painting for the predella of the Wittenberg altar (ill. 6b), never took their eyes off the preacher. To these scenes, a late sixteenth-century painting (ill. 7) forms a stark contrast by its realistic depiction of adult members sleeping during the sermon. Below the pulpit, a woman seems to pay more attention to her baby than to what is going on during the service. The painting, still on display today in St. Maria zur Wiese, a Lutheran church in Soest, Westphalia, depicts the church interior during the pastor's sermon. Although the artist gives the pastor an engaging rhetorical gesture, the reaction of the congregation is not uniform: some listen

8. The Sleeping Congregation. The subject selected by the eighteenth-century English inventor of the modern satirical cartoon needs no comment. We must beware of looking at the Sprenger memorial painting (ill. 7) through William Hogarth's eyes: whereas the sixteenth-century memorial painting represents the preacher's experience frankly, Hogarth satirizes it. William Hogarth, *The Sleeping Congregation*, 1736.

attentively, others do not seem to care, and some even sleep. No doubt the pastor of St. Maria was not spared Luther's experience.

People prefer, Luther is quoted as remarking in his Table Talk, to be entertained with good stories. "If you preach the article on justification, people sleep and cough. But when you start telling stories and examples, then they prick up their ears." So the woodcut in Luther's catechism represents the ideal, not the reality. By contrast, the artist of Soest wanted to represent real life in the style of Pieter Brueghel or perhaps Laurentius de Voltalina, who in the fourteenth century painted students sleeping during a university lecture given by a German professor. However, realism or even a sense of humor do not seem to provide the full explanation of this unusual painting. Reference to the Bible can help us to see what the artist had in mind. In the parable of the sower, a peasant went out, took a handful of seeds, and scattered them. Some seeds fell upon the path, and some fell on rock, while others fell into good soil and brought forth fruit. The artist seems to explain that the reaction to the preaching of Johannes Sprenger, the church's pastor in 1567–81, corresponds to what is said in the gospel: some listen to the word of God, and others don't. Some just sit and doze. The painter challenges the viewer to make sure that his or her own reaction to preaching will be adequate.[49]

It was only two centuries later that the theme of "sleeping in church" became a favorite subject of satirical comment. We must beware of looking at the Sprenger memorial painting with the eyes of Jonathan Swift (author of *Gulliver's Travels*) or William Hogarth (father of the modern cartoon) (ill. 8). The satirical attitude would make us miss the subtle message conveyed by the sixteenth-century artist.[50]

3. Patterns of Protestant Preaching in the Modern World

The Protestant reformers' enthusiasm for preaching created a form of worship dominated by the sermon, with the Eucharist given much less emphasis and generally omitted from the normal Sunday service. The ministers or pastors were preachers in the first place, for they considered the delivery of the Sunday sermon—and sometimes additional weekday sermons—their essential duty. The Protestant decision to give priority to word-centered worship gave birth to a new and very rich culture of preaching and an equally rich culture of homiletic reflection on the aims and strategies the responsible and successful minister has to pursue. At the most general level, one can say that the aim of the sermon coincides with the aim of worship, namely, to bring both the congregation as a whole and its individual members closer to God. The underlying idea is that believers, although baptized and instructed in basic Christian doctrine, are still lacking something: the fervor of faith and commitment, adequate knowledge of the scriptures and Christian teaching, or the courage to fight against sinful inclinations. Preachers wage war against ignorance, immorality, and lack of trust in God and Christ.

In the nineteenth and twentieth centuries, three outstanding and influential schools or movements of Protestant preaching can be identified: evangelism, liberalism, and neo-orthodoxy. Evangelism, a movement originating in the eighteenth century and boasting such names as Jonathan Edwards, John Wesley, and Billy Graham, aims at promoting faith and conversion as emotional events and thus continues the preaching tradition initiated by Martin Luther. Neo-orthodoxy, a twentieth-century theological school dominated by Karl Barth, does not believe in instant conversion and therefore defines explanation of the scriptures and their doctrine as the central subject of the sermon. The classical model of scriptural learning we found in Luke and Origen is taken up. Liberalism, a movement originating with Friedrich Schleiermacher in early nineteenth-century Germany, refrains from making precise doctrinal commitments and prefers the preaching of a spirituality that helps one cope with life and find inner peace. Theological liberalism both continues and modifies classical faith preaching and moral exhortation. In the present chapter, we will present the homiletic ideas of the evangelistic movement, the neo-orthodox theologian Karl Barth, and the liberal preacher Harry Emerson Fosdick.

9. Early Evangelistic Preaching Satirized. George Whitefield (1714–70) can be credited with the invention of a new type of preacher: the actor-preacher who addressed the audience directly and began to endanger the traditional role of the scholar-preacher who lectured from notes. In this celebrated cartoon, Hogarth depicts Whitefield as a preacher under whose gown one can see the harlequin's dress and under whose displaced wig the tonsure of the friar becomes visible. Hogarth no doubt knew that in eighteenth-century continental Europe Catholic orders—Franciscans, Jesuits, Redemptorists, and others—practiced an equally dramatic preaching style when they visited parishes for a week to reinvigorate religious life. William Hogarth, *Enthusiasm Delineated* (detail), 1739.

Evangelistic Preaching: From Jonathan Edwards to the Twentieth Century

Luther's enthusiasm for leading his audience to a response of faith found little support in the sixteenth century. His fellow reformers, though articulate and successful preachers, tended to be more focused on instruction than on warming up the heart to faith. Rather than inspiring new Christian enthusiasm, they created a Protestant orthodoxy. The eighteenth century, however, saw a revival of affective preaching which still shapes the pulpit today, especially in American Protestantism. The new affective preaching, today known as evangelism, emerged in the 1730s with the "Great Awakening" in America, led by Jonathan Edwards and George Whitefield (ill. 9), and in English Methodism led by John Wesley. In the nineteenth century, Charles Finney continued and promoted its cause. The most famous preacher of twentieth-century America, Billy Graham (b. 1918), belongs to the same tradition. All evangelistic preaching is based on two related discoveries: the discovery that within the Christian community, many lack the fervor of true faith, and the discovery that new strategies of bringing home the Lord's saving message can convert the lukewarm.

Among the first to discover the problem of nominal Christians was Increase Mather, one of the most prominent Puritan divines of seventeenth-century New England. He realized that inveighing against moral laxity, delight in wearing fashionable clothing, disobedience of inferiors to superiors, and ruthless profiteering in trade did not suffice. In fact, it treated the symptoms rather than the disease. He discerned a more basic sin underlying that moral laxity: the waning of faith and spiritual fervor. "Where is the old New England spirit that was once amongst us?" he asked in 1674. "Where is our first love? Where is our zeal for God, especially in matters respecting the first table [of the Ten Commandments], which once was our glory?" Faith, not just morality, was lacking, and under the very eyes of the Puritan pastors, the once ideal community of the committed dissolved into a small minority of saints surrounded by a majority of cold, dead Christians. The very existence of the lukewarm in the church was a scandal, and something had to be done about it. Ministers felt responsible for bringing the lukewarm back into the fold of the true believers.[51]

Once they had realized the problem, ministers developed new strategies of preaching to handle it effectively. Here the pioneer was Jonathan Edwards (1703–58), whose sermon on "Sinners in the Hands of an Angry God" (preached at Enfield, Connecticut, in 1741) has become the supreme example of colorful emotional rhetoric, ending on a note of urgency: "Therefore let everyone that is out of Christ, now awake and fly from the wrath to come. The wrath of almighty God is now undoubtedly hanging over a great part of this congregation. Let everyone fly out of Sodom." The new type of preaching invited the lukewarm to a new conversion or recommitment to the Lord, and it was often very successful, leading to a series of spiritual "awakenings," of which the first broke out in December 1734; this was in Northampton, Massachusetts, the town pastored by Edwards. The "awakening" approach resonated with developments on both sides of the Atlantic, and within a few years, an entire new style of preaching and concomitant new theologies emerged. Three roles for the preacher became increasingly visible and shaped what came to be called evangelism: the *spiritual engineer*, who relies on emotional appeal; the *Lord's attorney*, who emphasizes the rational arguments; and, as a subsidiary role, the *personal counselor*, whose advice individuals appreciate.[52]

As a *spiritual engineer*, the preacher first of all has to realize that humanity can be divided into three groups: nonbelievers, lukewarm Christians, and true believers. Many if not most of those who care to listen to him (or her) belong to the middle group; they are "unregenerate" or "nominal Christians." They may outwardly be good Christians, attend church, and obey the moral commandments. Yet, lacking real commitment and piety of the heart, they must be considered "unsaved." The preacher's main task is to warm up the heart to faith. In his *Treatise concerning Religious Affections* (1746) Jonathan Edwards began to develop this insight. The mature and refined theory of conversion and affective preaching was developed in England by John Wesley (1703–91). For Edwards, sudden conversions were somehow a miracle wrought by God among those whom he had chosen or "predestinated" for life everlasting in heaven. Wesley shed the Calvinistic framework of Edwards's theology and insisted on the transforming power of love. He adopted an essentially "female" definition of faith: it is a relationship of love and trust in God and thus a matter of the heart. According to Wesley, people acquired eternal life more through the human heart's commitment to Christ than through knowledge of and intellectual assent to the subtleties of doctrine. As John Wesley wrote: "We may die without the knowledge of many truths and yet be carried to Abraham's bosom," provided that we do not die without a loving commitment to the Lord.[53]

The preachers' appeal to the emotions did not fall on deaf ears, for it resonated with the general appreciation of the sentimental life, especially in the nineteenth century. Although historians fail to agree on the exact nature or timing of what Lawrence Stone calls the "affective revolution," most would acknowledge that during the nineteenth century sex, love, family, and sentimental religion were accorded greater attention in literature, the arts, and the realities of everyday life. Religious emotionalism was in tune with the general cultural climate.[54]

The key to successful spiritual engineering is emotionalism, for only powerful preaching (sometimes accompanied by choir singing and music) can establish an atmosphere conducive to conversion. The emotional atmosphere, designed to make sinners—and not only sinners—break down and weep, can be created through extemporaneous preaching which is more conversational in tone and more personal and immediate in style than carefully prepared sermons. Fervor and enthusiasm are favored over learned arguments, theological jargon, and pleasing rhetoric. The sinner has to be addressed directly, key ideas and phrases must be repeated until they are understood, and references to the possibility or even likelihood of eternal damnation should punctuate the discourse. Preachers never leave any doubt about the urgency of their message. In a 1741 sermon, Edwards argues that the dreadful reality of hell demands urgent, lively pleading. As an analogy, he asks if parents in his audience, seeing their child in a burning house, "would speak to it only in a cold and indifferent manner." Music and singing also play a crucial role in creating a devotional atmosphere. Beginning with English Methodism in the eighteenth century, singing has always figured prominently in the various "awakening" movements. By the end of the nineteenth century, new "inspirational" songs and hymns had become a trademark of religious revivalism. In the 1870s, preachers like Dwight L. Moody began to team up with music directors, singers, and choirs. Enhanced by music, the magnetic atmosphere of worship sometimes takes precedence over the precise content of what is preached. Everything must combine to produce the effect of "winning" souls or "saving" them—individually or, better still, in large numbers.[55]

Not all evangelistic preachers want to be spiritual engineers relying on emotionalism. In nineteenth-century America, Charles Finney (1792–1875), a lawyer-turned-preacher, developed another, alternative role: that of the *Lord's attorney*. Here the church serves as the Lord's courtroom, the congregation is composed of individuals accused of unbelief, and the preacher pleads the Lord's cause and sometimes presents witnesses who give testimony by speaking of their own conversion. Instead of mounting the pulpit, Finney sometimes stood among the people, made sure that there was eye contact, and did not spurn addressing and even physically touching individuals. Commitment or recommitment to Christ had to happen not in private some time after the service of worship, but immediately in a public act. Many preachers follow Finney in urging sinners to come forward to the platform to make some definite, formal act of confession and committal. Attorney-evangelists want to see results and count their converts in the courtroom-church.[56]

In order to initiate the process of conversion or recommitment, both preacher and audience have to realize that faith involves a personal decision to accept Christ as one's savior. Faith must not be seen simply as a gift of God, given to some and denied to others. Evangelistic preachers tend to disagree with the traditional Calvinistic emphasis on predestination and the utter helplessness of human subjects. The preacher's job is to challenge the audience to come to the decision of faith. Finney entertained a predominantly "male" view of faith: faith involves a rational decision to submit to the authority of the Lord. While the Wesleyan school anchored religion in emotion and tears (to love Christ is a matter of the heart), the followers of Finney gave preference to reason and logic (it is rational to obey God and thus avoid eternal damnation). The Finney approach was in tune with the general optimism of the nineteenth century, which can be seen in the belief of President Andrew Jackson (1829–37) in the ordinary citizen's ability to govern him- or herself, in the temperance movement, and in numerous other causes like women's rights and education that found promoters in North America and elsewhere. The message of all these movements is that the individual can change for the better. The preacher assures his listeners that they *can* do something about their lives—irrespective of the constraints of their pasts, of the limitations of their individual characters and social backgrounds. God has endowed people with "free will," that is the ability to change one's life once and for all. As to the moment when the decision should be made, opinion shifted between the eighteenth and the nineteenth centuries. Preachers like Whitefield were sending people away to pray for a change of heart through new birth, and to keep praying and partaking of the Lord's Supper as a means of grace. They believed in Christian nurture and in the slow, gradual working of the Holy Spirit. By contrast, nineteenth-century evangelists like Charles Finney and most of their twentieth-century emulators believe in instant conversion. Commitment to Christ in faith and repentance has to be made *now*, at the very moment of preaching—not the next day or later. As a favorite verse of scripture quoted by evangelists explains, "See, now is the acceptable time; see, now is the day of salvation!" (2 Cor. 6:2). Does not even common sense tell us not to put off till tomorrow what we can do today? Some evangelistic preachers like Billy Graham have refined the Finney-style definition of conversion. They know that after a commitment to Christ has been made, it has a tendency to lose its freshness; it must be periodically renewed, because Christian life is a process that is punctuated by crisis. All believers have to deepen their relationship with Christ and to mature in their faith. Graham defines his audience not as nominal Christians but as believers in need of spiritual renewal.[57]

In both Wesley's "emotional" and Finney's "rational" camp of the evangelistic ministry, it was understood that the preacher's task did not end with the "Amen" at the end of the sermon. The ministry of the word must be supplemented by that of the *counselor*. Once a preacher has won the heart and the intellect of the hearer, he or she is the ideal person to step into that supportive role. Individuals disturbed or made anxious by preaching must never be left alone and unattended. Someone must listen, must understand. Personal contact with others and perhaps individual counseling are needed to bring deliverance to sinners, to quiet agitated souls, and to restore people's inner balance. Finney understood this elementary psychological law quite well and held so-called "anxious meetings" at which those who wished could get advice and be prayed for. He also visited people in their homes and made himself available for personal consultation; later evangelists like Charles Spurgeon (1834–92) in England and Samuel Keller (1856–1924) in Germany made it a rule. "If you wish to see results from your sermons," Spurgeon told candidates for the ministry, "you must be accessible to enquirers" and "continually invite such to come and speak with you." In addition to this, Spurgeon envisaged group meetings of the kind Finney had held in America. He described these as "enquirers' meetings" at which the pastor would "assist the troubled and guide the perplexed," pronounce fervent prayers for the individuals present, and invite recent converts to present short, encouraging testimonials. Finney's "anxious" Americans and Spurgeon's English "enquirers" seem to have been individuals shocked and disturbed by the preacher's message and in this situation needed spiritual advice. The Germans seeking Samuel Keller's advice seem to have been different, and Keller describes them more as standing at the beginning of a longer spiritual journey. After reading an American book on evangelism—a German translation of Reuben A. Torrey's *How to Bring Men to Christ* (1893)—he decided that Germans are not quite as quickly brought to their knees as their transatlantic contemporaries. Conversion, though initiated by emotional appeals, is often a slow process. The preacher, according to Keller, must exercise a time-consuming pastoral ministry to help people on their way to Christ. Many evangelists believe that their counseling ministry is as important as it is successful. In his autobiography, Samuel Keller proudly refers to having talked, individually, to 24,000 men and women and to having written almost 70,000 letters of advice. Evangelists like Keller in Germany and Billy Graham in America assumed the role of the spiritual advisor. The preacher acts as therapist who helps with the process of conversion and guides the "anxious" through their spiritual crisis. Evangelistic preaching, especially in the twentieth century, does not promise only eternal salvation. Generally, it makes another quite important promise: that inner peace will be experienced immediately and permanently in the present life. Once a person has been "born again" by conversion, that person's conscience is no longer troubled by cares and anxieties; instead, he or she enjoys an overwhelming feeling of inner peace. The Lordship of Christ provides protection, courage, strength, spiritual health, and calmness. Through the act of faith, Satan's spell is broken, and the human person is free at last. In order to find this peace and freedom, pastoral help is needed and must be offered by the preacher.[58]

During the nineteenth century and beyond, evangelistic preaching made a tremendous impact on both American and European Protestantism, giving it a new face. It made Protestant Christianity more emotional, attracted increasing numbers of women, led to the neglect of social issues, and promoted a certain loss of interest in church and congregational life.

Not all evangelistic preachers share Wesley's emphasis on the emotional side of religion, and Charles Finney actually opposed the "affective revolution" promoted by the Methodists and their many followers. For him, as we have seen, faith and commitment to Christ are a thoroughly rational affair, and emotional preaching is nothing more than a means to awaken the sinners and get their attention. Despite Finney's warning against too much emotionalism, Protestants increasingly adopted the view that religion was a matter of the heart, of feeling and sentiment, and therefore particularly fitting for women. Unwittingly, evangelistic preaching promoted the sentimentalization and feminization of religion, especially in the nineteenth century. With feminization and emphasis on the emotions came loss of interest in social change. Preachers set out on crusades against individual sin and aimed at reforming individuals, not society as a whole. They wanted to produce "perfect selves"—often female selves—"in the midst of an imperfect society."[59]

How does evangelistic preaching fit in with traditional organized Christianity, with regular church-going and life in the parish community? Methodists and Catholics always thought in terms of renewed ecclesiastical fellowship and parish life as the intended effect of their preaching ministry. Wesley started his career within the established church, and eventually formed his own group, the Methodist church. When Jesuits or Redemptorists as "missioners" visit a Catholic parish for a week and, through emotional preaching (ill. 10) (and, less successfully, through the singing of sentimental mission hymns), aim at

10. Dramatic preaching at a Catholic Popular Mission. When Jesuits and other religious orders in early modern Europe sought to reinvigorate Catholic life, especially in rural areas, Baroque preaching assumed dramatic forms and impressive theatricality, paralleling that of Protestant revivalists. Italian etching, eighteenth-century.

reinvigorating faith, they motivate their audience to active participation in the church's ritual life, especially going to confession, Mass, and holy communion. However, evangelistic preachers generally departed from the Wesleyan and Catholic pattern. They overheard Finney's injunction never to leave converts without regular teaching and church fellowship. Reluctant to rely on traditional or organizational patterns of life and authority, they preferred to act as what the sociologist Max Weber calls "charismatic leaders." From Whitefield in the eighteenth to Oral Roberts and Billy Graham in the twentieth century, evangelistic activists want to stay outside organized churches or denominations; they assert their independence, for they feel called "to deal with individuals and not the denomination." As preachers have increasingly emphasized individual commitment to Christ, they have downplayed the ecclesiastical values of liturgical fellowship. Salvation is not through participation in church life, but through personal faith in Christ and sometimes also in the preacher. In certain cases, commitment to the evangelist can overshadow even commitment to Christ, as was the case with Benjamin Franklin, who made friends with Whitefield but was never "converted." Evangelistic activity "crafted a new religion out-of-doors, beyond parish boundaries and clerical authority," an individualistic Christian subculture that placed the convert before the

11. Two Preaching Styles. "You'll all be d[amne]d," says the impassioned evangelistic preacher who raises his fist in a gesture of condemnation. The ascetic figure is contrasted with a priest of the established church who calmly addresses his "Dearly beloved brethren." The British cartoonist's two characters represent two different contents: preaching the gospel and lecturing about the gospel, and two different aims of the sermon: conversion and transmission of knowledge. British satirical print, 1818.

itinerant preacher whom he met in a tent, a football stadium, a concert hall, or in the media—religious magazines, radio and television programs. Participation in the evangelistic popular culture overshadows and weakens, and sometimes replaces, local and denominational affiliation.[60]

Not all observers have been happy with evangelistic preaching and the increasing impact it has made (ill. 11). In his novel *Elmer Gantry* (1927), the Nobel-prize-winning writer Sinclair Lewis denounced it as a mixture of fraud, credulity, religious hysteria, and superstition. Both liberal and neo-orthodox theologians proposed and practiced other models and aims for the sermon. One of them was Karl Barth.

Neo-Orthodox Preaching: Karl Barth

The Swiss Reformed theologian Karl Barth (1886–1968) ranks as one of the foremost theologians of his time and has been called a twentieth-century church father. His fame is based on his early rejection of liberal nineteenth-century-style theology in his *Commentary on Romans* (1922) and on his role as the theological leader of the "Confessing Church's" opposition to National

Socialism's attempt to rule the German church. This leadership led to his dismissal, in 1935, from his chair of Protestant systematic theology at the university of Bonn. Offered a position in the university of Basel, he spent the rest of his life in Switzerland where he produced the huge and verbose volumes of his *Church Dogmatics*. He left no theological problem untouched, and his long list of publications includes sermons (many of them delivered in the Basel jail) and treatises on homiletics, i.e., the theory of preaching.

The main concept of Barth's theology is that God acted and revealed himself in Jesus Christ. The original act of revelation cannot be explained; it can only be stated and accepted as a fact recorded in scripture. God has reconciled himself with human beings; they were sinners, but through God's grace they have been saved. It is this event, and nothing else, that the preacher has to explain in the sermon in which worship culminates. The act of preaching shares the sudden and miraculous character of the original event itself. Preaching therefore comes to the congregation "truly from on high, from above, in fact *vertically from above*: just as grace comes to nature, just as a miracle enters our world!"[61]

Despite the relevance of "sacred" scripture for preaching, Barth understands the central act of worship as a thoroughly secular activity. There is nothing particularly sacred about preaching. Even the Bible itself, for Barth, lacks the aura of sacredness. The Bible, often called the "word of God," is in fact only the word of human authors and thus shares all the weaknesses of human writing: error, inaccuracy, disobedience, sinful distortion. Sometimes Barth criticizes biblical authors like Paul for not saying exactly what they should have said in their endeavor to proclaim and elucidate the meaning of God's initiative in revealing himself and in sending his son. The biblical authors have no part in the process of revelation; they have a function similar to the bells the altar boys ring in a Catholic Mass: they do so not as part of the sacred act, but to draw the congregation's attention to this event. However, Barth fully acknowledges biblical authority. What gives the Bible its unique position in worship is that it alone points unerringly to God's revelation in Jesus Christ. While being the normative and standard record of revelation, the Bible must not be confused with divine revelation itself. And the same is true of preaching: based on the Bible, it shares all its weaknesses and errors. To identify human preaching with the word of God is a common error among theologians; however, that identification must be qualified as the ultimate presumption and the ultimate kitsch, i.e., the human attempt to reduce the divine to the human level. "At best," he explains, "human words can be an echo, a witness, a mirror image of the word of our God that will stand for ever." Preaching, then, is an activity as secular as the Bible itself.[62]

Still, the preacher's word, like the biblical text, can have revelatory force and lead the hearer to an act of faith. Challenged to expect and experience a new revelation, the congregation may actually experience it. Only insofar as this happens would Barth speak of the preacher's word as the word of God. What the preacher says does not *per se* have the objective quality of God's word, but it can acquire this quality when received and responded to in faith and obedience. What in the preacher's mouth was an entirely human word may be completely divine in the hearer's heart. In this case, God has made use of the preacher's human word to bring his own divine message to an individual. When this happens, it is not owing to the preacher's genius, wit, power of persuasion, or captivating rhetoric, but owing alone to what Calvin called the "internal testimony" of the Holy Spirit. Without spiritual illumination the act of faith can never happen. Thus preaching is only a preparation for the act of faith, an "instruction in listening to the Word of God" or "the announcement of what people will have to hear from God himself." For Barth, therefore, "the central key to an understanding of preaching" is "the understanding of it as provisional, as heralding." A herald is not a master. "The Word of God must remain sovereign and free . . . , for God will speak his own Word to the congregation."[63]

If we ask what type of preaching Barth favors—the instructional, the ethical, or the evangelistic—then the answer must be the instructional. "Doctrine," he explains, "means instruction, teaching, the giving of lessons. . . . This is what Christian preaching must accomplish." For all its existential dimensions, faith is also "a form of knowledge" that can be transmitted in an educational process. The church is a "school." Here Barth stands in the tradition of the Reformed church in which, ever since the days of John Calvin, giving a sermon has meant instructing a congregation in biblical matters. By describing the church's preaching as "doctrine," Barth wants to express "a certain reservedness" about the high claims sometimes made. Doctrine, even pure doctrine, will never be equal to what God does when he speaks his own word. Doctrine, moreover, cannot bestow the Holy Spirit, awaken someone to faith, or contribute to maintaining or advancing faith. Doctrine, of itself, cannot establish contact with Jesus Christ or produce the union of God and human beings. Those who expect these things to happen, expect too much from the unpretentious act of preaching. Preachers, according to Barth, have the task of explaining how God acted in Jesus Christ, and they are to use scripture as their exclusive basis and text. Barth defines the sermon as "the attempt, by someone authorized in the church, to explain a section of the biblical record of revelation with the intention to say in his own words and elucidate for contemporaries the promise of the revelation, reconciliation, and calling of God, to be expected here and now." Preachers who wish to be true to their vocation must resist the temptation of playing the intellectual who knows better, the spiritual engineer who leads to Christ, or the priest who creates a world of liturgical splendor.[64]

The role of the *intellectual* comes as the first temptation to preachers. When dealing with scripture, they know better than anyone else and display their knowledge, referring as they do to philological, historical, archaeological, and circumstantial detail—Jerusalem during the Syro-Ephraimite War in the days of Isaiah, scriptural scholarship at the time of Jesus, or factions in Paul's Corinthian community. Intellectuals also like the thematic approach; rather than explaining a biblical text, they speak about the Jews or the problem of prayer. As soon as a sermon becomes "thematic," the preacher is likely to lose contact with scripture and deliver his or her own, personal message. Responsible preaching, for Barth, involves the exposition of scripture rather than the exposition of one's own favorite ideas. Intellectuals also like to "apply" the biblical text to the lives of their audience, giving practical advice on how to survive the modern world and its temptations. They offer their personal reflections and instruct in matters pertaining to psychology, sociology, ethics, or political science. Or, worse, they comment on contemporary events. Barth admits to having made the intellectualist mistake in his early ministry. In 1912 he once preached about the *Titanic*, the English ship which on its first voyage to America hit an iceberg and sank, with more than 1500 people being drowned. And in 1914, when the war broke out, he made it the subject of another of his Sunday sermons. But Barth later explained that current affairs were not the proper subject of Christian preaching. His published sermons show Barth faithful to his own standards. Scripture always dominates. Although he would sometimes quote a poem, mention a conversation with a taxi driver, or refer to current events and newspaper articles, such matters have a purely illustrative function. They never take over. In his later sermons, Barth would never make the sinking of the *Titanic* the actual subject of his preaching.[65]

According to Barth, the preachers who have cultivated the intellectual approach are responsible for "the lukewarm tediousness and irrelevance of Protestant worship" which culminates in mere—and often boring—"friendly religious sayings."[66]

The second role to beware of is that of the *spiritual engineer*. It is in many disguises that the spiritual engineer enters the Protestant pulpit. The most common in Barth's generation was that of the evangelistic preacher. Evangelists with divine authority urge people to convert instantly. Preaching, according to their tradition, "has the task of building up the kingdom of God, of converting, of leading to decision. It must confront us with the reality of God. It must be vital and communicate an experience. It must bring to light our situation and set us before God." The preacher has the sacred task of representing—making present—the authority of God to the congregation, and leading them, individually and as a community, to faith.[67]

Barth never felt tempted to play the spiritual engineer. Indeed, he positively hated the role. He reports how he had once listened faithfully to a visiting evangelist and was dismayed by the rhetoric of hellfire, the uncompromising insistence on immediate conversion, and the unrefusable invitation to subscribe to a magazine called *Tabernacle Greeting*. The Swiss theologian did not feel at home with the evangelistic media-oriented, "print and preach" strategy that aimed at creating a community of readers (or viewers of a television program) and not at educating members of a local parish community. He disliked this "bad form of religious mechanics" and felt the absence of any reference to the joys of heaven. Barth never believed in the instant conversion urged by evangelistic preachers. Even the "sudden conversion" (*subita conversio*) John Calvin claims to have had did not impress him. In one of his early lectures, Barth went out of his way to prove that Calvin's conversion must have been a longer process of spiritual reorientation. Barth, the rational thinker, mistrusts all suddenness and all surges of enthusiasm in matters of faith.[68]

Conversion, awakening, and decision: all of this may well happen in a preaching situation, but according to Barth it is not the preacher's task to bring it about. The preacher must not interfere with what God has reserved for himself to do. "There is no place at all . . . for the aim of directing listeners to a certain type of conduct." Far from being a kind of spiritual engineer, the preacher has to expound a biblical text and "give witness to the congregation concerning the redemption and the reconciliation of God that has [already] taken place in Christ." Preaching has to explain the act of God in Christ, which is an act that happened in the past. What God wants to do today with those who hear the preacher's voice is none of the minister's business; it must be left to God himself.[69]

Preachers, therefore, must abstain from all pious wishes to produce "faith" in their audience. God can of course act, and often does act with those who hear a sermon. However, Barth uses guarded language in describing what God does. In traditional theological rhetoric, God works through the sermon to lead those who hear it to faith. For Barth, the act of faith must not be confused with God's original revelation in Christ. Correct theology must therefore avoid speaking of faith as a final decision, or a saving deed of God. Ultimately, it is not "faith" that saves, but God's sending of his Son. Barth admits that he does not know how our own life actually relates to the coming of Christ. His emphasis on the original divine act forces him to speak here of a mystery, a veiled reality God has chosen not to reveal to us before death. Only in heaven will the hidden links between our lives and the life of Christ eventually become clear.[70]

How does God speak his word to the congregation? According to one common view, propounded by Gijsbert Dingemans, he does so individually. God also respects the freedom of the individual. Under the guidance of the preacher, "those who listen develop their own, individual relationship with the scriptural text, with the gospel message, and with God himself," observes Dingemans. "Thus they compose their own sermons!" Preaching proceeds in such a way as to give the listener something to think, to feel, to decide, to do. It presupposes the listener's freedom to respond. Just as it is up to God to use the preacher's word, so it is up to the listener to open his or her heart to God.[71]

Superficially, Barth's theory of preaching comes close to that of Dingemans. For Barth, just as for the Dutch theologian, the congregation consists of individuals. If God speaks to them, then a sacred bridge between the divine and the human has been formed. However, here Barth and Dingemans part ways. While Dingemans insists on the free decision of God's human partners, Barth's theology does not include such a decision. According to Barth, the bridge may lead to faith and obedience, because God himself can lead to faith and obedience. Far from leaving individuals to decide about a divine offer, God guides, decides, and leads to faith. Barth's theology of preaching rather surprisingly echoes that of Thomas Aquinas, for whom the preacher acts as a mere teacher helping the audience to dispose itself to belief. The preacher can do nothing but bring the word of God before the congregation; with the help of their natural intellects and, especially, through God's intervention in moving their wills, people can finally come to the act of faith and be saved through it. Barth does not seem to be interested in this sacred and essentially individual encounter. His theology deals exclusively with the preparatory, objective teaching of the biblical word. This teaching, although an indispensable preparation for the sacred event, stays outside the realm of the sacred. Barth believes that the preacher's task is not itself sacred, but is instead purely secular.[72]

The third role dear to preachers is that of the *priest*. Priests cultivate a special relationship with Christ and as spiritual people proclaim Christ's word. The Benedictine theologian Anselm Günthör (b. 1911) explains that the priest must be "ever more filled with Christ" in order to be able to make himself a good instrument for the Lord. "The preacher's word is the instrument by which Christ makes his own word present. For this reason, the priestly word of the sermon, spoken out of union with Christ, cannot remain without power and strength." Priests give their sermons an elaborate liturgical setting. They use architecture, artistic decoration, and liturgical music to create a truly sacred environment which inspires religious feelings.[73]

Barth never felt attracted to the role of the priest. He disliked priestly presumption and arrogance. For Barth, preachers must remain humble heralds. They "must not be 'clerics' who, puffed up with the sense of their mission, office, and theology, and perhaps 'full of the Holy Ghost,' attempt to represent the interests of the good Lord to the world." By emphasizing the importance of the message, Barth downplays the personality of the preacher, never allowing him priestly status. Barth also rejects liturgical pageantry. "From my very youth I had a dislike of all ritual solemnity," including organists' preludes and postludes to congregational singing. The organ must not be considered a "second pulpit." The organ, he insists, must support singing, and music as an end in itself has no place in Christian worship; it is not allowed to compete with the preacher, let alone with the biblical text. Just as Barth could never warm up to the priestly role and to liturgical splendor, so he remained cold to the vanities of sacred architecture. When in 1952 certain windows of

Basel cathedral had to be replaced, Barth succeeded in preventing the insertion of stained glass windows with pictures. He voted for utter simplicity. Asked his opinion on church building, Barth blended theology with practical advice. Like preaching itself, according to Barth, its liturgical setting must be simple, artless, and profane. For the Reformed tradition, the church building has no particularly sacred qualities. Barth wants the church to have a central hall in which the congregation meets. This hall should be closed rather than open, shutting out the outside world and permitting full concentration. People would sit in a semi-circle around a simple wooden table (not an altar, he insists), placed on a raised platform. This table would serve as the communion table, the place of baptism, and, with a lectern placed upon it, as the pulpit. "The simple functionalism of style, size, and color of doors, walls, and windows, like those of the pews, all can and should contribute to the concentration of those who participate in worship, and should direct them toward the message and the devotion which unite them. Herein lie their dignity and beauty."[74]

In 1967, when he received a pamphlet showing pictures of the newly built Christ Church of Eiserfeld, Germany, he responded with enthusiasm. The stark, tent-shaped structure with a free-standing bell-tower was perched on a steep hillside overlooking a valley. In the pentagonal worship hall—an auditorium seating 160 people—a simple table bearing an open Bible provides the central focus around which the Reformed congregation gathers (ill. 12). Neither an altar nor a pulpit separates the minister from the worshipers. The preacher enters through the same door as everyone else. No piece of art distracts the attention, no stained glass inspires a sense of the sacred. The wood-paneled high ceiling, the red covering of the chairs, the arrangement of the lamps, and the wide windows betray a careful, aesthetically satisfying design. In Barth's view, the room seemed to have too many windows, which risked diverting the congregation's attention; the Swiss theologian nonetheless approved. In its simplicity and lack of artifice, the church approximated to his ideal.[75]

Although Barth was never attracted to liturgical and architectural splendor, he appreciated music and paintings. In his youth he had seen the work of Beethoven and Michelangelo as sources of genuine revelation. Later he enjoyed the work of Grünewald and placed a reproduction of the Isenheim altarpiece in his study. He celebrated Mozart's music in various essays, and even his *Church Dogmatics* includes passages on his favorite composer. Nevertheless, he wanted to keep art out of church. However clearly Barth may perceive the religious message of art (as he does in the case of Mozart and Grünewald), for him all art remains ambiguous. Even specifically religious themes in art can be grossly misunderstood. Barth gives examples. A crucifix showing the tortured, dying Christ could make us neglect the message of resurrection and inspire questionable piety that focuses on Christ's—or even our own—suffering. Albrecht Dürer's etching *Knight, Death, and Devil* repre-

12. The Church as Lecture Hall. Chairs and—almost invisible—a simple table. Built in 1967, the stark sobriety of the Reformed Christuskirche in Eiserfeld, Germany, attracted the attention and approval of Karl Barth, the foremost Reformed theologian of the twentieth century. Barth agreed with John Calvin that there should be no ornaments, let alone pictorial representations, in the room in which Christians assemble for listening to their preacher. Christuskirche, Eiserfeld, Germany.

sents the Christian soldier who, armed with the shield of faith and the breast-plate of righteousness, is able to stand against the wiles of the devil. Now this engraving, although based on Ephesians 6 and Erasmus's *Manual of the Christian Soldier*, was often taken to depict the truly Germanic hero or even the Nietzschean superman. With good reason, Barth withstands the temptation of "confus[ing] the history of salvation with any part of the history of art."[76]

As a further example of the way in which the aesthetic dimension may distort God's word, Barth refers to the traditional hymns sung in Protestant churches. Early Protestant hymns were soundly biblical and included little lyrical ornamentation. Later, however, they became increasingly subjective, concentrating on the pious feelings of the faithful at the expense of glorifying God and praising Christ's work of salvation. With such hymns, a certain un-Christian spirit entered communal worship. Barth wants congregations to sing hymns whose content corresponds to revelation and therefore can be justified theologically. Here, as in preaching, Barth calls for vigilance and constant testing for doctrinal purity.[77]

Barth's efforts to keep aesthetics out of worship are certainly not rooted in a lack of sensitivity to art. Rather, the rejection of pictorial representations and the hesitant, qualified acceptance of music must be seen as a conscious decision, based on careful theological reasoning. For Barth, liturgy and its spatial setting have to remain sober, simple, and profane, so that no one would confuse emotions with faith and the message of music or paintings with the word of God. True: "God may speak to us through Russian communism, through a flute concerto, through a blossoming shrub or through a dead dog," but Barth feels that when people go to church, they must leave behind the vague sentiments of God's presence inspired by art, nature, history, or work; somehow, these natural possibilities are "exhausted." What counts, and what conveys definitive clarity, is God's word. So we must first of all be able to recognize the divine word. This ability can be acquired only in a clean, aseptic laboratory situation in which the pure word of scripture is read and the uncontaminated message of Christ proclaimed. In worship, we must be exposed exclusively to divine revelation in its normative, Christ-centered form. Even the finest, classic works of art are individual responses to revelation, not revelation itself:

> Irrespective of how pious one's representation of Christ may be conceived, no one has the authority and privilege to focus the congregation's attention on just this particular work. This would be granted by installing pictures at the place where the congregation meets for listening to scripture, for praying, for celebrating baptism and the Lord's Supper. Proclaiming Christ is a living event; from Sunday to Sunday, from preacher to preacher, from century to century it must be renewed, enlarged, deepened, clarified and purged of unauthorized ideas that may have crept in.

God speaks only in words; the rest is mere sentiment. We must form our faith and belief in response to Christian preaching rather than in response to works of art, which always remain a secondary kind of witness. Confined to the private space of the home, art may have its message; but it should never become a publicly displayed, iconic embodiment of the sacred. So even a Grünewald, according to Barth the best of all Christian painters, would not be allowed to decorate a church. Although God, in his omnipotence, may speak to us through nature, our own heart, through good art, and the enticing sweetness of Handel's *Largo*, worship is not the place for this to happen.[78]

Worship, as Barth understands it, must be a Bible-based, word-centered event in which God's revelation in Christ is explained and proclaimed. In order to safeguard its exclusively Bible-based character, all potentially "numinous" elements—music and works of art—have to be absent. Since neither preaching nor celebrating the Lord's Supper can represent (let alone manipulate) Christ's or God's active presence, worship remains a secular activity. Paradoxically, God commanded his church to engage in the completely worldly activity of preaching so that he himself could convey his own sacred and saving message to those who listen to it in faith and obedience.

Barth's theology has made much impact on twentieth-century preaching. Many have hailed him as the conqueror of a liberalism that exchanges the word of God for its own, human word. His theology has earned him the title of father of neo-orthodoxy, of the right Christian faith restored and defended. However, Barthian-style preaching has also found its critics. One the one hand, without Barth, present-day preaching would not be "so pure, so biblical, and so concerned with central issues, but on the other hand, it would also not be so alarmingly correct, boringly precise, and remote from the world." This remoteness from the world has always scandalized Barth's critics. Adolf von Harnack, who had been one of Barth's teachers at the university of Berlin, never appreciated his student. "This sort of religion," he commented, "is incapable of being translated into real life; so that it must soar above life like a meteor rushing towards its disintegration." Under the spell of Barth, Paul Tillich reports, many pastors "turned away from the great social problems created by the catastrophes of the War and settled back in their sanctuaries of theological discussions." Other pastors, however, resisted the neo-orthodox temptation of withdrawal by insisting on close encounters with real people and the real world. One of them was Harry Emerson Fosdick.[79]

Liberal Preaching: Harry Emerson Fosdick's Program of Honesty and Therapy

Between 1922 and his retirement in 1946, Harry Emerson Fosdick (1878–1969) ranked as one of America's most famous Protestant preachers. A best-selling author and pastor of Riverside Church in New York, he was known for his radio ministry, his long-term association with millionaire John D. Rockefeller, and his program of pastoral counseling. Fosdick stands in the tradition of liberal Protestantism which originated in nineteenth-century Germany and become a major movement in American Christianity from around 1870. From its founding father Friedrich Schleiermacher (1768–1834), liberalism had inherited the emphasis on religion as a disposition present in every human being; if adequately developed, that disposition leads to a clear consciousness of being connected and in harmony with the divine and transcendent reality of God. The religious sentiment, when properly stimulated in worship, especially through the sermon, leads to peace and composure of mind. In a published sermon on "The Value of Public Services of Worship," Schleiermacher calls the sermon the "medicine" (*die Arznei*) that helps restore the inner balance of those who have lost it, and will lose it again, in the many worries and troubles of occupational and domestic life. Schleiermacher's notion of religion represents his attempt to describe and conceptualize his own experience of finding a peaceful mind in the company and worship of the German Moravians with whom he went to school and whose democratic, edificatory, and spiritually elating worship he appreciated even later in life. The religious education

Schleiermacher received with the Moravians proved to be lasting. Although he revolted against the obscurantist theology of the Brethren, he retained a deep regard for their sincere piety and warm personal faith. Throughout his life, he remained close to his sister Charlotte who joined a celibate Moravian order. He remained, as he later admitted, "a Herrnhutter [Moravian], though of a higher kind." Along with Schleiermacher, all liberal theologians, both in Europe and America, remained Moravians of a higher kind, i.e., men and women interested not so much in Christianity as a body of doctrine but in a practical spirituality that helps one to cope with life.[80]

Fosdick studied at Colgate Seminary in Hamilton, NY, and Union Theological Seminary in New York City. In Hamilton, it was William Newton Clarke and in New York George William Fox who made the liberal tradition vivid to him, and he fully identified with it, sharing, for instance, Schleiermacher's belief in the joyful experience of the divine presence in the human heart. He became a Baptist minister, and in 1915 he exchanged his pastorate for a chair in practical theology at Union Theological Seminary. An experienced preacher and author of best-selling devotional books, he was also invited to serve at the First Presbyterian Church in New York, and it was there that he exercised his extraordinary gifts, attracting large crowds every Sunday in the 1920s. As a liberal pastor and preacher, Fosdick acted in the three roles of intellectual, priest, and counselor, and they came to him successively in his long New York-based ministry.[81]

The role of the *intellectual* came to Fosdick quite naturally. Right from his student days he had embraced biblical criticism, intellectual honesty in matters of belief, the idea of biological evolution, and the nondogmatic, experiential nature of Christian teaching. One of Fosdick's early sermons received national attention and made him a famous man whose views were discussed in the newspapers. Entitled "Shall the Fundamentalists Win?" (May 21, 1922), it commented on and contributed to the debate between liberals like Fosdick himself and the ultra-conservatives ("fundamentalists") who had begun to attack the teaching of Darwinism in American schools. Fosdick accepted Darwinism, rejected belief in the Bible's literal inspiration, and pleaded for "an intellectually hospitable, tolerant, liberty-loving church." He called fundamentalism an "immeasurable folly." Historians remember Fosdick's speech as "the most sensational and widely publicized sermon of his generation." A realist, Fosdick knew that liberalism had its perils, and he named irreverence toward and bias against the hallowed traditions of Christian belief as examples. The greatest peril of liberalism, however, was not this critical attitude in matters of belief, but "ethical disloyalty to Jesus." Accordingly, the preacher's task must be defined as the application of Jesus' "ethical teaching to the personal life, social customs, economic systems, racial problems and international needs of this generation." Fosdick preached sermons on all of these issues, and he became particularly well known as an ardent pacifist as a result of his comments during the Second World War.[82]

The second ministry, that of the *priest*—not as a formal title, but a liturgical role—came to Fosdick as a surprise, and was due to his association with John D. Rockefeller, Jr. (1874–1960). The Rockefeller family was one of the world's richest families, and they invested greatly in philanthropy. They restored the gardens of Versailles, the cathedral at Reims, the château of Fontainebleau, and erected the New York Public Library. John Rockefeller supported the ecumenical movement, the establishment of the (US) National Council of Churches, and the World Council of Churches. He also became involved in an experiment to create an ecumenical model community, one that would prefigure Christian unity by admitting members with a diversity of Christian backgrounds, ranging from Baptist to Congregationalist and Quaker (but not Catholics). Rockefeller launched this project, which entailed the building of a new, nondenominational church—Riverside Church. Fosdick accepted the invitation to be its first pastor. The huge and beautiful Gothic Revival structure became the center of Fosdick's activities from its inauguration in 1930 until his retirement in 1946. At the request of Fosdick, the architects designed more than a huge lecture hall complete with recently invented electrical sound-amplifying equipment (ill. 13). In tune with the taste of his day, Fosdick wanted a *cathedral,* where "not the pulpit but the high altar would be central and where beauty of proportion and perspective, of symbolism and color would speak to the soul even when the voice of man was silent." As one of Fosdick's contemporaries pointed out, the days of the ugly meeting house were over, and church architecture had to follow the general historical movement "from the crudities of the frontier to the refinements of culture." A hundred years earlier, Ralph Waldo Emerson had developed a taste for sacred architecture as he traveled in Europe. He hated the "grand granite piles" of America and longed for churches with carved, painted, and inscribed walls. Now, in Riverside Church, Emerson's dream had come true. In the new, dignified environment, regular Sunday worship assumed a splendor that sometimes bordered on liturgical vanity. The stained glass windows, the huge Gothic nave, the altar, the pulpit (ill. 14), the well-dressed ushers, the robed choir, and of course the solemn organ music all conspired to create a sacred atmosphere—much to the liking of the chief minister, Dr. Fosdick. Although sacred architecture may not be able to replace the saving word, it can at least supplement and support it or prepare for its reception. Fosdick even expressed doubts about "sermon-ridden Sunday mornings" spent in "glorified lecture halls." Accordingly, Riverside Church from the beginning of its existence in the 1930s had a "liturgical service without sermon" celebrated every Sunday afternoon. It consisted entirely of music and singing, no spoken word being uttered except the final benediction.[83]

13. The Preacher's Loudspeaker. In the early twentieth century, technology began to invade the cathedral. "Alle Hörer sollen der Predigt ohne Anstrengung folgen können" (all hearers should easily be able to follow the sermon). Interestingly, this 1929 advertisement juxtaposes the old and the new device: while the preacher speaks into the microphone, his pulpit is still furnished with a canopy that serves as a sounding board. Early advertisement for loudspeakers, Austria, 1929.

The third role, that of the *counselor*, overshadowed both his priestly and his intellectual ministry. What made Fosdick uniquely qualified for this role was not the theoretical study of psychology, but his own background and experience. When he was a young man, he interrupted his studies for a year in order to earn some money, for his father, a schoolteacher, had a nervous breakdown and could no longer support the family. Later, as a student, he worked on volunteer projects in the slums of New York City (1901). He also went through a nervous breakdown himself and had suicidal thoughts, which forced him to suspend his studies for several months. These he spent in a sanitarium and on a trip to Europe, where he slowly, though not completely, recovered. During this period, Fosdick had an overwhelming experience of divine help: "I learned that God, much more than a theological proposition, is an immediately available Resource; that just as around our bodies is a physical universe from which we draw all our physical energy, so around our spirits is a spiritual Presence in living communion with whom we can find sustaining strength." Thus his audience found in him an understanding interlocutor, familiar with poverty, despair, dependence on the help of others, suicidal impulses, and the complete hell of neurotic agony. And they found a man who knew the power of spiritual

14. Sacred Space. Patterned on the medieval cathedral of Chartres, France, the Riverside Church of New York City (1931), within walking distance of Manhattan's bank and business area, was designed to give tangible expression to the spiritual world. "This church believes in the ministry of beauty, and makes no apology for building as impressive a sanctuary as it was able. In a city whose secular business is so dramatically housed it is glad to have erected this temple of the spirit," explained the church's handbook in 1931. Riverside Church celebrates Christ as "the Great Physician, the Humanitarian, and the Lover of Beauty." This photo shows a view of the pulpit from which Harry Emerson Fosdick preached to the large crowds that flocked to hear him there. The Riverside Church, New York.

reality. A pastor with Fosdick's experience and pastoral sensitivity could hardly fail to give good advice.[84]

Fosdick wanted to respond to people's needs by "bring[ing] the saving truths of the gospel to bear on them . . . creatively." For him, a sermon was meant to serve people, and he referred to it as "personal counseling on a group scale." Therefore he started a sermon not by analyzing and commenting on a biblical lesson, but by presenting a real problem experienced by real people which he then discussed in the light of the Bible. In the pulpit, scripture served as "an amazing compendium of every kind of situation in human experience with the garnered wisdom of the ages to help in meeting them."[85]

Of course, this approach to preaching has its difficulties and risks. Although ministers may know their audience well, they have to guess what their real problems are. To speak to a congregation can be compared, writes Fosdick, to discharging a pipette of eye medicine from a third-story window into a crowded street in the hope of hitting someone in the right place. However, Fosdick did know his audience, and he met many of them in his office for personal counseling. The key to being a good preacher for him was to make himself available as a counselor to his parishioners, his audience, and whoever approached him.[86]

In his autobiography, Fosdick recalls how, early in his ministry, he had come

to feel the lack of "a Protestant version of the Catholic confessional," especially in a large city like New York. Soon, he established regular hours and began his extensive career as a counselor. He absorbed as much psychological literature as he could, and he discussed problems and cases with a professional psychologist. He also relied on the help of organizations like Alcoholics Anonymous, a self-help group that emerged in the late 1930s as "a godsend to us ministers." Although his plans to establish a professional counseling center or clinic at Riverside Church never materialized, he very much emphasized this side of his work. "I am commonly thought of as a preacher," he reports, "but I should not put preaching central in my ministry. My preaching at its best has itself been counseling on a group scale." His ministry in the pulpit was supported and nourished by his counseling experience. Here a steady flow of troubled people confronted him with their doubts, attempts at suicide, anxieties, depression, and guilt, and he could get first-hand experience of the way lives came under the rulership of Christ and were actually transformed. Here, in its individual application, the gospel demonstrated its healing power. It was in his self-devised "confessional" that Fosdick found as much if not more satisfaction than in the pulpit. "Of all the rewards of my work," he wrote in his autobiography, "I prize nothing so much as the remembrance of miracles I have witnessed as the result of Christian truth brought to bear privately on individuals." Was not Christ himself ahead of his time in insisting that "the sinner is sick, he needs not so much a Doctor of Laws than a Doctor of Medicine"?[87]

The preacher of Riverside Church considered himself less a successful man of the pulpit than a successful pastor in vital, caring, and curing contact with individuals. "Indeed, I distrust a preacher to whom sermons seem the crux of his functioning." To Jesus, Fosdick insists, individuals and their stories mattered. Like the Master (and, we may add, like the Catholic confessor), the Christian minister must touch lives, must deal directly with individual needs. Only his contact with individuals can prevent him from living isolated and aloof from life's real problems. And, of course, the pastoral ministry reflects back on the preaching. If "the firsthand experience with individuals" functions as "the creative center" of someone's ministry, this pastor's sermons will be saturated with life, spiced with stories, and never lack human appeal.[88]

"Human biographies and indeed the chaos of the entire world supply the problems, and Christianity has the answers." Can we reduce Fosdick's approach to his ministry to this easy formula? Although he sometimes comes close to saying just this, things are not quite so simple. Since Fosdick does not take Christianity as a fixed set of theoretical teachings and ready practical commandments, he relies on what he considers the essential biblical experience. Common sense and psychological insight, for him, count as much as what he learns from the Bible about, for instance, the soothing force of personal prayer. A close reading of Fosdick's book *On Being a Real Person* (published in

1943, then a national bestseller in the US) reveals that the author did not believe in a particularly Christian variety of counseling and therapy. In order to become "a real person," neuroses and other obstacles have to be dealt with and optimism must be inspired so that a "basic faith" can develop. In all his writings Fosdick emerges as an incorrigible optimist, a person for whom hopeless cases simply did not exist. His attitude borders on naïveté, so that his biographer Robert Miller likens him to Dr. Pangloss, Voltaire's famous—and foolish—believer that ours is the best of all possible worlds. With more reason, Fosdick can be compared to one of his younger fellow-ministers in New York City, Norman Vincent Peale, whose *Power of Positive Thinking* (1952) was a bestseller for several years (and is still in print today). The two ministers had much in common: a pastorate in New York, a lively interest in psychology and counseling, an unbounded optimism, the use of the radio as a medium of Christian ministry, the reputation of being among America's best preachers, and the authorship of bestselling religious books. Their common message was that with some optimism, and much faith, everyone's problematic life can be transformed and healed. Listen to your preacher, read his books, get his personal advice if you feel you need it, and you can be a healthy person. Yet, a characteristic difference separated the thinking of the two ministers. For Fosdick, the American dream was fulfilled in "being a real person," i.e., in psychological well-being, and religious energies were to be mobilized to that end. Peale did not share the sobriety and modesty of Fosdick's pastoral goals; he promised that "positive thinking" would lead not only to health but also to wealth and success in life (a message that found an eager readership that outnumbered that of Fosdick).[89]

While Fosdick extolled faith as indispensable for the integration and health of the human personality, he defined it in very vague terms. Faith means accepting oneself as "a being of divine origin, nature, and destiny." Healthy people somehow believe in their own, God-given worth and vocation. If a man or woman finds this basic faith, a faith that helps to cope with life, then Fosdick feels that he has succeeded in his ministry.[90]

If Fosdick is to receive a place in twentieth-century church history, he must be remembered as one of the first to design a new version of faith, one in tune with psychological experience and sensibility. With the American pragmatist and psychologist William James (1842–1910), whose work he admired, he shares insight into the vital biological function of religious faith, its contribution to a person's health and wholeness. However, his interest is not theoretical but eminently practical. While James remained in his study at Harvard to collect and analyze masses of autobiographical documents, people crowded in front of Fosdick's office. He dealt with real people in a counseling situation.

Fosdick saw himself as a doctor rather than as a philosopher or theorist. "Were I not a minister," he once mused, "I should probably be a psychiatrist." As a popular psychiatrist, he explained to a wider, more general public what it

means "to be a real person." His concern about people's spiritual health, his belief in healing faith, and his commitment to a liberal, therapeutic Christianity must be seen in the context of a trend in Western culture, a movement "away from its former configuration, toward one in which old ideological contents are preserved mainly for their therapeutic potential, as interesting deposits of past motifs of moralizing." In the final analysis, according to cultural psychologist Philip Rieff, the emerging post-Freudian "psychological man" no longer commits himself to any definite religious creed and no longer relies on orthodox traditions and canonical scriptures; instead, he is "a user of any faith that lends itself to therapeutic use." Naturally, Fosdick's therapeutic sermons did not meet with unanimous approval. A young German student, who in 1930–31 attended Fosdick's Union Theological Seminary class on "Brief Sermons," deplored the state of preaching in America. "In New York City," Dietrich Bonhoeffer (1906–45) wrote,

> you can hear sermons on almost any subject, with one notable exception. I myself, at any rate, have not succeeded in hearing a single sermon on the gospel of Jesus Christ, on the cross, sin and forgiveness, life and death. In Dr. Fosdick's homiletic seminar, forgiveness of sins and the cross figured at the very end of the assignment list as examples of more "traditional subjects"!

As a follower of Karl Barth, Bonhoeffer identified preaching with biblical exposition and would have none of Fosdick's strange, modernistic emphasis on experience. Five years after having studied with Fosdick, Bonhoeffer taught his own course on homiletics and told his students to refrain from thematic preaching in answer to contemporary questions. He moved as far away from his American teacher's program as possible. Bonhoeffer wanted his students to give lectures on scripture in the pulpit and to "educate the congregation to follow the sermon with opened Bibles." Unlike Fosdick, he wanted to be a Christian teacher, not a religious therapist.[91]

4. Conclusion: The Authority of Preaching

We have identified three great preaching traditions. Each of them pursues a different aim. A first group of ministers and priests defines their task as that of teachers whose instructional sermons impart saving knowledge. Others prefer the role of pastor and advisor, whose ethical preaching makes their audience fit for life. And again others emphasize the centrality of the act of faith as the adequate response to affective preaching. In other words: preachers may address the head, the hands, or the heart of those who listen.

Now we should of course beware of overstressing the exclusivity with which preachers identify with any of our three preaching traditions. While some preachers and movements show a clear preference for one of the traditions, others mix them or design preaching programs that include more than one type. A blend of the various kinds of sermon seems quite sensible if preaching aims at promoting the soul's mystical progress toward union with God. Following the model of Neoplatonic philosophy, classical Catholic mysticism has argued that union with the deity constitutes the highest stage that can be achieved by a mature Christian man or woman. This stage is reached through preparatory stages termed "purification" and "illumination." First, one has to be freed from grave sins and lead a morally unobjectionable life. As the Neoplatonic philosopher Hierocles put it, "practical philosophy," often embodied in "the laws that are generally in force," serves to "purify us of the irrational by means of the virtues." Once the foundation of a holy life has been established through the exercise of the virtues, one can expect to get more and more acquainted with God by studying scripture and life in the light of scripture, and thus advance to knowledge and illumination. At that stage, one learns to see everything in the light of God's relationship with humankind. The following, final stage, that of friendship and indeed union with God, crowns one's spiritual journey. It seems that the three preaching traditions correspond to the three stages of spiritual development. Ethical preaching is essentially designed to purify one's life and soul; instruction serves to illuminate; and affective preaching aims at producing faith and love of God.[92]

Once we accept this analysis, we can see why Gregory the Great and Harry Emerson Fosdick engaged in ethical preaching. They were dealing with large audiences that lacked even the rudiments of a spiritual life. So purification was called for, and it could be promoted by ethical and therapeutic preaching.

Origen's audience of catechumens—those who demanded admission to the Christian community—was of a different kind. The catechumenate presupposed certain moral qualities; otherwise one was not received into this kind of preliminary membership. In fact, many preachers, from Origen to Karl Barth, have assumed that most people are in fact striving for moral purity, and do so by natural inclination. What they are lacking, however, is instruction in the stories, mysteries, and particular beliefs of Christians. What they need is doctrine rather than moral inculcation, and, as Origen asserts, being exposed to the word of scripture means being exposed to its purifying force: scripture both purifies and illuminates. The third group of preachers dares to invite their audience even beyond the stage of illumination. Luther, Schleiermacher, revivalist and evangelistic preachers all share a similar theological background in mysticism or pietism, i.e., in movements that emphasize the immediacy of the believer's experience of God. Nurtured in an elevated spiritual climate, they share the aim of leading their audience to a union with God or Christ. As is to be expected, the audience of an "affective" preacher are not always prepared to follow their pastor's invitation. Standing at a different, much lower level of spiritual development, they just cannot understand what their preacher is talking about. It has no relevance for them. This is why, when Luther starts to speak about God's justifying love, they begin to sleep or to cough.[93]

Clearly, the preacher's aim, whether purifying, illuminating, or mystical, would have an impact on the content of his message. In addition to the preacher's aim, there is another important factor that affects the content: the *authority* on which the speaker bases his argument. Here we can again distinguish a variety of ways in which the three preaching traditions define their ultimate basis.

The first basis of authority is of course the book. Ezra's Jewish preaching in Jerusalem in the fifth century BCE has much in common with Christian intellectual worship as practiced in Origen's community in Caesarea. In both cases, preaching was not only based on a book—that of Moses or that of the apostles—but it also served to inculcate the traditional values laid down in the sacred volume. The patristic church, like Ezra's Judaism, is a book religion. Its sacred scripture serves as a canonical repository of rules, beliefs, and stories that have to be known, appreciated, and respected in life. Worship serves to publicize, to repeat, and to inculcate the contents of scripture. Both Jews and Christians attribute their books to authorities who lived, if not in the mythic past like Moses, then in the already distant days of the apostles. Far from teaching new doctrines, the preacher relies on ancient, unchanging, and canonical scriptures. Moses and the apostles (those "sent out" by the Lord himself) serve as father figures whose authority is established and beyond dispute, for God or Christ had spoken to them. As authority figures, they participate in or stand for divine authority.

The earliest Christian preaching as recorded by Luke is of a very different kind. While the liturgical setting, the presence of a text, and the endeavor to explain it are identical, the text as such has lost much of its authority. Christ himself speaks authoritatively and merely uses the text in order to illustrate what he does and who he is. In a similar manner, Paul, when addressing a congregation assembled in a Diaspora synagogue, applies a prophetic message to the present with reference to the figure and mission of Christ. Here a new teaching, aptly termed the newly revealed "word of God," disrupts what people were accustomed to hearing. The mixed response that ensues shows what the preacher aimed at: not an understanding of traditional stories and an obedience to codified law, but the acknowledgment of a new leader in a redefined situation. The earliest gospel, that of Mark, characterizes Jesus right from the beginning as a teacher with a difference: "They were astounded at his teaching, for he taught them as one who had authority, and not as the scribes," that is, not as Ezra, Justin, and others (Mark 1:22). "What is this?" people asked, "A new teaching—with authority!" (v. 27). The earliest Christian preaching shared the provocation and the nontraditional, charismatic nature of Jesus' own message. While the audience of Ezra and Justin would generally accept the teaching on the authority of Moses and the apostles, the earliest Christian audience had a different reason for its belief. They were shocked, shaken, touched, and overwhelmed by the new message. "He believed," reports Luke of a Roman proconsul, "for he was astonished at the teaching about the Lord" (Acts 13:12).[94]

In order to have a handy terminology for describing the preacher's strategy and intention, we can use—and adapt to our purposes—Max Weber's well-known distinction between traditional and charismatic authority. Traditional authority rests upon a belief in the sanctity of "the laws that are generally in force" (to quote Hierocles again), the rules that guide, and have always guided, everyday behavior; it is closely connected to patriarchal structures and to institutions—like scripture—that were established in the distant past and therefore belong to the basic structure of the world. Charismatic authority, by contrast, rests on the belief in the supreme sanctity or value of the extraordinary, of a new leader with a new message and new demands. Ezra and Justin preached in the "traditional" mode, while Jesus and Paul represent the "charismatic" way, with its denial of and opposition to traditional rules, opinions, and values.[95]

"Traditional" preaching fits well in the structure of religious ritual. It shares its nonhistorical, atemporal nature, for it repeats, almost mechanically, the same message, the same teaching, and the same, unchanging story about the same, unchanging acts of God. Since God acted in the past, his story can be told as a complete narrative. Like all ritual events, the sermon remains free from surprises and avoids reference to current affairs. "The doctrine delivered by all preachers is the same," asserted Jonathan Swift in the eighteenth century. Preachers like Karl Barth take care to screen out the present with its conflicts and problems. No "dialogue" with the modern mentality is attempted. Understandably, this kind of rhetoric will always frustrate people like Paul's Athenians and foreigners who spend their time in telling and hearing something new (Acts 17:21). It can be described using a phrase often used in Catholic liturgy: "as it was in the beginning, is now, and will be forever." Charismatic preaching, by contrast, breaks out of the comfortable cage of ritual: it announces something new, something that no longer confirms and perpetuates tradition. As we see in the case of Jesus and his early followers, the sermon can be a creative instrument of subversion and propaganda. "When no one disagrees," mused the Russian historian Diakonoff, "there is place for ritual but not for propaganda." In Luke's reports on early Christian preaching, we can see how the calmness of ritual was upset as propaganda invaded the liturgy of the synagogue.[96]

We know, of course, of the instability of the charismatic situation. With time, as the initial excitement vanishes, more stable and permanent structures appear. True charismatic preaching again gives way to its traditional counterpart. Despite their interest in the new and unexpected, in the long run people prefer security and stability. All propaganda, including that of religion, aims at establishing a new stability.

Instructional preaching rests firmly on traditional authority. Origen considered his teaching as a faithful transmission of traditional doctrine, originating with the apostles and deposited in sacred scriptures. "The teaching of the Church," he states, "has indeed been handed down through an order of succession from the Apostles, and remains in the churches even to the present time." And he adds: "That alone is to be believed as the truth which is in no way at variance with ecclesiastical and apostolic tradition." As a scholar and former "grammarian" (teacher of pagan literature), Origen naturally relies on the written record of tradition. He is one of the first Christians to discuss the scriptural "canon," the list of authoritative books to be used in worship, preaching, and theological scholarship. Origen reports having carefully studied books like the gospel according to the Egyptians and the gospel according to Thomas. "But among all of these we approve none others except those, the four only gospels, which are received by the church."[97]

Karl Barth, though famous for insisting on the supreme, exclusive lordship of Christ, in fact based his theology and preaching on ecclesiastical tradition. His view is nuanced, but he goes far in his acceptance of the institutional church and its history:

> The Bible is given to the community of the Church. Tradition helps us toward sound exegesis, and tradition includes the whole history of the Church (including the nineteenth century!). Confessions also help, but none of these is an absolute criterion. In interpretation, tradition and Church Fathers and confes-

sions are our "parents" whom we must respect and honor, but there are times when a breach must be made (Reformation!).

For all his independence and critical spirit, Barth would never develop a theology without paying close attention to confessional statements and the views expressed by theologians of the past. Theology has to respect the "fathers."[98]

While ethical sermons can be distinguished from instructional ones as performing a different task, they generally share the same traditional basis and enjoy the same type of authority. Medieval theorists of moral exhortation like Alan of Lille state clearly that their preaching derives "from the fountainhead of authorities," that is from the biblical books:

> This should be the form of preaching: it should develop from, as it were, its own proper foundation, from a theological authority—especially a text from the Gospels, the Psalms, the Epistles of Paul, or the Books of Solomon, for in these, in particular, edifying instruction resounds. Texts should also be taken from other books of Holy Writ if necessary, and if they have a bearing on the theme in hand.

Interestingly enough, Alan refers to the biblical books of Solomon which include Proverbs and Koheleth, writings known for their moralizing wisdom and philosophy, developed from observation and experience. Koheleth, in particular, insists on personal experience which he uses to criticize and subvert traditional ethical discourse.[99]

However, it is not only implicitly that medieval theologians refer to experience and reason as belonging to the foundations of the pulpit. Humbert of Romans insists that "experiential knowledge" is an invaluable asset of the preacher. "Those who have had much experience in dealing with the state of the human soul can say much more about the affairs of the soul." For Alan, preaching "derives from the path of reason and from the fountainhead of the authorities." The ethical sermon can thus depend on the possibility of an altogether different, modern type of authority which Weber termed "rational." While traditional morality rests on the belief in the sanctity of inherited values, its modern, rational successor establishes new, empirically and scientifically tested ideas. Traditional ways of behavior may be retained in rational ethics, but they must first pass the test of being functional in the present situation. The new ethics, especially visible in Fosdick, does not take the past and its canonical repositories as its basis; instead, it looks to the "rational" ideal of "being a real person." In his therapeutic preaching, Fosdick draws on personal experience and psychology to construct the rational and emotional resources that help the individual to solve his or her problems. In 1924, a journalist called

15. "The First No Sermon Church of Rocky Knoll." Sermons are not always popular with church-goers, so why not suppress them altogether? *New Yorker* cartoon by Henry Martin, 1986.

Fosdick "a preacher who reaches the heart through the brain." In his preaching, Fosdick also invoked the Bible more as a rationally justifiable authority than as a mere repository of tradition. In his *Modern Use of the Bible*, Fosdick carefully distinguished the traditional, culture-bound thought forms from the experientially verifiable, rational, and timeless message. Religion, as he believed and preached it, had an entirely rational basis. In the words of Fosdick's colleague at Union Theological Seminary, Reinhold Niebuhr: "He challenged theological obscurantism as a basis for faith and made it possible for the cultured classes to appreciate the 'intellectual respectability' of the Christian faith."[100]

Compared to Origen, Barth, and the medieval theologians—"traditional" preachers who based their teaching and moral exhortation on inherited patterns of belief and behavior—Fosdick emerges as an example of the modern, "rational" preacher.

Weber's charismatic authority represents what we have termed the affective mode of preaching. As a reformer who broke away from the constraints imposed by scholastic theology, monastic discipline, and papal rulership, Luther naturally preferred the affective sermon. Like his successors in revivalism and evangelism, he would rarely if ever refer to any other authority besides scripture, which, when faithfully preached, became the word of the living God. Ruling out all tradition and transcending any rational discourse, the divine word requires immediate submission in faith and obedience. Charismatic preaching enjoys charismatic authority only for those whom it moves to the act of faith, and for them, it is never boring.

Schematically, then, we can summarize our interpretation as follows:

stage of purification: ethical preaching based on traditional or rational authority;

stage of illumination: instructional preaching—based on traditional authority;

stage of union: affective preaching—based on charismatic authority.

Whether charismatic, traditional, or rational and modern, all preaching requires the minister's careful thought and argumentation as well as the congregation's undivided attention. If not their eternal, then at least their temporal life, their faith, their belief, their world view, their spiritual and moral well-being are at stake. A "no-sermon" church would not be a church at all, but would represent Satan's attempt to abolish it. Only the frivolous (and people too deeply rooted in the faith to be irritated by a little tap from Satan's hammer) can smile at Henry Martin's cartoon (ill. 15).

In some Protestant churches, regular Sunday worship culminates in the sermon. Framed by other oral rites—prayer and praise—it often gives worship a distinctly intellectual note. For others, however, the service continues with another sacred game that relies more on gestures and the use of food: that of giving to God and receiving from him in sacrifice.

The Fourth Game: Sacrifice
Giving to God and Receiving from Him

Une religion qui n'a pas de sacrifice, n'a pas de culte proprement dit.[1]

François-René de Chateaubriand, 1802

Ante agnus offerebatur, offerebatur et vitulus, nunc Christus offertur.
(Formerly a lamb was offered, and a calf; now Christ is offered.)[2]

Ambrose of Milan, ca. 390

The priest: Orate, fratres: ut meum ac vestrum sacrificium acceptabile fiat apud Deum Patrem omnipotentem.
The people: Suscipiat Dominus sacrificium de manibus tuis ad laudem et gloriam nominis sui, ad utilitatem quoque nostram, totiusque Ecclesiae suae sanctae.
(Pray, brethren, that your and my sacrifice may be acceptable to God, the almighty Father. May the Lord accept the sacrifice at your [priestly] hands, to the praise and glory of his name, for our benefit also, and that of all his holy Church.)

Roman Mass, eleventh century

1. On Sacrifice

Whether in the form of the offering of vegetables and flowers in a temple, or of the burning, complete or in part, of a slaughtered animal, sacrifice during antiquity figured prominently in daily life, private as well as public. Priests engaged in regular sacrifices on behalf of the state, individuals brought their offerings to temples, and in a national crisis a mass assembly of the citizens might be ordered "to beg peace from the gods by sacrifice." As so often, Plato offers the most succinct definition: "There is also the priestly class, who, as the law declares, knows how to give the gods gifts from men in the form of sacrifices which are acceptable to them, and to ask on our behalf blessings in return from them." The sacrificial gift served to enlist divine help and protection.[3]

Sacrificial Reciprocity

Deeply rooted in human behavior, the logic of gift-giving can be observed even in small children. Starting from their second or third year of life, children give gifts to adults and other children, usually objects without value. My mother told me that I was a true champion in finding ever new gifts for her: fallen leaves, tiny stones, feathers, flowers, dead insects and, live worms. Far from being intended to negotiate immediate exchanges, these gifts serve to establish or foster relationships. Nevertheless, even small children are already familiar with the mechanism of exchange. Psychologist John Bowlby reports of a boy of three years who offers his teddy bear to his mother to get back the knife she had taken away. The giving of gifts—to do homage to others or to negotiate exchange—belongs among the earliest gestures of childhood. Elaborated later in life, it forms the foundation of social and religious behavior.[4]

Reduced to its key idea, sacrifice means *do ut des*, "I give in order that you give [in return]." The ancient Romans knew this, and the same idea can be found with the Greeks and in the Bible. In the Old Testament, the book of Proverbs puts it bluntly in a word of advice to the peasant: "Honor the Lord with your substance, . . . then your barns will be filled with plenty" (Prov. 3:9–10). Among the many stories told in ancient Israel was one concerning the prophet Samuel's sacrifice. When Israel's enemies, the Philistines, gathered to attack them, Samuel "took a suckling lamb and offered it up as a whole burnt offering to [the god] Yahweh." At the same time, he "cried out to Yahweh for

Israel" (1 Sam. 7:7–11). Now Yahweh heard the prophet. He responded by sending a mighty thunderstorm that confused the Philistines and made them flee. God had granted the request, it seems, because the prophet had followed a traditional ritual procedure, one in which the deity received a special gift. But not only in wartime did the ancient Israelites and Jews offer sacrifices on behalf of the community. According to the Jewish historian Josephus, when people offer sacrifice at the Jerusalem Temple, then "prayers for the welfare of the community must take precedence over those for ourselves [as individuals]; for we are born for fellowship, and he who sets its claims above his private interests is specially acceptable to God."[5]

From their school days, the ancient Greeks were familiar with the same pattern. Many—including some educated Jews—could certainly recite these lines from the first page of Homer's *Iliad*:

> Over and over the old man prayed as he walked in solitude
> To King Apollo, who Leto of the lovely hair bore: "Hear me . . .
> If ever it pleased you that I burned all the rich thigh pieces
> Of bulls, of goats, then bring to pass this wish I pray for:
> Let your arrows make the Danaans pay for my tears shed."

The old man's sacrifices were not in vain: "So he spoke in prayer, and Phoibos Apollo heard him." Apart from private sacrifices, the Greeks celebrated public ones on behalf of the city. When Herodotus, the fifth-century BCE traveler and historian, learned that the Persians actually prohibited private sacrifice, he appreciated their love of the community. Among the Persians, Herodotus notes, "to pray for blessings for himself alone is not lawful for the sacrificer; rather he prays that it may be well with the king and all the Persians, for he reckons himself among them." An echo of the Persian insistence on the state, rather than the individual, as the exclusive recipient of sacrificial benefits can be found in the Bible. King Darius made constant donations of animals, wheat, salt, wine, and oil to the Jerusalem Temple, so that the priests "may offer pleasing sacrifices to the God of heaven, and pray for the life of the king and his sons" (Ezra 6:10). As we can see here, the state has an interest in ensuring that sacrificial benefits are not diverted to private advantage, but are made available to the community and, especially, to the king, its chief representative.[6]

The Greeks were a people not only of poets like Homer and historians like Herodotus, but also of philosophers and satirists, and some of them questioned the practice of sacrifice. Ridiculing the popular attitude, the satirist Lucian caricatured sacrificial activity as an exchange procedure with more or less fixed prices. "It looks," he wrote in the second century CE,

> as if the gods do nothing at all *gratis*, but offer their commodities for sale to
> humans. One may buy of them health, for instance, at the cost of a calf, wealth

for four oxen, a kingdom for a hecatomb, a safe return passage from Ilium to Pylos for nine bulls, and the crossing from Aulis to Ilium for a princess—a high price certainly. . . . One must suppose, however, that they [the gods] have plenty of things to dispose of at the price of a cock, a garland, or even a stick of incense.

Long before Lucian, the philosopher Plato was familiar with this kind of argument and dismissed it as the product of frivolous and immature minds. Gods cannot be bribed. Older and experienced people, Plato argues, do not hold such cynical ideas. Writing in the context of Emperor Julian's fourth-century pagan revival, the philosopher Sallustius explained, quite simply, that "without sacrifice, prayers are only words; prayers with sacrifices are animated words," i.e., powerful words that work.[7]

The Romans also believed in the power of sacrifice. In one of his *Elegies*, Tibullus imagines himself to be a simple peasant who offers a lamb to his household gods while the youngsters shout, "Huzza! Send us good crops and wine!" (*Io, messes et bona vina date*). The traditional formula used in Roman private sacrifice is more restrained: "In offering this cake, O Jupiter, I humbly beg that thou, pleased by this offering, wilt be gracious and merciful to me and my children, my house and my household." The deity honored with a gift—or the promise of a gift—was expected to reciprocate. Without the expectation of a counter-gift, sacrifice would be meaningless, useless. Lactantius, a Christian philosopher who flourished around 300 CE, captured the pagan mind quite well: "For if God confers nothing good on any one, if he repays the obedience of his worshiper with no favor, what is so senseless, what so foolish, as to build temples, to offer sacrifices, to present gifts, to diminish our property, that we may obtain—nothing?"[8]

Gift-giving in the divine–human relationship must not be mistaken for trading. A world of difference separates trading and giving. A gift involves a social relationship between giver and recipient. No law or obligation can govern the gift which, by definition, must be unsolicited. Trading, by contrast, is contractual, regulated by laws and customs, and enforced with the threat of punishment. It implies not a long-term, close social relationship, but an impersonal business relationship lasting hardly any longer than the actual transaction. Generally, religious thinkers insist on understanding sacrifice as expressing a social relationship rather than as trading goods for benefits that are received or expected. In practice, of course, the gift may degenerate into a bribe and people may think of sacrifices as investments or as a kind of insurance. If the gods are thought of as distant and difficult to approach (as in the religion of ancient Rome), then their human partners are likely to see their offerings as tribute paid to distant lords. Or they see them as goods exchanged in return for benefits, knowing that "commerce is a form, even though it be the lowest form, of communion." However, if sacrificers have a good, direct, and emotionally strong relationship to a deity or familiar spirit (as was the case in ancient Greece and Israel), they will refuse to think of their gifts as prices to be paid. In any case, sacrifice links the human and the divine world by establishing a common ground of action and reaction. As Jan van Baal has aptly observed, "all communication begins with giving, offering."[9]

Ancient Jewish Sacrifice, Private and Public

If we take the biblical development as typical, we can see how sacrifice had "primitive" origins in remote days in which people began to slaughter some of their domesticated animals for the benefit of the gods. The offering of food to the gods affirms the deity's belonging to the community. Whenever the deity is offered food, the act of offering carries with it the message: "You are a member of our community. You have the right to partake of our food." Those who partake of the social group's food are of course expected to contribute to the well-being of that group, and in this sense one may invoke the New Testament dictum: "Anyone unwilling to work should not eat" (2 Thess. 3:10). The world in which animal sacrifice seems to have originated was one that no longer depended on the varying chances of finding food through hunting and gathering. It was the world of pastoralists and agriculturists who domesticated animals and cultivated plants. These people relied on regular work, planning for the future, and investing in close social relationships which they negotiated through gift-giving. Especially in times of need they would reaffirm social relationships—hence the practice of offering special sacrifices in situations of crisis or before going to war. These remote origins have cast a long shadow, right down from prehistory into history. Originally, the head of a household would do the sacrificing whenever the need arose and wherever he may have thought it appropriate. Later, local or regional shrines served as places of sacrificial worship. At the third stage, a professional class develops. Now priests begin to take care of the sanctuary and sell their ritual expertise, as well as access to the altar on which a victim, or part of a victim, was burned. Priests dominate sacrificial practice, codify the increasingly elaborate ritual proce-dures, and train their sons to succeed them in their ritual office. A fourth and final stage involves the rise of a centralized state temple. Priests not only sell their ritual knowledge; they also now carry out certain regular and complex sacrificial rituals on behalf of the entire community. Sacrifice has become an institution controlled by a trained clergy and protected by the state. People still bring occasional sacrificial gifts to the temple in order to implore God or the gods; but the clergy has developed its own, independent daily routine of establishing contact with the divine. Sacrificial worship has emancipated itself from the irregular nature of individual need, personal taste, and local custom. The history of sacrifice is a story of increasing institutionalization.[10]

    Sacrificial practices and institutions in the eastern Mediterranean world had much in common. Sacrifices in Homer's *Odyssey* and *Iliad* look very much like their biblical equivalents, and they both reflect a common heritage: certain parts of an animal were burned for the deity, and what was not burned was consumed in a joyous feast. Or the entire animal, rather than only a small symbolic portion, was placed on a pyre and burned. The two traditions also share the notion of inviting the deity to the table and offer food for consumption. The chief difference between the two traditions was monotheism. While the Greeks would sacrifice to a variety of gods and goddesses in many temples, Israel's Yahweh-alone movement promoted worship of a single deity in a single temple. By New Testament times, monotheistic Judaism had replaced earlier Hebrew polytheism.

Most Jewish communities recognized the Temple in Jerusalem as the exclusive, and very vital, center of sacrificial worship. In New Testament times, many Jews had only rare opportunities to attend a sacrificial ritual, and many never had the opportunity at all. Because many Jews were living in the Diaspora far away from Jerusalem, they probably had more knowledge and experience of pagan sacrifice than of Jewish sacrificial worship. Yet, they felt they should make a pilgrimage to Jerusalem in order to fulfill their vows, to give thanks, or simply to engage in traditional rites. Aristeas, a noble and wealthy Jew living (presumably) in second-century BCE Alexandria, visited Jerusalem and its high priest on behalf of the Jews living in Egypt. In a letter sent to his brother, he describes what he saw in Jerusalem and how he was received by the high priest Eleazar. The latter allowed Aristeas and his companions to climb a citadel tower near the Temple so that they could see the magnificent buildings and watch the spectacle of the burning of sacrifices. Since a festival was being celebrated (no doubt one of the great pilgrim festivals), they witnessed a busy scene: more than 700 priests and their attendants were occupied with their various tasks: some carrying wood to the pyres, others oil, others flour or spices, again others offering burnt offerings of the flesh of the victims, and again others killing and dividing "with unerring accuracy" bulls, sheep, and goats. "Everything is carried on with reverence and in a manner befitting supreme divinity. It was an occasion of great amazement when we saw Eleazar engaged in his ministry, and all the glorious vestments." Aristeas ends his description by asserting that anyone who observed this spectacle would feel as if they had been transported into another world and experience "astonishment and amazement beyond words."[11]

The most common sacrificial act witnessed by Aristeas consisted of the killing of an unblemished sheep (by a priest or an assistant), the tossing of the blood against an altar (always by a priest), and the burning of the animal, either in part or as a whole. An open-air platform made of a heap of unhewn stones served as the altar; it was located in front of a building referred to as the sanctuary. Jews believed that their deity resided in this sanctuary, a building inaccessible to the lay person.[12]

Sacrifices were either public or private, depending on how the animal was obtained. For public worship, priests bought the animals with funds collected as an annual tax from all Jews. In private worship, individuals brought an animal from their own flock or bought one in Jerusalem. In public sacrifices, only young, unblemished sheep or goats could be used. In private worship, by contrast, the quality was of less importance—an ox or a lamb that had a limb that was too long or too short qualified as a suitable victim. Generally, the priestly law considered male animals more suitable for sacrifice than female ones.[13]

Public worship was carried out as a daily routine with groups of priests taking shifts. The culmination of the daily morning sacrifice was the slaughter and complete burning of a one-year-old lamb. Before the slaughtered animal was burned, a group of five priests pronounced the priestly blessing on the people who watched from the surrounding court (with women relegated to a court further removed from the sanctuary than the men). After the various parts of the divided body of the lamb had been thrown into the fire, a temple choir sang the psalm of the day, and at every pause in the singing two priests blew silver trumpets. At every blast of the trumpets, the congregation prostrated themselves. People prayed for themselves and for the common welfare of the community. In the afternoon, at around three o'clock, the priests repeated the ritual with little variation. Sacrificial activity tolerated no interruption. From Plato we know how the ancients thought about public sacrifices: they should be offered daily "on behalf of the city, and the citizens, and their possessions." It is through "prayer and sacrifice" that the well-being of "households and cities" is secured. The community's welfare depended on daily acts of worship.[14]

Ideally, public sacrifice would involve the presence of "all Israel," because the entire people acted as the official sponsor of public worship. In order to ensure the presence of a congregation, the priests devised a system of inviting representatives from all regions. Thus "all Israel" was represented by official lay delegations coming from all over the country. The presence of these delegations and the large numbers of priests—Paul Billerbeck speaks of eighteen men officiating at the altar, and refers to a choir of at least twelve persons—contributed to the solemn and official character of the event.

Public worship culminated in the Day of Atonement (*Yom hakippurim*) celebrated in September or October. The ritual, performed by the high priest himself, involved two central acts: (1) the sacrifice of a bull as atonement for the sins of the priests, including the high priest; (2) the sacrifice of a goat for the sins of the people. In both cases, the blood served an important ritual function: the high priest took it inside the Temple building in order to sprinkle it on an aniconic ritual object, possibly to be identified as God's throne. The greater part of the blood was applied to the foot of the altar in front of the sanctuary (and then drained away by an invisible drainage system, much admired by Aristeas). When the high priest entered into God's presence in the Temple, all feared for his life, and he himself felt enveloped in awe and mystery. Returning in triumph he resembled, in his majesty, the morning star: "Emerging from behind the veil of the sanctuary, he was like the morning star appearing through a cloud" (Sir. 50:5–6, REB). The blood ritual served to cleanse both the sanctuary and the altar, for both of these had attracted the impurity caused by the people's sins. Restored and renewed by the cleansing, the sacred place of contact between God and his people could again serve its purpose.

The Day of Atonement ritual also included the curious item of transferring the people's sin onto a goat—the scapegoat—which, by being driven out of the Temple precinct, symbolically takes away the people's sins. While the blood ritual performed at the sanctuary seems to reflect specifically priestly notions (the cleansing of the sanctuary), the scapegoat rite apparently echoes more popular ideas about the people's separation from sin.

Despite its frequency and splendor, the public practice of sacrificial worship remained in the shadow of *private offerings*. From morning until night, large crowds of individuals or small groups brought their sacrificial gifts and made the Temple a busy place. The animal could be any from the flock or herd, male or female. The worshiper placed his hands on the victim's head, thus designating the animal to be his own victim. The killing followed, usually carried out by a priest or some other Temple official. Originally, the worshiper himself would have done the slaughtering (women could at times enter the sacred area, but were not allowed to slaughter). But by New Testament times, the ritual had been thoroughly clericalized and become a priestly privilege. The blood was given to the priests to be thrown about the altar. The fat parts of the animal, including the kidneys, the liver, and the fat tail of a lamb, were burned. All fat, like blood, belonged to the Lord. The breast and the right thigh were the priests' portion and constituted part of the priestly income. The rest of the meat was to be cooked and eaten by the worshiper, his family, and guests. The joyous eating constituted part of the celebration, and people would say that the Lord himself invited them to his table. Although there were various types of private sacrifice, the one described, called a "peace offering," seems to have been one of the more frequent ones.

Like public worship, private sacrificial activity also culminated in a feast. In contrast to the public nature of its fall counterpart (the Day of Atonement), it was the more domestic celebration of Passover that gave spring its distinctive character. Passover originated as a domestic ceremony in a nomadic milieu. By New Testament times, part of the ceremony had been transferred to the Temple, for by then, legitimate sacrificial worship was only permitted there. Many Jewish families made their pilgrimage to Jerusalem, purchased their lambs, and took them to the Temple. Coping with huge numbers of animals in a single day called for considerable organization. Priests would deal with worshipers and their lambs in three sessions. After each group had entered the Temple court, the doors were closed.

Unlike on other occasions, in the Passover ritual the laity was permitted to participate in the sacrificial procedures. "The whole people sacrifice," reports the Jewish philosopher Philo of Alexandria, "every member of them, without waiting for their priests, because the law has granted to the whole nation for one special day in every year the right of priesthood and of performing the sacrifices themselves." As each man killed his own lamb, a priest caught the blood in a silver or golden bowl. Passed along by a chain of waiting priests, the bowls would reach the altar where they were emptied out at the base. The animals were skinned and the sacrificial portions removed. Horns were blown and the Temple choir accompanied the ritual with the singing of psalms. When the first group left, each person carrying a slaughtered animal, the second group would follow, and eventually the third one. All who had sacrificed stayed within the Temple precincts until nightfall, when they went to their homes or lodging places to feast. The domestic ceremony included the drinking of wine, possibly the recitation of the story of Israel's flight out of Egypt, and the feast ended with the same psalms earlier sung in the Temple. The domestic part of the ritual as well as the individual purchase of the animal underscore its private nature.[15]

In ancient Judaism, Christianity's parent religion, sacrificial worship played an important role. Like the Hebrew Bible, the synagogue, and scriptural scholarship, it constituted one of its pillars. The Temple of Jerusalem, considered by many Jews the only place of legitimate ritual, had a large priesthood, an impressive daily routine of worship, and enjoyed enormous prestige among the faithful and even among many pagans (whose offerings the priests also willingly accepted). The story of Christian sacrifice must therefore begin with its founder's attitude toward the Temple.

2. Jesus and the Origins of the Eucharist

In the present chapter, we will argue that the Eucharist as "instituted" by Jesus and celebrated by his early followers belongs to the category of sacrifice. Jesus does not seem to have "invented" the ritual handling and consumption of a token piece of bread and the drinking of wine; arguably, what he did was transform a well-known and often practiced form of sacrifice celebrated at the Jerusalem Temple in his period. We will develop our argument in three stages. First, we will offer a detailed description of a standard private sacrifice as it was celebrated at the Jerusalem Temple. Then we will show how Jesus and his movement designed the Eucharist on the basis of some of the elements of this Temple ritual. A third section will present a hypothetical account of the reasons why Jesus designed a new ritual. Our fresh (and to some readers no doubt rather daring and surprising) reconstruction rests on earlier historical scholarship, especially on the solid work of Hartmut Gese and Bruce Chilton. These two biblical scholars were the first to explain the Lord's Supper in terms of sacrifice. In so doing, they demonstrated that the origins of one of the central acts of Christian worship are not lost in the darkness of legendary accounts.[16]

Private Sacrifice in Jesus' Time

In order to thank God for benefits received—recovering from illness, returning home safely from a long journey, and the like—Jews took a lamb or a goat, went to the Jerusalem Temple (ill. 16), and presented themselves to a priest, who then saw to it that the animal was slaughtered, certain parts being burned on the altar. A feast was then arranged for the sacrificer and the latter's guests. While this description may give a first idea of what happens when a sacrifice is offered, it remains too sketchy for our purposes. There are many more acts involved, and biblical as well as some other sources can help us to reconstruct many of the exact procedures and their arrangement as a sequence of sacred acts. The insert that follows overleaf lists the most important acts referred to in the ancient sources and tries to reconstruct the "ideal type" of a private sacrifice. In order to sketch the full picture, we also make an effort to fill some of the gaps in the historical record.

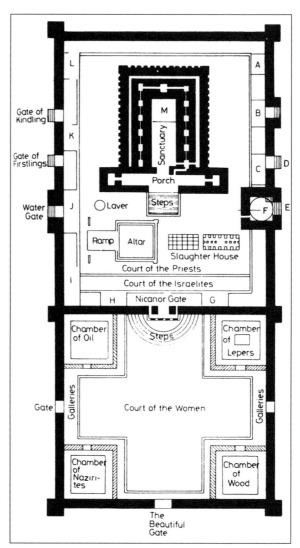

The following labels appear on the Temple plan:

L · A

Gate of Kindling · K · B

Sanctuary · M

Gate of Firstlings · C · D

Water Gate · J · Porch · Steps · F · E

Laver

Ramp · Altar · Slaughter House

Court of the Priests

Court of the Israelites

I · H · Nicanor Gate · G

Chamber of Oil · Steps · Chamber of Lepers

Gate · Galleries · Court of the Women · Galleries

Chamber of Nazirites · Chamber of Wood

The Beautiful Gate

16. The Temple, Place of Sacrifice. An ancient temple was not just a building but a vast complex of buildings and courts. Animals were killed in the slaughterhouse, then the priest presented the victim's blood and corpse at the altar in front of the sanctuary. Modern plan of the first-century CE Jerusalem Temple.

The Six Steps of Sacrificial Procedure (Privately Offered Sacrifice)

The principal characters	The sacrificing lay person (a man or a woman), here called "sacrificer"; the victim (an animal, normally a lamb); the priest.
The place	The courts of the Temple of Jerusalem, especially the "court of the Israelites" and the court of the priests.
The time	First century CE (before 70 CE, date of the Temple's destruction).

Step I	*Preparation.* The sacrificer brings the animal and some other gifts, including bread and wine, to the Temple and presents them to a priest.
Step II	*Slaughtering.* The priest slaughters the animal and separates "blood" and "body."
Step III	*Offering of the blood at the altar.* The priest tosses the blood against all sides of the altar. We conjecture that before the blood is tossed, the priest presents it to God, pronouncing a formula: "This is N's blood," N being the name of the sacrificer.
Step IV	*Presentation of the body and the bread at the altar.* The sacrificial material brought before the altar is presented and dedicated to God with a gesture of elevation. We conjecture that at the presentation at the altar, the priest pronounces these words: "This is N's body," N being the name of the sacrificer.
Step V	*Disposal of the wine.* The priest presents the wine at the altar, elevating the cup and invoking the name of God. The concluding ritual act is the pouring out of the wine at the foot of the altar.
Step VI	*Communal meal.* The sacrificer receives the body of the slaughtered animal back and prepares a feast to which guests are invited.

Sacrifice must be thought of as a costly meal in whose preparation priests are involved and which requires a particular sequence of acts taking place in the Temple. At the first stage, which we may term the preparation, someone takes an animal to the Temple and presents it to a priest. The sacrificer declares which kind of sacrifice he or she wants to offer. The sacrificer also puts his hands (with force) on the head of the animal. Slaves and women were not allowed to perform the hand-leaning rite. In addition to the animal, the sacrificer also brings wine and four kinds of unleavened and leavened bread.[17]

The slaughtering of the animal (step II) follows immediately. The priest or the priest's attendant slaughters the animal and separates "blood" and "body." The blood is collected in a bowl. The sacrificer watches from the "court of the Israelites," while the priest does the slaughtering in the sacrificial court. During the following steps, the sacrificer stays in the court of the Israelites.[18]

The following two steps seem to be the culmination of the ritual. First comes the offering of the blood at the altar (step III). The priest tosses the blood against all sides of the altar. We conjecture that before the blood is tossed, the priest presents it to God at the altar, pronouncing a formula: "This is N's blood," N being the name of the sacrificer. The sacrificer still watches. Then, the victim's body and some bread are presented at the altar (step IV). The

17a. Offerings Presented to the Deity (1). Sacrifical ritual, as understood by many religions, culminates in the presentation of gifts to the deity. This ancient Egyptian relief shows the king as he presents a tray with gold, silver, and copper ingots to a statue of the goddess Hathor. The walls of ancient Egyptian temples are full of scenes that depict the pharaoh acting as priest and offering gifts—often food and drink—to a deity. Ancient Israelites and Jews never depicted any ritual scenes. However, Jewish priests seem to have presented their offerings with a similar gesture of elevation at the altar. Relief in the Hathor temple of Dendera, Egypt, first century CE.

17b. Offerings Presented to the Deity (2). The time-honored gesture of presentation (ill. 17a) survives in the Catholic Mass. This 1950s photo shows a priest presenting the host (a wafer in disc form), placed on the paten, to God. The paten served as an offering tray; the reformed Roman Mass of 1970 simplified the liturgical equipment and now uses a larger bowl in which not one, but all the hosts consumed at Mass are elevated in a similar gesture. Early 1950s.

sacrificial material brought before the altar consists of part of the bread, the slaughtered animal's breast, and certain parts of the entrails (essentially the kidneys and the fat covering the entrails). All of this is presented at the altar and dedicated to God with a gesture of elevation (ills. 17a and 17b). Then the entrail parts are thrown onto the pyre that burns on the altar, whereas the breast and the bread remain with the officiating priest who consumes them later. We conjecture that at the presentation at the altar, the priest pronounces these words: "This is N's body," N being the name of the sacrificer. The sacrificer watches.[19]

After the offering of blood, meat, and bread, the priest takes a cup of wine, elevates it, utters an invocation to God, and then pours it at the foot of the altar (step V). The sacrificer still watches.[20]

After the priest has poured out the wine, he returns the slaughtered animal to the sacrificer for consumption. The communal meal that follows (step VI) no longer takes place at the altar, but nonetheless near the Temple. Since the meat has to be consumed on the day of sacrifice, the sacrificer immediately prepares a feast to which guests are invited (people who had been present all along, together with the sacrificer watching the priest officiate). Bread and wine are also consumed.[21]

The ritual as we have reconstructed it has a beautiful, symmetrical design with a beginning, a middle, and a conclusion. The preparatory stages (I and II) are followed by the offering of bread and the animal's body (IV), which is framed by two libations, first of blood (III) and then of wine (V). A joyous meal forms the conclusion (VI). The main sacrificial material is the slaughtered animal's blood and body, but this material is doubled in unbloody form with bread and wine.

For the words with which the priest presents the sacrificial gifts at the altar, no ancient sources are available. Here our reconstruction relies on the words that Jesus used in his redesigned ritual: "This is my body" and "This is my blood." Placed in a concrete ritual situation, these words lose their enigmatic quality and sound quite natural. In an earlier period, when the sacrificer, and not the priest, officiated at the altar, these could have been the formulae of sacrificial presentation. When the sacrificer approached the altar with his slaughtered animal, he uttered the words: "This is my body," i.e., here I bring my sacrificial body; it belongs to me and I place it on your altar. Similarly, when offering the victim's blood, he would say, "This is my blood," i.e., here I offer the blood of my sacrificial victim. Unfortunately, this interpretation must remain conjectural. Yet, we can point to three sacrificial formulae found or alluded to in the Old Testament. The book of Deuteronomy prescribes a text to be pronounced by the peasant as he presents his harvest gifts to the Temple. It includes a presentation formula, to be said at the handing over of the basket to the deity, represented by a priest: "Now I bring here the first fruits of the land which you, Yahweh, have given me" (Deut. 26:11). This example shows that the bringing of a gift to the Temple involved a formal act of presentation in which it was customary to use certain prescribed words. Formulae pronounced by priests and related to the ritual use of blood bring us closer to "eucharistic" language. In the book of Exodus, there is an expression that Moses used when applying sacrificial blood to people: "Behold the blood of the covenant that Yahweh has made with you" (Exod. 24:8). A third example comes again closer to the words spoken by Jesus. An Old Testament legend recounts how King David, during a war, makes a sacrifice to Yahweh in the abbreviated, substitute form of a libation. As no animal could be slaughtered, water serves as a substitute for blood. David pours out the water in the name of the men who in a daring act have fetched it from a cistern under the enemy's control. In the absence of an altar he pours the water out onto the ground and says: "This is the blood of the men who went at the risk of their lives" (2 Sam. 23:17). Priests may have used similar expressions when tossing sacrificial blood at the altar, presenting the victim's breast or bread and wine, or when throwing parts of the victim into the fire burning on the altar. A sacrifice must be formally presented and the sacrificer identified. Actually, the presentation, and not the killing of the victim, seems to have been the central ritual act.[22]

Jesus' New Sacrifice

The earliest form of the Eucharist, as far as we can reconstruct it, consisted of three simple parts. First, a communal meal was eaten by a small number of people; here we may of course think of Jesus and his narrower circle of the twelve as mentioned in the gospels. Then, the presider presented some bread to God in a gesture of elevation, saying, "This is my body." Those present shared the token piece of bread offered to God. The third and concluding act repeated the bread rite with a cup of wine. Here again, the words of presentation were pronounced, "This is my blood," and the cup was shared by those taking part in the celebration. What we have here is patterned on private sacrifice as celebrated at the Temple. We can best understand Jesus' new sacrifice as an abbreviated form of the six-step ritual described above. One item remained essentially unchanged: as in the Temple ritual, bread was presented to God with the formula, "This is my body," and was then eaten (without being burned on the altar). Other features were changed. Jesus introduced two main alterations: (1) He transferred the ritual to the realm outside the Temple; as a consequence, every act involving the co-operation of a priest had to be omitted. Since no priest was involved, no animal could be slaughtered, no blood could be sprinkled, and nothing could be burned on the altar. (2) Jesus reduced the Temple ritual to its unbloody part, and here he reversed the order of the various ritual acts: the meal no longer formed the conclusion, but was now placed at the beginning and was followed by ritual gestures with bread and wine. There is some ambiguity as to the sequence of these gestures. The gospel of Luke places the wine rite first, whereas Mark and Matthew place it after the bread rite. Both sequences make sense. The sequence wine rite—bread rite may be seen as replicating the original sequence of the animal sacrifice which required the quick disposal of the victim's blood (which had to be tossed against the altar before congealing). Those placing the wine rite last no doubt simply imitated the priests who concluded sacrificial celebrations with a libation of wine.[23]

The new, unbloody ritual, while completely redesigned, still served the same purpose of honoring God with a present and giving him thanks for benefits received. Therefore Christians often called it by its old name of *eucharistia*, the Greek term for thanksgiving. The central rite by which God was honored consisted of a gesture of elevating bread and wine and presenting these gifts to God saying, "This is my body—This is my blood." Neither an accompanying prayer (as in later Christian worship) nor the eating and drinking formed the core. The sacrifice of Jesus consisted exclusively in the very rite of presentation, i.e., the elevation and the words accompanying this gesture.[24]

Why should the abbreviated, unbloody sacrifice replace the elaborate, expensive, and time-consuming priestly celebration at the Temple? The idea of replacing a standard sacrifice by something else is not entirely new, but has precedents in actual ritual practice. In anthropological literature, the classical example of sacrificial lenience comes from the Nuer, a black cattle-herding people living in the Sudan. When someone cannot afford to slaughter an ox, a tiny little cucumber will do as well, at least as a temporary expedient. The Nuer treat the cucumber as though it were an animal victim: it is presented and consecrated, an invocation said over it, and eventually slain by the spear. A similarly striking instance of sacrificial substitution can be quoted from ancient Egypt. A priest or a scribe could honor a deity or a deceased person by pouring some water and uttering the formula: "A thousand loaves of bread, a thousand jugs of beer for N." The water replaced the large amount of bread and beer referred to by the sacrificer. In Israel, private sacrifice, like its public counterpart, normally required the killing and offering of a domestic animal. Frequently, the entire animal was burned "for the deity," so that the sacrificing individual or community did not have the benefit of a joyous meal. Only the well-to-do could afford frequent sacrifices. One Old Testament story contrasts the poor man, who owned only one little ewe lamb, with a rich person, who had very many flocks and herds. We can see why the lower classes were excluded from frequent participation in private sacrificial worship. In certain cases, they were allowed to offer a pair of pigeons or turtledoves instead of a lamb; and if they could not afford to buy these, an offering of some flour (about 4 kg) would do as well. The most common substitute for sacrifice, however, was prayer, which ranked as a kind of "offering of the poor." Visitors to the Temple were ideally expected to bring an offering to Yahweh, but if they came empty-handed they were at least supposed to prostrate themselves and utter a prayer.

Such an understanding of prayer is reflected in the book of Psalms, the collection of Jerusalem Temple prayers. Thus we find a supplicant asking that his prayer "be taken like incense" before the Lord, and his "upraised hands" (that is, the palms raised upward in a customary gesture of prayer) be accepted "like an evening grain offering" of the public cult. When the psalmist says, "accept, O Yahweh, the free-will offering of my mouth," the poor person actually expects his words to be as acceptable as an animal sacrifice. When he declares that "a broken spirit is a sacrifice acceptable to God" and proclaims that God "will not despise a broken and contrite heart," he has no intention of renouncing sacrifices as such, but merely indicates the fact that a broken spirit, expressed in song or prayer, is all he can offer. He expresses the hope that this spirit will count for him as if it were a "real" sacrifice. A post-biblical Jewish text sums the matter up quite succinctly: "If a man has a bullock, let him offer a bullock; if not, let him offer a ram, or a lamb, or a pigeon; and, if he cannot afford even a pigeon, let him bring a handful of flour. And if he has not even any flour, let him bring nothing at all, but come with words of prayer."[25]

The last quotation seems to imply that an animal constitutes the original and real sacrificial material, whereas everything else counts as a substitute. However, not all Jews may have looked at it this way. The French scholar Alfred Marx has suggested that in early Judaism there was an emphasis on the unbloody part of the sacrifice, and possibly certain circles saw it as more important than the actual animal sacrifice. In the cultural world in which early Judaism developed, a certain opposition to animal sacrifice and its replacement by offering of bread and drink was known. This was the ritual option of some of the ancient Zoroastrians whose god Ahura Mazda was recognized as the state god of the Achaemenid empire. According to inscriptional evidence dating from ca. 500 BCE, Ahura Mazda was honored with daily gifts of bread and wine. At least some Jews admired and emulated Zoroastrian monotheistic belief, insistence on ritual purity, and expectation of resurrection after death. They would even go as far as adopting a vegetarian diet. While the Zoroastrian connection with Jewish Temple ritual and its understanding by those who practiced it remains conjectural, there is evidence for the prominence of the libation rite that formed the conclusion to both the public and the private sacrifices. The oldest description we have of public sacrificial worship at the Temple refers to the high priest who "held out his hand for the cup and poured a drink offering of the blood of the grape; he poured it out at the foot of the altar" (Sir. 50:15). The description seems to imply that the gesture of pouring out "the blood of the grape" was more visible and more solemn than the sprinkling of the animal blood (not mentioned at all in this source). One of the Psalms refers to a private sacrifice of thanksgiving as follows: "I will lift up the cup of salvation and call on the name of the Lord . . . I will offer to you a thanksgiving sacrifice" (Ps. 116:13.17). Here, the gesture of presenting the cup of wine can sum up the entire celebration.[26]

Why did Jesus design this new form of sacrifice? It is tempting to see him as the prophet who wanted to bring the Temple ritual and its spiritual benefits within the reach of the poor who could not afford to buy and sacrifice a lamb. It is also tempting to see Jesus as the legislator who abolished animal sacrifice, replacing it by simpler, unbloody gifts, thus (perhaps unknowingly) adopting Zarathustra's attitude and promoting the Persian prophet's ritual reform. However attractive these interpretations may be, they are based on ideas foreign to the mentality of Jesus and his early followers. We have to look for different reasons why Jesus felt he should design a new program of sacrifice.

While the well-known gospel legend places Jesus' birth in Bethlehem, a small town near Jerusalem, Jesus was a Galilean, born and raised in the northern part of Palestine. To be a Galilean meant being recognized by one's particular dialect, and by one's lack of interest in the priestly worship celebrated at the far-away Jerusalem Temple. Jesus seems to have belonged to those Galileans who refused to conform to the priestly demands. Horrified at the thought of expressing the relationship to God in a monetary transaction, he opposed the way public sacrifice was organized.[27]

Private sacrifices, by contrast, meant much for Jesus. During his lifetime, his followers, or at least those who listened to him, went to the Temple to offer their sacrifices. In one instance, after a healing, Jesus sent the healed person to the Temple: he did not tell him not to bother about sacrificing. Rather, he would instruct him: "Go, show yourself to the priest, and offer the gift that Moses commanded" (Matt. 8:4). Jesus respected the law that prescribed a series of offerings that reintegrate a formerly "leprous" and "unclean" person into full membership of the community (Lev. 14). He addressed all those who wished to sacrifice and insisted on a very particular preparation: the restoration of social harmony among people. This injunction is contained in a well-known passage from the Sermon on the Mount: "So when you are offering your gift at the altar, if you remember that your brother has something against you, leave your gift there before the altar and go; first be reconciled to your brother, and then come and offer your gift" (Matt. 5:24–25). Disharmony would spoil the sacrifice, make it ineffective, and presumably offend God, provoking his wrath. Here the attitude of Jesus echoes the psalmist's conviction that only someone "who has clean hands and a pure heart" can legitimately sacrifice in the Temple (Ps. 24:4).[28]

Jesus, as we saw, accepted the institution of animal sacrifice. He also endorsed the biblical legislation regulating it. But he had his own ideas about the personal situation of the sacrificer. He criticized the procedures involving the actual offering at the Temple. His critical stance culminated in a dramatic action generally referred to as his "cleansing" of the Temple.

All four gospels report how Jesus, in an angry demonstration, disrupted the transactions at the Temple. Mark's report is believed to be the oldest one:

Then they came to Jerusalem. And he entered the Temple and began to drive
out those who were selling and those who were buying in the Temple, and he
overturned the tables of the money changers and the seats of those who sold
doves; and he would not allow anyone to carry a vessel through the Temple. He
was teaching and saying, "Is it not written, 'My house shall be called a house of
prayer for all the nations'? But you have made it a den of robbers." And when the
chief priests and the scribes heard it, they kept looking for a way to kill him; for
they were afraid of him, because the whole crowd was spell-bound by his
teaching. And when evening came, Jesus and his disciples went out of the city.
(Mark 11:15–19)

While historians would generally agree that the report reflects a historical
event, they are less sure about what actually happened and what Jesus' intention may have been. For readers unfamiliar with the cultural and religious
world of ancient Judaism, the incident suggests that the market place had
spilled over into the Temple in the way it often invaded the interiors of
medieval cathedrals. In his dramatic action, Jesus restored the original function
of the Temple, making it a house of prayer again. However, this reading
ignores the cultural setting of the report. The "buying and selling" does not
refer to just any transaction done in a market place; rather, we have to think of
the buying and selling of sacrificial animals which include the pigeons mentioned in the passage. Does the report indicate, then, Jesus' rejection of sacrifice (for which animals had to be bought) and his preference for the more
spiritual act of prayer?[29]

Two facts militate against this interpretation, making us aware of quite
different implications. As we have seen, Jesus was far from condemning private
sacrifice as such; in fact, he endorsed and even recommended it. It also seems
that the selling of animals had been introduced into the Temple precinct only
recently and did not meet with general approval. Caiaphas, high priest between
ca. 18 and 36 CE, was apparently the first to authorize the sale of sacrificial
animals within the Temple precincts, presumably within the outer court. What
Jesus wanted, then, was to change what went on in the Temple, to bring it
closer to the ideal of unmediated, direct worship of God. He invoked a passage
found in the prophecy of Zechariah: "There shall no longer be traders in the
house of the Lord of hosts" (Zech. 14:21). His bold action may have appealed
to popular sentiment, even among the Temple personnel, so that no one
bothered or dared to take action against him. If they had indeed been offended,
one would expect the Temple police to have taken immediate action, and Jesus
would have been challenged and arrested on the spot.[30]

We could stop here and admit that any further interpretation borders on
mere speculation. Recent scholarship, however, seems to permit at least tentative suggestions about what Jesus had in mind when "cleansing" or

"occupying" the Temple. Although some details of our reconstruction may seem unusual, they can be put forward as at least plausible.[31]

By Jesus' day, laypeople wishing to present a private sacrifice seem to have been reduced to the role of paying sponsors. They would pay, in the court of the Gentiles, for a sacrificial animal which was then handed over to the Temple personnel. Sponsors would probably wait for some time until they got certain parts of the slaughtered victim (in the case of so-called peace offerings and thanks offerings). Paying, laying hands on the animal's head, and receiving part of a slaughtered animal: this was all that happened in the foreground. Slaves and women sacrificers were not allowed to perform the laying-on of hands. The actual sacrificing—the slaughter, the collection of the blood, the ritual disposal of blood and fat, sometimes even the laying-on of hands—happened far away, hardly visible to the sponsor. Not being permitted to enter the Temple's court of the priests (where the animals were slaughtered and where the altar was located), he or she stood in the "court of the Israelites" and simply watched: this was all that a sacrificing man or woman could do. This reduced, minimal involvement of laypeople naturally made sense: it facilitated the performance of a large number of sacrifices by priestly specialists, especially on festival days when the Temple became crowded. The practice also kept non-Jews out of the sacred areas, while allowing their sacrificial gifts, simplified to payment or the handing-over of an animal, to be accepted. Now, Jesus objected to reducing the sacrificial procedure to a financial transaction in which someone would pay for a sheep and then have little to do with the actual sacrifice. In ancient times the actual slaughtering had been the task of the offering person himself. A priest would step in only if the offerer found himself in a state of ritual impurity. For Jesus, God's people were pure, and thus should have had more involvement with the sacrificial procedure than the Temple establishment granted them. People should buy their animals on the Mount of Olives, where the market was located prior to its transfer to the Temple area itself. They should actually own their victim.[32]

Sacrificers should also be present at the actual slaughtering and the ensuing ritual acts. Tradition acknowledges that someone's offering cannot be made "while he is not standing by its side." But mere presence, in the eyes of Jesus and other teachers, would not suffice. We can invoke the Talmudic tradition of Rabbi Hillel, almost a contemporary of Jesus, who also objected to the impersonal, clericalized manner of sacrifice. According to Hillel, offerings should not simply and informally be given to the priests for slaughtering. Rather, the owners should always, even during busy festival days, lay their hands on their animals' heads prior to handing them over to the officiating priest. Apparently this ritual gesture, prescribed by law (Lev. 3:2), indicated both the ownership of the sheep and served as a gesture of offering. Hillel's suggestion made such an impact on one Baba ben Butha that he had large numbers of animals brought to the Temple and gave them to those willing to lay hands on them in advance of sacrifice.[33]

Jesus, like Hillel, wanted people to participate more in their offering. As a theurgist involved with arcane sacramental procedures (see part V of the present study), he had a strong sense of the need to perform a ritual in the proper way. If people bought their animals on the Mount of Olives (rather than in the Temple area), they would actually own them and bring them to the Temple themselves. Jesus may have been aware of the strict rule governing the foremost private sacrifice, that of Passover. The law prescribed that prior to offering the Passover lamb, the sacrificer must own it for four days. Owning the victim, then, must have been important for Jesus. While we do not know anything about Jesus' view of the laying-on of hands on the animal's head, we can at least speculate about a formula with which he wanted people to designate a sacrifice as their own. Perhaps they should offer the various parts of the slaughtered and cut-up animal using the formula, "This is my body," i.e., here I bring my sacrificial body; it belongs to me and I place it onto your altar. Similarly, they should offer their blood saying, "This is my blood," i.e., here I offer the blood of my sacrificial victim.[34]

The rest of the story about Jesus and the Temple is quickly told. Jesus' occupation of the Temple did not lead to any changes in the traditional ritual procedures. Everything stayed the way the priestly establishment had determined. His action had no immediate impact; like Hillel's, it remained an episode remembered by his disciples, passed on orally, and eventually recorded in a few puzzling lines of literature.

Although the priestly establishment may have disagreed with Rabbi Hillel's view on the laying-on of hands, we hear of no action against him. Why, then, were the priests so enraged with Jesus that they wished to kill him? The reason must be sought in another offense and not in this one—an act that threatened their very existence.

Historians of early Christianity have long argued that Jesus was killed because he committed an act of provocative disobedience to Israel's sacred law, an act of blasphemy punishable by death. Bruce Chilton has persuasively argued that this act had to do with Jesus' disillusionment with Temple sacrifice. After realizing the impossibility of reforming the sacrificial procedure at the Temple, he came to oppose private sacrifice. He thought of it as procedurally deficient and hence ineffective and invalid. He was not the only one to protest against ritual abuses surrounding sacrifice: the Essenes rejected Temple worship as then practiced (though for reasons different from those of Jesus: they held the contemporary high priesthood to be illegitimate).

Unlike the Essenes, Jesus did not consider sacrificial worship as impossible to perform. Rather, he created his own substitute for it. He continued the already well-established tradition of joyous meals. These he shared with large crowds, with "publicans and sinners," with his wealthy sponsors, and with the narrower circle of his disciples. He began to introduce into these meals a new and unprecedented ritual action, one that involved the use of sacrificial language. Jesus declared the eating of bread and wine a new sacrifice. Bread would stand for the sacrificial body of the slaughtered animal and wine for the blood tossed at the foot of the altar. The declarative formulae, "This is my body" and "This is my blood," designate bread and wine as unbloody substitutes for private sacrifice. We must beware of reading any hidden meanings into this symbolic gesture. Bread and wine neither take on special, magical qualities, nor is there any link to the (sacrificial) death of Jesus. A simple and straightforward declaration said over bread and wine had, in the minds of Jesus and his followers, *replaced* private sacrifice as performed at the Temple.

The priestly establishment could have ignored a Galilean rabbi's private cult. Yet, they vented their anger on him and were successful in their plan to have him killed.

The rest of the story is known. Jesus introduced his new ritual in secret among the most intimate of his friends. He practiced it occasionally if not frequently, and the new ritual meal demonstrated his decision not to live in compromise with the Temple establishment of his day. The authorities got wind of it. Wishing to be sure about what was going on, they looked for a witness. A man called Judas betrayed his master's "sacrifice." Jesus had added to and indeed surpassed his earlier extravagant behavior, which had already led to accusations of blasphemy. Now that the crime of blasphemy had been established definitively, the Temple authorities had little difficulty having Jesus executed by order of the Roman procurator, Pontius Pilate.[35]

Our tentative reconstruction visibly departs from what we find in the gospels. This departure can hardly be avoided if what we are looking for is the true course of events. The account in the gospels blends reliable information with legendary accretions and shapes them so that they speak meaningfully to Christians of the second or third generation. Yet, there are enough historical facts that can be discerned in the gospel account of the "Last Supper" to suggest some kind of introduction of a new ritual. Viewed against the background of Jesus' original endorsement and eventual rejection of private sacrifice, his ritual of bread and wine makes sense.

After Jesus: Christian Sacrifice in Jerusalem, Antioch, and Lyons

Jesus died a martyr's death in Jerusalem in 27 or 30 CE. His followers created a movement or, more precisely, a number of movements that continued and propagated his message as well as his preferred ritual, the offering of bread and wine in the context of meals held outside the Jerusalem Temple. Early Christian texts dating from the first and the second centuries CE allow us to reconstruct how in Jerusalem, Antioch, and Lyons the members of these movements engaged in sacrificial worship.

For *Jerusalem*, most of our information comes from Luke's Acts of the Apostles. "Day by day, as they spent much time together in the Temple, they broke bread at home and ate their food with glad and generous heart, praising God and having the goodwill of the people" (Acts 2:46–47). Luke's report about the Jerusalem community's two meeting places must be taken literally. They met at the Temple, and they also met in their homes for private rituals patterned on the "bread sacrifice" inaugurated by Christ. But what would the early community do at the Temple? The book of Acts implies their involvement with Temple worship, public and private. "One day," we are told, "Peter and John were going up to the Temple at the hour of prayer, at the ninth hour" (Acts 3:1). This is the hour of the afternoon sacrifice, celebrated at about three o'clock. Like many other Jews, the members of the new community would go to the Temple to watch how the smoke of the holocaust ascended upward, to join in the general murmur in which everyone present uttered his or her personal prayers, and to receive the priestly blessing. The book of Acts also mentions four Christians who were under a vow that involved certain sacrificial obligations. Because these men were poor, Paul sponsored their sacrifices and accompanied them to the Temple.[36]

Although Christian participation in sacrificial Temple rituals continued during the first generation after the death of Jesus, it received two devastating blows. The first came from Christian intellectuals who argued that Christ had abolished sacrifice, so that participation was simply superfluous. The other came from politics: when the Romans destroyed the Temple, sacrificial activity had to cease.

The critique of Christian intellectuals focused on the most solemn of the public rituals: that of the Day of Atonement (*Yom hakippurim*). The Atonement ritual involved two main ritual acts, performed by the high priest with two goats. He symbolically transferred the sins of the people to the first goat, traditionally called the scapegoat, and the animal was then chased out of Jerusalem and pushed down a precipice so that it died. After the second goat was slaughtered, the high priest took its blood into the Temple's sacred chamber, the "holy of holies," and applied it to a ritual object traditionally referred to as the "mercy seat." The scapegoat was said to eliminate the impurity from the people, and the second goat to purify Temple and country, but one may consider the two ritual acts simply as synonyms aiming at cleansing the people from the stain of the sins they had committed during the past year. When Christians spoke of the atoning death of Christ, their language echoed ideas connected with the Day of Atonement. Christ could be said to be the scapegoat that bears our sins, or the source of atoning blood, or even the high priest who, with his own blood, enters the sanctuary. While the identification of Christ with the high priest presumably belongs to the daring thought of the epistle to the Hebrews, the other ideas—the human scapegoat and the purifying force of human blood—were no doubt well known even outside

Christian circles. What was special, however, was the finality of Christ's atonement: Christ atoned "once for all," making any further ritual pointless. Thus
the entire system of sacrifice could vanish. In the words of Hebrews: "What is
obsolete and growing old will soon disappear" (Hebr. 8:13). Public Temple
rituals of atonement could not add anything to what Christ had already done,
once for all.[37]

Although some first-generation Christians continued to sacrifice at the
Temple, that form of worship had lost much of its attraction. If one takes Paul
at his word, let alone Jesus, it had certainly been superseded. James, the brother
of Jesus, went to the Temple for his frequent prayers, but apparently not for
sacrificing—if we can trust a tradition recorded by the church father Eusebius.
In the early community a prophetic dictum circulated that was very critical of
sacrifice: "I have come to abolish sacrifices, and if you do not cease sacrificing,
the wrath [of God] will not cease from being upon you." Attributed to Jesus in
an early non-canonical gospel, this tells us how some Christians imagined the
opinion of their master.[38]

When the Romans responded to a Jewish rebellion by destroying part of
the Jerusalem Temple in 70 CE, sacrificial worship received a serious blow.
Although the priests seem to have resumed sacrificial activities in a limited
way, presumably only for private sacrifices, they lacked the means to restore the
previous Herodian magnificence of Temple and ritual. The Romans appropriated the Temple tax, which the Jews had used to support their public worship.
Instead of supporting their own worship, they had to contribute to the cult of
Jupiter Capitolinus in Rome. Deprived of financial support, the priestly cult of
Jerusalem appeared to be an ailing institution. For more than theological
reasons, Hebrews could state that "what is obsolete and growing old will soon
disappear" (Hebr. 8:13), and that is what happened soon thereafter. When the
Jews risked another anti-Roman rebellion in about 130 CE, the Romans reacted
with uncompromising brutality. Emperor Hadrian's troops razed hundreds of
villages, sold thousands of Jews as slaves, cleared Jerusalem and its environs of
all Jewish inhabitants, and renamed the city Aelia Capitolina. The establishment of a pagan temple at the ancient sacred site ended Jewish sacrificial
worship permanently. Jupiter had replaced the Jewish god. After the collapse
of sacrificial worship in 135 CE, Christian anti-sacrificial ideas inevitably dominated Christian practice. While many Jews felt deprived of their central ritual,
Christians felt little remorse. Already powerless, anachronistic, and obsolete
before the second Jewish rebellion, the Temple ritual vanished, never to be
restored and never to be regretted. Thus, the new movement developed not
only into a new religion; it also started its career as a new type of religion—one
without sacrificial slaughter.[39]

When we move from Jerusalem to *Antioch*, we move from a Jewish city
centered on a temple to one in which temple sacrifice was not an issue. Antioch,
the capital city of Syria, was the third largest city in the Roman Empire,

surpassed only by Rome and Alexandria. It boasted a substantial Jewish community. Josephus reports that the Jews were granted equal privileges with the Greek citizens. It is not surprising to find an important early Christian community there, a community that included leading theologians whose ideas on Christ's sacrifice found important echoes in the New Testament. When Paul as a new convert came to Antioch some time in the 30s CE in order to meet with Christians, they instructed him about the meaning of the Lord's Supper which they celebrated. Into one of his letters, Paul inserted a tantalizingly brief passage in which he explains what he was told:

> The Lord Jesus on the night when he was betrayed took a loaf of bread, and when he had given thanks, he broke it and said, "This is my body that is given for you. Do this in remembrance of me." In the same way he took the cup also, after supper, saying, "This cup is the new covenant in my blood. Do this, as often as you drink it, in remembrance of me." For as often as you eat this bread and drink the cup, you proclaim the Lord's death until he comes. (1 Cor. 11:23–26)

Although echoing what we consider to be Jesus' own words ("This is my body; this is my blood"), the passage as a whole does not reflect the historical meal of Jesus. Instead, it reflects the way the Christians of Antioch celebrated the Lord's Supper and how they understood it. Although this understanding is expressed with a minimum of words, one can recognize its outline. The key idea is that two levels of ritual action must be distinguished: what Jesus did and what the celebrating community does. As for Jesus, he performed a ritual action with bread and wine in order to indicate that his own death would be a sacrifice. By virtue of the sacrificial blood shed in a violent death, a covenant with God is established, comparable to the covenant Moses once established over an animal sacrifice. The words transmitted by Paul clearly echo the Old Testament account of the Mosaic covenant, especially the words, "This is the blood of the covenant that the Lord makes with you" (Exod. 24:8). In other words: according to Antiochene theology, Jesus' death concluded a covenant between a community—the true believers—and God.[40]

Who devised the Antiochene Eucharist? Unfortunately, we do not know. Clearly, the Antiochene Eucharist and its theology were designed by a great theologian, no doubt a man of Jewish background and well versed in the Jewish scriptures; a man who certainly rivaled other early Christian thinkers and their scriptural knowledge, including Paul and the anonymous author of the epistle to the Hebrews.

While we cannot but admire the boldness and creativity of the Antiochene thinker's argument, we note (and regret) his failure to conserve the original meaning of Jesus' cultic act. Jesus had never thought of himself as a source of sacrificial blood, and now, this idea was not suggested just in a learned homily, but came to be the main notion of the central ritual act performed by the community. When the three gospels of Mark, Matthew, and Luke were compiled, their authors used an essentially Antiochene account of the Lord's Supper. However, their Eucharist reflects one further idea. They added one more level of meaning to the "blood" mentioned in the Antiochene text. They used theology derived from the Day of Atonement ritual. In addition to being the blood of the covenant, the blood was understood as the purifying blood of the sacrificial goat of atonement, and the eucharistic bread was viewed as the goat's meat which people ate. According to the developed post-Antiochene theology of the gospels, Jesus' death concluded a covenant between the community —the Christian believers—and God; at the same time, that death purified them from the stain of sin.[41]

When we move from Antioch in the east to *Lyons*, the metropolis of Gaul and one of the largest cities in the western Roman Empire, we find again a substantial Christian community led by important theologians. In the mid-second century, Lyons was the home of one of the most important early theologians, Bishop Irenaeus (ca. 140–200). For Irenaeus, the Eucharist was a non-animal sacrifice offered to God. He wrote extensively against Gnostic Christians who felt that the present world was intrinsically bad and presumably the work of an evil deity; for this reason, they argued, it is sinful to offer to the true, spiritual God "the fruits of ignorance, passion, and degeneracy," i.e., polluting material things. Irenaeus affirmed the goodness of creation and the appropriateness of sacrifice against this anti-sacrificial "heresy". In his infinite bounty, God gave humanity the blessings of nature. It is precisely in sacrifice that Christ demonstrated his solidarity with the Creator and that Christians acknowledge the goodness and purity of natural things and indeed the entire created world. Christ's sacrifice consisted in the offering of "bread, a part of creation," and "wine, likewise a part of that creation to which we belong." Bread and wine are to be considered the "first fruits" which one should offer to God in acknowledgment of the gifts that he gives us through nature. In offering bread and wine, Christ "has given directions to his disciples to offer to God the first fruits of his own created things." This sacrifice, moreover, he "taught to be offered throughout the world"—in Palestine as well as in Gaul. Christ gave the precept to make offerings; indeed, "it is also his will that we should offer a gift at the altar, frequently, and without interruption." Irenaeus carefully avoids any sense of special petitions connected with the offerings made at the altar; rather than being given to elicit a divine counter-gift, they simply thank God for the blessings already bestowed on humanity.[42]

Irenaeus does not tell us how exactly the Christian sacrifice was celebrated in Lyons. However, we are no doubt justified in assuming that the Christian ritual shared the generally complex nature of ancient ritual. Among the ancient Hebrews, for instance, an animal sacrifice was normally accompanied by an offering of bread or grain and by a libation of wine, and on solemn occasions, carefully arranged series of animal sacrifices were offered. From hints made by

Irenaeus the three stages of a complex Christian ritual can be reconstructed. The *first* stage was the people's offering of gifts of food. In Irenaeus' community, Christians respected the biblical precept, invoked by the bishop, "not to appear in the presence of the Lord your God empty-handed" (Deut. 16:16). In preparation for the service of worship, people "set apart all that they have for the Lord's purposes, giving joyfully and freely." Irenaeus wanted those who could afford it to give more than just one tenth of their income. When the people, laity and clergy alike, came to the assembly, they brought all they had saved, placing it on the common table that served as the altar. While Irenaeus does not specify what Christians brought to church, other early Christian sources imply that people supplied everything needed for a common meal— bread, wine, oil, water, fish, fruit, and so on. Either with an oblatory gesture or a prayer, or both, the bishop presented these gifts to God. The *second* phase of the complex ritual proceedings involved the bishop's celebration of Christ's offering of bread and wine. At this point, commemoration was made of Christ, who singled out just bread and wine as special gifts to be offered to God, and these were taken to symbolize Christ's body and blood. Interestingly enough, Irenaeus has much more to say about the goodness of creation, the people's own gifts, and their pure minds and fervent love, than of their bishop's celebration of Christ's sacrifice. Even without and apart from the special, "phase-two" offering of bread and wine in commemoration of the Lord's Supper, the gift of food was understood to be a complete sacrifice. Far from being the only sacrificial gift offered to God, bread and wine served as a model or paradigm for the other and more common "phase-one" offerings. During the *third* and concluding part of the service, bread and wine and other foods that had been offered were consumed in joyous table fellowship. According to common Christian practice, the left-overs were given to the poor and needy.[43]

Comparing the ancient ritual laws of the Jews and the new Christian practice, Irenaeus states that "oblations in general have not been done away with, for there were oblations then, and there are oblations now; there were sacrifices among the [Jewish] people, there are sacrifices also in the church." And this has never changed since.[44]

After Irenaeus, four trends developed: the first enhancing the idea and the practice of what we have termed the first stage of the sacrifice; the second restricting it to the priest's offering of bread and wine; the third abolishing the idea of an offering of natural gifts altogether, limiting the idea of sacrifice to the offering of consecrated bread and wine; and the fourth rejecting any idea of sacrifice. Those who felt that the offering of food should be developed gave it an *elaborate ritual structure* called "offertory." It began with the laity's bringing of their gifts, sometimes in solemn procession, during which one respected the ancient Greco-Roman custom of being silent during the offering of sacrifice. The officiants took the gifts, presented them to God with a gesture of elevation, and spoke prayers that avoided reference to the sacrifice instituted by Christ.

One reads: "Holy Father, almighty, everlasting God, accept this unblemished sacrificial offering, which I, thy unworthy servant, make to thee . . . for my countless sins . . . and on behalf of all who are present." In some churches the names of the donors were read out from a list, and, in imitation of both Old Testament and pagan ritual, incense was burned. However, a *more restrictive view* developed. While for Irenaeus and those who thought along similar lines, the Lord's own gifts of bread and wine were just one special, paradigmatic case of a more diverse range of cosmic offerings, the office holders of an increasingly institutionalized church came to devalue the people's gifts, robbing these of their sacrificial dignity. The laity may put money on the collection plate in all simplicity, whereas the clergy celebrate the Lord's own sacred ritual with much ceremony. Medieval scholastic doctors such as Thomas Aquinas and John Duns Scotus appreciated the laity's bringing of gifts, but they considered only the priest's formal offering of bread and wine a real sacrifice. In our century, Bernhard Durst (d. 1966), a German Benedictine abbot, took up the medieval idea and argued that the central part of Mass begins with the church-instituted sacrifice of bread and wine (which was then followed by a second sacrifice, that of Christ). While not many theologians hold this view today, the 1992 *Catechism of the Catholic Church* seems to allude to it. *A third, mostly modern group* of Catholic theologians, led by the Jesuit Francisco de Suárez (1548–1619), has come to look with suspicion at the offertory, arguing that only the Lord's Supper, with the words of consecration ("This is my body—This is my blood") should be considered a sacrifice, offered by the officiant on behalf of the community. There should be only one offering, not two. For them, the "offertory" counts as a preparation of the ritual, not as part of the sacred ceremony itself. For this reason they prefer to minimize all solemnity prior to the actual sacrificial phase of Mass. To complete the picture, mention must be made of a *fourth group*, for, beginning in the sixteenth century, Protestants have rejected everything that smacks of sacrifice as a blasphemy, designed to detract from the one, true sacrifice—Christ's death on the cross. Satan, they argued, "has blinded nearly the whole world with a most pestilential error—the belief that the Mass is a sacrifice and offering."[45]

By way of conclusion, we can state that the three communities of Jerusalem, Antioch, and Lyons continued the sacrificial ritual inaugurated by Jesus. Apparently, the theologians of Antioch focused exclusively on the ritual offering of bread and wine, which they saw as an act celebrated in memory of Christ's sacrificial death. The Christians of both Palestine and Gaul had a broader interest in sacrificing. In Jerusalem, many participated still in Temple rituals, and in Lyons, they brought all kinds of food offerings, including bread and wine, to the Lord's table at which the bishop offered the people's gifts to the Lord. All early Christians were involved in some kind of sacrifice.

3.   Sacrificial Receiving: The Career of an Idea

The giving of a gift usually entails the receiving of a gift. It establishes reciprocity and creates an atmosphere of mutual trust and friendship. Within that relationship, gifts and counter-gifts flow constantly.

Sacrifice, understood as the giving of a gift to God, initiates or maintains a reciprocal relationship between God and the church, or between God and the individual worshiper. Certain theologians, Cyprian and Augustine, for instance, emphasized the human side of that relationship. For them, the idea of Christ's offering of himself to God, and the believer's joining with Christ in this offering, formed the key to understanding the Eucharist. Respecting the Lord's dictum that "it is more blessed to give than to receive," they neglected the divine response to the sacrificial giving (Acts 20:35). However, theologians like Cyprian and Augustine represent only one current of thought. There were many for whom it appeared logical to think about sacrificial benefits. When we offer a gift to God, comments John Chrysostom, "then we even have God for our debtor." God must respond to our sacrificial action.[46]

The story of sacrificial receiving is as long as the history of thought about the Mass. Yet, this story may be told as one with a beginning, a middle, and an end. Bishop Eusebius can be credited with the invention of the new state sacrifice that secured divine blessing for the fourth-century Roman Empire. Around 600 CE, Gregory the Great invented or at least promoted what became the "sacrificial machine" of the Middle Ages. Finally, Gabriel Biel, author of a late medieval theological textbook, developed the theory of the fruits of sacrifice, a theory known to and rejected by Luther, but considered orthodox in the Catholic church well into the twentieth century.

Eusebius or the Invention of the New Imperial Sacrifice

With Constantine (312–37), the Roman Empire had its first Christian leader, and he not only put an end to persecution, but also legalized Christianity, donated churches, and sought the support of bishops. While he did not take any measures to abolish paganism, he began to rely on bishops like Eusebius of Caesarea for the creation of a ritual that would secure divine blessings for the state.

Eusebius' theology of sacrifice is revealed in his reports on the dedication of the newly built, magnificent churches in Tyre (ca. 313) and Jerusalem (335). Eusebius' dedication speech for Bishop Paulinus of Tyre calls the bishop the high priest, Mass a sacrifice, the table an altar, and the church building a temple. Now publicly acknowledged in the empire, the Christian priesthood and sacrifice replaced the ancient Jewish, Old Testament institutions. In imitation of the (no longer existing) Jerusalem Temple, the high priest, the clergy, and the faithful all had their assigned places in the new cathedral. By 313, the church had its priestly and sacrificial institution in place. Two decades later, when the emperor-sponsored Church of the Holy Sepulcher in Jerusalem was dedicated in September 335 (the month being chosen to coincide with the dedication of King Solomon's temple), Bishop Eusebius was also present. The bishop's report reveals further, quite radical ideas incorporated in Christian worship. Acting as priests, some of the bishops present "propitiated the Deity with unbloody sacrifices (*thysiai*) and secret rites, fervently praying to God for the general peace, for the church of God, for the emperor himself as the one who had sponsored [the building], and for his pious sons." While the eucharistic ritual remained inaccessible to the pagan public (hence Eusebius' insistence on the "secret rites"), it had become an eminently public affair, endowed with the splendor of the imperial cult which involved solemn processions, the use of lights, and incense. And, what is more, Christian worship had become the state cult. By 335, the Eucharist had not only replaced Jewish sacrifice; it also functioned as (and later came to replace) the official state sacrifice.[47]

Bishop Eusebius' interest in sacrificial benefits responded to the needs of a specific cultural and political situation. When in the early fourth century the Roman Empire made Christianity an officially recognized religion, and the emperors themselves became Christians, eucharistic rites came to be seen as the Christian substitute for pagan sacrificial ritual. Eusebius is remembered as the "court bishop" of the first Christian emperor, Constantine. Although residing in Caesarea in Palestine rather than in Rome, Eusebius nonetheless helped to forge the idea of a Christian empire. State and church would be two mutually supporting institutions. While the empire would protect the church, the church would supply spiritual benefits, secured by its regular eucharistic sacrifices. The Eucharist gained political importance. "The Church presents the unbloody, reasonable sacrifice to God," is one of Bishop Eusebius' standard ways of referring to the Eucharist. In order to understand the significance the Eucharist assumed in Constantine's empire, three facts have to be considered: the meaning of sacrificial worship in the Roman state ideology; the new imperial policy of suppressing and eventually prohibiting pagan sacrifice; and the state's recognition of the Mass as the official state sacrifice.[48]

Although the pagan empire of Rome did not have a clearly defined "state religion," it did have public sacrifices. On certain occasions, priests offered animals on public altars for the benefit of the empire. In his attempt to revive paganism in 361–63 CE, Emperor Julian "the Apostate" staged huge sacrifices in which such large numbers of oxen were slaughtered in restored temples that people thought livestock would become scarce. For Julian, the safety of the state depended on the sacrificial bull, as portrayed on his large bronze coins. While Julian seems to have exaggerated his duties toward the gods, public rituals of this kind were so "normal," so intrinsically bound up with Roman religion, that ancient authors rarely refer to the fact, let alone explain the theory guiding such a practice. However, when the Roman system came under the attack not only of radical Christians, but also under that of Christianized political authorities, pagan apologists became more vocal. One of them, the pagan orator Libanius, addressed the emperor Theodosius I in 386 CE. Asking for tolerance, he takes care to explain the benefits brought by the sacrifice. He says quite bluntly that the stability of the empire depends on sacrificial worship: "If the stability of the empire depends on the sacrifices performed there [in the city of Rome], we must consider that sacrifice is everywhere to our advantage. The gods in Rome grant greater blessings, those in the countryside and the other cities, lesser ones, but any sensible man would welcome even such as these. . . . One supports the might of Rome, another one protects for her a city under her sway, another protects an estate and grants it prosperity." Stability and prosperity depend everywhere on sacrificial worship! Therefore, suppression of pagan sacrifice creates a huge vacuum.[49]

Christians considered pagan sacrifices, whether public or private, idolatrous acts that should be abolished. For them, they counted as superstition and had never had any claim to legitimacy. According to Eusebius, Constantine initiated the policy that aimed at reducing and eventually prohibiting traditional pagan sacrifice. The Emperor, so Eusebius tells us, issued a decree which "provided that no one should erect images, or practice divination and other false and foolish arts, or offer sacrifice in any way." Unfortunately, we do not know whether the decree sought the abolition only of public pagan worship, or already included private rituals. Whatever the precise meaning of the emperor's anti-pagan legislation, it clearly favored Christian worship. However we may feel about the reliability or proper interpretation of the Eusebius passage, pagan sacrifice came to be restricted by 341, and by the end of the century, Emperor Theodosius I, presumably under the influence of Bishop Ambrose of Milan, had it suppressed. In 391–92 Emperor Theodosius completed anti-pagan legislation by issuing three edicts that banned all pagan sacrifices and ordered temples closed: "No person shall pollute himself with sacrificial animals; no person shall slaughter an innocent victim; no person . . . shall wander through the temples, or revere the images formed by mortal labor, lest he become guilty by divine and human laws." Pagan ritual continued to be tolerated locally, because the fines imposed were not prohibitive and the authorities shrank from strict enforcement; nevertheless, pagan worship had lost its legitimacy.[50]

As we have seen, Eusebius could speak quite naturally of the Eucharist as a sacrifice for the benefit of the empire. For him, the unbloody Christian sacrifice had superseded pagan sacrificial cults. Not only bishops thought along these lines, but also the representatives of the state. Emperor Constantine acknowledged the public role of Christian priests by exempting them from other public duties, "for when they render supreme service to the Deity, it seems that they confer incalculable benefit on the affairs of the state." By the early fifth century, during the time of Theodosius II (402–50) in the East and Valentinian III (425–55) in the West, state recognition of the new sacrifice had long since become a matter of fact. The two emperors state it quite unambiguously in a common edict of 438 CE geared toward prohibiting pagan ritual:

> We decree by an unshakable order that if any person of polluted and contaminated mind should be apprehended in making a sacrifice in any place whatsoever, Our wrath shall rise up against his fortunes, against his life. For We must give this better victim, and the altar of Christianity shall be kept inviolate. Shall we endure longer that the succession of the seasons be changed, and the temper of the heavens be stirred to anger, since the embittered perfidy of the pagans does not know how to preserve the balance of nature? For why has the spring renounced its accustomed charm? Why has the summer, barren of its harvest, deprived the laboring peasant of his hope of a grain harvest? Why has the intemperate ferocity of winter with its piercing cold doomed the fertility of the lands with the disaster of sterility? Why all these things, unless nature has transgressed the decree of its own law to avenge such impiety [of the Jews, Samaritans, pagans, and heretics]?

The decree issued in 438 CE sums up the new state cult: pagan sacrifice has been replaced by the offering of "the better victim," i.e., Christ, on Christian altars; pagan and heretic rituals can only provoke God's anger and upset the balance of nature supported and guaranteed by Christian rituals. Although some pagans still continued their idolatrous practice, Bishop Augustine could say of the Eucharist: "To this supreme and true sacrifice all false sacrifices have given place."[51]

In the era of Constantine, the concept of the Christian liturgy as a sacrifice of propitiation for both church and empire gained acceptance. We are fortunate to know how Cyril, one of the first bishops to teach in the Church of the Holy Sepulcher, spoke about the Eucharist to those receiving their elementary instruction in preparation for their first communion.

> Then, after the spiritual sacrifice and bloodless service is completed [by invoking God to send his Holy Spirit on the bread and wine], over that sacrifice of propitiation [*thysia tou hilasmou*] we entreat God for the common peace of the churches, for the welfare of the world, for kings, for soldiers and allies, for the sick, for the afflicted, and in a word for all who stand in need of succor we pray

and offer this sacrifice. Then we commemorate also those who have fallen asleep . . . believing that this will be of the greatest benefit to the souls of those on whose behalf our supplication is offered in the presence of the holy, the most dread sacrifice. . . . We sacrifice the Christ who was slain for our sins, thus propitiating the merciful God on behalf of those who are gone before and on our own behalf.[52]

Bishop Cyril of Jerusalem offered this explanation at the very end of his instruction, given in preparation for the novitiates' participation in the sacrifice. Although converts still underwent a lengthy course of instruction before baptism and admittance to eucharistic worship, that worship had lost its flavor of secrecy and its exclusive, "inner-circle" character. The Christian sacrifice had become a publicly recognized means of propitiating the deity and began to supersede the pagan sacrifices offered for the benefit of the empire. With its regular and prominent reference to the departed, it also became a substitute for ancestor worship. As in much of ancient tradition, the dead were thought of as weak and in need of support and nursing—just like the elderly; the cult of the dead prolonged the care for older generations beyond physical death. The Christian sacrifice, like pagan ancestor worship, could supply whatever the dead members of a family needed. Relevant to both the private and the public sphere, the Eucharist served as a truly universal ritual.[53]

Interestingly, both Eusebius and Cyril refer to the expiatory character of the Christian sacrifice. Cyril's words imply that our sins must be atoned for. In the case of the departed, for whom prayers are offered during the ritual, God is expected to mitigate their sentence, and the same is of course also hoped for the living. For Cyril, the eucharistic sacrifice "activates" the atoning sacrifice of Christ's death on the cross.[54]

One of Cyril's contemporaries, John Chrysostom, gives even more prominence to propitiation. He also expresses himself with greater precision. When Cyril wrote of "propitiating the merciful God," he concealed the fact that God, before being merciful, was actually angry. To propitiate means to appease someone's anger and thus to render him merciful. In ancient thought, both biblical and nonbiblical, human sacrifice serves as the most powerful means to avert divine wrath. According to John Chrysostom, God "was wroth against us, and displeased [with us] as being estranged [from him]." The death of Christ "has stopped divine wrath." Now every eucharistic celebration renews the sacrifice of Christ and, having no less efficacy than the original sacrificial act, stops divine wrath. Every Eucharist, therefore, serves to propitiate God and to restore the original peace between the human and the divine, the peace created by Christ.[55]

Here we get a glimpse not only of Cyril's and John Chrysostom's personal beliefs, but also of the importance of sacrifice in the ancient world as a whole. The wrath of the gods plays a very important role in ancient Greek and Roman history, religion, literature, and philosophy. While philosophers often insisted on the gods' freedom from the uncontrolled feelings characteristic of people and went as far as denying them any passion, most of the ancients thought otherwise. Storm and pestilence, deformity and sickness, drought and famine, as well as military defeat and political evils such as civil war and mutiny, were all plain evidences of divine wrath. God or the gods could be angry because of whatever sins the people, knowingly or unknowingly, have committed. Moreover, divine ire may result not from some transgression of the moral code, but from a lack of attention to a god's cult. Or gods could be capricious, or their majesty could be seen as awful, exploding into anger and blind rage, and at any rate as inspiring fear. Hence, the deity has to be appeased so that disaster will be averted. When the Goths had entered and vandalized Rome in 410 CE, the non-Christian population blamed the Christians. "As long as we could offer sacrifices to our gods," they claimed, "Rome stood upright, Rome flourished." To them, Christian sacrifice seemed powerless; it could not avert divine anger. "Any account of ancient pagan worship which minimizes the gods' uncertain anger and mortals' fear of it," explains Robin Lane Fox, "is an empty account. This fear did not preclude thanksgiving, but thanks, in Greek prayer, were interwoven with ideas of propitiation. These ideas centered on the offering of gifts." In fact, the "worship of angry divinities" by way of sacrifice can be identified as "the dominant piety" of late antiquity. Part of the appeal of the Christian eucharistic sacrifice in late antiquity was based upon its propitiatory power.[56]

One might offer God a gift in order to propitiate him because he was angry or hostile; or to please him so that one could persuade him to act—a very different kind of propitiation, not to be confused with the payment to avert wrath. Whichever conception predominated in the mind of the ancient worshiper, the intended aim was identical: to make the deity "propitious," that is favorably disposed and graciously inclined. When Celsus, an enemy of the Christians, summarized the religious duties the ancients felt they had, he simply stated that "we must believe in [the gods], sacrifice to them according to the [traditional] laws, and pray to them that they may be propitious." Christian worshipers, not unlike their pagan neighbors, approached God with a gift in hand—the unbloody sacrifice—and then asked him to bestow his favors on all humankind.[57]

Sacrifice, for the ancients, involves the violent extinction of a victim's life. "An awful thing is death, and very full of terror," comments John Chrysostom, and this is especially true of the sacrificial death of Christ. Echoing Christ's sacrifice, the Eucharist also shares that event's quality. The Eucharist's awful nature, however, does not rest on the experience of death alone. Even more numinous is the meeting between mortals and the angry, majestic God. For both Cyril and John Chrysostom, the Christian celebration assumes a sacred, numinous quality. "That most awful hour," says Cyril of the liturgy, and

Chrysostom speaks of "that fearsome, awful sacrifice." The laity must "attend with piety our awful mysteries" that are celebrated in the presence of a non-rational numinous power to which we can only relate with fear and trembling.[58]

In the ancient world, pagan state religion served to propitiate the gods and procure divine blessings that ensured public welfare. Priests and temples procured that blessing through sacrificial worship. With the decline of paganism, the sacrificial task fell to the church. A religion without an institutionalized sacrifice would no doubt have seemed unequal to the church's new task of supplying imperial rituals destined to "propitiate the deity." What had begun in New Testament Christianity as a substitute for sacrifice had become, by the age of Eusebius, Cyril, and John Chrysostom, a new sacrificial institution.

Gregory the Great, or The Invention of the Sacrificial Machine

The eucharistic sacrifice, as understood by the fourth-century bishops, secures benefits on behalf of the entire church and the Roman Empire. By the early fifth century, in addition to being the state sacrifice, Mass had also taken on the meaning of private sacrifice, offered for the benefit of individuals. Augustine hints at the fact that people go up to the altar with a gift, wishing to appease God because of their sins (*placare Deo pro peccatis*). At Mass, the celebrating priest announced the names of those who had brought their offerings:

> Remember, Lord, your servants, men and women [whose names are here inserted] and all here present. Their faith and devotion are known to you. They offer you this sacrifice of praise: for themselves and for all who are theirs, for the cleansing of their souls, for the hope of safety and well-being. They bring their gifts to you, the eternal, living, and true God.

While to us the language of this terse prayer seems almost impenetrable, it was quite clear to the ancients. "To bring a sacrificial gift for safety and well-being" (*reddere vota pro salute et incolumitate*) was the normal Latin way of referring to private sacrifice and the benefits expected from such offerings. Here the church's liturgy had simply adopted the traditional terminology of pagan religion. Pagan sacrifice did not exist any more, and so the church felt free to use its language. And, what is more, it felt free to offer to Christians all the blessings pagan individuals had secured from their sacrifices. The Mass became the supreme occasion for everyone to bring gifts to God and ask him for favors. In Christian worship, the pragmatic spirit of the ancients entered and prevailed. What this new development meant can be seen in the work of Gregory the Great.[59]

Gregory, elected bishop of Rome in 590, administered an Italian church troubled by political instability, military invasions, and economic stress. In 568, the Lombards, a fierce tribe, had crossed the Alps, disrupting political and

ecclesiastical life. Some forty bishoprics disappeared. Gregory assumed many
responsibilities in the secular realm: maintaining supplies of food and water,
paying soldiers, negotiating treaties, administering estates and charitable
funds. The political unrest and especially the invasion of the Lombards created
a tense climate of fear; people believed they were living in the apocalyptic days
of the final tribulation which would be followed by the end of human history.
The Lombards seemed to be the instruments of divine wrath and punishment.
In this distressing atmosphere, the church multiplied its ritual efforts. Mass
was changed from a weekly liturgy (in which people handed their lives to God
in an act of sacrificial offering) to a daily ritual of expiation in which one atoned
for sins and propitiated the angry deity. In one of his homilies, Gregory likened
the priests saying Mass to ambassadors sent out to meet an approaching army
to negotiate peace with a mighty king. However, Gregory's priests are not
negotiating peace for the entire church. Since peace is negotiated on the basis
of the sacrificial gifts brought by individuals, i.e., tears of repentance and works
of mercy, the benefit concerns individual Christians.[60]

Gregory's entire spiritual writing, especially his *Moral Commentary on the
Book of Job* and his *Pastoral Rule*, focuses on the individual believer. Although
Gregory's Italian audience is Christian, he sees them as being in need of true
conversion, spiritual growth, and a life informed by the metaphor of sacrifice,
that is by abnegation and the surrender of the self to God. The end of human
history was believed to be imminent, and the closeness of the Last Judgment
gave particular urgency to each individual's spiritual struggle and responsibility. The believer's spiritual struggle is complex and involves recurring
alternation between progress and regress. Therefore constant divine assistance
is needed and can indeed be procured through daily Mass. In other words:
Mass, as a means of procuring divine favor, prepares for the imminent Last
Judgment. Those who possess the divine gift procured at Mass will certainly
escape God's wrath.[61]

God was therefore expected to respond to the eucharistic sacrifice not just
globally, but also and especially individually. On account of the Eucharist,
Cyril had explained, God would help "all who stand in need of succor." While
Cyril spoke of those needing divine help in the plural, Gregory often uses the
singular. For him, the priest can actually celebrate his ritual on behalf of an
individual. When Christ is "again immolated for us in this mystery of the holy
oblation," then this sacrifice often produces an immediate effect, benefiting
an individual.[62]

Reading Gregory's *Dialogues*, a collection of edifying stories about Italian
saints, his contemporaries enter a world in which miracles can be produced at
will—by priests saying Mass. Gregory reports the story of a wife who had
Masses read for her husband who had been imprisoned by enemies. When the
priest celebrated Mass on his behalf, the prisoner was miraculously freed from
his fetters. In another account, Bishop Agatho of Palermo said Mass for a

shipwrecked person. Through a miracle, the unfortunate man received some bread which restored his physical strength to the extent that he was able to swim and eventually find a safe shore.[63]

Gregory did not originate the concept of the Eucharist as a sacrifice that produces immediate and tangible effects. One and a half centuries earlier, Augustine had spoken of the Eucharist in a similar fashion. In the *City of God*, he included a story about a Christian man whose family, cattle, and servants "suffered from the malice of evil spirits." When a priest came to their home and "offered there the sacrifice of the body of Christ, praying with all his might that the vexation might cease," the demons left. Augustine's story shares the spirit of Gregory's miracles and could indeed find a place in the *Dialogues*. But we must not overlook the differences. In the *City of God*, the story is isolated. In Gregory's *Dialogues*, by contrast, the effects of the eucharistic sacrifice abound and impress by their number and exaggerated miraculous quality. Gregory's readers are almost led to expect miracles produced by priests.[64]

In a context in which the end of history was imminent, and therefore each individual must be prepared to go before the throne of the divine judge, accounts of miracles had a reassuring force. They demonstrated the power of the divine gift received at Mass. The visibility of these miracles enhanced the credibility of the claim that Mass could produce the ultimate miracle: sparing the individual from divine wrath and thus secure eternal life after death. Here, too, Augustine provided the authoritative statement. "The souls of the dead benefit from the piety of their living friends, who offer the sacrifice of the Mediator," i.e., the sacrifice of Mass. But what in the work of Augustine remains an isolated statement was elaborated by the generation of Gregory and illustrated with edifying stories.[65]

A particularly interesting story is set in the monastery in which Gregory himself served as the abbot. A monk named Justus receives and keeps for himself three gold pieces. When he hides the money, he commits a grievous fault against his vow of poverty. Upon being discovered, Justus is excommunicated. The penalty makes him reflect, and some time later he dies in true repentance. Nevertheless, Gregory, in order to inspire the monk's brethren with a lively horror of the sin of avarice, does not withdraw the sentence of excommunication. So Justus has to be buried apart from the other monks, and the three pieces of money are thrown into his grave, while his fellow monks repeat the words of St. Peter to Simon the Magician, "May your money perish with you!" (Acts 8:20). Some time afterwards, Gregory reconsiders. Judging that the scandal was sufficiently repaired, and moved with compassion for the soul of Justus, he calls the prior and declares sorrowfully, "Long enough has our brother been tortured in the flames; we must through charity make an effort to deliver him. Go, then, and take care that from today the sacrifice be offered for him for thirty days. Let not one morning pass without the Victim of Salvation being offered up so that he will be forgiven." The prior obeys

18. Out of Purgatory. According to Catholic doctrine, the celebration of Mass is one of the means of helping souls leave the place where they are purged before their admission to heaven. The "poor souls" leave purgatory in return for the priest's sacrifice of the Mass and the payment of alms that were regularly given to the poor right after Mass. This fifteenth-century Yorkshire drawing depicts the priest and the alms-giver as those who lift the souls out of purgatory with the help of a huge wooden tub and tackle, fixed in heaven. English manuscript illumination, fifteenth-century.

diligently. The thirty Masses are celebrated in the course of thirty days. When the thirtieth day arrives and the thirtieth Mass is ended, the deceased appears to a brother saying, "Until now, I suffered badly; but now I am well, for today I have received communion." The Masses said on the deceased monk's behalf have freed him from the place of torment.[66]

The story demonstrates much more than the intense, vision-producing religious atmosphere of the sixth-century Italian monastery. It shows that the divine gift received at Mass worked for the dead just as it worked for the living. Priests could make the divine gift available to the dead and thereby free them from whatever divine punishment they had to endure for their sins (ill. 18). In Gregory's words: "This sacrifice in particular saves the soul from eternal damnation." But, of course, this requires not one sacrifice, one Mass, but multiple sacrifices, in this case thirty Masses.[67]

The *Dialogues* became one of the favorite books of the Middle Ages. The prestige of the *Dialogues*' author—a bishop of Rome—contributed to their fame and influence. Both priests and lay people understood their message quite well. God responds to the eucharistic sacrifice by bestowing special gifts upon the person for whom the sacrifice is offered. This view of the tremendous power of the Mass shaped medieval eucharistic practice in four ways: it motivated bishops to compile Mass books with prayers for special purposes, lay people to pay priests for having a Mass said on their behalf, priests to say more than one Mass each day, and architects to furnish churches with an increasing number of altars.

Soon after Gregory, bishops began to compile Mass books with special prayers. A priest would recite these to procure certain divine favors for the living and the dead. By the seventh century, ritual books like the "old Gelasian" sacramentary of Rome included 59 formularies for Masses said for special purposes. In eighth-century Gaul, sacramentaries included 96 Masses, and by the early tenth century, the number of Masses found in Carolingian manuscripts had climbed to 278. Among these were: 62 Masses for the benefit of certain individuals: the pope, bishops and their flocks, kings, priests, monks, and nuns; 53 Masses which request particular favors—charity and peace in a community, patience and humility, help for friends, benefactors, physically or mentally suffering persons; 29 Masses for help in private matters—forgiveness of sins, for the deliverance from sickness or infertility, for the protection of sailors; 56 Masses for the dead—bishops, abbots, priests, monks, including Masses said on the anniversary of a death and ones for the dead in general. Priests and lay people alike believed in the enhanced efficacy of Masses designed for special purposes. A votive Mass with special prayers for the dead, for instance, was thought to be more powerful than the ordinary Mass commemorating the martyrdom of a saint; in the Middle Ages, Thomas Aquinas explicitly endorsed this view. Asked by a lay person to celebrate the Eucharist on his or her behalf, the priest could choose a ritual that was fitting for the exact occasion or purpose.[68]

While bishops and priests endeavored to have the proper formula for celebrating the sacrifice on someone's behalf, the pious laity strove to have these "votive Masses" (as they came to be called) performed for them. Individuals and groups began not only to ask a priest, but to pay him for saying Mass on their behalf. *Missam comparare*, "to buy a Mass," belongs among the standard expressions found in medieval texts. In the late Middle Ages, Mass said for a specific purpose generally involved three kinds of expenditure: the celebrating priest had to be given a honorarium, several candles (up to twelve) had to be brought and lit during the celebration, and, after Mass, alms (generally given in kind) had to be distributed to the poor, sometimes in fixed amounts. Some priests actually lived from the honorarium they received. They would rarely, if ever, say Mass for a congregation assembled in church. Accompanied by just one person—normally a layman, called a "server"—he would use one of the numerous side altars or side chapels of a church to say "private Mass." By celebrating "privately," he would secure spiritual or even tangible benefits for whomever hired him: a wealthy merchant, a guild of artisans, or someone who bequeathed funds so that Masses could be said for the rest of his or her soul.[69]

Specially designed votive Masses and lay payment for their performance were only part of the huge "sacrificial factory" developing between the seventh and the tenth century. Monasteries had many priests to work in this factory. While at the time of Gregory monasteries had only a few priests, their number began to increase steadily. Around 800 CE, under Abbot Angilbert, the Centula monastery near Amiens, France, had only twenty-two priests among its three hundred monks. By the tenth century, about 55 per cent of the monks were priests—a huge Mass-celebrating force, prepared to meet all the requests of a devout laity. A book of rules dating from the late ninth century states that a priest should say no more than seven Masses a day. However, if he is asked to say Masses on feast days, "he may say as many as are requested, even if the number exceeds twenty."[70]

Churches built or remodeled in late antiquity and the Middle Ages usually included more than just one altar for the celebration of Mass. In fact, between the fifth and the ninth century, altars proliferated. Before this period, a church normally had just one altar, in keeping with the one heavenly altar seen by the visionary in the book of Revelation. However, multiple altars became increasingly fashionable for both symbolic and practical reasons. Symbolically, they represented the presence of the saints, for they were furnished with relics. Relics—remains of the bodies of saints, usually martyrs—were believed to enhance the sacred quality of the altar and distinguished it from a normal table. A church with numerous altars came to symbolize the community of the saints. At the practical level, multiple altars facilitated the celebration of multiple Masses. The number of Masses that were said correlated to the number of altars available, for a general rule allowed only one Mass (or perhaps two) to be said at a particular altar on any given day. "It is illegal to say two Masses at one altar each day" (*non licet super uno altario in una die duas missas dicere*), insisted a synod at Auxerre, France, in 578. But by the tenth century, the celebration of three Masses was granted. Naturally, the solution was to build as many altars as possible. Some time in the late sixth century, Bishop Palladius of Saintes, France, had thirteen altars built in one church; as he did not have enough relics to furnish them properly himself, Pope Gregory the Great supplied the missing pieces (596 CE). Around 800 CE, the convent of Saint-Vaast near Arras, France, had thirty-six altars, while the church of the Holy Savior in Le Mans, France, boasted only twenty-eight. In the Benedictine abbey of Centula, near Amiens, the altars found in its various churches and chapels added up to thirty. On the famous Carolingian plan of the St. Gallen monastery, there are nineteen altars (ill. 19). Some theologians frowned on the multiplying altars and in 804 persuaded the Emperor Charlemagne to legislate against the abuse: "there must not be an excessive number [of altars] in the churches" (*ut non sint superflua in ecclesiis*). But apparently, to no avail: the number of altars kept multiplying.[71]

Unrestrained altar-building and the saying of excessively large numbers of Masses each day by individual priests combine to evoke the image of churches resounding all day with the hum of Mass being recited without interruption. When one priest had finished, the next would be ready to do the same job. "We are led to believe," explains Cyril Vogel, "that the monk-priest, when not reciting the Office or working, spent all his time repeating Mass indefinitely."[72]

The Sacrifice of the Mass in Medieval Practice and Theology

Medieval priests, when saying Mass at the numerous altars erected in monasteries, chapels, and cathedrals, took a great interest in receiving a counter-gift from God. When they offered Christ as a sacrifice to the heavenly Father, would not God respond by giving something in return? They had inherited the idea of sacrificial receiving from patristic authorities like Gregory the Great, whose prestige as the Roman pontiff placed it beyond doubt. Far from belonging only to theological speculation, the idea had practical implications. For the priests, the sacrifice of Mass served as an opportunity to secure divine benefits and to pass these benefits on to the laity, often in return for payment. The idea of gift and counter-gift operated not only between God and priest— the priest offers Mass and receives grace, but also between clergy and laity— the clergy secure spiritual benefits and receive material goods. How did this system work in practice?

19. The Many Altars of a Medieval Church. According to medieval canon law, only one Mass a day was to be said at any particular altar. In order to enable all priests to say Mass each day, churches were filled with numerous altars. This plan shows the location of seventeen altars, each marked with a cross, in a Swiss ninth-century monastery church. There were two more altars in the round towers (left). Benedictine monastery of St. Gallen, Switzerland, ca. 820.

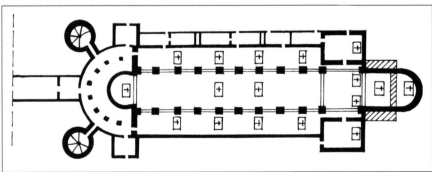

Since the early Middle Ages a system of benefices had been in force. Churches acquired income-producing property to support the clergy who served in them. While in theory every spiritual office was to be supported by an income-producing unit called a prebend or a benefice, in practice the number of prebends were too few to match the clergy. In certain cases, the prebend would not be an income-producing piece of land, but a foundation which required the cleric to say Mass for the benefit of a guild, a pious association or, most often, for the soul of a deceased person who had established a regular Mass or even a chaplaincy. Suffering from a shortage of income from too small a prebend, priests appreciated being approached by someone expressing the wish to establish a Mass: "I will give you such-and-such a field, a house, or a tithe, and ask you to persolve [say] an anniversary [Mass] for me and my friends in such a fashion." Such requests reflected the common opinion, shared by priests and laity alike, that a single Mass was of little help to a sinner's soul. In order to be sure that God would indeed release someone's soul, transferring it from purgatory to heaven, a large number of Masses was needed—thirty (as Gregory's *Dialogues* have it) or one hundred or an even higher number, for instance an annual or daily Mass celebrated in perpetuity, until the Last Judgment. The higher the number of Masses, the shorter would be the time one had to suffer in purgatory before being admitted to heaven. As a result, the laity deluged their priests with requests to say Mass for them. The numbers of Masses established by testament were sometimes so high that the clergy felt unable to persolve all of them—and so some people felt they should increase payment to have their Masses actually said for them. (It was not until 1575 that a generous pope established the possibility of having a soul liberated out of purgatory through just one Mass celebrated at a specially privileged altar. Such a measure was bound to upset the medieval priestly economy.)[73]

There were not enough benefices to support the numerous clergy. The shortage was aggravated by the presence of "unbeneficed" clergy, i.e., by priests who had no regular income at all. This clerical proletariat often outnumbered the regular clergy, especially in the cities. In 1377, for instance, the English city of Lincoln had 189 unbeneficed clerics who lived chiefly from honorariums they received for saying Masses at the request of lay sponsors. These sponsors did not have the means to endow perpetual chantries and chaplaincies, i.e., establish pious foundations that would provide regular, long-term income for a priest who was given a house to live in and who had no other obligation than saying Mass; instead, they would prefer to pay a priest a small sum for saying just one or a few Masses according to their intention. Thus two financial systems existed at the same time: (1) an "aristocratic," traditional, and more stable financial system based on benefices and pious endowments, and (2) a more recent, "democratic," flexible, market-oriented system based on affordable rates paid by lay sponsors to unbeneficed clergy for their services. These affordable rates made the unbeneficed clergy very popular with a middle class hungry for the spiritual benefits produced by having Masses said for them. While both systems depended on saying private Masses—endowed Masses in the "aristocratic" system, individual Masses in the "proletarian" one—it was chiefly the latter system that promoted the saying of multiple Masses by one priest.[74]

In the early Middle Ages, the number of Masses a priest said each day was left to his discretion, and those who wanted to say many Masses could invoke the example of Pope Leo III (795–816), who celebrated up to nine per day. Later, popes like Alexander II (1061–73) and canon lawyers changed their mind. They wished to prevent excesses. One Mass was considered normal (the Mass of the day that commemorates a saint or some event in the life of Christ), and another one (a votive Mass) could be conceded, grudgingly:

> It is enough for a priest to celebrate one Mass per day, for Christ suffered only once, and thereby redeemed the whole world. To say one Mass is not a small matter, and blessed is he who can celebrate this one Mass with dignity. One may say one Mass for the dead, and the [regular] Mass of the day in addition, if there is need. However, those who presume the right to say several Masses a day for the sake of making money or as a courtesy to lay people, those I think, will not evade [eternal] damnation.

Not only canon lawyers, normally priests with sufficient income, were horrified at the thought that a priest or a monk would say ten or more Masses a day in order to earn his living. In the sixteenth century, Martin Luther deplored that the Mass "has been turned into mere merchandise, a market, and a profit-making business. Hence . . . intercessions, merits, anniversaries, memorial days and the like wares are bought and sold, traded and bartered in the Church. On these the priests and monks depend for their entire livelihood." The archbishop of Canterbury, Thomas Cranmer (1489–1556), joined the disaffected Augustinian friar in his assessment that the endless number of private Masses sprang up because of "lucre and gain." Here the reformers had much to deplore, to criticize, and to abolish. Among the Catholic leaders, Ignatius of Loyola had the wisdom not to allow paid Masses to form a source of income for Jesuits.[75]

Certainly greed or, perhaps more often, poverty made priests sell the "fruit" of Mass. But an equally strong, if not stronger, motivation was the wish of the laity to acquire the merit of a Mass and have their name pronounced (though in a low voice) at Mass, before the consecration if they were living, or after the consecration if they were dead. Having their names so closely attached to the most sacred action conceivable hypnotized the faithful of the Middle Ages. There were also the fascinating stories, found in prestigious books and told by their preachers: accounts of the miraculous effects of Masses said for a person, living or dead.[76]

The medieval churches can be seen as huge sacrificial factories in which laborers—the priests—worked to secure spiritual benefits for themselves and for the laity. In late antiquity and throughout most of the Middle Ages, theologians felt little need to develop theories supporting the system of honorariums given to priests in exchange for spiritual benefits derived from Masses. Theories explaining how exactly the sacrificial mechanism worked were also rare. Mass renewed or repeated the sacrifice of Christ; and since Christ's original sacrifice had an effect, why should not its repetition also have an effect? Rather than being explored in detail, the efficacy of the sacrifice of Mass was simply taken for granted. Nevertheless, some authors such as John Duns Scotus (ca. 1265–1308) in Paris and Gabriel Biel (ca. 1418–95) in Tübingen, Germany, did offer their reflections, and from their work we can reconstruct the theoretical foundation on which the sacrificial system rested. That foundation consisted of three doctrines: there is a divine treasure of grace to which the clergy give access; one of the main forms of access is by way of the sacrifice of the Mass; the clergy can rightfully claim payment in return for their spiritual work.

According to medieval theology, Christ's life of obedience and humility, and especially his death on the cross, established a *meritum infinitum*, an inexhaustible treasure or stock of merit. In order to make his treasures available to, and his merits affect, the faithful, Christ instituted a priesthood by endowing some of his disciples (and their successors, the Christian priests) with special powers. These powers enable the priests to give divine grace and favor to all Christians. In baptism, the priest cleanses the new-born or newly converted of the stains of estrangement from God. In the sacrament of penance, for example, the priest bestows divine forgiveness on the repentant person confessing sins. The priest's most noble power and privilege consists in the celebration of Mass. Here he draws from the boundless resources of Christ's merits, applying them to the entire church, to the living as well as to the dead. While God can bestow his grace apart from the clergy's mediation, priestly mediation is the most common and most certain way of securing divine favor and help.[77]

At Mass, the priest makes the grace of God available in two ways, termed sacrament and sacrifice. Using his power of consecration, he presents the risen, heavenly Christ under the veil of bread and wine. When the faithful partake of the bread (the wine being reserved for the priest), their soul is nourished with divine grace. This *sacramental* reception of divine favor is supplemented by the *sacrificial* mediation of divine benefits. Like the sacrament, the sacrificial mediation also rests upon the real presence of Christ under the guise of bread and wine, now thought of as the presence of Christ's earthly body which is offered up to the Father. The sacrificial presence of Christ is related not to the glorious, heavenly Christ, but to Christ's humility, to his suffering and death on the cross. By reminding God of Christ's unique sacrifice, the priest secures much divine grace, which he passes on to the faithful. In the words of Gabriel

Biel: "Whatsoever Christ our Savior merited when he offered himself on the cross for all [human beings]: liberation from evil and bestowal of good for the wayfarers, those in purgatory, and the blessed, through this sacrifice [of the Mass] it is applied to each in particular."[78]

Medieval theologians prized communion highly and recommended it to the faithful. The sacramental reception of divine grace is regarded as the best, most noble, and most intimate way to relate to God. At most Masses, however, only the priest would take communion, for the faithful felt unworthy to approach the altar and to receive Christ's body from the priest's hand. The sacrificial way, though more general, less intimate, and somewhat less effective, was thought to require less "purity." Thus, sacrifice came to be understood as the normal way of getting in touch with the divine.

Whereas the total amount of grace acquired by Christ forms an infinite, inexhaustible treasure, the benefit God grants in return for the sacrifice is a small, finite entity. Mass is only a representation or image of the original, powerful sacrifice, and pales in comparison with its larger, divine model. Just as Cicero's statue represents the Roman statesman without being identical to him, so Mass commemorates Christ's death without being the same event. To this principal and metaphysical limitation of the value of Mass, Biel adds a second determining factor. The amount of grace God returns in answer to the sacrifice also depends upon the church's degree of worthiness at the moment of the offering. The worthier the church is, the larger the quantity of grace that is bestowed.[79]

Does the acquisition of grace depend also on the worthiness of the celebrating priest? According to medieval theology, a sinful priest, if rightfully appointed by the authorities, neither spoils the sacrifice nor reduces the quantity of grace acquired. At Mass, the priest acts not in his own name but in the name of Christ who remains the "invisible and principal priest." Christ's offering cannot be rejected by the Father to whom it is offered. Consequently, theologians say that the sacrifice of Mass works *ex opere operato*, on the basis of the act itself, rather than *ex opere operantis*, by virtue of the individual priest who happens to say Mass.[80]

Whatever the quantity of grace acquired through Mass may be, it must be passed on to others. Although medieval theologians did not define the quantity of grace, they developed precise notions about the relationship between that grace and its recipients. John Duns Scotus, the first to develop this relationship systematically, followed tradition in speaking of three different "fruits" (*fructus*) that were acquired through each celebration of the holy sacrifice and that were acquired by three recipients. The first fruit was acquired for the benefit of the entire church, the second fell to the celebrating priest, and the third was given either to the parishioners in general or to those whom the priest has the authority to name. Mass, then, benefits first of all the entire Christian church, but especially those of the faithful who happen to be present at the celebration. Their spiritual state and devotion determine how the divine grace meant for them can enter and influence their lives. Gabriel Biel identified the expiation of sins as the most common effect the first fruit of Mass has on those who attend. The recipient of the second fruit is the celebrating priest himself. If he is worthy, free from unrepented sins, and in a state of grace, God will bestow this most special fruit on him. Although the Mass is valid and effective even when celebrated by an unworthy priest, the unworthy celebrant at least would forego the acquisition of grace.[81]

It is from the third fruit (also called the "special fruit") that votive Masses draw their power and efficacy to help individuals or communities. In his *Exposition of the Canon of the Mass*, Biel discusses the allocation of the third fruit from the perspective of the priest. The following questions dominate his exposition: (1) To whom can the special fruit of Mass be given? (2) Can it be given to more than one person? (3) Is it legitimate for a priest to receive a honorarium for applying the special fruit to someone?

Biel answers as follows:

(1) Normally, the parish priest is obliged to give the special fruit of the daily Mass to the parishioners in general. But if the celebrating priest is free from this obligation, he can dispose of it freely. The special fruit can be given to any Christian who has not been excommunicated and who is not a heretic. Biel singles out some cases for special comment. The "fruit" can be applied to a sinner—for his or her betterment. It can also be applied to someone who is dead; in which case that soul's stay in purgatory will be shortened. Biel inserts at this point a story—one of many of its kind—in which a pope, after having said five Masses for a deceased relative, has a vision of Mary drawing the relative's soul out of purgatory. (Sometimes we hear Biel the popular preacher, not Biel the professor.) When a priest says Mass for someone who has died, this person may also be a saint residing in heaven. In this case, the saint's "joy" grows. Biel qualifies this statement by defining the new joy as one secondary to the joy experienced through the vision of God. Yet, the new joy is real.[82]

(2) The special fruit acquired at Mass must be thought of as a finite, limited good, even though we cannot measure it. Consequently, the fruit can be cut up into pieces and given to any number of people. These portions can also be arranged in a hierarchical order. Thus, a priest can have three intentions in the same Mass, establishing, for example, three degrees. He could apply the fruit in the first degree to his father, in the second to the founder of his church, and in the third to a good friend. In this way three persons would share, albeit in different degrees, the special fruit.[83]

While Biel accepts the partitioning of the fruit as a common practice, he knows its problems. A Mass said for just one person is, of course, more effective than a Mass said for several people. Therefore, it amounts to spiritual fraud to say a Mass with several intentions where a Mass with the application of the entire special fruit was promised or legitimately expected.[84]

(3) Since Masses were a source of income, priests might try to say more than one a day out of greed—if not out of poverty. Here the question was one of legitimacy. Because the fruit of the Mass-sacrifice was something spiritual, a gift bestowed by God out of the merits of Christ, it could not be sold. Theologians insisted on the impossibility of selling spiritual goods. They quoted the Acts of the Apostles where a certain Simon is chided for his attempt to buy from St. Peter the power to confer the Holy Spirit by the laying-on of hands. "May your silver perish with you, because you thought you could obtain God's gift with money!" (Acts 8:20). Money cannot buy what God has given for nothing. "Simony" was used as a term denouncing such transactions as trafficking in sacred matters. Biel knows well what many say: "This [priest] celebrates Mass because of money, or else he would not celebrate. Therefore he is a simoniac priest." Nevertheless, Biel defends the practice of payment. According to him, a gift given to a priest for saying Mass establishes a binding contract. "It is legitimate and reasonable," writes Biel, "that someone who gives alms should ask for a prayer [in return]." As long as a priest performs Masses for individuals correctly, Biel approves of the honorarium. He knows well that "without temporal goods, the spiritual cannot exist for a long time in the misery of earthly life." This insight notwithstanding, Biel supports the standard view defended by medieval canonists and theologians: "non . . . celebrat sacerdos missam pro pecunia," priests do not celebrate Mass for money. While making money *can* be a reason for saying Mass, it qualifies only as a secondary reason. But no one should doubt the legitimacy of receiving temporal goods which provide sustenance, in exchange for the administration of spiritual goods. Does not scripture itself support this view by stating that "the laborer deserves to be paid"? (Luke 10:7).[85]

"Gold is most excellent," a famous contemporary of Biel wrote. With it "treasure is made, and he who possesses it can do as he wishes . . . and even drive souls into Paradise." Buy Masses and thus liberate souls from Purgatory, helping them on their way to Paradise! Biel would agree with this popular sentiment expressed by the explorer Christopher Columbus.[86]

However, while Biel defends the principle, he does not always defend the practice. He warns priests of greed, the accumulation of benefices, and the harmful, disturbing effects of inequality among the clergy. In Biel's experience, clerical wealth seems to be more problematic than clerical poverty. When speaking about "those simple priests who have no pastorate" (*simplices sacerdotes non curati*), he does not think of their poverty, but rather of their freedom from obligations. As the freest clerics, they can apply the special fruit of Mass one day to their parents, another time to a benefactor, and yet another for a sinner's conversion. A priest without defined Mass obligations can do what seems to be Biel's ideal: "potest applicare cui voluerit," he can apply the fruit of Mass to whomever he wishes. The free priest can dispense the divine benefits freely.[87]

In his *Exposition of the Canon of the Mass*, Biel speaks to priests and his Tübingen students who are preparing for the priesthood. Eager to instruct them in the details of priestly knowledge and liturgical behavior, he lectures with all the thoroughness and pedantry of a German professor. Mass should make sense to priests; they should not celebrate it without knowing what they are doing. The doctrine of the three "fruits" received at each Mass as taught and elaborated by Duns Scotus and Biel served as the standard theological opinion for centuries. It has been consistently maintained since the sixteenth century by all schools of Catholic theology, up until the twentieth century.

4. Sacrificial Giving in Carthage, Hippo, and Suburban Paris

The history of Christian spirituality cannot be written without reference to sacrificial giving. To lead a life shaped by the spirit of sacrifice, a life culminating in the self-immolation at the Eucharist, was for many centuries considered an ideal for members of religious orders, priests, and laypeople alike. Tears shed at Mass served to emphasize one's contrition and devotion, and people felt that the tearful prayer was more likely to reach the Father than any other kind. Often one of the penitential psalms was quoted: "A sacrifice to God is an afflicted spirit: a contrite and humbled heart, O God, thou wilt not despise" (Ps. 51:17). Even Gregory the Great, a bishop otherwise more vocal on receiving gifts from God than giving to him, alludes to this biblical verse which came to be a leitmotif of true spirituality. For many centuries, this ideal was recommended in sermons, books of counsel and consolation, and explanations of the Mass.[88]

The present chapter will explore the historical roots of the idea of Mass as an occasion of the participants' self-immolation to God. The first to suggest the idea was Bishop Cyprian who preached it in times of persecution to his flock in Carthage, North Africa. With Augustine of Hippo, the idea hardened into a major theological doctrine. Chiefly transmitted in Augustine's writings, it shaped the spirituality of those who adopted as their master the author of the *Confessions* and a huge corpus of sermons. Among Augustine's followers, we will single out Jean-Jacques Olier who served as a parish priest in seventeenth-century suburban Paris.

Cyprian of Carthage, or The Sacrifice of the Martyrs

Some early Christians used water instead of wine when celebrating the Eucharist, as was their custom, in the early hours of the day. They were afraid, Cyprian tells us, of being "recognized by its fragrant odor, perceived by unbelievers." Pagan persecutors detected them by this token when interrogating them.[89]

Cyprian, bishop of Carthage from 248 until his martyrdom in 256 CE, urged the clergy of North Africa not to tolerate this error. Celebrated properly, the Eucharist must correspond to what Jesus did before he was betrayed and handed over to his enemies. Since Jesus used wine, only wine was acceptable.

At least some wine should be added to the water consumed in the ritual. Addressing this issue in a long letter written around 255, Cyprian left us the first monograph on the Lord's Supper.[90]

Cyprian's extensive correspondence—some sixty letters plus additional pieces—shows him to have been an indefatigable pastor and administrator who controlled his own flock in Carthage and influenced Christian communities in many other areas, including Rome and Spain. The experience that shaped his entire work and outlook was the persecution of Christians in 250, at which time he went into hiding. His reasons for doing so are clear enough: he had heard of the emperor's command to take action against the church by arresting and executing Christian leaders. Bishop Fabian of Rome was the first victim, killed several days after the emperor had given the order. Historians now consider Emperor Decian's persecution to have been relatively mild in North Africa, since the death penalty was the exception rather than the rule; however, the general fear was great and the entire experience traumatic for Cyprian. The fear was not entirely unreasonable: another persecution followed in 252, and in Emperor Valerian's persecution of 257–60 Cyprian died a martyr.[91]

When Cyprian came out of hiding he found the church of Carthage disorganized and his personal standing low. Many members of the community had acquiesced and sacrificed to Jupiter as required by the emperor's decree. Although "lapsed," they still considered themselves Christians. The church's disciplinary system lay in ruins. It was uncertain who should be considered church members and who should not. It was also uncertain who would decide. Artisans and small traders, like Solassius the mule-keeper and Paula the mat-maker, had become influential, and these "confessors" had assumed the leadership. Their claim to authority rested on the fact that they had risked death when confessing their faith to the imperial authorities. Although he respected these confessors, Cyprian would not allow them to determine who among the "lapsed" Christians could be re-admitted to full membership. He preferred to integrate them into the existing hierarchy, having them start with the humble office of the *lector*, the one responsible for reading scripture to the congregation. Cyprian also asserted his authority by prescribing acts of penance to the lapsed Christians. He called for strict discipline in the case of former heretics who wanted to be received into the larger church. He declared the earlier, heretical baptism invalid; it had to be repeated. Rallying thirty-seven North African bishops in 254, and a total number of eighty-seven in 256, he advanced his position even against the new bishop of Rome. Within a few years, Cyprian controlled his church; his influence was unrivaled and extended beyond North Africa. More than a century later, he would be an authority for Augustine, and later historians agree that his power could almost be called papal.[92]

Descended from an aristocratic and wealthy family and having received an earlier education in rhetoric, Cyprian was well suited to the task. However, it would be mistaken to see in Cyprian only the aristocrat for whom the emerging

Catholic church offered a career fitting his personal taste. Authority and order, for Cyprian, were part of the divine order and had to be maintained, at all costs, in the face of a world that was out of joint. In a treatise with which Cyprian defended his conversion to his fellow aristocrats of Carthage, he is quite explicit on this: "The world is now reaching its old age," and everything is beginning to fall apart in both nature and society—the showers of winter fail for nourishing the seeds, the trees of autumn are barren, the mines exhausted, the arts without skill; friendship is without love, justice absent from the courts, and there is no discipline in human conduct.[93]

When addressing his fellow Christians, Cyprian translates the Stoic theme of the "aging world" into that of the Antichrist's final assault against the church:

> You ought to know and believe, and hold it for certain, that the day of affliction has begun to hang over our heads. The end of the world and the time of Antichrist draw near, so that we must all stand prepared for the battle. Do not consider anything but the glory of life eternal, and the crown of the confession of the Lord; and do not regard those things which are coming as being such as were those which have passed away. Now a more serious and ferocious battle threatens, for which the soldiers of Christ ought to prepare themselves with uncorrupted faith and sturdy courage.[94]

Cyprian speaks of the courage to die in a spiritual battle, not of the valor needed in a fight with real arms. The armies of Hell could only fight a losing battle. Killing the Christian martyr's body only seemed a victory to their foes' blind eyes. What actually happened remained hidden from view. Gushing forth, the martyr's blood would "quiet with its glorious flood the flames and fires of Hell." In and beyond death, the martyr triumphed with the risen Christ.[95]

The martyr imitates Christ. Martyrdom establishes such an intimate relationship with Christ that one can say he or she is possessed by him. This idea can be traced back to the New Testament's assertion that Christians do not need to worry about what to say when being questioned by their persecutors, for the spirit of Christ will answer through them (Mark 13:11). When a Christian suffers, it is no longer he or she who suffers, but Christ who suffers in them. Cyprian refers to "the passion of Christ in the persecutions" that we have to endure. A more graphic—and touching—expression of the idea can be found in the account of the martyrdom of Felicitas, a woman slave killed in Carthage in 203. When the pregnant woman was in labor, "one of the prison guards said to her: 'You suffer so much now—what will you do when you are tossed by the beasts?' 'What I am suffering now,' she replied, 'I suffer by myself. But then Another will be inside me who will suffer for me, for I shall be suffering for him.'"[96]

The suffering and death of the martyr blend with the suffering and death of Christ. Cyprian's view can be illuminated by a well-known theme of Platonic philosophy. Every act of love or justice done on earth corresponds to an ideal pattern of love and justice established in the eternal and divine world of pure ideas. Every act of justice provides the transcendent idea of justice with a tangible form in our world; thus the divine is no longer distant and separated from the human but actually dwells among us, giving our actions meaning and substance. In the same way, Christ, who dwells with the heavenly Father in the realm of the transcendent, is present in a life of suffering and martyrdom.[97]

In Cyprian's theology, the relevance of imitating Christ extended beyond martyrdom. It included the liturgy. Those who do not literally obey Christ's clear command, "Do this in remembrance of me," cannot claim to celebrate the Lord's Supper. Thus, one has to celebrate it exactly the way Christ himself celebrated it, that is, with bread and wine (not with bread and water). Only if done properly would Christ be present when the bishop or the presbyter conducted the liturgy. Any deviation from the prescribed procedure nullified the rite.

For the Bishop of Carthage, the Eucharist is a ritual repetition and imitation of the Last Supper of Jesus. Since the subsequent history of the Lord's Supper follows Cyprian's conception, this statement may appear banal. However, the novelty of Cyprian's understanding deserves to be highlighted. Before Cyprian, the Eucharist was not so much a replication of the Last Supper of Jesus as a ritual that either commemorated Christ's death or produced sacred food. With Cyprian, the biblical context of the Last Supper and the connection with Jesus' death are given prominence. Like the original Last Supper, the Eucharist was now celebrated in an atmosphere of "tribulation," the foes' assault upon Christ and his followers. With bread symbolizing Christ's dead body and wine his blood, the ritual commemorated the Passion and death of Christ. "As often as you eat this bread and drink the cup, you proclaim the Lord's death." Cyprian quotes and accepts this dictum of Paul's.[98]

Unfortunately, we know little about the prayers and words said during Cyprian's eucharistic liturgy. However, we do have evidence enough to speculate. In Justin's liturgy of the mid-second century, the New Testament text of Christ's "institution" of the Eucharist was not recited. The invocation of the divine "Word" (*logos*, i.e., Christ) served to consecrate the elements. In Cyprian's ritual, on the other hand, such recitation would seem to be an essential reminder to do exactly what the Lord did, with the *sacerdos* acting in Christ's place. It would be the bishop, then, who would pronounce the sacred words, "This is my body," and "This is my blood," over bread and wine. The very words of Christ replace the invocation of the Holy Spirit or the Logos.[99]

Aware of the novelty of his approach, Cyprian develops his view in a long letter. He sets out to prove his point from scripture, piling reference upon reference. Even before Christ, the Lord's Supper was prefigured, for instance by the priest-king Melchizedek, who had offered bread and wine to Abraham. (Cyprian's view of scriptural typology, based on a quasi-Platonic model of history as imitating the ideal and eternal, has no difficulties with the concept of Old Testament figures foreshadowing Christ.) In his treatise, the bishop not only argues from scripture, but also hints at a personal revelation. The Lord himself instructed him, presumably in a dream. To break away from the established tradition of celebrating the Eucharist only with water, the appeal to scripture had to be supplemented by an appeal to a new revelation—"an inspiration and command of God"—in tune with the witness of the Bible.[100]

Cyprian uses sacrificial language to explain the precise import of the celebration. "To sacrifice" (*sacrificare*), for him, means "to celebrate the Eucharist," and "those who sacrifice" (*sacrificantes*) are Christians assembled for worship. The Eucharist is *oblatio et sacrificium nostrum*, "our offering and sacrifice," i.e., a precious and pure gift offered to God the Father. Christ himself gave his life as a sacrifice to the Father. Since bread and wine correspond to the body and blood of Christ, "the Lord's passion is the sacrifice (*sacrificium*) we offer." Cyprian was not the first, of course, to apply sacrificial terminology to Christian worship. His work, however, is different from that of his predecessors in that it applies sacrificial terminology consistently as well as systematically, making it the leading concept in its theology of worship. Only the *sacerdos*, i.e., priest, can preside over the Christian liturgy. This would normally be the bishop, rarely a presbyter, and certainly never a woman. With disgust Cyprian recalls an incident that occurred some time before in Cappadocia. Suddenly, a certain woman "in a state of ecstasy announced herself a prophetess, acting as if she were filled with the Holy Spirit." Not only would she "walk in the keen winter with bare feet over frozen snow," she would also deceive many, pretending that "with a powerful invocation she could sanctify bread and celebrate the Eucharist." For Cyprian, the sacrifice must be offered by the *sacerdos*. Otherwise, it would not be accepted by God.[101]

How can we account for Cyprian's insistence on calling the Eucharist a sacrifice? Must we look for the origins in the Roman idea that contact with the gods is established chiefly by way of sacrifice, offered in the ritually correct way by the (pagan) priest? Or shall we recall the fanatical aspects of the old Carthaginian religion which involved suicide and human sacrifice as means of securing divine favor? A continuing nocturnal sacrifice in early third-century Numidia, with its substitution of a lamb for a human victim, suggests the persistence of the idea that human life might be sacrificed to appease the deity. For whatever reasons Cyprian favored the sacrificial pattern of worship, his choice would make sense in the ritual milieu of his North African home.[102]

A sacrifice does not only establish contact with the deity: once it is accepted by a god, it calls for a corresponding gift from the divine side. Sacrifice is an exchange. *Do ut des*—I give in order that you give to me—is the rule, and Cyprian does not need to invoke it explicitly. His contemporaries lived in a world in which sacrificing animals was an everyday affair; its implications were understood as well as taken for granted. In the case of the Christian, eucharistic sacrifice, people expected God to reciprocate by giving them eternal life after death. "We shall drink new wine . . . with Christ in the kingdom of the Father," writes the bishop, echoing the biblical text.[103]

Eating the sacred bread and drinking the sacred wine, Christians are assimilated with their Lord and thus made ready to follow him even unto death. Since theirs is a time of persecution, they have to be prepared for death every day, and thus the Eucharist should be celebrated daily (or more precisely, every morning). "Give us this day our daily bread!" When Cyprian's community pronounced the fourth petition of the Lord's Prayer, it had an unambiguous eucharistic meaning for them: people wanted to partake of the sacred bread every morning, and they prayed for it. "We ask that this bread should be given to us daily, that we who are in Christ, and daily receive the Eucharist as the food of salvation, may not . . . be separated from Christ's body," and thus live in the danger of forgoing salvation. The incorporation of the eucharistic sacrifice into daily morning prayer is mentioned in other contemporary sources and seems to represent a general trend of liturgical development in the third century. Cyprian had a good reason to promote this trend, for in times of crisis, religious people in all ages have tended to multiply and intensify their observances in order to stay in uninterrupted contact with their god.[104]

Prior to Cyprian's time, that contact was generally established through the domestic use of eucharistic bread. In Cyprian's Carthage, this custom was still practiced. But the bishop seems to have regarded the private consumption of the eucharistic bread as insufficient. The Lord told his disciples to partake of both bread and wine, and this was only possible during communal worship. Eucharistic bread and wine were to be available every day for all believers (including children!), hence the daily sacrifice led by the bishop or a presbyter. While Cyprian wanted his fellow believers to have all the benefits of the Christian sacrifice, he also wanted to be in total control. Nothing should happen without the bishop's presence or consent.[105]

Not all Christians were willing, or even able, to follow Cyprian's advice to attend the eucharistic celebration every day. We hear of those who had second thoughts about drinking wine in the morning, and wished not to advertise their faith by the odor of their breath. Others—like those sent to the mines, far away from their fellow Christians—did not have the chance. It would certainly not occur to Cyprian to let these wretched people celebrate their own Eucharist without the presence of an approved minister, and without wine. They live, as he carefully puts it, "where there is no opportunity to God's priests (*sacerdotes*) for offering and celebrating the divine sacrifices (*sacrificia*)." We note that Cyprian here—as elsewhere—applies the pagan term for priest, *sacerdos* ("sacrificer"), to the Christian minister, or more precisely to the bishop who alone can preside at the Eucharist. In one of his letters addressed to Christians sent to the mines, Cyprian faces the problem, offering a solution which again reveals his enthusiasm for martyrdom. The absence of the sacrament, he writes, constitutes no threat to church or faith. "You celebrate and offer a sacrifice (*sacrificium*) to God equally precious and glorious," he declares. "And that will greatly profit you for the retribution of heavenly rewards. . . . You offer this sacrifice (*sacrificium*) to God; you celebrate this sacrifice (*sacrificium*) without intermission day and night, being made victims to God, and exhibiting yourselves as holy and unspotted offerings." Here Cyprian draws from the well-established Christian theology of martyrdom to be found, for instance, in the book of Revelation, a book often quoted by the bishop (Rev. 7:9). But his own reflections take him further: to sacrifice one's life for the sake of Christ can actually replace the Eucharist.[106]

Whenever possible, however, Cyprian would insist that even martyrs should participate in the ritual. Even though Cyprian acknowledges the presence of Christ in the martyrs and indeed their being "sacrificial offerings to God" (*hostiae Deo*) and "holy and immaculate victims" (*immaculatae victimae*), he would normally insist on the use of the sacrament. Had not Abel first sacrificed to the Lord, and then died a martyr under the blows of his brother Cain? The bishop urges Christians to drink the blood of Christ: "Now a more serious and ferocious battle threatens, for which the soldiers of Christ ought to prepare themselves with uncorrupted faith and sturdy courage, considering that they drink the cup of Christ's blood daily so as to be able to shed their blood for the sake of Christ." When martyrs suffer, it is Christ who suffers in them, and when they shed their blood, it is the blood of Christ.[107]

If Cyprian's correspondence reveals his enthusiasm for martyrdom, it reveals an even greater devotion to the Eucharist. In Cyprian's Africa, the church began to commemorate the days on which martyrs died. On his or her day, a martyr's triumphal death and entry into heaven was celebrated, and people honored the saint who could now act as their intercessor with God. Although Cyprian shares his contemporaries' veneration of the martyrs, he mitigates the theological claims connected with them. Martyrs, for Cyprian, are not automatically saints and perfected beings. It was not until much later that another North African, Augustine, would call prayer on behalf of martyrs an "insult" or "crime" (*iniuria*), since martyrs should not be prayed for, rather they should be interceding with the Lord for us. But unlike Augustine, for whom martyrs have become venerable and superhuman figures of the heroic past, Cyprian has no illusions about the spiritual state of his martyred contemporaries. Were the martyrs any different from the confessors or near-martyrs who survived their tortures—and then often stained their lives by all kinds of "dishonesties, rapes, and adulteries"? The community still has to pray for the martyrs as it does for all dead Christians. "We offer always, as you remember, sacrifices for them every time we celebrate the days of the sufferings of the martyrs and anniversary commemorations." Even after their glorious deaths, the martyrs cannot achieve salvation without the eucharistic sacrifice. Thus Cyprian insists on the absolute superiority of Christ's sacrifice over all heroic human achievement.[108]

We can reconstruct what Cyprian means when he says that the eucharistic sacrifice is offered "for" the martyrs. The martyrs, like all other believers, belong to the church of sinners whose sins the Lord bore on the cross. Although a martyr's death does have atoning, purificatory force, that force is limited and does not work apart from Christ. When the drama of our salvation is mystically re-enacted on the altar, the church is again joined to the Lord. Without our being united to the Lord, there can be no salvation for us, he asserts. This union of the church and the Lord is symbolized—magically, we might say—in the mixture of water and wine, water symbolizing the people and the wine, Christ. Only for those who are symbolically "mingled with Christ" can the Lord's sacrifice accomplish the hallowed act of redemption.[109]

Although the water corresponds to the imperfect and indeed "sinful" Christians to whom the martyrs belong, Cyprian does not think of the worshipping community as one of grave sinners. Since only something pure and unblemished can be offered in sacrifice, the worshiping individuals, who are included in Christ's offering on the altar, have to be as pure and perfect as possible. A sign of sufficient purity seems to be general peace and harmony in the community. Unworthy individuals are not seen as disrupting the harmony and spoiling the sacrifice as such; they only harm themselves. Participation in the ritual by a grave sinner, especially by someone who has denied Christ and worshiped the idols of Roman religion, is punished by God himself, and the punishment may be meted out instantly, even during worship. Cyprian reports several cases of unworthy participation. When a baby girl refused to partake of the eucharistic cup and, after having been forced to drink, sobbed and vomited, it was found out that she had eaten bread soaked with some wine used in a Roman ritual. "In a profane body and mouth the Eucharist could not remain; the drink sanctified in the blood of the Lord burst forth from the polluted stomach." An unworthy man, who was about to partake of the sacred bread, discovered that in his hand the morsel had turned into ashes. A sinful woman, who "secretly crept in among us when we were sacrificing," was worse off: "As if taking some deadly poison into her jaws and body, she began presently to be tortured, and to become stiffened with frenzy. Suffering the misery no longer of persecution, but of her crime, shivering and trembling, she fell down." Cyprian did not have to recall Paul's warning that a profanation of the Lord's bread and cup might entail sickness and even death; his community had seen what unworthiness might entail, and Cyprian himself was present when the little girl vomited in church. Such incidents were a warning for those who adopted a cavalier attitude to the magic substance consumed during the Christian sacrifice.[110]

The bishop's preference for and praise of the sacrifice of Christ, however, must not be misunderstood. What looks like a strictly theological or Christ-centered argument—the superiority of the Lord's sacrifice over human achievement—also has a strong episcopal side to it. As chief celebrant of the Eucharist, the bishop asserts his own authority against that of confessors and martyrs. He takes a rather critical stance toward the private cult of martyrs and the veneration of the confessors. For Cyprian, there can be no religious authority apart from Christ and his bishop.[111]

Whatever personal advantage Cyprian may have derived from his eucharistic practice, he gave it a unique and attractive interpretation. It could claim a firm basis in those biblical texts that relate Jesus' own Last Supper to the Passover sacrifice celebrated during a time of persecution. And, more importantly, he made Christian worship meaningful in a time of severe crisis. Partaking of the body and blood of Christ, Christians prepare for their own death. They will be swallowed up and perish in the general turmoil—in the hope, of course, of living forever with their Lord. Even after their death, the eucharistic sacrifice, celebrated in the Christian community, would help them to attain this end.

Augustine, or The Believer's Union with Christ's Sacrifice

Although developed in and congenial to an age of persecution, Cyprian's conception of the eucharistic sacrifice survived that age. The authority that Cyprian's name enjoyed beyond the confines of Africa did not fade after his death. His stern piety, his eagerness to communicate with other bishops, and his well-written letters and treatises all combined to establish the fame both of Cyprian and of the African church. The Bishop of Carthage was the first figure in early Christianity whose life became the subject of a biography. He also came to be remembered as the greatest and most influential Latin-writing theological authority before another North African—Augustine of Hippo—became an even more imposing figure. Augustine had no ambition to minimize Cyprian's merits; in fact, he adopted and developed Cyprian's teachings, making them relevant after the Roman state had stopped its persecutions and converted to Christianity. Thus Augustine contributed to the continuing influence of the Bishop of Carthage.[112]

Following Cyprian's teaching, Augustine considered the Eucharist to be an eminently personal ritual, allowing the individual to include himself or herself in the sacrifice offered to God. The Bishop of Hippo, however, did not simply repeat Cyprian's formula of the sinner's union with Christ in the atoning sacrifice, symbolized in the mingling of water and wine. Augustine rethought Cyprian's teaching and gave it a new direction.

Sacrifice, for Augustine, defines our proper relationship to God. "A true sacrifice," he explains, "is every work which is done that we may be united to God in holy fellowship." Such "work" (*opus*) constitutes fellowship itself; it is not done to overcome estrangement or atone for sins, or the like—this would be to misconstrue Augustine. Nor does sacrificing involve the giving of some material or even spiritual object; to sacrifice, for Augustine, means to dedicate oneself to God, to give oneself to him as a present. Here Augustine echoes traditional Neoplatonic philosophy which understood sacrifice as a means of

being joined to God as to our ultimate "cause" of existence. Here is how the
fourth-century philosopher Sallustius explains sacrifice:

> The happiness of anything lies in its appropriate perfection, and the appropriate
> perfection of each object is union with its cause. For this reason also we pray that
> we may have union with the gods. So, since though the highest life is that of the
> gods, yet man's life also is life of some sort, and this life wishes to have union
> with that, it needs an intermediary (for objects widely separated are never united
> without a middle term), and the intermediary ought to be like the objects being
> united. Accordingly, the intermediary between life and life should be life, and
> for this reason living animals are sacrificed by men, both by those who are now
> among the blessed and by all the men of old, not in a uniform manner, but to
> every god the fitting victims, with much other reverence.

The philosopher's statement includes all the elements we find in Augustine's
theory of sacrifice: the wish to be joined to God and the need for mediation. We
can see how easy it is to graft Christian ideas onto the structure of Neoplatonic
philosophy. Augustine has no difficulties in using the Neoplatonic definition
for speaking about the significance of sacrifice for the entire human history. As
a personal act of love, sacrifice existed in paradise, where our first parents could
give themselves to God: "Intact and pure from all stain and blemish of sin, they
offered themselves to God as the purest sacrifices." And in heaven, too, the
angels join themselves to God by offering themselves. For us, however, who no
longer live in paradise and do not yet live in heaven, to sacrifice involves
renunciation which may amount to giving one's life in martyrdom.[113]

In Augustine's day, martyrdom no longer represents a commonly experienced Christian ideal. The place of the martyr is now taken by the ascetic.
When Augustine quotes Paul's letter to the Romans (12:1)—"I beseech you,
brothers, by the mercy of God, that you present your bodies a living sacrifice,
holy, pleasing to God, your reasonable service"—Augustine does not think of
martyrdom, but of asceticism and restraint. "Our body too is a sacrifice when
we discipline it by self-control." Just as martyrs gave up their life for the sake
of the Lord, so the ascetics give their possessions to the poor and offer their
own, self-inflicted sufferings and self-humiliation as a sacrifice to God.[114]

Although the ascetic's life as a whole assumes a sacrificial character, the
celebration of the Mass provides the ideal opportunity to bring this life before
God. In the Eucharist, the entire church—which ideally consists of ascetics—
offers itself to God: "Now we ourselves who are his City are his most splendid
and best sacrifice; such is the mystery that we celebrate in our offerings, which
are known to the faithful." In one of Augustine's sermons, this idea assumes a
graphic quality (comparable to that of Cyprian's identification of the faithful
with the water poured into the wine): "After all that fasting, after suffering,
after self-humiliation and contrition, you have come in the name of Christ, as

it were, to the Lord's chalice. Now here you are on the table, here you are in the chalice."[115]

Unfortunately, Augustine's sermon on this theme survives only as a summary. However, the theme of sacrifice figures so prominently in the bishop's work, that we can reconstruct his meaning. It is based on three key ideas: (1) Bread and wine represent the faithful; (2) more specifically, bread and wine stand for their sufferings; (3) the sacrificial gift, i.e., the faithful and their sufferings, must be joined to the Christ-victim.[116]

(1) In the Eucharist, bread and wine represent not only Christ's individual body which lived on earth and died on the cross. They also symbolize Christ's mystical body, i.e., the community of the faithful.

(2) In his sermons, Augustine often develops the equation of bread and wine with the faithful and their lives of ascetic trials as Christians. Like bread and wine, Christians are the end product of a long process of treatment. In wine-making, many ripened grapes are squeezed in the wine press, and after fermentation, the sweet liquid becomes wine. So with the making of Christians: gathered as grapes and crushed in the wine press of fasting and labor, of humility and sorrow for sin, they come forth from baptism as the wine which is the church.

(3) Our personal sacrifice must be joined to or included in the sacrifice of Christ. Augustine's logic again relies on the concept of the mystical body of Christ. Since the church is the body of Christ, our sufferings are Christ's and are offered to the Father. Christ's self-sacrifice, when represented on the altar and offered to the Father, includes the sacrifice of those incorporated into his mystical body. Augustine carefully points out that there could be no sacrifice to God without Christ's mediation as both priest and victim. As sinners, we cannot offer ourselves to God as a perfect and pure sacrifice. However, when joined to the purest and holiest victim, i.e., the Lord himself, the Father will accept us. Christ will make up for the imperfection. In this conception, we are not only imperfect victims, but also, stained by sin, imperfect priests. Only Christ, the true priest, can bring us as sacrificial gifts before the Father.

The Augustinian version of Cyprian's concept of the church's presence on the altar became one of the standard concepts of eucharistic theology and spirituality. How it worked in practice can be seen in a sermon Pope Gregory the Great delivered in 590–91. The pope recommends the devotion of a certain Cassius (d. 558 CE) to his Roman audience:

Many of you, my dearest brothers, have known Cassius, bishop of the city of Narnia [in Italy]. He used to celebrate the sacrifice daily so that there was hardly a day on which he would not have offered the sacrifice of propitiation to the almighty God. His entire life was shaped by the spirit of sacrifice. For he gave all he owned as alms, and at the hour of the holy sacrifice he immolated himself with a contrite and humbled heart, almost completely dissolved in tears.[117]

After Constantine, martyrdom was rare and no longer served as the superior form of "bearing the cross of Christ." It was replaced by asceticism, which now began to attract many committed believers. While living in the world, the ascetic would renounce its pleasures and delusions and thus follow the Lord. Although the ascetic stood at all times closer to God than other people, and would have easier access to the divine, he or she would still need the sacrifice of the church.

Concluding our patristic survey, we must once again look back to Jesus and try to assess what some of the early theologians did with his thought and practice. For what they did has become foundational for most of the subsequent Christian thought and remains influential to our own day. Without exaggeration, one can say that contemporary eucharistic thought is more influenced by Cyprian than by the original practice of Jesus.

Jesus, as we have seen, presented to God some bread and wine in a sacrificial gesture accompanied by words of presentation: "This is my blood. This is my body." By so doing, he offered a substitute sacrifice, i.e., something smaller than a lamb, a goat, or an ox which would be slaughtered before being offered in a "real" sacrifice at the Temple of Jerusalem. Simple, inexpensive, not bound to a particular sacred place, and not involving the services and the specialized knowledge of a priest, Jesus' sacrifice was a truly popular version of an otherwise complex ritual. Everyone could afford and perform the new sacrifice and thus link himself or herself to God. The way Cyprian and, later, Augustine defined sacrifice, is quite unlike Jesus' understanding. In fact, it constitutes a real innovation, if not revolution, in Christian thought. Unlike Jesus, Cyprian took his idea of sacrifice not from traditional low-key animal sacrifice, but from that most qualified form of offering: human sacrifice. For him, bread and wine served as a substitute for Jesus' martyred body and the blood he had shed during his Passion. The material offered—bread and wine— still replaced an original sacrificial gift, but a very different gift indeed. It replaced a dead man's body and blood. How could theologians like Cyprian and Augustine discover and appreciate the value and meaning of human sacrifice?

If an answer is to be ventured at all, then it must be the following one: as North Africans, they lived close to and participated in the Semitic mentality, which they encountered both in their Punic neighborhood and, of course, in the Bible. Child sacrifice remained a conspicuous feature of Punic ritual down to the third century CE. Tertullian (ca. 160–225), who lived most of his life in Carthage, reports: "In Africa infants used to be sacrificed to Saturn, and quite openly, down to the proconsulate of Tiberius. . . . Yes, and to this day that holy crime persists in secret." Tertullian indicates that he knew soldiers who served under that Tiberius and who had crucified the wicked priests of Baal-Hammon, known to the Romans as Saturn. Archaeological finds as well as inscriptions indicate that occasionally children would be spared, an animal being offered to the deity as a substitute. However, there is ample evidence that children were actually killed and burned to appease an angry deity. The bulk of evidence comes from the Phoenician and Punic colonies in Sicily, Sardinia, and North Africa, especially Carthage. Archeologists have discovered large cemeteries containing the burial urns of sacrificial victims at all these sites. It has been estimated that between 400 and 200 BCE, a total number of 20,000 burial urns were interred in the cemetery of Carthage. Gustave Flaubert's historical novel *Salammbô* (1862) does not seem to be much exaggerated in its unflattering portrait of ancient Carthage as a city of horror, echoing with the cries of mothers as their children are torn from their arms and the sound of flesh sizzling on hot coals. The Bible includes several reports about the very same institution of child-sacrifice. In the ninth century BCE, King Mesha of Moab sacrificed his son and thereby motivated his god to overthrow the Israelites, Mesha's enemies. Although the Israelites seem to have practiced human sacrifice also, their tradition emphasizes that ritual's substitute forms: God accepts a lamb instead of Isaac's blood, and when in Egypt all the first-born infants are killed, the Israelites are allowed to redeem their own offspring with a lamb.[118]

Despite the possibility—and probably widespread practice—of substituting an animal for a human, the original Semitic ideology never faded. For many centuries, Moabites, Israelites, and the Punic population of North Africa knew that the most efficient sacrifice was that of a child—preferably one's own, first-born baby boy. The logic underlying this idea is clear enough: the ideal sacrifice would be to offer one's own life; in this way, Paul could say that he would "give away all my possessions, and deliver my body to be burned" (1 Cor. 13:3). But since people never actually sacrificed themselves and instead killed a child, then the infant can be seen as an equivalence of the sacrificer himself. By killing his own child and offering it to the deity, the sacrificer gives himself, his own life. The gift symbolizes or represents the giver, and the giver cannot be represented better than by his own child. Some of the ancient records clearly hint at the equality of victim and sacrificer: according to the Bible, the king of Moab sacrificed "his first-born son, who was to succeed him," and according to Philo of Byblos, the god Kronos once "arrayed his son in royal apparel, and prepared an altar, and sacrificed him." The reference to succession and royal apparel underline the identity of sacrificer and victim. In other words: if a gift can be considered as an extension of the giver's person, then this is especially true of someone's child and successor. By sacrificing his child, a father sacrifices himself. The Semites could not think of a more radical form of sacrifice (with the possible exception of self-sacrifice in martyrdom). They could not conceive of a deity that would claim more than the first—and therefore best—child. Their gods could not find a better way of asserting their superiority; faced with a severe crisis, or with the anger of a deity, the Semites gave up the lives of those dearest to them.[119]

According to another version of the Phoenician myth just quoted, the god Kronos not only sacrificed his son, but also resorted to the drastic measure of including himself in the offering. "At the occurrence of a fatal plague, Kronos immolated his only son to his father Ouranos, and circumcised himself, forcing the allies who were with him to do the same." Here, someone kills himself symbolically by circumcising his penis. The combined ritual of child-sacrifice and circumcision represents complete self-immolation.[120]

Seen against this somewhat disturbing background, we can understand why North African authors like Cyprian and Augustine could suggest and promote a sacrificial understanding of the Eucharist. For them, Christ's death was a human sacrifice, and in symbolically evoking that sacrifice, people should join Christ in offering themselves to God. Bread and wine, offered to God, stood as symbols for both Christ and the Christian believer. The idea of sacrificial giving has very deep roots in the religious history of the Semites and all those who still shared their culture and mentality.

The Spirit of Sacrifice in Suburban Paris: Jean-Jacques Olier

In the Middle Ages, sacrificial giving of oneself to God, so forcefully established by Cyprian and Augustine, was overshadowed by the notion of sacrificial receiving. Yet, the idea was never completely forgotten. It found an advocate in Thomas à Kempis, whose *Imitation of Christ* (1420–27) ranks among the most widely read devotional guides. "There is no offering more worthy, no satisfaction greater for the washing away of sins than to offer yourself purely and completely to God at the same time that the Body of Christ is offered in the Mass and in Communion." In the seventeenth century, with the revival of mysticism and the renewed interest in Augustine, the notion of self-sacrifice received much attention and began to appear in catechisms. The faithful, it was taught, when offering Jesus Christ to the Father through the hands of the priest, "s'offrent aussi à Dieu conjointement avec Jésus-Christ" (offer themselves to God, together with Jesus Christ). The notion of sacrifice epitomized Christian spirituality, especially in France, and began to captivate clergy and laity alike. Among the clergy, Jean-Jacques Olier (1608–57) revived and adapted the mentality of Cyprian, Augustine, and Thomas à Kempis.[121]

Olier's liturgical spirituality can best be approached from two experiences that resonate through his writings and biography: the experience of living in a hostile, often atheist world, and the feeling of being impure and worthless before God.

In 1642, at the age of thirty-four, Olier was appointed parish priest (*curé*) of Saint-Germain, one of the big suburbs of Paris. The young priest was extremely pious, zealous, authoritarian, and devoted to the liturgy he conducted at his small church of Saint-Sulpice (now replaced by a majestic structure that rivals Notre Dame). Legally, Olier's parish was outside the control of the French bishops, and the abbey of Saint-Germain, to which it belonged (and which was controlled only by the Holy See), did not interfere with his work.

Olier appreciated his independence, which enabled him to pursue his own pastoral program. He wanted to rid the neglected suburb of its atheists and Huguenots, and to transform the quarrelsome inhabitants, many of whom were given to dueling, into solid parishioners. Although the young priest managed to renovate the church, to reinvigorate the liturgy, and to establish a pious *fraternité* called *La confrérie du très-Saint Sacrement* (Company of the Most Blessed Sacrament) to which he invited noble ladies like the Princess of Condé, he experienced little success from his tireless labors. In fact, there was growing opposition from many sides toward his reforms. Even his legal title to the pastorate came under dispute. Olier did little to ease the tension. When he received word of a possible attack on his life, he took no precautions and followed his routine of saying morning Mass at Saint-Sulpice. "He repaired to church, wearing his surplice as usual, and celebrated the holy sacrifice, offering himself with our Lord, in order to be immolated for the glory of his Father, rejoicing in being able to partake of that chalice, after which he had languished so long and so ardently." The year before, Olier had pronounced a private vow in which he declared himself a host-victim to God. This vow implied his willingness to suffer, and now, on June 8, 1645, he was ready to sacrifice his life. After Mass, an angry mob stormed and pillaged the rectory. Olier was dragged through the dirty streets and beaten. Rescued by friends, he found shelter in the Palais de Luxembourg where he had his bruises bandaged. His enemies hoped he would either resign from his pastorate or at least relax his aggressive style of tending his flock. They were to be disappointed. Returned to his parish, Olier continued his reforms with as much zeal as before.[122]

The incident of June 8, 1645, was typical of the seventeenth century, and we can think of it as a small, telescoped reflection of the religious and social unrest of the period. Historians describe the European dimensions of this unrest as the "crisis of the seventeenth century." A long period of economic stagnation, depression, and poverty succeeded the prosperity of the sixteenth century. These economic difficulties combined with growing social tensions to spark local disturbances and even wars; these were so terrible that they forced many to sail for the New World. During the same time that Olier's rectory was vandalized, the Thirty Years' War was raging in Germany (1618–48) and the Civil Wars were being fought in England (1642–46). Although both of these wars had a number of causes, religious factors were powerful if not decisive. What men like Olier feared most was neither war nor poverty, but unbelief and laxity in Christian practice. In France, the new and developing class of physicians, lawyers, civil servants, and merchants involved with capitalist enterprise had lost its traditional, unquestioned adherence to the Catholic faith. Olier's own family belonged to the *noblesse de robe*, the new emerging nobility, so named because their power came from their role as magistrates and counselors, not from traditional inherited lineage. Rationalism and skepticism emerged in this class, leading to anti-clerical sentiment or even outright hostility to the church. The libertine became a prominent figure. As the Age of Reason advanced upon them, men like Olier found themselves in a hostile world in which they were prepared to struggle—and to suffer—for God and his church.[123]

The second factor that shaped Olier's thought was human unworthiness and impurity, feelings that his spiritual director Charles de Condren (1588–1641) had instilled in him. Since impurity prevents humans from being linked to God properly, the spiritual goal must be to annihilate oneself before God and so find him. *Anéantissement*, for Condren, is an act of sacrifice. The twin themes of impurity and sacrificial self-annihilation resonate through much of Olier's writing. The human heart is "an inexhaustible well of impurity, completely filled with self-love" (*JC* 118). Very little remains of the original goodness our first ancestors enjoyed in Paradise. Our heart is "Satan's own empire" (*JC* 131). Olier finds ever new expressions for describing our estrangement from God and our hostility toward him. "It is the true sign of our religion to offer everything in sacrifice to God and thus to testify how vile and despicable all things are in his presence. In this way we value and respect nothing other than him alone" (*IVV* 9). To practice religion, for Olier, means to center one's life on God, to join oneself to him, to give oneself to him alone. In order for us to become victims worthy of him, we must be purified and sanctified. With divine help we can, if not conquer, then at least control the evil side of ourselves and join "the purest part" of our souls to God (*JC* 123). Olier uses sacrificial language for the act of abnegation and mortification. "The Christian, in the spirit of penitence . . . must sacrifice everything that is impure to God and his holiness" (*JC* 191). Olier recommends, and practices himself, a harsh régime of asceticism. We know of his frequent flagellations (ill. 20) and the primitive sack of hay that served as his bed.[124]

Christian existence involves a constant effort to achieve holiness and means an incessant struggle against the lures of the flesh. In our lifetime, self-denial and mortification will never be complete. Only after our death, after being purged in purgatory, and only after the final destruction of our sinful and impure side, will we be able to give ourselves to God in a complete act of sacrifice. For Olier, this final act transcends the individual by involving the universal scenario of the Last Judgment. Only a final destruction of the universe can remove all the obstacles that divert us from God or obstruct our way to him. Then we will be true "victims of love" and can forever be consumed by the "fire of his love." Like many theologians of his time, Olier believed in a "worldless" heaven and an eternal life in which the blessed would have nothing but God to enjoy.[125]

While Olier's general sacrificial theology echoes the Augustinian thought of Charles de Condren, his theology of the Mass must be acknowledged as his own contribution. But he did not form it independently. He again relied on Augustine, developing the Augustinian notion that Christ instituted the

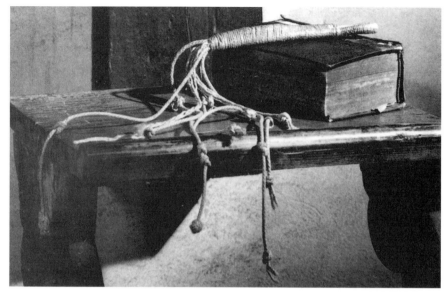

20. Promoting the Spirit of Sacrifice. Traditional Catholic asceticism involved self-flagellation to promote the "spirit of sacrifice." In his 1609 *Introduction to the Devout Life*, Francis de Sales recommends the "discipline's" moderate use to the laity, to both men and women. This photo showing the "discipline"—hemp ropes with knots—was included in a 1955 coffee-table book illustrating monastic life. Today, the scourge no longer seems to be in use. "Discipline" or penitential scourge, 1950s.

Eucharist as a daily sign of his sacrifice to the Father. Celebrating the sacrifice, "the Church learns to offer herself through him [Christ]" to God.[126]

In Olier's theology, as in the standard Catholic theology of the seventeenth century, consecration and, more visible to the people, elevation are the central acts of Mass. Pregnant with meaning, these acts represent condensed statements of the entire theology of sacrifice. When the priest consecrates bread and wine, he represents Christ's sacrificial death, signified by the separation of body and blood. The words of consecration, pronounced by the priest, are "like a sword that cuts" (*un glaive tranchant, EC* 331). However, Christ's death is so intimately linked to his resurrection that the consecration actually makes the resurrected, glorified Lord present in bread and wine. The two elements of bread and wine conceal the glorified reality of the risen Christ. With the gesture of elevating the host before the congregation, the priest offers the consecrated food—that is, Christ himself—to God. For Olier, this symbolism involves a complex, two-stage sacrifice, consisting of an immolation (on earth) and a union (in heaven). In the first sacrificial act, human life is given up and destroyed; in the second, the glorified person is united with God. In other words, the sacrifice has two dimensions: a horizontal and a vertical. Horizontally, Mass reaches into the past, commemorating the death of Christ; vertically, it reaches up to heaven, joining us to Christ's self-oblation to the Father. The prayer "*Unde et memores*," which the priest says immediately after the consecration, appears to indicate this double connection: "Calling therefore to mind [1] the blessed passion of this same Christ, thy son, our Lord, and also [2] his resurrection from the grave, and glorious ascension into heaven, we thy servants, Lord, and with us all thy holy people, offer to thy majesty . . . a sacrifice."[127]

While the Middle Ages would see in the elevation a magic moment in which the blessing of Christ could be experienced, Olier followed a tradition that saw it as an oblatory gesture. A thirteenth-century illumination (ill. 21) captures the moment by representing the priest as handing over the Christ-child to an angel (who is thought to transport the sacred gift to the heavenly Father). The priest, in one of the prayers said at Mass, actually asks the Father that the gift "be carried by the hands of thy holy angel up to thy altar on high, into the presence of thy divine majesty." The priest holds the sacred elements up, offering the body and the blood of Christ to God—or rather, because he acts in the place of Christ, he represents Christ's giving of himself. The gesture of the oblatory elevation reminds Olier of the flames that once consumed animal sacrifices,

21. Christ-Child Presented to God. Some medieval theologians considered the elevation of the consecrated host a gesture of sacrificial offering. With artists and visionaries, the presentation assumed visual qualities; where others saw the host, they saw the Christ-child. "When the abbot elevated the host with his hands, presenting and offering it to God, the virgin [Alpais of Cudot] saw him holding a most handsome boy. . . . And the heavens above opened, and two of the blessed spirits—ones that were of superior majesty and authority—descended above the altar. With highest reverence they took this heavenly boy from the abbot's hands and presented him before the divine majesty to God the Father." Although the twelfth-century vision of the French peasant girl Alpais of Cudot and the Bavarian illumination are unrelated, they express the same idea. Breviary of Aldersbach, Bavaria, ca. 1260.

sending them upward to heaven. The flames of the Father's love consume the offering.[128]

Elevation, then, symbolizes the second act of sacrifice. Here we are shown how Christ is united to his Father. And here, according to Olier, we can look beyond the small earthly congregation and join in the everlasting heavenly liturgy:

> To understand the mystery of the most holy sacrifice of the Mass and to open at one stroke the curtain that hides it from our view, we must know that this sacrifice is the sacrifice of heaven. And we must be well instructed in what that sacrifice of paradise consists and how it is done. To most people—I am speaking of the common folk—it seems strange to suggest that there is a sacrifice in heaven. Others, however, who have a better knowledge of the meaning of religion and its first duty, i.e., sacrifice, will never doubt the existence of sacrifice in heaven—for even on earth the one who believes in the existence of God offers sacrifices: *sacrificat qui putet esse Deum*. . . . No one can doubt the existence of sacrifice in heaven, which is the place of the perfect religion and the most sublime veneration of God. It is really there that sacrifice must be offered incessantly, so that religion itself is not interrupted. (*EC* 287)

For Olier, the life and death of Jesus epitomize the essence of religion: sacrifice. Jesus sacrificed himself to God. In heaven, he continues this religion, offering himself to the Father in all eternity. As the eternal priest, Christ implies in his sacrifice all the sacrifices ever offered to God. Together with these, he offers his entire church, dedicating it and handing it over to the Father.[129]

The idea of the heavenly sacrifice of Christ (a sacrifice renewed on the occasion of every Mass celebrated on earth) is traditional and has its roots in an exegesis of the New Testament epistle to the Hebrews. Seventeenth-century theologians like Olier seem to have found it in biblical commentaries or perhaps also in the church fathers who often commented on Christ's heavenly sacrifice. One of Olier's English contemporaries, Bishop Jeremy Taylor (1613–67), developed a sacrificial understanding of the Eucharist that paralleled that of the parish priest of Saint-Sulpice. He extolled Christ's heavenly priesthood and sacrifice and inspired the frontispiece of a commentary on the Book of Common Prayer published in 1710. The frontispiece (ill. 22) depicts the communicants kneeling on the chancel floor before the rails of the altar at which the celebrant is preparing the elements. Above him in a cloud of glory stands the Savior, hands raised before the heavenly altar. A halo contains the lettering "Hebr IX 11.23 VII 25." These references to passages in the seventh and ninth chapters of Hebrews are taken to assert that Jesus is the heavenly high priest who, by offering sacrifice, "ever liveth to make intercession" for the faithful.[130]

Olier takes great care to show that every detail and every gesture performed during Mass must be understood in terms of sacrifice. While the consecration

22. The Earthly and the Heavenly Sacrifice. The sacrifice of the Mass, celebrated at the altar in church (*bottom*), corresponds to and indeed joins Christ's self-sacrifice in heaven (*top*). The idea of the heavenly altar at which Christ offers himself to the Father was based on the medieval reading of the epistle to the Hebrews. English devotional engraving, eighteenth-century.

and the elevation represent Christ's sacrifice to the Father, the priest's communion stands for the Father's acceptance of the offering. The Father consumes the body and blood of Christ, thus uniting his Son to himself in unsurpassed intimacy. (At Mass, the priest is generally understood to represent Christ; for Olier, the role of the priest changes from representing Christ in the consecration and elevation to the role of the Father in taking communion.)[131]

At Mass, Christians are not mere spectators of Christ's sacrifice; they participate in it. In his priestly function, Christ offers both himself and his church "as a holocaust to God" (*EC* 287). As in Augustine's theology, we cannot offer ourselves to the Father, but Christ can do so.

In Olier's parish, people were exhorted not only to attend and "hear" Mass, but also to receive communion, and to do so frequently, as was the wish of the Council of Trent.[132]

Unlike the priest's communion, the laity's eating of the body of Christ does not symbolize the Father's acceptance of the sacrifice. In communion, the resurrected, glorified Christ visits the human soul. That visit can be experienced at two different levels of intensity, depending on the communicant's spiritual development.[133]

For many, communion is an experience that leads to an inner purification. At the reception of communion, the first reaction to the Lord's visit of the soul is the soul's feeling of utter unworthiness. "My God, I am an abyss of impurity, why are you descending into it? O my all, O my good, tolerate that I recede from you rather than approach you. At least, O my all, let me keep an inner distance from you out of a sincere respect. If I am approaching you, I do so because I am bound to obey you and your Church" (*JC* 134). Olier's model prayer reveals a tormented soul, deeply aware of its unworthiness, its ugliness, its sinfulness. "O my Jesus, leave me, O my Lord and Master, go and take your abode in God your Father, in that adorable bosom that fills you with glory and makes you perfect in majesty" (*JC* 135). Eventually, the communicant may become accustomed to and appreciate the Lord's presence. Christ's eucharistic presence in the human heart helps to subjugate our evil inclinations and to mortify our old, unregenerate being. "So come to us, O Lord [Jesus] . . . , come to annihilate in us the empire of Satan, [the Father's] sworn enemy. Come to annihilate in us the sinful flesh with its evil desires and base attachments. Come and establish in us the kingdom of God the Father, and make everything in us obedient to him" (*JC* 131). Olier knows that often the effect of this mortification, purification, or inner restructuring remains minimal, especially when communion is a merely "spiritual" act rather than the sacramental reception of the transubstantiated bread. The action of God is typically "very rare and very feeble; the creature spoils all, impeding God's great designs for us" (*CC* 66).

A deeper experience can be had by those advanced in their spiritual development. When they receive communion, the distance between the human soul and Christ, characteristic of the first stage, is overcome. Now the soul no longer runs away from Christ but finds herself in his embrace. "He embraces her strongly, as if to make her enter into himself" (*L* 1:354—letter no. 145). Drawing on the mystical tradition, Olier speaks of a marriage of Christ and soul and can refer to communion as the wedding banquet. "In his nuptial banquet, he [Christ] entertains the soul, treating her as a spouse" (*CC* 63). For Olier, the most important effect of the love relationship is the soul's assimilation to and indeed transformation into Christ: "for our Lord penetrates the entire soul, as it is indicated by the term of communion which refers to a union of the soul with Christ and of Christ with the soul, a union so complete that the soul is possessed by Christ, and the entire soul is transformed into Christ." The mystical bond involves the soul's complete transformation, and the soul thereby acquires Christ's own attitudes and dispositions. This process orients

23. The Christ-Lamb in the Host. The host, held by a Baroque ostensory, represents the Christ who, like a lamb, is presented to God as a sacrifice. Jean-Jacques Olier, parish priest of Saint-Sulpice in seventeenth-century suburban Paris, had this print designed and engraved by celebrated contemporary artists Charles Le Brun and Claude Mellan. It served as a devotional aid and reminded people of the spirit of Christ's sacrifice which they were to imitate. Charles Le Brun and Claude Mellan, devotional print, 1642 or 1643.

the soul toward God the Father, making her share Christ's spirit of humility and sacrifice. Herself Christlike, the human soul participates in and is drawn into Christ's sacrifice to the Father.[134]

For Olier, the soul's enjoyment of her intimate union with Christ is only one stage in a process that culminates in a self-sacrifice offered to the Father. Christ does not draw the soul to himself without drawing her to the Father. By joining Christ at communion, the faithful become part of his sacrifice. Communion "is nothing else than a union with the host-victim [i.e., Christ], so that it is expanded and made into a greater sacrifice. It makes of all the offerers and worshipers as many victims for God" (*EC* 434). Thus, to receive communion is nothing short of joining Christ's sacrifice in an act of self-oblation. With communion, "the concluding part of the sacrifice," Mass has reached its climax, its goal, and its end (*EC* 434).

As a parish priest and preacher, Olier felt the difficulties involved in explaining his sacrificial theology to his parishioners. Abstract reasoning was of little help, and not many read the pious books available at his specially established bookstore. His solution was to present his theology in visual form (ill. 23).

He sketched and had engraved an ostensory which showed the host with an immolated lamb, offered to the Father who floats above the scene, his arms wide open in a gesture reminiscent of Michelangelo's work, ready to accept the sacrifice. The ostensory is surrounded by rays of light and inscribed with what Olier perceives to be "the state and the occupations of Jesus in this mystery" of the Eucharist: "sacrifice, oblation, immolation, self-annihilation, penitence." Designed by Charles Le Brun and engraved by the famous French artist Claude Mellan (1598–1688), the print was frequently imitated. Nineteenth-century adaptations served as holy cards for devotions and sometimes included texts that celebrated Olier as a leader of spiritual renewal.[135]

The original print, a large leaf measuring 29 × 44 cm, was given as a present to the members of the *Confrérie du très-Saint Sacrement* which Olier established in his parish. In his book *La Journée chrétienne* he included a series of prayers to be said when meditating on the picture. "O eternal Father, I adore the acts of homage and the duty which your Son in his soul pays to you in the most holy sacrament. I beseech you to accept them from him on my behalf, for he pays them in my intention and in my place" (*JC* 161). After having asked the Father to accept the homage paid by Jesus, the meditating individual addresses the Son: "I ask you, Son of God, to establish in my heart the same sense of love and veneration of your Father, for I cannot hope to have any true feeling of fear and respect for you unless I participate in your inner being which is the fullness of Christian perfection" (*JC* 161).

Once Christ has made the praying person like himself, that person can offer him- or herself to God as a sacrifice:

> I also dedicate myself, O God, to you as a host-victim that presents itself to your majesty in order to be sacrificed in your honor and to be annihilated for your glory. At this very moment I offer myself to you and consecrate myself to your altars, in order to be immolated at the time you have chosen in your providence. . . . I give you my body so that it may be immolated in suffering, and my spirit so that it may be immolated in the experience of inner pain. (*JC* 162–63)

At this final stage, the believer imitates Christ in surrendering him- or herself completely to God. In doing so, the believer hopes to be incorporated into, or swallowed up by, the deity: "I give you my heart so that it may be consumed in your love. Make of it a holocaust that makes me pass over into your divine being (*passer dans votre Etre divin*)" (*JC* 163). Thus, the self-sacrifice again culminates in the mystical moment in which the human soul is united with God in unsurpassed intimacy. This moment, however, does not belong to our lifetime and earthly circumstances. On earth Christians can only hope to acquire Christ's spirit of sacrifice and accept a life of suffering.

The engraving centers on the sacrificial connection between the Christ-lamb and God the Father. The burning lamb is consumed in flames that are reaching up to God the Father and to the Holy Spirit, the latter represented as a dove. Originally, Olier had planned to include another theme: the priest as the mediator of the spirit of sacrifice taught by Christ's offering. He wished to have a priest depicted standing at the foot of the ostensory. The priest's heart would receive Christ's emanations of love and devotion to the Father, in order to pass it on to his parishioners. Charles Le Brun, the artist Olier commissioned, may have omitted the priest figure in order not to overload the picture and to attain a perfect and convincing symmetry.[136]

In a later pictorial project the priest was to assume center-stage. He wanted to print and distribute an engraving depicting Holy Mass. Olier's early death, at the age of forty-eight in 1657, prevented him from realizing his wish. However, a nineteenth-century drawing, apparently based on Olier's description, gives us an idea of what he had in mind. It shows the priest as he elevates the host, offering it to the Father who floats, his arms opened wide, in the high vault of heaven. The celebrating priest is joined not only by the faithful, who crowd around the altar, but also by the saints and angels in heaven, as well as the poor souls suffering in the flames of purgatory. The sketch includes a legend to be printed at the bottom: "At the moment of the elevation, the heavenly Church descends on the clouds, uniting itself with the one on earth in order to offer itself to God as a single host-victim with Jesus Christ." Olier's view of the Mass, like his entire theological reflection, can be condensed into one word: sacrifice.[137]

5. Conclusion: Two Theologies of Sacrifice

Sacrifice, in the ancient world, meant the slaughtering of an animal and the ritual handling of its body and blood by a priest. The sacred act culminated in the presentation of blood and body at the altar; the priest handed them over to the deity. Christianity inherited this notion from the cult conducted at the Temple in Jerusalem, and at least some early Christians actually participated in certain sacrificial rituals. Jesus himself apparently showed much interest in the Temple cult, to the point of attempting its reform in a bold occupation of the Temple. He used sacrificial language in a ritual he established after having failed to reform the procedure of private sacrifice at the Jerusalem Temple. In this new ritual, inaugurated shortly before his death and presumably not celebrated very frequently, a simple meal replaced the private sacrificial worship other Jews continued to celebrate at the Temple. The polemical replacement itself was expressed in the identification of bread with the victim's slaughtered body and the wine with its blood—hence the bold reuse of the sacred words with which the Jewish sacrificer presented his victim at the altar: "This is my [animal's] blood—This is my [animal's] body." With the partial destruction of the Temple in 70 CE and its complete removal in 135 CE, however, all Jewish sacrificial activity ceased, and so Christian involvement with sacrifice in the literal sense also came to an end. Judaism lost its major traditional ritual, and it was never restored. It could not be restored, for its legitimate celebration was thought to be permitted only at the Jerusalem Temple. The end of Jewish animal sacrifice and Jesus' use of bread and wine as a substitute for the animal victim combined to produce a lasting effect on Western religion: animal sacrifice disappeared from its repertoire of rituals. While Jesus may have meant his substitution only as a temporary measure, his "unbloody" celebration actually created a new, nonsacrificial religion. Sacrifice, in the literal sense of killing an animal victim, became obsolete. Here we can witness how particular historical circumstances, how an "accident" rather than actual decisions, produced a religious revolution of world-historical significance.

Christians gave up killing animal victims in a ritual context and felt that this should never be restored. Nevertheless, they continued the practice of material (but non-animal) offerings, and their leaders developed sacrificial theologies. The earliest sacrificial theology that we can tentatively reconstruct is that of

Irenaeus of Lyons. Although this theology is expressed in vague terms, it implies the presence of two sacrifices: one in which people offered material gifts to God and one in which the priest offered bread and wine, identified with Christ's own body and blood. No major theology of the people's gifts emerged, for there was no need for it. In accordance with ancient pagan thought, gifts were given in return for divine blessing. While the clergy took much interest in the gifts themselves (for they contributed to their livelihood), they rarely acknowledged these gifts' sacrificial dignity. They focused on Christ's bread and wine, whose offering they understood as a commemoration of the dying Christ's self-offering to the Father. In the patristic period, two interpretations of this commemorative, unbloody sacrifice emerged. According to the first, the faithful must include themselves in Christ's sacrifice so that he may offer them to the Father. The second view concentrates on the benefits which God gives in return for the sacrificial gift (Christ's, not the people's) he receives.

For Cyprian and Augustine, who developed the first interpretation, the faithful present at the Eucharist somehow include themselves in Christ's self-giving. Together with Christ, they offer themselves to the Father; or rather, Christ, when approaching the Father, offers both himself and the faithful. Christian theologians, though often more interested in other aspects of the eucharistic ritual, never lost sight of the idea of sacrificial giving. In the sixteenth century, Martin Luther found the idea of the Christian sacrifice acceptable, as long as it is clear "that we are not offering Christ, but Christ offers us [to God], and in this sense it is tolerable, even profitable to call Mass a sacrifice," for "we offer ourselves with Christ, i.e., we place ourselves on Christ, firmly believing in his promise." However, since people tend to misconstrue the meaning of sacrifice, both Luther and his followers generally avoided the term, leaving it to Catholics to rediscover Augustine's theology in the seventeenth century. Jean-Jacques Olier, a priest in seventeenth-century suburban Paris and a devotional author, served as our main example for the modern spiritual ideals of self-oblation and adoring abandonment to the divine.[138]

Reinvigorated by spiritual authors like Olier, the view survived the seventeenth century. Theologians and spiritual directors continued to recommend the "sacrificial communion" at which "the truly perfect communicant places himself entirely on the cross with Jesus so as to form one victim with him." The doctrine came to be adopted as part of official Catholic teaching. Pope Pius XII, in a 1947 encyclical letter, explains the meaning of the Mass with explicit reference to Augustine, as does the 1994 *Catechism of the Catholic Church*. Pius XII also seems to echo the mind of the parish priest of Saint-Sulpice. Not only should Christians strive to have "the same dispositions as those which the divine Redeemer had when he offered himself in sacrifice," that is the humble attitudes of adoration, honor, praise, and thanksgiving; they should also "undergo with Christ a mystical death on the cross" and thus assume "the character of a victim." Without the faithfuls' offering "themselves, their cares, their sorrows, their distress, and their necessities in union with their divine Savior," Mass would be incomplete.[139]

While Olier's view reflects a standard doctrine in Catholicism, sacrificial self-giving also receives the attention of other churches and sometimes forms part of their liturgies. In one of the eucharistic prayers used in the Church of England, for example, self-oblation is explicitly mentioned: "Through him [Christ] we offer you our souls and bodies, to be a living sacrifice." In response to Christ's self-sacrifice, the faithful are called to offer themselves to God. Kenneth Stevenson, a priest in the Church of England, admonishes his congregation to remember the cost of sacrifice: "Sometimes it would be a sobering experience," he reflects, "if those going so cheerfully away from our warm and comfortable fellowships were to feel and breathe the air of hostility and persecution faced by so many Christians in many parts of the world." In the rhetoric of the preacher we can hear an echo of Cyprian's voice speaking to persecuted congregations in third-century Africa, exhorting them to prepare for martyrdom. From Cyprian to Olier and Stevenson, sacrificial self-oblation must be more than the inner movement of the devout spirit; it includes the preparedness to shed one's blood for the sake of Christ.[140]

Even though sacrifice must be more than an inner movement, it certainly starts with an inner awareness or a ritual act helping worshipers to find the proper, sacrificial state of mind. The Catholic liturgy defines that state as one of purity and therefore begins Mass with a rite of purification: the sprinkling of holy water as a cleansing agent, the singing of Psalm 51—"purge me with hyssop, and I shall be clean; wash me, and I shall be whiter than snow"—or a simple confession of sins followed by the priest's words of absolution. As we have seen, a sacrificial victim must be pure, and only in a state of maximal purity can the faithful join the sacrifice of the One who was without the stain of sin.

Those Christians who hand themselves over to God in a sacrificial gesture, must not even secretly expect to get a divine gift in return—this at any rate is the implication of the Augustinian point of view. Any expectation would destroy the purity of their intention of loving God for his own sake. They must agree with Carl Gustav Jung who argued that "a gift" is not automatically a sacrifice, for "it only becomes a sacrifice if I give up the implied intention of receiving something in return."[141]

Not all theologians shared this harsh Augustinian view of self-effacement before God. For them, it made sense to ask whether God granted any benefits in return for Christian offering. In the Christianized Roman Empire, this question received a positive answer. For bishops Eusebius and Cyril, the Eucharist functioned as a universal sacrifice that secured divine help for church, empire, and the individual believer. Because of its powerful effects, it superseded and eventually replaced pagan sacrificial worship. Owing to its powerful effects recorded in the writings of Augustine and Pope Gregory the Great, it also developed into "private Mass." By saying a private Mass, the priest applies some of the Mass's sacrificial benefits to an individual or a group in need of help. Increasingly, people would pay priests for "saying Mass on their behalf." In the late fifteenth century, the German theologian Gabriel Biel still found this an acceptable practice, though his subtle account is hedged with caution.

Protestants, starting with Luther, generally rejected the Catholic method of securing and applying sacrificial benefits. Especially unpopular with them is the idea of "payment." Today, however, after Catholic theologians themselves have abandoned the details of Biel's system (while still retaining its essence), some Protestants no longer feel hostile to the idea of sacrificial receiving. In 1982, the Protestant monk Max Thurian of Taizé composed a text for an ecumenical celebration of the Eucharist. He felt that the ecumenical climate now permitted the use of sacrificial language: "United in Christ's priesthood, we present to you [Father] this memorial: remember the sacrifice of your Son and grant to people everywhere the benefits of Christ's redemptive work." No doubt, Eusebius, Gregory, and Gabriel Biel would have found this prayer congenial to their view of the eucharistic sacrifice.[142]

The balance of sacrificial giving and reaping of benefits may seem theologically satisfying. Yet, modern spirituality as represented by Olier seems to have a clear preference for the aspect of giving, of self-oblation, of binding oneself to the bleeding, painfully suffering, dying Christ. Stevenson, the Anglican priest quoted above, appreciates the offering of one's own person as a supremely appropriate metaphor for reminding people of the existential challenge involved in worship. Far from building on "an instinct within the human person," self-offering requires an act of renunciation. "Communion costs" serves as the slogan of Stevenson's eucharistic theology, and his favorite hymn is Isaac Watts's invitation to complete self-sacrifice:

Were the whole realm of nature mine
That were an offering far too small.
[Christ's] Love so amazing, so divine,
Demands my soul, my life, my all.

Christian life, like eucharistic celebration, culminates in a complete self-offering to God.[143]

While priests like Stevenson and Augustine and Jean-Jacques Olier and many others have spoken of the Eucharist mainly as the sacred game of sacrifice, other Christians have come to see it from a different perspective. Rooted as they were in the world of ancient magic, they could not avoid playing it as a magical game to which they gave the name of sacrament.

The Fifth Game: Sacrament
Meeting Christ at the Lord's Supper

Very truly, I tell you, unless you eat the flesh of the Son of Man and drink
his blood, you have no life in you. Those who eat my flesh and drink my
blood have eternal life, and I will raise them up on the last day.

> Jesus (John 6:53–54, NRSV)

Come, Holy Ghost, thine influence shed,
And realize the sign;
Thy life infuse into the bread,
Thy power into the wine.
Charles Wesley (1707–88), Eucharistic hymn no. 72

Quand l'hostie fut déposé sur mes lèvres, je me sentis comme tout éclairé en
dedans. Je tremblais de respect. (As the host was placed on my lips, I felt as if
enlightened from within. I trembled with awe.)[1]

> François-René de Chateaubriand on his first communion, 1781

1. On Magic: A Rehabilitation

Being rooted in magic, the sacrament, like the practice of animal sacrifice, has the ring of something primitive, superstitious, and utterly irrational. In medieval scholasticism, when the ancient magical roots of Christian rituals, such as the holy bath (or washing) of baptism or the Lord's Supper, had long been forgotten, even a sophisticated, rational theory could not ignore the basic components that define both Aladdin's Lamp and the Lord's Supper: a visible action, a tangible object, a sacred word uttered, and a secret, invisible power set in motion. The Lord's Supper, known to most Christians, reminds them little of the occult arts (though belief in the power and possible intervention of the dead, an assumption basic to ancient magic, is common to both). But many would agree that exorcism, in which a twentieth-century priest commands evil demons to leave a human being, smacks of arcane knowledge, the occult, the archaic, and the shaman's craft, and leaves them with an uneasy feeling. As part of contemporary Christian ritual, magic survivals constitute a rather embarrassing subject, out of tune with the enlightened mentality of our age. However, if we want to understand the meaning of the sacrament as a central act of Christian worship, we simply cannot avoid the subject of magic.[2]

The best way to introduce ancient magic is to discuss some of the relevant received ideas, and to show how scholarship has begun to abandon them.

The Received View of Magic vs. the Greek Magical Papyri

For millennia (so runs the received view) human cultures have perceived their environment as being haunted by supernatural powers: gods, demons, good and evil spirits. People lived in an enchanted forest whose glens and groves swarmed with superhuman, divine beings. In this world, reality was charged with a magical power that erupted here and there to threaten or benefit. Properly managed and utilized, this invisible energy could be supplicated, warded off, or channeled, and people did so with the help of gods and spirits. At an early period, two ways of dealing with the world of supernatural powers emerged. While the early priests humbled themselves before the gods, imploring them and seeking their friendship, the early magicians resorted to a harsher régime: they sought to control gods and spirits by threatening them. These two attitudes, though initially often confused, became increasingly distinct. As the two attitudes crystallized into religion and magic, a fundamental conflict developed. Since time immemorial, explains the anthropologist Sir James Frazer,

> the haughty self-sufficiency of the magician, his arrogant demeanor toward the higher powers, and his unabashed claim to exercise a sway like theirs could not but revolt the priest, to whom, with his awful sense of the divine majesty, and his humble prostration in presence of it, such claims and such demeanor must have appeared an impious and blasphemous usurpation of prerogatives that belong to God alone.

In the ancient world of paganism, the priestly religion fought against magic by outlawing it and by pushing it to the periphery of ritual behavior. It became the underground religion of the sorcerer who for payment offered his services to those who hoped to gain advantage by using his expertise. It was not before the advent of biblical religion that the conflict between religion and magic was finally resolved. The prophets abolished magic by promoting a thoroughly rational religion, based on the obedience to and love of God, and under the impact of Christianity, even pagan magicians gave up their superstitious craft and burned their books (Acts 19:19). Christianity is—and should be—free of magic.[3]

When Sir James Frazer wrote *The Golden Bough* (1890) and the Protestant theologian Harvey Cox published *The Secular City* (1965)—the two books we have used to present the "received view" of magic—they had little knowledge of ancient magic and its practice. Like many of their contemporaries, they had not studied the remnants of ancient magical lore accessible to twentieth-century scholarship mainly in an ancient library found in Thebes, Egypt. A Scandinavian merchant by the adopted name of Giovanni Anastasi (1780–1857) bought this unique collection of eight scrolls and fifteen codices in four languages and scripts (hieratic and demotic Egyptian, Greek, and Old Coptic). A good businessman, Anastasi divided his treasure into various lots which he sold to the national libraries in London, Leiden, Paris, and Stockholm. Only very slowly and hesitantly did European scholars take a closer look at the new source material, for it seemed to contradict the lofty notions they had of the enlightened Greek mentality. Only finally edited and translated in the twentieth century, Anastasi's treasure is known as the *Papyri Graecae Magicae* (*PGM*). Contemporary scholars who have studied these papyri together with other ancient sources such as the fragments of the third-century CE *Chaldean Oracles*, the philosopher Iamblichus' treatise *On the Egyptian Mysteries*, and the Coptic texts recently edited as *Ancient Christian Magic*, have come to a different assessment from those who despise the esoteric arts as belonging to the realm of superstition and the "magical underworld" of late antiquity. "Magic in the ancient world," explains Cyril Richardson, "comprehended so much we would denominate as mystical, charismatic, and psychical, that such a [negative] view is really untenable. Our attitudes derived from the Enlightenment need serious revision." Ancient magic neither aimed at "coercing" the gods, nor was it generally outlawed and considered a superstition.[4]

Despite the seemingly ineradicable, nineteenth-century notion that magicians "force" supernatural powers to conform to the petty wishes of men and women, the magical attitude is generally one of humbleness and pious devotion. The ancient practitioners of magic prayed to deities and spirits, imploring their help. One prayer included in *PGM*, presumably composed by a first-century Jew living in Egypt, summons the Father by a long list of magical names in order then to ask him quite humbly: "Fill me with wisdom! Strengthen me, Master; fill my heart with good, Master, as a terrestrial angel, as one who has become immortal, as one who has received this gift from you." (The papyrus carries the instruction to utter the prayer seven times.) True, there are ancient magical spells in which evidence for humility is lacking and the practitioner converses with the gods on equal terms. However, the magician's lack of humility, evident in some of the ancient sources, should not be misunderstood. When in some ancient documents the magician gives orders instead of imploring humbly, one has to keep in mind an ancient ritual pattern that modern scholars have termed the *unio liturgica*, the "liturgical union" with a supernatural being. Just as today's Catholic priest assumes the role of Christ when pronouncing certain words at Mass, so the ancients often identified with gods when performing ritual acts. The ritual acted out on earth replicates, in the form of a sacred drama, events happening in the realm of the gods. Whether humbly imploring or giving a command, the magician hopes the deity will "descend" from the supernatural realm and show its presence or work its miracles here—in the magician's kitchen, on the roof of his (or her) house, where roads cross, during the day or at midnight. With the divine agent's arrival, the ritual act has attained its goal.[5]

In order to understand magic as found in *PGM*, the distinction between its three main varieties must be kept in mind. Following ancient terminology, we may call them thaumaturgy, black magic, and theurgy. *Thaumaturgy*, the first kind, serves to produce more or less tangible miracles. It is here that country magic for the crops and love charms for the languishing heart belong. They may be (in the minds of some) as superstitious as other ritual acts, but they were never classified with *black magic* (i.e., black thaumaturgy, also called sorcery or witchcraft), done for treasonable or murderous purposes. When the ancients outlawed witchcraft, sorcery, and similar business, they tried to suppress the harmful rather than the helpful or "white" rituals. Although a thaumaturgist could be suspected of misusing his powers for evil purposes, "black" and "white" rituals were clearly distinguished. The third kind of magic, *theurgy*, was given its name by third-century CE Neoplatonic philosophers like Porphyry, who in his commentary on the *Chaldean Oracles* emphasized the unique and lofty character of their ritual acts. The term means "divine operation" and can be paraphrased as "sacred ritual" which involves someone's "being worked upon by the gods" (and has nothing to do with "urging" occult forces or "working upon the gods"). It refers to actions that bring about the presence of a divine being or supernatural power in a material object such as a statue or a person, resulting in a state of trance. As an "honorable" and "laudable" art, ancient theurgy placed its practitioners above the suspicion of performing harmful or at any rate questionable rituals for selfish purposes. Unlike the black or white thaumaturgist, the theurgist was exclusively interested in the saving or therapeutic experience of the divine; any other, "secular" advantage—taking vengeance on an enemy, procuring love, fertility, or wealth—did not come into the equation. Theurgy is magic applied to a religious purpose. According to Iamblichus, the foremost ancient theorist of sacred magic, "theurgists do not address the divine intellect [i.e., the deity] over trifling matters but only concerning things that pertain to the purification, liberation, and salvation of the soul." Theurgy, as understood by Neoplatonic philosophers, also relied on a world view different from that of earlier magic. Before the emergence of Neoplatonic theurgy, magicians had sought to enlist the help of demons and disembodied souls residing in the underworld. Theurgy, by contrast, placed the power the magician sought in the celestial realm. The demons and deities who help the theurgist were imagined to dwell in the air between the earth and the moon. Thus, theurgy inherited all the prestige invested in the traditional cults venerating celestial gods. The new magic of theurgy no longer had to do with the impure realm of the dead.[6]

Thaumaturgy and Theurgy in Jewish and Christian Practice

The diligent study of the Greek magical papyri not only dispelled certain received ideas about pagan magic; it also led scholars to reconsider the involvement of ancient Judaism and early Christianity with thaumaturgy and theurgy. In fact, a look at the sources reveals that Christians from their early history on shared the thaumaturgical beliefs and practices with which their cultural world was saturated. As Homer tells us, the friends of young Ulysses treated his hunting wound with both a bandage and a charm that stopped the bleeding. Around 205 CE, Tertullian reports how his fellow Christians deal with a scorpion's sting: by "immediately making the sign [of the cross] and adjuring, and besmearing the heel with the [gore of the] beast." Nothing had changed since Homer's day: the magic gesture and the healing charm had not disappeared from "first aid." Thaumaturgical magic had a firm and unchallenged place both in ancient Judaism and in early Christian practice. Josephus (37–100 CE), a contemporary of the apostles, talks about Jewish magicians and includes an eyewitness report on one of them, a man called Eleazar. He also explains that these figures considered King Solomon the first man to apply exorcisms and magical cures; as their founding father, Solomon had initiated an art still practiced by many. According to popular tradition, no one could surpass Solomon's wisdom, for "God granted him knowledge of the art against demons for the benefit and healing of men. He also composed incantations by which illnesses are relieved, and left behind forms of exorcisms with which those possessed by demons drive them out, never to return. And this method of cure is of great force unto this day." In the Roman world, Christian clergy had the best access to secret powers which they could mobilize on behalf of the faithful. Christians like Augustine made full use of the widespread fascination with miracle and magic. In the *City of God*, he devotes an entire chapter to miracles, some of which he had witnessed himself, and occasionally shares the recipe with his readership. Why should one not rely on the application of oil, mixed with the prayerful tears of a priest (a prayer made tangible), as an ointment against demonic possession? Magic's visible success attracted attention and won converts. Edward Gibbon, in his celebrated *Decline and Fall of the Roman Empire* (1776–88), mentioned exorcism and magic cures among the main causes contributing to the unprecedented growth and eventual victory of the new religion. In our century, Adolf von Harnack's *Mission and Expansion of Christianity* (1902) has affirmed Gibbon's claim: while some intellectuals like Origen preferred Christ the Teacher, Christ the Savior or Healer was more popular with the masses, and his priests knew how to make his power available. Recent scholarship has continued Harnack's interest in magical Christianity by describing how it developed after the third century, when Harnack's study ends. Theologians and churchmen like Augustine, Gregory the Great, and Caesarius of Arles all helped to forge a specifically Catholic variety of magic, one that established the medieval apparatus of weather blessings, miraculous relics, holy water, crosses (as a gesture and as a sacred object), exorcisms, and display of the consecrated host in a monstrance (for the altar and for processions outside the church), together with the supporting belief in demons, angels, and saints. What intellectual Christianity today plays down, hides, ignores, or disdains as superstition, served then as its most powerful propaganda.[7]

While ancient communal ritual often included a certain amount of what Sir James Frazer defined as "public magic, that is, sorcery practiced for the benefit of the whole community," its use intensified in the Hellenistic period and developed quite distinctive forms. As the rule of Alexander the Great and his followers put an end to the political independence of practically all the Near Eastern peoples, their religions underwent a period of crisis and transformation. The veneration of deities and the observance of traditional rites no longer seemed natural and unquestionable. In particular, ethnic gods lost much of their prestige, because they had not been able to protect their nations and prevent their being absorbed into the political system established by the Greek overlords. One looked for deities that were able to offer better protection and guidance. People were more and more prepared to rethink and even change their cultic affiliations. The idea of "conversion" to a particular deity or cult became fashionable, and cults tended to become local or even international fellowships into which one could be received, irrespective of ethnic background or social class. Many of the new cults came to be called "mysteries." Typically, there were no "born" members; one had to be initiated, for only after initiation could one be admitted to participation in certain theurgical rituals and benefit from its promise which often meant life after death. According to the new mentality, people no longer felt born into a divinely established and protected land with stable institutions of political leadership, priesthood, and temple. Instead, they felt they should be initiated into a new relationship, with a divine protector no longer tied to a particular land. In contrast to the public celebrations of traditional state cults concerned with national prosperity, mystery religions were voluntary associations whose cult focused on individual salvation brought by theurgy.[8]

The rituals of "mystery cults," though far from being uniform, nevertheless generally culminated in a sacramental drama that brought the initiates into close contact with the deity of the cult: with Isis, Mithras, Dionysos, or the Jewish god. Since the participants were generally placed under a vow of silence, we know very little about the rituals celebrated. Apparently, they included magic manipulations of objects, food, or water, and took place in a highly charged emotional atmosphere. Some of the mystery associations, especially the one venerating Mithras, included communal meals which the ancient author Pliny called "magical banquets" (*magicae cenae*).

> Tense mental anticipation, heightened by a period of abstinence, hushed silences, imposing processions and elaborated pageantry, music loud and violent or soft and enthralling, delirious dances, the drinking of spirituous liquors, physical lacerations, alternations of dense darkness and dazzling light, the sight of gorgeous ceremonial vestments, the handling of holy emblems, autosuggestion and the promptings of the hierophant [priest]—these and many other secrets of emotional exaltation were in vogue.

Emotional atmosphere, magical apparatus, and the aim of a mystical encounter with the deity or with the realm of the gods, characterize the sacrament celebrated in the mystery cults.[9]

First-century CE Judaism, while largely remaining an ethnic cult even in the Diaspora, nevertheless developed certain features of the mystery religions. This development was in a way inevitable, for Judaism had long since lost its national institutions and had become a belief system and way of life that could be practiced irrespective of whether one lived in Palestine, Egypt, Rome, or Spain. The Jewish god, moreover, was eminently suited to a mystery cult: the creator of the universe, he was a powerful deity whom the entire cosmos had to obey. Whatever their local origins may have been, all deities venerated in mystery cults transcended local particularism and the limited tasks assigned to them in earlier religious systems. While the existence of a mystery variety of Judaism is a matter of scholarly debate often hinging on definitions, we can point to the existence of sacred meals apparently held in small groups.[10]

In Old Testament times, some of the rituals priests celebrated in the Temple were not public. Not everyone could participate, presumably only priests, the king, and some of the elders. According to a legendary account, Moses was not alone on Mount Sinai when he conversed with God. On one occasion, he was accompanied by priests and the elders of the Israelite tribes, seventy men; all of them "beheld God, and they ate and drank" (Exod. 24:11). This biblical story may echo theurgical rites during which God was made present in a cloud of smoke, produced by the burning of incense. Participants had visions of the Lord and held a meal in his presence. Gerhard von Rad, one of the foremost twentieth-century interpreters of the Old Testament, postulated the existence of "an inner circle of rites, mysteries, and cultic events, to which many would have liked to be admitted," but which were celebrated in restricted circles of specially privileged persons.[11]

In the Hellenistic period, however, participation in Jewish mystery rites was less restricted; even pagans, duly converted, could attend. Readers versed in ancient religions have often suggested that the story of Joseph and Aseneth, a Jewish Diaspora novella dating from New Testament times, reflects a "mystery" understanding of Judaism. The story tells how a beautiful Egyptian lady, Aseneth, converts to Judaism and then marries Joseph, a Jewish man. This "mystery novel" permits us to reconstruct an elaborate ritual used for the reception of a convert into full membership. It begins with the convert's confession of sins before the congregation, in which pagan ritual is denounced as defiling. After the announcement that God has received him or her into Judaism, the new member is renamed, anointed, and puts on a new garment. Then the officiant pronounces a word of praise and congratulation: "Happy are you, N., because the ineffable mysteries of the most High have been revealed to you, and happy are all who attach themselves to the Lord God in repentance." The "ineffable mysteries" are no doubt the honeycomb and the cup which the convert is now given to eat and drink. After the convert has done this, the officiant explains: "Behold, you have eaten bread of life and drunk a cup of immortality, and been anointed with ointment of incorruptibility." The ceremony ends with everyone present kissing the new member.[12]

While this "mystery" reading of the Jewish story seems attractive, some have been reluctant to accept it. Christoph Burchard, a severe critic, nevertheless accepts the fact that here we have an echo of a magical Judaism. According to Burchard, the story implies that any Jew can act as a magician when blessing a meal. The biblical figure of Joseph is here presented as "a man who blesses with his mouth the living God and eats blessed bread of life and drinks a blessed cup of immortality and anoints himself with blessed ointment of incorruptibility."

The blessing spoken over food and over the daily ointment confers a special quality on them; no longer normal bread, blessed bread is the bread of life—food not only preventing the human body from becoming weak but also guaranteeing everlasting life. "The idea seems to be," explains Burchard, "that the benedictions will somehow imbue food, drink, and ointment with the spirit of life, making them the earthly substitute for celestial manna which is the spirit of life by essence. The spirit will in turn permeate a person as he or she consumes blessed food and drink and applies blessed ointment to the skin." Decisive for a Jewish blessing is the use of the appropriate, and sometimes complicated, form of the divine name, such as (in Hebrew) "Creator of the fruit of the tree" or "Lord our God, God of Israel, God of the Hosts who sits upon the Cherubim." Whoever knows how to pronounce a proper blessing over food can enjoy its secret and sacred properties at any time; and he or she can do so alone or in the company of others.[13]

The sacrament at the center of Christian worship, known as the Lord's Supper, involves prayers said over bread and wine and the consumption, generally communal, of a simple meal. In preparing the food and drink, the celebrant invokes the name of the Lord Jesus, a martyred being who resides in the beyond and whose earthly presence is brought about by this ritual. In order to understand the sacramental meal, we have to start with the founder of Christianity—with Jesus the Magician.

2. Inventing the Magical Celebration

The first three centuries of our era—the time in which Christianity emerged as a new religion in the Roman world—boasted an important magical culture. Babylonian, Egyptian, Greek, and Jewish magical lore flourished, and often met and blended to create new forms. In was in this context that early Christians developed their own magical liturgy, the Eucharist. In doing so, they stood under the influence and inspiration of Jesus, the Jewish magician of first-century Palestine. After the death of Jesus, his early disciples became increasingly involved with their master's art, and they redefined his sacrificial meal to suit their own theurgical and thaumaturgical preferences. This development is echoed in the New Testament, whose writings date from the second half of the first century. In the early third century, under the patronage of Julia Mamea and Julia Domna (two members of the Roman emperor's household), a wave of renewed enthusiasm for arcane ritual lore swept the empire. Christians proudly celebrated their increasingly organized sacramental liturgy, which one of their leaders, Bishop Hippolytus, codified in the *Apostolic Tradition*. In discussing first Jesus and his early disciples, and then the two Julias and Hippolytus, we move from East to West and from obscure origins to a well-established pattern of worship.

Jesus and the Magical Meal

The Lord's Supper originated as a simple ritual gesture in which men and women, instructed by Jesus, offered bread and wine to God as a substitute for an animal sacrifice (see the present study's part IV, above, pp. 215–27). In order to perform this gesture, nothing other than bread and wine were needed. People could have taken the lesson taught by Jesus and simply continued the ritual offering of bread and wine, without thinking much of the teacher. We may be grateful to those who taught us the ABC, but when writing, we rarely pause to marvel at how much time someone has invested in instructing us. However, the early Christians felt that in following the example of their master, they simply could not avoid thinking of him. The Lord was dead but his memory was alive, and also alive was the ritual he had performed with bread and wine. Whenever they offered bread and wine to God, they did so in remembrance of Jesus. Later, some of their leaders actually thought that this had been the Lord's very wish, and when telling the story of how Jesus taught the ritual, they made the Lord say, "Do this in remembrance of me" (1 Cor. 11:24; Luke 22:19). Since this particular saying is absent from Matthew and Mark, but not from Paul and Luke, it may well be that this particular version of the story represents a local development, possibly beginning in the city of Antioch, where Paul had lived before embarking on his missionary career.

When remembering a special person or moment, we do not remain unaffected, but often find ourselves in a melting mood. We may relive some past experience and feel joy or gratefulness, love or regret, or all of these at the same time. Memories may create a very special kind of pregnant atmosphere in which the past enriches and transfigures the present. The hearts of those who remembered the Lord were not cold but "burning within them" (Luke 24:32). Among the early believers, these feelings and the ensuing charged emotional atmosphere reached their peak during their eucharistic celebrations. Something special happened when Christians met to offer cup and bread. The atmosphere reminded them strongly of something they had felt earlier, when their master had engaged in rituals of spiritual healing and mystical contact with the divine reality.

The most ancient and most common image of Jesus found in biblical and nonbiblical tradition is that he acted as a healer, an exorcist, a miracle worker. "He healed many who were sick with various diseases, and cast out many demons," reports Mark in what is generally considered the oldest of the gospels (Mark 1:34). Mark also reports that it was his power to perform miracles that made Jesus famous throughout Galilee, the country where he was born and where he lived. People considered him an exorcist "greater than Solomon" (Matt. 12:42)—a man standing in Solomon's tradition but surpassing the legendary founder of Israel's magical lore. Jesus understood his exorcisms and healings as visible signs of God's rulership; they indicated that God himself worked through Jesus in driving out "unclean spirits." Arcane healing procedures did not exhaust the repertoire of Jesus. In fact, they represent only one side of his complex activity. In addition to performing "miracles," Jesus was involved with ritual practices belonging to the kind known from mystery cults.[14]

In mystery-like celebrations he initiated some of his disciples into the heavenly realm. One theurgical rite is known under the name of baptism. Apparently, Jesus and his followers were not satisfied with the "baptism" (the sacred bath) in which John the Baptist prepared people for God's kingdom. In the Jesus movement, baptism apparently involved a longer period of preparation; the sacred bath led to the candidate's endowment with the divine spirit and having a visionary experience. While the early sources supply little information about baptismal theurgy, we can learn more from the gospel story of Christ's "transfiguration." Jesus took three of his disciples and led them up a mountain, presumably after a six-day period of preparation. During a ritual séance, whose details are not told, the white garment Jesus wore for the occasion began to shine, a heavenly voice was heard, and Jesus spoke to two heavenly figures: Moses and the prophet Elijah (Mark 9). This initiation was meant only for a spiritual elite for whom Jesus would make heavenly beings descend and appear on earth. At another time, when Jesus was praying in the presence of his disciples on the Mount of Olives, an angel appeared. A similar scene, included in the Hebrew Bible, may have served as a precedent: Moses had taken Israel's elders to the top of the sacred mountain where they "saw God" (Exod. 24:9–11). Seeing Moses, Elijah or an angel in an hypnotic state was presumably the first stage in an ascent that would eventually lead to "seeing God."[15]

Unlike earlier critics, recent commentators no longer dismiss the story of Christ's transfiguration as a mere legendary fabrication. They can quote ancient sources to support the view that the account echoes ritual practice. Conversing with heavenly beings (angels, gods, or deceased humans), the assimilation of a human person to the gods' luminosity, and the demonstration of these theurgical achievements to others all have their equivalents in ancient theurgy. Particularly instructive is the fourth-century CE report about the Christian monk Anatolius. This holy man of eastern extraction, presumably from Beirut, who now lived in a monastic community near Tours in Gaul, would not have attracted much attention if he had only claimed to converse with angels and other heavenly beings. For Jesus the same claim was made, and both Paul and Bishop Martin of Tours (Anatolius's contemporary) made it for themselves. One cannot doubt that they refer to actual experience (which, for us moderns, invites a psychological rather than a supernatural explanation). Anatolius's second claim—"in me dwells the power of God"—was much rarer, though not unheard of. According to the gospel of John, Jesus had spoken of himself in this way, and so had the Teacher of Righteousness (founder of the Qumran sect) as well as the high priest Enoch (a legendary figure). Of Simon Magus, a representative of Samaritan theurgy, people said, "This man is the power of God that is called great" (Acts 8:10). It does not come as a surprise that not many of these holy men revealed their higher, luminous nature to others and demonstrated their skill of communicating with supernatural beings. In fact, only reports on the actual demonstrations of Jesus and Anatolius survive. Anatolius succeeded in showing his white, shining garment to some of his fellow monks and convinced them of his extraordinary abilities; others, however, rejected his theurgical arts as diabolical. Anatolius shares Jesus' roots in the religious culture of Syria-Palestine and therefore his case helps to elucidate early Christian involvement with eastern theurgy and mystery cults.[16]

How did Jesus develop an interest in practicing rituals reminiscent of a mystery cult which was complete with initiation and sacred teaching? The answer to this question can of course only be tentative, for the gospels tell us very little about the early career of Jesus. We know, however, that he was involved with John the Baptist, the leader of a movement on the way to becoming an organized mystery religion. Jesus' interest in cultic matters may have been inspired by his teacher John the Baptist. Jesus, like John, had followers or, in more mundane terms, a clientele. They must be seen as representatives of a social type well known from ancient sources: the itinerant practitioner or craftsman of the sacred. Although the wandering magician may have had a circle of friends and supporters, such a group must not be mistaken for a cultic association or a church. Although mystery cults often took the form of clubs, Jesus does not seem to have intended to establish one. The consolidation of the Jesus-movement into a series of local, synagogue-like associations represents a later development, born of the wish of those who knew Jesus to perpetuate his teaching and mysteries. Most scholars agree with Walter Burkert that, while many mystery cults originated with itinerant practitioners and achieved some stability in the form of associations, the process of social organization was never as successful as it came to be in the Christian case.[17]

While some of the details remain obscure, the early sources reveal to us a consistent image of a Jesus involved with two kinds of "white" magical procedures: healing and bringing others into contact with the divine world. Remembering their Lord's thaumaturgy and theurgy, the early believers used these patterns to explain what happened when they celebrated the Lord's Supper and ate the Lord's food.

There is a world of difference between two groups of early Christian writings. According to the gospels of Mark, Matthew, and Luke (the "synoptic gospels"), Jesus is the healer, the exorcist, and miracle worker, and his followers benefit from and participate in their Lord's healing ministry. The kingdom of God has come, when the blind see, the lame walk, and the demons are forced to leave tortured human bodies and enter into a herd of swine. By contrast, in the letters and Paul and the gospel of John, Christ is the risen Lord to whom his believers are united in faith and love and want to be filled with his spirit. They want to develop spiritually so that they can state with Paul that "it is no longer I who live, but it is Christ who lives in me" (Gal. 2:20). The difference between the two groups of writings can be defined in terms of thaumaturgy and theurgy. While the synoptic gospels focus on the thaumaturgical (miracle-working) ministry of Jesus which is continued by his disciples, John and Paul indicate that Christian existence culminates not in outward demonstrations of miraculous power, but in an inner, theurgical experience. Paul indicates the possibility of being caught up to the third heaven and hearing things that are not to be told, and in John, Christ promises that his disciples will "see him" a short while after his death, presumably in the kind of visionary experience described in the book of Revelation. Interpreters of Paul and John have often tried to define their theology in terms of mysticism. Albert Schweitzer wrote a book on *The Mysticism of Paul the Apostle* (1930), and John's gospel, with its message of love between Christ and the paradigmatic "beloved disciple," has often been termed "the gospel of mysticism." In accordance with their general thaumaturgical and theurgical perspectives, the two groups of New Testament writings propose two different perspectives on the Eucharist. While John and Paul speak of the Lord's Supper as a theurgical celebration, the synoptic gospels give it a decidedly thaumaturgical orientation.[18]

The first pattern, that of *thaumaturgy*, dominates the way the synoptic gospels tell the story of the Last Supper at which Christ "instituted" the celebration. They depict this story against a dark background which serves as its narrative framework. Following apocalyptic tradition their authors believed that the coming of God's kingdom would be preceded by a terrible time of war, social and political upheaval, famine, persecution, religious controversy, and apostasy—falling away from the true faith. Both the imprisonment and eventual beheading of John the Baptist and the execution of Jesus were taken to be clear evidence of the "great tribulation." The biblical account of the passion and crucifixion of Jesus includes a description of the last meal that he shared with his most intimate group of followers: his disciples. This meal is known as the "Last Supper," and it is said to have taken place in some "upper room" in a house in Jerusalem. According to the gospels of Mark, Matthew, and Luke, the most important features of this meal are as follows: (1) Jesus ate the meal knowing that it would be the last formal and festive meal before his death; (2) it was a Passover meal, i.e., a highly ceremonial meal which involved the consumption of bread, wine, and a lamb that had been ritually slaughtered by Jesus' disciples at the Temple; (3) Jesus presided over the meal and gave bread and wine to his disciples saying "this is my body" and "this is my blood poured out for many (or: for you)."

The meaning of the symbolic identification of bread and wine with Jesus derives from both the Passover context and the expectation of the death of Jesus during the tribulation. As part of the banquet, the story of the original, "first" Passover was recounted. During the time of Moses, when the ancient Israelites were held captive in Egypt, their God sent terrible calamities to punish the country. In order to avoid being harmed by one of the ten plagues sent against the Egyptians, the Israelites were told to sacrifice lambs and mark the entrances of their homes with the blood. This sign would ward off all evil and protect the homes of the Israelites. Just as all the plagues were initiated by magical means such as touching water with a magic wand or throwing dust in the air, so this magical mark indicated the houses that would remain unaffected. No doubt, a story so visibly magical attracted the attention and captured the imagination of a community involved in similar practices. Jesus' community was in a situation similar to that of the Israelites; like them, they were surrounded by hostile powers. Apparently, the ten plagues of the Exodus story were seen as the prototype of the calamities that were to occur during the tribulation. Anticipating his death in a symbolic gesture with bread and wine,

Jesus put himself in the place of the slain lamb. He used bread and wine to stand for "flesh" and "blood" separated in sacrificial slaughter. The bread was for consumption as the sacrificial meat. No Jew would drink blood, of course, but it would be natural to drink wine. In the oldest of the gospels, that of Mark, Jesus identifies the wine with his blood only after his disciples had shared the cup; thus the idea of actually "tasting" blood was avoided or at least made less prominent.[19]

Just as the sacrificial blood of the first Passover protected the Israelites in Egypt, so the blood/wine of Jesus would ward off the evil powers attacking his disciples. Protected by the blood of Jesus, the disciples would be able to survive the coming calamities, the foremost of which would be their master's death. Their protection did not imply that they were to be unconcerned bystanders of the terrible things to come. Jesus himself predicted the disciples' "falling away" and "being scattered" (Mark 14:26–27). However, they would be scattered only temporarily, and the community would soon be restored for the celebration of the final victory of God's kingdom. Jesus thus predicted that he would die, and that his death would usher in both a terrible crisis and, ultimately, the divine kingdom. His death, therefore, would not simply be one of the terrible losses characteristic of the tribulation; producing the protective blood symbolized by the wine, the master's death would also be a gain. Serving, for the disciples, as a protection against the ever-threatening powers of evil, it would benefit them greatly.

The atmosphere in which Jesus celebrated Passover was characterized by the expectation of his violent death. The tribulation, in fact, was felt as invading the room itself in the figure of Judas, the disciple who would betray Jesus. Whether the presence of the betrayer is a strictly historical feature of the biblical account or not, it certainly captures the imagination. Betrayal and hatred between brothers are included in the narrators' list of the tribulation horrors.[20]

Some early Christians recognized the apotropaic—danger-averting— meaning of their use of the Passover wine. Origen, one of the foremost of the early theologians, explains: "By drinking his blood as a true drink, they [the faithful] anoint the lintels of the houses of their souls." While Origen speaks of an inner "anointing" as a result of the drinking of the eucharistic cup, other early Christians actually moistened their foreheads with the eucharistic wine. The magical mark formerly placed at the lintels of real houses is now used to designate the protection of the human person, or at least of the soul. Did not Jesus himself mean the same thing when he suggested that those who persecute his followers can "kill the body but cannot kill the soul" (Matt. 10:28)?[21]

According to the second, *theurgical pattern*, the Lord's Supper makes the Lord present to those participating in the celebration and forges an enduring relationship between Christ and the believer. In the New Testament, evidence for the theurgical understanding of the Lord's Supper comes mainly from the letters of Paul and the gospel of John. In Paul, we find that the Lord's presence is somehow tied to bread and wine, termed "the Lord's food" or "spiritual food" and "spiritual drink." The eucharistic species serve as mysterious "vessels" or "carriers" of the Spirit of Christ, and by consuming them, the faithful are filled with the Spirit. If they partake of the magical meal in an unworthy manner, they may be severely punished. Rather than conveying the life-giving Spirit, the meal may in fact make them "weak and ill," and they may die (1 Cor. 15:45; 11:27–30). As long as individuals enjoy a harmonious relationship with Christ, they can greatly benefit from the Lord's spiritual presence in their body. To be possessed by Christ's angry Spirit, by contrast, may lead to death. It may well be that Paul or his contemporaries remembered the story of the Last Supper: all of Jesus' companions ate the blessed bread and drank the blessed wine; most received the blessing, but one did not and died—Judas, who had betrayed the Lord.[22]

The drinking of a magical substance that could help or harm was known in Jewish tradition. A good example of this is the ordeal procedure practiced in the Temple, designed to establish someone's innocence or culpability. Given wine to drink, the righteous would benefit from drinking it and the sinners would be harmed by it. The "cup of salvation" may turn into the "cup of wrath." The possibility of a negative and possibly even lethal effect of the eucharistic food and drink seems to echo these ancient ordeal procedures.[23]

For Paul, bread and wine represent—literally: make present again—the absent Christ or Christ's Spirit. More precisely, the eucharistic food is "possessed" by the Spirit, so that those who consume the magic substance will be possessed by the same Spirit. Paul did not invent the idea of the use of food and drink as carriers of some supernatural agent; rather, it corresponds to standard magical practice and has parallels in several ancient sources, including the Bible. Jesus himself reportedly used magical food: he gave a morsel of bread to Judas and so made "Satan enter into him," commanding "Do quickly what you are going to do." (The command to do something "quickly" also belongs to standard magical practice.) One of the Greek magical papyri gives instruction for making a special bread from barley, formed in the shape of a female figure and symbolizing the moon goddess, Selene. This bread is supposed to embody the essence or power of the goddess. Eaten every month on a particular night after fasting, this bread conveys special power. Drink also qualified as a carrier of supernatural power. In this case, a good example comes from a Jewish spell which asks the heavenly spirit of David to "come down upon this cup which stands before me! Fill it with grace and a holy spirit, so that it become for me a new plant within me." When Hellenistic Christians like Paul developed their eucharistic teaching, the idea of food serving as a vessel for supernatural powers came to them quite naturally. Those Christians who remembered—

and cherished—the venerable tradition of Jesus the Theurgist would not hesitate to practice a kind of magic that was so similar to that practiced by their Lord.[24]

With the gospel of John, we enter a theurgical world different from that of Paul. In the only passage in which John refers to the Eucharist, he has Jesus say: "He who eats my flesh and drinks my blood has eternal life, and I will raise him up on the last day. . . . The one who eats this bread will live forever" (John 6:54.58). Ignatius, bishop of Antioch ca. 100–17 CE, uses equally succinct words to sum up the same doctrine: "the one bread which is the medicine of immortality"; elsewhere he adds that the Eucharist helps to break the powers of Satan. Scholars studying Hellenistic paganism have often quoted statements that are exact parallels to these expressions. Thus, the Egyptian goddess of magic, Isis, is said to have used "the medicine of immortality" to bring her son Horus back to life and thereby annul the destructive action of Seth, an evil spirit. Although Christians would never indulge in pagan rituals, the Eucharist flourished in the same milieu: that of thaumaturgical magic.[25]

The idea of life-giving magical food was not peculiar to Christians. As we saw in the previous chapter, Hellenistic Judaism could understand even the most ordinary, everyday meal as having special, magical properties, giving everlasting life. The gospel of John not only emphasizes the life-giving quality of the eucharistic food; it also states that it creates a special bond between Christ and the faithful: "Those who eat my flesh and drink my blood abide in me, and I in them" (John 6:56). Much of ancient magic served to create a bond of love, generally between a man and a woman. In ancient magic, bread could be used as a "philter," a means to promote love. When in late antiquity Christian priests distributed "blessed bread" (*panis eulogias*) to those who did not partake of communion proper and sent it to the homes of friends, they performed a ritual of "connective magic." When in North Africa around 400 CE Augustine sent some "blessed bread" to a woman (presumably Theresia, the wife of his friend Paulinus of Nola), he was accused of trying to get involved with her by using *amatoria maleficia*, "love spells."[26]

Interestingly, wine was also used in love magic, and could even be equated with blood. In the Greek magical papyri, there are recipes and spells for magical potions reminiscent of the Eucharist. The magician concocts a potion made up of wine and other ingredients, calls it his or her blood, and gives it to someone who is then expected to love the magician. The magical spell pronounced over the potion or the food often addressed deities, and sometimes these would include the names of the Jewish god: Iaô, Sabaoth, or Adonai. The name most often employed is Iaô.[27]

One (first-century CE?) pagan charm involved the manipulation of wine which a lover would give to his beloved in order to bind her to himself. As part of the ritual, the magician recounts a mythical precedent: the god Osiris once gave wine, which he called his blood, to Isis. The ensuing love was so strong that after Osiris' death, Isis, the goddess of magic, revived him. The mythical pattern is quite clear: a stronger and a weaker partner are joined together in a kind of blood bond. While the ancients distinguished, as we do, between erotic love and other kinds of attachment, the magical recipe parallels John's idea that the sacred meal joins the Christian believers to their powerful Lord.[28]

The gospel of John is full of references to the love between Jesus and his disciples as well as between Jesus and his heavenly Father. The logic behind these assertions is clear enough: "He who loves me will be loved by my Father" (John 14:21). The bond of love between Jesus and his followers allows them to participate in the bond between Jesus and God himself. All those who share in this bond will have eternal life.

Jews do not drink blood; nor do they consume blood at all. One of their strictest customs forbids them to touch blood: "It shall be a perpetual statute throughout your generations, in all your settlements: you must not eat any fat or any blood" (Lev. 3:17). That the faithful did not drink real human blood in the Eucharist, but only wine representing the blood of Christ, could have made a difference. The gospel of John reflects the attitude of Christians with a Jewish past when it relates that Christ's teaching about the drinking of his blood was met with much opposition. "This teaching is difficult; who can accept it?," people asked. "Because of this, many [!] of his disciples turned back and no longer went about with him" (John 6:60.66). The Johannine Jesus is depicted as a lonely man, on the verge of being deserted even by his circle of immediate disciples. The new magical understanding of what used to be a sacrificial meal seems to have led to a severe crisis; many believers with strong Jewish backgrounds may have preferred to leave the group. They did not wish to be involved with a cultic meal that included even the symbolic consumption of blood. Nevertheless, in the end, the magical understanding triumphed, and the authority of the disciples to determine not only the details of the ritual, but also its interpretation, was accepted.

The two major sources attesting a theurgical understanding of the Lord's Supper are supplemented by an isolated passage found in the gospel of Luke, a passage with a decidedly Johannine flavor. This text moves beyond the thaumaturgical orientation of the synoptic gospels' account of the last supper the Lord celebrated with his disciples. According to the gospel of Luke, two of the earliest followers of Jesus encountered their Lord after the resurrection, but without recognizing him at first, for he was disguised as a traveling stranger. As they walk, he explains the scriptures to them, and later, having arrived at an inn, he "breaks the bread" for them in a gesture that makes them recognize the stranger's identity (Luke 24:30–32). The legend may echo a pattern of worship that consisted of scriptural preaching followed by a theurgical act which conjured up the real, though fleeting presence of the Lord. The discussion of scripture serves as a mental preparation for the sacred act by revealing higher wisdom and creating a charged emotional atmosphere: the text says that the disciples' hearts were burning as they came to understand the hidden meaning of scripture. Once the leader has prepared the theurgical group, which may have consisted of just two people as in the legend in Luke, the Lord himself is made present in a ritual of breaking the bread, i.e., the speaking of a prayer followed by a communal meal. How the Lord relates to the bread, and how precisely a prayer evokes the Lord's presence, remain unclear. Nevertheless, the account of the two disciples of Jesus encountering their Lord has the ring of a magic night-time meeting. If our reading is correct, we can take the passage as the earliest reference to a ritual sequence still used today: the combination of an explanation of scripture with a eucharistic rite.[29]

The Eucharist echoed in Luke 24 seems to culminate in a "hallucinatory rite" in which Christ becomes present in a way that makes him visible, at least to the eyes of those who believe or who possess special visionary gifts. Hallucinatory rites belong to well-established magical tradition. The Bible relates two incidents in which a magician conjures up the spirit of one or even two deceased prophets. While the spirit of Samuel was only visible to the witch of Endor and not to her patron, three of Jesus' disciples allegedly saw Moses and Elijah. Hallucinatory rituals practiced by the first generation of Christians are likely to be the historical basis of the New Testament legends about Christ's "being seen" after his death. However, hallucinatory rites are precarious as no one can be sure of their success. If those present fail to see the Lord, they may begin to suspect that the ritual does not work. The dilemma of the unsuccessful hallucinatory rite resulted in the more general assumption of Christ's invisible presence at the Eucharist. The routinized theurgical rite no longer aims at producing a miracle. (Much later, theologians would do much to defend the idea of an invisible miracle happening at each celebration of the Eucharist.)[30]

Very early on, and not without precedent in the magical ministry of Jesus, a sacramental meal became a central Christian ritual. Its benefits ranged from protection to making the deity present and from forging a bond of love to conveying eternal life. Later Christian authors did much to elaborate the sacramental legacy left by the biblical tradition. They also developed the organizational structure that provided the setting for the magical meal. Christians formed local cult associations, reminiscent of, if not inspired by, the mystery clubs flourishing in the Hellenistic cities. Anyone could join the club, irrespective of ethnic origin. The initiation through baptism, the possibility of everyone joining, the sacramental union with Christ, and the promise of life after death all had relatively close equivalents in contemporary mystery cults. The Gnostic branch of Christianity in particular adopted the idea of secrecy, most likely in imitation of the mystery cults; members recognized each other by certain signs and excluded nonmembers from the sacred celebrations in which their club life culminated. Of course, early Christians knew and commented on the similarities between mystery celebrations and their own rituals. Present-

day scholarship explains these similarities in terms of the common ritual family
to which both Christian and pagan mysteries belong. The ancients never
attempted such an objective evaluation. For them, it was a matter of legitimate
divine institution versus illegitimate imitation, inspired by the devil. The
Christian apologist Justin, for example, writes about the Eucharist "of which
no one is allowed to partake except one who believes that the things we teach
are true, and has received the washing for forgiveness of sins and for rebirth";
he then adds that "this also the wicked demons in imitation handed down as
something to be done in the mysteries of Mithras; for bread and a cup of water
are brought out in their secret rites of initiation, with certain invocations which
you either know or can learn." According to the early theologians, idolaters
imitate Christian ritual and fail to notice that evil demons deceive them with
empty forms.[31]

As cult associations, Christian groups had a concept of membership, a ritual
of initiation (baptism), a central ritual that was celebrated regularly (the sacramental meal), and office holders. It was around 200 CE, in the age of Julia
Domna and Julia Mamea, that both their social organization and their worship
assumed increasingly fixed forms.

*Bishop Hippolytus, or The Magical Meal in the Age of Julia Domna and
Julia Mamea*

Although he was presumably born in the Greek-speaking East, Hippolytus
flourished in Rome between 190 and 238. In a little book now known as the
Apostolic Tradition, he has left us a description of certain vital aspects of the
liturgical life of the Christian community which must have been considerable
in his days. In Hippolytus' time, Roman Christians met frequently and enjoyed
communal meals in some of which religious rites figured prominently.
The *Apostolic Tradition* distinguishes between two kinds of religious meal;
for the sake of convenience, we may call them the Lord's Supper and the
Blessing.[32]

The *Lord's Supper* starts with a ceremonial dialogue in which the bishop bids
those present to focus their minds on the Lord, saying, "Up with your hearts!"
to which the others respond, "We have them with the Lord." The group's
well-focused attention as well as their united and concentrated will are a
prerequisite for the sacramental action to succeed. In keeping with established
magical practice, the *Apostolic Tradition* prescribes the words with which to
consecrate the elements of bread and wine. The bishop's consecration begins
with a description of how these sacred words came into human possession:

We render thanks to you, O God, through your beloved child Jesus Christ,
whom in the last times you sent to us as savior and redeemer. . . . You sent him

from heaven into the Virgin's womb; and, conceived in the womb, he was made flesh and was manifested as your Son, being born of the holy Spirit and the Virgin. Fulfilling your will and gaining for you a holy people, he stretched out his hands when he should suffer, that he might release from suffering those who have believed in you.

When he was betrayed to voluntary suffering that he might destroy death, and break the bonds of the devil, and tread down hell, and shine upon the righteous, and set up a boundary [against the infernal powers], and manifest the resurrection, he took bread and gave thanks to you, saying, "Take, eat; this is my body, which shall be broken for you." Likewise also the cup, saying, "This is my blood, which is shed for you; when you do this, you make my remembrance." Remembering therefore his death and resurrection, we offer to you the bread and the cup, giving you thanks because you have held us worthy to stand before you and minister to you. And we ask that you would send your holy Spirit upon the offering of your holy Church; that, gathering them into one, you would grant to all who partake of the holy things to partake for the fullness of the holy Spirit for the strengthening of faith in truth. . . . Amen.[33]

The *Apostolic Tradition* defines the consecrated species as "the symbol (*antitypus*) of the body of Christ" and "the image (*similitudo*) of the blood." When giving the bread to communicants, the bishop says, "The bread of heaven in Jesus Christ," to which each partaker responds "Amen" (*Apostolic Tradition* 21).

The *Blessing*, the other sacred meal, receives much less attention in the *Apostolic Tradition*. One may call it a lesser Eucharist. It seems that in this case a wealthy patron invites members of the community to share a meal in the evening. Before people eat, the bishop and other office holders—presbyters and deacons—hold a little ceremony. They say an evening prayer and recite psalms. A small quantity of bread and wine is also consumed by everyone present. Wine, it seems, is not distributed in any formal way. Everyone, including the bishop, says his or her own blessing over the wine before drinking. The bishop distributes morsels of bread, and again, everyone seems to pronounce a blessing before eating. The morsel, explains Hippolytus, "is a *eulogia* [i.e., a Blessing] and not a [real] Eucharist, which [latter] is a symbol of the Lord's body" (*Apostolic Tradition* 26). The catechumens are given a different morsel, called the "exorcized bread," over which the bishop himself has said a blessing. After this opening ceremony, the actual evening meal starts. After dinner, prayers are said, and children and young women recite psalms.

While Hippolytus' descriptions are terse and not always easy to understand, it is clear enough that the Lord's Supper embodies the magical paradigm we discussed earlier. The Blessing must no doubt be understood along similar lines, even though in this case the magical element is visibly diminished and perhaps even consciously played down. How to account for the two sacred meals? There seem to be two possible explanations: (1) The Blessing represents the old tradition of the Christian meal where people met in small groups in the home of a member. The Lord's Supper, by contrast, is something new: a more elaborate celebration under the full control of the emerging clergy, held in a larger building, presumably in a church building and on Sunday. While the bishop concentrates on celebrating his own Sunday ritual which requires (ideally) the presence of the whole community, he also tries to establish his control over the smaller, home-based communal meals, where he asserts his authority. Only when the bishop is present does the home-based meal become a ritual event, termed the Blessing. In the bishop's absence, it is "just a meal." (2) In Roman society, the wealthy patrons occasionally invited their clients, treating them to a free supper. When a Christian patron invited his Christian clients, the clergy tried also to be present. Competing with the patron's authority by asserting their own, superior rank, they set the secular supper within a religious frame by celebrating a lesser Eucharist, the Blessing, which they invented for the occasion.[34]

Whatever the proper interpretation, it is clear that the generation of Roman Christians living around 200 CE were caught up in the dynamics of institutional growth. They abandoned the earlier presbyterial form and adopted an episcopal constitution. While there were still many "house churches" or "house schools" led by presbyters and teachers, several smaller communities combined to form larger churches under one bishop. Elected by the faithful, he was the leader of the local church (and soon after Hippolytus, there was only *one* bishop of Rome). The differentiated structure of offices and sacraments is by no means peculiar to the city of Rome and the *Apostolic Tradition*; it can also be found in the contemporary *Syrian Didaskalia*, a document that originated in the East. Church buildings, the bishop, and a ranked system of sacred meals all emerged together and form part of the same development.[35]

The emergence of the episcopal office no doubt strengthened the magical side of the Eucharist, for the church now had someone endowed with prestige and eminent ritual expertise and authority. These sacred meals were shaped and consolidated not only by the institutional dynamic, but also by the general religious climate and Zeitgeist. At the time of Hippolytus, the empire's "first ladies," Julia Domna and Julia Mamea, set the fashion. Daughter of a prince-priest to the Sun god of Emesa, Julia Domna was born in Syria. As spouse of the emperor Septimius Severus, who reigned from 193 to 211 CE, her interest in religion and magic made a tremendous impact. Under Julia Domna's influence, Eastern magic became fashionable in the western parts of the Roman Empire. The emergence of the Severan dynasty (193–235) as rulers of the Roman world ushered in a period of dynamic change and brought about a new cultural climate and, indeed, a revival of magic. Septimius Severus opened the way for the rule (after his death in 211) of a Semitic, female-dominated dynasty with a religious cast of mind. For forty years, Eastern cults flooded the West in general and the city of Rome in particular, and two of the Severan emperors, Elagabalus and Severus Alexander, seem to have been favorable to Christianity. Julia Domna did not work as a magician, but she surrounded herself with philosophers and literati interested in the magical arts. Her son Caracalla delighted in wizards and later erected a shrine to Apollonius, the famous first-century philosopher, miracle man, and healer. On Julia's request, the Athenian author Philostratus wrote *The Life of Apollonius* in 217. Modern scholars have often compared this book with the New Testament gospels and still debate the question whether Philostratus had access to Christian traditions. While this issue remains controversial, scholars agree that the cultural climate in which *The Life of Apollonius* originated was favorable to Christian as well as pagan magical lore. Many Westerners read about Apollonius and came to admire the higher wisdom of the Eastern cults, and that wisdom often comprised magic. One of the successors of Septimius Severus, the emperor Severus Alexander (222–35), a man born in Phoenicia, is reported to have furnished his domestic chapel with statues of Apollonius (the magician), Christ, Abraham, and Orpheus. Although dismissed by some modern historians, this report sheds light on the Severan court's ecumenical perspective on religion. While nothing is known about Bishop Hippolytus' relationship with the court, he may have entertained friendly relations with the emperor's mother, Julia Mamea, known for her interest in religion and for talking to theologians like Origen; at any rate, Hippolytus dedicated one of his theological writings—a treatise on resurrection—to her (forgetting for a moment, it seems, his otherwise negative attitude toward the Roman Empire which he identified with the prophet Daniel's "wild beast that rules now").[36]

We know very little of the magical milieu in which Julia Domna and her niece Julia Mamea grew up in Syria, but we can at least speculate that it did not differ much from that of other Eastern cults. We are relatively well informed about Jewish magic of the period. The Babylonian rabbi was not only a thaumaturgist who could bring rain or knew incantations for cures; he was also a theurgist "apt to be visited by angels and to receive communications from them. He could see demons and talk with them and could also communicate with the dead." Among Eastern Jews and gentiles, magic flourished in all its forms.[37]

In the days of the Severans, Christianity, as a tradition rich in magical lore, appealed to the taste of many, to pagans and Christians alike. In the generation around 200 CE, explains William Frend, Christianity had moved "to the position of one of the major religions of the Roman world."[38]

As a Christian leader, Hippolytus both profited from and was shocked by the new Severan revival of Eastern cults. This brought new respectability and new converts, but it also brought problems. As a Christian philosopher and magician, Hippolytus definitively rejected pagan and unorthodox magic. A passage in his *Apostolic Tradition* seems to imply that many magicians were anxious to be admitted among the Christian catechumens, presumably in order to learn new rituals and powerful charms which they would add to their repertoire. Although the approach of such people was more subtle than that of Simon the Magician who, according to the Acts of the Apostles, offered money for ritual power, Hippolytus would not admit them among those who prepared for baptism: "A magician shall not be brought for examination. A charmer, an astrologer, a diviner, an interpreter of dreams, a mountebank, a cutter of fringes of clothes, or a maker of phylacteries [amulets]: let them be rejected." Hippolytus would also have nothing to do with the "magical arts and incantations, love potions and voluptuous feasts" of a Christian group called the Carpocratians. His account of the fraudulent Eucharist of one Marcus is fairly detailed. Pronouncing incomprehensible words and secretly using a drug, Marcus makes water first assume a red color and then, by some trick, makes the bowl appear to overflow with the sacred drink. Hippolytus reserved his severest criticism for the pagan magic arts, which he rejected as completely fraudulent. He devoted an entire book of his multi-volume *Refutation of All Heresies* to these arts and also to astrology. His descriptions of the ritual procedures, the recipes, and the roles of the master-magician and his assistants, as well as the credulity of a committed clientele are all clear evidence of Hippolytus' expertise. His most vivid polemical description is that of a séance in which, on a moonless night, the magician invokes a blood-thirsty deity. Hekate, the goddess invited, roams the earth in the company of baying dogs and the hungry spirits of those who were not ready to die, or were murdered, or not given the appropriate burial rites. A goddess of Semitic origin bearing an Egyptian name denoting "female magic," Hekate epitomizes the occult powers invoked by sorcerers. The details are precise enough to warrant the warning that one should not try to perform this and other rituals discussed in the *Refutation*. Although Hippolytus seems to have relied on written sources, he no doubt also had first-hand, eyewitness knowledge of pagan magical practices.[39]

   In the third century, Christians, Jews, and pagans shared an intense interest in magic. Theoretical knowledge no longer sufficed. A true philosopher or religious scholar did not confine his expertise to book learning. He was supposed to show that knowledge meant power—magical, superhuman power. Rather than knowing abstract, theoretical truth, they were expected to know the proper charm, the right ritual, the efficacious magical potion. Hippolytus' worship has a decidedly magical quality. In the *Apostolic Tradition*, scriptural reading and preaching receive practically no attention, though they must have formed part of the ritual. For Hippolytus, the making of the sacred food and its consumption assume center-stage. It is not difficult to identify in Hippolytus' description the elements of all theurgical ritual: the spell, the rite, and the person of the sorcerer. The magician is none other than the bishop; as has been observed, the complicated nature of ancient magic requires the full-time specialist. Moreover, as Frazer explains, "the magician does not doubt that the performance of the proper ceremony, accompanied by the appropriate spell, will inevitably be attended by the desired result." In magical procedures, exact words have to be used. The recitation of a story telling the fate of the deity or spirit involved is also characteristic. "Magic is the bridge between the golden age of primeval craft and the wonder-working power of today. Hence the formulas are full of mythical allusions which, when uttered, unchain the powers of the past and cast them into the present." The "Amen," spoken by the congregation in response to Hippolytus' eucharistic prayer, is a magical word of assent. In Hippolytus' Greek-speaking community in Rome, the Semitic word had a foreign and—therefore—most powerful ring.[40]

Can we assume that the actual consecration is accomplished as the bishop speaks the very words Jesus himself had used: "This is my body," and "This is my blood"? While the *Apostolic Tradition* lacks precision on this point, Hippolytus' contemporary, Tertullian, indicates such an understanding. However, there is also an invocation of the Holy Spirit, who is petitioned to "descend upon the offering." Which words are decisive in actually operating the consecration: the words of Jesus or the invocation of the Spirit? As the text stands now, the bishop-magician duplicates the consecration, drawing upon two different traditions. The invocation makes the eucharistic elements, which are, by then, already the flesh and blood of Christ, into carriers of the divine Spirit. When consuming the elements, people also partake of the Spirit. But what exactly is meant by the Spirit? Is he the Christ (or Logos)? Or is he identical with the heavenly "Father" of Jesus who, in the form of the Spirit, impregnated the Virgin? Unfortunately, neither the *Apostolic Tradition* nor other works of Hippolytus give us a clear answer.[41]

There can be no question about the special magical properties of the consecrated elements. They share in Jesus' power to "destroy death, and break the bonds of the devil, and tread down hell, and shine upon the righteous." After the ritual, people take some of the consecrated bread with them in order to be able to eat a morsel of it every morning before eating anything else. This custom, also attested to elsewhere, was believed to provide special protection: "If you partake of it in faith, then not even a deadly poison given to you will do any harm to you." Appended to this somewhat fantastic promise are the more down-to-earth instructions not to offer the sacred bread to unbelievers (as medicine?) and to put it out of the reach of mice.[42]

In 235 CE, when Severus Alexander died and Severan rule was discontinued, things changed dramatically. The emperors increasingly came to see magicians as endangering their own monopoly of power, and Christians were suspect. In the very year 235 the new emperor Maximinus tried to suppress Christianity, which he considered a strange and illegal cult. Hippolytus was sent to Sardinia where he died in a Roman prison. Yet, the persecution did not destroy the church or affect its liturgy. Despite increasing imperial strictures on magic and divination, the days of the magical renaissance were not gone. The bias toward magic not only endured, but became even stronger. Magic and theurgy, whether Jewish, Christian, or pagan, were both feared and respected, and attracted an increasing number of intellectuals.[43]

3. Christ's Sacramental Presence

Like all magic, the Christian sacrament implies some kind of theory of how the procedure actually produces the desired results. Thus, the idea of a life-giving bread in the gospel of John ("Those who eat my flesh and drink my blood have eternal life," 6:54) obviously reflects the experience that bread sustains life; sacramental bread does the same in a mysteriously, magically enhanced way. Often, implicit theories of this kind suffice because people rarely reflect on the abstract principles involved in their actions. However, the day comes when thinkers no longer take a book like the third-century *Apostolic Tradition*, with its implicit sacramental theory, to be an exhaustive treatment. They want to know more than can be said in a simple, prescriptive manual of canon law (of which the *Apostolic Tradition* is a precursor). They want to know how Christ is present when the community celebrates the Eucharist.

Over the many centuries, as Christian practiced, thought and speculated about the Eucharist, three major orientations emerged: one that focused on the Eucharist as the performance of a sacred drama, one that placed the emphasis on the sacred substances of consecrated bread and wine, and a third that focused on the intervention of Christ at the time of the eucharistic celebration. The action-related model, which is characteristic of Eastern Christianity, is best demonstrated by the work of Pseudo-Dionysius, a Greek-speaking author who lived around 500 CE. The second, substance-related paradigm was developed in particular in medieval Western theology, and we will look at how it was explained by its major representative, Thomas Aquinas. The third paradigm, originally developed by Augustine, re-emerged in the sixteenth century as a Protestant alternative to the Catholic teaching, and we will study its manifestation in the work of John Calvin.

*The East-Side Story: Mass as a Sacred Drama according to
Pseudo-Dionysius*

Nothing is known about Dionysius the Areopagite, the Athenian whom the apostle Paul converted to Christianity. In the early sixth century, some Greek authors started to refer to, and quote from, a number of books allegedly written by Dionysius, and subsequently these became both influential and classic. The author hiding behind the pen-name Dionysius remains unknown. Modern scholarship thinks of a Syrian bishop (ca. 500 CE) who must have considered himself a converted Athenian, i.e., a pagan philosopher who had come to embrace the Christian faith. Fortunately, scholarship agrees about Pseudo-Dionysius's philosophical roots in fourth- and fifth-century Neoplatonism.[44]

In order to understand the Areopagite's sacramental theology, we have to look at the theurgy as taught and practiced by Neoplatonic philosophers. In late antiquity, all followers of Plato defined the aim of philosophy as overcoming the estrangement from the divine world. They had tried study and rigorous asceticism, and even thought about establishing a city to be named Platonopolis (a project never realized) as a possible means of purifying souls and thus preparing them for postmortem heavenly ascent. By the fourth century, the followers of Plato had discovered a new—though actually quite old—means of salvation: the way of religious ritual. The promise of ritual was quite unlike the promise of asceticism. Philosophers advocating the latter assumed that by refraining from too much involvement with the world and by concentrating on meditation, the soul could somehow get closer to the world of the divine, a world attainable only after death. No, countered Iamblichus (ca. 250–330), a Syrian-born adept of the Platonic way; we should not ascend to the gods but invite the friendly, world-loving deities to join us here on earth and be uplifted by them. "Intellectual understanding does not connect theurgists with divine beings. . . . Rather, it is the perfect accomplishment of ineffable acts religiously performed and beyond all understanding, and it is the power of ineffable symbols comprehended by the gods alone that establishes theurgical union." According to Iamblichus, the means to invite the gods successfully has already been known for a long time by priests and magicians. Their ritual knowledge and experience enables them to make the gods come to those who want the benefit of their presence. Iamblichus, the Syrian who proudly kept his foreign-sounding Semitic name, reminded his fellow philosophers of a truism familiar to all who had any knowledge of Greek or Near Eastern religions: the gods, when approached humbly and with the help of the proper ritual words and devices, would come and bless and be friendly with humans.[45]

As far as we can judge from the surviving documentation, Neoplatonic theurgists valued all traditional rituals that survived from paganism in the increasingly Christian culture of the fourth and fifth centuries. They also seem to have had certain favorite rites, and one of them may give us an idea of what they were like. The goddess Hekate herself reportedly gave the following instructions for meeting her. First of all, an image of Hekate must be made from wild rue, a woody, strong-scented dwarf-shrub sacred to the goddess. Then a rite of consecration must be performed to draw her into the doll. The consecration involves the decoration of the image with small animals, the burning of a mixture of fragrant essences and ground lizards, and the saying of a certain prayer in the open air under a waxing moon. The instruction ends with the goddess's personal promise: "And when you then address the image in fervent prayer, you will see me in your sleep [trance?]." While modern as well as ancient rationalists would dismiss this kind of rite as superstition, Neoplatonists defended its efficacy on the basis of a subtle philosophy. They assumed, in true Platonic fashion, that our material world is somehow deficient when compared to its transcendent, ideal model. However, the material world also echoes something of its ideal, divine prototype. These hidden, often hardly perceptible echoes or signs of divine splendor can be captured and concentrated in specially prepared concoctions. By the proper manipulation of certain theurgical substances, one can reconstitute pure and unified divine matter that corresponds to its original idea. That divine matter also corresponds to the transcendent deities that preside over it. Hence, by virtue of the network of forces linking image to archetype and divinity, manipulation of the appropriate material objects brings the theurgist into contact with the deities they represent—for instance, with the goddess Hekate.[46]

The recipe for making and animating the likeness of Hekate comes from a book called the *Chaldean Oracles*. This is a collection of turgid and obscure hexameter oracles originating in the trance-revelations of a second- or third-century Syrian prophet or prophetess. The Neoplatonist Porphyry (ca. 232–303) was the first to write a commentary on this book, which came to be received into the canon of texts studied and believed in by many of the followers of Plato. One of the latter was Proclus (412–85), the last head of the Neoplatonic school of Athens, whom his ancient biographer Marinus presents not just as a deep thinker and dedicated teacher, but also as a pious pagan and a theurgist. Marinus refers to him as an active member of a group whose "Chaldaic gatherings and meetings" engaged in theurgical rites. Presumably with the help of a rite like the one we have referred to, Proclus was able to converse with the luminous apparitions of Hekate. "Whenever Proclus spoke to us about these things that he saw," Marinus reports, "he would be brought to tears, so great was his affinity for what was divine." Although Athens had become a Christian city by the mid-fifth century, the authorities tolerated Proclus and the pagan rites that were celebrated in private in the home or at some of the old shrines. Scholars have often commented on Pseudo-Dionysius' indebtedness to Proclus, and the pseudonymous author seems to refer to Proclus' book *Elements of Theology* by title.[47]

Readers of Dionysius' work have often complained about the author's obscurity, and a first look at the *Ecclesiastical Hierarchy*, his treatise on the sacraments, leaves most of them puzzled. Yet, his description of what happens at the Eucharist is straightforward: after the catechumens have been sent away, the baptized members of the congregation exchange the kiss of peace and stay to witness the most sacred rite celebrated by the bishop. Bread and wine are brought, presumably veiled, words of praise are sung by the celebrant, and after the celebrant's own communion, the faithful partake. The description is followed by a dense and seemingly impenetrable philosophical analysis. However, when we take a standard theurgical rite like the conjuring of Hekate as our guide, a striking parallelism emerges and leaves no doubt about what Dionysius had in mind. For him, the Christian sacrament was a theurgical rite that forged the link between the faithful and their heavenly lord. In what follows, the parallels between the two rites—the conjuring-up of Hekate and the Eucharist—are set out in detail.[48]

The *first* feature of the Hekate text is its claim to have been revealed by the goddess; it is she who takes the initiative by telling the theurgist to make an image of her. Dionysius explains that the bishop celebrates the Eucharist at Christ's explicit command. "He apologizes, as befits a hierarch [bishop], for being the one to undertake a sacred task so far beyond him. Reverently he cries out: It is you who said, *Do this in remembrance of me*" (441 D). This is the only text uttered in the liturgy that Dionysius explicitly quotes; there can be no doubt about the importance he attributes to the divine command. For both the Hekate rite and Dionysius, the divine command is fundamental. Both are revealed and commanded by the deity.

Both rites use material substances: this is the *second* shared feature. For the Hekate rite, the theurgist needs a whole list of things: the wood of wild rue, lizards, and a mixture of myrrh, gum, and frankincense. The rue is essential, for it provides the substance for the goddess's image or likeness; the rest is needed mainly for the rite of consecration. Dionysius' rite involves the use of bread (a large loaf, later broken and distributed), a cup of wine, water and some incense. As in the Hekate rite, modern ritualists would differentiate between primary and secondary materials: rue, bread, and wine belong in the first group; incense, lizards, and so on in the second, for they have a supporting function. To the ancients, however, everything seems to be of almost equal importance. In the terminology of the ancient theurgists, all the objects used are called *synthêmata* or *symbola*, i.e., "agreed signs" or "tokens" of divine presence: signs that belong to or are in a special relationship with the deity and signal his or her presence. "The Paternal Intellect has sown symbols throughout the world," reads one line of the *Chaldean Oracles*, a book held in esteem by theurgists. According to Iamblichus, theurgical symbols are charged with "the ineffable power of the gods"; indeed, "in some way they have the same power as the gods themselves." Dionysius refers to bread and wine as the "holy symbols" (437 D) or "the reverend symbols by which Christ is signaled and partaken" (437 C). For him, the incense is also a symbol.[49]

The *third* shared feature is the use of the material symbols in a rite consisting of words and actions. At the beginning of the eucharistic rite, the entire church is filled with the perfume of burned incense. Bread and wine are unveiled, shown, and then distributed for communion; water serves for the bishop's washing of hands. The Hekate rite uses the rue for making an image and the other objects either for decorating it or for the burning of incense at the consecration. These actions are accompanied by or alternate with words being spoken. Hekate teaches a prayer to be said at the consecration of her image (which unfortunately has not been preserved in the ancient sources), and indicates that the adept addresses the consecrated image with another fervent prayer. Dionysius also refers to spoken parts of the eucharistic celebration, especially the bishop's hymn that celebrates "all the work of God on our behalf" (435 C). Both Dionysius and the ancient theurgists use a specific terminology for designating the acts performed and the words spoken. The words are called symbols, i.e., they are given the same designation as the material objects used. Dionysius calls the bishop's hymn a "symbol of adoration" (436 C), and the theurgist Iamblichus refers to the prayers as *synthêmata*, tokens revealed by the gods themselves. The entire ritual procedure, with all the words uttered and the actions performed, is known as *theourgia*, "divine operation," or *hierourgia*, "sacred operation." Dionysius uses *theourgia* exclusively for the acts of God and Christ; when speaking of the actions of Christ in instituting the Eucharist (to quote but one example), he calls them *theourgiai*, "divine operations" (441 C). The essential *theourgia* is, of course, the coming of Christ into the material world: "Out of love he has come down to be at our level of nature and has become a [human] being. He, the transcendent God, has taken on the name of man." The rites that the bishop performs in imitation of the *theourgiai* are called *hierourgiai*, "sacred operations," a term Iamblichus uses in the same sense. Again, the similarity between pagan theurgy and the Christian sacrament is striking.[50]

At first sight, the effect of the two rites seems to be very different: Hekate appears to the theurgist in a dream or trance; Christ appears but remains concealed under the guise of bread and wine which are consumed. Before communion, the priest shows bread and wine to the congregation and offers them for partaking with the words, "Holy things for the holy." A close reading of Dionysius reveals that, for the Areopagite, it is not the partaking of the sacred symbols that carries the importance, but the looking at them. He quotes scripture as saying, "Taste and see" (Ps. 34:8; 445 C), and we know that this quotation from the Psalms was sung as the invitation to partake of the bread and wine. Dionysius clearly places the emphasis on seeing. For him, the Eucharist culminates in the opening of the curtain behind which the priest prepared bread and wine; once the curtain is opened, the sacred symbols are lifted into view. "Those fond of visions reverently behold the most holy of sacraments" (436 C) and thereby act as eyewitnesses of the coming of God out of heaven into the material world. Thus, a visual experience of the divine is the *fourth* and final feature common to Dionysius' Eucharist and the Hekate rite. The ancients appreciated sight more than the other bodily senses; for them, it ranked as the most noble and sublime sense; standing closer to the intellect than taste and touch or hearing, and therefore particularly appropriate for perceiving the divine within the realm of the senses. When speaking of the sacred gaze (*epopsia*) of those admitted to the eucharistic celebration, Dionysius uses a variation of the Greek standard term for the visual experience in some of the ancient mystery cults. The most ancient of all mystery cults, that of Eleusis in Greece, culminated in the *epopsia* or *epopteia*, the silent gazing at a single head of grain, symbol of the goddess Demeter, the "Grain Mother." Lifted into view, the sacred object represented the goddess as she manifested herself in a visual epiphany. Elevation, as a gesture of presentation, is one of the most archaic rites we know in religious history. "To show something ceremonially—a sign, an object, an animal, a human being—is to declare a sacred presence, to acclaim the miracle of a hierophany. This rite, which is so simple in itself, denotes a religious behavior that is archaic." Mircea Eliade does not hesitate to postulate its use before the development of human language: "Perhaps even before articulate language, solemnly showing an object signified that it was regarded as exceptional, singular, sacred." Apparently, the gesture of elevating the sacred symbols began to be practiced in the time of Dionysius, no doubt under the influence of ancient mystery cults which the Eucharist had come to replace.[51]

The idea of a divinely instituted rite, the use of symbolic substances, the utterance of prayers, and the visual epiphany of the deity belong to the shared features of the two rites. Nevertheless, certain differences cannot be overlooked. Neoplatonic theurgy emphasizes the use of magical substances, objects in which sacredness is inherent. In the Eucharist, on the other hand, the rite itself defines the sacredness of the elements. Although serving as carriers of the divine, bread and wine seem to be of little importance for Dionysius. Whereas the theurgist's sacred substances must be combined in a procedure reminiscent of chemistry or alchemy, Dionysius' Eucharist re-enacts a sacred meal in which Christ symbolized his descending into the world. The Eucharist is a sacred drama, and herein differs essentially from the theurgic alchemy of the Hekate ritual.

While the theurgical paradigm of eucharistic theology has left its mark on the way in which some of the Eastern churches celebrate the Eucharist to this very day (e.g., the orthodox churches of Greece and Russia and the Coptic church), the West came to develop a very different model.

The West-Side Story (1): The Medieval Doctrine of Transubstantiation

In the thirteenth century, with Thomas Aquinas (1225–74), a sophisticated new paradigm of eucharistic thought emerged in the Latin-speaking West where the leading theologians lived in Italy and France. Like all medieval theologians, Aquinas found the raw material of his theology in the existing tradition, or more precisely in the manuscripts available to him in the monastery libraries of his day. He drew from two traditions: Carolingian theology and early scholasticism.

Carolingian theology was available to Aquinas in the first eucharistic treatise a theologian had produced in the West, a book entitled *On the Body and Blood of the Lord*, written in the 830s by Paschasius Radbert, a Benedictine monk living in the abbey of Corbie near Amiens in northern France. One cannot say that Radbert had a theory about Christ's presence at Mass. He simply stated that when the priest pronounced the words of consecration—"This is my body; this is my blood"—the elements of bread and wine were changed into something else, namely the body and blood of Christ. He was not concerned about explaining how this could happen; he simply stated what for him was a fact. All who doubt the literal realism of the words of consecration must yield to Christ's unambiguous explanation recorded in the gospel of John: "My flesh is meat indeed, and my blood is drink indeed" (John 6:56). Moreover, to change bread and wine into something else must be quite easy for Christ the Creator. In the work of Radbert we can see a mentality quite different from that of the Eastern theologians. He had a pragmatic, extroverted cast of mind, interested in the concrete and tangible. Sophisticated Eastern ideas about how the sacred is present and at the same time is not present in material objects (for instance in the sacred paintings known by the name of icons) were beyond his grasp. To be sure, certain Western theologians opposed Radbert's crude materialism, most notably Berengar of Tours (ca. 1005–88), but the realist account of the Eucharist prevailed and Berengar had to revoke his error.[52]

Of course, not all medieval theologians were satisfied with the mere assertion of eucharistic realism. In the newly created cathedral schools and emerging universities of the eleventh century, theologians wanted a more detailed, philosophically refined account of the apparent paradox of bread and wine which had been transformed, and yet looked and tasted as before. In this atmosphere of learning, a new level of eucharistic speculation was reached. Scholastic teachers (as they came to be called) used philosophical language to elucidate the paradox involved in sacramental worship. The first to refine "realistic" eucharistic thought with the help of sophisticated philosophy were Lanfranc (1010–89) and Guitmund of Aversa (d. ca. 1095), two Benedictine scholars. Drawing on language they found in the writings of the ancient philosopher and theologian Boethius, they distinguished between the "substance" and the "outward appearance" of things. Scholastic doctors adopted this philosophical language, and in around 1140 the Parisian master Robertus Pullus coined the term *transubstantio* (change of substance). By the early thirteenth century, a council held in Rome had used the new terminology in a doctrinal statement. Christ's body and blood "are truly contained in the sacrament of the altar under the appearances of bread and wine, the bread being transubstantiated into the body by the divine power, and the wine into the blood" (Lateran Council of 1215).[53]

Medieval eucharistic theology reached full flowering when the scholastic doctors refined their philosophical thinking on the basis of books freshly translated from Arabic and ancient Greek. These new books often supplied more detailed information than the short and often enigmatic books of Boethius.

Theorizing about the Eucharist culminated in the work of Thomas Aquinas, the undisputed prince of scholasticism whose theology served as the quasi-official doctrine of the Catholic church for many centuries. Aquinas relied on Aristotle as his ultimate philosophical authority. The ancient Greek philosopher's work had been lost to Latin-speaking thinkers for many centuries. In the twelfth century, however, much of Aristotle's work began to be translated into Latin, and scholars started to study it with enthusiasm. By Aquinas's time, Aristotle's authority had been established in many circles, and Aquinas's fellow Dominican William of Moerbecke was involved in producing fresh translations and revising existing ones. Aquinas himself produced massive commentaries on some of Aristotle's books, and his theological writings include many references to "the philosopher." Among the books included in the Aristotelian corpus and commented upon by Aquinas is the *Metaphysics*, a book in which the philosopher provides a vocabulary with which reality can be described, and Aquinas used that vocabulary in his analysis of the Eucharist. One of the basic ideas found in the *Metaphysics* is the distinction between the "substance" of something and certain secondary things that can be said about it. Now, a "substance" may be a table, a horse, an apple, or an individual person like Socrates. A substance is in a definite place, moves or rests, has a certain color and is in a relationship with other substances. While a substance is independent and in a way self-sufficient, the things we attribute to it—movement and color and so on—refer to something dependent on it and as it were secondary. Aristotle calls them "accidents," as they belong merely accidentally to the substance. These "accidents" are components of a complex reality the philosopher attempts to grasp with the help of a sophisticated language.

When medieval theologians began to use Aristotelian vocabulary to analyze the Eucharist, they realized that what we experience are the "accidents," while the substance somehow hides beneath them. The accidents may change—a person may stop walking or shave off his beard, a fruit may change its color—but the underlying substance provides continuity and remains the same. Socrates remains Socrates, whether he stays married to Xanthippe or sends her away, terminating his conjugal relationship with her. Socrates remains himself, whether he is young or old, whether he walks through the streets of Athens or fights on the battlefields of the Peloponnesian War. The substance of the apple does not change, although the fruit changes color and size in the process of growing and ripening. In this last example, we have a particularly apt demonstration of the invisibility of substances that remain the same during a process of outward change.

According to the Aristotelian way of looking at things, bread and wine may decay, but they can never change into something completely different. They are substances, and as such they stay identical with themselves. The color, quantity, odor, and taste may change, but what we have is still in essence the same wine or bread. Theologians like Aquinas were intrigued not so much by the essentially static character of the substance as by its hiddenness and invisibility. The substance of things, for them, is beyond the reach of our five senses: sight, hearing, smell, taste, and touch. "The senses cannot judge about the substance, only about the sense-related forms." We cannot touch a substance, we can reach it only with our faculty of reasoning. Although substances are material, they are also somehow spiritual: mysterious realities hidden under appearances and grasped only by thought.[54]

When, in the Eucharist, the divine words of consecration (seen as the Creator's own command) change bread and wine into the human body and blood of Christ, there is no visible change. What we see, feel, and taste is still bread and wine. It is as if nothing has happened. At this point, Aquinas admits a paradox into his reasoning. He severs *all*, not just some, of the "accidents" from the "substance," exaggerating, as it were, Aristotle's merely conceptual distinction (which would make little sense in the philosopher's original thought). In the Eucharist, it is not the "accidents," the outer qualities of bread and wine, that change. Rather, the food changes inside and from the inside. The hidden, invisible substance changes. Now a new and different substance—Christ's body and blood—is present beneath the old and unchanged "accidents." God, who is somehow present in everything he has made, has absolute control over all created substances, and if he wished, could change the substance of bread into any other substance, e.g., into the substance of a *lapis*, a stone or rock. There are no limits to God's power: he is omnipotent. "Like all the other miracles," transubstantiation must be "attributed to God's omnipotence."[55]

While Aquinas included the argument about God's power to "transubstantiate" something into a stone in his earlier *Commentary on the Book of Sentences*, he omits it from his *Summa theologiae*. Although the reference to God's power is certainly apt, it may be confusing. Does God actually change substances very frequently? How can we be sure about the substances hidden under "accidents"? Does God create, by way of transubstantiation, an entirely different world, imperceptible to us? Aquinas does not wish to confuse his readers. For him, the process of "exchanging" the substance of a thing is absolutely unique; far from happening in other cases and contexts, it is confined to the sacrament. Beyond the Eucharist, God never changes the substances that underlie and constitute things, objects, or persons. There is an essential order, solidity, and stability in the world. Sacramental "instability"—the fact that here substances change—must be seen as something unique, as an exception through which God makes a transcendent, spiritual reality present in our material world. In other words: the Eucharist must be appreciated as a real miracle in which God changes the rules that operate under normal circumstances. The question of whether God can or indeed does change substances has often puzzled theologians. While Thomas Aquinas limited transubstantiation to the eucharistic miracle, Robert Holcot (d. 1349) declared that we do not know whether God actually does such transubstantiations all the time, and so we cannot trust our senses: "God could change the entire world and make it exist under the species of a single mouse." Later, John Calvin rejected the whole notion of transubstantiation as contradicted by the fact that God fixed the structure of things at creation, once and for all.[56]

According to Aristotle, all knowledge is based upon our senses, upon seeing, hearing, tasting, and so forth. Usually, we can rely on the impressions we get from our senses and derive valid knowledge from them. In the case of the Eucharist, this rule does not apply. Here our senses fail, for they cannot reach "beneath" the outer appearance, philosophy's "accidents." Hence, Aquinas distinguishes between sense-impressions and true, spiritual understanding. The presence of Christ's body and blood "cannot be detected by any sense, nor understanding, but by faith alone, which rests upon divine authority." Just as God changes the usual rules of nature, so must we change the rules of perception, if we are to penetrate into and appreciate the mystery of the Eucharist.[57]

Thomas Aquinas explores the philosophical and theological implications of his theory. For him, two main philosophical problems are implied in the eucharistic changes in substance. What happens to the substance of bread and wine? And how can the "accidents" of bread and wine stay intact when the underlying substance disappears? With regard to the substances of the eucharistic elements, Aquinas thinks that they do not disappear as if they were annihilated and reduced to nothingness. Rather, the eucharistic miracle involves a transformation of the substances themselves. Thus, there is no waste involved in the process. With regard to the accidents, Aquinas has a trickier problem to deal with, for an accident is always inherent in a substance and disappears together with its underlying substance. In order for the accidents of bread and wine to stay, must they be given a new foundation? Aquinas answers: "The accidents continue in this sacrament without a subject [substance]. This can be done by divine power," for God can "by his unlimited power preserve an accident in existence when the substance is withdrawn." The preservation of the accidents, like the eucharistic change of substance, is an effect of special divine intervention.[58]

Eucharistic bread and wine, even after being deprived of their original substance, retain all their original qualities. Not only do they retain their former taste, shape, and color, but they also continue to have a nourishing quality and can be corrupted. Thus, if someone ate large quantities of eucharistic bread, he or she would be as satisfied as after a normal meal. Consecrated wine can turn sour, and the holy bread can get moldy or be burned.[59]

The doctrine of transubstantiation involves as many theological problems as it does philosophical difficulties. The main ones discussed by Aquinas are concerned with the relationship between the resurrected Christ and Christ's body and blood as present in the Eucharist. Resurrected and enjoying his glorified human body, Christ lives and reigns in heaven. Can Christ have many bodies—one in heaven and numerous other ones on numerous altars upon which priests celebrate the Eucharist, often at the same time? Aquinas's answer to this question is complex. Christ's body is in heaven "under its own species"; upon the altars, Christ's body and blood are present in a special, "sacramental" mode. We cannot picture to ourselves the way in which Christ's body and blood are present in the sacrament. The seeming incompatibility of Christ's large "real" body and his "small" sacramental body in a piece of bread only teaches us that Christ's sacramental body lacks the quality of dimension.[60]

Christ, though present with us in the eucharistic bread and wine, never leaves his heavenly abode. Only in heaven can Christ's full presence be experienced. Under the species of bread and wine, his presence always remains incomplete. Although Christ's eucharistic body and blood are somehow related to Christ in heaven, this relationship does not make Christ sacramentally present in his full person. Not even the Lord's body and blood are made present in their whole being, but only in their substance (which is something less than the full reality). Thus, Christ's sacramental presence, as the presence of the substance of his glorified human body and blood, is more impersonal than truly personal. We can add here a thought suggested by a modern scholastic doctor. Christ's eucharistic body, according to Michael Schmaus, is not a means through which the heavenly Christ gets sensual impressions from earth. In other words, although Christ's ears are part of his glorified body, they do not hear us through the host. Christ's eyes, though also part of his body, do not look at us through the host (though at least one scholastic doctor had defended this view and some later theological writers insisted on this point). Nor does he feel our teeth when we consume the host that contains his body. When leaving us his body and blood in a sacramental manner, Christ did not give us himself as a complete person; rather, he gave to his faithful a token of himself. Although that token is physical, it cannot be touched. For what we touch with our hands and feel on our tongues, are only the "accidents," the outer qualities of bread and wine. Under the disguise of these elements, the substance of Christ's body and blood remains concealed. However, Aquinas concedes that God occasionally lifts the veil, so that "by miraculous apparition" of flesh or the Christ-child (ill. 24), God shows "that Christ's body and blood are truly in this sacrament."[61]

Finally, there is a minor but quite significant problem involved with the doctrine of transubstantiation. According to the words of Jesus ("This is my blood"), wine is transformed into blood. But what about the water which the priest usually adds to the wine before consecration? There were real theological debates about what happens to the water which had an uncontested place in the rite. No one suggested that they circumvent the problem by using just plain wine for Mass. For some, the words of consecration affect only the wine; water simply stays water. Although we may be inclined to take this to be the obvious answer, Aquinas thought it could not stand. If priest and congregation really worship the contents of the chalice, that chalice should contain only the blood

24. The Elevation of the Christ-Child. In the presence of King Edward the Confessor (d. 1066), the elevated host was for a moment changed into the Christ-child. This is not a unique miracle, but just one in a long series, meant to strengthen belief in the real presence of Christ under the veil of eucharistic bread. The normal explanation, given by Thomas Aquinas, was that God works the miracle not in the priest's hands but in the eye of the beholder (*Summa theologiae* III 76:8). English illuminated manuscript, thirteenth-century.

of Jesus, nothing else. Should one identify the water in the chalice with the water that flowed from the Lord's side as he was crucified? This suggestion, too, does not satisfy the scholastics, for if it is taken seriously, then there should be a further act of consecration, in addition to the words said over bread and the words said over wine: an act changing the water into the water that flowed from Christ's side. Aquinas's solution runs as follows: when the words of consecration are spoken over the mixture of wine and water, the water is first changed into wine and then the wine into the Lord's blood. Although Aquinas fails to tell us whether the water is invisibly changed (i.e., transubstantiated) into wine or visibly changed, he seems to have believed that it changed visibly—as visibly as water was changed into wine at the wedding of Cana! However, Aquinas is prudent enough not to tempt his fellow priests to test the idea empirically, for he also says that just a little water should be added. If too much water dilutes the wine, the whole ritual won't work, for too much water would destroy the substance of the wine. Here we can see that scholastic speculation could discover—or invent—ever new problems and test ever new solutions. In the seventeenth century, a Spanish Jesuit theologian and cardinal, Juan de Lugo, rejected Aquinas's extra little miracle, for transubstantiation works without it; later theologians, presumably knowing more than Aquinas about the chemical properties of wine, have dropped the issue from the list of items to be discussed in sacramental theory.[62]

In addition to philosophical and theological questions, the scholastic doctors also dealt with a number of practical ones. Some hardly needed discussion, e.g., that consecrated bread that was not consumed at Mass should be kept in a safe place (the tabernacle) for later consumption. There were, of course, more difficult questions. For example: What does a mouse get (*quid sumit mus*) when it happens to nibble at a consecrated host? Is Christ's body in a poisoned host? Can a priest consecrate all the wine in a cellar? What happens to the body of Christ when the host is eaten and Christ's blood drunk? As to the question of what the mouse gets, the twelfth-century theologian Abelard had the wisdom to answer that only God can know. According to scholars with more imagination, the mouse gets nothing but bread, for an automatic reverse-consecration brings back the original substance, while Christ's body leaves the host just before the act of desecration. Aquinas, on the other hand, argued that a mouse or dog, when eating the host, would actually consume the body of the Lord. As for the priest's power of consecration, we also have Aquinas's unambiguous answer. Communion can indeed be misused to poison someone. By consecrating "all the bread sold in the market and all the wine in the cellar," the priest can misuse his power to ridicule the sacrament. Although this is sinful, the sacred words he utters nevertheless transubstantiate any amount of bread and wine. As ordained priests, most scholastic doctors firmly believed in the powers they and their sacerdotal confrères were endowed with.[63]

The question about digestion and communion lent itself to ridicule. In one of the worst blasphemies to come from his pen, the French Enlightenment philosopher Voltaire made fun of it. In Catholic countries, he writes, "one sees every day priests and monks who, leaving an incestuous bed and without so much as washing their hands soiled with impurities, manufacture gods by the hundred, eat and drink their god, shit and piss their god." Theologians have seen the problem and have decided that the blood and body of Christ do not survive digestion. Christ's presence is linked to the existence of bread and wine, and digested bread and wine are no longer to be called bread and wine. While Aquinas refrains from calculating the length of the sacramental moment, i.e., the time during which the bread is not fully digested, the subject received much attention from later authors. Writing around 1700, the Italian Jesuit Domenico Viva referred to contemporary medical opinion on the digestive process; according to the foremost authorities, once the bread is in the stomach, it takes no longer than a minute—the sixtieth part of an hour, as he specifies—

to dissolve. Twentieth-century authors tend to be more generous, allowing for a sacramental moment of eight to ten minutes. This is the time communicants physically touch the resurrected Lord.[64]

It is precisely this physical contact with Christ that was vital in the thought of Aquinas. For him, Christ was the friend of his followers, for he had declared that they were no longer servants, but friends. Now friends, as Aristotle said, want to live together, and Aquinas adds the insight that friendship culminates in the pleasures derived from physical touch. But how can we touch Christ, and how can he touch us after his death? The paradox of the dead friend leads straight into eucharistic speculation: it is in bread and wine that Christ makes himself bodily present to his friends. Mystics, who presumably never cared to read Aquinas's *Summa theologiae*, would certainly have delighted in this thought; it would have fueled their imagination and inspired ecstasies of love. Early sources indicate that at Mass and when receiving communion Thomas could be moved to tears; but these rare feelings had little if any influence on his essentially rationalist theology. However, shortly before his death, he had a strange and overwhelming experience when celebrating Mass, an experience that made him stop writing, so that he left his celebrated *Summa theologiae* unfinished. When urged to explain, he said, "Everything I have written seems like straw by comparison with what I have seen and what has now been revealed to me." While this looks very much like a pious invention, scholars agree that the story must be true. In an extraordinary moment of rapture, Thomas seems to have experienced what St. Paul had experienced before him and Pascal after him: Christ's friendship and love, a love that makes theological speculation look rather dull and unattractive to someone who has finally been touched by the Lord himself. Aquinas must have felt overjoyed, but utterly inadequate and helpless. He could not bear the burden of Christ's presence, and so the exhausted scholar preferred to retire and die.[65]

By way of conclusion, we can say that the medieval doctrine of transubstantiation, with its insistence on the presence of Christ's glorified human body under the species of bread and wine, made Mass into a celebration of divine epiphany. Although he is in heaven, Christ somehow also resides on the altar and, since some of the consecrated bread is kept in a tabernacle, in church. In the thirteenth century—the century of Aquinas and of the origin of the feast of Corpus Christi—the custom of having an "eternal light" became widespread: a perpetually burning candle or oil lamp was placed near the tabernacle to indicate the presence of Christ's body.

The West-Side Story (2): Calvin's Theory of Christ's Spiritual Presence

The sixteenth-century reformers consistently rejected the scholastic theory of transubstantiation. "It is certainly a piece of magic and sorcery (*incantatio magica*), when the consecration is addressed to a dead element," insisted John

Calvin, the French reformer of Geneva. In Germany, Martin Luther concurred. Christ, when instituting the sacrament, spoke to people, not to "a stick or a stone." For twelve hundred years, he states, the church had managed without "transubstantiation," that "monstrous word and monstrous idea" invented by the "Aristotelian church" which gave undue prominence to philosophical speculation. Transubstantiation belongs to the errors "the devil sowed to corrupt this holy mystery." For Luther, transubstantiation was not only monstrous, but also simply wrong and based on questionable philosophical assumptions. The denial of the chalice to the laity amounted to clerical malpractice, and the doctrine of transubstantiation reflected misused and misunderstood philosophy. "This opinion of Thomas," he thunders, "hangs so completely in the air without support of Scripture or reason, that it seems to me that he knows neither his philosophy nor his logic." Aristotle, as Luther knew quite well, "speaks of subject and accidents so very differently from St. Thomas" that "it seems to me this great man is to be pitied not only for attempting to draw his opinions in matters of faith from Aristotle, but also for attempting to base them upon a man whom he did not understand."[66]

While the reformers identified the eucharistic bread with Christ's body, and wine with his blood, they insisted that the bread and wine remain what they are: real food. Beyond this assertion, they failed to produce a generally accepted Protestant alternative to the traditional, Catholic theory. In the sixteenth century, Calvin and Luther were unable to find common ground in their eucharistic teaching. Luther himself had no philosophy to offer. He accepted Christ's identification of bread with his body, and of wine with his blood. This is what scripture says, and we must accept it even though we do not understand how this can be true. The bread and the wine, of course, remain fully intact.

The most prominent, and ultimately the most influential, eucharistic doctrine is that of Calvin. For him, bread and wine serve as symbols. When we partake of them in eucharistic worship, Christ feeds our soul with his true body and blood. The two actions—our eating and Christ's feeding—happen in parallel on two different levels of reality. While Christ himself never leaves his heavenly abode, God's Spirit establishes a personal, intimate relationship between Christ and ourselves, forming a kind of channel or bridge that connects heaven and earth. "We maintain no other presence [of Christ] than that of relationship," wrote Calvin. "Christ is not visibly present, and is not beheld with our eyes, as the symbols are which excite our remembrance by representing him. In short, in order that he may be present to us, he does not change his place, but communicates to us from heaven the virtue of his flesh as though it were present." Christ, of course, makes himself available only when the recipient truly believes in him.[67]

While later Protestants sometimes claim that the sixteenth-century reformers went straight back to the Bible to construct their doctrine, this is not quite true. Calvin defended his eucharistic teaching by arguing that "Augustine had felt and spoken the same way." And behind Augustine stood the authority of Plato's philosophy. Like many humanistic thinkers of his time, Calvin felt more at home with Plato than with Aristotle, the favorite philosopher of scholastic theologians. And like many humanists (including Erasmus), he preferred Augustine to Thomas Aquinas. In his main work, the *Institutes of the Christian Religion*, Calvin often quotes Augustine and Plato as authorities. His teaching on the Lord's Supper simply restores Augustine's Platonic view by renewing the distinction between the visible sacramental sign and the invisible sacramental reality, a distinction scholasticism had blurred.[68]

One of the basic doctrines of Plato is that material objects represent, under the unfortunate conditions of the material world, ideas at home in a superior, higher world. Material objects are real in that other world, and what we experience is only a shadow of "the real thing." Yet there is a strong continuity between the upper realm and the terrestrial world, which allows a reciprocal relationship between them. Although we cannot reach "the real thing" with our senses, it can be reached spiritually by our thought. In his theory of the Eucharist, Calvin made use of some elements of this doctrine. Bread and wine represent the body and the blood of Christ, and by partaking of these signs, we can actually participate in Christ himself, who remains in the higher and more perfect realm of heaven. Calvin, of course, understood the difference between Platonic metaphysics and Christian doctrine: while the relationship between a normal object and its transcendent idea is altogether natural, the relationship between the eucharistic elements (bread, wine) and Christ is supernatural. The Holy Spirit joins the earthly, material signs to the heavenly, divine realities. While the Holy Spirit does not actually fit into a Platonic world view, the distinction and continuity between two realms as well as the symbolic nature of tangible reality enabled Calvin to speak meaningfully of Christ's double presence: in heaven and in the sacrament.

	Plato	Calvin
metaphysical realm (superior realm)	form or idea of an object	the resurrected Christ
	linked by natural participation to	linked by the Holy Spirit to
earthly realm (inferior reality)	tangible object	bread and wine

By following Christ's commandment, "Do this in remembrance of me!" (1 Cor. 11:25), in the eucharistic celebration, the sacramental action reaches into heaven and enables the celebrating community to come into mystical contact with the Lord. Somehow bound to the elements of bread and wine, Christ is spiritually present only at the moment of consumption, defined as the moment of the divine–human encounter. Protestants have consistently rejected the veneration of what Calvin called the "dead element" of bread. Unlike Catholic churches, Protestant houses of worship never include a tabernacle in which consecrated bread is kept for veneration. And a Protestant would never kneel in front of a Catholic tabernacle, for this would amount to idolatry: the veneration of a created reality as if it were Christ himself.

Throughout the centuries, the Protestant bias against sacralizing the eucharistic elements has remained consistent. Protestants shy away from making Christ tangible; for them, his body and blood must remain intangible spiritual realities. Like Luther, they refrain from speculating how exactly the invisible reality of Christ's body and blood can associate with the visible reality of bread and wine. There are exceptions, however, and Jacob Boehme is the most prominent thinker to develop a detailed theory of Christ's spiritual presence.

No other Protestant thinker has ever associated the spiritual and the material realms more closely than Jacob Boehme (1575–1624). For this Lutheran artisan, merchant, and mystic, bread and wine constitute what one may call a natural sacrament even outside Mass. Unlike other edible materials, they are made of more than the four elements of earth, water, air, and fire that nourish our physical body. They also include a mysterious fifth element to which he gives the name of "tincture," a term borrowed from alchemy. The tincture constitutes the active principle inherent in a chemical substance. According to Boehme, the tincture of bread and wine is a spiritual principle that serves to nourish the human spirit in a natural way; hence we are justified in referring to bread and wine as natural sacraments. In the Eucharist (the supernatural sacrament), Christ associates his glorified flesh and blood with the tincture. Being the most spiritual part of bread and wine, the tincture can serve as a carrier for Christ's supernatural and intangible reality. In this way, bread and wine remain what they are—they are not transubstantiated; and Christ's body is not made tangible. The supernatural body of Christ touches the spiritual side of bread and wine, but never becomes drawn into the realm of the created world. Although willing to associate himself with the tincture, Christ remains free to withdraw his power from bread and wine, which he does when an unworthy person partakes of the Lord's Supper. In such a case, the communicant eats mere bread and wine. For all his mystical realism, Boehme shares and affirms the Protestant bias against the sacramental materialism of Catholic teaching.[69]

Ironically, it was a Catholic Romantic theologian who in the early nineteenth century renewed Boehme's view. Like Boehme, Franz von Baader (1765–1841) argued that Christ's presence in the eucharistic species must be thought of as some kind of energy that can be made to reside in them, in much the same way we would say an electric battery can store energy. Von Baader took his inspiration from Boehme, whose views he updated on the basis of a then famous medical theory, developed by the physician Franz Anton Mesmer (1734–1815). Mesmer not only devised a new technique of spiritual healing, he also supplied an explanatory theory. According to this theory, a power he termed animal magnetism (in distinction from magnetism in iron) resides in every human body. By touching a patient in the right way, the physician's own magnetism can serve to readjust the patient's damaged magnetic harmony. Mesmer also argued that doctors can store their magnetic power in material substances, especially in water. Von Baader compared Christ's eucharistic presence to the stored form of Mesmer's magnetic power. Just as the magnetizer transfers his personal power to the material substance to make it available to the patient, so Christ transfers his divine power to bread and wine. Magnetized by Christ, the eucharistic substances serve as a bridge that renews and maintains the rapport between himself and the believer. For all their graphic qualities and romantic plausibility, neither Boehme's nor von Baader's eucharistic theories have ever gained much currency.[70]

The Twentieth-Century Story: Minimalist Options

In the late twentieth century, many Catholic and Protestant theologians have abandoned traditional explanations of the special relationship that may exist between Christ and the Lord's Supper. Most Protestant theologians reject all traditional ideas that theorize about such a relationship. Catholic scholars have generally been less radical, but most of them are dissatisfied with traditional notions of transubstantiation; their eucharistic theologies tend to abandon them in exchange for minimalist positions. This can be shown with respect to Karl Rahner and the widely influential personalist account of the Eucharist taught by some Dutch theologians.[71]

The German Jesuit Karl Rahner did not avoid the most difficult subject of Catholic eucharistic teaching: the conversion or "transubstantiation" of the substance of bread and wine into the substance of Christ's body and blood. In a famous lecture given in 1958, Rahner suggested that it was possible to get rid of many, if not all, difficulties inherent in this obscure and problematic notion by introducing a helpful distinction. He distinguished between: (1) the dogmatic use of the term transubstantiation simply as a linguistic gloss on the words of Christ, "This is my body; this is my blood"; and (2) the philosophical and often obscure speculations about the actual physics of what happens at the Eucharist. The first usage was actually the one employed by the Council of Trent in 1551:

> Because Christ our Redeemer said that it was truly his body that he was offering under the species of bread, it has always been the conviction of the church of God . . . that, by the consecration of the bread and wine, there takes place a change of the whole substance of bread into the substance of the body of Christ our Lord. . . . This change the holy Catholic church has fittingly and properly named transubstantiation.

The second usage was of course never taught by the church. It would take the following form (never decreed by any council): "Because medieval theologians like Thomas Aquinas, basing their view on the sound philosophy of Aristotle, explained how, by the consecration of the bread and wine, there takes place a change of the whole substance of bread into the substance of the body of Christ our Lord. This change theologians have fittingly and properly named transubstantiation." Rahner suggested retaining the Council of Trent's philosophically innocent linguistic use of the term and argued that the church never adopted any particular philosophy to explain what "really happens" at the eucharistic consecration. In other words: the sacramental philosophy of Thomas Aquinas and its details do not belong to what the church has to teach and its members are expected to believe. The Catholic church urges its members to use certain traditional terms like transubstantiation, but as philosophers and theologians they are free to decide for themselves rationally what this term refers to.[72]

In 1969, a decade after his lecture on transubstantiation, Rahner returned to the subject. Now he departed from traditional doctrines in an even bolder way. Theologians, he argued, have made the mistake of postulating too many mysteries; for them, everything smacks of miracle and mystery, so that dogmatic theology resembles a never-ending catalog of essentially incomprehensible facts and ideas. For Rahner, there are only two mysteries: God himself and the incarnation of Christ. Good theologians, according to him, apply Ockham's razor, the famous law that exhorts philosophers to avoid invoking a plurality of principles when a single one will suffice. Instead of multiplying miracles and mysteries, they should reduce their number. Accordingly, there is no need to postulate that a miracle termed transubstantiation happens whenever a priest celebrates Mass. If there is anything mysterious about it, it derives from God's becoming a human person in Christ. It is entirely sufficient to contemplate this essential mystery.[73]

Rahner was not, of course, the only theologian to advocate—and practice— free research into the meaning of traditional eucharistic doctrines. Many Catholic theologians, especially those with some competence in philosophy, have felt that the scholastic teaching about transubstantiation has its defects. They have increasingly expressed their distaste for an outmoded Aristotelian view of "substance" and Thomas Aquinas's "nonsensical abuse of Aristotelian terminology." The Thomist view, explains the English priest-philosopher P.J. FitzPatrick, leads to nothing but absurdities. Once the consecrated bread and wine are consumed, what remains is some liquid and some ashes that remain forever "accidental," that is without real substance. "My only comment," he explains,

> is that if all this ingenuity be so, we have the somewhat eerie result that there are, scattered through the world, the products of past corruptions of consecrated material, apparently substantial but really accidental; that any further corrup-

tion of these will leave them accidental; and so that the general category of things is, slowly but surely, slipping from Substance to Accident. It is a speculation worthy of Jorge Luis Borges, and I was delighted to find I had been eloquently anticipated as long ago as 1704 in framing it, by the Cartesian philosopher Sylvain Régis.

The progressive insubstantiality of the world, so admired by Teilhard de Chardin and Rudolf Steiner, is in this case used to ridicule an outdated and positively misleading doctrine.[74]

Criticism of traditional notions of transubstantiation, of which FitzPatrick's is only the most recent example, necessitated the development of an alternative, more viable theory of the Eucharist. The theory that was most widely discussed originated in Holland and came to be called the theory of transignification. Its chief proponents, Luchesius Smits, Edward Schillebeeckx, and Piet Schonenberg, wrote and published on the question between 1959 and 1969.

The Dutch theory replaced the traditional emphasis on the eucharistic "elements" (i.e., bread and wine) with a more appropriate emphasis on the "person" whose presence the Eucharist celebrates: the person of Christ. When speaking of the Eucharist, we should speak of Christ, not of the metaphysical structure of bread and wine. Smits explained the personalist theory in terms of the phenomenology of the gift. The Dutch theologian relies on a captivating analogy. Imagine being welcomed by a housewife who offers you a cup of tea and a biscuit. The tea now is nothing but tea and the biscuit does not change on being offered to you. Yet, they are different, redefined by the situation. Given the situation, they incarnate the woman's welcome. If we take a closer look, gifts serve as means of communication, and what is communicated is nothing else than the very person. The welcoming woman communicates as it were herself; she embodies herself in the tea offered. The gifts serve as an extension of herself. The woman might, of course, have expressed her welcome in words only, but she feels that things cannot stop there. Naturally, she cannot give herself physically to the visitor. So she prefers to embody her feelings in these gifts. "Food and drink take over the role of the body itself, the welcome becomes tangible in the gifts. What I could originally call no more than a snack and a drink, in the material and biological sense of the expression, I can no longer indicate by the word 'snack,' because its activity is no longer part of a relationship that is biological; it is part of one that is personal." A gift, there-fore, is an extension of the giver, even of a physically absent giver. (One can imagine that the woman cannot be at home and so has a neighbor serve you tea; she will join you later.) Every gift can be said to embody the giver. Jesus, by saying "This is my body, this is my blood," said, quite simply: this is myself, my person. (Ancient Semites often said things twice, in parallel expressions: blood and body stand for the person.) In these eucharistic words, Jesus simply stated a fact, the truth of which can be understood using the analogy of the tea and the biscuit. Jesus in fact stated the truth not only about his special gift of bread and wine, but about all gifts, for every gift offered out of love embodies the giver him- or herself. Smits does not hesitate to call the gift of tea "a kind of mystical body" (Dutch: *een soort mystiek lichaam*) of the woman who offers it . Now, if the giver—Christ—is just a human person, then the gift would be the token or embodiment of his humanity; but if Christ indeed is the God-man, then his gift embodies his divine-human nature.[75]

Bread and wine, if they are considered at all, are therefore understood as symbols. And what is a symbol? Material objects, through human intention, often become something very different from what they were before: they assume a special meaning which transcends their mere materiality, they become symbols of something. A variety of flowers, gathered into a bouquet, may express love and serve as a tangible token of it. One can thus understand how bread and wine become "transignified." If the Eucharist is set in a framework in which people interact rather than one in which objects are handled, it makes little sense to continue traditional Catholic notions of transubstantiation. Personal relations must not be reified and treated as objects. The liturgy thus redefines the meaning of bread and wine, and they become symbols of Christ himself, in very much the same way that a bouquet or tea and a biscuit symbolize love.

Interestingly, the Dutch eucharistic theory comes close to that of the great sixteenth-century reformer, John Calvin. He, too, thought of the Eucharist as uniting the communicant with Christ symbolically rather than physically. "We must not suppose that there is any change in the substance, but must only believe that it [eucharistic bread] is applied to a new purpose." Like Calvin, the Dutch theologians and their followers insist that at Mass, "nothing is changed." At the material level, bread remains what it is outside the ritual. As in Calvin, the connection between the heavenly, living Christ and the human consumption of symbolic food is defined in terms of a relationship.[76]

Although Pope Paul VI did not like the Dutch approach and in 1965 wrote an encyclical letter against it, the personalist theory of the Eucharist remains popular with Catholic theologians.[77]

4.   The Benefits of Partaking

Like all magic, the Christian sacrament aims at producing certain results. The New Testament accounts include no more than hints at what those effects might be. The story of the Last Supper as told by Matthew seems to imply that the eucharistic wine procures "the forgiveness of sins" (Matt. 26:28). In the gospel of John, Christ asserts that "those who eat my flesh and drink my blood have eternal life" (6:54). Often, these scriptural promises have sufficed for clergy and laity alike. However, the time comes when people begin to describe what they feel at communion, and what impact it makes on their spiritual and even physical lives. Theologies of eucharistic participation are then explained in sermons, and developed in learned treatises, theological manuals, and popular books of spiritual direction. Ideas about the effects and benefits of the Eucharist are also embodied in liturgical behavior. In this chapter we will first look at the Eastern theology of which the fourteenth-century spiritual writer Nicholas Kabasilas provides an excellent example. While the "East-side story" demonstrates a continuing concern with speaking of all the eucharistic benefits, the "West-side story" shows a different picture. Here the various traditions of Catholicism, Protestantism, and mystical elitism developed individual emphases. Finally, we will look at twentieth-century theologies with their conflicts between minimalist and maximalist views.

The East-Side Story: Pseudo-Dionysius (ca. 500) and
Nicholas Kabasilas (ca. 1350 CE)

According to Pseudo-Dionysius, the Syrian bishop living ca. 500 CE, the Eucharist holds a firm place in a series of ritual acts that bring human beings closer to God. That series begins with various rites that make up baptism, the task of which is to purify and illuminate. Once duly prepared through purification and illumination, the believer can be brought into contact with the deity in order to reach the third and final stage of spiritual development, the stage of "perfection" or "divinization." This stage is reached by means of a theurgical celebration to us known as the Eucharist. It serves to align believers with God's being, transforming them into new, godlike creatures. The closeness of Dionysius' eucharistic celebration to pagan theurgical rites, which we pointed out earlier, also applies to the benefits derived from the Eucharist. According to Iamblichus, for instance, "the manifold sacred rites of the hierurgies purify or lead to perfection that which is in us or about us; they also give us proportion and order and deliver us from mortal errors and put everything in concord with all the powers superior to us." Or again, "The coming of the gods gives us physical health and virtue of the soul, purity of mind, in short, an ascent of our whole inner existence toward its proper principles." What Dionysius says about the effects of the sacraments amounts to very much the same.[78]

Whereas the focus of Dionysius was on the realignment with God (called "divinization") of those present at the eucharistic celebration, later Eastern theologians complicated the picture by arguing that the eucharistic celebration has at least a fourfold effect. The first effect is that the elements of bread and wine are themselves transformed and divinized. The theologians' eucharistic realism focused on bread and wine as sacred food that had been mysteriously transformed. They understood this sacred food to be Christ's glorified human body which was penetrated by divine energies. The second effect is that in partaking of the sacred food, the believers are themselves penetrated by these energies and thereby purified. The third effect is that communion, far from simply purifying the believers, also illuminates them. And, finally, the fourth effect is divinization. Thus, the Eucharist conferred not only one benefit—divinization—but a multiplicity and thus contributed to all the stages of the mystical ascent: purification, illumination, and perfection. In the work of the fourteenth-century Greek author Nicholas Kabasilas (ca. 1320–95) we find a compendium of Eastern thought on the effects of holy communion.[79]

Among mystical writers it has become an established tradition to use Dionysius' "three ways" to describe the stages of mystical ascent to the divine. Spiritual progress may of course be more complex, and in the work of Kabasilas, one can recognize at least four stages (some names of which differ from those used by Dionysius): purification, restoration, indwelling of Christ, and finally, deification. However, Kabasilas rarely distinguishes these stages very clearly; he happily mixes them, and we may account for this by referring to the Dionysian idea that the superior stages somehow include and perfect the previous ones. As the most powerful sacrament, the Eucharist recapitulates, sums up, and completes the entire sacramental process: it perfects the exorcistic purification and the baptismal illumination and leads to the union with God. Kabasilas's failure to distinguish the various elements of sacramental experience thus finds an easy explanation. In what follows, we try to put some order into the rambling meditations of Kabasilas.[80]

However the details of the sacramental ascent are presented, *purification* always comes first. When the faithful approach the sacred table, they realize their unworthiness, but they also know that the sacred food purifies them. The faithful must partake of the sacred food frequently, because they often fall into the traps of sin and thereby obscure the light baptism has brought to their souls. "The Eucharist is a means of purification and ordained as such from the beginning; it frees us from all defilement." It serves "to wipe out the disgrace which comes from sin." It may be added that the traditional Greek liturgy of St. John Chrysostom, which is the subject of Kabasilas's commentary, refers to the purifying effect of communion in unambiguous terms. When the celebrating priest gives communion to the deacon (who partakes after the priest has partaken), the priest echoes a passage from Isaiah: "This has touched your lips and shall take away your iniquities and your sins." Just as the angel in the prophet's vision purified Isaiah's mouth with a burning coal, so does the host purify the communicant.[81]

After purification comes *restoration*. Sin not only defiles; it also weakens and makes the faithful "fade away and die" spiritually. Kabasilas speaks of the human condition as "a disease in need of a cure." Christ, of course, heals. He gives himself to the faithful as a "medicine and diet and whatever else is conducive to health." Searching for an analogy, Kabasilas describes Christ as a potter who sits by the clay and repeatedly restores the shape which is being blurred. Since Christians constantly lose their spiritual form, the sacred food helps them to recover their proper shape.[82]

In a particularly dense and speculative passage, which is unfortunately very brief, Kabasilas speaks of two persons within one human body. The one is the "old Adam whose body was formed from the earth." The other one, the "new Adam," is born from God and sustained by the Eucharist. "Earthly nourishment," he explains, "pertains to the former life, while the heavenly table feeds the new man with its own proper food. Therefore, when they come to an earthly end, the one life goes back to the earth from whence it came, while the other goes to Christ from whom it was taken." Communion restores the immortality originally intended by the Creator. At death, the Christlike, heaven-oriented, immortal nature of the frequent communicant asserts itself.[83]

Kabasilas was of course not the first to refer to the restorative and life-giving force of the Eucharist. "Whoever eats of this bread will live forever," says the gospel of John (6:51). In the second century, Irenaeus repeated the idea with much emphasis on the physical reality of the life promised by the sacrament: "Our bodies, when they receive the Eucharist, are no longer corruptible, but have the hope of the resurrection to eternity." The eucharistic bread itself is not only a pledge of resurrection and life everlasting; it actually begins a real transformation that makes us Christlike and therefore incorruptible. This idea figures prominently in the Greek patristic authors. In the fourth century, for instance, Gregory of Nyssa uses medical terminology to describe how the Eucharist serves to heal our ailing bodies. For him, communion does not serve as food for human souls; rather, it benefits the body exclusively and restores its paradisal health.[84]

After purification and restoration, the third stage is the *indwelling of Christ*. Restoration, it seems, "does not improve the soul," but as the Lord "pours his own blood into the hearts of those who have been initiated, he makes his own life to dawn upon them." Through communion, the faithful now become a "dwelling place" for Christ. "He dwells within the house and wholly fills it with himself." Once we have reached that stage, our human mind is mingled with Christ's mind, our human will blended with that of Christ, our human body with the divine body, and our human blood with the divine. Now the divine mind obtains control, and Paul's dictum applies: "It is no longer I who live, but Christ lives in me" (Gal. 2:20). At this stage, the faithful must "constantly partake of the table, so that the law of the Spirit might be active in us and that there be no place left for the life of the flesh, nor any opportunity to fall back to the earth, like heavy bodies when the support is withdrawn." If they frequently go to partake of the Lord's table, the faithful are uplifted, i.e., more closely linked to heaven than they are linked to earth. Communion "makes us more akin to Christ than birth makes us akin to our parents."[85]

At the *final stage*, the sacred food—that is Christ himself—transforms faithful communicants, making them Christlike and "participants of the divine nature" (2 Peter 1:4). "By his divinity he is able to exalt and transcend our human nature and to transform it into himself." Borrowing the language of Augustine, Kabasilas refers to a paradoxical form of spiritual digestion. Whereas normal food is assimilated to our body, we are ourselves assimilated to the sacred food of Christ. Kabasilas searches for new analogies to explain this final stage of human divinization. As fire changes iron by penetrating it with its heat, so we are penetrated by Christ; or we are dissolved like a drop of water when it is poured into an immense sea of ointment. When Christ "has led the initiate to the table and has given him his body to eat, he entirely changes him, transforming him into his own state. The clay is no longer clay when it has received the royal likeness but is already the body of the king." Kabasilas's teaching on the ultimate effect of the Eucharist can be summed up in the same word Pseudo-Dionysius had used: *theôsis*, deification. It is impossible, he adds, "to conceive of anything more blessed than this." And, indeed, "after the Eucharist, then, there is nowhere further to go." The communicant is transformed as much as is possible under the conditions of the present life.[86]

Communion, then, has a wide range of possible effects. It supplies the specific help the individual needs at his or her stage of spiritual development. "Holy communion confers on everyone who partakes that which he needs," explains a marginal note found in several fifteenth-century manuscripts of *The Life in Christ*.[87]

Throughout the centuries, Eastern theologians have defined deification as the aim of sacramental worship and indeed as the aim of all religion. The human being, according to them, is essentially vulnerable and weak, and mortality is its chief and most fundamental defect. Mortality is reckoned as the greatest of evils, and to live forever as the greatest of all blessings. God transcends mortality in his inexhaustible abundance of life. The essential task of religion is to bridge the chasm that separates the human and the divine, and here God himself has taken the initiative. He sent his own son, who lived among the mortal beings and began to impart divine life to them. He began to elevate them to immortality, a state in which they participate in the divine abundance of life. And he continues to do so through the Eucharist that serves as a carrier of divine life. As Adolf von Harnack, the great historian of Christian doctrine, has pointed out, Eastern theology presents redemption "in a wholly realistic fashion, as a pharmacological process—the divine nature has to flow in and transform the mortal nature." The sacred food of consecrated bread and wine serves as the *pharmakon* or medicine that initiates and promotes the process of deification.[88]

The West-Side Story: Catholic Empowerment, Protestant Purification, and the Elite Spirituality of Mystical Union

The eucharistic theology of Kabasilas is representative not only of the orthodox tradition; both Catholics and Protestants share the idea and indeed the experience that the Eucharist contributes to the mystical ascent that leads from purification to spiritual empowerment and the indwelling of Christ. Here, Thomas Aquinas, Martin Luther, and John Calvin all agree with Kabasilas. Western theologians, especially Protestants, have been reluctant to speak much about the human person's ultimate assimilation to Christ and deification, but the theme is not completely lacking. Otherwise, when they explain the effects the Lord's Supper has for those who partake of it, they stay fairly close to the common Christian tradition represented by Kabasilas. When they differ, it is never a matter of principle but rather a matter of emphasis. Thus one can say that Lutherans consistently emphasize the effect of spiritual purification, while Catholics expect to be empowered by the sacred repast. For the spiritual and mystical elite of all traditions, purification and empowerment do not suffice: those who love the Lord want to be led to personal union with Christ himself.[89]

The idea that the Eucharist strengthens, nourishes, and sustains the soul, restoring it to its full power, is a commonplace of *Catholic* theological manuals, spiritual writing, and popular imagination. Communion transforms the essentially fragile human person into a spiritual hero who, being united to Christ and assimilated to Christ's sinlessness, cannot commit any sins, either in thought or in deed. Of course, all spiritual writers know that while some saints have approximated this ideal, it does not correspond to the way normal people are. Thomas Aquinas sees the human person involved in a daily struggle for spiritual perfection, and sins—so-called venial sins—diminish their spiritual strength, making them weak and frail. Through sin, "something is lost daily" of our spiritual strength, and this loss lessens "the fervor of our love [for God]." The ideal would be to partake of communion daily (as priests do), for the "daily bread" of communion can be our "remedy against daily infirmity." Aquinas has no doubt about the empowering benefits of communion. Serving as a "medicine given to strengthen" and to provide spiritual refreshment, the Eucharist helps us to avoid sins and protects us from the assaults of the devil. Specifically, communion helps to diminish impure sexual desires, and "one is even preserved from being harmed bodily (*a noxibus corporalibus*) through the healthy exercise of the sacraments."[90]

Catholics often partake of communion with great expectations pertaining both to the spiritual and the physical realm. As early as the patristic period, popular miracle stories explained how the host can influence the human body in significant and surprising ways. Two types of story figure prominently in the repertoires of those who have collected them: the story of the person, typically a woman, who gives up normal food in order to live exclusively on the host; and the story of someone who has been severely ill and is miraculously cured upon reception of the sacrament. Alpais of Cudot, a French peasant girl who died in 1211, was often mentioned as a woman who had lived upon the eucharistic bread for many years (forty, according to one source). Among those whom communion healed from a severe ailment was Louis the Fat, king of France (1081–1137). The medicinal effect of communion became a commonplace of preaching, prayer, and pious writing. It also became a theme of Christian iconography, especially in the seventeenth and eighteenth centuries. One example, an eighteenth-century painting, presumably of Austrian origin and believed to have belonged to a monastery's pharmacy, shows "Christ the Pharmacist" (ill. 25) as he stands in front of shelves with medicine bottles labeled "holiness, perseverance, mercy," and so on, but also "eye water, stomach water, heart water, strengthening water." In order to underscore the physical dimension of Christ's healing, a painting within the painting shows Christ as he touches the eyes of a blind man. But how can present-day believers be touched by Christ in the most immediate way? Here, too, the painting has a clear answer: through holy communion. The white circle of the host with its green, radiant aureole balances the figure of Christ himself and provides the painting's main focus. The painting must be seen as an invitation to partake of the Lord's Supper. The large sheet lying on the desk below the chalice has Christ's own invitation inscribed: "Come to me, all who labor and are heavy laden, and I will refresh you!" (Matt. 11:28). This biblical quotation has traditionally been associated with the eucharistic bread. For instance, in the *Imitation of Christ* we read: "I thank you, good Jesus, eternal Shepherd, for choosing to nourish us with your precious Body and Blood and for inviting us by your own words to share in these mysteries, saying: Come to me, all who labor and are heavy laden, and I will refresh you." In a manner reminiscent of the painting, the *Imitation of Christ* calls communion a *remedium*, i.e., a medicine. Accordingly, "this most high and worthy sacrament is the health of the soul and body, the medicine that cures every spiritual illness. In this sacrament my weaknesses are cured and my passions are held in check, my temptations are overcome or they become less burdensome, grace is more greatly infused,

25. Christ the Pharmacist. Christ's medicine is the Eucharist. The large sheet lying on the desk below the chalice reads: "Come to me, all who labor and are heavy laden, and I will refresh you" (Matt. 11:28). The motif of "Christ the Pharmacist" was popular with both Catholics and Protestants in the seventeenth and eighteenth centuries. Our example is Catholic and believed to come from the pharmacy of an Austrian monastery. Anonymous Austrian painting, eighteenth-century.

virtue once started now increases, faith is made firm, hope is strengthened, and love's embers are fanned into flames, spreading ever wider." This traditional "trinity" of religious virtues, faith, hope, and love, is also present in the painting: "love" is inscribed on the heart, "faith" on the lid of the chalice, and hope is represented by the anchor.[91]

While theologians insist that the empowering and healing effect of the Eucharist depends on actual partaking, the laity have often thought otherwise. According to popular opinion, the benefit of communion may be obtained right after the consecration when the priest elevates the consecrated host and the entire congregation sees and welcomes the body of Christ. Looking at the consecrated host could be a powerful experience reminiscent of an Old Testament episode. In the days of Moses, many Israelites, after having been bitten by snakes, were healed by looking at a "brazen serpent" set on a pole (Num. 21:8). Catholic popular piety attributes a similar curative force to the act of looking at the elevated host. Miraculously, even blind eyes may see the host and be healed. In fifteenth-century England, such miracles were attributed to the intervention of St. Osmund and King Henry VI. Miracles of this kind are not, of course, confined to the distant past. They happen even in the twentieth century. People tell the story of Eric Malene, a young piano virtuoso who went blind. Though a Protestant, he went to a Catholic Mass at Christmas. At the elevation, Eric saw a great light emanating from the host (ill. 26), and that light restored his vision. This miracle happened in the church of Our Lady in Prestwich, England, on December 25, 1937.[92]

Another, more arcane gesture to contact the power-giving host was restricted to deacons and altar-servers. After the consecration, when the priest genuflects to honor Christ and then elevates the host, the serving deacon or altar boy lifts, holds, or touches the priest's chasuble. Although this gesture has recently disappeared from Catholic liturgy, it is worth studying. To hold the priest's chasuble is a gesture of venerable antiquity; it goes back at least to the late thirteenth century. Around 1285, a ritual book from Liège in Belgium refers to it. Soon after, it appears in art: it can be seen in an illuminated French breviary of 1323–26 (ill. 27a) and in paintings in the San Francesco church of Assisi (1320s) (ill. 27b) and the cathedral of Florence, Italy (ca. 1340). As for the meaning, a twentieth-century popular book on the Mass quotes the woman of the gospel who, after having touched the hem of Christ's garment, was healed of an ailment from which she had suffered for twelve years: "If I but touch the hem of his robe, I shall be healed" (Matt. 9:20). Ancient and medieval Catholics were fascinated by this account (ill. 28), and stories about women

26. A Eucharistic Miracle. The elevated host emits light and restores the eyesight of Eric Malene, a blind young pianist. The miracle happened in the Church of Our Lady at Prestwich, England, on December 25, 1937, and is chronicled in Catholic devotional literature. Popular book on eucharistic miracles, 1960s.

being healed after touching the cape of a saint, such as Martin of Tours and Thomas Aquinas, circulated widely. The server, then, performs a symbolic gesture. The server who knelt close to the priest was unable to see the elevated body of Christ. The holding of the hem or the touching of the chasuble could be understood as indirect, but real physical contact with the sacred substance (ill. 29). Touching the priest's chasuble no doubt compensated for the lack of visual contact with the body of Christ. As the popular book explains, the altar boys who touch the priest's robe represent the congregation. The priest's fingers touch the body of the Lord. Through this touch, "the stream of grace shall flow from the Lord, through the priest and to the people." In the gospel story, Christ realizes that "power had gone forth from him" (Mark 5:30). Whenever someone touches Christ or his eucharistic body, he or she comes into contact with a vibrating source of power.[93]

Among the *Protestants*, Luther and certain Puritan theologians spoke of the eucharistic benefits not as empowerment but as *purification*. For Martin Luther, the principal benefit of the Lord's Supper, clearly stated in the gospel (Matt. 26:28), is the forgiveness of sins:

> What is the use or fruit of the sacrament? Listen to this: "given for you"; "shed for you." I go to the sacrament in order to take and use Christ's body and blood, given and shed for me. When the minister intones, "This cup is the New Testament in my blood," to whom is it sung? Not to my dog, but to those who are gathered to take the sacrament. These words must be apprehended by faith. Therefore I use the sacrament for the forgiveness of my sins.

For Luther, the remission of sins is the most important effect of the Lord's Supper, and this corresponds to his basic theological concern. In his conception, the human being is utterly sinful and, if sensitive enough, guilt-ridden. The burden of unworthiness, of sin and guilt, made Luther an unhappy, continually frustrated friar who resorted to ever new practices of asceticism and "good works" which he carried out to please God. The discovery of the merciful, forgiving God stands at the beginning of his career as an independent theological thinker and reformer. His experience led him to see the sweet promise of the sacrament in Christ's words reported in Matthew's gospel and repeated at each Mass: "This my blood of the new testament, which shall be shed for many unto remission of sins" (Matt. 26:28). Luther, in the ups and downs of his moods, in ecstasy and despair, needed the consolation that sins are forgiven and that the human being is mercifully accepted by God.[94]

Luther's emphasis on the purificatory effect of communion became the essential characteristic of his eucharistic teaching. But it was not appreciated by all his contemporaries. Zwingli did not like to hear that "the mere eating of the body of Christ remits sins" (this is how he summarized Luther's view), and he accused Luther of superstition. Catholics also had problems with it. According

27a. Holding the Priest's Chasuble (1). At the elevation, the deacon or the server held the Catholic priest's chasuble, presumably to be close to the host and capture some of the sacred power emanating from it. The illumination seems to be the earliest representation of the gesture which echoes a gospel passage according to which a woman was healed after having touched Christ's cloak. Also note the curious motif of Christ celebrating Mass, served by an angel. Bréviaire de Belleville, ca. 1323–26.

27b. Holding the Priest's Chasuble (2). St. Martin, after giving half of his coat to a beggar, celebrated Mass with bare arms which were then covered by angels. Whereas most artists depict the server holding the hem of the priest's chasuble, Simone Martini shows him touching it at the center. The Italian artist—or the server whom he painted—presumably knew that according to Mark's gospel, the woman touched Christ's cloak itself (*vestimentum*, Mark 5:27), not just the fringe or tassels of his cloak, as Matthew and Luke specify (*fimbria vestimenti*, Matt. 9:20 and Luke 8:44). Fresco by Simone Martini, San Francesco, Assisi, ca. 1320–25.

28. Touching the Hem of Christ's Garment. The inscription accompanying the scene explains that a woman touched the fringes of Christ's garment and was healed of a serious infirmity (Matt. 9:20–22). The mosaic follows the gospel in integrating the woman into the crowd that surrounds Jesus. It completes the biblical text by having Christ look and stretch his arm toward her in a gesture of blessing. He comes close to returning her touch, as if the artist were saying: if you touch Christ in a humble gesture, he will touch you. The invisible healing power emanates not only from Christ's garment, as in the scriptural text, but also from his hand and his face. Mosaic, Cathedral of Monreale, Sicily, ca. 1182–90.

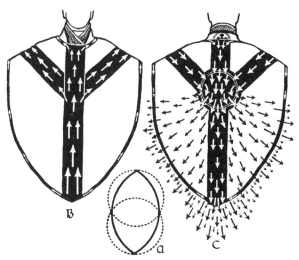

29. The Priest's Chasuble as Conductor of Sacred Forces. According to the Anglican priest and theosophist Charles Leadbeater (1854–1934), the consecrated eucharistic elements bread and wine radiate sacred forces. These forces are caught up by the front part of the priest's chasuble (left) and radiate from its back (right). Leadbeater claimed to have seen the radiation and included the drawing in his book, *The Science of the Sacraments*, 1920. Theosophist drawing, 1920.

30. Communion for Souls in Purgatory. The benefits of Mass are not only for the living, but also for the dead. When the priest says Mass "for the deceased," angels administer communion to suffering souls. The host serves as a medicine that purifies the soul from the stain left by venial sin and thus shortens the stay in purgatory. Tyrolian altar painting, ca. 1525.

to Luther, communion brings about the forgiveness of all sins, not just the venial ones, as Aquinas had stated. For the latter, light, "venial" sins (often sins caused by "seminal loss" in men or by sexual intercourse) should not prevent anyone from receiving communion, for the sacrament purifies the soul from the stain acquired by "light" sinning. Catholic art depicting angels who bring the host to the suffering souls in purgatory (ill. 30) echoes the belief in the purificatory power of communion. The fire of purgatory serves to purify from the stain left by venial sins, and communion can speed up the process. (Christians guilty of mortal sins would go straight to hell, and for them, purification comes too late.) Luther's Catholic opponents understood the difference between Luther's and Aquinas's view quite well, and they were alarmed by the extraordinary claim made by the reformer. They feared he would abolish the sacrament of confession (which he did not; nevertheless, it soon dropped out of much Protestant practice). In 1551, the Catholic Council of Trent condemned those who followed Luther in saying "that the principal fruit of the most holy Eucharist is the forgiveness of sins, or that no other effects come from it." After the Council of Trent, Catholics came to consider confession, rather than communion, the chief sacrament of spiritual purification.[95]

Not only Luther and his followers, but also Puritans considered purification the first and foremost benefit of communion. In the Puritan imagination, the purificatory effect of communion could assume quite graphic qualities, at least in the second part of Bunyan's *Pilgrim's Progress* (1684). Little Mark, son of Bunyan's Christiana, has eaten green plums from the trees in the devil's orchard. The suffering boy will certainly die without the intervention of Mr. Skill, the physician. The doctor knows that the boy's stomach must be purged, and he tries to do this, but to no avail. So eventually he applies the strongest and best medicine he has, a special pill made *ex carne et sanguine Christi* (from the flesh and blood of Christ—"you know physicians give strange medicines to their patients"). Mixed with much salt, the sacred substance was formed into pills, and the boy swallowed three. "So with much ado, after a short prayer for the blessing of God upon it, he took it, and it wrought kindly with him. It caused him to purge, it caused him to sleep and rest quietly, it put him into a fine heat and breathing sweat, and did quite rid him of his gripes." We may laugh at Bunyan's strange allegory of communion as purgative medicine, but we should realize that preachers have never spurned even the strangest illustrations to make their point. Christiana does not leave Mr. Skill without taking a supply of twelve boxes of the pills, for "it is an universal pill; 'tis good against all the diseases that pilgrims are incident to, and when it is well prepared it will keep good time out of mind." More than a purgative, the sacred food can serve many purposes; "a universal pill," it restores health.[96]

Whereas the purificatory and the empowering force of the sacrament can be appreciated by the majority of ordinary Christians, the idea of *personal union with Christ* is more at home with the *spiritual elite* of Catholic saints and nuns, Protestant pietists, and those committed to a sentimental spirituality that borders on mysticism.

Hadewijch, a Flemish *béguine* of the early thirteenth century, belonged to those female mystics who simply could not live without communion. She describes a vision of a heavenly encounter with Christ using eucharistic symbolism. First, she reports, "he gave himself to me in the shape of the sacrament, in its outward form, as the custom is." But then, she continues, "he came himself to me, took me entirely in his arms, and pressed me to him, and all my members felt his in full felicity." The Eucharist functions as a symbolic beginning, foreplay to a more immediate, erotic encounter. The "customary" rite leads to something less customary. Hadewijch's vision no doubt echoes what mystics often felt when they took communion at Mass: as they fell into their trances or ecstasies, they met the Lord himself. Communion was simply an entrance rite to a full spiritual encounter. In the work of Gertrude of Helfta (d. 1302), we find similar and even more daring confessions. Gertrude asked the Lord about the gift she would receive at communion, and hears this answer: "[I will give myself to you] entirely, with all my divinity, just as my Virgin Mother received me." Here we have the intimation of a spiritual pregnancy. One of

31a. The Sacred Kiss (1). "Ah! how sweet was the first kiss Jesus gave to my soul! Yes, this was a kiss of love, and I felt I was loved." This is how Thérèse of Lisieux, now a canonized Catholic saint, described her experience of first communion (May 8, 1884). Contemporary French holy cards express the same sentiment. First preached by Ambrose of Milan (*On the Sacraments* 5) in the fourth century, the idea was popularized by Catholics in the nineteenth century. Inscribed "le baiser de paix" (the kiss of peace), the holy card depicts a communion scene in which Christ replaces the priest. French holy card, 1882.

Gertrude's visions is yet more explicit. In a vision, she attends a Mass which is said not by a priest but by Christ himself, accompanied by angelic hosts. When the time comes for communion, Gertrude asks the Lord what the "feast" (*convivium*) will be. There is no communion rite; instead, Christ embraces Gertrude, and she feels his "caresses," his "penetration," and "influx." Normal communion, Gertrude explains, entails a similar intimate union with the Lord: his "most affectionate embrace" (*amicissimi affectûs amplexus*) and "sweet kiss of peace" (*pacis osculum suave*).[97]

We can readily understand this peculiar fantasy that originated in a convent in which the nuns received "the blood of Christ" at communion and also identified male semen with human blood. Perhaps we should not be shocked by the boldness (or perversity) of the nun, but instead appreciate her radical female love of the male Christ. We should also realize that it is traditional to identify communion if not with copulation then at least with marital closeness. A century before Gertrude, the Benedictine abbess Hildegard of Bingen had actually dressed her nuns as brides when, on feast days, they went forward to receive communion. For twentieth-century Catholics, this does not sound so extraordinary, as they may remember having seen ordinary parish girls, at age

31b. The Sacred Kiss (2). Christ and the communicant are united as lover and beloved. The girl's halo indicates that, at least at the moment of communion, the communicant can be considered a saint. French holy card, twentieth-century.

nine or twelve, dressed as little brides of Christ on the Sunday of First Communion. But in the Middle Ages, bridal symbolism and spirituality were known only among the spiritual elite in the monasteries. It was not before the nineteenth century, that bridal mysticism—and fashion—came to be recommended to the laity (ills. 31a, 31b, and 32).[98]

Similar notions can be found among the elite of German Lutheran pietists and a variety of English-speaking Protestants. The idea that the communicant and Christ are united as bride and bridegroom is common to Jeremy Taylor (1613–67) in England, Count Nicholas Ludwig von Zinzendorf (1700–60) in Germany, and Jonathan Edwards (1703–58) and John Williamson Nevin (1803–86) in America. A particularly valuable account comes from William McCulloch, an eighteenth-century Scottish minister who, in an early attempt at doing fieldwork in religious psychology, collected the spiritual experiences of over one hundred people; from the McCulloch papers in New College Library, Edinburgh, it is clear that female communicants especially thought of themselves as brides of the Lord, sick with love. According to Nevin, "the mystical union with Christ is more intimate and real than any union that is known in the world," though marital intimacy, apparently, comes close. Some eighteenth-

32. Fashion for First Communion. In the nineteenth century, first communion became a big family celebration for bourgeois Catholics. Here an artist in a French fashion magazine shows a mother taking her children to church. In Catholic France, as elsewhere, it became fashionable to dress girls as brides for the occasion. French fashion magazine, 1850.

century German pietists took the biblical comparison of the husband–wife and the Christ–church relationship (of Eph. 5:1–32) so literally that sexual intercourse in wedlock was not practiced for begetting offspring but for celebrating "communion" with Christ, just as in the Lord's Supper![99]

A classic expression of Protestant eucharistic eroticism can be found in the lyrics of Johann Franck, a seventeenth-century German hymn writer. In a hymn still familiar among German Protestants today and known among English-speaking Christians in Catherine Winkworth's rendering, Franck calls upon his soul to open her house to the Savior:

Hasten as a bride to meet Him,
And with loving reverence greet Him,
For with words of life immortal
Now he knocketh at thy portal.
Haste to ope' the gates before Him,
Saying while thou dost adore Him,
"Suffer, Lord, that I receive Thee,
And I never more will leave Thee."

Singing about communion as the consummation of a mystical marriage attracted German Lutherans more than other groups. Franck's hymn happens to be the one that has survived changes of taste. Many other seventeenth-century mystical hymns on the Lord's Supper no longer figure in the Protestant repertoire. However, the personal coming of the Lord to the individual's soul is a way many Christians—Protestants and Catholics alike—have thought of and experienced communion.[100]

The Twentieth-Century Story (1): Teilhard de Chardin and Rudolf Steiner

Around 1900, the general theological mood was inclined toward accepting the Kantian notion that God and therefore human contact with God can be spoken of only in a cautious and tentative manner. Since we have no immediate experience of the divine, rationalist theologians preferred not to make bold claims about what happens at worship. Of course such theological modesty provoked a reaction from those who thought otherwise. Among them, two stand out for their boldness of thought and the wide influence of their theologies: the ex-theosophist Rudolf Steiner (1861–1925), co-founder of a Christian church in Germany, and Pierre Teilhard de Chardin (1881–1955), a French Jesuit priest, scientist, and controversial theological writer. During the years of the First World War, both Steiner and Teilhard decided that the advance of humankind was in a real sense affected by the Eucharist. For Teilhard, the Eucharist promotes the spirit of human community. For Steiner, the sacrament helps the human individual to transcend the material world and to belong to a higher, spiritual universe, yet to be formed. For both, the Eucharist also affects the entire universe.

During the First World War, three worlds met in *Pierre Teilhard de Chardin*: the religious world of the Jesuit priest who had been ordained in 1911; the world of the young scientist who had begun to study geology and paleoanthropology in Paris; and the world of the soldier who enthusiastically participated in the defense of his country against the Germans and who celebrated the war as a revelation of human co-operation and community. Committed to his religious vocation, Teilhard worked out a theory of the Eucharist that united his three worlds in a meaningful way. He expressed his views of communion in a note entitled "Le Prêtre" (1918) and later in "La Messe sur le monde" (1923), as well as in *Le Milieu divin* (1926/27), texts published only after his death. These essays reflect the love Teilhard had for stones, geological formations, and prehistoric finds. As one who studied and took pleasure in the realm of the material, Teilhard could not identify with a complete, ascetic rejection of the world (of which the Christian tradition includes so many examples). He saw the birth of Christ as an event of truly universal implications. In Christ, the material world received an impulse or force that functions as the physical center of the evolutionary movement. After Christ's resurrection, the church had to link humanity with the impulse imparted by and somehow identical with Christ. Teilhard defines the priest's task as bringing both the material and the social world closer to Christ. For him, eucharistic communion contributes to the assimilation of both the human and the material world to Christ, the aim of all social and biological evolution. In taking communion, the faithful incorporate something into themselves that both symbolizes the direction of evolution and promotes the process. Teilhard expressed his view of the Eucharist in many different ways. His early essay, "Le Prêtre" includes the following passage:

> When Christ, carrying farther the process of his incarnation, comes down into the bread in order to dwell there in its place, his action is not confined to the particle of matter that his presence is at hand, for a moment, to etherealize. The transubstantiation is encircled by a halo of divinization—real, even though less intense—that extends to the whole universe. From the cosmic element into which he has entered, the Word [i.e., Christ] is active to master and assimilate to himself all that still remains [of the universe].

In his later treatise *Le Milieu divin*, he argued that through communion "the human layer of the earth is wholly and continuously under the organizing influence of the Incarnate Christ." However, this organizing influence extends "to the less luminous regions that sustain us," so that "at every moment the Eucharistic Christ controls . . . the whole movement of the universe." Step by step, the eucharistic energy invades the universe, creating what Teilhard calls "le milieu divin."[101]

Traditional Catholic teaching identifies eucharistic wine with the blood of Christ and bread with his body. For Teilhard, the traditional Catholic doctrine of the transubstantiation represents only a first step. Transubstantiation at Mass sets the stage for a more universal transformation in which the entire universe becomes Christ's body. In the language of scholastic doctrine: every eucharistic transubstantiation eliminates the substance of a small amount of created matter (bread and wine), turning it into Christ. After consumption, what remains of bread and wine is no longer substantial, but only accidental. Thus, the human body, due to its use and assimilation of consecrated matter, becomes in part "accidental." It gradually loses its substance, retaining only its accidental qualities. Eventually, the entire universe will be accidental, and behind all things visible is only one true substance: Christ. Then, Christ's words "This is my blood" and "This is my body" will identify the entire creation as belonging physically to him. Thus, the entire material world will lose its opacity, and humans will realize Christ as the true substance of all created matter. Christ will shine through all things in a universal epiphany or, as Teilhard says, "diaphany." Here Teilhard joins—or presumably is inspired by—ancient Neoplatonic and alchemical thought which sees nature primarily as a spiritual reality. Its material opacity, which prevents the Creator's ideas from shining through and being perceived, is not permanent, but can be overcome. Those who see beyond material opacity must initiate the great process of transformation.

During his lifetime, most of Teilhard's theological writings remained unpublished. In the decade following his death in 1955, however, they became available in print. Bestsellers avidly read by progressive Catholics in the 1960s, they stimulated theological discussion. Although theologians admitted that they did not know exactly how the Eucharist affects the human person and the material world, at least some, like Alfons Auer (b. 1915) of Tübingen and Henri de Lubac (1896–1991) of Paris, hailed Teilhard's view. De Lubac, in his appreciation of Teilhard's thought, quoted a passage from Augustine's *Confessions*, a text apparently supporting the Jesuit's view. At one point of his career, Augustine felt he had heard Christ's voice from on high: "I am the food of the fully grown; grow and you will feed on me. And you will not change me into you like the food your flesh eats, but you will be changed into me." In other words: the Eucharist incorporates the communicants into the body of Christ, and they are actually transformed into the substance of that body. They become "Christified," even physically! According to Auer, a new appreciation of the material character of the Eucharist could help to overcome the traditional Catholic devaluation of the material world and provide lay people with a new spirituality characterized by a radical openness to secular activities and professions. Far from separating the faithful from their daily tasks, the celebration of the Eucharist and the reception of communion could give them a new sense of their vocation and provide moral and even tangible, physical strength. The new, Teilhardian spirituality enabled Auer to preach a secular gospel that resonated with the radical generation of the 1960s, while at the same time remaining faithful to Catholic sacramentalism. Ideally, in Auer's view, every Christian believer should follow Teilhard who, as a Jesuit and a paleontologist, combined a priestly career with a secular vocation. While of course not everyone can study theology and become ordained, everyone must strive to achieve a new wholeness in understanding the hidden eucharistic center of secular existence.[102]

While Teilhard's alleged pantheism came under attack from the Catholic hierarchy, his philosophy still enjoys great prestige. Recent years have actually seen a Teilhardian renaissance among those who seek to include "nature" in a new Christian spirituality or who believe in evolution and universal progress. Christians, according to the American Jesuit Peter Fink, expect "the transformation of all creation into Christ"; for him, "bread and wine, as bits of creation converted into Christ, announce the destiny of all creation, and serve as sacrament (*sacramentum*, seal) of that transformation yet to be realized." Although now little known among the general public, Teilhard's cosmic vision has left its mark on Catholic theology.[103]

The world of *Rudolf Steiner*, the Austrian Goethe specialist, philosopher, and founder of the "anthroposophical society" (1913), is hard to define. From his numerous books and published lectures (some three hundred volumes), three key ideas stand out: there is a higher, nonmaterial world of which one can gain knowledge through intuition; the coming of Christ into the world is a decisive event in the evolution of humankind and the universe as a whole; in religious mystery cults, people can gain access to higher worlds and link themselves to the power of Christ. In several of his lectures and books, Steiner spoke about the Eucharist as the mystery celebration adequate for the present age. Steiner, unlike Teilhard, has a wide following among Christians with esoteric leanings. While Teilhard's views remain controversial among specialists and practically unknown among the laity, Steiner's romantic vision continues to shape the lives of many. His theological legacy survives in a church that he helped to found in the 1920s and that still exists as the "Christian Community" (*Christengemeinschaft*). This church's life culminates in its sacramental worship, and its members do not hesitate to speak of their community as a sacramental association.[104]

Steiner, who grew up a Catholic, compiled a book of worship for the Christian Community, based on and preserving the essential structure of the traditional (medieval) Mass. In the Christian Community, Mass (which they call "the Act of Consecration of Man") is celebrated every day, and celebration focuses on the sacrament. The Christian Community's theologians make a great effort to explain the meaning of the sacrament to their congregations. Drawing upon the thought of Steiner, they describe it as a supernatural, yet very real, event. The sacrament consists of two magical acts: transubstantiation and communion. In the first act, the priest's words bring the cosmic power of Christ into relationship with material reality or, more precisely, with the special food of bread and grape juice. These substances are pervaded by the power of Christ and thus transformed into the glorified elements of Christ's body. In communion, the second act, the faithful eat transformed bread and drink transformed grape juice. By partaking of the sacred food, the communicants are themselves transformed, at least in a preliminary manner. Invoking Paul's metaphor of "putting on Jesus Christ" and his reference to Christians belonging to a "new creation," Hans-Werner Schroeder emphasizes the supernatural reality of what happens at communion. According to him, the sacred food is the "eternal medicine" for the "cure of the sickness of sin." Although the faithful remain mortal, they become absorbed into a higher reality which is both spiritual and physical. This reality consists of a "finer materiality" permeated by the spiritual power of Christ, and it assimilates the faithful and begins to heal their defects. The communicants enter this new reality not merely with their mind and emotions, but with their entire being of spirit, soul, and body.[105]

If Christian believers partake of the sacred food frequently, their whole existence will be made more and more Christlike. At death, when Christians shed their mortal husk, their material remains still bear the marks of the higher world. They are as it were transfigured by heavenly light. When given back to nature, even the dead body contributes to the universal process by which Christ transforms not only people, but nature as well—indeed, the entire universe. With its cosmic dimensions, communion has an effect that transcends both the individual and the community of believers.

The Christian Community's priests are trained in Steiner's theology, the complexities of which are hard to master and even harder to explain to the uninitiated. Nevertheless, we can at least attempt to sketch some of Steiner's ideas that develop traditional Christian notions by blending them with concepts borrowed from Indian philosophy and nineteenth-century theosophical thought.[106]

Basic to Steiner's theology is his view of evil and corruption. He sees the human being as deficient and corrupted by the Satanic stain of sin. Given the human predicament, the central task of spiritual life is to overcome the state of evil and thus to reach the state of "being like God." This new and higher state is produced neither by a natural process nor by mere human action. In fact, only once in the entirety of human history has this divine, godlike state become fully realized: in Jesus Christ. What has become real in a unique way in Christ is a possibility for all humankind. Every human being can follow him and enter into the process that leads to deification. Although that process involves human effort and determination, believers do not depend exclusively on their own resources. Objective forces that promote spiritual advancement and salvation radiate from the Christ-event and can reach and gradually transform the individual person. These healing forces aim at spiritualizing and eventually deifying the believer; as "heavenly forces" they are present and effective in the sacraments, especially in the Eucharist. Steiner suggests that people say the following prayer after receiving communion: "Your body, O Christ, that I received, and your blood that quickens me, these shall penetrate me, so that the sickness of sin may be healed through the healing medicine, the sacrament." This is, of course, patterned after the prayer the Catholic priest uttered (in Latin) in the traditional, pre-Vatican II Mass: "May your body, Lord, which I have taken, and your blood, which I have drunk, cleave to my innermost being [literally, entrails]. Grant that no stain of sin may be left in me, now that I am renewed by this pure and holy sacrament."[107]

Steiner's teaching about the effects of the Eucharist cannot be separated from his view of the destiny of the universe and his idea of reincarnation. In fact, his cosmology and his doctrine about life after death combine to give his vision a unique character. The two substances used in the ritual—bread and wine (actually, grape juice)—not only promote the spiritualization of those who partake of them; they also affect the extra-human material world. The transubstantiation involves the entire material world in a process of spiritualization that aims at uniting the entire universe with Christ. The eucharistic transformation initiates a process in which a new, spiritual creation emerges. According to Steiner, the godlike human being needs a congenial spiritual environment. Sacramental magic contributes to the building of a new creation that transcends ordinary materiality. The new creation will also survive the eventual dissolution and dissipation of what now constitutes our physical environment.[108]

Of course, the universe's transformation into a Christlike structure will take time and can only be achieved over millennia. And just as the slow cosmic transformation remains almost invisible to us, so the individual's transformation transcends the short space of an earthly existence between birth and death. In order to achieve the final state of apotheosis, a sequence of several human lives is needed. Therefore, Steiner suggests that human beings are reincarnated: after physical death, people may return to this world in order to work out their salvation and to expose themselves again to the saving impulse that radiates from the Christ-event. In working out their salvation, reincarnated human beings do not have to start from the beginning again; instead, they retain the measure of conformity with Christ that they have achieved in previous lives. In other words, the state of spiritual health each person has acquired in the course of an earthly existence has a great influence over their next incarnation. By taking the spiritual medicine of communion, the faithful actually prepare themselves for another life. Communion can improve their "karma," their spiritual inheritance.

The Twentieth-Century Story (2): Minimalist Options

In a century marked by theological pluralism, it is not surprising that there are not only enthusiastic promoters of the teachings of Steiner and Teilhard, but also theologians who reject these views and propose what we may call minimalist interpretations of the eucharistic benefits. The Lutheran Paul Althaus (1888–1966) and the Jesuit Karl Rahner (1904–84) have written critiques of the Steiner–Teilhard approach, and their minimalist views have become very popular among twentieth-century Christians.

According to Althaus, "a Christian realism, that teaches certain sacramental effects . . . has betrayed the clear teaching of the gospel to gnosticism and theosophy." The gospel, as Althaus reads it, "does not legitimate us to expect the comprehensive and penetrating operation of Christ and his Spirit specifically from the sacraments." Evidence of special sacramental effects, moreover, does not exist. In receiving communion, the faithful do not receive any special "gifts" from their Lord. The benefit of meeting Christ in the sacrament is to receive the Lord's legal promise of forgiving sins and granting eternal life. This transcendent legal act must be believed but cannot be experienced in a process of sanctification. The Lord's Supper, for Althaus, is simply a sign of faith. This view has a long Protestant tradition. Luther, for instance, compared the sacrament of bread and wine to a legal document. When a Christian believer receives the sacrament, "it is as if a citizen were given a sign, a document, or some other token to assure him that he is a citizen of the city." According to the *Heidelberg Catechism* (1563), the Eucharist places a "seal onto the promise of the gospel." The promise, of course, is the remission of sins and consequently the admission to heaven. A seal validates and confirms, without adding anything to the contents of a document, i.e., to the promise of life everlasting. The Eucharist, therefore, can be called "the most holy seal of the divine promises which we can present at the Last Judgment. Having this pledge we may exult with joy and be sure of eternal life." When partaking of the Lord's Supper, we receive *tessera resurrectionis ad vitam aeternam*—"the ticket to resurrection and eternal life."[109]

Karl Rahner, the famous German Jesuit, was a master of minimalist theological notions. Most of his writing aimed at pruning traditional religious notions, cutting them down to a size that seemed more rational, more acceptable to twentieth-century Christians. Thus, he attacked the popular Catholic notion of communion "as a friendly state visit, accompanied by tokens of grace and favor," and "as the time when the Lord begins 'to be there,' to hold audience so to speak, so that one can now start to talk to him" in a special way. This view is common in Catholic spiritual writing, and, in particular, French spiritual directors like Pierre-Julien Eymard (1811–68) and Adolphe Tanqueray (1854–1932) extolled and recommended it as a form of eucharistic mysticism possible for all Catholics. Rahner can refer to it only in an ironical way; he refuses to accept sentimental notions of Christ's presence. And—what is a particularly devastating blow against Catholic popular piety—the Jesuit asserts that the Lord's sacramental presence actually ceases at the very moment the host is placed into the mouth and consumed (ironically, this is what according to some scholastic doctors happens when an impure person or a mouse eats the consecrated host). Rahner also insists on the absence of any tangible effects of communion. The reception of the consecrated bread "does not set up a reciprocal physical influence between the body of Christ and the communicant in the realm of experience." He comes close to denying the special character of communion. In order to communicate with Christ in prayer and meditation, the faithful do not have to wait for a priest who has the power to conjure up the Lord for them and put him into their mouths.[110]

How Rahner's sacramental minimalism weakened, if not actually destroyed, Teilhardian notions can be studied in a letter written to the famous Jesuit theologian in 1962. "I should like to imagine that my body will gradually consist of nothing but hosts and thus be the body of Christ," reflected Rahner's correspondent Luise Rinser. However, she checked her Teilhardian wish by adding: "Well, dogmatically speaking, this cannot be the case. What a pity. You don't turn into an apple by eating nothing but apples. And, besides, I eat many other things also, not just hosts." She also echoed Rahner's minimalism by restricting the Lord's presence to the short moment of eating the host: did not Jesus himself say, "Take, eat; this is my body"? At all other times, the host can stand as a symbol for Christ, but it cannot be identified with his body. The wish for a Teilhardian experience of eucharistic transformation is made nonsensical as soon as it is touched by the kind of rational thought that is characteristic of Rahner and his circle.[111]

While the Europeans Althaus and Rahner stay at the level of criticism and fail to develop new theories about the eucharistic benefits, American theologians go one step further. Gordon Kaufman (b. 1925), Charles Baker, and Matthew Fox (b. 1940) suggest truly modern accounts that are in tune with late twentieth-century sentiments. Kaufman and Baker sketch a eucharistic theology comparable to American "civil religion," while Fox proposes an "ecological" view.

In order to understand Kaufman's and Baker's view, one has to start with Ulrich Zwingli, the sixteenth-century reformer of Zurich in Switzerland. Zwingli, like Kaufman and Baker, had given up all magical notions connected with the Lord's Supper. But he knew that there was something fascinating about the congregational celebration of it. Zwingli likened the enthusiasm Christians experienced when celebrating the sacrament to the Swiss feeling of national pride. Just as the Swiss have their national sentiments and celebrations, so Christians have the Lord's Supper. In the Lord's Supper, the faithful commemorate their Lord's death; this is all. And they draw much enthusiasm from this commemoration. People like to demonstrate their allegiance to Christ in the same way in which they demonstrate their allegiance to the Swiss confederacy by wearing certain badges or visiting Nähenfels, the place where the Swiss defeated the Austrians in 1388. Baker echoes Zwingli in saying that "bread and wine are blessed or consecrated to be the symbols of the body and blood of Christ in somewhat the same sense that a flag of red and white stripes with fifty stars on a background of blue has been dedicated to represent all that the USA stands for." From participating in such a celebration, national or religious, no magical benefits can be derived. While Baker simply reiterates Zwingli, Kaufman spells out the implications of the Zwinglian doctrine. Far from suggesting the celebration's worthlessness, the Zwinglian paradigm actually reveals its true meaning. Just as visiting Nähenfels relates the national community to a victory of historic importance, so the religious celebration relates the church to its formative events. The Lord's Supper is a significant, yet merely emotional event in the life of a Christian congregation. While preaching instructs the intellect, the sacrament appeals to our "deeper levels." Since faith involves not only the appropriation of ideas, but also a reorientation of the whole person, the sacramental drama is indispensable. Kaufman rejects only the exaggerated claims and reifications of traditional theology. He retains the sacramental act itself, an act whose emotional qualities he appreciates. For him, the sacramental act has the same advantage a kiss has over a mere word of love: the advantage of touch, immediacy, and completeness. If we accept the view that all magic has its roots in our exuberant and unsatisfied emotions—a theory proposed by the anthropologist Malinowski—then even Kaufman remains faithful to the very essence of magic.[112]

The most recent attempt to redefine eucharistic theology in a decidedly minimalist way follows Kaufman in denying any supernatural implications of the Lord's Supper. Matthew Fox wants to explain the material, and not the supernatural, qualities of eucharistic bread and wine. Christians must realize the intrinsic, natural sacredness of the eucharistic food. In developing a new, "natural" theology of the Eucharist, Fox appeals to a generation that loves nature and fights against its ecological deterioration through pollution and exploitation, a generation attracted to religious ideas that emphasize the sacred character of Mother Earth. He sets his sacramental thought firmly within a theology of creation and ecological consciousness. He is fascinated with the vast dimensions and the wild beauty of the universe with its ever-expanding galaxies and solar systems that form and eventually disappear. For him, any theology that forgets the cosmic dimension and has a narrow focus, e.g., on the human person, can never do justice to God the creator of the universe and to the cosmic Christ whom he identifies in an almost pantheistic way with the universe. Fox abhors the human destruction of the ecological balance of our own planet through ruthless exploitation of the earth, overpopulation, extinction of certain species of animals, and the ever-increasing pollution of forests, rivers, and seas. Nature is endangered because the human race exaggerates its dominant position on planet earth. Humans have lost a sense of their proper place in the universe. Here a new eucharistic spirituality can help us to realize our proper place.

Communion, according to Matthew Fox, establishes contact between a human individual and the universe. "What is more grounding, more intimate, more local, and more erotic than eating and drinking?" he asks. Fox rejects much of modern theology with its demythologized, empty, and inherently meaningless universe. As Christ's creation, the universe must be seen as grounded in God and thus echoing something of divine goodness and beauty. Communion should make the faithful feel at home in the cosmos because the sacred food consumed is "in fact the *real* . . . eating and drinking of the cosmic body and blood of the Divine One present in every atom and every galaxy of our universe." Bread, in the Eucharist, is truly understood when "it is seen for what it is: a cosmological gift, twenty-billion-years old, a gift of the earth, air, fire, water, of photosynthesis and the sun, of supernova explosions and of original fireballs." However, in communion, Christians not only reaffirm their magical bond with the universe. They also establish contact, and indeed a bond, with a particular part of that universe, the "wounded earth," because "Jesus Christ is Mother Earth crucified." While at an intellectual level communion provides an orientation in the universe, at a deeper level it also links us to the suffering, the death, and the resurrection of entire galaxies and solar systems. In celebrating the Eucharist, we are drawn not only into the drama of the life and death of Jesus, but also into the drama of the cosmic Christ, i.e., the entire universe.[113]

Certain contemporary theologians, then, have done much to attenuate the magical view of the Eucharist. They will never claim that the Eucharist transforms the communicant's life by mediating special supernatural powers that can be experienced and that initiate an ongoing process of sanctification. What communicants can experience and identify is a fleeting moment of being touched by the divine. Despite its divine nature, this moment shares the fragility of our existence and defies any dogmatic definition.

The "minimalist" and "maximalist" views of the Eucharist that we have presented were formulated in the twentieth century. It must be pointed out, however, that they have long prehistories. The two views echo the Romantic and the Enlightenment attitudes toward religion which emerged in the eighteenth century and subsequently became characteristic of the Western mind. The maximalist view has its roots in the visionary, Romantic tradition associated with names like Swedenborg, Oetinger, Herder, and Novalis; this tradition appreciates religion as a dominant force in human life, and some of its representatives developed a sacramental realism and a eucharistic enthusiasm. The Enlightenment tradition, by contrast, which we associate with names like Voltaire and Immanuel Kant, confines religion to the realm of morality and wants to speak about it "within the limits of reason alone." In the rationalist atmosphere of the Enlightenment tradition, the sacraments and sacramental theology cannot flourish. Wherever theological thought is tinged by rationalist sentiments, its sacramental theory tends toward minimalism. The divine presence, as traditional believers have experienced it in the sacred meal, has become problematic for the modern mind.

5.   Conclusion: The Christocentric Sacrament

As far as we can reasonably conjecture, Jesus himself performed the magical rite of baptism (an ablution with water for purification). The meals he shared with his followers and friends had a ritual character, but they were marked by sacrificial rather than magical ideas. Very shortly after his death, however, the ritual meals of Christians assumed a magical character. Far from being new and peculiar, the sacred meal shared its magical character with baptism, exorcism, and healings performed by Jesus, whose activities are rooted in the ancient and Jewish magical milieu. Thus, some of Jesus' early followers brought their master's sacred meal into line with many of his other activities. One of the most prominent magical reinterpretations of the sacred meal involved that meal's identification with a Jewish Passover celebration. The food consumed at the ritual meal, and especially the wine, came to be seen as providing protection during the "great tribulation," a time of war, persecution, and crisis in which Christians had to fear for their lives. But the thaumaturgical (or, more precisely, apotropaic) interpretation had no claim to be the only possible one. Others preferred to celebrate the Lord's Supper as a meal with different miraculous effects: as sacred food, bread and wine mediate eternal life and, comparable to love magic, establish a link with Christ. And again, this thaumaturgical variety did not displace other possible meanings. Eventually, a third interpretation emerged as the dominant and indeed abiding one. Ancient magic includes one specific sub-type, theurgy, and if we want to define the Eucharist in ancient terms, we cannot but call it a theurgical ritual. Theurgy and the Eucharist share the following characteristics: (1) Theurgical and eucharistic rites both aim at making a deity present to the worshiper; (2) unlike other magical rites, theurgical and eucharistic rites never aim at harming anyone or at promoting selfish aims; (3) while the practice of magic was ubiquitous in the ancient world, theorizing about its nature was rare. The exceptions are Neoplatonic theurgy and Christian sacraments; they both became the subject of much theoretical speculation.[114]

Even after the theurgical idea had become firmly established, Christian theologians were by no means satisfied. They sought to define how the Lord is made present in the Eucharist. Two classic interpretations of the sacred meal emerged. According to the first, used mainly in the Eastern churches and connected with the name of Pseudo-Dionysius the Areopagite, the Eucharist commemorates the life and death of Jesus in a sacred drama. This drama re-enacts the story of Jesus, making its benefits available through a symbolic performance. The symbolic action makes the truth, the value, and the power of Jesus' original coming present to the congregation. In the Western church, scholastic theologians like Thomas Aquinas developed another, rival interpretation of the meal. It focuses on the "elements" of bread and wine; as sacred substances they not only represent and symbolize, but actually are (by way of a theurgical operation) the living body and blood of Christ. Recently, Pope Paul VI, in his encyclical letter *Mysterium Fidei* (1965), reaffirmed Catholic commitment to traditional notions of transubstantiation, by which in "a unique and truly wonderful change" a new reality is created. (Paul VI also appreciated the lesser eucharistic miracles commemorated in places like the cathedral of Orvieto, Italy.) While sixteenth-century reformers like Martin Luther and John Calvin rejected the scholastic doctrine of transubstantiation, they still shared the Western focus on the sacred food. According to both Catholic and mainstream Protestant teaching, bread and wine serve as the visible and tangible point of contact with the living Christ.[115]

Often, theologians went further than merely explaining how Christ is made present and contact is established with him. When identifying certain benefits that resulted from sacramental contact with the Lord, they regularly resorted to apotropaic and thaumaturgical notions found or hinted at in the Bible: the Eucharist purifies from sin, strengthens the soul (and even the body), and may extend its transforming force to the entire material universe. However, all theologians agree that union with Christ ranks as the Eucharist's supreme benefit. The Eucharist establishes contact and leads to union with the living Christ: this is the most important definition given to the eucharistic celebration. Historically, we can call this the abiding theurgical nature of the Lord's Supper, for ancient theurgical rites aimed at making a deity present to the worshiper. The truly distinctive nature of the eucharistic meal is to be sought in its focus on Christ. Although at first sight this statement may seem to be almost meaningless—doesn't all Christian worship have to do with Christ?—it is actually a very significant point. As a matter of fact, not all Christian worship has a clear Christocentric orientation. The sacrificial mode of worship, for instance, has a decidedly theocentric orientation: Christians offer to God the Father, and it is from him, not from Christ, that they expect to get returns. Prayer and praise are mostly directed to God rather than to Christ. The word read from scripture and explained in homilies represents "the word of God," not, or not so much, the word of Christ. In ecstatic worship, the Holy Spirit is sometimes understood as the Father's spirit, sometimes as representing Christ in spiritual form, and sometimes as a distinct divine person. There can be no doubt: the Eucharist is the only type of worship with an exclusive and distinctive focus on the person of Christ.

As we have seen, the biblical account of the "institution" of the Lord's

Supper by Christ cannot be taken at face value. It already reflects more than one meaning given to the celebration; we are confronted with sacramental (magical) notions grafted onto an earlier sacrificial sense. The original sacrificial meaning of the Lord's Supper was not focused on Christ, for what Jesus offered to the Father was wine and bread, understood as substitutes for the animal sacrifices controlled by the Jerusalem Temple and its priesthood. Although we must admit that historical scholarship leaves much room here for a diversity of opinion, all historians agree on one fact: that the ritual as it came to be celebrated in the church is oriented to Christ. However the various theological traditions have defined the relationship between the sacred substance consumed and the resurrected, living Christ, they insist that there is such a relationship. At the moment of communion, when the priest or minister gives consecrated bread and wine to the faithful, he or she recalls the Christ-orientation of the sacrament. The Church of England's traditional Book of Common Prayer uses the following formula:

And, when he delivereth the Bread to any one, he shall say, The Body of our Lord Jesus Christ, which was given for thee, preserveth body and soul unto everlasting life. Take and eat this in remembrance that Christ died for thee, and feed on him in thy heart by faith and thanksgiving.

And the Minister that delivereth the Cup to any one shall say, The Blood of our Lord Jesus Christ, which was shed for thee, preserve thy body and soul unto everlasting life. Drink this in remembrance that Christ's Blood was shed for thee, and be thankful.

When the Catholic priest gives communion to the faithful, he does so uttering the formula: "The body of Christ" and "The blood of Christ." To which the communicant responds: "Amen." (Priests never say: "The body of God" and "The blood of God.") When the communicant receives the sacred food, the name of Jesus Christ is mentioned again, and again there is no reference to God. While we may say that Christian worship, in general, is directed toward God, the Eucharist is a significant exception. Being the one exclusively Christ-centered form of worship, the Eucharist has a central and irreplaceable function within the canon of liturgical patterns. In a fifteenth-century prayer Thomas à Kempis tells Christ, "Give yourself to me and that will be enough, for no comfort satisfies me apart from you. I cannot live without you; without you, I am unable to exist. Therefore, I must come to you often and receive you as the medicine of my salvation, lest, deprived of this heavenly food, I should faint on my journey [through life]." In this prayer, the medieval mystic summed up well how most Christians have felt about the Eucharist: it unites them with Christ, and only united with him can they exist as Christians.[116]

A final confirmation of the thoroughly Christocentric nature of the eucharistic celebration comes from an unexpected source: the celebration of Mass by groups of "progressive" Catholic priests and lay people in the 1960s and 1970s in France, Germany, and the Netherlands. In the aftermath of the Second Vatican Council (1962–65) and the turmoil of liturgical reforms, these groups designed their own, unofficial liturgy which culminated in a Eucharist whose sacramental significance was neglected, minimized, or practically denied. Although frowned upon by the ecclesiastical hierarchy and sometimes positively forbidden, these informal liturgies did exist "in the underground." Some young priests celebrated them outside church settings, for instance in homes or in school classrooms, without altar, sacred vessels and vestments, and on the basis of unauthorized prayers. The participants were young people, often university students. Such celebrations were modeled on the community meals Jesus has shared with his friends and his audience, not on a sacred act instituted at the Last Supper. The purpose of the eucharistic rites was to keep alive the memory of Christ, the man who lived and died for the community. The celebrating priests took great pleasure in transgressing liturgical rules; they felt close to Christ who himself had spurned the religious establishment of his day. The French social psychologist Jean Milet, who reports on these Masses, refers to the presiding priest's "constant talk of Christ, the human Christ, who lived in Galilee, who suffered and died." In his description of such a Mass ("if one can call it that"), he notes "that the priest pronounced the name of Christ one hundred and thirty times, and did not mention the name of God at all. Do I need to add that in each one of these allusions the Christ was seen from a human perspective, under a social and humanitarian aspect?" Even those who no longer believed in traditional theologies and liturgies made Christ the center of their post-Catholic celebrations.[117]

We will conclude this section with the definition Pope Pius XII gave to the church's liturgy. He quite sensibly defined it in terms of its double focus on God and on Christ, as "the public worship which our Redeemer as head of the church renders to the Father, as well as the worship which the community of the faithful renders to its Founder." While the former—the honoring of the Father—is done through sacrifice, prayer, and praise, the latter—homage paid to Christ—is done in the Eucharist when an ancient theurgical rite makes the Lord present.[118]

Divine presence is also the key to the next and final one of the sacred games discussed in the present study: the game of spiritual ecstasy. This complex game includes several rites already familiar to us—praise, prayer, and sermon, but these do not exhaust its ritual repertoire. Its distinctive mode derives from features like "speaking in tongues" and trances. To these we will now turn.

The Sixth Game: Spiritual Ecstasy
Exercising the Gifts of Glossolalia, Prophecy, and Healing

Indeed, these are not drunk, as you suppose, for it is only nine o'clock in the morning. No, this is what was spoken through the prophet Joel: "In the last days it will be, God declares, that I will pour out my Spirit upon all flesh, and your sons and your daughters shall prophesy, and your young men shall see visions and your old men shall dream dreams. Even upon my slaves, both men and women, in those days I will pour out my Spirit; and they shall prophesy."

Acts 2:15–18 (NRSV)

Some of the most common events taking place at a renewal are laughing, crying, fainting, trembling, convulsing, seeing visions, prophesying, jerking, running (sometimes called "Jesus leaps"), falling (being "slain in the Spirit"), staggering (getting "drunk in the Spirit"), and whooping, trilling, roaring, barking, mooing and making other animal noises.[1]

B.J. Oropeza, 1995

The ultimate objective of worship in the Sanctified church tradition is some form of spirit possession.[2]

Cheryl J. Sanders, 1996

1. On Ecstatic Worship

Plato and his school distinguished two kinds of behavior that neglected or violated generally accepted norms. One kind of madness or ecstasy could be a sure sign of disorder, mental derangement, and illness; it is "filled with foolishness and delirium." The other kind, by contrast, is "a divine release of the soul from the yoke of custom and convention." It shows the soul in contact with the divine realm and therefore "imparts goods more honorable than human wisdom." Indeed, "humankind's greatest blessings come by way of madness." People all over the world and throughout history have felt the same way. Many have sought to gain a particular religious experience by stimulating their bodies. In the state of ecstasy, or so they believe, they feel the presence of the divine power within themselves as an overwhelming, tangible, and pleasant reality. Typical means of stimulation include dancing, as used by the whirling dervishes, a Muslim sect; the making of or listening to the rhythms of music, as in certain ancient Israelite prophetic groups; and the use of certain drugs such as peyote, among Mexican Indians and in some modern experimental cults. Historians of religion have pointed out that as an experience, ecstasy is universal, coextensive with human nature and history. Only the religious interpretations and ritual elaborations vary, and the techniques designed to facilitate it are historically conditioned. Its universality has been underlined by the English writer Aldous Huxley. Even before his own experimentation with drugs, Huxley made ecstatic trances, induced by a mild stimulant, a regular feature of the ritual celebrated by men and women in his futuristic novel *Brave New World* (1932).[3]

The present chapter explores ecstatic religion as it was practiced in the world in which Christianity originated. As a matter of fact, ecstatic rituals flourished throughout antiquity, and their legacy can be seen in both early Christianity and modern Pentecostalism.

Ecstatic Worship in the Ancient World

Many "real" religions (of which Huxley's is but a caricature) include rituals that involve similar bodily movements, comparable states of excitement, and produce almost identical altered states of consciousness. They often belong to the worship of divine figures that also have much in common: the Indians call their mad lord of the dance Shiva, the Greeks give him the name of Dionysos. In ancient Greece, women considered madness an important aspect of their worship of Dionysos. They formed associations and at one, fixed time of the year, they left their husbands and families to celebrate their wild rituals. In and through their frenzy, the maenads—"mad women"—honored "him of the orgiastic cry, exciter of women, Dionysos, glorified with mad honors."[4]

Dionysos was the god of wine and ecstatic vitality, in whose honor "orgies" were held. Besides drinking, these included lively dancing, with women clashing cymbals to produce noise and rhythm, as can be seen in a first-century BCE painting in Herculaneum, Italy (ills. 33a and 33b). Euripides' stage-play *The Bacchae* gives us a glimpse of the atmosphere typical of the frenzied cult of Dionysos. When its chorus shouts "Ho! ho! our Lord! our Lord!" (line 582), we hear the cry of enthusiasm that initiates and heightens the frenzy and raving as the ecstasy seizes those participating in the ritual. Strabo, in his *Geography*, explains how popular writers describe women as they celebrate the Bacchanals:

> They represent them, one and all, as a kind of inspired people and as subject to Bacchic frenzy. In the guise of ministers, they inspire terror at the celebration of the sacred rites by means of war dances accompanied by uproar and noise and cymbals and drums and also by flute and outcry.[5]

Under the name of Bacchanalia, the Greek cult of Dionysos traveled west and attracted Roman followers until it was, finally, severely restricted by the Senate of Rome. The Roman historian Livy, in his report about the senatorial debate of 186 BCE, gives us interesting information. From him we know that by the second century, men were also admitted to the cult, and that their ecstatic behavior rivaled that of the women. "Men, as if insane, with fanatical tossings of their bodies, would utter prophecies (*vaticinari*)." However, the senatorial decree did not mean the end of the cult and its orgies. Noisy dances were at least remembered in art—witness the cymbal player from Herculaneum (ill. 33a) and the typical Bacchic scene of flute player and dancing girl with a tambourine (bas-relief from Herculaneum). Herculaneum, like the entire area around Mount Vesuvius, had Bacchus as its patron deity. No public authority can ultimately suppress, let alone eliminate, the ecstatic religion in which Friedrich Nietzsche saw a fundamental and eternal attitude toward life. If there is a rational Socratic attitude and an aesthetic Apollonian way, there must also be an irrational, Dionysian mood.[6]

The ancients knew, of course, that ecstatic cults were vastly different from other kinds of rituals. The important thing was, as the philosopher Aristotle said, "not to learn, but to experience something and be put into a [special] state." Apparently, Aristotle preferred learning to ecstatic experience; but he certainly understood the latter.[7]

Judaism also had a long and significant ecstatic tradition, although it is little

33a. Clanging Cymbals. (*left*) In the world of classical antiquity, Greek women were known for their ecstatic celebrations, and some Roman women imitated them, as does the dancer in this first-century BCE painting found in Herculaneum, Italy, a city associated with Bacchus, god of wine and orgies, the patron deity of nearby Mount Vesuvius. The cymbals she clangs to produce a ringing sound are also mentioned in the New Testament in the context of Christian ecstatic rituals held in Corinth, Greece (1 Cor. 13:1). Wall-painting in Herculaneum, Italy, first-century BCE.

33b. (*right*) Ancient cymbals consisted of two bronze dishes or cups with handles. Modern drawing of ancient cymbals.

known to us. Scripture itself refers to the music and the dervishlike dancing of prophetic circles. A familiar sight was the band of prophets coming down in frenzy from the shrine with harp, tambourine, and lyre playing in front of them. In their ecstasy, each of them was "turned into a different person" (1 Sam. 10:6 NRSV). The most interesting examples of ecstatic Judaism date from the first century CE. According to the *Testament of Job* (late first century CE?) certain individuals in an ecstatic state utter incomprehensible, glossolalic words understood as the language of the angels. Significantly, these individuals are women rather than men. Before his death, Job bequeathed to his daughters "multicolored strings" of miraculous power which they should wear as girdles or sashes around their breasts. Job had been cured of his ailments by them, and they also conveyed prophetic power to see into the future. Presumably, these stringlike girdles are a garment angels and other spiritual beings wear in heaven in addition to their white robes. When the daughters put these cords on, their hearts are transformed and they are able to speak in a heavenly tongue:

> Accordingly, the one called Hemera arose and wound the rope about her, just as her father had told her. And she assumed another heart, no longer minding earthly things. She gave utterance in the speech of angels, sending up a hymn to God after the pattern of the angels' hymnody. And as she spoke ecstatically, she allowed "The Spirit" to be inscribed on her garment. (*Testament of Job* 48:1–3)

Job's other two daughters shared their sister's ecstatic experience. In the language of the "archons" and the "cherubim" they extol the work of the heavens and the glory of the heavenly powers. Unlike the cult of Dionysos, Jewish ecstasy enables its practitioners to speak in unknown, angelic tongues, so that the contents have to be interpreted to the community.[8]

Rather than being a mere legend, the story of Job's belt most likely reflects ritual practice. In Judaism, magical garments have a long tradition; the ephod King David wore when leaping and dancing before God's sacred ark, the high priest's elaborate breast-piece that apparently ensured the divine oracles he had to pronounce on certain occasions, and the phylacteries (tefillin) Jewish men wear at prayer all seem to belong to it. A magical belt such as that of Job was presumably used in a community of Jewish ecstatics. In their ritual, someone would be given a special garment inscribed "The Spirit." That garment would link the individual to the divine spirit and enable her or him to fall into ecstasy and use the angelic speech for praising God. As we shall see, it was on such models that Paul relied when he and his communities developed their own variety of an ecstatic ritual. Paul and his group did not of course use a miraculous belt or sash; for them, the spirit-filled substances of eucharistic bread and wine had the same function. And Jesus, rather than Job, was considered the ritual's founding father.[9]

A second description of ecstatic ritual can be found in Philo of Alexandria's book on the Therapeutae, a Jewish sect living in Egypt. Philo, who flourished between 10 and 40 CE, reports on an all-night festival with which the sectarians celebrated Pentecost, the fiftieth day after Passover. In Jewish custom, this festival celebrated the completion of the wheat harvest. Philo's report is very detailed. The group, which includes men, women, novices (as servants), and the president, meet in the evening for a service of prayer, scriptural exposition, and singing, followed by a communal meal at which only bread, water, salt, and hyssop are served. After this simple dinner, the rest of the night is spent singing and dancing (ill. 34). In the morning, the festival is ended with a ceremonial salutation of the rising sun. While Philo emphasizes the orderliness of the proceedings, it is clear that the dancing gets quite ecstatic. Here is part of his report:

> All rise together, and in the middle of the banquet there are formed, at first, two choruses, one of men, the other of women, and a guide and leader is chosen on either side who is one most held in honor and most suitable. Then they sing hymns composed in honor of God in many measures and strains, sometimes singing in unison, and sometimes waving their hands in time with antiphonal harmonies, and leaping up, and uttering inspired cries, as they either move in procession or stand still, making the turns and counterturns proper to the dance. Then, when each of their choirs has had its fill of dancing by itself and separate from the other, as if it were a Bacchic festival in which they had drunk deep of the Divine love, they unite, and form a single choir out of the two. . . . As the deep tones of the men mingle with the shriller ones of the women in answering

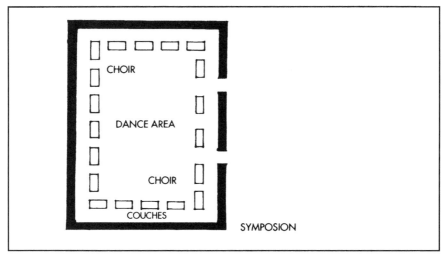

34. Ancient Hall of Ritual Dancing. The first-century CE Jewish sect of the Therapeutae celebrated ecstatic rituals during which the female and the male group united to form a single choir. They had specially designed halls for their sacred dances. This modern plan is based on Philo of Alexandria's description. Plan of ancient Jewish dancing hall.

and antiphonal strains, a full and harmonious symphony results, and one that is veritably musical.

The dancing is supposed to imitate the dancing of the prophet Moses and the prophetess Miriam after the crossing of the Red Sea, and the Therapeutae imitate not only the dancing, but also the prophetic frenzy and their being "rapt with the Divine spirit." This "godly drunkenness," reminiscent of Bacchic behavior, comes to an end only in the morning. When celebrating their festivals, some Jewish groups developed a taste for ecstasy, and their "inspired cries" may well have had glossolalic quality. The Therapeutae considered it their "greatest festival." Their taste for ecstasy may have led them to celebrate their all-night festival not only on the eve of Pentecost, but every fiftieth day and therefore seven times a year. This is how some scholars have read Philo's text. If we accept this reading, we may assume that the Therapeutae relied on a calendar which Palestinian peasants seem to have used until recently as they divided the year into seven fifty-day periods.[10]

All-night celebrations were, of course, nothing unheard of in the Hellenistic world. Some of the Greek festivals such as the Panathenaea culminated in a *pannychis* ("vigil"), a joyful event at which choirs performed hymns, round dances were danced, and cries of enthusiasm could be heard. According to Plutarch, the *pannychis* and the dance also belonged to Bacchic festivals. Interestingly enough, Philo likens the Therapeutae's all-night celebration to a Bacchic orgy (which is just another name for a Dionysian revel) and thus assimilated it to the most famous ecstatic cult of antiquity. Apparently, the dances, singing, and the shouts were similar. Recent research on Greek maenadism demonstrates that Philo was even more justified in making the comparison. While earlier research presented Dionysian ritual as an annual event, celebrated outside the city and out of doors, culminating in the maenadic romp through the hillsides, recent authors have emphasized that the members of Dionysian groups also had banquets, held in the city and indoors. Some Greek vase paintings (ill. 35), rather than depicting frenzied outdoor scenes, are evidence of a somewhat more sedate ritual: some maenads leisurely recline on comfortable couches, while others spend their time dancing. (In the next section, we shall see how Christian ecstatic worship in the city of Corinth included some of the features familiar from a Dionysian banquet.)[11]

Theories of Ecstasy

Celebrations like those typical of Greek maenadism and those mentioned in the Jewish *Testament of Job* have been given the name of ecstatic rituals (although some would prefer to speak of trance rituals, reserving the term of ecstasy for the solitary experiences of mystics and individuals who deprive themselves of food and leave society on a vision quest). Ecstatic behavior, in its most pro-

35. Honoring Dionysos in Maenadic Dance. Pagan maenads, here depicted on an ancient Greek vessel, provided the model for some early Christians who celebrated the presence of the Lord with comparable movement and enthusiasm. The sitting woman plays the tambourine to whose rhythm another woman dances. One woman is clearly exhausted. Ancient Greek ritual scene, Athens, ca. 420 BCE.

nounced form, typically involves: (1) mild body convulsions (jerking of the neck, bending of the trunk and legs); (2) prolonged dancing, usually to music, in what appears to be a semi-stuporous state; and (3) falling to the floor, either with body contractions or remaining still as in a faint. Convulsions, dancing, and fainting may also occur independently, without being linked to the other features. Often tears flow. Sometimes strange words are uttered, incomprehensible to outsiders. During such rituals or at their high points, according to a standard religious interpretation, a supernatural being is felt to be present. Participants are in intense communion with a deity or spirit, which may also "descend into" and "fill" an individual. The person is "possessed" by some divine agency—a spirit, a god, or a demon. The human individual is no longer present; rather a different, supernatural agency acts through that person, expressing itself in movement, dance, song, or speech.[12]

"Possession" by a spirit, god, or goddess can be initiated in various ways: by fasting, by drinking a specially prepared wine or some other stimulant, by eating magic food, or by wildly dancing to the sound of music or monotonously beaten drums. It can also be produced through listening to an exciting sermon. The person possessed may be an individual—a shaman, a prophet, or a medium—or a larger crowd, often, as anthropologists have observed, with a majority of women. If the supernatural agent expresses itself in some form of speech, then the utterance can be either an articulate, clear oracle, or the wordless language known as glossolalia or "speaking in tongues." Possession, ecstasy, glossolalia, and healing in a state of trance were often thought of as belonging to the strange features of "primitive" religion. However, it has also been reported from cultural areas not normally classified as archaic, such as ancient Greece. In our century, Christian Pentecostals have made us more familiar with the ritual pattern of ecstasy, and an expression comparable to glossolalia is familiar from certain half-articulate vocal parts of jazz singing known as "scat" (of which Louis Armstrong and Cab Calloway were masters, matched only by a character in George Gershwin's musical *Porgy and Bess*).[13]

Challenged by such strange behavior and ceremonies so unlike those Western academics identify as normal, psychologists and anthropologists have done much to elucidate if not explain ecstatic rituals. Psychologists have developed the concept of dissociation to describe states in which ordinary, waking consciousness ceases to control someone's behavior, feelings, and perception of the outside world. These states, while being "abnormal," may be experienced by almost everyone and are not necessarily symptoms of illness. Anthropologists have looked at the social and cultural contexts in which dissociation occurs and is appreciated, ritually induced, and cultivated as a meaningful religious experience.

Ecstatic ritual, according to anthropological research, is often practiced by the lowly and the oppressed for whom participation produces a temporary respite from the pressures of life. People whose lives are given little structure because they have been denied participation in well-defined, socially acknowledged roles seem to be especially prone to experiences of trance and possession. They even welcome those experiences, deriving much satisfaction from them. Likely to be oppressed members of society, women are never absent from the cults of frenzy. In ancient Greece, female participants dominated in the cult of Dionysos, the god of wine and vitality, in whose honor "orgies" were held. Specialists tell us that in the case of the Dionysian associations, the members called "maenads" actually came from the upper classes, for only these could afford to go to the mountains for a couple of days, leaving their children at home with their slaves. The ecstatic celebration offered them a respite from daily routine, domestic confinement, and isolation. When the dances and trances were over, they returned home to resume their dull and isolated existence, which the maenadic ritual helped them to endure.[14]

While Greek maenadism was of course a female affair, ecstatic behavior may also occur irrespective of gender, social class, and ethnic origin. Whatever their social or ethnic background, in the state of ecstasy, all men and women are equal and discover their shared humanity. "There is neither Jew nor Greek, there is neither slave nor free, there is neither male nor female; for you all are one," explains Paul referring to those who are possessed by Christ (Gal. 3:28). One who utters prophetic oracles, receives and exercises the power of healing, or overwhelms others with glossolalic speech, may also acquire an acknowledged social status within the ritual community.

In ecstatic worship, participants not only find an outlet for accumulated, dammed-up frustration. They may also discover their shared humanity, which allows them to interact with other members of the ritual group in a friendly, supportive way. In ecstatic dances and trances, everyday roles are shed and distinctions melt away, and then all are equal, and elementary bonds of friendship and sharing can be created—at least according to a theory dear to some anthropologists. Whether this is a valid theory or not, all agree that the very performance of ritual promotes group solidarity. This solidarity provides moral support and perhaps at times also real support, a home for the homeless, and may even become the basis of social protest. Ioan Lewis aptly comments: "However seemingly satisfying the play of such cults, the potentiality for deeper and more radical outbursts of pent-up resentment is always there."[15]

The attraction of ecstatic rituals has been given a third interpretation, which may in fact supplement those that emphasize compensation and protest. After listening to music, after singing and being excited, many feel emotionally released, liberated, and somehow healed. Did not David's playing of the lyre soothe King Saul's tormented soul? When David played, "Saul would be relieved and feel better, and the evil spirit would depart from him" (1 Sam. 16:23). In the third century CE, the Greek musicologist Aristides Quintilianus proposed a modern-sounding interpretation: "This is the purpose of the Bacchic initiation, that the depressive anxiety of less educated people, produced by their state of life, or some misfortune, be cleared away through the melodies and dances of the ritual in a joyful and playful way." Enthusiastic cults provide a cathartic experience, sobering one's mind and leading it to tranquility and balance. Like psychotherapy, the intense experience of the spirit can give one's life new joy, a new meaning and direction. Christian believers themselves often resort to expressions like "therapeutically liberating" or call their church a "hospital for the soul." According to one anthropological theory, trance is a necessary precondition not only of psychological reorientation but also of many kinds of physical healing. Trance helps the brain to overcome our status quo and to reorganize vital functions of our body. Whether one agrees with such strong claims or not, one can at least assert its therapeutic value.[16]

Glossolalia, "speaking in tongues," has also been discussed by those who emphasize the therapeutic value of trance behavior. Glossolalia, according to Wayne Oates, reproduces the language of infants or, more precisely, the "babblings" that announce and foreshadow speech. The strange sounds of glossolalia belong to the primary language which precedes definite linguistic structures that subordinate sound to sense. The "regressive return" to someone's earlier lack of linguistic competence can be obtained only in particular mental states in which learned structures can be shaken off. Once that state is attained through a special process of unlearning, glossolalia indicates a release from tension, personal stress, and trauma.[17]

In addition to explaining ecstatic ritual as congenial to the oppressed, as a means of creating elementary solidarity, and as producing therapeutic trances, one can also ponder the merits of a fourth theory. People seem to be hungry for religious experience, and ecstatic rituals, like mysticism, promise that experience. During an altered state of consciousness, the "possessed" person experiences something extraordinary, something different, something to be identified with the divine reality. The new experience, however, tends to be short-lived. People lose the ability to get into trances. As the effervescence ends, ecstatic sects assume churchlike features and the spirit wanes. Unlike non-Western cultures, traditional Christianity seems to include a strong mechanism that serves to suppress ecstatic disorder. Some day, though, the cycle will begin again: people rediscover the sweetness of ecstasy and their enthusiasm draws others into the experience and its ritual repetition.

In Christianity, ecstatic worship is more firmly rooted than mainstream Protestantism with its calm, intellectual worship might lead us to expect. If mainstream worship represents the Apollonian side of Christianity, ecstatic cults reveal its Dionysian aspects. Christian ecstatic worship has a long history as well as a noble, biblical pedigree. While the following sections will recall only parts of that history, its New Testament beginnings must be analyzed in detail.

2.   Paul the Possessed and the Lord's Supper in Corinth

In the spring of 55 CE, when the Christian missionary Paul was active in the city of Ephesus in Asia Minor, he received visitors from the distant Christian community of Corinth in Greece, which he had founded several years earlier. The visitors brought him a letter written by some of the members of the Corinthian group; they also talked to him about problems in their church. There were factions and quarrels, and some members were concerned about ritual matters that had apparently run out of control. When Stephanas, Fortunatus, and Achaicus (1 Cor. 16:15–17) returned home, they carried Paul's response. This response is the First Letter to the Corinthians, and from it we can see what some of the problems were. Many of them have to do with the chief Christian ritual, "the Lord's Supper" (*to deipnon kyriakon*), as Paul calls it. And since this is the case, Paul provides us with information that allows us to reconstruct the Corinthian service of worship, in fact the earliest Christian worship about which we have any amount of knowledge. The most distinctive feature of this worship, in which Greek and Judaeo-Christian elements blend, is its ecstatic and charismatic nature.

The Ecstatic Banquet (1): What Paul's Letter Reveals

The setting and general outline of the Lord's Supper as celebrated in Corinth is Greek in style. It parallels a banquet held in the home of someone who would invite friends and guests and who might or might not bring their own food in potluck fashion. Since the Greek *deipnon* ("dinner, supper") implies an evening meal, we must assume that the group assembled in the evening, most likely on Sunday night after normal working hours. In the Greek cities, people had supper when it was getting dark. (A free Sunday did of course not exist at that time; it dates from the fourth century CE.) The ritual follows the two-phase pattern typical of the Greek banquet. At a formal banquet people would first recline—not sit—at table and eat. People did not drink with the meal, for wine was served after dinner, at the second event, the symposium, where people drank and talked in a relaxed atmosphere. It was here that glossolalia and prophecy occurred.[18]

Some members of the congregation boasted the gift of prophecy. A man or a woman would utter a word of Christ, possibly introducing it by saying "Thus says the holy Spirit" (as reported of an early Christian prophet in Acts 21:11). This formula would be followed by a word of instruction, exhortation, or consolation believed to be communicated by the risen Lord Jesus using the prophet as his messenger or mouthpiece. In addition, a prophet might also speak of other matters. The congregation accepts the prophet's revelation of the spiritual state of someone present, presumably the revelation of a particular sin or some other "secret of the unbeliever's heart" (1 Cor. 14:25). Unfortunately, the biblical text remains vague, and it is understandable that scholars continue to come up with new suggestions. According to Thomas Gillespie, Paul's first letter to the Corinthians actually includes the complete text of a ten-minute prophetic discourse by Paul himself. In this prophetic statement, he explains why those who argue that there is no resurrection are clearly wrong; to this he adds a new insight that he received through divine inspiration: not all of the present generation will die; some will see the Lord return in glory (1 Cor. 15). Had Paul been present in Corinth, he would have delivered this prophetic speech orally; his absence made him write it down, presumably to have it read at a meeting. According to another scholar's recent suggestion, some members of the congregation asked the prophets to respond to questions about personal matters: whether to get married, to venture on a voyage, to risk a loan, to buy a slave, what sex a child would be, whether the child a woman was bearing was her husband's or someone else's. Such questions were commonly asked at pagan oracular sessions, and the Genesis story of Rebekah asking the oracle about the twins she was pregnant with may have served as a precedent for Christians. Although these scholarly suggestions remain speculative, they can at least stimulate our historical imagination.[19]

While prophets enjoyed some prestige, the congregation did not simply accept their utterances. A prophet was tested by those known for their ability to "discern the spirits" (1 Cor. 12:10; cf. 1 John 4:1). These would presumably ask questions to identify whether the spirit that possessed the prophet or prophetess was the spirit of Christ or some intrusive, undesired agent, foreign to the ritual situation of the community and presumably to be identified as the spirit of some other dead person. The spirit of the Lord, unlike other spirits, would never say, or respond to an invitation to say, "Jesus be cursed!" (1 Cor. 12:3). Whenever prophecy was uttered during the ritual, such a test would be applied.[20]

The testing procedure, whose details Paul fails to report, shows the esteem early believers had for a message from Christ. But it also shows that prophets did not dominate the Christian meeting. Apparently, they did not enjoy the absolute authority claimed by the apostles and by Paul. On the scale of actual power, they ranked low. As a recent biblical specialist has conjectured, the early community had a rather nuanced understanding of prophetic charisma. While an apostle's word counted as the literal word of Christ, a prophet spoke merely human words to report something Christ's spirit had brought to mind. After being tested, a prophetic oracle was to be recognized as true and authentic; but it lacked authority. Prophets, it seems, could never attain the more dignified and powerful position held by the apostles. Being confined to speaking in ritual situations, they remained under the control both of the apostles (in our case, Paul) and the congregation. They enjoyed some ritual prestige, but apparently had little or no independent power in the community.[21]

Prophetic voices and the voices of those who tested oracles were not the only ones heard in the ecstatic meeting. More ecstatic than prophetic speaking was praising the Lord "in tongues," i.e., with singing or shouting, using a language incomprehensible to everyone present, including the glossolalist. The importance attached to glossolalia becomes intelligible only when we recognize that for Jews and Christians possession of the divine spirit expressed itself in states that implied the inactivity of the human mind. "The human mind," writes Philo, "is evicted at the arrival of the divine spirit." "One who speaks in a tongue speaks not to men but to God," explains Paul; "for no one understands him, but he utters mysteries in the Spirit" (1 Cor. 14:2).[22]

Glossolalists praised God by speaking and singing in the dialect of the angels, and that language was sometimes put into intelligible human words (1 Cor. 13:1). To do this involved the performance of hymns of praise that would be sung by a gifted individual in response to and as a verbalization of the glossolalic praise. We do not know whether those who generated such "interpretations" had to produce new hymns or could rely on set texts like the biblical psalms and Christian hymnody. The congregation would respond to this intelligible singing with the traditional Hebrew "Amen," meaning "This is true," and thus express their assent and applause (1 Cor. 14:16). Interpretation, in Paul's day, was often found in ritual situations. "Revelations," people believed, were often given in archaic language or incomprehensible speech. In the synagogue, the Hebrew of the biblical lessons was translated into the Aramaic or Greek vernacular. Greek oracles were known for their obscurity and, as Plato tells us, they were regularly judged and interpreted by experts called "*prophêtai.*"[23]

The Ecstatic Banquet (2): Filling in the Gaps

What we have said thus far about the Lord's banquet can be gleaned from Paul's letter in a more or less straightforward way. However, questions remain. Was there some sort of consecration of bread and wine, corresponding to or foreshadowing later Christian practice? Why did some of the Corinthian Christians think that the Lord's banquet was the ideal time to utter prophecies or praise God in angelic tongues? Twentieth-century scholarship has tried to find tentative answers. Some of them merit our attention.

When Paul reminds the Corinthians of the sacred character of their banquet, this does not preclude the assumption that some sort of blessing was pronounced. Someone must have conducted the ritual act, presumably one of the older members of the community or the owner of the house in which the meal was held. He would speak a blessing over a large loaf of bread which was then broken up, so that everyone present would receive a morsel. Later, at the symposium, when people began to drink, the sharing of the bread was followed by the sharing of a cup of wine, over which a blessing was also pronounced. Unfortunately, Paul does not give us the wording of the blessing used. He takes its knowledge for granted. "The cup of blessing which we bless, is it not a participation in the blood of Christ?" (1 Cor. 10:16). There must have been some act of consecration or invocation of the Spirit. Most likely, the Corinthian community used a prayer that asked the Lord to send his Spirit upon, or into, bread and wine. Such prayers were common in later eucharistic practice.[24]

For the Corinthians, the bread was "spiritual food" and the wine "spiritual drink." This meant that it communicated the presence of Christ. The dead Christ was thought of as a living spirit, an idea not foreign to ancient thought. In accordance with Semitic (but not Greek) belief, his spirit could possess people, and the eating of the Lord's spiritual food filled them with the Lord himself. An interesting analogy is provided by an ancient Coptic charm (presumably of Jewish origin) in which the spirit of David is asked to "come down to this cup which stands before me! Fill it with grace and a holy spirit, so that it become for me a new plant within me." The long spell, of which we quoted only a small part, considers David (here called Davithea Eleleth) a mighty spirit who stands just below the Father in the heavenly hierarchy. The person using the charm asks David to put his spirit into a cup of drink, so that the petitioner can drink and be full of David's spirit. The expected result is that the person drinking gets a "voice without hoarseness, without cracking, without harshness, which goes up to the heights, and a tongue which blends with every instrument . . . one which gives forth a musical sound." The petitioner hopes to be able to sing as sweetly as David and the heavenly beings. This analogy demonstrates that the idea of a drink as the carrier of the spirit of a heavenly being—David or Christ—was not foreign to the religious world in which Paul lived. In true magical fashion, bread and wine serve as a vessel for supernatural power.[25]

Not only the "sacramental," eucharistic dimension of the Lord's banquet, but also the "ecstatic" one can be filled out with some more detail. Ancient sources include a great deal of information about the entertainment patrons offered their guests at symposia. A typical report reads, "As soon as they had had enough to eat and drink they wanted music and dancing, which are the crowning embellishments of a banquet." At a Greek banquet, respectable women would not be present. If the sponsor of a banquet was wealthy or ambitious, however, he might arrange for female musicians, singers, and prostitutes to be present. While wine and women sufficed to make a Greek symposium a success, it might actually develop features of a Bacchic revel. In this case, one would see women dancing and raving to celebrate maenadic madness. They did so without wearing a veil, letting their hair flow freely after the fashion of the devotees of Dionysos or Isis: "Necks bare, and hair left free to the winds . . . they fill the air with whimpering cries," runs a typical ancient description of women hailing Dionysos. "Her hair became loose and flew around wildly as her head whirled around and around," runs a typical description of female possession in present-day India. In a state of frenzy or possession, not only women, but also some of the "men, as if insane, with fanatical tossings of their bodies, would utter prophecies (*vaticinari*)." A "maenadic" symposium would fill much of the night, entertaining its guests with wine, women, music, and prophetic voices.[26]

Many parallels between the "mad" pagan symposium and Corinthian worship suggest themselves. The biblical text clearly implies drinking, and Paul even refers to people getting drunk. A special feature of Corinthian ecstatic worship is the conspicuous participation of women. They pray and prophesy, which means they fully and legitimately participate in the entire ritual, including the more ecstatic phases (1 Cor. 11:5). The singing of praise and thanksgiving, both in "tongues" and in comprehensible language, was possibly accompanied by music, so that a joyful noise would enhance the excitement. Paul's reference to the "resounding gong," the "clanging cymbal," as well as to harp and flute can be thus understood (1 Cor. 13:1; 14:7). Christians, like the Temple singers of old, would "prophesy to the accompaniment of lyres, harps, and cymbals" (1 Chron. 25:1). The Pauline injunction that women should be veiled while they pray or utter prophecies almost certainly presupposes the fact that some women did prophesy with disheveled hair; it may well be that in so doing they simply copied standard maenadic behavior. The outbursts of frenzy among both the devotees of Dionysos and those of Christ make the conclusion inevitable that the early liturgy of Greek Christians had forms resembling those of Dionysian ritual. The consumption of wine must have facilitated if not induced the charismatic activities of glossolalia and prophecy. The ancient Greeks considered intoxication a mantic state, and to be filled with wine doubled as being filled with Dionysos. In view of the accord between the Pauline description and that of the ancient authors who report on or echo Greek maenadism, and Paul's use of the Greek technical term for ritual raging (*mainesthai*, "to be mad, to rave, to be in a state of mania," [1 Cor. 14:23]), one begins to wonder whether some of Paul's Corinthian converts might have previously belonged to a Dionysian association or were at least familiar with that kind of ritual behavior.[27]

Just like a Greek symposium, the Christian meeting could take up much of the night. Eventually, the drumming ceases, the cymbals fall silent, the solemn noise of glossolalic utterance dies down. People awaken from their trances. They return to their homes very late at night or early the next morning, certainly edified but also exhausted.

Paul's Response

Paul had no objections to these ritual procedures as such. Most likely it was he who had taught them to the community. The letter he received from Corinth, however, did not make him entirely happy with recent developments. The apostle objected to certain features of the final, ecstatic phase of the ritual. Unhappy with ecstatic excesses, he wanted things to proceed in a more orderly fashion. Women should not unveil their hair; speaking in tongues should be restricted to "two or at most three, and each in turn" (1 Cor. 14:27), and there should also be someone to interpret the utterance. "In church, I would rather speak five words with my mind, in order to instruct others, than ten thousand words in a tongue" (14:19). As for prophecy, which Paul deemed a gift higher than that of glossolalia because it is more articulate, the same rule should apply: two or three may communicate the Lord's word to the assembly, and the others must "weigh what is said" (14:29). In all of this, speakers are asked not to interfere with someone else's singing, praying, or prophesying, and to yield the floor to others upon demand.

In Paul's letter we can perceive a certain antagonism between the two main types of ecstatic expression: glossolalia and prophecy. While both of these are ecstatic and inspired by the Lord's spirit, they differ significantly. Singing or speaking in tongues, unintelligible in terms of normal human language, may contribute to the atmosphere of worship, but does not have a rational, edifying message. Glossolalists produce sounds but not words and speech. Prophecy, on the other hand, addresses the congregation with clear and intelligible words. Scholars agree that prophecy here means prophetic instruction and exhortation in the name of the Lord. Although we must not think of it as the delivery of a set sermon, it may have come close to preaching and seemed to create a temporary division between the audience and the speaker. Paul's clear preference for prophecy reflects his own background; he was an educated teacher and presumably also a prophet. The glossolalists were most likely not the educated but the illiterate converts, the slaves and harbor workers who found in this gift a convenient and powerful means of expression in ecstatic worship. Since Paul never made an attempt to suppress glossolalia, ecstatic worship must always have consisted of a mixture of prophecy and tongues, with the tongues often dominating and giving the service its distinctive tone and flavor.[28]

Paul warns the Corinthians not to overestimate the manifestations of the spirit. Christ's spiritual presence, visible in glossolalia and ecstatic prophecy, is something essentially incomplete and provisional. The Lord's Supper is to be celebrated "until he comes," i.e., until he comes to rule in person (1 Cor. 11:26). Then the ecstatic symposium will no longer be celebrated: "As for prophecies, they will pass away; as for tongues, they will cease; as for knowledge, it will pass away. For our knowledge is imperfect and our prophecy is imperfect; but when the perfect comes, the imperfect will pass away" (1 Cor. 13:8–10).

The Lord's banquet, for Paul, was not peripheral to Christian life. In fact, it epitomizes that life because in the Lord's Supper, Christ himself is present and reigns. His spirit is tangible in bread and wine, he is audible in glossolalia and prophecy, his rule visible in ecstasy and trance. The worshiping group is the Lord's visible body, animated by his spirit, that is, by himself. "It is no longer I who live, but Christ lives in me," is how Paul describes his personal religious ideal (Gal. 2:20). The presence of Christ swallows up his worldly identity, putting him completely under the control of the divine spirit. During the ritual each individual can realize and experience the ideal of his own body serving as "a temple of the Holy Spirit which is within you" (1 Cor. 6:19). That this kind of the Lord's manifestation with his followers and believers was imperfect and would not endure forever is really a minor point. For the time being, Paul appreciates ecstatic behavior: "So, my brethren, earnestly desire to prophesy, and do not forbid speaking in tongues" (1 Cor. 14:39). And again: "Do not quench the Spirit, do not despise prophesying" (1 Thess. 5:19–20).

After Paul: The Eclipse of Ecstasy, or From Paul the Possessed to Timothy the Teacher

Paul's first letter to the Corinthians, in spite of being a quite unsystematic writing closely tied to a specific (and not easily discernible) situation, was often read and seems to have served as a guide to proper liturgical behavior. At least at one point we can actually see how a later generation has interpolated a section in which it articulates its own concerns. This is the famous passage about women being silent in the assembly: "The women should keep silence in the churches. For they are not permitted to speak [shout?], but should be subordinate." The passage, if genuine, may simply tell women not to shout as women do in Dionysian celebrations. However, a different reading seems possible and may indeed be preferable. It assumes the secondary, interpolated nature of the command.

The secondary nature of the line is not only evident from the implied contradiction to Paul's statement earlier in the text (women may contribute their prayers and prophecies; 1 Cor. 11:5), but also from its uncertain location in the Pauline letter (some manuscripts place it at 1 Cor. 14:34–35, others after v. 40 of the same chapter). The problematic passage seems to echo Pseudo-Paul rather than Paul; see the injunction Pseudo-Paul gives to Timothy: "I permit no woman to teach or to have authority over a man; she is to keep silent" (1 Tim. 2,12). The interpolation was discovered long before contemporary feminists—women who want to serve in churches as ministers or priests— rediscovered the forgery. The interpolation reveals both the authority Paul's word enjoyed in the church and the continuing issue of order and decency

36. Early Christian Women, Prophesying and Teaching. While Paul restricts the participation of women in worship, early Christian art seems to tell a different story. The woman standing at the center speaks with arms outstretched, while her head is veiled to conform to the Pauline injunction (1 Cor. 11:5). She prays and presumably also prophesies. The woman sitting, also veiled, holds a scroll and speaks, no doubt addressing an assembly in the same way male members of the community would preach. The woman who stands and prays with arms outstretched is one of the most frequent motifs of early Christian art. The earliest example is a fresco in the Roman catacomb of Callistus, dating from between 190 and 220 CE. The most elaborate examples—like the one shown here—are from sarcophagus reliefs (third/fourth-century CE). Early Christian sarcophagus, Rome, ca. 270 CE.

during the ecstatic symposium celebrated as the Lord's Supper. The study of ecstatic rituals in African Zâr associations, the ancient Greek cult of Dionysos, and among many similar groups has led specialists to conclude that ecstatic behavior is more likely to attract women than men. If Paul's ecstatic community was no exception to this rule, it would seem that the interpolation silencing the women reflects a stage in which the ecstatic elements were either controversial or had already been toned down. Early Christian iconography with its frequent depiction in the third and fourth centuries of veiled women who pray with both arms outstretched (ill. 36) may well echo the post-Pauline situation. These women follow Paul's injunction to be veiled and not to engage in any particularly ecstatic movements; yet they are present when the community celebrates its worship, and, like the male members, they speak up to deliver prayer and prophecy. One of them, the fourth-century "prophetess" (*prophêtissa*) Nanas, received a funeral inscription that celebrates her in florid Greek as a woman noted for her powerful prayer and praise as well as her visions of angels and her strong voice. But as the interpolated Pauline passage shows, women were far from equal with men. Men had established their leadership in ritual matters, a leadership that had not existed in Paul's original congregation. And these men did not like their womenfolk to take on leading roles in the congregation; hence the interpolated injunction that women should remain silent, either completely or, as Witherington suggests, when the men test and weigh the prophecies that have been proclaimed. Paul's call for order was reinterpreted to suit a new situation, one in which ecstatic prophecy and speaking in tongues no longer shaped Christian worship. Whatever the precise meaning of the interpolated passage may be, the artists creating the catacomb frescoes and coffin reliefs depicting the veiled women had no objections to women appearing and speaking up in public. Like the women, they relied on 1 Cor. 11:5 rather than on the interpolated passage in 1 Cor. 14.[29]

There is not much evidence for post-Pauline versions of Paul's ecstatic Eucharist. It would be wrong, however, to think that it did not survive its founder. Occasional echoes found in scattered sources permit the conclusion that some of its features did not disappear or were at least remembered for some time. Luke, the evangelist who in the late first century belongs to the Pauline trajectory, still writes of praise, prayer, and prophecy inspired by the Holy Spirit. In the book of Acts, Luke tells the story of how fifty days after Christ's resurrection the Spirit came over the apostles as they were assembled in Jerusalem. He connects the apostles' glossolalic ecstasy with the hoped-for and expected "outpouring of the Holy Spirit," for which he quotes an Old Testament prooftext from the prophet Joel: "And in the last days it will be, God declares, that I will pour out my Spirit upon all flesh, and your sons and daughters shall prophesy" (Acts 2:17, quoting Joel 3:1 [Eng., 2:28]; note the daughters). This well-known legend of Pentecost is told as a one-time event, but it seems to have originated with a regular celebration. Some of the early Christians no doubt followed Jewish groups like the Therapeutae in having a "sacred all-night festival" on the night of Pentecost, a celebration with singing and dancing in almost Bacchic frenzy. The general excitement led to glossolalic ecstasy. When Luke compiled his gospel, the "sacred all-night festival" had presumably ceased to exist. Thus we find traces of ecstasy in Luke, but no longer evidence of ecstatic practice. Moreover, Luke does not seem to connect the Spirit with the Lord's Supper.[30]

The *Didache*, a manual of church discipline dating from between 110 and 160 CE, tells the community to "permit the prophets to give thanks as much as they will" (or "in their own way") after the meal. Here free, if not ecstatic, prayer was still considered a possibility, although apparently not one appreciated by everyone. Interestingly, enthusiastic if not ecstatic thanksgiving after receiving the Eucharist is depicted in the Codex Pupureus of Rossano (ill. 37), an illuminated Greek gospel manuscript dating from the sixth century. In a scene depicting how Christ gives communion to his apostles at the Last Supper, one of them, after having partaken of the bread, throws his head back and raises his arms in a joyful gesture of enthusiasm. While we cannot be sure of the exact meaning of the scene, it seems plausible to think here of an outburst

37. Rejoicing after Communion. Christ offers communion to an apostle, while another, having partaken, throws his arms up in an enthusiastic gesture of thanksgiving. Most depictions of the Last Supper show Christ and his disciples at table; this manuscript illumination, however, echoes how the Lord's Supper was celebrated in the early church. *Codex Pupureus Rossanensis*, Constantinople or Antioch, sixth-century CE.

of prophetic thanksgiving. Filled with the divine Spirit, the apostle acts out his gratefulness in movement, song, and prophecy. In the manuscript illumination, the grateful apostle's erect standing and joyous gesture stand in contrast to the others who approach the Lord with their heads bowed down in humility. As they receive the sacred repast, they move from silence and humility to song and dancelike gestures. The illumination is accompanied by a biblical quotation: "Then flew one of the seraphim unto me, having a live coal in his hand and said: This has touched your lips; and your iniquity is taken away and your sin is purged" (Isa. 6:6–7). The Isaianic passage is actually quoted in the traditional Greek liturgy to indicate the purifying effect of communion; the illustrator of the Codex Purpureus moves beyond this by suggesting that the communicant, just like the purified Isaiah, can now prophesy. The Greek codex originated in the East, possibly in Antioch or Jerusalem, and may reflect an old iconographic tradition based on liturgical practice.[31]

The Eucharist as celebrated in North Africa ca. 200 shows even clearer traces of the Pauline pattern than do the *Didache* and the Codex Purpureus. This is evident in Tertullian's description of what comes after the sacred meal: "After manual ablution and the bringing in of lights, each is asked to stand forth and sing, as he can, a hymn to God, either one from the holy scriptures or one of his own composing—a proof of the measure of our [restraint in] drinking. As the feast commenced with prayer, so with prayer it is closed." The Corinthian pattern of a meal followed by worship has been retained, and the call to stand forth with a hymn clearly echoes the Pauline text (1 Cor. 14:26). Yet, much has changed. The service has been stripped of its more spontaneous and ecstatic features. Women no longer sing their songs, nobody falls visibly into a trance or proclaims a word received from the Lord. No one is drunk or behaves as if he or she were. Tertullian reports of a woman, a prophetess, who often has visions during worship, but will not speak about them until afterwards. "After the people are dismissed at the conclusion of the sacred services," she reveals her experiences to only a few. Tertullian's North African contemporaries certainly fulfill both the apostle's wish for order and the Pauline interpolator's injunction to prevent women from speaking in the assembly.[32]

Unfortunately, we know very little about how liturgical life developed in the communities Paul had founded or at least strongly influenced in Corinth, Thessalonica, Philippi, and Ephesus. All available sources indicate the replacement of Paul's democratic structures with a strong episcopal leadership. This is what post-Pauline literature attests at least for Corinth and Ephesus. The bishop's task is clearly defined as one of teaching. A pseudo-Pauline letter exhorts Timothy, bishop of Ephesus, to read scripture in public, to exhort, and teach his community. A salaried staff of elders helps the bishop to fulfill his task. Belief in the divine status of the sacred writings plays a major role. Not people, it seems, but the scriptures count as inspired by the Holy Spirit. The high regard for biblical exposition and learning, coupled with the absence of any hint of ecstatic inspiration, points to a worship dominated by preaching and teaching. Even though Paul does not provide any information about it, we may assume that his congregations knew forms of worship that culminated in the teacher's discourse. Most likely, Pauline communities had two kinds of worship: ecstatic rituals and teaching rituals; this at least would correspond to the liturgical life we found among the Therapeutae, a contemporary Jewish group in Egypt. If this assumption is granted, we must think of a gradual decline of ecstatic phenomena and an increasing emphasis on teaching in post-Pauline worship. By the end of the first century, the communities founded by Paul had abandoned their earlier charismatic, free-style worship altogether. Paul the Possessed no longer served as the model of worshipful behavior; he had been succeeded by Timothy the Teacher.[33]

While Timothy the Teacher rather than Paul provided the pattern for mainstream Christianity, ecstasy all but disappeared from worship. However, occasional revivals rediscovered the ecstatic mode. In antiquity, the most famous ecstatic movement developed in Phrygia, Asia Minor. It was there that the generation living around 200 CE witnessed a powerful prophetic movement initiated by the prophet Montanus and the two prophetesses Maximilla and Priscilla. Writing from the point of view of that movement's enemies, Bishop Epiphanius reports about their worship: "In their assembly it often happens that seven virgins carrying torches enter dressed in white to prophesy to the people. Displaying a sort of frenzy, they manage to deceive the people present and they make everyone weep as though brought to the lamentation of repentance; they shed tears and make a show of bewailing human life." Against such practice, the bishop invokes Paul, "I do not allow a woman to speak or have authority over a man" (1 Tim. 2:12). For Epiphanius and many others, Paul and Timothy spoke with one voice—against ecstasy.[34]

3. The Rebirth of Pentecostal Worship in Twentieth-Century America

In the early 1900s, originating in various places in Europe and especially the United States among "holiness churches" of Methodist and Baptist origin, a Pentecostal and charismatic movement swept the entire Christian world. It began like earlier revivals, but soon two distinguishing features appeared. The first of these was "speaking in tongues," something that may have occurred during earlier revivals but went virtually unnoticed. Now it became the new revival's most distinguishing mark. But the second, no less astonishing and equally visible (though perhaps less miraculous) feature must not be forgotten: the formation of new churches and denominations that adopted and perpetuated a new, ecstatic style of worship. At the end of the twentieth century, Pentecostalism has become a major force in Christianity. No longer a fringe phenomenon, the Pentecostal movement now claims to represent almost a quarter of organized Christianity: one recent source speaks of 332 million, that is about 21.4% of all Christians (1988), another refers to 23.2% (1990). Since the 1960s, its doctrines and practices have made a tremendous impact on established mainstream churches; now Catholic, Lutheran, Baptist, Presbyterian, and other groups have developed their own charismatic movements. To name Catholicism and Protestantism as the two major forces in Christianity no longer corresponds to reality; a "third force" has established itself: the Pentecostal movement.[35]

The present chapter tells the story of the forms of worship that emerged in the new movement. This story begins with a brief look at two traditions that combined to produce and to shape Pentecostal worship: the emotionalism of white Protestants in the eighteenth and nineteenth centuries, and the ecstatic rituals African-American Christians have developed since colonial times.

The White and the Black Roots of Pentecostalism

After Paul, ecstatic worship ceased to be common among Christians, but the ecstatic experience survived. Men and women like Meister Eckhart, Mechthild of Magdeburg, Teresa of Avila, and other medieval and early modern mystics cultivated this mode of religion. Unlike in the Pauline communities, mystical ecstasy was not public but private; experienced in the solitariness of the monk's or nun's cell, it was whispered about in the confessional rather than spoken about in the congregation. With the advent of Protestantism, a new quest for religious experience made itself felt. In the seventeenth century, some of the radical Puritans and the Quakers came to believe in the Spirit's almost tangible reality, a reality to be experienced apart from holy scripture and ecclesiastical tradition. Unwittingly and despite their sobriety and restraint, the Puritans, in their quest for "immediacy in relation to God," prepared the way for a new charismatic movement and new ecstatic forms of worship. When in the 1650s the Englishman George Fox began to invite the members of his Society of Friends to worship with him, the seemingly strange behavior of "quaking" occurred. Members would frequently experience what they called an "agony of the soul" so painful that it had an external effect. The convert's body was shaken with "groans, sighs, and tears." These outward signs bespoke an inward struggle between the forces of darkness and those of the light, often culminating in a victorious "sweet sound of thanksgiving and praise." There was so much ecstatic turbulence and "quaking," that Fox himself advised restraint; somewhat like St. Paul, he wanted his disciples to "love gravity, and soberness, and wisdom." Yet, charismatic phenomena like healing, glossolalia, and the utterance of prophecies abounded in Fox's circle and were apparently encouraged by the leader. The quaking behavior gave the movement its popular name: the Quakers.[36]

The most conspicuous group to adopt ecstasy as their leading ritual pattern were the Shakers, a group that originated in eighteenth-century England, but only flourished when transplanted to the New World in the 1770s. Their leader and prophetess, Mother Ann Lee (1736–84), promoted singing and dancing in worship. An early apostate, William Haskett, has left us a graphic report on a service in which he no longer wished to take part. The elder (he reports) began a certain phase of the service by remarking that every good believer was known by his or her gifts. Shouting "Shake off the flesh!", he began stamping and shaking violently. In an instant, the Spirit seized the entire congregation, making all stamp and shout. Later, women began to talk in unknown tongues, while others shook, stamped, and turned.

> Now was heard the loud shouts of the brethren, then the soft, but hurried note of the sisters, whose "gifts" were the apostolic gifts of tongues. These gently gestured their language, waved themselves backward like a ship on the billows of a ceased storm, shook their heads, seized their garments, and then violently stamped on the floor.

In 1828, when Haskett published this report, the United Society of Believers (as the Shakers called themselves) had this fairly uncommon, charismatic style of worship, characterized by group dancing and ecstasy. However, the Society's spiritual potential had not yet arrived at its full flowering.[37]

In the late 1830s, and lasting for about a decade, a revival began in

Watervliet, Ohio, and spread to all the Shaker communities. Men, women, and children saw visions, talked to those who had gone to heaven, and proclaimed inspired messages. The enthusiastic nature of Shaker worship intensified. We hear of "powerful shakings and quakings, testimonies, promises, threatenings, warnings, predictions, prophecies, trances, revelations, visions, songs, and dance." When the spirits of the other world—the souls of the departed persons, residents of heaven—took over leadership of worship, the proceedings bordered on the bizarre. Some brothers and sisters were blessed with the gift of perpetual laughter. Others performed a sacred theater, miming, under the impulse of spirits, everyday activities like drinking, washing, and fighting. Yet others sang or performed like native Americans, adopting their wild ways under the impulse of "native spirits." Unusual spirit visitors filled the meeting houses week after week—angels with strange names, natives speaking foreign tongues, biblical figures from ancient times, political heroes from America's past. For more than a decade, Shaker meetings came to be punctuated by the delivery of prophetic messages, the singing of new, inspired songs, and the performance of new dances (ill. 38).[38]

38. Ecstatic Dance of the Shakers. Even before twentieth-century Pentecostalism, ecstatic worship was practiced by certain Christian fringe groups like the Shakers, a group founded in eighteenth-century Britain and brought to America in 1774 by Ann Lee Stanley. Some Shakers had the "whirling gift": they whirled so rapidly that they eventually fell prostrate on the floor. American etching, nineteenth-century.

While the outburst of the Spirit among the Shakers soon came to an end, it showed dramatically that American worship could be as ecstatic as any "native cult" was imagined to be.

Shaker emotionalism must not be thought of as an isolated matter. By the end of the nineteenth century, Protestantism had lived through various "awakenings" and revivals of which the Shaker experience was only one example. Between 1800 and 1835—during the generation preceding the Shaker revival—Methodists, Presbyterians, and Congregationalists had their own revivals with emotional open-air preaching and the singing of hymns. Powerful revivals peaked in the United States in 1857–58 and again in the 1880s. Maria Woodworth-Etter, a prominent woman preacher in the late nineteenth century, recalls her childhood days in the state of Ohio. "When I was a girl the Methodist church was the most powerful and the most spiritual. The people fell under the power of God, shouted, danced, got healed from diseases and did lots of other things." It was this thrilling atmosphere that she wanted to recreate in her campaigns as an adult preacher. On the platform of Mrs. Woodworth's tent, people often fainted. "To be slain by the Spirit" or "to be under the power" came to be one of the hallmarks of her meetings. A 1890 drawing from a St. Louis newspaper (ill. 39) shows one of these exciting incidents.[39]

Not only white Anglo-Saxon Christians had their emotional and ecstatic religious tradition. Among America's black population, trance, emotionalism, and spirit possession had even deeper cultural roots and were not limited to occasional outbursts as they were in the "white" revivals. When they were transplanted as slaves to America, West Africans (especially the Yoruba and the Fante-Ashanti) brought with them a culture of spirit possession. Western Christians have traditionally associated spirit possession with evil demons and hostile Satanic powers, and have fought against possession through prayer and priestly exorcism. West Africans, on the other hand, have a positive view of possession: some of their rituals aim at inviting benign spirits to enter humans and to communicate their supernatural power to them. Ecstatic trance, in West Africa, is not associated with illness and evil, but counts as evidence for the presence of divine forces. Now most of the black slaves brought to colonial America in the late seventeenth and eighteenth centuries came from there, and in the New World they continued some of their rituals in secret. In the nineteenth century, Peter Randolph, a former slave in Virginia, described a typical secret meeting on a Southern plantation. When the slaves meet, usually before dawn, "they first ask each other how they feel, the state of their minds, etc. The male members then select a certain space, in separate groups, for their division of the meeting. . . . [Then they pray and sing] all around, until they generally feel quite happy. The speaker usually commences by calling himself unworthy, and talks very slowly, until feeling the Spirit, he grows excited, and in a short time there fall to the ground twenty or thirty men and women under

39. "Being Slain in the Spirit." While Maria Woodworth-Etter stands with arms raised and hand outstretched, a woman and three children faint on the platform of the American charismatic tent-evangelist. From around 1883 people in her meetings began to go into trancelike states which she described as the baptism of the Holy Spirit. Healings also occurred. Pentecostal authors and historians see her meetings as having all the characteristics of Pentecostalism, except for speaking in tongues. A St. Louis journalist's view of a revivalist scene, 1890.

its influence." While a visitor might have found this form of worship strange, if not ridiculous, "the worshipers, perspiring at every pore, were never more serious." Of course, Randolph's plantation slaves no longer considered themselves pagans; with Christianity they had adopted belief in the Holy Spirit. Here we have a Christianized version of an African ritual that aims at getting into trance, evidence of being possessed by the Holy Spirit. Slaves and ex-slaves like Randolph did not invent the new Christian interpretation of "growing excited" and "falling to the ground." They took it over from white Methodists who promoted emotional religion, enthusiastic singing, and who in ca. 1800 still followed John Wesley in believing that conversion may manifest itself in "falling to the ground."[40]

The combination of African and Methodist elements created new rituals of which the most conspicuous is known as the "shouting." Both white and black people have reported on this ritual event, characteristic of Christian slave culture. Although "shouting" was not the same as yelling, the ceremony thus named did include singing, handclapping, and making a loud noise. Shouting denoted a form of communal ritual dance of men and women to the rhythm of hand-clapping, foot-stomping, and the singing of spirituals. The feet were not supposed to cross each other or to leave the floor, for such acts would be secular dancing, and secular dancing was regarded as sinful. So the foot is hardly taken from the floor, and the progression is mainly due to a jerking, hitching motion which agitates the shouters. Certain movements have been described as reminiscent of the "Charleston." The shouters stand in ring formation and move energetically, often for several hours, which may lead to trances and spirit possession. As anthropologists have pointed out, the shouting echoes the West African ring-dance. The slaves improvised a substitute for the drums, with rhythmic hand-clapping and foot-stomping. They also Christianized the ensuing trances, which they understood as being filled with the Holy Spirit. We can see that black ecstatic worship predates Pentecostalism and prepared its way.[41]

Historians trace the origins of American Pentecostalism to a revival that broke out in Los Angeles in 1906 and boasted black as well as white leaders, with the black side apparently dominating. A closer look at the relationship between black and white Pentecostals in Los Angeles in the movement's early days is quite revealing. In 1906, the Asuza Street mission—the place where the movement originated—had a black leader, William Joseph Seymour (1870–1922). Seymour had studied under a white pastor, Charles Fox Parham, at a Bible school in Houston, Texas. Among Parham's students, ecstatic experience and glossolalia had made an appearance in 1900, and some historians consider Parham the founder of the Pentecostal movement. However, when Parham visited Seymour's Azusa Street mission, he was horrified at what he saw and denounced Seymour for involvement in Spiritualism and hypnotism, that is in non-Christian, presumably Satanic matters. Parham was unable to appreciate the wild, ecstatic features of the new forms of worship and healing practiced by his black student. Did Seymour's African soul come to the fore at Azusa Street and create that unique blend of African and Christian elements?[42]

A careful reading of the early sources strengthens the view that the Azusa Street revival was originally a black event. "Whites came to an already black Azusa Street revival," concludes historian Leonard Lovett. According to Frank Bartleman, white eyewitness of the revival, blacks and whites mixed easily under Seymour's leadership. "The 'color line' was washed away in the blood [of Christ]," Bartleman explained. Later, a black participant recalled that "in Los Angeles . . . everybody went to the altar together. White and colored, no discrimination seemed to be among them." However, Seymour's dream of an interracial Pentecostal movement did not come true. Despite his efforts, segregation soon made itself felt. By 1914, with the outbreak of the First World War, his Asuza Street mission had become a local black church with an occasional white visitor.[43]

Recently, the Harvard theologian Harvey Cox celebrated the African-American origins of and contributions to the Pentecostal movement. He argues that black Pentecostalism has revitalized Christianity in the same way, and at the same time, as jazz has revitalized music. Originating around 1900 in two American urban centers—New Orleans and Los Angeles—jazz and Pentecostal Christianity share two features: their preference for spontaneity and love of trance. They constitute a great gift first to American, and then to international culture.[44]

Early Pentecostal Ritual: The Account of Frank Bartleman

One of the early leaders of the movement was Frank Bartleman (1871–1935). His activity as an author of tracts, newspaper reports, and autobiographical books makes him the ideal guide to what came to be the distinctive Pentecostal way of worship. In 1909 he began to publish a series of autobiographical works which he sold or gave away, as he did with his religious tracts. In these books he recounts his life and spiritual experience as a traveler, missionary, and religious inspirer of a movement that despised organized leadership. In *How Pentecost Came to Los Angeles* (1925), Bartleman looks back at the beginning of the charismatic experience he shared with other Christians in 1906. Although one would suspect retrospective romanticizing of the "truly wonderful days," Bartleman's report is free from such distortion. His account is based on his personal diary as well as on numerous newspaper clippings which he had collected throughout the years. Here it is a participant who reports, sharing with us his memories and documents and, above all, his enthusiasm.[45]

In Los Angeles, Bartleman made friends with the Englishman Joseph Smale (1867–1926), minister of the First Baptist church. He came to share Smale's interest in and enthusiasm for the frequent prayer meetings, mass conversions, and the general excitement that suddenly filled the churches during the religious revival in Wales in 1904–6. Smale had actually traveled to Wales and spoken to Evan Roberts (1878–1951), the simple miner who became one of the leaders of the Welsh revival. Through these contacts, Bartleman received five thousand pamphlets on "The Revival in Wales," which he distributed among Los Angeles churches. He exhorted people to pray "for a revival like they had in Wales" (*PLA* 18). Bartleman also exchanged letters with Roberts.[46]

Bartleman often went to prayer meetings in Smale's church, because he admired the minister's ability to inspire the meetings with the spirit of charismatic revival. He wrote an article on Smale for the *Daily News* of Pasadena. Entitled "What I Saw in a Los Angeles Church," it described a typical revivalist service of 1905. Here is Bartleman's report:

The service of which I am writing began impromptu and spontaneous, some time before the pastor arrived. A handful of people had gathered early, which seemed to be sufficient for the Spirit's operation. The meeting started. . . . By the time the pastor arrived the meeting was in full swing. Pastor Smale dropped into his place, but no one seemed to pay attention to him. Their minds were on God. . . . The pastor arose, read a portion of the Scripture, made a few well chosen remarks full of hope and inspiration for the occasion, and the meeting passed again from his hands. The people took it up and went on as before. Testimony, prayer and praise were intermingled throughout the service. The meeting seemed to run itself. (*PLA* 23)

Bartleman was indeed impressed with the communal nature of the service. Having neither opened the meeting nor served as a leader nor contributed the central ritual act, "the pastor was one of them" (*PLA* 23). The congregation balanced the pastor's short sermon with their own testimony in which they spoke of their own religious experience. For Bartleman, the lack of formal leadership meant that "the Spirit was leading." The Holy Spirit inspired and controlled what everyone spoke, sang, and did. The pastor, like the people, would just surrender himself to the Spirit. Bartleman quotes and endorses these words of the Welsh revivalist preacher Evan Roberts: "I have been asked concerning my method. I have none. I never prepare what I shall speak, but leave that to Him" (*PLA* 36). Neither leadership nor preparation held a prominent place, for direction came immediately from heaven. "The meeting gives one a feeling of 'heaven on earth,' with an assurance that the supernatural exists, and that in a very real sense" (*PLA* 23).

Smale held his prayer meetings in the First Baptist church every day for fifteen weeks. The officials of the church came to oppose his innovations, and so he left their church, assembling his revivalist congregation elsewhere in Los Angeles—a measure Bartleman fully approved of. "Cold intellectualism, formal ecclesiasticism, and priestly domination are altogether outside the genius of the Gospel," he commented (*PLA* 29).[47]

The separation from more traditional communities could not extinguish the enthusiasm. Rather, it served to heighten the sense of being chosen for something special. When several revivalist preachers set up their own churches in Los Angeles, hope for a general and powerful religious revival increased. Smale called his new community the New Testament church, and it met at Burbank Hall. It was at this time that the black Baptist preacher, William Seymour, left his church to set up a worship center in an abandoned Methodist church at Azusa Street, which had been previously used for storing lumber. As for Bartleman, he rented a church building at the corner of Eighth and Maple Streets. These churches stayed in close contact with each other. Bartleman "kept going day and night to different missions, exhorting to prayer and faith for the revival" (*PLA* 38).

As the atmosphere of prayer intensified, worship became increasingly fervent. In 1906, ecstatic forms began to make their appearance in all three communities. People started to speak "in tongues," anywhere from "fifteen minutes" to "five full hours" (*PLA* 76. 102). With this extraordinary manifestation of the Holy Spirit, the revival reached its peak. A new Pentecost seemed to repeat the ecstasy and enthusiasm known from the book of Acts. And as in Acts, some observers ridiculed the religious fanaticism and thirst for the miraculous. Trying to make fun of the new service of worship, intruders disturbed certain prayer meetings by bringing in kittens who "began crawling into view from everywhere." The cats were meant to underline what seemed obvious to the enemies: the entire movement must not be taken seriously. Bartleman and many others, however, rejoiced, believing that "Pentecost has come to Los Angeles, the American Jerusalem," as it had come to Wales just a few years earlier (*PLA* 63). People knew that "in Wales, colored lights were often seen, like balls of fire, during the revival there" (*PLA* 38). Although no "tongues of fire" were experienced in Los Angeles, some claimed to have seen the Lord's luminous glory by night over the church at Azusa Street (*PLA* 60). An additional sign that proved God's presence was the terrible earthquake that shook California in April 1906, claiming many lives in San Francisco. Paralyzed with fear, people flocked to the prayer meetings. God made his voice heard in mighty signs, exhorting the people to surrender their lives to him.[48]

What did regular worship look like in such an atmosphere of Pentecost, an atmosphere "almost too sacred and holy to attempt to minister in" (*PLA* 69)? Bartleman describes the prayer meetings held in his church at Eighth and Maple several times. The most detailed report, however, comes from the pen of a visitor whose report was published in the *Way of Faith*, a journal widely read by the early Pentecostals. "I had the rare joy of spending last evening at Pastor Bartleman's meeting, or more correctly where he and Pastor Pendleton are the nominal leaders, but where the Holy Spirit is actually in control. Jesus is proclaimed the head, and the Holy Ghost His executive" (*PLA* 86). Dr. W.C. Dumble of Los Angeles, author of the report, could not conceal his admiration for Bartleman's prayer meeting held one night in September 1906. He begins his account by contrasting the meeting with regular Protestant services held in other churches. Unlike in the typical Protestant service, "there is no preaching, no choir, no organ, no collection, except what is voluntarily placed on the table or put in the box on the wall" (*PLA* 86). This is how Dr. Dumble describes one of Bartleman's services:

singing	Someone begins to sing: three or four hymns may be sung, interspersed with hallelujahs and amens.
lay testimony	Then some overburdened soul rises and shouts, "Glory be to Jesus!" and amid sobs and tears tells of a great struggle, and a great deliverance.

prostration	Then three or four are on the floor with shining faces.
extemporaneous prayer, glossolalia	One begins to praise God, and then breaks out with uplifted hands into a "tongue."
pastor's testimony	Pastor Pendleton now tells how he felt the need, and sought the "baptism" [of the Spirit] and God baptized him with such an experience of his divine presence and love and boldness as he had never had before. The officials of his church therefore desired him to withdraw, and a number of his people went with him and joined forces with Pastor Bartleman.
lay testimony	Then a sweet-faced old German Lutheran lady told how she wondered when she heard the people praising God in "tongues," and began to pray to be baptized with the Spirit. After she had gone to bed her mouth went off in a "tongue," and she praised the Lord through the night to the amazement of her children.
glossolalia, going to the altar	Next an exhortation in "tongues" comes from Pastor Bartleman's lips in great sweetness, and one after another make their way to the altar quickly, until the rail is filled with seekers. (*PLA* 86–87)

Dr. Dumble's report includes all the elements characteristic of the early Pentecostal ritual. There is first of all singing, with which the service usually starts and which can occur time and time again throughout the service. No hymn books are used, and the interjected "amens" and "hallelujahs" contribute to the spontaneity and freedom of expressing people's joy. "All the old, well-known hymns were sung from memory, quickened by the Spirit of God" (*PLA* 57). Whereas standard hymns like "The Comforter Has Come" and "The Life Is in the Blood" were sung communally, singing could also be individual (*PLA* 57). "A young lady of refinement was prostrate on the floor for hours," reports Bartleman, "while at times the most heavenly singing would issue from her lips. It would swell away up to the [divine] throne, and then die away in an almost unearthly melody. She sang 'Praise God! Praise God!' All over the house men and women were weeping" (*PLA* 61).[49]

People prayed spontaneously, without using a book or a fixed text. "Prayer was not formal in those days. It was God [who] breathed. It came upon us, and overwhelmed us. We did not work it up" (*PLA* 35).

Glossolalic utterances were understood as the result of an experience in which the Holy Spirit inspired the receiver of this "baptism in the Spirit" to bring messages or to praise God, or both. Bartleman tells of a Methodist preacher's wife who "came through to a mighty 'baptism', speaking something like Chinese" (*PLA* 70). Another young lady also "spoke fluently in a strange tongue" (*PLA* 87). "A colored sister both spoke and sang in tongues" (*PLA* 52). "Tongues," a spiritual gift often given to women and more rarely to men, were appreciated as the most tangible and overwhelming sign of an individual's contact with God or Christ. It brought the divine presence to the community.

Much time was given to "real testimonies, from fresh heart-experience," in which individuals gave short, spontaneous accounts of their conversion, their spiritual experience, or some mighty act the Lord had wrought for them. The speaker "might be a child, a woman, or a man. It might come from the back seat, or from the front. It made no difference" (*PLA* 59). These testimonies took the place formal preaching would have taken in the traditional Protestant service. Pentecostals needed no preacher, prepared sermon, or Bible. Spiritual experience was not confined to biblical times. Full of miracles and moving spiritual surprises, the life of the faithful itself provided enough edifying "text."

Prostration and going up to the altar were frequent features of the prayer meetings. Both meant adoration and complete surrender to God. "The altar was full of seeking souls all day," writes Bartleman. "There was hardly a cessation of the altar service. Souls were coming out and going through, while the meeting went on. Men and women lay around the altar, stretched out under the power [of the Spirit] all day" (*PLA* 70). "Men would fall all over the house, like the slain in battle. . . . Such a scene cannot be imitated" (*PLA* 60). "Such a divine 'weight of glory' was upon us [that] we could only lie on our faces. For a long time we could hardly remain seated even. All would be on their faces on the floor, sometimes during the whole service" (*PLA* 69).

The coming forward of some people to kneel at the altar rail was not invented in the Pentecostal movement. For a long time, revivalist preachers had invited "sinners" to come forward to the altar, the communion table, or simply the open area in front of the congregation. Through their coming forward, "sinners" demonstrated their repentance or conversion and renewed the handing-over of themselves to Jesus. Among Pentecostal believers, it also served as a multi-purpose expression of special devotion and adoration. The altar area, although not permanently invested with sacred qualities, became a place of encounter with the divine as well as a stage for demonstrating one's submission to God.[50]

A formal liturgy did not exist. Although the elements were repeated—singing, praying, prostrating, and giving testimony—"no two services were alike," because worship, led by the Spirit, remained spontaneous (*PLA* 103).

Bartleman held his prayer meetings every day in the evening, and on Sundays all day long. "On Sabbath last the meeting continued from early morning to midnight," reports Dr. Dumble (*PLA* 87). Occasionally, people would prefer staying in church to going home, and Bartleman found them at odd hours, "lost to all but God" (*PLA* 102). True worshipers lost their sense of time, with a whole night seeming like half an hour. Bartleman never says anything about how a prayer meeting ended. Prayer, in the enthusiastic and charismatic community, could never end.[51]

Worship, for Bartleman and the early Pentecostals, was strictly theocentric, focused on the trinity of God, Christ, and the Holy Spirit. As Dr. Dumble reported: "Jesus is proclaimed the head, and the Holy Ghost His executive" (*PLA* 86). During the service, people experienced the powerful presence of God. More than once, Bartleman tells us that the prayer meeting meant "heaven on earth," and that people felt the glory of God dwelling among them. "The whole place was steeped in prayer. God was in His holy temple. It was for man to keep silent [Hab. 2:20]. The *shekhinah* glory rested there," he explained, using a learned Hebrew term for the divine presence (*PLA* 60). "The Lord seems almost visible. He was so real" (*PLA* 70). "The presence of the Lord was wonderfully real. . . . And this condition lasted for a long time" (*PLA* 83). As if to make the Lord's presence more dramatic, Bartleman illustrated his point with the following anecdote. One night at church, "the Lord came suddenly so near that we could feel His presence as though He were closing in on us around the edges of the meeting. Two thirds of the people sprang to their feet in alarm, and some ran hurriedly out of the house, even leaving their hats behind them, almost scared out of their senses" (*PLA* 38). One day, when Bartleman and one of his friends were in a Pasadena church, crying and praying for a revival, they had a special experience of Jesus. "Suddenly, without premonition, the Lord Jesus revealed himself to us. He seemed to stand directly between us, so close we could have reached out our hand and touched him. But we did not dare to move. I could not even look. . . . His presence seemed more real, if possible, than if I could have seen and touched Him naturally" (*PLA* 19–20).

The focus on God meant that little attention was given to other worshipers. In a way, everyone present worshiped the Lord alone, being involved with their own spiritual struggle. True, on one occasion, someone got up filled with love and "ran all over the place, hugging all the brethren he could get hold of" (*PLA* 61). However, this was exceptional. Generally, people would focus their attention on God rather than on the faithful who were assembled. "When we first reached the meeting we avoided as much as possible human contact and greeting. We wanted to meet God first. We got our head under some bench in the corner in prayer, and met men only in the Spirit, knowing them 'after the flesh' no more" (*PLA* 59). The more intensely the divine presence was felt, the less would people be aware of others.[52]

The spiritual struggle aimed at being completely open to the divine, the believer's "old self" (Rom. 6:6) being buried and forgotten. That struggle consisted of two stages. The first involved handing oneself over to God in an emotional, conversionlike experience. Ritually, this was expressed in or supported by frequent and long prostrations in personal prayer. Believers had to humble themselves. Often, this would involve groaning and weeping. Surrender to God or Christ was also expressed by going up to the altar, a movement symbolic of one's willingness to approach the divine and to sacrifice oneself. In the second stage the struggle came to an end in an event sometimes referred to as "baptism in the Spirit." Suddenly, the individual would feel a great joy and strength. Overwhelmed by and filled with the divine Spirit, he or she would burst forth and speak or sing in "tongues." As a new creature in the Spirit, the "old self" no longer resisted the divine impulse. The human being could now serve as a pure vessel of the Spirit.

Though most people would go through the spiritual struggle of humbling themselves alone, someone else could help them with it. Pastor Bartleman developed some skill in doing this. In a prayer meeting he saw a woman whom he knew as a former volunteer worker for the mission. The young woman "had been backslidden for several years." After eleven o'clock at night, as the service drew near its end, she still sat unmoved. He spoke to her, warning her it might be her last chance. As she still sat indifferent, he started pleading with her. A full hour he battled with her (and with others present who tried to prevent him from being too hard on the woman). Finally, he fell to the floor "under a real travail of soul for her," his life being almost pressed out of him. This helped. Now the woman also fell to the floor, struggling with herself and weeping for nearly three hours. At about three o'clock in the morning, she arose, "with the very shine of an angel on her face" (*PLA* 94). She no longer resisted God. The battle was won.

For the next stage, the "baptism in the Spirit," we have Bartleman's account of his own experience. He had a great hunger for the gift of speaking in tongues. Having been present when others spoke in tongues, Bartleman realized one day that "the Spirit [had] dropped the heavenly chorus into my soul" (*PLA* 56). He joined those who sang in ecstasy. This was on Friday, June 15, 1906—Bartleman carefully chronicles the experience. However, he did not yet have the full experience of speaking in tongues. This happened two months later, "in the afternoon of August 16" in his church at Eighth and Maple in Los Angeles (*PLA* 71). During a prayer meeting with only seven participants, Bartleman spoke in tongues "possibly for about fifteen minutes" (*PLA* 76). Here is his report:

> After a time of testimony and praise, with everything quiet, I was softly walking the floor, praising God in my spirit. All at once I seemed to hear in my soul (not with my natural ears) a rich voice speaking in a language I did not know. I have later heard something similar to it in India. It seemed to ravish and fully satisfy the pent-up praises in my being. In a few moments, I found myself, seemingly without volition on my part, enunciating the same sounds with my own vocal organs. (*PLA* 71)

Rather than speaking or singing himself, Bartleman felt that he remained absolutely passive during the experience, which he described as thrilling and blissful. Language seems inadequate to describe the unique event: "it must be experienced to be appreciated" (*PLA* 71). The divine Spirit, he later reflected, had gradually prepared him through his own prayer and that of others. One day, he was ready, so that the Spirit could speak and operate through him. He had become an instrument of the Spirit, completely obeying His will.

Going through this two-stage process did not create complete saints who would stay filled with the Spirit at all times. Spiritual experience would come and go. So each individual would always have to go through the ritual process again, would humble him- or herself before God and eventually again reach the peak experience of ecstasy, rapture, and glossolalic expression. However, if a person had received the "baptism of the Holy Spirit" once (that is, the gift of tongues), the process would be shorter and, presumably, easier. People would get used to the experience and acquire the ability to repeat it more frequently, especially in the heated, excited atmosphere of an ecstatic prayer meeting.

The Pentecostal effervescence did not last forever. To his disappointment, Bartleman saw the excitement pass as more regular, routine forms of worship developed. Some, for a time, would try to continue the earlier spontaneous forms, but without much luck. The result was inauthentic, fake Pentecostalism, involving "spurious tongues" and "imitated" singing in the Spirit (*PLA* 160). Such nostalgic attempts to recreate the original experience, for Bartleman, produced services that remained empty and "without the Spirit" (*PLA* 160). The spiritual experience no longer originated in people's hearts. It tended to be induced with the help of music and singing. Bartleman, like the Welsh leader Evan Roberts, fought against "too much singing" (*PLA* 36). Earlier, singing had been rare, spontaneous, and unaccompanied by instruments. The spontaneous singing of the early days came to be replaced by singing from hymnals. Where was the original "gift" of the "new song," exercised at the prompting of the Spirit? "They drove it out by hymn books, and selected songs by leaders. It was like murdering the Spirit" (*PLA* 57). "There is very little real spirit of worship" in the new hymn-book songs; "they move the toes, but not the hearts" (*PLA* 57). Gone were the days of not speaking above a whisper; pastors now tried to move seekers by "jazzing them through" to counterfeit spiritual experience (*PLA* 55).[53]

While some churches made an attempt to keep the original spirit of revival alive (though by questionable means), others came to abandon the Pentecostal model of worship altogether, replacing it by traditional forms (ill. 40). Bartleman reports how at the old Azusa Street mission in Los Angeles, the place where the original excitement had begun, the Spirit went out of fashion. The leaders of worship deliberately suppressed the once powerful evidence of spontaneity:

40. The Idolatry of Organized Christianity. According to Pentecostal Christians, traditional churches worship two idols: high-powered organization and formal worship. King Jeroboam of northern Israel made two shrines with golden calf idols to prevent people from worshiping in the Jerusalem Temple. Pentecostal cartoon, 1939.

Old Azusa Mission became more and more in bondage. The meetings now had to run just in appointed order. The Spirit tried to work through some poor, illiterate Mexicans who had been saved and "baptized" in the Spirit. But the leader deliberately refused to let them testify, and crushed them ruthlessly. . . . Every meeting was now programed from start to finish. (*PLA* 140)

In some of the poor and deprived, like Bartleman himself, the Spirit lingered on. But for most leaders, the ecstatic pattern of worship had lost its attraction. Pentecostalism began to develop new, churchlike features.

Contemporary Charismatic Ritual

Pentecostalism has changed appreciably since the early 1900s, the days of Frank Bartleman. It has not only settled into more organized forms, but has also recognized and cultivated a greater variety of spiritual gifts. The interest of Bartleman and some of his contemporaries focused quite narrowly on fervent prayer followed by outbursts of glossolalia. However, even in the early days, speaking in tongues was not the only way in which the Spirit manifested itself. Sarah Covington, who participated in the Azusa Street revival, speaks of "prophecies that came true, healings, revelations, miracles." In addition to glossolalia, other spiritual gifts, present from the beginning, have become characteristic of the movement: effective prayer, especially prayer that heals the sick; prophetic utterance in the name of God; and fainting, styled as "being slain in the Spirit." While these are the most characteristic manifestations of the Holy Spirit, they do not exhaust the possibilities, for one can also observe dancing, jumping up and down, laughing, and, according to recent reports, also the making of animal noises, such as roaring, barking, and mooing.[54]

Pentecostal and charismatic ministers never conduct worship according to a fixed pattern, established by an ecclesiastical authority and fixed in an official prayer book. Like Bartleman, they are horrified at the very thought of having to follow prescribed, unalterable liturgies. These would prevent the Spirit from asserting its rulership and from guiding people in their congregational devotions. This does not mean, however, that the congregation would not know what to expect. A loosely defined, very flexible, oral rather than written agenda exists. In many charismatic groups, a standard ritual pattern comprises three parts: praise, preaching, and altar service. In the first, introductory part, the singing of hymns, the saying of prayers (that are never read out of a book), and the giving of lay testimonies (volunteered or called out) are normal. There is also much rousing instrumental music, and a choir often alternates with or supports lively congregational singing. Among the many persons active during the first phase of the service—the preacher who says an opening prayer, one or more members who give testimonies, musicians and choir members—the song leader stands out as the person responsible for a smoothly flowing experience of worship.[55]

Preaching, the second part, forms the middle section of the service. Often, a short biblical passage is read, which is selected by the minister and not taken from an established lectionary. The sermon may be rather long, taking the best part of an hour. Again, no written medium is involved; the preacher never uses notes, though he or she may occasionally quote from the Bible. Typically, the congregation interacts rather energetically with the preacher: by giving assent through shouts of "Yes" and "Amen," by applauding, or by giving choral responses to questions asked by the preacher. A prayer follows. The third and final part of the service begins with an "altar call." The preacher or worship leader invites some individuals, if not the whole congregation, to come forward onto the platform—to the area in the sanctuary where traditional, liturgical churches would have an altar. Here they praise the Lord in special ways, are given special blessings, are prayed for, or pray for others—whatever the leader announces or members of the congregation request. Eventually, hymns and prayers conclude the service.

We must not think of the service thus outlined as culminating in some sort of sacramental act placed at the end. For some participants, the end can be the most meaningful part, the time in which they feel the touch of the Spirit most clearly. However, at least in theory, the entire service is felt to be a preparation for the manifestations of the Holy Spirit, and the expected event—the individual believer's experience of the Spirit—may happen at any time during the service: at the time of praise, during the sermon, or at the altar. The service has to allow for spontaneity, because it is primarily in spontaneous expression that the Spirit is felt to act. Usually, a balanced blend of planned and unplanned elements creates the worshipful atmosphere valued by Pentecostals as being conducive to spiritual experience. For Pentecostals and charismatics, this means being possessed by or filled with the Holy Spirit. The observer can distinguish various forms of possession. A weak form can be described as little more than a heightened state of enthusiasm and concentration in which the believer has full control of him- or herself (though not always of the tears that may flow). A strong possession, by contrast, involves an actual trance and an altered state of consciousness in which a divine force seems to displace the believer's self-control. Typically, the state of possession or trance is short, rarely lasting longer than a quarter of an hour.

In contemporary charismatic practice, one can distinguish four main forms in which the Spirit manifests itself during worship. (1) Worshipers may experience a sudden surge of joy and *excitement*, accompanied by singing, dancing, glossolalic utterance, or a combination of all of these. (2) Another kind of spiritual manifestation is the *effective prayer*. Individual or communal prayer, pronounced by spirit-filled worshipers, produces certain effects of which instant healing is the most spectacular (though perhaps the rarest) type. (3) A third form of spiritual manifestation is the *revelation*. Here someone feels inspired to transmit a prophetic message or a dream to the congregation or to an individual. (4) The charismatic worshipers' contact with the divine power may finally manifest itself in his or her "*being slain in the Spirit*," i.e., in an altered state of consciousness that normally leads to falling on the ground. Descriptions of each these forms will provide a fuller picture of what happens in charismatic assemblies.

The first manifestation of the Spirit is *excitement*, often culminating in glossolalic utterance. Typical charismatic worship features a long period (perhaps thirty minutes) of singing. A "worship leader," backed up by other singers and a "stage band," leads from chorus to chorus according to a well-planned but seemingly spontaneous progression, encouraging the congregation to "abandon themselves to the Spirit" in singing, clapping, and dancing. The service begins rather quietly at first with muted instruments and the congregation seated. Gradually the tempo picks up, the decibels increase, and soon the congregation is often clapping and jumping more than singing. Sometimes, songs are followed by prolonged clapping, shouting, and whistling. Finally, the repeated songs give way to a hush of awe, and in silence or quiet songs believers may enter the very presence of God, the Holy of Holies, where (according to their definition) "worship" finally takes place. In this most intimate experience of relationship with God, believers may express their adoration however the Spirit leads them. In communal ecstatic praise, people raise their arms in a gesture of adoration and say a diversity of individual prayers aloud, so that their voices blend to form the sound of a huge polyphonous choir. Many of the congregation would pray in English, but some use what they call prayer language in which they utter random combinations of sounds, interspersing their vernacular with incomprehensible, sacred, glossolalic sounds. "An important aid in worship for the Spirit-filled believer is his prayer language, by which he is able to worship God more perfectly than he can by the sole means of the human intellect," explain the authors of *Foundations of Pentecostal Theology*. The "spoken" delivery of communal prayer may give way to chanting or singing. A beautiful intertwining of melodies and harmonies, called "Spirit singing," may ensue.[56]

Especially in black congregations, the Spirit may manifest itself in an even more intense way. Invited by the minister and lured by rhythmic music and the beating of drums, they perform the "holy dance," generally at the end of the service. Adults, young people, children, and even some of the elderly get up from their seats, raise their hands, and start to make all kinds of body movements. A large number of worshipers dance, moving in and out of the aisles. Some clap, others sing "Yes, yes!," and again others speak or sing in tongues, some with a trancelike, lost expression. After a period of dancing, some individuals retire to their seats exhausted. The dancing, accompanied by instrumental solos on the tambourine, the trumpet, the guitar, and the saxophone, may continue for the better part of an hour.[57]

Charismatic outburst in speaking or singing in tongues, in movement, music, and dance celebrates the presence of the Spirit. Touched by the Spirit, the faithful cannot but celebrate and make, as they say, "a joyful noise." (This quaint expression can be found in the King James Version of the Bible, but has disappeared from some of the more recent translations.) Pentecostal doctrine privileges glossolalia as an activity based on and encouraged by scripture over other forms of expression in worship.[58]

When people give testimonies in which they make public and celebrate the favor the Lord has shown them in their lives, the sequence is that of event and praise. The event (for instance, having recovered from some illness) is recalled in worship and thus the Lord's saving act is acknowledged and praised. In glossolalic praise, by contrast, the event—the powerful presence of the Spirit in the believer—and the act of praise coincide in time. Glossolalic praise is pure praise that fully concentrates one's mind on God, abandoning all earthbound thoughts. In the words of one Pentecostal pastor: "Praying in tongues is the only way to get the human mind out of it."[59]

While the Pentecostals of Frank Bartleman's day never doubted the genuineness of the outburst of the Spirit, some present-day charismatics are more critical of their own experience. "Some of our worship services are completely earthbound, based almost entirely on fleshly construction," explained one Assemblies of God minister. He criticizes worship designed to make an emotional impact and produce an emotional response. Emotionality all too easily poses as a genuine spiritual experience. A congregation, he argues, might as well "move into true spiritual worship without being told to raise their hands and without any musical backup at all." Worship can happen in a quiet, non-emotional atmosphere, because authentic spiritual excitement does not depend upon singing and upbeat music. Another minister, also belonging to the Assemblies of God, commented on a new understanding of glossolalia. While earlier Pentecostals saw it as happening in a trancelike state, it is now acknowledged to be learned behavior. People move easily and at will in and out of this expression. Both ministers agree that the Spirit can manifest itself in a quiet atmosphere. At least in the Assemblies of God, worship seems to move away from the noise and the trances characteristic of the early days of Pentecostalism and still typical of many black charismatics.[60]

Although some Pentecostals have become suspicious of emotionality induced by music, that suspicion has little basis in the Methodist tradition from which much of their music derives. John Wesley, in his "Thoughts on the Power of Music," praises simple, melodious, moving music, preferring it to the sterility of unemotional productions based on academic ideas of harmony. Music, for Wesley and the classical Pentecostal tradition, must charge the atmosphere, stir up emotions, and thus open people's hearts to God. Another tradition present in Pentecostal circles is that of Spirit-filled singing, an idea inherited, it seems, from German pietism. Filled or even "inebriated" with the divine Spirit, the human heart begins to sing with much enthusiasm—hence the pietists' traditional *Singstunden*, lay meetings dedicated to spiritual singing.[61]

The second, quite characteristic feature of charismatic worship is *effective prayer*. Charismatics believe in the power of prayer. A supplication spoken by someone filled with God's Spirit cannot fail to produce effects. The standard scriptural reference is to the letter of James: "The prayer of the righteous is powerful and effective" (Jas. 5:16). Charismatic believers take "the righteous" to refer to all Christians, especially those who have been "baptized with the Spirit." Like prophecy, effective prayer exists in two forms, which may be termed "weak" and "strong." Certain individuals have been given the special gift of "strong," powerful prayer. Their prayers rarely fail to be answered, and some of them are known as healers or exorcists. These gifts, however, are infrequent. Confined to "faith healers" like Oral Roberts (b. 1918) and some others who figure prominently in the (American) media, spectacular healings owing to "strong" prayer seldom if ever occur in a normal service of worship. All believers who have been "baptized by the Spirit" and thus been filled with supernatural power enjoy at least the "weak" variety of effective prayer. Although they may not produce instant healings or immediate deliverance from demonic forces, their prayers are seen as effective, powerful, and indeed indispensable.

Now it must be pointed out that not all prayers pronounced at a service of worship qualify as effective prayer. Three distinguishing marks of effective prayer can be listed: (1) They are petitionary prayers in which something specific is asked for—healing from an ailment, empowerment for a task, divine help in a family crisis or for a student's examinations, and the like; (2) the recipient of divine help typically moves onto the platform to be visible to all, and he or she may be touched by some of those who pray; (3) the prayer is pronounced in a heightened form and often includes glossolalia and the use of oil and cloth. If the desired effect is physical healing, many pastors anoint the sick person with oil "in the name of the Lord"; in so doing they follow the instruction of the New Testament (Jas. 5:14–16). If the person who needs to be healed is not present, prayer may be said over a piece of cloth; consecrated through communal prayer (and perhaps the additional touch of a particularly gifted healer), the cloth is believed to carry a healing power. The *Foundations of Pentecostal Theology* quotes the scriptural basis of the "prayer cloth": "And God wrought special miracles by the hand of Paul: so that from his body were brought unto the sick handkerchiefs or belts, and the diseases departed from them, and the evil spirits went out of them" (Acts 19:11–12). If cloth in Paul's day transmitted healing powers, why should this not also be possible today?[62]

The gift of powerful prayer must be exercised by and be put at the disposal of the community. In the structure of a worship service, effective prayer has its most common place in the third and final part, the one often referred to as "altar service." Typically, the minister calls those who are sick or those who have special needs to come forward to the platform. There they stand or kneel, with their backs to the congregation. Usually, people's special needs are announced, so that everyone knows what to pray for. The entire congregation follows the minister's invitation to a few minutes' prayer "in concert." Just as in general, congregational praise, individuals address Jesus or God—first with murmurous petitions said in unison and then raising their voices into clamorous shouts. As prayerful noise rises, the atmosphere is heavy with glossolalia, petition, and an impressive solidarity. At a sign from the prayer leader, the corporate prayer ends abruptly.

As an alternative to communal prayer, the congregation may form small groups of six to eight people. In these groups, people make their needs known and then pray for each other. It is common to see an individual surrounded by some of the faithful who touch this individual's shoulder or place hands on his or her head while uttering their prayers of intercession, prayers in which they blend the use of English with that of glossolalic "prayer language." A rite of anointing may also be administered. In this case, the pastor places a drop of oil upon the forehead of a congregation member who requests it, while other members circle him or her and begin to pray loudly, or shout, and some may speak in tongues.[63]

The typical situation of effective prayer involves not just an individual speaking to God on behalf of someone; instead, a group of several people (if not the entire congregation) performs this task. As often, Pentecostalists invoke a scriptural passage that establishes the precedent: "Truly I tell you, if two of you agree on earth about anything you ask, it will be done for you by my Father in heaven" (Matt. 18:19). There is also a strong sense of community, and the members identify with the problems of others who belong to the group. In touching each other at the moment of prayer, the corporate character of the congregation assumes visibility. "The laying on of hands," explains Steven Land, "is not so much to transmit healing virtue as it is a sign of identification of the body of believers with the suffering and the need of the one anointed. They are healed together, and they rejoice together." The Spirit, one might say, sometimes prefers to touch the group rather than just an individual.[64]

For charismatic Christians, effective prayer functions as the most important activity in which all the members exercise a "priestly" function. Although some members may have special spiritual gifts (like the gift of healing), in principle they are all equal. Thus, people never leave a service of worship with the idea of having simply received spiritual blessings; they are also convinced of the relevance of the contribution they made through their own prayer.

The Spirit not only manifests itself in excitement and effective prayer, but also in *revelations* communicated by individuals. These form the third kind of spiritual manifestation in worship. Revelation can happen in two different ways. Ideally, the minister's preaching should always be "anointed," that is, the Spirit should guide and inspire him. The congregation expects him "to convey a divine message or oracle, some word of Scripture that comes to fresh life as it is made the vehicle of what the Lord wants to say now to this set of people." The minister never speaks in his own name but steps back "to let the Lord speak his Word for the present time." In a more intense way, the Spirit may address the congregation or individuals through revelations transmitted by the minister or by lay members of the congregation. Speaking through an individual, a man or a woman, the Spirit can communicate its own prophetic message.[65]

According to prevailing Protestant doctrine, the scriptures constitute the word of God, given for once and for all, and to which individual thought or inspiration is to be strictly subordinated. Certain charismatic circles accept this view by speaking of two types of prophetic authority: whereas the Bible enjoys universal, eternal, and objective authority, post-biblical prophetic messages are considered particular and subjective and therefore of more limited value. Many Pentecostal believers qualify this teaching. For them, the scriptures constitute *a* word of God, one instance or a series of instances (albeit a most important one) of divine revelation. That revelation cannot and must not stop. It is realized as an ongoing process in people endowed with the gift of prophecy. For both prophet and audience, the immediacy of a new revelation surpasses the impact of the biblical text. A Catholic lay woman, a mother of several children and member of a prophetic group, observed in the 1970s: "God's word, in a sharper way than just by reading Scripture, really penetrates through and speaks out."[66]

A prophecy can address the entire community and announce some event, sometimes in language borrowed from Old Testament prophecy. A typical example is the following oracle of salvation, loosely patterned on the prophet Ezekiel:

> Mark down this day and remember it. . . . Call to mind; declare it publicly. Have no fear, because I am faithful to my word, and I will fulfill it. I am going to restore my people and reunite them. I am going to restore my people the glory that is mine, so that the world will not mock or scorn them, but so that the world might know that I am God and king and that I have come to redeem and save the earth. . . . I am restoring my people, bestowing upon them honor and glory, bringing back to them the glory that is proper to my people, and making them look again like a kingdom, the kingdom of God on this earth.

Some Pentecostals celebrate such an oracle as a genuine renewal of Old Testament prophecy and its language (although charismatic oracles rarely announce the doom so often prophesied in the Bible). However, it seems that general, Bible-like revelations are relatively rare and not particularly appreciated. People seem to be less interested in "general" prophecies; they prefer to listen to more specific revelations, especially those that address individuals and announce God's help.[67]

Many prophecies transmitted through the pastor, a guest evangelist, or a member of the congregation address everyday matters concerning individuals who are present. A common kind of prophecy, often called a "word of knowledge," is a divinely given insight into the presence of people with this or that specific complaint, which God can or indeed will heal. A typical "word of knowledge" sounds as follows:

> God is showing me that there is a woman somewhere in these first three rows on the left side of the church who is suffering from a stomach disorder. God wants to heal you.
> I see a couple in the balcony whom God has revealed are having serious marital problems. God wants to restore your relationship.

The pastor would call for such people to come forward for prayer or ask the congregation to heal them through their intercession.[68]

Those enjoying the gift of prophecy need not pronounce their revealed messages of help and encouragement publicly. The loose structure of the service and the seating arrangements often allow them to approach the Spirit's addressees directly. A forty-year-old white woman, an experienced and frequent prophetess whom the present writer interviewed, avoids speaking in public. Since she receives messages for individuals, she prefers to address them privately, though during the service. "Once the Spirit has started to use you for transmitting messages, he rarely stops," she explains. Easily excited by a worshipful atmosphere, reluctant Deborah often uses earplugs to prevent the Spirit from seizing her. In order not to impose herself too often and not to make a fool of herself in the congregation, she tries to restrain her prophetic activity. Although she thinks of prophecy as a precious gift, she wants to use it with as much discretion and restraint as possible.

Some of the Assemblies of God pastors welcome revelations in their worship, considering them a forceful expression of the Spirit that should be encouraged. Others, by contrast, show a preference for preaching. Although they would not deny the validity and actual occurrence of revelations through members of the congregation, they opt for a restrained exercise of that gift. If it degenerates into a routine exercise, it loses its authenticity and promotes the caricature of charismatic worship as a meeting of unbalanced, if not actually lunatic, people. Some congregations have established an elaborate procedure to prevent the delivery of offensive or meaningless prophecies. A prophecy must be shared with a representative from the prayer gathering who, in turn, clears it with the leader. The leader then selects the prophecies that may be given to the entire congregation.[69]

A similar development can be reported in Catholic charismatic communities. Like the Assemblies of God, the "Word of God" community of Ann Arbor, Michigan, has brought the prophetic gift under the firm control of its leadership. While the group recognizes and appreciates the gift, it prevents it from being exercised spontaneously. Before a woman or a man proclaims a prophecy in public worship, he or she has to join the community's prophetic team and undergo special training. The idea of having a team seems to echo a biblical institution: the board of "prophets and teachers" which the book of Acts speaks of in the early Christian community at Antioch, Syria (Acts 13:1). In order to discern and develop their gifts, the team members practice in small groups. They can rely on the experience, guidance, and advice of their master Bruce Yocum, who has also written a manual entitled *Prophecy: Exercising the Prophetic Gifts of the Spirit in the Church Today*. Even the trained prophetess or prophet, however, must first consult the leader of a prayer meeting before speaking up. Revelation must be hedged with rules in order not to become offensive, inauthentic, or worthless. It seems that Catholic charismatics develop a sense of control faster than their Protestant fellows. The Catholic charismatic community of Ann Arbor originated in the late 1960s; by the mid-1970s, prophecy was already under the firm control of leadership and was being exercised according to codified rules.[70]

Rules and the strict adherence to them present a problem for charismatics, including those with a Catholic background. An anonymous letter-writer complains to the Catholic magazine *New Covenant* that at prayer meetings "people who prophesy infrequently must submit their prophecy in writing to a member of the word-gift ministry. This rule has inhibited many people from giving prophecies." The responding Father Bertolucci admits that too much legislating is out of place: "In general, I believe easing up restrictions allows people the freedom to develop the gift of prophecy." The priest is inclined to let the entire congregation hear the prophecy and "test it," that is, comment on it and decide about its validity. While priests and lay people have few problems with prophecies of encouragement, they often feel uncomfortable about words that address individuals, command specific actions, and call for immediate obedience. Comments Sister Nancy Keller: "Personal prophecy is very, very dangerous. I have seen individual lives really destroyed and set in the wrong direction when they have taken a prophecy given to them and directed their lives by it." Revealing a divine message involves a risk, both for the prophet and those who are addressed.[71]

A prophetic group active in Kansas City (ca. 1990) recommends limiting public prophetic pronouncements to words of edification, encouragement, and consolation. Other prophecy, such as the exposure of sin or exhortations about the church's future, should be brought to the leaders who will then decide about delivery. Ideally, a prophet not belonging to the leadership should be humble and share his revelations in a low-key, behind-the-scenes way with a leader who serves as his or her advisor. The leader would also help to clarify the meaning of obscure images or words occurring in revelatory experience, much as a therapist would help to find the meaning of a dream. One of the Kansas City prophetic pastors requires his followers to write out in full any prophecy they wish him to receive. He gives them full instructions: it must be typewritten and accompanied by a brief summary, typed on another clean page. The "lay" prophet must also indicate the date of the prophetic experience and give his or her address and phone number. "Having given the prophecy to the leadership, the hands of the sender are now clean. The responsibility is with the leadership. They will call if they want further elucidation." In other words: prophetic leaders wish to keep all revelatory pronouncements under their firm control, so that nothing they have not endorsed reaches the public. Despite its modern and seemingly repressive details, the rule here applied can actually be found in one of the letters of St. Paul: "Do not despise the words of prophets, but test everything; hold fast to what is good" (1 Thess. 5:20–21).[72]

In the 1970s and 1980s, certain charismatic communities moved away from the earlier emphasis on glossolalia as one of the foremost manifestations of the Holy Spirit with the individual believer. Instead, they came to believe in an experience they termed "*being slain in the Spirit*" or "resting in the Spirit," which is the fourth and final spiritual manifestation discussed here. Although this was a traditional feature of charismatic services, it had previously received little notice, but was now rediscovered and gained new visibility.[73]

Overwhelmed by divine power, individuals fall in a semi-swoon either on the floor or into their chair, remaining there in a state of complete peace and relaxation, typically for a few minutes, but sometimes for hours. Some people fall when the minister walks through the congregation, so that one can speak of a spontaneous experience. More often, however, the experience is explicitly "staged" and forms part of a prayer ritual that aims at inducing an altered state of consciousness. The charismatic pastor or priest as well as helpers randomly chosen from the congregation surround and touch an individual for whom they pray. The pastor sometimes anoints the individual's forehead with blessed oil. The group and the person prayed for stand. All of a sudden, the individual loses control of him- or herself and falls backwards, with knees unbent—not to the ground but into the arms of a "catcher" who prevents the "slain" person from being hurt. The catcher places the Spirit-controlled person on the ground, where he or she rests for some time. The feelings reported range from total consciousness to complete unconsciousness. People regularly describe the state of "resting in the Spirit" as being pleasant, enjoyable, peaceful, calm, and relaxed. They feel as if they are in another dimension, with waves of peace and love permeating their body.

Interpreting the experience, both ministers and lay people refer to giving up one's will and resistance. Abandoning themselves to the divine power, they fall into "the invisible nurturant arms of the deity." While in prophetic inspiration, charismatics are empowered to be active and to get involved with others whom they dominate, resting in the Spirit represents the passive side of the spiritual economy. "Slain" members of the congregation do not minister to others; they are ministered to, both by the community and by the Spirit itself. They feel touched by the transforming power of God. They invoke certain states reported by mystics like John Tauler and Teresa of Avila; but far from being the privilege of a few saints, the glories of mystical union with God are for all the faithful. In more recent religious history, the fainting and sinking down is recorded particularly in the early Methodist tradition, with the first references dating from 1739 in John Wesley's journal. In the nineteenth century, the fainting of individuals often accompanied the preaching of the itinerant American evangelist Maria Woodworth-Etter (1844–1924). These people, she said, were "slain in the Spirit" (ill. 39).[74]

The recent history of the charismatic movement shows that not all the four gifts—excitement in the Spirit (with dancing and glossolalia), effective prayer, prophecy, and being slain in the Spirit—are always appreciated and used in the same way. The 1940s and 1950s saw a great healing revival, followed, in the 1970s and 1980s, by a prophetic revival. Holy laughter seems to be typical of the 1990s. Certain gifts can be more or less "fashionable." But all the spiritual gifts have all left their mark on worship, making contemporary charismatic services rich and varied.[75]

The Doctrinal Basis of Pentecostal Worship

Pentecostalists have never spent much time in writing up systematic accounts of what they believe and teach. Their writing focuses on the biographies of their spiritual leaders or on compiling testimonies written by members of their denominations. Lived life and communal worship take clear precedence over theological reflection. It would be wrong, though, to assume that Pentecostal worship lacks a doctrinal basis. Although their theology may be undeveloped and lack the large tomes characteristic of other Christian groups, Pentecostalists have precise notions of the basis of their worship. That basis can be found in the first letter to the Corinthians in which we get a glimpse of how some early Christian communities worshiped (see above, pp. 372–78). Their worship was lively, noisy, and Spirit-filled. Speaking in tongues and prophecy figured prominently in Pauline worship.

If we compare Pauline and standard Pentecostal services, one major difference cannot be overlooked. Unlike the Corinthians, Pentecostalists take little interest in eucharistic rituals. While in Corinthian worship the Spirit was made present through the bread and wine that served as his vessels, Pentecostalists believe in Christ's unmediated coming. For them, a sacred meal that "commemorates" the death of Christ ("do this in memory of me") somehow implies that the original event belongs to the past. The sacraments, as celebrated by non-charismatics, reflect a routinized stage of a religious group's development. Pentecostalists, of course, have little interest in commemorating activities. They believe in original, new events effected by the presence of Christ's Spirit, not in weak echoes captured in commemorative meals. The nineteenth-century "holiness" movement in American Protestantism, out of which Pentecostalism developed, was known for its opposition to "sacramentalism." Frank Bartleman's detailed accounts of early Pentecostal worship include only one reference to a eucharistic celebration. Visiting India as an itinerant preacher, he once helped a Pentecostal pastor to administer "the Communion to the girls in the afternoon" (*WF* 68). While Pentecostal churches occasionally do celebrate the Eucharist, it does not hold a central place in their ritual life, as it does for instance in Catholic practice.[76]

In addition to Paul's first letter to the Corinthians and its report on early Christian worship, Pentecostalists also rely on another New Testament book, the Acts of the Apostles. The very name of Pentecost is derived from this important source.

Literally designating the "fiftieth (day)," Pentecost is the Greek name for one of the Jewish religious feasts celebrated in June in biblical times. Fifty days after another feast, that of Passover, it celebrated the harvest of wheat, the last of the cereals to ripen in Palestine. Thus, it marked the closing of the grain harvest with a celebration of joyous thanksgiving. For Christians, the name of Pentecost came to stand for an important event in their early history. According to the Acts of the Apostles, some of the followers of Jesus met in Jerusalem shortly after their master's death. As they were together, they had the overwhelming experience of a divine gift being bestowed upon them. In the words of the book of Acts:

> When the day of Pentecost had come, they were all together in one place. And suddenly from heaven there came a sound like the rush of a violent wind, and it filled the entire house where they were sitting. Divided tongues, as of fire, appeared among them, and a tongue rested on each of them. All of them were filled with the Holy Spirit and began to speak in other languages, as the Spirit gave them ability. . . . All [those who witnessed the event] were amazed and perplexed, saying to one another, "What does this mean?" But others sneered and said, "They are filled with new wine." (Acts 2:1–4.12–13)

In Acts, the event of Pentecost marks a new phase in the development of the early Christian community. Before Pentecost, the community had a membership of about 120 individuals; at Pentecost, about 3000 more joined the rapidly growing church.

The Pentecost experience was not an isolated event. On a later occasion, when a group of Christians met for worship, it happened again: "When they had prayed, the place in which they were gathered together was shaken; and they were filled with the Holy Spirit and spoke the word of God with boldness" (Acts 4:31). Being filled with the Spirit, praising God, speaking in tongues, and prophesying are all characteristic of the early Christian community. For Luke, being filled with the Spirit functions as a prophetic gift with which God endows individuals or groups for special tasks. Although some nonbelievers are on one occasion also seized by the Spirit, the gift is normally given to believers as something special, as something given in addition to their general calling into the Christian community.[77]

Pentecostalists draw a threefold lesson from their favorite book, the Acts of the Apostles. It teaches them that religion has to do with experience or, more precisely, with visible experience; that the Pentecostal experience of the Spirit can and indeed does happen over and over again; that the experience marks a decisive, final stage in the spiritual development of the Christian believer.

The notion of religious "experience" has never been absent from Christianity. Mystics like Teresa of Avila, Puritan divines like Jonathan Edwards, German pietists like Count Zinzendorf, and Methodists like the Wesley brothers all agreed that religion has to do with an inner feeling and sentiment. And all of them ascribed religious experience not to every believer but only to an elite. Catholic tradition finds this elite among its canonized saints and feels that a monastic, ascetic lifestyle serves as its foundation. People with real religious experience were rare and could be found in monasteries and nuns' convents. Protestants, by contrast, include a much larger group in the elite; in fact, they consider every believer a potential candidate for that spiritual elite. In the seventeenth century, American Puritans took great care to have only "experienced" believers admitted into their congregations—individuals who had had a powerful conversion experience. One sign of its authenticity was a moral, saintly life. The Puritans knew, however, that saintliness remains invisible in this life. In the words of Samuel Willard (1640–1706), the great Puritan divine: "Their glory for the present is within. Outwardly they look like other men, they eat, drink, labour, converse in earthly employments, as others do. The communion which they have with God in all of these, is a secret thing."[78]

How can the truly converted be recognized under such unfavorable circumstances? The seventeenth-century American Puritans saw no other possibility than to rely on their fellow Christians' "relations," that is on their orally delivered conversion reports. Only those whose relations seemed to echo authentic religious experience were admitted to the community.

Pentecostalists share the Puritan emphasis on spiritual awareness and generally want their members to have had a conversion experience before being admitted to full membership through baptism. Conversion, however, marks no more than the first step in one's spiritual development. A second and final stage must be attained, and this happens in the "baptism with the Holy Spirit." Like conversion, Spirit-baptism comes from God and does not grow out of free human deliberation. Also like conversion, it is something felt and acknowledged by the believer. But unlike conversion, Spirit-baptism is visible to others, having an outburst in glossolalia as its physical, objective sign. In this outburst, according to Pentecostal belief, "we may unequivocally and without reserve identify an act of God himself."[79]

Glossolalic expression, when first uttered by a believer, qualifies as a real miracle. Like Catholics, Pentecostalists reject the common, chiefly Protestant rationalism, with its theory of the "cessation of miracles" at the end of the apostolic period. According to this theory, God used miracles in order to impress his message onto the untrained minds of the early believers; later, as Christianity had outgrown its formative phase, miracles were no longer needed. Such a rationalist view angers Pentecostalists. They believe that miracles continue even today. Although it may be true that God's Spirit only rarely manifested itself during long periods of Christian history, this must not be taken as evidence of its inactivity. Miracles, of which glossolalia is but one kind, can happen today—and in fact do happen—as they happened in biblical times. The creedal statement of the Assemblies of God, the largest American Pentecostal church, teaches the ongoing relevance of speaking with tongues. Glossolalia not only functions as the "initial physical sign" of "the baptism of believers in the Holy Ghost." It also continues with them, adding "a necessary dimension to worshipful relationship with God." As one Assemblies minister explains, glossolalia "should be an experience that is perpetuated personally and publicly."[80]

Glossolalia, as we have seen, is not the only, and often not even the most prominent, form of spiritual expression in worship. Prophecy has come to play an important role. The book of Acts refers quite explicitly to revelations received by believers. On the day of the Pentecost miracle, the apostle Peter is reported to have preached to the crowds. In his sermon, he quotes an Old Testament prophecy that he thinks of as having been fulfilled. That prophecy, given through the prophet Joel, announced generalized prophethood for all members of the community; indeed, all humankind is said to be gifted with the prophetic Spirit and invited to exercise it: "In the last days it will be, God declares, that I will pour out my Spirit upon all flesh, and your sons and your daughters shall prophesy, and your young men shall see visions, and your old men shall dream dreams. Even upon my slaves, both men and women, in those days I will pour out my Spirit; and they shall prophesy" (Acts 2:17–18). For charismatic believers, the gift of prophecy includes that of healing. While the Pentecost story as told in the book of Acts does not explicitly refer to healing, it hints at the subject by reporting that "wonders and signs were being done by the apostles" (Acts 2:43). That book repeatedly refers to the subject. In chapter 3, apostles Peter and John heal a lame man in Jerusalem; in chapter 4, a prayer mentions the fact that Christian preaching is accompanied by healings, signs, and wonders, performed in the name of Jesus. Christians, according to the book of Acts, are indeed called to the double ministry of healing and prophesying.

Noncharismatic Christians generally argue that at some point in the early church, God decided to stop making his will known to his people. There was no need for new revelations, for believers could rely on earlier prophecies that had been written down and formed the sacred scriptures. Pentecostals call this the "cessationist error"; for them, God has not ceased to make his will known through men and women called into prophethood. One apologist explained that cessationists argue like a spouse who tells her husband: "From now on, you can keep quiet. At any rate I won't listen to you any more, for I have the letters that you wrote me long ago. All you can possibly mean to say can be found in them." When speaking about the presence of the Spirit in glossolalia, ecstasy, prophetic revelation, and effective prayer, the Bible documents the beginning, not the end.[81]

The public stage on which glossolalia and other gifts of the Spirit are exercised, is the worship service:

> If a church believes that God reveals himself through the Holy Spirit, that people can be converted and transformed, that He heals men, that people can be baptized in the Holy Spirit, that love and forgiveness are possible—then the

church must expect these things to occur in its worship service, and allow opportunity for them to happen.

The author summarizes the Pentecostal mind well. "Our integrity is questioned," he adds, "if we proclaim these important deeds of God, and yet it remains but words and nothing happens in our gatherings." For him, as for all Pentecostals, the image of a "dead" congregation in which "nothing happens," in which the Holy Spirit no longer "fills" its members, no longer dances, speaks, laughs, heals, praises, and sings through them, cannot be but the final, Satanic threat.[82]

4.   Conclusion: A Story with Two Endings—Ritual Intellectualized and Charisma Routinized

Sociologists have studied typical histories of groups and found certain patterns that help the historian to understand what happens as they grow and take on more definite forms. Typically, groups have "charismatic" beginnings with great formal flexibility; later, they settle for stability and order. According to one of the "laws" of social development first described by Max Weber, charismatic fluidity wanes. In the light of Weber's law, we would expect that Paul's charismatic and ecstatic ritual did not survive for a long time. We might have the same expectation with regard to modern Pentecostal worship. Charismatic groups have a precarious existence and are generally short-lived. If they do not simply dissolve, sooner or later they are supplanted by more organized, less spontaneous structures. The charismatic phase, according to social scientists, is followed by a calmer one, and the ecstatic movement or sect gradually becomes an organized church—not unlike a pair of lovers eventually settling for a marriage and setting up a regular household. What happened in the early church and in the twentieth-century Pentecostal movement certainly follows the outline indicated by this pattern.

Despite their general similarity, however, the stories of Pauline ritual and Pentecostal worship have different endings, representing the two possibilities for the "second stage" expected after the waning of original charismatic effervescence. The "second stage" may be either the gradual (though complete) replacement of charisma by something else, or it may be characterized by the continuation of charisma in a new, "routinized" and less spontaneous form. *Replacement* involves the abandonment of earlier ritual forms that are now seen as rudimentary and inadequate; their place is taken by new ones that are deemed more appropriate, more advanced, or more "authentic." New tastes and new insights demand new ways of worship. In the case of *routinization*, by contrast, things stay as they were in the beginning, which is seen as the ideal time. Routinization involves the conscious, faithful repetition of what people did at the beginning, at the period of excitement. By repeating what the fathers (and mothers) did at the beginning, *in illo tempore*, people express the wish to share in and re-live the original excitement—and they may actually recreate some of it. Now, the first or "replacement" variety can be seen in the early church as Pauline ecstasy was suffocated and extinguished and replaced by the intellectual, instructional type of worship. The process of routinization, with its attempt to keep alive the original inspiration, characterizes much of the development of Pentecostal ritual.

Unfortunately, the scant evidence—interpolations in the Pauline text, a few lines in Tertullian's *Apology*, and the possible representation of ecstatic behavior in early Christian art—does not allow us to get much insight into the afterlife of early Christian enthusiasm. The emergence of a nonecstatic form of Christian worship is equally obscure. It is already in existence in the pseudo-Pauline letters to Timothy and in the work of Justin, and most likely does not represent an innovation of these authors.

While the character of the Eucharist itself did not change fundamentally during the first three centuries, this cannot be said of the ritual framework into which it came to be embedded. The main change that occurred was the addition of scriptural reading and preaching. In Paul's writings, the sacred meal preceded and actually induced glossolalic and prophetic speech, in which the Lord made his presence visible and audible in a powerful way. By the end of the first century (Timothy) and, better documented, by the middle of the second (Justin), the ecstatic ritual had given place to a calmer service of worship, one dominated by intellectual concerns. Thus, we can compare the following patterns:

Paul: sacred meal—sacred word (inspired utterance)

Justin: sacred word (scripture)—sacred meal

Transferred from the end of the ritual to its beginning, the sacred word changed its character: it moved from ecstasy to rational discourse, from Paul the Possessed to Timothy the Teacher, or, in the words of Nietzsche, from the Dionysian to the Apollonian. In Paul's communities, Christ's reign would be most visible in the ecstasy of trance, possession, and glossolalic utterance. For Justin, on the other hand, Christ's rule has a different character. According to him, the Old Testament phrase, "The Lord will send forth the rod of power from Jerusalem, and dominate" is "a prediction of the mighty word which his apostles, going forth from Jerusalem, preached everywhere, and which . . . we everywhere both receive and teach." Christ rules through the word of his teachers who explain scripture. Hence the dominating position of scripture in the intellectual variety of Christian worship. In Pauline ecstatic ritual, on the other hand, no one would even consider reading a text from scripture. Why would anyone rely on something written, which only indirectly testifies to the Lord, when the Lord's Spirit is present, and thus the Lord himself?[83]

When the Corinthians arrived at a Christian meeting, they had to wait for some time until the Lord manifested himself in the ecstatic speech of some of the participants; in Justin's community, by contrast, the word of God was present even before people arrived. Available in scripture, its presence was quite independent of any ecstatic mood. The divine word was no longer a living reality manifesting itself spontaneously; instead, it was found enshrined in a book. It was not the ecstatic lay person, possessed by the Holy Spirit, who would utter the sacred word, but the teacher who, by reading and explaining, brought it to the community. In the words of Charles Chauncy (1705–87), a bitter enemy of eighteenth-century religious emotionalism: "Where God really works on their hearts, by his Spirit" people will get "an enlightened mind, and not raised affections." The emergence, by the time of Hippolytus (ca. 220 CE), of biblical commentaries and, at least in the case of Origen, of the exegetical sermon (which would explain the scriptural text rather than offer random reflections) continued the trend begun by people like Justin and enhanced the intellectual aspect of the ritual. Here we can recognize the origins of what came to be the shape of the Christian liturgy as it exists to this day in many churches.[84]

Ironically, Paul, who defended if not promoted ecstatic worship in New Testament Christianity, contributed to its decline. He did so by insisting that glossolalic speech be accompanied by an "interpretation," i.e., by rationally understandable discourse that translated the angelic language into understandable Greek discourse. Although he appreciated glossolalic utterance, he was unable to tolerate its autonomy and independence. He did not accord it an independent status in the repertoire of ritual acts. He also preferred prophetic, i.e., articulate, utterance. Here Georges Bataille, the French essayist, can help us understand the tension if not contradiction between rational discourse and essentially untranslatable ecstatic utterance. "A few Christians have broken from the language of the word and come to the ecstatic one. In their case, an aptitude has to be supposed which made mystical experience inevitable in spite of Christianity's essential reliance on speech." Christians like Paul rely on speech and thereby compromise glossolalic utterance and ecstasy. It seems that Paul actually tended to relegate ecstatic behavior to the private realm, so that in public—"in church"—rational speech prevailed: "I thank God that I speak in tongues more than all of you; nevertheless, in church I would rather speak five words with my mind, in order to instruct others also, than ten thousand words in a tongue" (1 Cor. 14:18–19). Paul, moreover, must actually be considered the founder of a literate Christianity. Historians of early Christianity point out that Paul, in 55–57 CE, wrote and edited most of his letters—notably the ones sent to the Galatians, Corinthians, and Romans—in a short period of time during which he was based in Ephesus. Paul the charismatic missionary had become Paul the pastor who aimed at safeguarding what he had accomplished. In his letters he appears as a systematic thinker who delights in teaching and writing. His editing of the first set of his letters made him the father of the emerging Christian book culture. (A generation after Paul, that culture was flourishing, and the authors of the four gospels were writing up the traditions concerning Jesus.) Pseudo-Pauline literature is presumably right in depicting Paul as a book-lover who travels with a portable library. When he insists on glossolalic utterance being "interpreted" and calls for order in worship—"all things should be done decently and in order" (1 Cor. 14:40)—he paves the way for those later church leaders who suppressed charismatic worship, replacing it with more stable forms that feature reading and instruction.[85]

Whereas in the early church, charisma eventually gave way to more stable, institutional forms of intellectual worship, the modern Pentecostal movement developed along different lines. Although it shares the instability and precariousness of early Christian enthusiasm, its charismatic ritual was not replaced by intellectual or any other kind of worship. Rather, Pentecostalism's original charismatic outburst became routinized, subordinated to institutional regularities and constraints. Despite having lost some of its original effervescence, third-generation Pentecostal worship still retains its charismatic features. Services of worship provide fresh religious experience when they allow the congregation (or at least some of those who attend) to be filled with the Holy Spirit and to exercise supernatural gifts like prophesying, healing, speaking in tongues, or pronouncing effective prayers.

Routinized features of present-day Pentecostal worship are easily visible to any observer. Trancelike states, typical of the early period, have become rare. The ease with which participants move in and out of glossolalic expression demonstrates that for them, "the understanding of what 'praying in the spirit' is has changed somewhat." No longer the spontaneous outburst of someone in the "dissociated" state of trance, it is a learned behavior exercised at will. Trance is generally replaced by a milder state that can be termed enthusiasm. Emotional preaching, loud instrumental music, and a regular choir's singing all contribute to an atmosphere of enthusiasm. Effective prayer, too, shows signs of being toned down, losing the tinge of the supernatural and spectacular. Effective prayer, the laying-on of hands, and anointing may make people "feel better" rather than cure them right away. "Therapy" tends to supplant "healing." While some of the Pentecostal ministers deplore the waning of the Spirit, others encourage the more respectable, sedate forms. The ecstatic "Africanisms," so typical of early Pentecostal worship, no longer enjoy general support. "Speaking in tongues is not spooky," explained Jean Stone in 1964,

> it's wholesome, good, clean, beautiful. We use no weird positions, no peculiar gymnastics. Don't add your own little goodies to it. If you make it sound peculiar, you'll scare people pea-green. . . . Don't moan or shriek. . . . And beware of personal prophecy, or prophecy about catastrophic happenings. If we seem too strange to outsiders, we're not going to get many outsiders to become insiders. You'll only attract desperate people.

Here the charismatic style of worship has been accommodated to white middle-class tastes and made palatable to almost anyone.[86]

As the typically charismatic features of worship are toned down, certain elements of mainstream, institutionalized liturgy re-enter the sanctuary. The initial unwillingness to celebrate the Eucharist, characteristic of the early twentieth-century Pentecostal movement and its nineteenth-century "holiness" predecessors, no longer exists. For Pentecostal leaders like Bartleman, the Eucharist simply played no role at all. In their enthusiasm, Bartleman and his contemporaries relied on their immediate access to the Holy Spirit. Any mediation through carefully designed liturgies, ordained clergy, and sacramental mediation, was suspect. It belonged to the ways of the "old" churches that had not tasted the Spirit. Today, this attitude has changed. Although the Eucharist cannot be said to play a major role, it has found a place in charismatic worship. The Assemblies of God, for instance, offer communion services four times a year. Although they have not developed a full-blown sacramental system and theology, they have moved one step away from the original position. Pentecostal worship has adopted more traditional, noncharismatic forms.[87]

Despite all routinization and compromises with more traditional, non-ecstatic forms of worship, the Spirit still operates in charismatic meetings. People often feel its active presence. Still filled with the Spirit, they rejoice in the Lord who works wonders among them.

Our analysis has stressed two possible developments typical of ecstatic worship. The ecstatic side may be completely suppressed in a process in which calm, intellectual forms come to dominate. If the ecstatic side is appreciated, it must be made permanent by introducing regularity and controlled forms. In discussing these two developments, we must not forget their common beginning: the powerful manifestation of the divine in and through worship. At any stage of the movement that leads away from an original charismatic inspiration, a new beginning can be made. At least in worship, no "entropic" tendency inevitably dissipates *all* spiritual energy. It seems that there is always a tiny, almost imperceptible particle of the spiritual glow, hidden, perhaps, under heaps of cold ashes. From there, the fire can start again, and the cycle can be repeated.

Epilogue: Divine Meekness, Divine Majesty
The Familiar and the Awesome Deity

In the foregoing study, we have dealt with six major ways in which Christians approach their God. We have spoken about praise, prayer, preaching, sacrifice, sacrament, and ecstasy as the "sacred games" of worship. These games are the instruments or mechanisms by way of which the faithful establish and maintain contact with their Lord. At the end of our extended essay on the "instruments" of worship, we feel we should say more about the Lord to whom worship is directed.

The practice of Christian worship reflects two basic orientations that correspond to two different experiences of the divine. God may be experienced as majestic and superior, or as familiar and loving: as God the Father, or Christ the Son. These conceptions, closeness and distance of the divine, reveal two theological temperaments and, indeed, world views. One view emphasizes the superior aspect of God: "It is he alone who has immortality and dwells in unapproachable light, whom no one has ever seen or can see; to him be honor and eternal dominion" (1 Tim. 6:16). And the other insists on the Lord's own promise: "Where two or three are gathered in my name, I am there among them" (Matt. 18:20).

A good example of a twentieth-century theologian preferring the veneration of a majestic God is Rudolf Otto (1869–1937). With a huge apparatus of comparative material, the eminent German historian of religions and theologian advocated what he termed "numinous" worship. In his *Idea of the Holy* (1917), Otto tried to evoke and explain the majestic side of God. Among the divine attributes discussed in theological manuals, he selects incomprehensibility, omnipotence, and holiness as the most characteristic ones, concentrating them in a Latin term: *tremendum*, the reality that makes one tremble. He perceives the biblical god as an awful, majestic power, beyond human comprehension and rational calculation. Even the angels do not immediately relate to God. They can only acknowledge his otherness by shouting their "Holy, holy, holy." The biblical prophet Isaiah, who in a vision finds himself transported into the presence of God, stammers, "Woe to me! I am lost, for I am a man of unclean lips, and I live among a people of unclean lips; yet my eyes have seen the King, Yahweh of hosts!" (Isa. 6:5). Before this God, "the soul, held speechless, trembles inwardly to the farthest fiber of its being." For Otto, the prophet's trembling was more than a story from distant biblical times. In May

1911, he experienced "a shock of solemn awe" (*ein feierlicher Schreck*) when he heard the angelic words—*Kadosh, kadosh, kadosh*—sung in a ghetto synagogue in Mogador, Morocco. He would never forget the experience which colored his perception of Christian praise.

> "I have heard the *Sanctus, sanctus, sanctus*," he reports, "sung by the cardinals at St. Peter's, the *Swiat, swiat, swiat* in the cathedral of the Kremlin, and the *Hagios, hagios, hagios* intoned by the patriarch of Jerusalem. These are the most sublime words that have ever come from human lips. In whatever language they are heard, these words never fail to reach the deepest level of the human soul, stirring up the sense of the great and awesome mystery of the transcendent, awakening it from its sleep."

Otto terms God the *mysterium tremendum*, the awful mystery. "The truly 'mysterious' object," he explains, "is beyond our apprehension and comprehension, not only because our knowledge has certain immovable limits, but because in it we come upon something inherently 'wholly other,' whose kind and character are incommensurable with our own, and before which we therefore recoil in a wonder that strikes us chill and numb."[1]

Worship, Otto felt, must always emphasize the sacred. As someone interested in the promotion and renewal of Lutheran worship, Otto devised new liturgies, for the new recognition of God's majesty required adequate forms of expression. His model liturgy was the Catholic Mass, though with a characteristic change. He left out the Eucharist, replacing it by silent adoration of the aniconic deity. The congregation would kneel in silence, contemplating, it seems, a huge stained glass window, inscribed with the word "Father," vaguely reminiscent of Gothic rose windows (ill. 4). Historically, Otto's inscribed window replaces *maiestas Domini*, the enthroned Christ often represented in the apse of Byzantine churches. Characteristically, Otto's worship was directed to God the Father, not to Christ, for the latter would be too close, too anthropomorphic, too familiar. For Otto, silence, a sublime gesture of submission, was the only adequate reaction to the majestic deity. Even in the human world, the presence of a person of superior rank commands silence. After a period of silence, Otto's service moves on to the Lord's Prayer: "Our Father in heaven, hallowed be your name, your kingdom come." In Otto's liturgy, even the term "Father," often taken to imply intimacy, reflects Old Testament notions of God's royal majesty, transcendent power, and remoteness.[2]

Sister Ann and Luise Rinser (an English nun and a German Catholic writer) have ideas about God and worship that differ very much from those held by Otto. Interviewed by an anthropologist in the early 1970s, Sister Ann explains that she has recently gone through a period of spiritual growth that led her to adopt a new view of God. "You see as a child I had always a great fear of the retaliation of God—I think this lies at the heart of the relationships with God, whether he is an awesome and wrathful figure or whether he is kind and forgiving." Sister Ann belongs to a group of nuns who live not in a convent, but in ordinary houses, often in run-down city areas. They have no purpose-built chapels, but invite priests to celebrate Mass with them in the house where they have a simple meal, then the Mass, and then a discussion. The ordinary table serves as the altar. They talk, drink communion wine out of a chalice which they pass around, and take the consecrated bread with their own hands. The atmosphere is relaxed, and the nuns enjoy the egalitarian relationship with the priest, who, like the local bishop, is "sympathetic" to their modern views. This relationship echoes, the anthropologist speculates, "their relationship with a close, friendly divinity in touch with humanity. It is a move to a more mature relationship in which the father is no longer to be feared."[3]

The friendly God stands at the top end of a great chain of benign beings. The divine Father is followed by a brotherly Christ, a sympathetic bishop, an understanding priest and, ultimately, the nuns themselves who sympathize with the sick and downtrodden among whom they engage in social work. The entire structure depends on the character of God whose compassion the nuns emulate.

In Germany, Luise Rinser went through a development comparable to Sister Ann's. When thinking of "God, the abyss," she felt the full impact of the divine majesty which made her tremble with fear (*Angst*). Only after realizing that Christ covers the abyss with his human qualities was she able to overcome her fearfulness and meet a human Christ. In a letter she sent to her friend and spiritual director, the Jesuit Karl Rahner, she reports her feeling of divine closeness at communion and her being overwhelmed with tears ("but no one saw the tears").[4]

Sister Ann's and Luise Rinser's spiritual journeys must be seen in the context of shifts that in the 1960s changed the spiritual climate of the Catholic church. We find evidence of new sensibilities at all levels: in official statements of the council, in catechisms approved by national episcopal conferences, and in opinion polls. According to a statement adopted in 1964 by the Second Vatican Council, Christ, though "sitting at the right hand of the Father," is "continually active in the world," guiding people and nourishing them through his sacrament. Christ seen as a close being has revolutionized Catholic sensibilities. "Scripture does not speak only of God's inaccessible distance. It proclaims still more insistently his closeness. He is not far from each of us, for in him we live and move and have our being (Acts 17:28)," explains the *Dutch Catechism* (1967). When in the early 1980s the American Jesuit-sociologist Andrew Greeley asked respondents to choose from a list of divine attributes those closest to their own ideas and experiences, he found the same new spirituality: images, pictures, and stories of God were generally more benign, more gracious, and more affectionate than the judgmental and legalistic set of ideas promoted in pre-Vatican II days. God had a softer image. Catholics now tended to imagine God as "mother, lover, spouse and friend," the sociologist found. For them, God resembled more the jovial, democratic Pope John XXIII than the stern, aristocratic Pius XII. Something fundamental had happened in the Catholic "religious imagination" which had aligned itself with and echoed "the Sixties Spiritual Awakening." Catholics both contributed to and were influenced by a larger movement that promoted racial equality, the end of the Vietnam War, non-Western spiritualities, and a new democratic practice in universities and churches. With the old hierarchies, the old, dominating Father-God also lost his previously unquestioned place in the world view of many Christians.[5]

Otto's worship of the divine majesty forms a strong contrast to the two women's worship of the Lord's meekness. It is this twofold experience that we will now briefly look at from four angles. We will look at its background in Christian history, explore its pattern from the perspective of the history of religions, analyze its psychological structure, and, by way of conclusion, get a glimpse of its echoes in art.

Clerical Solemnity vs. Mystical and Popular Intimacy

First-century Christianity, which venerated a lowly Christ who had died the death of a criminal, provided a strong contrast to the solemn sacrificial cult celebrated at the Jerusalem Temple and the pagan temples of the Greco-Roman world. Christ had been resurrected by the divine Father; however, the resurrection had not removed him from the community of believers. Christ was present in a tangible way in ecstatic rituals and magical meals. The heavenly Father, by contrast, remained in the background; yet, even he could be drawn into closeness, because Christians felt they shared Christ's high degree of intimacy with the Father, for they considered themselves to be his children.

During the first generations of Christianity, there is little recorded about numinous feelings that may have accompanied their services of worship. One of the isolated references is in the epistle to the Hebrews. This source advocates worship with awe, though without specifying its ritual setting: "Let us give thanks, by which we offer to God an acceptable worship with reverence and awe; for indeed our God is a consuming fire" (Hebr. 12:28–29). The God worshiped by the early Christians is none other than the Old Testament God, whom the book of Deuteronomy calls "a consuming fire" (Deut. 4:24). "The general atmosphere of Hebrews is . . . one of awe before the divine majesty, before that dark and blazing power, which it likes to evoke in terms of fire."[6]

One of the earliest theologians to promote liturgical solemnity was John Chrysostom (ca. 350–407), and Otto does not fail to quote him as an authority. John's promotion of a majestic, numinous liturgy, celebrated in honor of a majestic deity, is closely related to the clericalization of worship, i.e., to its being organized and controlled by a professional priesthood. The full divinity of Christ, according to John Chrysostom, is not only present in the consecrated bread and wine, but also in the celebrating priests. Christ, the divine person, acts as the chief officiant at the eucharistic celebration. The visible, human priests who celebrate Mass manifest the invisible, divine consecrator, i.e., Christ himself. Those who receive communion must behave as if the Lord himself gave them the sacred food: "When you see the priest administering the Eucharist to you, do not think that the priest does this, but consider rather that it is Christ you see stretching out his hand."[7]

John Chrysostom's identification of the priest (or bishop) with Christ must be seen as the final outcome of a liturgical development that had begun as early as the second century. Whereas the first Christians celebrated the Eucharist without a presider, that role had gradually emerged and finally established itself firmly. The presider, often called *presbyteros* ("elder") or *episkopos* ("overseer") and always a man rather than a woman, had a regular office surrounded with much dignity. He stood closer to God than the rest of the Christian believers, and was the only one who could approach and truly worship the deity. Through elaborate rites of consecration, the bishop assumed a superior, quasi-divine status. The lay congregation, although attending the service and occasionally responding to the presider's prayers, were reduced to the role of spectators watching a sacred activity. The clericalized ritual did much to balance the popular notion of Christ's sacramental closeness with ideas of dignity, distance, and awe. Far from being easily available and accessible, the divine is located at the far end of a cosmic hierarchy, and the distance can only be bridged with much caution by specially trained and consecrated intermediaries: priests and bishops. These protect the sacred from being in the hands of ordinary men and women who have (supposedly) little understanding of the divine mysteries.

In the fourth century, numinous vocabulary begins to appear in descriptions of Christian worship. Cyril of Jerusalem speaks of "that most awful hour" of the eucharistic liturgy, and the sermons of John Chrysostom are full of references to the numinous, "awe-inspiring" character of the Christian liturgy. Chrysostom's theology and liturgical practice blend to create a charged, numinous atmosphere. The evidence is overwhelming. Now liturgy itself is referred to in numinous language: the priest celebrates "that fearsome, awful sacrifice" or "this most awe-inspiring rite," and the laity must "attend with piety our awful mysteries." Chrysostom's priest, when offering the sacrifice, is attended by angels who fill the entire sanctuary. The church father assures us that a credible witness had actually been allowed the privilege of seeing the otherwise invisible spirits—"a host of angels clad in bright robes, encircling the altar and bowing their heads, as you would see soldiers bow, when they stand in the presence of their king." During part of Mass, the altar was made invisible through the closing of curtains, possibly to protect the sacred rite from profane eyes. At certain moments, the curtain was opened to dramatic effect: "Whenever you see the curtains drawn up, then consider that heaven is let down from above, that the angels are descending." He insists on the spiritual preparation of those who receive communion; to partake of the sacred food in an "unworthy" state can have terrible consequences. "Approach it with all awe and purity," he commands, for "those who partake unworthily will suffer the ultimate torments" in hell. As a bishop, Chrysostom prefers martyrdom to giving Christ's "awesome blood" to an unworthy communicant. He instructs the faithful to help the clergy in their effort to prevent unworthy communicants from profaning the fearful mystery: "If you see that someone, though being a member, commits fornication and yet approaches the mysteries, then you shall say to the deacon: This one is unworthy of the mysteries. Turn away his impure hands!"[8]

According to John Chrysostom, the faithful encounter Christ's full deity as they worship their Lord. He insists on the divine nature of Christ. The Lord must never be considered a mere creature, as Arius the heretic (ca. 260–336) had done. In the fourth century, when the church decided not to adopt the view of Arius and when the Eucharist came to be the official state ritual of the late Roman Empire, liturgy assumed an increasingly numinous character. By 400 CE, the Eastern as well as the Western liturgies included an explicit acknowledgment of the awesome nature of the sacrifice by placing the Sanctus, the singing of "Holy, holy, holy," at the beginning of the central act of sacrificial consecration.[9]

The numinous atmosphere the priests established in the fourth century continues to shape worship, especially in the liturgical traditions of Catholicism, Eastern Orthodoxy, high-church Anglicanism, and Episcopalianism: the prominence of the priest as presider, the wearing of vestments, the burning of incense, the use of costly chalices, the Catholic priest's celibacy, the solemn and archaic language (even after Vatican II's abandonment of Latin in the Catholic liturgy), reference to arcane theological doctrines like transubstantiation, and so on. A recent advocate of liturgical solemnity and "triumphalism" insists that at Mass, kneeling, reverent inclinations of the head, kissing the altar, and the humble folding of hands should not be considered irrelevant; they are nothing but adequate behavior in the context of standing before God's majesty. He agrees with Francis de Sales who in the seventeenth century reminded his fellow Christians that at worship "we are standing before the same God before whom the angels tremble." Rudolf Otto would certainly have agreed with the Catholic saint.[10]

The theocentric conceptions of authors like Otto focus on the divine as majestic, distant, and impressive. They can invoke a long and important theological tradition as well as a diversity of ritual patterns. In what we have called the "minimalist" version of the eucharistic sacrament, the distant majesty of God is strongly underlined. Unapproachable and transcendent, God does not mingle with humans; he stays away from them, granting only brief and "minimal" contact which is more often intellectual than physical and real. Even in the sacrament of his earthly presence, God does not make himself really visible and available. Rituals of instruction are frequently based on the same idea of the distant God, especially in Karl Barth's theology of preaching. God's coming can be announced and heralded in a process of teaching, but that teaching does not bring about his closeness. If God uses the word of scripture and the preacher's word to bring someone to faith, he reaches out of the distance, acting as Barth says "vertically from above." Praise, finally, can rest on a similar conception. If God is extolled in an absolute manner by those angels who sing their "Holy, holy, holy" without reference to any saving act, then he also stays distant from merely human concerns. He is praised for himself, for having the greatest value in the universe. According to the theocentric experience in worship, God, though somehow present, maintains his distance. Human beings sense their unworthiness, their smallness, their need to realize their humble, subordinate place in the hierarchy of being.

Certain experts on worship in Germany have accused the liturgical committees of their churches of promoting too much elitist solemnity, too much clerical "Byzantinism" on Sunday mornings. Liturgy should be more popular. Rather than elevate the congregation to join the angels in praising the divine majesty as described by Rudolf Otto, one should bring God into people's everyday lives, making worship meaningful to them. There can be little doubt that Sister Ann and Luise Rinser would agree.[11]

Whereas clerical theologies emphasize the distance that separates creator and creature, biblical realists (as we may call them) underline God's closeness to humankind. God is not a retired, distant Lord, but a present power. God constantly intervenes with his creation, caring for and helping his creatures. Not only the existence, but also the intervention of God in history and individual lives are taken to be empirical facts. The early Christian view of the close God has always been present in Christianity and has often helped to mitigate, if not actually to subvert, clerical notions of the distant, majestic deity. Four movements have specifically tried to give prominence to the meekness of God and Christ: medieval mysticism, the Protestant Reformation of the sixteenth century, twentieth-century Pentecostalism with its wide ecumenical echoes, and the Catholic reform movement generally associated with the Second Vatican Council (1962–65).

Mystics, in their raptures and ecstasies, have always experienced God or Christ as a dear father or as the soul's sweet friend and bridegroom. In the twelfth century, Bernard of Clairvaux expressed mystical sentiment in his sermons on the Song of Songs. He reads the Song as an allegory of the love relationship between God and the human soul, a relationship intensified by Christ's teaching. In the Cistercian abbot's rhetoric, God's majesty belongs to the Old Testament, whereas the New Testament reveals his fatherly closeness: "Where now is that thundering cry which used to sound so frequently and so alarmingly in the days of old, *I am the Lord, I am the Lord*? Now I am given a prayer whose very beginning charms me with the name of *Father*, which fills me with confidence that I shall obtain what I ask for." In Bernardian mysticism, the Our Father invokes God's paternal love rather than his patriarchal majesty. The mystics appreciated God as "the father of mercies and the God of all consolation" (2 Cor. 1:3).[12]

Fourteenth- and fifteenth-century popular mysticism, especially in the form of the *devotio moderna*, not only continued Bernard's theology; it also preluded and indeed prepared the way for whatever reforms were to be accomplished subsequently. Originating in the Netherlands, the new spirituality de-emphasized the clerical church and fostered the individual's direct contact with God. Its classic statement is *The Imitation of Christ*, compiled between 1420 and 1427 by Thomas à Kempis, an Augustinian canon living in a monastery near the Dutch town of Zwolle. Besides teaching Christlike humility as the supreme virtue and as a way of life, the *Imitation* recommends adopting Christ as a friend and ever-present protective spirit and receiving him in the holy sacrament. While Thomas encourages his readers to "approach this sacrament with profound awe and reverence" and states that "God—eternal, boundless, and of infinite power—does great things in heaven and on earth that are a complete mystery to us," he actually moves away from traditional notions of clerical superiority and the concomitant idea of God's majesty. Christ, the friend, is more important than God, the Father almighty. The basis of Thomas's treatise is biblical. The book reads like a tapestry of scriptural allusions—but never quotes any other authors.[13]

By rejecting priestly mediation, emphasizing "the priesthood of all the faithful," and making the Bible available in vernacular translations, the Protestant reformers promoted the worship of a God who stands close to humankind. Although Luther and Calvin are known for their preaching of a majestic God, they also emphasize his love for humankind. He is ultimately a loving and forgiving spirit. Luther's *Small Catechism* (1529) insists that "God, the Father almighty" provides his faithful daily and abundantly with all the necessities of life, protects them from danger, and preserves them from evil; "all this he does out of his pure, fatherly, and divine goodness and mercy." Luther's doctrine of the sinner's "justification" also works with a maternal, nurturing image of God: God is like a mother who lovingly accepts her naughty children. In America, we find a similar emphasis in the work of Jonathan Edwards. He could preach on "Sinners in the Hands of an Angry God" (1741) and wanted to "lie low before God, as in the dust." But he also wishes nothing more than to become "as a little child" before a caring and nurturing God. In a mystical moment, he was led to feel God's majesty and grace "in a sweet conjunction; majesty and meekness joined together; it was a sweet and gentle, and holy majesty; and also a majestic meekness; an awful sweetness; a high and great, and holy gentleness." Whenever Edwards speaks about God's majesty, he is quick to add an attenuating qualification. God "is indeed possessed of infinite majesty, to inspire us with reverence and adoration, yet that majesty need not terrify us, for we behold it blended with humility, meekness, and sweet condescension." Despite Edwards's insistence on God's supremacy, the balance is always tipped toward meekness and accessibility. In twentieth-century Protestant theology, Karl Barth emerged as a leading voice preaching the "humanity of God" and the closeness of Christ as "our brother." By doing so, Barth revised the exaggerations he had indulged in when, as an angry young man, he had promoted nothing but God's majesty. The mature thinker admitted that the idea he had preached earlier went too far. He even denounced Calvin's over-emphasis on God's independence and omnipotence. Had Calvin avoided his exaggerations, then Geneva (the city Calvinism ruled, or rather terrorized) "would not have become such a dismal affair."[14]

Clerical theologies often work with an implicit distinction between the sacred period of Christ and the apostles, during which the divine was close and miracles did happen, and the post-apostolic period of the church in which God is essentially absent or his presence more veiled than before. By contrast, Pentecostalism rejects that distinction: today, God is as close as in the days of the Bible, and miracles continue to happen. By sending his Spirit to manifest itself among his faithful, God never leaves his people alone.

While notions of the distant deity favor forms of worship that focus exclusively on God, the alternative idea of divine accessibility promotes forms in which the human person has the place of a partner. One might speak of "desacralization," the shift from "theocentric" to "anthropocentric" forms. "Anthropocentric" ideas of worship, which bring the divine close to the human, are quite unlike those suggested by the representatives of deistic, liberal theology. Like their opponents, biblical realists can invoke a long history as well as a diversity of ritual patterns. As a partner, God can be drawn into an interaction of giving and taking, and because Christ gave much, his friends can receive from the inexhaustible treasures. At the sacrifice of Mass, the interaction functions smoothly and almost without effort. Christ has made God benign, merciful, helpful, even indulgent. He will never withhold his gifts from his people. The reception of the sacrament, too, more encouraged than ever before in twentieth-century Catholicism, brings Christ close to his believers. As an anthropologist has observed among "modern" Catholic nuns, the Eucharist can forge a "relationship with a close, friendly divinity in touch with humanity. It is a move to a more mature relationship in which the father is no longer to be feared." In ecstatic rituals, the human and the divine almost merge, for Christ can speak, heal, and act through men and women, and he does so with astonishing frequency, even today. Christ is readily available for the faithful who celebrate the "real presence" which for them is tangible. Christ, though divine and the Lord, also appears as a brother, friend, and familiar spirit. This is why he can be approached with confidence in childlike prayer. In preaching, especially in evangelistic and therapeutic preaching, the divine word comes within the reach of all believers. Everyone can experience the transforming, existential quality of God's call to conversion. Everyone can feel the transforming, healing power of the sacred word interpreted and applied by the preacher-therapist. Praise, as concrete thanksgiving for divine favors received, reflects the same theological orientation. It is based on a relationship with a loving and kindly deity who is always prepared to help the individual.[15]

It is fascinating to see how the two ideas—of the more distant and majestic, and the close, intimate deity—structure Christian worship. Can we explain their appeal and their pervasiveness throughout Christian history? It seems that at least some insight can be gained from the study of the history of religions.

High God vs. Personal God

Christianity originated in a world inhabited by gods and goddesses and marked by religious institutions, teachings, and traditions. Although in many ways it constituted a new beginning and appeared to some early observers as an "atheistic" movement, i.e., as a movement not participating in the polytheistic cults of the ancient world, it did carry with it traditional notions of familiar and awesome deities. We can discern two experiences that came to structure Christian worship: the Hebrew experience of a high god who is the creator and the owner of the universe, and the polytheistic experience of each individual having a personal god, that is a protecting familiar spirit and friendly helper. These notions form the historical basis of how Christians thought of the God they related to in their spiritual and ritual life.

Otto's worship focuses on a high god. In religious history, high gods are typically related to the sky and head a pantheon, as Jupiter and Zeus do in the classical world, or they are the subject of monotheistic developments, such as Ahura Mazda in Persia and Yahweh in biblical Israel. High gods are the "owners" of the universe, and often the act of the first creation is attributed to them. In Israel, he is called "God Most High, owner of the heavens and the earth" (Gen. 14:19). In many traditions, their character is ambivalent. Enlil, the principal god of the ancient Sumerians, has two sides. On the one hand, he causes trees and plants to spring up from the earth and fashions agricultural implements to use in tending them. People invoked his name in prayers for abundance and prosperity. On the other hand, he can bring destruction, famine, chaos. Yahweh is also an ambivalent being. He punishes the wicked masses by sending the flood and saves one family to ensure humanity's survival. He can be a savior and protector, but he can also be an inimical force. Yahweh can be termed "merciful and gracious, slow to anger, and abounding in steadfast love. . . . As a father has compassion for his children, so Yahweh has compassion" (Ps. 103:8.13). But he can also be angry and act as an evil deity;

like a lion, he will "maul the prey" (Hos. 5:14). Two priests once approached Yahweh, offering him a sacrifice which he had not commanded them to offer; the result: "Fire came out from the presence of Yahweh and consumed them, and they died" (Lev. 10:2). So we can understand why the manifestation of Yahweh's majesty inspires fear and trembling. "Woe to me, I am lost," exclaims the prophet Isaiah when he sees the Lord (Isa. 6:5). At times, the Bible juxtaposes God's kindness and majesty, as if intending to point out the paradox: he can speak to Moses "face to face, as one speaks to a friend"; but no one can see him and live (Exod. 33:11.20). "Power belongs to God, and steadfast love" (Ps. 62:11–12). "He has sent redemption to his people; he has commanded his covenant forever. Holy and awesome is his name" (Ps. 111:9). Why not something like, "merciful and compassionate is his name"? To be sure, far from being irrational, the paradox has its logic: "Yahweh reproves the one he loves, as a father the son in whom he delights" (Prov. 3:12). Interestingly enough, certain parts of the Bible have not one but two names for the god of monotheism. The name Yahweh appears when the Bible presents God to us in his personal character and in direct relationship to human beings, especially to Israel as his chosen people; whereas Elohim occurs mostly when reference is made to the deity as the creator of the universe, a transcendent being that stands outside and above nature. So the Hebrews had two different names for different aspects of the same deity.[16]

Clearly, Otto is impressed with the majestic side of the Old Testament God whose worship he promotes.

As we have seen, the God dear to Sister Ann and Luise Rinser and encouraged by Vatican II Catholicism is of a different nature. Historians of religion are quite familiar with approachable deities, for these figure prominently in popular devotion and personal piety. While all gods and goddesses seem to have been eligible as personal protectors, the deities of personal piety are typically benign spirits of lower rank who serve as tutelaries and intercessors with higher gods, very much like the guardian angel of Catholic piety. In the ancient Mesopotamian and Israelite worlds, each individual had such a tutelary, often referred to as "my god, your god, the god of your father," or similar names. The "personal god," as specialists have come to call this type of deity, is well known from the biblical Psalms. Psalm 91 echoes particularly well what the ancient Israelites felt when reflecting about their personal god: the individual passes the night in his god's shelter, saying: "My refuge and my fortress; my God, in whom I trust." Elsewhere, the psalmist can sing: "It was you who took me from the womb; you kept me safe on my mother's breast. On you I was cast from my birth, and since my mother bore me you have been my God" (Ps. 22:10–11 [Eng., 9–10]). Some biblical authors considered Yahweh the personal god of the entire people, understood as one corporate person. The personal god can then be said to have formed Israel in the womb, just as the personal god forms an individual person in the mother's womb. He loves Israel more than a mother loves her child. In the nineteenth century, Ernest Renan understood that the Christian language of prayer reflects just these notions: "The way a pious Christian speaks to God would not be distinguished by such tenderness if behind the deity of three persons there would not be a more tangible God who held his tribe on his lap like a wet nurse, caressed them and talked to them as one talks to a child." Like Renan's insight, the most famous reference to the Bible's personal God also comes from France. It is in the *Mémorial*, Blaise Pascal's 1654 secret note on his conversion from the abstract God of philosophy to the living God of the Bible: "God of Abraham, God of Isaac, God of Jacob, not of philosophers and scholars . . . God of Jesus Christ . . . My God." Unlike the deistic *philosophes et savants*, whose deity had created the world and then left it alone, the biblical patriarchs and Jesus did have a close, personal relationship with God, a relationship that was paradigmatic for Pascal.[17]

In first-century CE Judaism, various groups had a "duotheistic" theology which involved the veneration of a creator-god along with a second, more approachable deity. While the Creator served intellectual needs by being the answer to the question of why the world exists, the personal deity as helper in everyday matters responded to emotional needs. In the book of Wisdom, the two deities are called God and Sophia ("Wisdom"); in the New Testament, God and Christ, with Sophia and Christ representing the approachable figure. When after Christ's death his spirit appeared to his disciples, even the doubting Thomas accepted him as his personal deity, saying: "My Lord and my God" (John 20:28).[18]

Throughout religious history, the almost universal notions of the close and the more distant, majestic deity have influenced ritual behavior. The distinction between the two accounts for certain ideas underlying Christian worship; especially the presence of Christ as the "personal god" who finds his place along with a high god and who serves as an intermediary. While the double focus of Christian worship involves both God and Christ, comparative religion reveals certain patterns of preference. In general, the learned elite prefers the veneration of majestic deities, while the people at large tend to concentrate their cults on the minor, more accessible gods. In ancient Greece, for instance, the simple folk directed their prayers and pious acts more often to the little gods who were nearer to their lives and hearts than the great deities of the state. When in need, people turned to Heracles and Asclepios, not to Zeus or Apollo, just as some Catholics are more likely to pray to a saint or the Virgin Mary than to God the Father.[19]

In eucharistic worship, the faithful meet Christ. However, the encounter can have two different qualities: it can be "numinous" in the sense of awe-inspiring, or it may be merely "solemn," unaccompanied by particular feelings of fear, utter dependence, or unworthiness. The "solemn" type, though recognizing worship as something special, involves a certain familiarity with the divine. The numinous, priestly type, by contrast, defines Christ as a mystery.

These two types can be described using the distinction between the "learned tradition" and the "little tradition." While intellectual, rational, literate versions of Christianity tend to emphasize Christ's majesty and mystery, the "little tradition" of popular religion concentrates on the experiential side: on Christ's real, effective presence. At communion, people expect to receive the Eucharist as real, nourishing food for life, not as food for thought and learned speculation. For popular Catholicism, the present Christ is an almost immanent power that can be experienced, loved, and talked to in an unceremonious way, and even manipulated. After all, Mass must be "good for something." While scholastic theologians discuss the mysterious way in which Christ can be present in a piece of bread and a cup of wine, others rejoice in the Lord's presence and profit from the occasion to approach him with specific requests and hopes, or simply enjoy the closeness of a divine friend. Catholic lore is full of stories about miracles that happen at Mass: Christ can act and does act, often to help people, but equally often to demonstrate his tangible presence to those who do not believe.

Not only in the popular experience of the Eucharist, but also in the charismatic trances, the distance between the human and the divine disappears. In ecstatic worship, the spirit of Christ can "possess" his devotees. To understand that it must be Christ's spirit or the Holy Ghost that enters the human body, a look at Hinduism can be illuminating. While the great gods of the Hindu pantheon do not generally possess their devotees, the lesser godlings do. In Christianity, too, those who feel possessed by a supernatural, divine force identify it as Christ or the Holy Spirit, never as the Father who remains more distant. Christians and Hindus agree: people do not generally become possessed or inspired by the distant deity. Interestingly, comparative research has also pointed out that those who become possessed by divine powers tend to be among the poor, the lowly, and the socially marginalized. Rarely do members of the learned elite participate in ecstatic rituals, which they often despise as undignified behavior. Rudolf Otto is an unlikely candidate for possession, but we may imagine Sister Ann moving toward a charismatic spirituality and trying Pentecostal forms of worship.[20]

The history of religions can indeed contribute to our understanding of the plain style of worship preferred by Sister Ann and the liturgical solemnity promoted by Rudolf Otto. However, there is another discipline that promises insight into the matter: psychology.

Father Worship vs. Mother Worship

The image of God is formed in childhood and somehow echoes the experience individuals have of their parents. As often in the young and controversial discipline of psychology, the truly fundamental insights go back to Sigmund Freud. Ever since Freud argued, in *Leonardo da Vinci and a Memory of His*

Childhood (1910) and *Totem and Taboo* (1913), that we tend to create God in our human father's image, this axiom has been widely accepted. From a psychological perspective, the duality of the close and the distant deity can be accounted for by the way small children experience their mother and father. Generally, they are in close contact with the nurturing mother. The father, by contrast, who is mainly absent at work or at any rate less accessible than the mother, may remain a more shadowy, distant figure. However, the father may also be the admired hero, the strong and omniscient figure who affords help and wards off the powers of evil. The awe-inspiring deity seems to be preferred by those who want to come to terms with the father-figure of their childhood. Others prefer the motherly side of the divine in their veneration of Christ.

Sigmund Freud felt that religion, as he experienced it in Judaism and as he saw it in the Christian world, cannot be understood apart from the divine Father it venerates. According to him, all religion reflects how children admire their human father and rely on his protection and power. "The derivation of a need for religion from the child's feeling of helplessness and the longing it evokes for a father seems to me incontrovertible, especially since this feeling is not simply carried on from childhood days but is kept alive perpetually by the fear of what the superior power of fate will bring. I could not point to any need in childhood so strong as that for a father's protection." Freud, who only late in life came to discover the relevance of the infant–mother relationship, considers religion a father-oriented infantile attitude.[21]

Some psychologists—for instance, Erik Erikson—argue that the real object of childhood nostalgia is not the father (as Freud had it), but the blissful, original symbiotic relationship between the mother and the infant. Even Freud had observed that as the infant "sinks asleep at the breast, utterly satisfied, it bears a look of perfect contentment." Had not the master himself stated that "if the infant could express itself, it would undoubtedly acknowledge that the act of sucking at the mother's breast is far and away the most important thing in life," for by this blissful act it satisfies its two basic needs: for food and love? Some of Freud's disciples realized that God is not necessarily created in the father's but often in the mother's image. According to Lou Andreas-Salomé, God is "the memory of the most intimate human tenderness whose sweetness a child was given to taste"—by the mother![22]

William James, like Freud a pioneer of psychology, once heard a lady describe the pleasure it gave her to think that she "could always cuddle up to God." For Freud, this was an infantile thought, not worthy of an adult person. James had a broader vision; he admired people of such a serene religion which he thought of as going hand-in-hand with a healthy, optimistic approach to life. Freud's disciples also re-evaluated the adult person's temporary return to childhood actions and attitudes. Return (or "regression," as the jargon has it) to childhood, far from being a mere strategy for avoiding confrontation with reality (again, as Freud had it), is of great therapeutic value. It enables people to find again their "basic trust" and their original creativity. The adult ego's control must be reduced in order to release creative energy and not to interfere with the act of thinking, writing, painting, and the like. The soul must step back in order to be able to move forward: *reculer pour mieux sauter*, as the French saying has it. Regression facilitates progression and healing. Having renewed their strength at the mother's breast, people can again confront reality. Oskar Pfister, Swiss pastor and a friend of Freud, did not hesitate to invoke Jesus as having recommended regression: "Truly I tell you, unless you change and become like children, you will never enter the kingdom of heaven" (Matt. 18:3).[23]

The angry deity that seeks justice and revenge, and the benign god who forgives, loves, and predestines to eternal felicity: this duality seems to reflect basic attitudes humans experience toward their fathers and mothers. From Augustine to Luther, sensitive souls have suffered from the idea of divine justice and lived in fear of punishment, until they came upon the other, benign, friendly, indeed motherly face of God. With this face, they discovered salvation in all senses of the term: reassurance in the battle of life, the courage to live and to confront the world, spiritual balance, confidence about their eternal destiny. According to Erikson, Luther's wish to restore the original biblical idea of faith as the trust in God's unconditional, maternal love reflects his wish to return to the basic trust of his early infancy, symbolized by the child's unity with the mother.[24]

Psychoanalysis not only elucidates the duality of Christian notions of deity but also helps us to understand certain elementary attitudes we find in liturgical behavior.

A first case in point is father-oriented worship. While the father affords protection, he also claims obedience and submission. Rudolf Otto, the most enthusiastic promoter of the worship of the majestic deity, pictures God in the form of a stern human father who asserts his superiority even in irrational acts of power. Deborah Tannen, the American linguist and bestselling author, has recently reminded us that men, mostly without knowing it, live in a world structured by hierarchical relationships. Male-to-male interaction in Western society, which Tannen has spied out with all the tools available to a contemporary socio-linguist (hidden tape-recorders, secret video cameras), is guided by the wish for domination, distance, and hierarchy. As soon as two men interact, one tends to dominate while the other accepts his subordinate position: even in friendship, it seems. Men seek acknowledgment of their power. Domination, for them, is a way of life. Therefore, as Freud has observed, "men cannot live together with their kind unless they develop a high degree of pliability." Otto, by acknowledging God's superiority, simply follows a well-established pattern of male behavior. And so do the Catholic boys whom Belgian researchers have found to think of the eucharistic Christ as a somewhat distant, awe-inspiring figure to whom we relate in a contractual, almost businesslike way.[25]

Belgian girls, by contrast, experience the eucharistic Christ as a more nurturing, protective figure, to whom they can relate in the way one relates to a
mother or a female peer. Here we can again invoke Tannen's research. She has
found that whether interacting with other women or with men, women typically seek intimacy, friendship, and understanding. With them, the wish to be
distant and to dominate plays a much smaller and often negligible role. Women
love to share secrets and seek to bind others to themselves as true friends and
confidantes. The wish to relate to a maternal, nurturing deity is of course not
confined to Belgian girls. Nor even to women in general, for all humans have
regressive wishes.

Eucharistic celebrations can be seen as ritual enactments of regression. They
appear to echo the ritual of the baby's crying and being fed. When the infant
cries, the mother comes and feeds the baby with her own breast, i.e., with
herself. So when called upon, a nurturing, loving Christ comes, giving himself
in the sacrament. Interestingly enough, this association between the communicant and the infant should not be seen as something new: as if it had been
invented by contemporary psychologists. It can actually be found in ancient as
well as in medieval sources. In the early church, newly baptized members
received not only bread and wine at communion, but also milk mixed with
honey and were thus, as Bishop Hippolytus stated, "nourished like little children" (*sicut parvuli nutriuntur*). While "milk communion" eventually disappeared from actual practice (except in Coptic and Abyssinian Christianity), the
underlying concept survived. Aelred of Rievaulx (1110–67), a Cistercian abbot
in Yorkshire, recommends his readers to meditate on the altar cross by saying
that Christ's "outspread arms will invite you to embrace him, his naked breasts
will feed you with the milk of sweetness to console you." The strange reference
to Christ's milk can only be understood in terms of a web of metaphors: Christ
is a motherly, caring figure; just as a mother's blood is transformed into her
breasts' milk, so Christ's eucharistic blood is the milk with which he nourishes
the communicants.[26]

What Aelred recommends as a theme of pious meditation, is acted out in the
liturgy, even in contemporary Christianity. When priests offer communion to
the members of Rudolf Steiner's Christian Community, they follow the medieval practice of feeding them as a mother would feed her child: by putting the
consecrated food and drink into the communicant's mouth. Steiner also taught
his priests to touch the communicant's cheek in a tender gesture of blessing:
just as a mother would caress her baby. So communicants return—ritually and
symbolically—to their early childhood. Other forms of ritual touching—the
laying-on of hands in charismatic prayer and healing—may be explained in the
same way. If it is true that tactile stimulation in childhood is important to
healthy development and that Western children do not get very much of it,
then one may indeed argue, as Thomas Csordas has done, that touching may
"compensate for a developmental deficiency."[27]

It is not only the sacramental contact with the divine motherly nourisher that can be appreciated as a true spiritual refreshment. Sacrificial notions of worship also involve the ego's "regression" to earlier stages of development. Jung understood and appreciated the Catholic sacrifice of Mass as a model of sacrificing the inflated adult ego and moving closer to the motherly realm of the unconscious. Olier's insistence that sacrifice implies the "annihilation" of the ego invites a Jungian reading. In more general terms, we can understand Augustine's view of sacrifice in terms of a regression to a state of blissful union with the idealized mother. Sacrifice, in Augustine's Neoplatonic philosophy, means joining oneself to one's ultimate cause, i.e., to God. Biologically speaking, the ultimate cause of a human person is, of course, that person's mother. It does not come as a surprise that God, for Augustine, often has maternal features: he feels like an infant sucking milk from God's breast. Joining oneself to God ritually can be seen as the wish to restore the symbiotic union with the mother.[28]

Moreover, from a Jungian point of view, trusting, childlike prayer to the benign heavenly Father can be appreciated as a ritual regression. And the same seems to be true of ecstatic worship, especially glossolalia and "resting in the Spirit." When glossolalic behavior is spontaneous, it must be seen as a dramatic regression. Then people resort to irrational, prelinguistic modes of expression; it is not the adult, language-dominated ego that is speaking, but the infant producing its first languagelike sounds. As all parents know, a baby needs no language to communicate with them. When in charismatic worship individuals faint and collapse as they are touched and prayed for, they typically fall into the arms of a "catcher" who prevents them from getting hurt; at the same time, they fall "into the invisible nurturant arms of the deity." At such a moment, the arms of the "catcher," the unconscious memories of the all-embracing maternal arms, and the arms of God all merge. So the mother–child relationship is almost ever-present in worship: in sacrifice, sacrament, prayer, and ecstasy.[29]

Images of the divine Father and the divine Mother are, of course, not confined to learned (and increasingly popular) psychological discourse. They also figure prominently in art.

Hieratic Art vs. Idyllic Art

In popular Catholic art, images of the Mass are not uncommon. If we place the Christ-child with the chalice next to the priest saying Mass, we can get a feeling for the two theological temperaments that inspire this kind of representation. The 1950s Christ-child from France (ill. 41) belongs to what most critics call "kitsch," though a more objective assessment might simply refer to folk art. The priest at the altar (ill. 44), painted by monks of the Benedictine monastery of Beuron, Germany (ca. 1900), conveys a rather different way of looking at

43. Playing the Mass. Catholic children play the Mass just the way they play school or wedding. The photo, presumably taken in a professional studio, shows a boy dressed for Mass and accompanied by an altar boy. Before the age of puberty, every Catholic boy can be seen as a little priest, for the innocence of the child equals priestly celibacy. From a Dutch magazine for Catholic children, 1914.

41. (*facing page, top*) Christ-Child with Chalice. Catholic popular art often represents Christ as a "cute" little child. While critics have often condemned the popular style as kitsch, the notion of the idyllic is presumably more appropriate. Religious idylls avoid hieratic distance by giving sacred scenes a homelike setting. French holy card, 1950s.

42. (*facing page, below*) Learning the Mass. Children educated in Montessori kindergartens are taught not to confuse religious games with secular ones. For this reason, these kindergartens include a special room, called an "atrium," in which children are introduced to worship. This photo shows how four-year-old Christina familiarizes herself with the mixing of water and wine at Mass. The model kindergartens established by Maria Montessori (1870–1952) are based on the idea of "learning by doing," and the foundress insisted that this rule should apply to religious education as to all other branches of education. Private Montessori atrium, Rome, Italy, 1978.

Mass: offering the august sacrifice, he celebrates the sacred mysteries in the presence of angels.

The "cute," feminized Christ-child with his—or her—chalice is more reminiscent of Catholic children "playing priest" than of a real, male priest saying Mass. The open-air setting on a fresh meadow cannot but reinforce the notion of play. "Playing the Mass" as they would also play policeman or cowboy, children create their own world, drawing the odd world of the adults into their own realm. Naturally, Catholic adults are aware of their children's playing the Mass, and in the nineteenth and early twentieth centuries, Catholic toy stores offered Mass sets, apparently complete with cardboard home altar, chalice, chasuble, and priestly biretta. In the 1920s, Maria Montessori, the Italian educational theorist and founder of model kindergartens, promoted the use of Mass toys for introducing children to the liturgy of the church (ill. 42). Although some priests warned against these toys, for they feared these would ridicule or profane the sacred, children seem to have been fond of playing the Mass. Boys seem to be the leaders of the game, but girls willingly co-operate, as Luise Rinser recounts in her book of childhood memories. In the recent German film *Peppermint-Frieden* (Marianne Rosenbaum, 1983), some Bavarian boys stage Mass in their parents' bedroom and use an old curtain and underwear as vestments. Boys playing the Mass were also photographed, presumably even in the studios of professional photographers, and published, for instance, in *De Engelbewaarder* (The Guardian Angel), a religious magazine for Dutch children (ill. 43). Before the age of puberty, every Catholic boy can be seen as a little priest, and, as the editor of *De Engelbewaarder* points out, his sacred game may be the first sign of a priestly vocation. Although the photo of the boy-priest and the French artist's version of the playful Christ-child may not be to everyone's taste and some might argue that this is kitsch or "bad art for children," no one can fail to understand the easy familiarity with the divine these pictures capture so well. It is precisely this familiarity and homelike atmosphere that art critics find in what they term the "religious idyll." In a review of a series of paintings by Wilhelm Tischbein, Goethe celebrated his friend's idyllic paintings that showed men, women, and mythical animals arranged in peaceful scenes reminiscent of the Golden Age of ancient mythology. Reflecting on the merits of such art, Goethe explained its character:

> All artful, idyllic representations are held in high esteem, for they present natural, eternally recurrent, pleasing situations of human life in a simple, truthful manner, yet cleared of all that is cumbersome, impure, and disagreeable, with which it is clothed on earth. Motherly and fatherly relations to children, especially to boys, the little ones' play and fondness of sweet things, thirst for education, the adults' seriousness and care: all this is here reflected in most delightful ways. Accordingly, the so-called Holy Family can be an idyllic motif. Elevated to godly dignity, it appeals even more—twice or three times as much.

44. The Requiem Mass. As the priest says Mass, souls are liberated out of purgatory and ascend to heaven. The sober hieratic style promoted by the German Benedictine monk and artist Desiderius Lenz aimed at reinventing specifically Christian art. While even contemporaries of Lenz judged the Beuron style a failure, some Catholics adopted it as their canon of taste for decorating churches, illustrating missals, and designing holy cards for devotional use. By the 1960s, however, the style had lost its popularity among German Catholics. School of Desiderius Lenz, Beuron, Germany, ca. 1900.

While it remains doubtful whether Goethe really believed in the superiority of religious idylls over their ancient and secular equivalents, the prince of German literature certainly understood the style as well as the appeal of popular devotional painting.[30]

The Beuron painting (ill. 44) is quite unlike the one representing the Christ-child and the photo showing the boy-priest standing near the altar. Here we see not a feminized Christ child or playing children, but an adult priest engaged in the serious, sacred business of saying Mass for the departed. The idyllic world of the Christ-child, with its small, closed-garden cosmos, is abandoned for a symbolic representation of the real, huge universe whose heaven of light extends beyond the painting. Great care is taken that the altar boy, the suffering souls in purgatory, the saints ascending to heaven, and St. Peter and the angels awaiting them all look dignified and "masculine." Inspired by their fellow monk Desiderius Lenz, the artists of Beuron sought to renew Byzantine

45. Preaching in a Calvinist Atmosphere. Dutch seventeenth-century artists often depicted church interiors. Here one can see a preacher in the pulpit as he speaks to his congregation. The atmosphere is simple and sober, for all Catholic decoration was eliminated in the days of the Reformation. The medieval church was turned into a lecture hall in which no object of art distracts the congregation's attention. Pieter Saenredam, *Odulphuskerk at Assendelft*, Dutch painting, 1649.

and to imitate ancient Egyptian iconography, whose archaic purity, timeless beauty, canonical regularity, religious dignity, lack of interest in individuality, and unsentimental qualities their master admired. For Lenz, true Catholic art had to be objective rather than subjective, governed by strict rules rather than by spontaneity and arbitrariness, and display majesty rather than familiarity. In short, it had to be hieratic. If a religious representation or a ritual is termed hieratic, it has certain qualities that make it sacred, setting it apart from the profane and preventing it from becoming intimate, sentimental, or idyllic. In art, the hieratic style is one that has a nearly religious solemnity, majesty, and ritual stiffness. Implied in this characterization is the existence of a special language of form particularly appropriate to authentically sacerdotal content. Some of the qualities associated with the concept are frontality, stasis or at any rate measured, dignified movements, severity, and an emphatic reduction of pictorial illusionism known from Byzantine icons. As is the case with Beuron paintings, hieratic art typically originates in the stern, ascetic environment of monasteries. Created by a spiritual elite, it expresses this elite's particular theological values. While the Beuron art had lost its appeal by the 1960s and is now generally dismissed as a failed attempt at renewing Catholic artistic sensibilities, the very idea from which it sprang enjoyed and still enjoys wide acclaim. Spiritual leaders of twentieth-century Catholicism like Romano

46. Before the Sermon. This Dutch church interior invites comparison with Saenredam's
Odulphuskerk (ill. 45). While date and provenance of the two paintings are similar, they capture
entirely different atmospheres. The hieratic mood of Saenredam's church interior has given way to
an idyllic scene, complete with a dog (lower right). Here people feel visibly at home in their church.
Rutger van Langevelt, Dutch painting, 1669.

Guardini (1885–1968) in Germany and the American Trappist monk Thomas
Merton (1915–68) have not hesitated to voice their appreciation of the work of
those engaged in the production of "authentic" religious art. Guardini celebrated the cult-image's specific nature: transcending the limits of the mere
devotional picture, it defines a place at which the *tremendum* of God's divine

majesty can be felt. In a similar way, Merton preferred hieratic art because "of its power to convey the awesomeness of an invisible and divine reality, to strike the beholder with deep reverence and with the awareness of the divine presence, in mystery." The *Grand Larousse* associates the term hieratic specifically with worship; it denotes something as "deriving its form from liturgical tradition: the officiating priest's hieratic gestures." In church architecture, decoration, ritual objects, and vestments, as well as in liturgical gestures and words, the hieratic style or attitude serves to express the awesome side of the divine presence. Theocentric theologies, whether entertained by Catholics such as Guardini and Merton or by Protestants such as Rudolf Otto, have consistently preferred hieratic environments and supported hieratic styles of worship.[31]

The painting of the Assendelft Odulphuskerk (1649) can serve as another example of the hieratic style (ill. 45). Pieter Saenredam's painting echoes theocentric notions of worship, notions inspired, in this case, by the stern asceticism of the sixteenth-century reformer, John Calvin. Saenredam depicts a decidedly hieratic, awe-inspiring environment. However, not all seventeenth-century Dutch artists shared Saenredam's uncompromising attitude. When his younger contemporary, Rutger van Langevelt (1635–95) painted an imaginary church interior in 1669, he took an entirely different perspective—both visually and theologically (ill. 46). Rather than getting lost in the distance, minister and audience are here placed at the center; in fact, they form the actual subject of the painting. Though still dwarfed by the immensity of the sacred space opening up above them, they are not lost in it but assume full presence and visibility. The architecture no longer provides the central focus; relegated to the background, it forms the setting for something else—for people. One can discern more than forty individuals: women, men, children, all of various ages.

The artist has carefully chosen the moment depicted: the beginning of the service. This beginning allows the artist to avoid the frozen, formal postures of people who are listening intently to a preacher raising his hand in that hieratic gesture visible in Saenredam's painting. Van Langevelt creates an animated, vivid scene, reminiscent not only of Catholic Baroque painting of the same period, but also of reality. While hushed silence characterizes the behavior in many churches, the Dutch even today talk before the service starts, greeting each other and exchanging their news. The two figures appearing under the arch (left side of the painting) are just about to join the congregation. Most have settled into their chairs or benches, women in front of the pulpit and men on the right and left. We can easily discern two features characteristic of Dutch Calvinists: the presence of special benches (*herenbanken*) for city councilors and the men's wearing of hats even during the service (except for formal prayer). Some are still looking around or talking. One woman stands, receiving a Bible from another woman. Below the pulpit, the reader (*voorlezer*) is most likely not yet reading the day's scriptural lesson, but announcing it. As people open their

Bibles, the minister walks up to the pulpit. The members of the congregation focus increasingly on the pulpit. The service is about to start.[32]

A certain warmth and tenderness pervade the scene. Though we do not know their names, these are real people with all their individuality intact. One can clearly see men with long hair, which suggests their liberal attitude (some strict Calvinists protested against this custom). Reality invades the painting even in the form of a little dog. In the seventeenth century, Dutch churches had a *houndenslager*, a dog-hitter whose task it was to prevent dogs from entering. Van Langevelt allows the *houndenslager* to be inefficient; the presence of a dog betrays his inability to keep pets out of church. By discreetly allowing pets to mix with the congregation, van Langevelt domesticates the sacred space, making it tender, homelike. He reveals "a world in which the abstract order of the state, of collective life (represented by gigantic space) is so assumed, so successful, that it can be played with: by miniature elements that represent the incursion of the personal, the creaturely. Public order can be relaxed, can even be mildly defaced. The sacred and solemn can tolerate a bit of mild profanity." The dog, along with one or two distracted children, provides an element of charm and reassurance in the majestic environment of worship. Here, even a Sister Ann would feel comfortable enough.[33]

Although seventeenth-century preaching could at times be severe and denounce the extravagance of long hair or the abuse of alcohol, it aimed at popular appeal.

> After a biblical passage has been read from the lectern, the preacher mounts the pulpit and begins with announcements that sometimes involve the most profane matters: business activities of street vendors, neighborhood news. Then he preaches. Taking the biblical text as his basis, the speaker moralizes in a rich, colorful language, never spurning puns or the use of popular sayings. As a contemporary remarked jokingly: The preachers' word clings to the heart like ringworm to a sheep.

Paul Zumthor's description of a Dutch Sunday service and its popular mood can serve as an apt commentary on van Langevelt's painting. Here we see people who feel at home, and when they listen, God's word is close to them, touching their hearts with sublime tenderness. "The word is very near to you; it is in your mouth and in your heart"—and, of course, in the Bible that you are opening (Deut. 30:14). Saenredam said, "This is the awesome place where God's word is taught." Van Langevelt insists on the presence of people. "These are the people: children, women, and men like yourself and myself, who open their books and listen to their ministers." And some, as Samuel Pepys did in contemporary London, might even take notes on what the preacher said. Or they might sleep if the sermon was too long and uninspiring. With unrivaled candor, Pepys describes in his diary what he did one Sunday afternoon when sitting in the gallery of St. Margaret's: "I did entertain myself with my perspective glass up and down the church, by which I had the great pleasure of seeing and gazing [at] a great many very fine women; and . . . with that and sleeping, I passed away the time till sermon was done."[34]

From van Langevelt's painting, as well as from the many sources discussed in our book, we can learn that the closer we look, the more human the acts of worship appear. At times, people may be inclined to adore the majestic side of God. At other times, the same people may prefer to worship the divine as a loving, nurturing Christ. Worship, a communal, public, patterned, purposeful activity directed to and guided by the divine, is deeply human and embraces all the dimensions of the human soul. Whether we consider historical sources, whether we delve into comparative religion, psychology, or art, we find ourselves, our own faces, psychologies, and cultural habits at the center of one of the most common and most characteristic expressions of Christianity, its sacred games of worship.

Abbreviations

CC	Jean-Jacques Olier, "Catéchisme chrétien pour la vie intérieure." In: Olier, *Catéchisme chrétien et Journée chrétienne*, ed. François Amiot. Paris: Le Rameau, 1954, 9–92.
CCCM	Corpus Christianorum, continuatio mediaevalis.
CCSL	Corpus Christanorum, series latina.
CR	Corpus Reformatorum.
CSEL	Corpus Scriptorum Ecclesiasticorum Latinorum.
CWS	The Classics of Western Spirituality.
DH	Heinrich Denzinger and Peter Hünermann, eds., *Enchiridion symbolorum, definitionum et declarationum de rebus fidei et morum*, 37th edn. Freiburg: Herder, 1991.
EC	Jean-Jacques Olier, "Explication des cérémonies de la grand'messe de paroisse." In: *Œuvres complètes de M. Olier*, ed. Jacques-Paul Migne. Petit-Montrouge: Migne, 1856, 281–455.
GCS	*Die griechischen christlichen Schriftsteller der ersten drei Jahrhunderte*. Berlin.
IVV	Jean-Jacques Olier, *Introduction à la vie et aux vertus chrétiennes*, ed. François Amiot. Paris: Le Rameau, 1954, 7–159.
JC	Jean-Jacques Olier, "La Journée chrétienne." In: Olier, *Catéchisme chrétien et Journée chrétienne*, ed. François Amiot. Paris: Le Rameau, 1954, 93–247.
KD	Karl Barth, *Die kirchliche Dogmatik*. Zurich: EVZ-Verlag, 1932–67.
L	Jean-Jacques Olier, *Lettres*, nouvelle éd. par E. Levesque. Paris: J. de Gigord, 1935.
LCL	The Loeb Classical Library.
Mansi	Johannes Dominicus Mansi, ed., *Sacrorum conciliorum nova et amplissima collectio*.
NRSV	New Revised Standard Version of the Bible, 1989.
PG	*Patrologiae cursus completus, series graeca*, ed. Jacques-Paul Migne.
PGM	*Papyri Graecae Magicae: Die griechischen Zauberpapyri*, ed. Karl Preisendanz *et al.*, 2nd edn. Stuttgart: Teubner, 1973–74. 2 vols.
PL	*Patrologiae cursus completus, series latina*, ed. Jacques-Paul Migne.
PLA	Frank Bartleman, "How Pentecost Came to Los Angeles" (1925). Repr. in: *Witness to Pentecost: The Life of Frank Bartleman*, ed. Cecil M. Robeck. New York: Garland, 1985.
SC	*Sources Chrétiennes*. Paris: Cerf, 1941ff.
STh	Thomas Aquinas, *Summa theologiae*.
WA	Martin Luther, *Werke. Kritische Gesamtausgabe*. "Weimarer Ausgabe."
WA Br	Martin Luther, *Werke. Kritische Gesamtausgabe; Briefwechsel*.
WA DB	Martin Luther, *Werke. Kritische Gesamtausgabe; Deutsche Bibel*.

WA TR   Martin Luther, *Werke. Kritische Gesamtausgabe; Tischreden.*
WF   Frank Bartleman, *Around the World by Faith* (n.d.). Repr. in: *Witness to Pen-
           tecost: The Life of Frank Bartleman*, ed. Cecil M. Robeck. New York: Garland,
           1985.

Notes

Preface

1. Plato, *Laws* 803 D/E; 803 C, trans. A.E. Taylor. The philosopher envisaged a society where the young of both sexes are in the pink of condition, exempt from severe menial labor and where all participate in "a lifelong round of sacrifices and festivals and chorus performances" (835 E).
2. Guardini (1937), 102–3.

The First Game: Praise

1. Ruusbroec, *Spiritual Espousals* 2:14 = (1985), 80; *CCCM* 103:319.
2. White (1992), 117.
3. Westermann (1981), 25; for Greek notions, see Versnel (1981), 46–63.
4. Homer, *Iliad* 1:472–74. Aeschylus, *Suppliant Maidens* 694–97 = (1922), I:71. Plato, *Laws* (*Nomoi*) 800 C/D (trans. Benjamin Jowett). Aelius Aristides, *Speeches* 50:31–45 = (1981), I:324–27. Greek paean: Fairbanks (1900).
5. For the details on singing, we rely on Kleinig (1993).
6. Hezekiah and Psalms: 2 Chr. 29:30.
7. 1 Chr. 16:8.9.19–23.25.34. An expression in v. 9 and 23 is often rendered "sing to him" and "sing to Yahweh," which is obviously wrong; for the proper translation as "sing of him," see de Boer (1981).
8. Petition, followed by congregational Amen and praise: 1 Chr. 16:35–36. "Truly he is good": 2 Chr. 7:3, in the trans. of Kleinig (1993), 117; the Hebrew *ki*, normally rendered "for," can also serve as the independent word, "truly"; see the discussion in Miller (1994), 358–62. Prostration: 2 Chr. 25:29–30.
9. Thomas Hobbes, *Leviathan* (1651), chap. 31.
10. Epictetus, *Discourses* 1:16 = (1925), I:112.
11. Voltaire (1972), 176.
12. Origen, *On Prayer* 33:1 = *GCS* Origenes 2:401; (1979), 169.
13. Babylonian Talmud, *Berakhot* 32a.
14. Inferior: Pseudo-Basil, *Monastic Constitutions*, *PG* 31:1328. Luther, *Lectures on Genesis*, *WA* 43:81. Calvin, *Institutes* (1986), 68 (from the 1536 edn. of the *Institutes*; see later standard edn. at no. 3:20,8). Ritschl (1966), 67 (§ 79).
15. P. Brunner (1977), 173.
16. Caleb: Jdg. 1:12–13. Jud. 13:18ff. Hasmoneans: 1 Macc. 3:1–9; 14:4–15. Sir. 44–50.
17. Clapping, etc.: Ps. 47:1; 2 Macc. 10:7. Ps. 105 = 1 Chr. 16. For the theory of a festival of the ark, see the discussion of Ps. 132 in Kraus (1989), 475–79.
18. Luther, *WA* 31/1:247–48.
19. P.D. Miller (1986), 68. Paul: Rom. 15:11, quoting Ps. 117:1.
20. The usual translation of the introduction to the Sanctus in Isa. 6:3 ("one called to another") is misleading, see Weinfeld (1983).
21. Ps. 29:11 must be rendered not as a petition, but as a confident assertion: "Yahweh will give strength to his people, etc.," as in the New English Bible and the Revised English Bible. For the radiation of divine *shalom* onto earth, see also the hymn in Luke 2:14.

22. The Qumran text quoted is known to specialists as 4Q405:20 and can be found in Vermes (1995), 261.

23. Westermann (1978), 188.

24. John Chrysostom, *Homilies on Colossians* 9:2 = *PG* 62:363. Edwards (1959), 262–63; Edwards's distinction is no doubt derived from Thomas Aquinas, *STh* I 5:6 (*bonum utile, bonum delectabile*). On general rather than specific praise, see also Brueggemann (1988), 89–121; Guthrie (1981), 1–30.

25. Norden (1913), 220–23.

26. Stewart (1988), 85.

27. On liturgical connections between Christians and Jews, see Werner (1959; 1984), whose pioneering work is not always historically reliable. On the use of the Psalms in Jewish and Christian worship, see Maier (1983); Füglister (1988). Recent musicological research emphasizes the independence of Jewish and Christian psalmody: Randhofer (1995).

28. "The public": Gelineau (1992), 494. "The joyful; reminds us": Taft (1986), 357.345. "In its": Söhngen (1961), 133.

29. *Roman Missal* of Paul VI (1970), 4th eucharistic prayer. Didache 10 = *SC* 248:178/80; Richardson (1970), 175–76.

30. P. Brunner (1954), I:261.

31. *Apostolic Constitutions* 8:12, 6–37 = *SC* 336:180–96. Guéranger (1878), I:2–4.

32. "That are; so as to": Sacred Congregation for Divine Worship (1983), nos. 146.152.

33. "We celebrate": Liturgy of the Hours, antiphon of Vespers, Tuesday of week 1.

34. Vielhauer (1952), Winter (1954), Flusser (1988) have perceptively written on the pre-history of the Benedictus and the Magnificat; see also Radl (1996), 128–31 on the Benedictus. The reference to the Marseillaise is in Flusser (1988), 131. The targumic late first-century version of the Song of Hannah in 1 Sam. 2, the Magnificat's model and twin, is also a highly political, nationalistic poem; it includes the line: "Jeru-

salem, which was like a barren woman, is to be filled with her exiled people. And Rome, which was filled with great numbers of people—her armies will be desolate and destroyed'; Harrington *et al.* (1987), 106.

35. "A glorification": Taft (1986), 357.

36. James (Jacobus) of Voragine, *Legenda aurea*, no. 182: "De dedicatione ecclesiae" = (1846), 847–48; on the traditional nature of this kind of commemoration, see also Cyprian, *Lord's Prayer* 35 = *CCSL* 3A:112; John Cassian, *De institutis coenobiorum* 3:3 = *PL* 49:116–26; de Reynal (1978), 47–53. Bonhoeffer (1954), 40–41.

37. For the idea of the religious being "delegated," see Pope Pius XII, Encyclical Letter "Mediator Dei" (1947), no. 142 = Megivern (1978), 109 and Tanquerey (1924), no. 514. *Konstitutionen der Regulierten Chorfrauen* (1933), 87–88. Gertrude of Helfta, *Herald of Divine Love* 3:9 = *SC* 143:42. Schneider (1901), 967 comments on blasphemy.

38. Francis de Sales (1895–1902), IX:333; cf. IX:49–50.

39. "The Church's": Sacred Congregation for Divine Worship (1983), nos. 270 and 23. On recent Catholic attempts to make the Office a matter of the entire Christian community, see Kohlschein (1987).

40. *Regel des heiligen Augustinus* (1986), 33. Schneider (1901), 967.

41. *Apostolic Tradition* 41 = *SC* 11bis:124. Eusebius, *Commentary on Ps 64* = *PG* 23:630. For the early history of the Divine Office, see Taft (1986).

42. John Chrysostom, *Homilies on Acts* 18:4 = *PG* 60:147. Egeria, *Peregrinatio* 24 = *CCSL* 175:67–70.

43. De Vogüé (1966).

44. Benedict, *Rule*: eight times, 16; "nothing is," 43 = *SC* 182: 524.586.

45. This is the shift from the earlier and more common "responsorial" to the later "antiphonal" way of singing. An early source mentioning both kinds is Basil, *Letter* 207:3 = *PG* 32:764; see McKinnon (1987), 10 and McKinnon's text no. 139. Bradshaw

46. Didache 8 = SC 248:174; Richardson (1970), 174. Origen, *On Prayer* 33:1 = GCS Origenes 2:401; (1979), 169.

47. On the early history of doxologies, see Jungmann (1989), 172–90. On Jewish connections, see Werner (1959), I:273–312; (1970).

48. The development of monastic psalmody is discussed in Verheul (1990); Dyer (1989, 1989a). On paying attention to the meaning of what is sung, see Butler (1919), 68–69. According to Thomas Aquinas, *STh* II II 83:13 (and 91:2 ad 5), a general awareness of the meaning of a prayer suffices to make its recitation meritorious. See also John Chrysostom, *On Psalm 41:2* = PG 55:158: one should sing the Psalms even if one does not understand the meaning of the words.

49. Commentator: see the reference to Paul the Deacon in Lackner (1972), 52. Butler (1919): "the proper," 30 (quoting Abbot Paul Delatte, OSB); "the daily," 31 (quoting Francis A. Gasquet, OSB).

50. On the *laus perennis*, see Hallinger (1977). That "138 Psalms" were at times recited at the abbey of Cluny is mentioned by John of Salerno, *PL* 133:57. Peter Damian, *PL* 145:873–74. On adding ever more psalms and prayers to the various canonical "hours," see Lackner (1972), 53–54.

51. Möbius (1984), 35.

52. Leuenberger (1990), 146. The memorial service for Miss Pearse was celebrated on October 23, 1993 and announced in the *Guardian* (London) of September 18, 1993.

53. The testimony quoted is included in Plüss (1988), 324–28.

54. Augustine, *City of God* 22:8,21 ("to publish"); 22:8,22 ("the whole congregation") = CCSL 48:824.826. The text of the miracle story read out by Augustine is included in the bishop's collection of sermons as *Sermo* 322 = PL 38:1443–45.

55. Indonesia: C.D. Grijns, Leiden, and formerly of Jakarta, in a letter to the author.

56. On the Puritan admission procedure, see Caldwell (1983), 45–80; Adams (1981), 40–50. The relevant passage of the "Platform" can be found in C. Mather (1853), II:226; Mather dates the beginning of public testimony-giving to 1634 (II:244).

57. "Useful; tyranny; nothing": C. Mather (1853), II:246.244.246. Experience meetings: Caldwell (1983), 76.79. "I do": Wigglesworth (1970), 113.

58. Synod of 1679: Pettit (1966), 202–3. Edwards (1959), 416.

59. "We had; the very": John Wesley (n.d.), IV:439.470, July 19, 1761.

60. "Commence": John Dungett as quoted in Church (1949), 240. More than twenty: W.R. Ward (1976), 21; F. Baker (1957), 29. "Generally": Jonathan Crowther, 1813, as quoted in H. Davies (1962–75), IV:262.

61. Methodist love-feast in the twentieth century: Burdon (1988). "Celebrates": Punshon (1990), 19.

62. Finney: Finney (1989), 136; for the local Methodists of the 1825 revival at De Kelb, see Hardman (1987), 66–67. The 1824 report is quoted by Bruce (1974), 83. National Methodist camp-meeting: McLean *et al.* (1869), esp. 106–14.155.

63. Knapp (1868), 136; for the tradition of lay preaching, see Adams (1981), 98–99. Palmer: Wheatley (1881), 238–57. White in Methodist "class meeting": E.G. White (1948), I:35–37 (White's autobiographical sketch). "Interesting; short; holy": E.G. White (1920), 114–16; the text is from her book *Experience and Views*, 1851. "All have": E.G. White (1948), II:579 (from Testimony no. 20 of 1871). "Full of": E.G. White, letter of April 7, 1889 (unpublished); see the archival file "The Ellen G. White 1888 Materials," p. 287.

64. Eddy (1960), 47.

65. For the dream-revelation, see R.W. Tyson (1988), 110–11. The psychology of religious perceptional sets has been studied by Sundén (1982), 33–66.

(1995), 16–21.78–81 comments on the ascetical nature of early monastic prayer.

66. For Puritan and Methodist ideas about personal covenants, see Hambrick-Stowe (1982), 248–53; Zaret (1985); Tripp (1969). Albanese (1992), 420.

67. For a history of the Sanctus, see Spinks (1991). Words shouted by the crowd: Matt. 21:9. Augustine, *De doctrina Christiana* 2:11 = *PL* 34:43.

68. This Charles Wesley hymn is included in *Hymns and Psalms* (1983), the hymnal of the British Methodists; the text is based on Gerhard Tersteegen's "Gott ist gegenwärtig."

69. John Chrysostom, *PG* 56:138. Sicardus, *Mitrale* 3 = *PL* 213:122, used in Durandus, *Rationale* 4:33,2 = *CCCM* 140:401. Augustine, *Sermon* 252:9 = *PL* 38:1176–77. John Ruusbroec, *Spiritual Espousals* 2:2 = (1985), 80. On the idea of a human-angelic community in worship, see Hofius (1992).

70. Whitehead: Price (1956), 223–24.

71. Otto (1950), 51–52. For a Catholic, almost scholastic version of Otto's argument, see de Puniet (1921). Kabasilas, *Commentary on the Divine Liturgy*, SC 4bis:102.

72. C.S. Lewis (1958), 95.

73. C.S. Lewis (1958), 96. Vatican II, "Constitution on the Sacred Liturgy" (1963), no. 84.

74. Schlink (1961), 82. "He would be": Kendrick (1984), 17.

75. Ratzinger (1987), 21: "Rechte Liturgie erkennt man daran, daß sie kosmisch ist, nicht gruppenmäßig."

76. Organ: Schuberth (1968), Williams (1993). For the medieval use of instruments at the Sanctus, see Hammerstein (1962), 37.

77. Hammer (1964), 407; on local Salzburg traditions, 3.

78. On the complement of choir and orchestra, see C.M. Brand (1941), 317–20.416–17.461.

79. On the imperial rulings about church music, see C.M. Brand (1941), 187–97. "I have heard": Landon (1977), IV:178; the unsigned article of October 5, 1803 is presumably by Friedrich Rochlitz.

80. "Adorning": White (1995), 43. "As long": A. Merz (1791), 8/1:15–16 from a "Schutzschrift für die Pracht beym Gottesdienste" (Essay in Defense of Splendor in Worship).

81. On Großgebauer, see Irwin (1993), 79–88. The quotation, trans. by Irwin 84–85, is from *Wächterstimme* 208–9.

82. On Mithobius, see Irwin (1993), 89–98; the quotation, trans. by Irwin, is from *Psalmodia Christiana* 180.

83. Hymns in eighteenth-century England: Arnold (1995). Victorian England: Gatens (1986), 18–32. Twentieth century: Kock (1989), Howe (1994).

84. "A confession": Wainwright (1992), 522. "We lay aside": Kabasilas, *Commentary on the Divine Liturgy*, SC 4bis:102. "There is a cutting": Buchanan (1977), 10.

85. "The singing": Hofmann (1957), 10. "Even when": Martin (1982), 28. Barth (1981), 9—letter of July 6, 1961.

86. Drewermann (1989), 177–80. Elaborated/restricted code: Douglas (1973), 40–58, based on the work of Basil Bernstein.

87. Adey (1988), 242.

88. Freud, *Moses and Monotheism* (n.d.), 78–79. Raffalt (1978), 238.

89. "Because of Who You Are," words and music by Bob Farrell and Billy Smiley (1982), quoted by Hustad (1992), 4.

The Second Game: Prayer

1. Theodore, *Homily* 15:31 = Mingana (1933), 88–89.

2. Luther, *Treatise on Good Works*, *WA* 6:236.

3. Peale (1992), 51.

4. Heinemann (1977), 28.

5. Aeschylus, *The Suppliant Maidens* 630ff. = Aeschylus (1922), I:67–71.

6. Inscription: trans. in Trombley (1993), I:4. Athenians: Marcus Aurelius, *Communings with Himself* 5:7 = (1930), 105. Priests: Aubriot-

Sévin (1992), 59–65. "Bless": from the Eighteen Benedictions, quoted after Heinemann (1977), 27–29; for the Eighteen Benedictions as an essentially Hellenistic "civic prayer," see Bickerman (1962).

7. Annual rite of atonement echoed in Ps. 51: Eaton (1976), 71–72.177–81. Enthronement request: Ps. 2:8. "Bountiful": Cleanthes, as quoted in Stobaeus, *Anthology* I, no. 12 = Long (1986), 147.

8. Rule of the Community (1QS) 1:24–2:3; *Hodayot* 16:12–13 = Vermes (1995), 71.232 (trans. modified). See the comments of Knohl (1996).

9. Proclus, *Commentary on Timaeus* 206–17 = (1967), II:27–39; with discussion in Esser (1967). Mystics: William of Saint-Thierry, *Song of Songs*, preface = *SC* 82:84–102.

10. A classic exposition of the difference between God's activity in deliverance and in blessing is Westermann (1978a).

11. Essenes: Philo, *On the Contemplative Life* 27 and 89; Josephus, *Jewish War* 2:128; both sources in Vermes *et al.* (1989). "An authentic": Heinemann (1977), 14–15. Studies of the absence of institutionalized regular prayer in the Bible and its beginnings in early Judaism include Talmon (1978) and Chazon (1994).

12. Aelius Aristides, see Behr (1968).

13. Version of the "international commission": *Prayers We Have in Common* (1975), 1; the text remains unchanged in *Praying Together* (1988), 1.

14. Heinemann *et al.* (1975), 23–24.

15. For the idea that certain prayers originated with either the scribal class or the priestly aristocracy, see Zahavy (1990), 87–101. On the distinction and shared concerns of the two institutions, see Urman (1993).

16. We quote the so-called Palestinian version found in a synagogue in Old Cairo: Heinemann (1977), 28.

17. Dan. 3:17–18.

18. Luke 11:1–2. Mell (1994) demonstrates that the Our Father has no clear links to the authentic Jesus tradition. The idea that the Our Father originated with John the Baptist was first suggested by Elliott (1973). Our explanation is indebted to three scholars who have explored the "baptismal" context of the Our Father without, however, attributing the prayer to John: Klein (1906), Swetnam (1972), Popkes (1990). On the historical relationship between John the Baptist and Jesus, see Murphy-O'Connor (1990).

19. Magnificat: Luke 1:47–55. Winter (1954); similarly Bammel (1984), 112–13 and Flusser (1988).

20. Josh. 7:9.

21. Akiba: Mishnah Yoma 8:9.

22. Ezek. 36:28.

23. Baptism in the name of God: it is not clear, though, whether this link to God was expressed in a formula or simply taken for granted; von Campenhausen thinks that baptism originally was celebrated as in Acts 8:38—without invocation of the name of Jesus; see von Campenhausen (1971). Ezek. 9:4.

24. *Praying Together* (1988), 2. For the manuscript reading of Luke 11:2, see Gregory of Nyssa, *The Lord's Prayer*, sermon 3 = *PG* 44:1157; Leaney (1956). Unlike most scholars, Leaney takes the alternative reading to be the original one. For "spirit" and "cleansing" in Ezekiel, see Ezek. 36:26.33.

25. "Father" used in prayer: 3 Macc. 6:3; Mark 14:36.

26. Davidic king: Ezek. 37:22–24.

27. Sirach on prayer: Sir. 7:14.

28. Josephus, *Jewish Antiquities* 18:116; see also Luke 3:10–14. Abounding Love: Heinemann *et al.* (1975), 23–24.

29. Tax-collectors: Luke 7:29.

30. Josephus, *Antiquities* 18:117. The New Testament reference to John's "baptism of repentance for the forgiveness of sins" (Mark 1:4) "Christianizes" John.

31. For the "trial/temptation" tradition, see e.g., Deut. 8:2.

32. On communal fasting in first-century CE Judaism, see Baumann (1993).

33. Origen, *On Prayer* 2:4 = *GCS Origenes* 2:302–3.

34. For the sequence of baptism and recitation of the Our Father, see *Didache* 7–8 (ca. 110/160 CE) = *SC* 248:170–74; relevant secondary sources include Rordorf (1980/81), 4; Popkes (1990). For a biblical text suggesting the sequence of baptism and prayer, see Luke 3:21. Jesus baptizes: John 3:22.

35. In the gospel of Matthew, the separation of Matt. 7:7–11 from the Our Father and the insertion of 6:14–15 obscure the unconditional promise attached to the Our Father.

36. "John performed no sign," John 10:41. "Mystery": Luke 8:10.

37. Mishnah, *Taanit* 3:8. Galilean magicians addressing God as "father": Safrai (1994), 6–7.

38. S.L. Davies (1995), 107–12.

39. M. Smith (1978), 132.

40. Naaman: 2 Kgs. 5.

41. All quotations are from Cyprian, *Lord's Prayer* 12 = *CCSL* 3A:96–97.

42. Ps. 22:29. In addition to Ps. 22 see especially Ps. 91; for the interpretation of these psalms, see Vorländer (1975a).

43. M. Smith (1978), 133.

44. Ethical preaching of John the Baptist: Luke 3:11–14.19.

45. Every believer a miracle-worker: Mark 16:17–18. Lindemann (1989), 91–100 explores the relationship between Matt. 4 and the Our Father.

46. Origen, *On Prayer* 30:1–2 = *GCS Origenes* 2:545/48; Tertullian, *On Prayer* 8:3–4 = *CCSL* 1:262; Cyprian, *Lord's Prayer* 27 = *CCSL* 3A:107. Odes of Solomon 14:5 = Charlesworth (1983–85), II:748. For the Evil One as Satan in ancient Jewish (apocryphal) sources, see Black (1990).

47. For the distinction between "traditional" and "utopian" religion in early Judaism, see J.Z. Smith (1990), 121–43. The importance of the distinction is underlined, though in dif-ferent terminology, by Cohn (1993); we disagree with Cohn's otherwise excellent study in arguing that Jesus does not seem to have held the "utopian" vision. For the "thaumaturgic response," we rely on Wilson (1973), 24–25.

48. Cyprian, *Lord's Prayer* 8 = *CCSL* 3A:93 (ca. 251/52 CE).

49. Saint Benedict, *Monastic Rule* 13 = *SC* 182:520.

50. On ancient, especially Roman notions of unchangeable ritual formulae, see Klinghardt (1996), 452–56.

51. Liturgical use of the Our Father: Augustine, *Sermon* 227:64 = *SC* 116:240. Eucharistic sense of bread-petition: Cyprian, *Lord's Prayer* 18 = *CCSL* 3A:101–2; Augustine, *The Lord's Sermon on the Mount* 2:7 [25–27] = *PL* 34:1279–81. (Pseudo-)Augustine, *Sermon* 6 (supplement) = *PL* 46:836; the same idea can be found in Augustine, *Sermon* 17:5 = *PL* 38:127. The emphasis on the petition for forgiveness can be documented from many patristic sources, see Furberg (1968), 50–56.104.109. "General Instruction of the Roman Missal," a text usually printed as the introduction to the Roman Missal of Paul VI (Eng. edn. 1974 and often); see also the *Documents on the Liturgy* (1982), 483 (no. 1446).

52. "Begs in the name": "General Instruction of the Roman Missal," see previous note.

53. Augustine, *Sermon* 59 = *SC* 116:186–99. On the date and provenance of the *Apostolic Constitutions*, see Marcel Metzger in *SC* 320:55–57; the relevant passage on baptism is 7:45 = *SC* 336:106.

54. Otto (1925).

55. Heiler (1920), 107. On the meaninglessness of the Our Father in worship, see Baumgarten (1914).

56. Cyprian, *Lord's Prayer* 9 and 28 = *CCSL* 3A:94.107.

57. All ancient healing cults include a rite of purification; for the classical world, see Burkert (1987), 16, for Judaism Sir. 38:9–12 and the apocryphal Prayer of Nabonidus = Vermes

(1995), 329. Oil of life, see *Life of Adam and Eve* 36 and 40–42 = Charlesworth (1983–85), II:272.274.

58. Name of Solomon: Josephus, *Jewish Antiquities* 8:46–49; Duling (1975). Jacob of Sama: Tosefta, tractate Hullin 2:22–23; cf. M. Smith (1978), 48–49 and Maier (1978), 182–92. Name of John: Acts 19:3. Simon: Irenaeus, *Heresies* 2:32,5 = *SC* 294:342; Simon is mentioned Acts 8:9, Menander and Carpocrates are known as Gnostic leaders, ca. 120 CE. Exorcism, baptism, and anointing in the name of Jesus: Matt. 7:22; Acts 2:38; James 5:14. Half-allegiance: Mark 9:39. Greek-speaking exorcists: Betz (1992), I:62 = *PGM* 4:1230ff. General discussions of the magic nature of the name of Jesus and of Christian prayer can be found in two older works, written in the wake of the German "history-of-religions" school: Heitmüller (1903), 257–65; Dibelius (1903), 14–17; see now also Aune (1996).

59. Origen, *Against Celsus* 1:24 = *GCS* Origenes 1:74–75; (1965), 23–24. On Origen's belief in Neoplatonic magic, see Dillon (1985); Shaw (1995), 181; Clerc (1995), 249–52.

60. Zechariah: Luke 1:9ff. Paul in the Temple: Acts 22:17–21. Light on the face: Exod. 34:29; Luke 9:29; see Reid (1994); Barker (1995a), 57. Thorn: 2 Cor. 12:7–9; on this text, see Price (1980).

61. Vision of Moses, etc.: Luke 9:28–36; on this passage, see below, part V, pp. 294–95. Messiah: Luke 9:18–20. "Opens up": Crump (1992), 115.

62. 1 Clem. 61; trans. after Lightfoot, *et al.* (1989), 63.

63. See Barker (1992) and Scroggs (1993).

64. Personal God: Vorländer (1975; 1975a). Hebrew Bible: Ps. 95:3.

65. "Those who invoke the name of Jesus": cf. Acts 9:14.21; 1 Cor. 1:2; Rom. 10:2; 2 Tim. 2:22. Bultmann (1951), I:128. The subject of prayer directed to Jesus has often been discussed; see Jungmann (1989); Hurtado (1988), 104–8.

66. Derrett (1979/80), 86.

67. Jungmann (1986), I:381–82. Schleiermacher (1928), § 147,1.

68. "Scrupulous; only to the God": Origen, *On Prayer* 15:2; 15:4 = *GCS* Origenes 2: 334.335; (1979), 113.114. St. Stephen: Acts 7:59. Breviarium Hipponense 21 = *CCSL* 149:39. Examples of early Christocentric prayer: Jungmann (1989); Hamman (1989), XX–XXI; Magne (1986).

69. Manual for clergy: Melanchthon, *CR* 23:LXXXIII–LXXXIX.67–75. *Loci praecipui theologici*: *CR* 21:955–84; 22:564–77. Pagans, Turcs: *CR* 23:LXXXIII.68; 21:955–56.974. Model prayer: *CR* 21:956–57. Our Father: *CR* 21:974.

70. Micklem (1936), 201.

71. "Thou, Heracles": Virgil, *Aeneid* 8:293–97 = (1934), II:81; further examples can be found in Frankfurter (1995). On the two styles, see Norden (1913), 220–23.

72. "Cold and dead; there is a certain": Addison in *Spectator* (1965), III: 514–15. For the history of the appreciation of the King James Bible and its language, see Norton (1993).

73. Seiler: quoted in Graff (1939), II:134.

74. Coffin (1972), 82–85. Episcopal Committee: McManus (1987), 206.

75. Legal background: Berger (1991); military use: 1 Kings 1:36. Egypt: Seybold (1992). Jerome, *Commentary on Galatians*, *PL* 26:355 (Roman basilicas) and Letters 75:3,1 = *CSEL* 55:32 (foreign-sounding word).

76. Amen in Corinth: 1 Cor. 14:16. Jewish prayers in the fourth-century *Apostolic Constitutions*: Charlesworth (1983–85), II:671–97. Justin, *First Apology* 65 = *PG* 6:428; Richardson (1970), 286. Revelation: Rev. 3:14. Augustine, *On Christian Doctrine* II, 11[16] = *CCSL* 32:42. "Do not so": Corpus Hermeticum 16:2 = (1960), 232. Amen: Stuiber (1985), 321–22. Brashear (1995), 3429 gives examples of the use of unintelligible sounds and foreign magical terms, from ancient Egyptian and Hebrew to Goethe (*Reineke Fuchs*, 11th song).

Amulet: Preisendanz (1973–74), II:219 = *PGM* Christian Papyrus no. 10.

77. "God give": H. Davies (1962–75), II:233. Miracles; "gradual": see the special issue of *Goodnews* (1992), 31–32. Rowell (1993) surveys "The Sacramental Use of Oil in Anglicanism and the Churches of the Reformation" from the sixteenth through the twentieth centuries. On healing services in the Church of England, see Lawrence (1976).

78. Luther's letter of December 4,1539 = *WA Br* 8:623, no. 3420. John Calvin, *Institutes* IV 19:19. For an in-depth study of the subject, see Ruthven (1993).

79. On the early history of praying for the dead, see Jungmann (1986), II:237–48; M. McLaughlin (1994), 178–249. Calvin, *Institutes of the Christian Religion* III, 5:10 = (1960), I:682. Luther, Gospel Sermon, First Sunday after Trinity (1522), *WA* 10/3:195.

80. Medieval traditions: Duffy (1992), 124.

81. Blessing used in the Roman Mass of Paul VI.

82. For the "solar" element in Num. 6:24–26, see Lev. 9:22–24, which refers to a literal manifestation of the divine "glory" after the priestly benediction had been pronounced. See also Keel and Uehlinger (1992), 420, who suggest that the implied reference may actually be to the mild light of the moon.

83. God's name placed on congregation: Num. 6:27. Magical link: cf. Num. 6:27 in the trans. of the Jewish Publication Society, 1967: "Thus they shall link My name with the people of Israel, and I will bless them." Amulets inscribed with the Hebrew text of the priestly benediction date from the sixth century BCE: Yardeni (1991).

84. Kant (1960), 161 (book 4, part 2:2). Voltaire, "Questions sur l'Encyclopédie," article "Prières" (1772) = (1879), XX:275–76.

85. Predestination: Thomas Aquinas, *STh* II II:832 = Albert and Thomas

(1988) 479–81. Thomas Aquinas, *Quaestiones disputatae de veritate* 6:6 = Albert and Thomas (1988), 419–24. *Liber de causis* = Brand (1981), 30.19–20.

86. Pittenger (1969), 155.

87. Schleiermacher (1987), 189 in the sermon "The Power of Prayer in Relation to Outward Circumstances." "Our primary": Schleiermacher (1928), 673 (§ 147:2).

88. Schleiermacher (1987), 192. Allowed in private devotion: Schleiermacher (1928), 675 (§ 147:3).

89. Franklin (1961), 95, in Franklin's list of virtues.

90. On Schleiermacher's attitude toward miracles, see C. Brown (1988), 122–23.

91. "The intentional; one who; when we": Pittenger (1974), 27.29.47. "Is a good; there are": Polkinghorne (1994), 9.

92. Cooper (1976), 422. Polkinghorne (1994), 7.

93. John Cassian, *Conferences* 9:27–28 = *SC* 54:63–64. Bonaventure, *Life of St. Francis* (Legenda maior) 2:1–2 = (1978), 191–92. Medieval nuns: Wilms (1923)197–98. Law, *A Serious Call to a Devout and Holy Life* (1728), chap. 11 = (1978), 158. Loyola, *Spiritual Exercises*, in De Nicola (1986), 164. Bossuet in Le Brun (1972), 239. Thomas à Kempis, *Imitation* 2:9 = (1989), 45. Pascal, *Pensées* no. 930 (513) = (1966), 320. A discussion of self-indulgent prayer can be found in Bremond (1928), VII:16–47.

94. "Fear; at all; if any": W. James (1958), 359.361.352 (lecture 19). "Exerts; something; a larger": W. James (1958), 394.394.396 (postscript).

95. James (1920), II:214.

96. "The Bible": D. Meyer (1988), 264. Peale (1992), 53 (chap. 4: "Try Prayer Power"). New thought: George (1993), 86–87.134–35. Shinn: Exoo *et al.* (1995). Kenyon and Hagin, see the polemical account of McConnell (1995).

97. James ([1902] 1958), 87–89. Women, see George (1993), 78–79.118–19.

98. Thipgen *et al.* (1957). Goodman (1988), 14–24. Allergy: Neal (1992), 117; for further material on personality-related diseases, see Coons (1988). Placebo: Messadié (1994). Peale (1992), 59 (chap. 4).
99. Yungblut (1991), 38.
100. "Is the place; to make; this is; the graces": Ulanov (1982), 20.43.43. 103.
101. Jung, *libido*: Ulanov (1994), 104.
102. Tillich (1952), 187.
103. "Receiving": Tillich (1967), 148. "We plunge": D.F. Strauss (1841), II:390 (§ 79).
104. Prayers attributed to authors: M. Smith (1978), 131–32.
105. For the "baptist" character of Luke 16:17, see Bammel (1958).

The Third Game: Sermon

1. Barth (1982), 51.
2. Plutarch, *Parallel Lives*: Numa 22.
3. Deut. 31:24–26; 2 Kings 22–23.
4. The expression and definition of "textual community" are from Stock (1983), 522; for the term "book religion," see Lang (1990). Josephus, *Against Apion* 2,175.
5. Hilkiah in Ezra's genealogy, see Ezra 7:1. The following account relies on Lang (1983), 141–48.
6. On the problematic issue of "translating" (?) the text read, see van der Kooij (1991). While according to van der Kooij the Hebrew term *mprs* implies carefully articulated reading, it can be argued that the last part of the relevant statement clearly implies an effort of explanation. According to Veltri (1993), Neh. 8 must be taken to refer to "explaining" rather than to translating the sacred text. The issue remains unsettled.
7. Scholars generally believe that Deut. 1–11 reflects the style of early preaching; see Westermann (1994), 125–45.
8. Israelite theory: Edelman (1991), 23. Persian theory: Blenkinsopp (1987). "This document": Pfeiffer *et al.* (1936), 103 (no. 51). "Three": Beckman (1996), 86. Assyrian vassal treaties: Holladay (1970), Weinfeld (1970), 64–65.
9. "So each": Philo, *The Special Laws* 2:62. "He [Moses]": Philo, *Hypothetica*, quoted in Eusebius, *Preparation of the Gospel* 8:7,12–13 = SC 369:74. Essenes: Philo, *Quod omnis probus liber sit* 81–82 = Vermes *et al.* (1989), 22. "In every": Acts 15:21; cf. Josephus, *Against Apion* 2:175.
10. Babylonian Talmud, Menahot 110a.
11. Morenz (1950), 714.
12. Justin, *First Apology* 67 = (1994), 129; Richardson (1970), 287.
13. For Justin's worship as a class of philosophy, see Clarke (1971), 87–88.123. On Taurus, see Aulus Gellius, *The Attic Nights* 17:20 = (1927), III:268–69. Assistant teacher: Grasberger (1971), II:144–48.
14. Sunday night, see the discussion in Klinghardt (1996), 502–3. Suetonius, *Lives of the Caesars*, Tiberius 32.
15. For Justin's tenement (?) apartment, see the Acts of Justin 3:1–3 in the A-recension = Musurillo (1972), 44. On the situation of "house churches" (Lampe) or rather "house schools" (Brent) in Justin's Rome, see Lampe (1989), 301–45; Brent (1995), 408.455. For Christianity as a philosophical school, see Wilken (1971); Brent (1995), 401–5.
16. Stock (1983), 522.524. Martha: Luke 10:38–42. Council of Basel: Mansi 29:163—"*theologum, qui sua doctrina et praedicationibus fructum salutis afferat.*" Hooker (1907), II:77–78 (book 5, no. 21).
17. Paul: 1 Cor. 4:20. "The hearts": Gregory the Great, *Moralia in Job*, on Job 12:15 = PL 75:960.
18. On the history of preaching during the first millennium CE, see R.E. McLaughlin (1991). Barth (1982), 51. Julian a Christian "reader"; his pagan project: Gregory of Nazianzus, *Oration* 4:23.97.111 = SC 309:118.244.266. It seems that Julian's project of a reform was supported by an apologetic treatise on pagan myth to be studied in the schools and, presumably, to be explained in the temples by qualified

teachers: Sallustius (1926). Revolution: Vovelle (1988), 160. Emerson (1903–4), I:150.

19. 2 Clement 19:1 = Wengst (1984), 264. Spurgeon (1954), 336. In a similar vein, the Council of Trent declared in 1563 that priests should be "equipped to teach the people what all need to know for their salvation," Tanner (1990), II, 749 (session 23, can. 14).

20. Inscription: The Theodotus inscription, on permanent exhibition in the Rockefeller Museum, Jerusalem, and now by certain scholars dated to the fourth (rather than the first) century, can be found in Greek in Schrage (1964), 811, n. 85 and is translated in Hestrin et al. (1973), 83. The early history of the synagogue is a heavily debated subject. Some recent contributions emphasize the "late" dating: there do not seem to be any synagogue buildings in Palestine dating from before the first century CE, and the idea of regular worship does not seem to antedate the destruction of the Temple in 70 CE; the debate can be followed in McKay (1994), Riesner (1995), Urman (1995).

21. For Jesus as a Cynic-style teacher, see F.G. Downing (1987).

22. Saul (Paul) as persecutor of the church: Acts 8:3; 9:1–2.

23. For privileges of the synagogues, see the discussion in Smallwood (1976), 120–43. Christian membership in the synagogue is discussed in Lang (1987), Stegemann (1991).

24. Earliest Christian sermon, apparently based on Isa. 54, see the Second Letter of Clement = Richardson (1970), 183–202; Wengst (1984), 238–69.

25. The two passages, Acts 4:42 and Luke 24, echo the two-part structure of Christian worship: preaching plus Eucharist. The allusion to the *Odyssey* 10:552–60 was detected by MacDonald (1994).

26. On the liturgical life in Origen's Caesarea, see Pierre Nautin in *SC* 232:100–91.

27. "Explains": Origen, *Against Celsus* 3:58 = *SC* 136:137. "Searches": Marrou (1981), II:253. Marrou (1958), 530 n. 2: "If we were to define the homily in terms of an ancient literary genre, we would have to refer to the explanation of texts as practiced by the *grammaticus*." For the "school" background of Origen's homilies, see Nautin in *SC* 232:132–36; Lang (1995); Scholten (1995).

28. Origen, *Homilies on Exodus* 12:2 = *SC* 16:246–47.

29. Epic version of the Pentateuch, etc.: Socrates, *Church History* 3:16 = *PG* 67:417–24. Julian, "Rescript on Christian Teachers" 423 D = (1923), III:120.

30. On Marius Victor, see Haarhoff (1958), 189. School at Nisibis: Junilius Africanus, *PL* 68:15 and Cassiodorus, *PL* 70:1105–6. Library: Marrou (1931). On Georgios Choiroboskos (who is often dated too early), the educator in Constantinople, see Glück (1967), 44–46; Kaster (1988), 234.394. The rise of schools in the West is discussed in Riché (1979).

31. Allusion to the woman of Luke 8:42–48: Origen, *Commentary on John* 10:28 [173] = *SC* 157:488.

32. "Purifies": Origen, *Commentary on John* 10:28[175] = *SC* 157:490. Stay at the beginning: Origen, *Commentary on Joshua* 20:1= *SC* 71:404/6.

33. Origen, *Homilies on Joshua* 19:4 = *SC* 71:402.

34. Origen, *Commentary on Joshua* 20:1 = *SC* 71:406–12.

35. For daily preaching during the weeks of Lent and Easter, see Kaczynski (1974), 69.126.

36. Gregory the Great, *Liber regulae pastoralis* = *SC* 381, 382. Humbert of Romans, *De eruditione praedicatorum* = (1982).

37. Gregory the Great, *Liber regulae pastoralis* 3:prologue = *SC* 382:258.

38. Gregory, *Liber regulae pastoralis* 3:1 = *SC* 382:262/66.

39. Tournaments, women: Humbert, *De eruditione praedicatorum* = (1982), 336–39.330–33.

40. Humbert, *De eruditione praedicatorum*

= (1982), 251; the quotation is from Gregory the Great, *Moralia* 18:39 = *PL* 76:58. On medieval sermon constructing, see Tugwell (1989).

41. For the medical metaphor in Gregory, see his *Liber regulae pastoralis* 2:10; 3:prologue; 3:2 = *SC* 381:240; 382:258.270. Ambrose, *Letters* 36:5–7 = *CSEL* 82/2:5–6. Augustine, Gospel of John 3:6 = *CCSL* 63:23. Gregory of Nazianzus, *Oration* 2:16–30 = *SC* 247:110–28. For the medical metaphor in ancient philosophy, see Malherbe (1989), 121–36. Gregory as a medical practitioner: J. Richards (1980), 47.

42. Humbert, *De eruditione praedicatorum* = (1982), 189.

43. "Sometimes": Humbert, *De eruditione praedicatorum* = (1982), 315.

44. "The chief; the final": Luther, *German Mass* (1526), *WA* 19:78.95.

45. Presence of families: *WA* 27:444.

46. "As a total": Bouwsma (1987), 238. On the rhetorical origins of Luther's notion of faith, see Dockhorn (1974).

47. *"Primo est"*: *WA TR* 4:479, no. 4765. The existential aim of Luther's preaching is analyzed by Rössler (1983).

48. Luther in a table talk of 1532 = *WA TR* 2: no. 2408 b. On Nikolaus Fabri, see N. Müller (1911), 282–83.316.

49. The woodcut's model is another woodcut, in which Cranach in the 1521 *Passional Christi und Antichristi* depicted the preaching of Christ, see the illustration in Groll (1990), 327, and what Groll writes about Luther being another Christ (72–77). For the crucifix which is now missing from the woodcut in the *Large Catechism*, see Grüneisen (1938), 32. Luther, *WA TR* 2: no. 2408 b. Laurentius de Voltalina, see Burke (1984), ill. no. 23: "Henricus de Alemannia lectures on ethics" (fourteenth century; painting on parchment in the Kupferstichkabinett of Berlin). Parable of the sower: Mark 4:3–8.

50. Jonathan Swift preached about "that luxury and excess men usually practice upon this day [Sunday], by which half the service thereof is turned into sin; men dividing the time between God and their bellies, when after a gluttonous meal, their senses dozed and stupefied, they retire to God's house to sleep out in the afternoon," i.e., during the sermon held on Sunday afternoon. Swift (1968), 218.

51. I. Mather (1978), 40 and 47.

52. Edwards (1834), II:12.

53. Against Calvinism, see Clapper (1989), 136–49. Wesley (1984), I:107.

54. Stone (1977).

55. Edwards, *Distinguishing Marks* (1741) = (1972), 247.

56. Preacher as lawyer; public act: Finney (1989), 83–86.306. For descriptions of Finney's performance, see Hambrick-Stowe (1996), 38.55.

57. Against Calvinism: Finney (1994), 303–21 and Hardman (1987), 279. Commitment now: Finney (1960), 206. Shift from Whitefield to Finney, see Finney (1989), 266–67; Packer (1995), 186–87. Jacksonian optimism, see J.E. Smith (1992). Graham, see Stackhouse (1992), 343–44.

58. Finney's pastoral efforts: Hardman (1987), 75.93–94.102–3; Hambrick-Stowe (1996), 40.108.213. Enquirers' meetings: Spurgeon (1954), 346; Keller (1924), II:171–83 and (1905), 11. American book: Keller (1910). Letters: Keller (1924), II:236.

59. Finney's intellectualism: Sweet (1976), Hambrick-Stowe (1996), 218. "Perfect": Sweet (1976), 219.

60 Catholic parish missions, singing: Dolan (1978), 82–83; Day (1990), 6–34. Finney: Hambrick-Stowe (1996), 218. "To deal": Meyer (1988), 354 (Oral Roberts). "Crafted": Lambert (1994), 97. On the de-emphasis on ecclesiastical values of fellowship, see Noll (1992), 92.95; Packer (1995), 188.

61. Barth (1971), 171.

62. Bells of altar boys: reported in Asendorf (1988), 20. Kitsch: Barth (1990), 90. "At best": Barth (1979a), 206.

63. "Instruction": Barth, *KD* I/2, 853 (§

22,2). "The announcement": Barth (1986), 30 [the English trans. (1991a), 44 is here not exact]; similarly, and with reference to the work of the Holy Spirit, *KD* I/2, 845 (§ 22,2) and Barth (1990), 455–57. "The central key; The Word": Barth (1991a), 74.80 = (1986), 58.63.

64. "Doctrine; a certain reservedness": Barth, *KD* I/2, 852 (§ 22,2). "A Form of": Barth in Godsey (1962), 87. "School": *KD* IV/3, 999 (§ 72,4). "The attempt": Barth, *KD* I/1,56 (§ 3,1); and, very similarly, Barth (1991a), 44 = (1986), 30.

65. Historical detail etc.: Barth, *KD* IV/3, 996 (§ 72,4). Thematic preaching: Barth (1933), 3–4; application: (1991a), 115 = (1986), 95. Taxi driver: (1979a), 208. *Titanic*, War: (1991a), 118 = (1986), 98.

66. Barth (1991), I:31.

67. Barth (1991a), 48 = (1986), 33.

68. Visiting evangelist, "bad form": Bowden (1983), 27. "Print and preach": Lambert (1994) discusses the eighteenth-century origins of this approach. Calvin, *Commentary on the Psalms*, preface; *CR* 59[31]:21. Barth (1993), 181–83.

69. Barth (1991a), 49.66 = (1986), 34.50.

70. Primacy of God's original revelation: Barth, *KD* IV/1, 858 (§ 63,2). Mystery: Barth (1967), 153.

71. Dingemans (1992), 25.

72. Thomas Aquinas, *On Truth* 27:3 ad 12 = (1980), III:169—"*praedicator autem se habet sicut disponens exterius ad fidem*"; see Moos (1993), 52–58. Recently, a Reformed theologian has claimed that Paul, in the New Testament, is a good Barthian who knows of no personal decision of faith but only of a creative act of God: Hofius (1991).

73. Günthör (1963), 25.

74. "Must not": Barth (1991a), 79 = (1986), 62. "From my": Barth (1979a), 283. Organ: Barth (1979), 489; *KD* IV/3, 994 (§ 72,4). Basel cathedral: Barth (1984), 294–97. "The simple": Barth (1984), 467–68. Barth here follows Calvin. For Calvin's opposition to "graven images," see the *Institutes of the Christian Religion* I, 11,13; for Calvin's opposition to applying the category of the "sacred" to the church building: see *ibid.*, III, 20,30.

75. Eiserfeld: Barth (1979), 380—Barth's letter of January 24,1967 to Otfried Hofius.

76. Beethoven etc.: Busch (1975), 69. Grünewald: Busch (1975), fig. 82 and Marquard (1995). Crucifix: Barth, *KD* IV/1, 379–80 (§ 59,3). Dürer etching: Barth (1984), 32. "Confus[ing]": Barth (1966), 71.

77. Barth, *KD* I/2, 275–80 (§ 16,2).

78. "God may speak": Barth, *KD* I/1,55 (§ 3,1). "Exhausted": Barth (1990), 75 ("The Need and Promise of Christian Preaching"). Nature, heart, Handel, etc.: Barth (1991), I:33–34. "Irrespective": Barth (1984), 296. Grünewald not allowed to decorate: Barth as quoted in Marquard (1995), 59.

79. "So pure": Zahrnt (1969), 118. Harnack in von Zahn-Harnack (1951), 415. "Turned": Tillich (1967), 240.

80. "Medicine": Schleiermacher (1970), I:219. "Herrnhutter": Schleiermacher to Georg Reimer, April 30, 1802 in Schleiermacher (1860), I:295.

81. Schleiermacher: R.M. Miller (1985), 52; Fosdick (1924), 264.

82. Fosdick's famous sermon can be found in Holland (1971), 338–48. "The most": R.D. Clark (1955), 425. "Ethical disloyalty; ethical teaching": Fosdick (1924), 206.205.

83. On Rockefeller's ecumenical activities, see Schenkel (1995), 121–96. "Not the pulpit": Fosdick (1956), 191. "From the": Scotford (1930), 890. Emerson, "Diary," February 16, 1833 = (1882), 95. "Sermon-ridden": Fosdick in R.M. Miller (1985), 230. "Liturgical service": Fosdick (1956), 202; see also R.M. Miller (1985), 240. Loudspeakers at Riverside Church: *Riverside Church* (1931), 40 and R.M. Miller (1985), 233. The history of loudspeakers installed in churches has never been recorded, but we have been able to get

the names of some of the churches that boasted such equipment at an early date: the Swedenborgian cathedral in Bryn Athyn, PA (1921), the Park Avenue Baptist church in New York (by 1926), the Catholic cathedral in Cologne, Germany (1926 or 1927), Notre Dame in Paris, France (by 1936).

84. Father; suicidal thoughts; "I learned": Fosdick (1956), 49–50.72–74.75.

85. Fosdick (1956), 94–95.

86. Eye medicine: Fosdick (1943), X.

87. "A Protestant; I am commonly; of all"; Alcoholics Anonymous: Fosdick (1956), 213.214–15.215.287. Counseling center; satisfaction: Fosdick (1943), VIII–IX. "The sinner": Fosdick (1949), 131 with reference to Luke 5:31.

88. "Indeed; the firsthand": Fosdick (1956), 216.218.

89. Pangloss: see Voltaire's novel *Candide* and R.M. Miller (1985), 69. Peale: George (1993).

90. Fosdick (1943), 263.

91. "Were I not": Fosdick in R.M. Miller (1985), 251. "Away from; a user": Rieff (1966), 25.27. "In New York City": Bonhoeffer (1958), I:94–95—formal report about his stay at Union Theological Seminary. "Educate": Bonhoeffer (1991), 129.

92. Hierocles, *On the Golden Verses* (1974), 118, see O'Meara (1994), 159.

93. Origen, *Commentary on John* 10:28[175] = *SC* 157:490.

94. Christian teaching called "word of God": Acts 13:5—Christian missionaries "proclaim the word of God in the synagogues of the Jews."

95. Hierocles, *On the Golden Verses* (1974), 118.

96. Swift (1968), 213. Diakonoff (1991), 62. The atemporality of traditional oratory, its avoidance of dialogue and reliance on ancestral authority are a well-studied anthropological subject, see M. Bloch (1974), Kuipers (1990).

97. "The teaching": Origen, *On the First Principles* 1:preface = *SC* 252:78. "But among": Origen, *Homilies on*

Luke 1 = *SC* 87:100. Origen on the canon: Eusebius, *Church History* 6:25 = *PG* 20:580–85.

98. Barth in Godsey (1962), 97.

99. "From the fountainhead; This should be": Alan of Lille, *The Art of Preaching* 1 = *PL* 210:111.113; (1981), 17.20.

100. "Experiential; Those who": Humbert, *De eruditione praedicatorum* = (1982), 217–18. "Derives from": Alan of Lille, *The Art of Preaching* 1 = *PL* 210:111; (1981), 17. Shepherd (1924), 28. Niebuhr (1953), 657.

The Fourth Game: Sacrifice

1. *Génie du Christianisme* [1802], IV, 1:5.

2. Ambrose, *De officiis* 1:238 = *PL* 16:94.

3. Livy, *Roman History* 3:3,7. Plato, *Statesman* 290 C/D (trans. Benjamin Jowett).

4. On early gift-giving, see Montagner (1988), 301–3.308. Bowlby (1969), 352—"a boy, just short of two years."

5. *Do ut des*: late Roman jurisprudence used the expression to define the business transaction as based on an implied bilateral contract (Corpus Iuris Civilis, Digesta 19:5,5). Josephus, *Against Apion* 2:196.

6. Homer, *Iliad* I:35–43, trans. Richard Lattimore. Herodotus, *Histories* I: 132.

7. Lucian, *On Sacrifices* 2 = (1974), II:114–15. Plato, *Laws* 885 B, 888 C. Sallustius, *Concerning the Gods and the Universe* 16:1; the opposite is also true: "the sacrifice of victims without a prayer is supposed to be of no effect," Pliny, *Natural History* 28:3 [10].

8. Tibullus, *Elegies* I,1:24. Traditional formula: Marcus Cato, *On Agriculture* 134. Lactantius, *On the Anger of God* 8:2 = *SC* 289:116.

9. "Commerce": Lawson (1910), 338. Difference between Roman and Greek relationship with deities, see Latte (1968), 51–52. Van Baal (1976), 178; the author also comments on the

difference between giving and trading, 165ff.

10. On the origins of sacrifice in the milieu of early sedentary people, see J.Z. Smith (1987), 197–202.

11. Letter of Aristeas 92–99 = SC 89: 148/52; English trans., here slightly edited, in Charlesworth (1983–85), II:19.

12. The description and interpretation of ritual acts rely on Billerbeck (1964), Milgrom (1976), and standard sources.

13. Quality of lifestock for sacrifice: Lev. 22:23.

14. Daily sacrifice: Num. 28:2–8. Josephus, *Against Apion* 2:196: prayer for common welfare. Plato, *Laws* 828 B and *Eutyphro* 14 B.

15. Philo, *De decalogo* 30 (§ 159); see also *De specialibus legibus* 27 (§ 145).

16. Gese (1981), 117–40. Chilton (1992; 1994).

17. Lev. 3:2; 7:12–13. Mishnah Pesahim 5:2; Mishnah Menahot 9:8.

18. Lev. 1:11; Mishnah Zebahim 2:1 and Mishnah Pesahim 5:5.

19. Step 3: Lev. 3:2. Step 4: Lev. 3:3–4; 7:12–14, 30; 8:25–29. Num. 15:8. The presentation of a live animal before God (i.e., before the altar) is referred to as an exception (Lev. 16:10). On the correct understanding of the "elevation" (Hebrew, *tenoufah*) gesture, see Milgrom (1990), 425–26.

20. Num. 15:10. Ps. 116:13. Sir. 50:15. (Ps. 116 implies that sacrificers, not priests, present the wine, but by New Testament times, this apparently had changed.)

21. Lev. 7:15.

22. The Old Testament does not include any prayer texts or words of offering recited at sacrifices. 2 Chron. 30:21–22 implies the existence of such prayers. For "body" (*sôma*) and "blood" (*haîma*) as belonging to the sacrificial vocabulary, see Hebr. 13:11.

23. Wine—bread: Luke 21:17–19; bread—wine: Mark 14:22–23 and Matt. 26:26–28.

24. For an early reference to the Chris-

tian sacrifice as *eucharistia* "thanksgiving," see Didache 9 = SC 248:174 (ca. 110/160 CE). See also the verb "to give thanks" (*eucharistein*) in the New Testament report on the Last Supper, Matt. 26:27.

25. Cucumber sacrifice: Evans-Pritchard (1956), 203. Egypt: Bonnet (1952), 425. Poor man: 2 Sam. 12:3. Pigeons, flour: Lev. 5:11; 12:8. Psalms: Ps. 141:2; 119:108; 51:19; our interpretation is indebted to Haran (1988), 22. Midrash Tanhumah Buber, Tsaw 8:9b, as quoted in Montefiore *et al.* (1974), 346. Lenience in Jewish sacrificial practice is discussed in Brin (1994), 74–81.

26. Marx (1994), 143–65. Zoroastrian state sacrifice: H. Koch (1988). The once popular idea that the prophet Zarathustra rejected animal sacrifice altogether is no longer maintained by scholarship.

27. This seems to be the implication of Matt. 17:24–27; see Chilton (1992), 129.

28. In Ps. 24:3, to "stand in Yahweh's holy place" seems to be a technical expression for the sacrificing layman's presence in the Temple.

29. The four reports: Matt. 21:12–13; Mark 11:15–19; Luke 19:45–48; John 2:13–17.

30. Eppstein (1964) reconstructs how the selling of animals was introduced into the Temple.

31. Recent scholarship: Chilton (1992), 91–111; (1994), 57–63.

32. Lay slaughtering of sacrificial animal: Lev. 3:2; priestly slaughtering in case of lay impurity: 2 Chron. 30:17. While the Mishnah (Zebahim 3:1) and Josephus' account of sacrificial practice in *Jewish Antiquities* 3:226–27 seem to imply that in the first century CE the layman killed his victim, Philo in *Special Laws* 2:145–46 denies this; presumably, practice varied. No laying on of hands by slaves, etc.: Mishnah, Menahot 9:8. When a woman's sacrifice was performed, she had access to the "court of the Israelites": Tosefta, Arakhin 2:1—"A woman would not be seen in the

court [of the Israelites] except during the offering of her sacrifice." People are "pure": Mark 7:14–23.

33. "While he is": Mishnah, Taanit 4:2. Hillel: Babylonian Talmud, Betsah/ Yom Tov 20a; as J. Milgrom pointed out to the author, this text implies the omission of the laying-on of hands only in the case of private mandatory sacrifices offered during festivals.

34. Ownership of Passover lamb: Exod. 12:3.6.

35. On the accusation of blasphemy, see Mark 2:7; 14:64.

36. General murmur: one should not think of silent prayer in the Temple, see van der Horst (1994), 25 n. 7. Vow: Acts 21:23–26.

37. Christ bears our sins: 1 Peter 2:24; John 1:29; is source of blood: Rom. 3:25; is high priest: Hebr. 9:25–26. For atoning human blood, see 4 Macc. 6:28–29; for human scapegoats in Greek rituals, McLean (1996), 88–100. The death of the goat slaughtered on the Day of Atonement may actually have symbolized the atoning death of the officiating high priest, see Barker (1996), 73.80. According to Rabbi Abbaye (fourth century CE), the high priest's death atones for others, though only for involuntary homicides, see Babylonian Talmud, Makkot 11b.

38. Eusebius, *Church History* 2:23,6 = *SC* 31:86. "I have come": gospel of the Ebionites, fragment 6 = Epiphanius, *Heresies* 30:16 = *GCS* Epiphanius 1:354. Judeo-Christians often adopted anti-sacrificial attitudes; in addition to the Ebionite fragment, one can refer to the Pseudo-Clementine *Recognitions*, a work dating from ca. 220 CE but based on earlier sources: according to this text, Christ came to abolish sacrifice, replacing it with baptism; see *Recognitions* 1:37,3; 39,1; 54,1 = F.S. Jones (1995), 67.69.87.

39. Scholars differ in their opinion about the date of the final cessation of Jewish sacrificial worship. Did it cease after 70 CE (Schwier 1989, esp. 335 n. 17)? Or did it continue until

135 CE (K.W. Clark 1980)? Or did only private sacrifice continue for some time after 70 CE (Guttmann 1967)?

40. Josephus, *Against Apion* 2:39.

41. Mark 14:24— "This is my blood of the covenant which is poured out for many." See Lev. 4:1–5:13 for the "sin offering" which scholars also term the "purification offering." Day of Atonement: Lev. 16. Eating of the atonement goat: Epistle of Barnabas 7:4 = *SC* 172:130; Mishnah, Menahot 11:7.

42. "The fruits; bread; has given; it is also": Irenaeus, *Heresies* 4:18,4; 17,5; 17,5; 18,6 = *SC* 100:608.590/ 92.590.614.

43. Complex ritual: Lev. 23:13; 2 Kings 16:13; series, see Lev. 9. Irenaeus, *Heresies* 4:18,1–2 = *SC* 100:596/98. For the interpretation, see Wetter (1922), 92–95; Gamber (1982), 32–37. A list of the varieties of gifts can be found in Jungmann (1986), II:10.

44. Irenaeus, *Heresies* 4:18,2 = *SC* 100:598.

45. "Holy Father": *Suscipe, sancte Pater* (Mass of Pius V, 1570); see Jungman (1986), II:54.57. Sacred silence: Christian, see Theodore of Mopsustia, *Homily* 15:28–29 = Mingana (1933), 87–88; pagan: Greek practice of *euphêmein*, see Stengel (1920), 111. Thomas Aquinas, *STh* III:83,4. Duns Scotus, see A. Clark (1950), 323. Durst (1963), 277–78. Catechism (1994), no. 1350. Suárez (1866), XXI:860 (no. 16). "Has blinded": Calvin, *Institutes* IV:18,1.

46. John Chrysostom, "Thirty-Third Homily on Hebrews," *PG* 63:230.

47. Temple, high priest, altar, sacrifice: Eusebius, *Church History* 10:4, 1.23.44.68 = *SC* 55:81.88.96.102. Solomon: Wilkinson (1981), 298–310. "Propitiated": Eusebius, *Life of Constantine* 4:45 = *PG* 20:1196.

48. "The Church presents": Eusebius, *Commentary on the Psalms*, *PG* 23:1096. Eusebius is one of the first theologians to make use of the expression "unbloody sacrifice" which

later became a standard formula; see Gesteira Garza (1989) and Stevenson (1991).

49. Julian, "Letter to Maximus, the Philosopher" = (1923), III: 24–25. Oxen becoming scarce: Ammianus Marcellinus, *History*, 25:4,17. Bronze coins: Sozomenos, *Church History* 5:19,2 = *GCS* Sozomenus 223; Frend (1984), 608. Libanius, *Oration* 30:33–34 = (1977), II:131.

50. "Provided that": Eusebius, *Life of Constantine* 2:45 = *PG* 20:1021. From Eusebius' perspective, pagan sacrifices had never been legitimate, and the Christian sacrifice superseded the bloody sacrifices of the Hebrews (rather than those of the pagan state), see Eusebius, *Demonstratio evangelica* 1:10 = *PG* 22:83–94. Cyprian, of course, also thought that "the ancient [Jewish] sacrifice should be made void, and a new one should be celebrated," *Testimonies against the Jews* 1:16 = *CSEL* 3:49. "No person": Codex Theodosianus 16:10,10 = Pharr *et al.* (1952), 473. For the anti-sacrificial legislation and the survival of pagan worship, see Trombley (1993), I:1–97.

51. "For when": Constantine to proconsul Anulius, quoted in Eusebius, *Church History* 10:7 = *SC* 55: 112–13. "We decree": Codex Theodosianus/Novels of Theodosius Augustus 3:8 = Pharr (1952), 489–90. Augustine, *City of God* 10:20 = *CCSL* 47:294.

52. Cyril of Jerusalem, *Catechetical Lectures* 23:8–10 = *SC* 126:156–61.

53. On the traditional character of the Christian prayer for the state, see 1 Tim. 2:2, the report on Cyprian's martyrdom in the *Acta Proconsularia CSEL* 3/3:CX, and Eusebius, *Church History* 7:11,8 *SC* 41:181 with n. 15. For the dead family members of Christians, see 1 Cor. 15:29—wishing to help their ancestors, some Christians have themselves baptized "on behalf of the dead."

54. Cyril of Jerusalem, *Catechetical Lectures* 23:10 = *SC* 126:158.

55. Human sacrifice: for the Bible, see Micah 6:7; for classical sources, Speyer (1989), 154–55. "Was wroth; has stopped": John Chrysostom, *Homilies on Hebrews* 16 and *Commentary on Galatians* 2:8 = *PG* 63:123; 61:646. No less efficacy: *Homilies on First Timothy* 5 = *PG* 62:530.

56. "As long": Augustine, *Sermon* 296 = *PL* 38:1356. R.L. Fox (1986), 38. On the wrath of the gods in ancient thought, see Speyer (1989), 140–59. Ire because of neglect, see Pleket (1981), 172.

57. For the various meanings of "propitiation" in an ancient sacrificial context, see Kirk (1981), 74. Celsus in Origen, *Contra Celsum* 8:24 = *GCS* Origenes 2:240.

58. Cyril, *Mystagogical Lectures* 5:4 = *SC* 126:150. John Chrysostom: *Homilies on First Corinthians* 24:3 = *PG* 61:203 and *On the Incomprehensibility of God* 3:375 = *SC* 28[bis]:218.

59. Augustine, *Enarrationes in Psalmos* 129:7 = *PL* 37:1701 (*accipit sacerdos a te quod pro te offerat, quando vis placare Deo pro peccatis tuis*). Public reading of names: Innocent I, *Letter* 25 = *PL* 20:553–54. "Remember": *Memento, Domine*; this prayer is reconstructed and explained by Stuiber (1954). Our translation of *pro redemptione animarum suarum* with "for the cleansing of their souls [from the stain of sin]" reflects Stuiber's explanation.

60. Ambassadors: Gregory, *Homilies on the Gospels* II 37:7–10 = *PL* 76:1278–81, commenting on Luke 14:31–32. On Gregory's sacrificial theology of the Mass, see Gramaglia (1991), esp. 242ff.

61. For sacrifice as the central notion of Gregory's theology, see Straw (1988), 20.179–93. Daily Mass: Gregory, *Dialogues* 4:60,1 = *SC* 265:200.

62. "Again": Gregory, *Dialogues* 4:60,2 = *SC* 265:200/2.

63. Gregory, *Dialogues* 4:59 = *SC* 265:196–200.

64. Augustine, *City of God* 20:8 = *CCSL* 48:820.

65. Augustine, *Enchiridion* 110[29] = *CCSL* 46:108-9.

66. Gregory, *Dialogues* 4:57,8–16 = *SC* 265:188–94.

67. Gregory, *Dialogues* 4:60,2 = *SC* 265:200.

68. On votive Masses, see Jungman (1986), II:129–32; Amiet (1987); see also Franz (1902), 115–291. Thomas Aquinas, *STh* Suppl. 71:9,5.

69. Candles, alms, see Franz (1902), 265.271–72.291. On the beginnings of "private Mass," see Angenendt (1983), who also comments on the honorarium priests received for saying Mass, pp. 167–74.

70. Statistics of priests: Vogel (1986), I. Müller (1962), 131. "He may say": Poenitentiale Vindebonense "A" in Wasserschleben (1851), 240.

71. Many altars: Bandmann (1962); I. Müller (1962), 129–34; Möbius (1984). Auxerre synod: *Mansi* 9:913. Gregory, *Letters*, in *Monumenta Germaniae Historica (Epistolae)* 1:422–23. Three Masses: granted under King Edgar of England (r. 959–75): *Mansi* 18:516. Charlemagne: *PL* 97:283.

72. Vogel (1986), 273. Möbius (1984) discusses the multiplication of altars as places for the celebration of private Masses.

73. "I will give you": Biel (1963–76), I:277/lecture 28 D. For the specially privileged altar of Pope Gregory XIII, see Göttler (1994); (1996), 54–88. Several recent studies are devoted to established Masses: Chiffoleau (1980)—Avignon, France, ca. 1320–1480; Eire (1995), 168–231—Madrid, Spain, sixteenth century; Kreider (1979)—England, with abolition by Act of Parliamant in 1545/47.

74. For unbeneficed clergy in thirteenth-century England, see McHardy (1987). On chaplaincies: Wood-Leigh (1965), esp. 235: "The great majority of founders . . . provided a house for the priest or priests as part of the endowments"; Avril (1993).

75. Up to nine Masses: Walafrid Strabo, *PL* 114:943 and Sicard of Cremona, *PL* 213:148. Canon law: Yvo of Chartres, *Decretum* and Gratianus, *Decretum* (*PL* 161:178; 187:1723); on the attempt to reduce the number of Masses said by priests, see Franz (1902), 73–77. Luther, *The Babylonian Captivity of the Church* (1520), *WA* 6:512. Cranmer (1846), I:353. Ignatius, *Constitutions of the Society of Jesus* VI:2,7; VII:4,4 = (1908), 187.216.

76. On medieval clerical proletariat, see e.g., Franz (1902), 294; on clerical dependence upon honorariums given for Mass even as late as the seventeenth century, see Venard (1980); Bremond (1932), IX:236. Stories: Ancient and medieval sources include Augustine, *City of God* 22:8,6 = *CCSL* 48:220; Gregory the Great, *Dialogues* 4:59 = *SC* 265:196–200; Bede, *A History of the English Church and People* 4:22 = *PL* 95:206–7; Caesarius of Heisterbach, *Dialogus miraculorum* 12:32–33 = (1851), II:342–44.

77. The "merit of Christ" is a standard subject of medieval theology, and it figures prominently both in the textbook of medieval scholasticism, Peter Lombard's *Sentences* (book 3:18–19; *PL* 192:792–98) and in Biel's notes on this book: Biel (1979), III:310–29. The idea of a "treasure" (*thesaurus*) was suggested by Wisd. 7:14 and was used in official statements, see *DH*, nos. 1025–27.

78. Biel (1963–76), IV:106/lecture 85 L: "Quicquid christus salvator noster meruit se offerens in cruce pro omnibus generaliter . . . hoc sacrificio applicetur particulariter singulis."

79. The issue of the "finite" value of Mass was widely discussed in the later Middle Ages, see Iserloh (1961). On the limited value of Mass and comparison with the statue, see Biel (1963–76), I:265/lecture 27 K and 4:101/lecture 85 F; the reference to the statue of Cicero is of course traditional, see Augustine, *Ad Simplicianum* 2:3,2 = *CCSL* 44:83 and Thomas Aquinas, *STh* III 83:1.

Holiness of the church, see 1:246/
lecture 26 J.

80. Impossibility of rejection, see Biel
(1963–76), IV:103/lecture 85 G; see
also I:245/lecture 26 G where the
expressions *ex opere operato* and *ex
opere operantis* are used.

81. John Duns Scotus, *Quodlibeta* 20:
1,4 = (1895), XXVI:299–300. Biel
(1963–76), I:246–47 and 250/lecture
26 K.P. For the traditional character
of the "three fruits," see Amalarius of
Metz (*PL* 105:1138), ninth century.
For the history of the doctrine, see
Iserloh (1961); Kilmartin (1966), esp.
50–53.

82. Parish priest's obligation: Biel (1963–
76), I:250–51/lecture 26 P. Heretic:
I:248/lecture 26 M. Story: II:403/
lecture 57 K; the entire lecture 57 is
devoted to the "Mass said on behalf
of the dead." Heaven: IV:106–7/lec-
ture 85 M.

83. Hierarchical order: Biel (1963–76),
I:251/lecture 26 Q.

84. Mass said for one person: Biel (1963–
76), I:263–64/lecture 26 J.

85. "This [priest]": Biel (1963–76),
I:278/lecture 28 E. "It is legitimate":
I:282/lecture 28 L. "Without":
I:277/lecture 28 E. "*Non . . .
celebrat*": I:276/lecture 28 C. Scripture: I:278/lecture 28 F with reference to Luke 10:7 and 1 Cor. 9:13.

86. Columbus (1982), 327.

87. "*Simplices; potest*": Biel (1963–76),
I:255/lecture 26 T.

88. Prayer with tears: Tob. 12:12
Vulgate. Gregory the Great, *Dialogues* 4:58:1 = *SC* 265:194, who also
refers to tears; tearful prayer as the
most effective kind is mentioned in
Justin, *Dialogue with Trypho* 90:5 =
PG 6:692. Sources on the sacrificial
self-offering of the faithful include
Gertrude of Helfta, *Mass, Celebrated
by the Lord Himself* 9 = *SC* 331:296/
98; Thomas à Kempis, *Imitation of
Christ* 4:7 = (1989), 142; Pope Pius
XII, *Mediator Dei* (1947), nos. 80–
81.98.103–4; Vatican II, *The Ministry
of Priests* (1965), no. 5: in the Eucharist, the faithful are "invited and led
to offer themselves, their labors, and

all created things together with Him
[Christ]."

89. Cyprian, *Letter* 63:15 = *CSEL*
3:713—variant reading.

90. This is Cyprian, *Letter* 63 = *CSEL*
3:701–17, of which an English trans.
can be found in *Cyprian of Carthage*
(1984–89).

91. On the relative mildness of the
Decian persecution of 250 in North
Africa, see Frend (1984), 334 n. 85.

92. It seems that Cyprian actually
enjoyed the status of a "patriarch,"
i.e. a leader of the North African
church. As such, his title was *papa* or
papas, see *Letter* 8:1 and the address
line of *Letters* 23 and 30, etc., also the
Acta proconsularia of Cyprian 3 =
CSEL 3:485.536.549; 3/3:CXII.

93. Cyprian, *To Demetrian* 3 = *CSEL*
3:352–53. For the stoic background
of the theme of the aging world and
Cyprian's indebtedness to the philosopher Seneca, see Koch (1926),
286–313.

94. Cyprian, *Letter* 58:1 = *CSEL* 3:656–
57.

95. Cyprian, *Letter* 10:2 = *CSEL* 3:491.

96. "The passion": Cyprian, *Letter* 63:15
= *CSEL* 3:713. *The Passion of
Perpetua and Felicitas* 15:5–6 = *PL*
3:48; Musurillo (1972), 123–25. An
earlier document, written in 177 CE,
refers to the glories the suffering
Christ has accomplished in the body
of Sanctus the martyr: Eusebius,
Church History 5:1,23 = *SC* 41:12.

97. For Cyprian's theology of martyrdom, see Laurance (1984), 181–
94. The theme of "imitation" is of
course not alien to both the New
Testament and popular philosophy,
see 1 Cor. 11:1 and Malherbe (1987),
52–60.71–72.

98. "As often": 1 Cor. 11:26; Cyprian,
Letter 63:10 = *CSEL* 3:708–9.

99. It seems that the dominical words
over bread and wine were first understood as the words actually effecting
the consecration by Tertullian,
Against Marcion 4:40,3 = *PL* 2:460.
This passage would imply that, by
the time of Cyprian, the African
church already had a tradition of

using the dominical words in its liturgy. Tertullian, although never mentioned by Cyprian, is considered to have been a major authority for the bishop. Jerome records the tradition that Cyprian read Tertullian daily and would call for his writings, *Da magistrum!*—Give me the master!, see Jerome, *On Famous Men* 53 = *PL* 23:698.

100. Melchizedek: Gen. 14:18. The hint at a revelation frames Cyprian's *Letter* 63; in the opening paragraph, he speaks of "the inspiration and command of God," in the conclusion of "the Lord's warning"; *Letter* 63:1.19 = *CSEL* 3:702.717.

101. "*Sacrificare*": Cyprian, *On the Lapsed* 25 and 26 = *CSEL* 3:255. "*Oblatio*": Cyprian, *Letter* 63:9 = *CSEL* 3:708. Christ gave his life: Cyprian, *Letter* 63:14 = *CSEL* 3:713. "The Lord's passion": Cyprian, *Letter* 63:17 = *CSEL* 3:714. "In a state": Cyprian, *Letter* 75:10 = *CSEL* 3:818. Cyprian applies the term of *sacerdos* almost exclusively to the bishop, rarely to presbyters, see Bévenot (1979), 413–29 and Laurance (1984), 198–200.

102. For information on third-century North African ritual, see Frend (1982), 154.

103. Cyprian, *Letter* 63:9 = *CSEL* 3:708, echoing Matt. 26:2.

104. "We ask": Cyprian, *Lord's Prayer* 18 = *CSEL* 3:280. Daily eucharistic worship is also implied by *Letter* 57:3 and 58:1 = *CSEL* 3:652.657. Daily eucharistic worship as a general custom is not attested prior to the third century; although the situation of persecution made the custom desirable, it was not introduced as a "crisis measure," see Klinghardt (1996), 521. For corporate morning prayer, see the *Apostolic Tradition* 41 = *SC* 11bis:125.

105. Domestic use: Hippolytus, *Apostolic Tradition* 36–37 = *SC* 11bis:119. Custom still practiced: Cyprian, *On the Lapsed* 26 = *CSEL* 3:256.

106. All quotations from Cyprian, *Letter* 76:3 = *CSEL* 3:830.

107. "Sacrificial; holy": Cyprian, *Letter* 76:3 = *CSEL* 3:830. Abel/Cain: Cyprian, *On the Lord's Prayer* 24 = *CSEL* 3:285. "Now a more": Cyprian, *Letter* 58:1 = *CSEL* 3:656–57.

108. Augustine, *Sermon* 159:1 = *PL* 38:868: *iniuria est enim pro martyre orare.* Cyprian, *Letter* 39:3 = *CSEL* 3:583. For the prayer for dead individuals who were not martyrs, see Cyprian, *Letter* 1:2 = *CSEL* 3:466. For the "dishonesties" of some of the confessors, see Cyprian, *Unity of the Catholic Church* 30 = *CSEL* 3:228.

109. "Mingled": Cyprian, *Letter* 63:13 = *CSEL* 3:711–12. On the limited atoning force of martyrdom, see Cyprian, *Unity of the Catholic Church* 14 = *CSEL* 3:222. Cyprian bases his symbolical interpretation of the water added to the wine on a series of correspondences which can be represented thus: water = God's people = sinful nations = those whom Christ bore along with their sins = "waters where the harlot is seated" = "multitudes and nations and tongues," with the quotations taken from Rev. 17:15; see *Cyprian of Carthage* (1984–89), 3:296.

110. On the peaceful community as a sacrifice to God, see Cyprian, *Lord's Prayer* 23 = *CSEL* 3:285; the punishment of unworthy participants is told in *On the Lapsed* 25–26 = *CSEL* 3:255–56. Paul's warning: 1 Cor. 11:29.

111. The above argument requires some detective work, which has been done admirably by Frend (1982),156–58, who comments on the specific meaning of sacrificing "for" the martyr. Interestingly, sacrifice on behalf of the dead is mentioned for the first time in a book deeply involved with martyrdom: 2 Macc. 12:45.

112. Pontius, *Life of Cyprian*; text in von Harnack (1913); English trans. in Deferrari (1952), 5–24.

113. "A true": Augustine, *City of God* 10:6 = *CCSL* 47:278—*Verum sacrificium est omne opus quod agitur, ut sancta societate inhaereamus Deo.* Sallustius, *Concerning the Gods and the Universe*

16. "Intact": Augustine, *City of God* 20:26,1 = *CCSL* 48:749. In heaven: Augustine, *City of God* 10:7 = *CCSL* 47:279.

114. Augustine, *City of God* 10:6 = *PL* 41:283.

115. "Now we": Augustine, *City of God* 19:23,5 = *CCSL* 48:694–95. "After all": Augustine, *Sermon* 229 = *PL* 38:1103.

116. (1) See Augustine's understanding of 1 Cor. 10:17, "We being many are one bread, one body" (*unus panis, unum corpus multi sumus*) in the *City of God* 21:25 = *CCSL* 48:794. (2) See Augustine, *Sermon* 227 = *PL* 38:1099–101; Sermons Denis 6 and Guelf. 7 = Augustine (1930), 30.463. (3) On Augustine's insistence on the purity of sacrifices, see Augustine, *On the Psalms* 149:6 = *PL* 37:1952–53 and *City of God* 20:26 = *CCSL* 48:748–51. That we need Christ as our priest is explained in *On the Psalms* 131 (Latin, 130):1 and 4 = *PL* 37:1704–6. For the church as incorporated into Christ's sacrificial body, see Augustine, *On the Psalms* 27 (Vulgate, 26), 2nd explanation, 2 = *PL* 36:200: "As he could not find a reasonable and pure victim besides himself, he, the immaculate lamb, redeemed us by shedding his blood and incorporating us into himself as his members, so that we should also be the Christ." A thoughtful interpretation of Augustine's view of sacrifice is Lécuyer (1955).

117. Gregory the Great, *Homilies on the Gospel* 37:9 = *PL* 76:1279; repeated in *Dialogues* 4:58:1 = *SC* 265:194.

118. Tertullian, *Apology* 9:2–3 = *CCSL* 1:102. Mesha: 2 Kings 3:27. Isaac, Egypt: Gen. 22; Exod. 12. Semitic child sacrifice is documented in Ackerman (1992), 117–43 and S. Brown (1991); for an interpretation, see Levenson (1993).

119. Philo of Byblos, as quoted in Eusebius, *Praeparatio evangelica* 1:10,44 = *SC* 206:204.

120. Eusebius, *Praeparatio evangelica* 1:10,33 = *SC* 206:198.

121. Thomas à Kempis, *Imitation of Christ*

4:7 = (1989), 142. Catéchisme (1679), 320. On the sacrificial spirituality in France, see Bremond (1932), IX:135–55; Galy (1950).

122. "He repaired": Faillon (1873), II:150. Vow: Dupuy (1982), 240ff.

123. For the "crisis of the seventeenth century" and the theocentric spirituality it promoted, see McDannell *et al.* (1988), 167–69.

124. For Olier's indebtedness to Condren, see Galy (1950), 331–32. Paradise: Olier, *JC* 97. On Olier flagellating himself, and on self-flagellation in his seminary, see Faillon (1873), I:175; III:125.

125. See Galy (1950), 302–8. For seventeenth-century views of a "worldless" heaven, see e.g., Fénelon (1851–52), VI:138 (*Instruction sur la morale et la perfection*) and McDannell *et al.* (1988), 167ff. Fénelon studied at Olier's Séminaire Saint-Sulpice.

126. Augustine, *City of God* 10:20 = *CCSL* 47:294.

127. The "sword that cuts," possibly based on Hebr. 4:12, is a traditional idea, see Gregory of Nazianzus, *PG* 37:281. On the consecration as producing the resurrected Christ, see *EC* 396 and *CC* 59. Compare the standard medieval view that "*corpus transfiguratum offerimus,*" *Decretum Gratiani, PL* 187:1778.

128. Olier, *EC* 404. For other authors who see the elevation as an oblatory gesture, see Honorius Augustodunensis, *Sacramentary* 88 = *PL* 172:793; Letourneux (1680), 130–31.

129. Christ's sacrifice implies all sacrifices: Olier, *EC* 289.

130. Taylor, *Rule and Exercises of Holy Living* 4:10,3 = (1900), II:123. On the frontispiece's standard seventeenth-century theology, see McAdoo (1994). On Christ's heavenly sacrifice, see Lécuyer (1949) and Symonds (1966); for early Latin authors, see Paschasius Radbert, *PL* 120:1315; Hincmar of Reims, *PL* 125:912. Modern biblical scholars read Hebrews differently: Christ's one sacrifice is followed not by ever

new heavenly sacrifices but by ever new non-sacrificial acts of intercession on behalf of his faithful, see Hebr. 4:16; 7:24–25 and Loader (1981), 142–60.

131. The Father consumes: Olier, *EC* 430.
132. Faillon (1873), II:91–92; Monier (1914), 530–31.
133. The two stages of the eucharistic experience (purification, union) as they are delineated below represent an attempt to systematize Olier's ideas. For Olier's own (unpublished) statements on stages of spiritual development, see Glendon (1979).
134. "For our Lord": Olier's spiritual diary as quoted by Chaillot (1984), 87.
135. Bookstore: Faillon (1873), II:61. "The state": Olier's spiritual diary as quoted by Chaillot (1984), 76. On the engraving (whose details must be studied on the original Mellan print in the Bibliothèque Nationale; even the print in Faillon (1873), II:opposite p. 124 has added details), see Simard (1976), 186–89; Préaud (1988), 89–90.
136. Original idea of engraving: Monier (1914), 343–45.
137. Nineteenth-century engraving: Faillon (1873), III:opposite p. 176. Purgatory: Christ, in offering himself to the Father, always prays for the souls in purgatory, and so we should also make mention of the suffering souls in our prayers at communion; see *L* II:121–25/no. 239 and Faillon (1873), II:80.
138. Luther, *WA* 6:369.
139. Sacrificial communion: Grimal (1911), 318–30 in a chapter entitled "La communion immolante": "au moment de la communion, le vrai, le parfait communiant se met tout entier avec Jésus sur la croix comme une seule et même hostie" (330). Pope Pius XII, "Mediator Dei," in Megivern (1978), 61–127: Augustine, no. 103; "the same," no. 81; "themselves," no. 104; incomplete, no. 98. *Catechism of the Catholic Church* (1994), no. 1372.
140. Stevenson (1989), 80.

141. Jung (1988), 152.
142. The text of the so-called Lima-Liturgy can be found in Thurian (1983), 225–46.
143. "An instinct; communion; were the whole": Stevenson (1989), 78.79.73. "Were the whole": Isaac Watts, "When I survey the wondrous cross" (1707/9).

The Fifth Game: Sacrament

1. Chateaubriand (1951), I:66 (book 2:6).
2. On the power of the dead in ancient magic, see Bernand (1991), 131–55.259–82.399–402.
3. Frazer (1922), 52. For Christianity, see Cox (1965), 21–22.
4. Greek magical papyri: Brashear (1995). *Chaldean Oracles*: des Places (1966), Potter (1991). Iamblichus: des Places (1971), Shaw (1995). Coptic texts: Meyer *et al.* (1994). Richardson (1974), 576–77.
5. "Fill me": Prayer of Jacob, *PGM* XXIIb:1–26 = H.D. Betz (1992), 261; Charlesworth (1983–85), II:722–23; for the dating, see M. Smith (1986), 461. Comments on the essentially "pious" nature of ancient magic can be found in Shaw (1985), 7ff.; Graf (1991). *Unio liturgica*: Assmann (1995).
6. "Honorable": Augustine, *City of God* 10:9,1 = *CCSL* 47:281, reports the pagan opinion which he rejects; by Augustine's time, theurgy had been outlawed by the Christian empire, see Clerc (1996). Iamblichus, *Mysteries of Egypt* 10:7 [293] = des Places (1966), 214. The world view of theurgy is explained by Johnston (1990), 76–89.147 and (1992), Markus (1994), Shaw (1995), and Clerc (1995), 248–96. On the distinction between "black" and "white" magic, see Clerc (1995), 155.172–92.
7. Homer, *Odyssey* 19:457. Tertullian, *Scorpiace* 1:3 = *CCSL* 2:1069. Josephus, *Jewish Antiquities* 8:45. Augustine, *City of God*, 22:8,8 = *CCSL* 48:821. Edward Gibbon, *The*

Decline and Fall of the Roman Empire (1776–88), chap. 15. Von Harnack (1924), I:129–50. For an up-to-date analysis of Christian thaumaturgy, see Flint (1991).

8. Frazer (1922), 45. On the magic element in mystery religions, see H.D. Betz (1991), 250: "Information about and relics from the Greek mystery cults definitely suggest that magic was a constituent element in the rituals of the mysteries." The general cultural mood out of which the "mystery cults" developed is sketched by J.Z. Smith (1978), xiii–xv.

9. According to Pliny, *Natural History* 30:6[17], an Armenian magician initiated the Emperor Nero into "magical banquets" (*magicis enim cenis eum initiaverat*). Mystery meals are surveyed in Klauck (1986), 91–233. "Tense": Angus (1925), 61.

10. The classic work on Hellenistic Judaism as a mystery religion remains Goodenough (1935). For a recent defense of including early Christianity and part of Diaspora Judaism among ancient mystery cults, see Koester (1995), I:189–96.

11. Theurgical rites: Lev. 16:12–13; H.-P. Müller (1964). Von Rad (1958), 239–40.

12. The reconstruction largely follows the one proposed by Sänger (1980), 174–87. The two quotations are from *Joseph and Aseneth* 16:14.16 = Charlesworth (1983–85), II:228–29.

13. *Joseph and Aseneth* 8:5 = Charlesworth (1983–85), II:212 with the interpretation of Burchard (1987), 117. Dschulnigg (1989) wants to confine the sacred and magical aspect of food to the Passover meal as understood by Diaspora Jews. The divine names quoted are from the Mishnah's section on "Blessings," *Berakhot* 6:1;7:3 = *Mishnah* (1988), 9;11. The idea of food as carrier of supernatural power is also evident from numerous other passages collected by Jeremias (1977), 233–36 and Klauck (1986), 166–205.

14. Miracles: Mark 1:28. Solomon: the exorcistic meaning of the dictum was recognized by Oegema (1994), 147. "Unclean spirits": Mark 1:23.26.27; 3:11, and often.

15. Jesus as performer of a baptismal ritual: John 3:22. Baptism and spirit, etc.: Luke 3:21–22; see also the "Secret Gospel of Mark" discovered by M. Smith, in Schneemelcher (1991), I:108. Transfiguration: Mark 9:2–8 and parallel report in Matt. 17:1ff. Six days: Mark 9:2. Mount of Olives: Luke 22:43. Hypnotic state: Luke 9:32; 22:45.

16. For recent commentaries on the transfiguration of Jesus, see Pilch (1995), M. Smith (1996), II:79–86. Anatolius: see Sulpicius Severus, *Life of Martin* 23 = *SC* 133:302/6; on Anatolius's eastern provenance, see Jacques Fontaine, *SC* 135:994–95. Conversing with angels etc.: see Luke 4:1–13; 14:43–44 (Jesus); 2 Cor. 12:7–8 (Paul); Sulpicius Severus, *Dialogues* 2:13 = *CSEL* 1:195–97 (Martin). Assimilation of theurgist to the deity: see John 14:10 (Jesus); M. Smith (1996), II:68–78 on the Qumran-text 4Q 491; 3 Enoch 12 = Charlesworth (1983–85), I:265. The classic statements on Jesus the Theurgist are M. Smith (1973), 220–37; (1978) 96–104.120–22.134ff. and Barker (1996), 1–55.

17. Jesus and John the Baptist: Murphy-O'Connor (1990). On various organizational forms of the ancient mystery cults, see Burkert (1987), 31–53.

18. Third heaven: 1 Cor. 12:2–4. Seeing Christ: John 16:19; Rev. 4–5.

19. Passover: Exod. 12. Repetition of the "ten plagues of Egypt" (Exod. 7–12): Apocalypse of Abraham 29:15 = Charlesworth (1983–85), II: 704 and Rev. 9 and 16; the idea that the plagues could be repeated and hit Israel can also be found in canonical literature: Exod. 15:26; Deut. 28:60. Magic wand, etc.: Exod. 7:20; 9:8. For the prohibition on drinking blood, see Lev. 3:17; Mishnah, Parah 4:3 = Mayer (1964), 59 (passage not in Mishnah 1988). Jesus identifies: Mark 14:23.

20. Hatred between brothers: Mark 13:12; Matt. 24:10.
21. Origen, *Commentary on Matthew* = *GCS* Origenes 11:21. The earliest reference to marking one's face with the eucharistic wine dates from ca. 150 CE: Justin Martyr, *Dialogue* 40 = *PG* 6:561; the subject is discussed in Dölger (1932), III:231–44.
22. "Lord's food": 1 Cor. 11:20, see Kremer (1996). "Spiritual food/ drink": 1 Cor. 10:3–4 is generally taken to imply a typological reference to the Christian Eucharist.
23. Van der Toorn (1988), 444–45.
24. Judas, see John 13:26–27. Quickly: H.D. Betz (1992), I:5 = *PGM* I:90 and often. Selene recipe: H.D. Betz (1992), I:28–29 = *PGM* III:410–23. Jewish spell: Goodenough (1953), II:166 = Meyer *et al.* (1994), 279 (no. 129), a Coptic text from London Oriental Manuscript 6794 (ca. 600 CE). This is a privatized Eucharist (Smith) that echoes an older Jewish magical spell (Goodenough), see Richard Smith in Meyer *et al.* (1994), 276.
25. Ignatius, *To the Ephesians* 20 (medicine) and 13 (Satan); these texts and a brief discussion of some parallels can be found in Schoedel (1985), 95–98.74; parallels are also discussed by Wehr (1987), 106–11. The Isis story quoted is from Didorus Siculus, *Library* 1:25,6, a work compiled in the first century BCE.
26. Augustine, *Contra litteras Petiliani* 3:16[19] = *PL* 43:357. "Blessed bread": Jungmann (1986), II:452–53.
27. Calling it blood: M. Smith (1978), 111.122–23. The magical text Smith quotes on p. 111 dates from the third century CE; Dölger (1922), II:502 n. 2 took this text to be an imitation of the Christian Eucharist. Smith must be credited with the more plausible suggestion of the opposite relationship: the magical idea forms the basis of the Christian ritual. For a first-century CE love spell which includes the unloved person's statement "I have tasted your blood," see H.D.

Betz (1992), I:317; Daniel *et al.* (1992), 109 (*PGM* 122).
28. The charm can be found in the demotic magical papyrus of London and Leiden; for a translation, see H.D. Betz (1992), I:220–21; for the first-century date of the magical texts written on this papyrus, see Griffith *et al.* (1904), I:10–13.
29. Johannine flavor of Luke 24:13ff.: see the shared name of Clopas/Cleopas and the motif of "recognition" (John 19:25; 20:11–18; 21:1–14). Crump (1992), 98–107 demonstrates that in Luke "breaking the bread" involves a prayer that opens up the channel to the divine world.
30. Samuel: 1 Sam. 28. Moses, etc.: Luke 9:28–36. M. Smith (1978), 122 and Shaw (1995), 219–22 discuss hallucinatory rites.
31. For Gnostic associations, see Rudolph (1983), 214–15. Justin, *First Apology* 66 = (1994), 127–28; Richardson (1970), 286–87.
32. The original text of the *Apostolic Tradition* is lost; the generally accepted reconstruction is that of Botte published as *SC* 11bis. An English version is Cuming (1976). The text as reconstructed by Botte (on whose work modern translations rely) may actually represent a fourth-century edition of the original document, see Edward C. Ratcliff's review in the *Journal of Theological Studies* NS 15 (1964), 402–7 and Brent (1995).
33. *Apostolic Tradition* 4 = *SC* 11bis:50–53. Cuming's translation has been modified. In translating "set up a boundary" I follow Lietzmann (1979), 131 and Easton (1934), 36 who point out the highly magical notion of the "boundary," reminiscent of Job 38:10; Prov. 8:29.
34. *First explanation*: Presence of the entire congregation for Lord's Supper, see Klinghardt (1996), 513. For Greek *ekklêsia* as "church building," see *Apostolic Tradition* 21.39.41 = *SC* 11bis:87.123.125. In his *Commentary on Daniel* 1:20 = *SC* 14:108, Hippolytus refers to the church building as the "house of God."

According to Klauck (1983), 74–77 this new meaning of *ekklêsia* emerged around 200 CE, i.e., in Hippolytus' generation. P.C. Finney (1988) argues that the transition from using private houses for the Eucharist to having separate structures for the same purpose was a gradual and geographically diversified process; there seems to be no evidence for Christian gatherings in non-residential buildings before ca. 200 CE. *Second explanation*: Bobertz (1993).

35. For the emergence of a "monoepiscopal" organization under Bishop Novatian (ca. 250 CE), see Brent (1995). The *Syrian Didaskalia* = Achelis *et al.* (1904) terms Hippolytus' *eulogia* a "friendship meal"; lacking a sacred character, it seems to serve for the redistribution of food collected in the community. Although not mentioning it by name, Cyprian also has a reference to the *eulogia* as an evening meal; see Cyprian, *Letter* 63:16 = *CSEL* 3:714 with explanatory note in *Cyprian of Carthage* (1984–89), III:299.

36. The religious and female dimensions of the Severan era are discussed by Santos Yanguas (1981/82); Cleve (1988), 196–206. Shiner (1995), 103–11 comments on Philostratos and Apollonius. Statues: Frend (1984), 275. Julia Mamea and Origen: Eusebius, *Church History* 6:21 = *SC* 41:121. Hippolytus, *Sermon on the Resurrection to the Empress Mamea*, *GCS* Hippolytus 1/2, 251. Hippolytus, *Commentary on Daniel* 4:8,7 = *SC* 14:276.

37. Neusner (1987), 213; see also 54–70.207–30.

38. Frend (1984), 272.

39. Simon: Acts 8:18–19. "A magician": Hippolytus, *Apostolic Tradition* 16 = *SC* 11bis:74. "Magical arts": Hippolytus, *Refutation of All Heresies* 6:20 = *GCS* Hippolytus 3:148. On the fraudulent ritual of Marcus, see Hippolytus, *Refutation of All Heresies* 6:39–40 = *GCS* Hippolytus 3:170–72, based on Irenaeus, *Heresies* 1:13,2 = *SC* 264:190/92. The Gnostic

magician Marcus flourished around 150 CE. Astrology: Hippolytus, *Refutation* 4:34–35 = *GCS* Hippolytus 3:61–62. On Hekate, see West (1995), 292.

40. "The endless complexity of directions to be followed makes one conclusion inevitable: magic is a full-time job," Burkert (1981), 133. Frazer (1922), 49. "Magic is the bridge": Malinowski (1954), 83; see also 141–42. Examples of myths providing a precedent for magical acts can be found in Frankfurter (1995). On the magical nature of foreign words used in ritual, see above, p. 453, n. 76. While contemporary anthropologists take Frazer's and Malinowski's assertions with a grain of salt, pointing out that the ancients were not nearly as superstitious as some scholars made them look, their classic analyses certainly apply to Hippolytus' ceremony.

41. According to available documents, the dominical words spoken over bread and wine were first understood as the words actually effecting the consecration by Tertullian, *Against Marcion* 4:40,3 = *CCSL* 1:656 (208 CE). According to Taft (1992), 497–98, the invocation is not a fourth-century addition to the text, but forms part of the prayer's original wording and must be understood as directing the Spirit not so much onto the eucharistic elements as onto the faithful communicants. On the identity of the Spirit in Hippolytus, see McKenna (1975), 20.

42. "If you partake": *Apostolic Tradition* 36 = *SC* 11bis:119. The "private" eating of the consecrated bread is also attested in Tertullian, *To His Wife* 2:5,3 = *SC* 237:138–39 dating from ca. 203 CE. He advises his wife in case of his death to remain a widow or marry only a Christian. A non-Christian husband would not understand her nightly prayers and her wish to partake of the sacred bread every morning.

43. Magicians as danger: Fögen (1993). On the growing impact of magic in

the third and fourth centuries CE, see MacMullen (1966), 95–127; Benko (1984), 103–39; Potter (1994).

44. Paul: Acts 17:34.

45. Platonopolis was to be in southern Italy; the death of Emperor Gallienus in 268 CE prevented Plotinus from realizing the project. Iamblichus, *Mysteries of Egypt* 2:11 [96] = des Places (1966), 96–97. For the theurgists' revision of Plotinus' philosophy, see Trouillard (1983), Berchman (1989), Shaw (1995). Truism of Greek and Semitic religions, see Latte (1968), 48–59; Vorländer (1975a).

46. The Hekate ritual is quoted in Eusebius, *Preparation of the Gospel* 5:12 = *SC* 262:312–15, part of which is counted as fragment no. 224 of the *Chaldean Oracles*. For its theoretical background, see Iamblichus, *Mysteries of Egypt* 5:23 [232–33] = des Places (1966), 178; Shaw (1995), 45–57.

47. *Chaldean Oracles*: Majercik (1989), Potter (1991). "Chaldaic; whenever": Marinus, *Life of Proclus* 28.32. Religion in Athens, see Trombley (1993), I:307–32. Dionysius and Proclus: Rorem (1993), 51.63.

48. The critical edition of the *Ecclesiastical Hierarchy* can be found in Pseudo-Dionysius, *Corpus Dionysiacum* (1991), vol. II. We use the 1987 translation by Colm Lubheid.

49. *Chaldean Oracles* no. 108 = Majercik (1989), 90. "In some; the ineffable": Iamblichus, *Mysteries of Egypt* 1:15[48]; 2:11[97] = des Places (1966), 66.96; see also Shaw (1995), 48.84. Incense: Dionysius, *Ecclesiastical Hierarchy* 429 A.

50. Incense, bread, etc.: Dionysius, *Ecclesiastical Hierarchy* 425 B/C. Prayers as nonmaterial *synthêmata/ symbola*, see Iamblichus, *Mysteries of Egypt* 1:15 [48] = des Places (1966), 66. "Out of love he": Dionysius, *The Divine Names*, PG 3:648 D. *Theourgia/hierourgia*, see Louth (1986). Iamblichus, *Mysteries of Egypt* 5:23 [232] = des Places (1966), 178 says "the sacred rites of the hierourgies."

51. Elevation of bread and wine before communion: Leipoldt (1961), 256–57; Taft (1996), 26–32; the earliest reference to this rite is in a commentary on Dionysius' *Ecclesiastical Hierarchy* by John Scholasticus, bishop of Scythopolis (ca. 535–50), *PG* 4:137. Ps. 34 sung at communion rite, see Cyril of Jerusalem, *Mystagogical Lectures* 5[23]:20 = *SC* 126:168/70. Visual experience: Dionysius, *Ecclesiastical Hierarchy* 505 D, 536 D. Vision as superior sense: Augustine, *On the Trinity* 11:1 = *CCSL* 50:333. The early history of concealing the altar behind a curtain is not quite clear; see Braun (1924), II:159–67; van de Paverd (1970), 41–47.340–44. Head of Grain, see Hippolytus, *Refutation* 5:8,39 = *GCS* Hippolytus 3: 96. *Epopsia* (*epopteia*), see Fascher (1962); the Neoplatonist Proclus also uses the term: Proclus, *Theology of Plato* 4:9 [193] = (1981), IV:30. Eliade (1958), 43.

52. Paschasius Radbert, *De corpore et sanguine domini* 4 = *CCCM* 16:27. Extroverted: Jung (1958–80), VI:23–26 comments on "extroverted" and "introverted" notions of the Eucharist.

53. On the beginnings of the doctrine of transubstantiation, see Jorissen (1965) and Goering (1991). The relevant text of the Lateran Council can be found in *DH*, no. 802.

54. "The senses": Thomas Aquinas, *Commentary on the Book of Sentences* 4:10,1,4–"*sensus non habet iudicare de substantia sed de formis sensibilibus.*"

55. God present in everything: Thomas Aquinas, *STh* I 8:1. For the argument about the *lapis*, see Thomas Aquinas, *Commentary on the Book of Sentences* 4:10,1 (answer to the 8th objection). "Like all": Thomas, *STh* II II 1:8 (last sentence).

56. Robert Holcot, *Questions on the Four Books of the Sentences*, quoted in Macy (1992), 113. John Calvin, *Institutes* 4:17,24.

57. Thomas, *STh* III 75:1.

58. "The accidents continue": Thomas, *STh* III 77:1.

59. Nourishing quality: Thomas, *STh* III 77:6; corruption: *STh* III 77:4.

60. "Under its; sacramental": Thomas, *STh* III 76:5. No dimension: Thomas, *STh* III 76:4.

61. Aquinas's insistence on the "incomplete" presence of Christ is discussed in Megivern (1963), 228–29. Schmaus (1952), IV/1:279. A different interpretation of Aquinas—one that emphasizes the idea of Christ's *complete* presence in the Eucharist—is given by Gy (1990), 263–83. At least one scholastic doctor: William of Ockham, *Quodlibetal Questions* (1991), I:300 (question 4:13); Ockham claims that "by means of an intellectual vision Christ in the Eucharist is able to see naturally the things that take place on the altar." "By miraculous": Thomas, *STh* III 76:8.

62. Thomas, *STh* III 74:8. Wedding: John 2. Juan de Lugo: Pohle *et al.* (1960), III:275.

63. Mouse: Thomas, *STh* III 80:3,3; see Landgraf (1952); Snoek (1995), 48. Power of consecration: Thomas, *STh* III 74:2; for other points of view, see Mangenot (1913), 1315–16.

64. Voltaire, *Philosophical Dictionary* (1767), article "Transubstantiation." Thomas, *STh* III 80:8. Viva (1757), IV/1: 77. Eight to ten minutes: Jone (1938), 404.

65. Not servants: John 15:15. Friendship, see Thomas, *STh* III 75:1; I II 31:7; Towey (1995). Tears at Mass, see Foster (1959), 46 and 55. Miracle at Mass, see Weisheipl (1974), 322.

66. "It is certainly": Calvin, *Harmonia evangelica*, *CR* 73[45]: 706—"*sane magica incantatio est, cum ad mortuum elementum dirigitur consecratio.*" "A stick": Luther, *Large Catechism*, *WA* 30/1: 429. "This opinion": Luther, *The Babylonian Captivity of the Church* (1520), *WA* 6:508.

67. "We maintain": Calvin, *Institutes* 4:17,13. "Christ is not": Calvin, *CR* 77[49]:489.

68. "Augustine had": Calvin, *Institutes* 4:17,21. The Platonic background of Calvin's thought in general and his sacramental theory in particular are discussed in Boisset (1959); McDonnell (1967), esp. 32–39.231; Partee (1977), 105–16.

69. Boehme (1957), VI: 96–97—"De testamentis Christi" (1624).

70. Von Baader (1854), VII:13, note (a text dating from 1815).

71. See also below, pp. 352–56.

72. Rahner (1966), IV:287–311: "The Presence of Christ in the Sacrament of the Lord's Supper." "Because Christ": *DH*, no. 1642.

73. Rahner, "Reflections on Methodology in Theology" (3rd lecture) = (1992), 343.

74. "Nonsensical": FitzPatrick (1991), 133. "My only": FitzPatrick (1993), 37 n. 9.

75. Smits as cited in FitzPatrick (1993), 58; FitzPatrick gives an account of the Dutch doctrine and its varieties, 49–107. Smits's own account can be found in Smits (1965), esp. 51–52 ("*een soort,*" 52).

76. "We must not": Calvin, *CR* 73[45]:706.

77. Paul VI, "Mysterium fidei," *DH*, no. 4410–13, with summary in P.H. Jones (1994), 206–8, who also comments on the influence of the Dutch approach, 197–242.

78. "Deification" (*theôsis*) as the benefit of the Eucharist, see Dionysius, *Ecclesiastical Hierarchy* 436 C. "The manifold; the coming": Iamblichus, *Mysteries of Egypt* 5:23 [232]; 2:6 [81] = des Places (1966), 177–78.86.

79. On eucharistic thought in Eastern theology, see Meyendorff (1974), 201–11; (1974a), essay no. 13.

80. "Three ways": Dionysius, *Ecclesiastical Hierarchy* 504 B and 536 D. For the background and early history of these stages, see Louth (1981), 57–59; Riedweg (1987), 127–30.142–43. Eucharist as sum of sacraments, see Dionysius, *Ecclesiastical Hierarchy* 508 C—the bishop, as master of the Eucharist, has the power to purify, illuminate, and perfect.

81. "The Eucharist": Kabasilas, *Life in Christ* 4:70 = *SC* 355:322. "To wipe": ibid., 4:52 = *SC* 355:310.

"This has": Brightman (1896), I:395, echoing Isa. 6:7, a verse applied to the Eucharist since patristic times, see Eschenbach (1927).

82. "Fade away": Kabasilas, *Life in Christ* 4:12 = *SC* 355:272. "A disease; medicine and": ibid., 4:88 = *SC* 355:338. Potter: ibid., 4:35 = *SC* 355:294.

83. Kabasilas, *Life in Christ* 4:99 = *SC* 355:348.

84. Irenaeus, *Heresies* 4:18,5 = *SC* 100:610/12. Gregory of Nyssa, *Catechetical Oration* 37 = *PG* 45:93–97.

85. "Does not improve": Kabasilas, *Life in Christ* 4:89 = *SC* 355:338. "Dwelling; he dwells": ibid., 4:7 = *SC* 355:268. Christ's mind mingled: ibid., 4:8 = *SC* 355:268. "It is no": ibid., 4:8 = *SC* 355:270. "Constantly": ibid., 4:34 = *SC* 355:294. "Makes us more": ibid., 4:46 = *SC* 355:304/6.

86. "By his divinity": Kabasilas, *Life in Christ* 4:27 = *SC* 355:288. Assimilation to the sacred food: ibid., 4:37 = *SC* 355:298 and Augustine, *Confessions* 7:10 = *CCSL* 27:104. 2 Peter 1:4, the classical biblical promise of deification, is used in a eucharistic context by Cyril of Jerusalem, *Mystagogical Lectures* 4[22]:3 = *SC* 126:136. Like fire: Kabasilas, *Life in Christ* 4:27–28 = *SC* 355:288.290. "Has led": ibid., 4:2 = *SC* 355:264.

87. Marginal note: Kabasilas, *Life in Christ* 4:31 = *SC* 355:292.

88. Von Harnack (1957), 232–33 (lecture 13).

89. The central biblical text on deification is 2 Peter 1:4; Protestant readings are discussed in M. Schmidt (1969), 238–98.

90. "Something": Thomas Aquinas, *STh* III 79:4. "Medicine": *STh* III 80:4. Desires: *STh* III 79:6. "One is even": *STh* III 61:1.

91. Alpais: Bynum (1987), 73. Forty: Stein (1995), 88. Suger, *Life of Louis the Fat* 21 = *PL* 186:1338. "I thank; this most; *remedium*": Thomas à Kempis, *Imitation of Christ* IV: 1.4.10 = (1989), 134.138.145; Matt. 11:28

also forms the epigraph to Book 4 and punctuates this book's text, see (1989) 131–32.139 (chap. 1 and 4). Painting: the motif of "Christ the Pharmacist," popular with German-speaking Catholics and Protestants, is studied by Hein (1974) and Herzog (1994), 421–29; not all paintings illustrated in Hein's book include a representation of the host which seems to be distinctive of Catholic iconography. For Protestants, "Christ the Pharmacist" offers not the sacrament but his word, see Luther, *WA* 48:153–54.

92. St. Osmund: Duffy (1992), 189. Malene: Haesele (1968), 240. On the traditional motif of light emanating from the host, see Snoek (1995), 326–28.

93. Liège: Jungmann (1986), II:213 n. 78. Painting in Florence: by Andrea Pisano in an "elevation" scene; see Schmitt (1990), 351, fig. 38. Popular book: Kunkel (1953), 37. Saint Martin, see Sulpicius Severus, *Dialogues* 3:9 = *CSEL* 1:207. William of Tocco, *Life of St. Thomas*, as quoted in Weisheipl (1974), 347.

94. Luther, *WA* 30/I:118–19; see also *WA* 6:358.

95. Zwingli, *CR* 92[5]:754—"corpus Christi naturaliter commanducatum peccata remittit." Catholic art: One wonders where the angels get the host: from the heavenly altar? or from the priest's chalice? or from the mouths of those who take communion vicariously for a suffering soul? See Jungmann (1986), II:311; Browe (1938), 165–74. Council of Trent: *DH*, no. 1655.

96. Bunyan (1965), 281.

97. Hadewijch (1980), 281 (vision 7). "I will give": Gertrude of Helfta, *Herald of Divine Love* 3:36 = *SC* 143:176. Mass: Gertrude, *Mass Celebrated by the Lord Himself* 13 = *SC* 331:302/4. Normal communion: Gertrude, *Herald of Divine Love* 1:14,23 = *SC* 139:198.

98. Male semen as blood: Thomas Aquinas, *STh* III 80:7 quoting Aristotle. Hildegard of Bingen, see letter

116, by Abbess Tengswich of Andernach, *PL* 197:336. On medieval eucharistic mysticism, see Bynum (1984). First Communion: Delumeau (1987).

99. Taylor (1900), II:132 (chap. IV, 10:14). Zinzendorf: see Gerland (1992), 103–4; Seidel (1983), 217–29. Edwards (1974), I:459 in *An Humble Enquiry into the Rules of the Word of God.* McCulloch: L.E. Schmidt (1989), 162–66. Nevin (1966), 172; as for the marital metaphor, see p. 265, where Nevin assumes that Eph. 5:30–32 compares the eucharistic communion with human marriage. Intercourse: Seidel (1983), 219.

100. Johann Franck, "Schmücke dich, o liebe Seele"; trans. by Catherine Winkworth as "Deck thyself, my soul, with gladness." On the mystical marriage theme in Lutheran hymns on the Lord's Supper, see Buchrucker (1987), 129–34.

101. "When Christ": Teilhard de Chardin (1965), 315 = (1968), 207 ("Le Prêtre," 1918). "The human": Teilhard de Chardin (1960), 103–4.

102. On de Lubac quoting Augustine, *Confessions* 7:10[16] = *CCSL* 27:104, see MacPartlan (1993). Auer (1962), 153–59.

103. Fink (1990), 446.

104. The *Christengemeinschaft* boasts a German membership of ca. thirty thousand people. Figures from other countries (including England, France, the Netherlands, South Africa, Switzerland, and the USA) were not available.

105. "Putting on": Schroeder (1990), 137–38. "Eternal medicine": Schroeder (1986), 260.

106. Central texts include Steiner (1982), 203–5; (1933), 270–71; (1965), 98–103.

107. "Your body": Steiner (1993), 472; Steiner's Latin model is the prayer "Corpus tuum, Domine, quod sumpsi," see Steiner (1993, supplement), 126 and Jungmann (1986), II:401.

108. Dissolution of the material world: Steiner (1965), 98–103.

109. Althaus (1972), 544. Luther, *The Blessed Sacrament of the Holy and True Body of Christ, and the Brotherhoods* (1519); *WA* 2:743. "Seal onto": *Heidelberg Catechism* (1563), question 66 (trans. of A.O. Miller altered). "The most holy seal": Johannes Gerhard, *Meditationes sacrae* (Jena, 1606), no pagination, meditation no. 20—"Hoc sanctissimum promissionum divinarum sigillum est quod coram judicio divino ostendere possumus." "Ticket": Gerhard, *Loci theologici* (1867), V:213.

110. "As a friendly": Rahner (1966), IV:319. Eymard (1887), 382. Tanqueray (1930), 148–49 (no. 285). Lord's presence ceases: Rahner (1966), IV:312–20. Scholastic doctors: Landgraf (1952), 49. "Does not": Rahner (1966), IV:293.

111. Rinser (1994), 82—letter of July 14, 1962. She also: Rinser (1994a), 142.

112. Zwingli, *CR* 91[4]:218. Baker (1971), 540. Kaufman (1968), 489–92 and 496. Malinowski (1954), 79–84: "Magic and Experience."

113. Fox (1988), 214.

114. On the rarity of theories about magic, see Markus (1994), 376.

115. Pope Paul VI, *Mysterium Fidei* (1965), no. 46: "conversionem, plane mirabilem et singularem," *Acta Apostolicae Sedis* 57 (1965), 766; the expression echoes a similar one used by the Council of Trent, see *DH*, no. 1652. For this pope's visit to Orvieto, see *Acta Apostolicae Sedis* 56 (1964), 751–57.

116. Thomas à Kempis, *Imitation of Christ* IV:3 = (1989), 136.

117. Milet (1981), 177 with n. 14. Two major Roman documents denounce the celebrants of "progressive" Eucharists: "Inestimabile donum" ("Instruction Concerning Worship of the Eucharistic Mystery") of April 17, 1980, issued by the Congregation for the Sacraments and Divine Worship; "On Certain Questions concerning the Eucharist" of August 6, 1983, issued by the Congregation for the Doctrine of the Faith. The texts can be found in *Acta Apostolicae*

Sedis 72 (1980), 331–43; 75 (1983), 1001–9.

118. Pius XII, *Encyclical Letter "Mediator Dei"* (1947), no. 20 = Megivern (1978), 68.

The Sixth Game: Spiritual Ecstasy

1. Oropeza (1995), 83.
2. Sanders (1996), 63.
3. "Filled with; imparts": Iamblichus, *Mysteries of Egypt* 3:25 = (1966), 133. "A divine; humankind's": Plato, *Phaedrus* 265 A, 244 A.
4. "Him of the": Plutarch, *Moralia/ Nine Books of Table-talk* IV:6,1 (671C). On women's devotion to Dionysos, see Kraemer (1992), 36–49.
5. Strabo, *Geography* X 3:7.
6. "Men, as if": Livy, *Roman History* 39:13. Bas-relief: Deiss (1966), 135. Patron deity: Herter (1957), 103. Friedrich Nietzsche, *The Birth of Tragedy* (1872).
7. Aristotle, fragment no. 15 = (1955), 84.
8. Prophetic dancing: 1 Sam. 10:5–13; 19:18–24. *Testament of Job*: Charlesworth (1983/85), I:829–68. Garment of angels: Rev. 1:13; 15:6.
9. David: 2 Sam 6:14. Breast-piece: Exod. 28:30, see Houtman (1990). For the ritual background of the *Testament of Job*, see van der Horst (1989).
10. "All rise; greatest": Philo, *Contemplative Life* 83–85.88; 65 = Vermes *et al.* (1989), 97/99; 90. Scholars: Klinghardt (1996), 188–90. Palestinian calendar: Dalman (1928), I:49–50.
11. Pannychis: Klinghardt (1996), 198–99. Plutarch, *Moralia/De curiositate* 3 [517 A]. Bacchanals: Bremmer (1984) presents a reconstruction of what happened out of doors; for banquets, see Bérard and Bron (1986).
12. The distinction between *ecstasy* experienced without music alone and *trance* experienced in a group with

the help of music is suggested by Rouget (1985), 3–12. Typical ecstatic behavior: Alland (1962).
13. Ancient Greece: Garcia Teijeiro (1992).
14. I.M. Lewis (1971) is a classic on ecstatic cults of the oppressed. See also Douglas (1973), chaps. 4 and 5. Ancient Greece: Bremmer (1984), 285–86.
15. Anthropologists: the reference is to Victor Turner; see B.C. Alexander (1989). I. M. Lewis (1971), 116–17.
16. Aristides Quintilianus, *On Music* 3:25; trans. in Burkert (1987), 113. The anthropological theory referred to is that of Goodman (1988). "Therapeutically": M.S. Clark *et al.* (1989), 150. "Hospital": Kliewer (1975), 124. General statements about the therapeutic value of ecstatic rituals can be found in Wilson (1961), 346 and Hollenweger (1968), 67ff.: "Ersatz für Gruppentherapie."
17. Oates (1967).
18. Structure of Greek symposium, see Plato, *Symposium* 176a. Potluck: Lampe (1994), 38–39; Philo, *On the Contemplative Life* 46. Sunday evenings: The evening is implied in the name "Lord's *Supper*" (1 Cor. 11:20), Sunday is generally suggested on the basis of 1 Cor. 16:2, see Salzmann (1994), 76.
19. Women as prophets: Acts 21:9; Wire (1990). Gillespie (1994), 199–235. Scholar's suggestion: Witherington (1995), 279–89; see the questioning of Christian prophets in the Shepherd of Hermas, mandate 11:4–6 = Lightfoot (1989), 230. Questions put to pagan oracles: examples given by Reiling (1973), 83–84. Rebekah: Gen. 25:22.
20. The meaning we attribute to the cursing of Jesus remains conjectural. Another possibility is that those who cursed Jesus followed a practice known from ancient Greek religion; people would curse a deity in order to avert evil from that deity or to indulge in camaraderie with it; for Greek cursing, see Farnell (1909),

V:104.211–12 and (1921), 156–59. According to an interesting interpretation of the difficult passage 1 Cor. 14:34–35, Paul here forbids a woman to test publicly the genuineness of prophetic speech, perhaps especially her husband's: Grudem (1988), 217–24.

21. Specialist: Grudem (1988).

22. Philo, *Quis rerum divinarum heres* 264–65.

23. "It is customary to appoint interpreters to be judges of the true inspiration. Some persons call them prophets," reports Plato, *Timaeus* 72 B; Fontenrose (1978),196–232 points out that there is no evidence for Plato describing the regular procedure at the Delphic oracle: here the Pythia spoke intelligible oracles and the prophet presided over the séance. In the Bible itself, there is no example of what Paul calls an "interpretation" of glossolalic praise. *Testament of Job* 49–50 = Charlesworth (1983/85), I:866, however, actually refers to collections of hymns that were understood as interpretations of glossolalic speech.

24. Sacred character: 1 Cor. 11:23–29. Bread broken: 1 Cor. 10:17. Hofius (1988), 403–5 comments on the possibility of an invocation of the Spirit as part of Paul's Eucharist. The two acts of blessing (first over bread, then over wine), seem to belong to the two parts of the proceedings, the banquet and the symposium; they do not appear to have been united in one single ritual act (as in later Christian practice). The report that Jesus took the cup "after supper" (1 Cor. 11:25) indicates that drinking belonged to the second part of the banquet, the symposium. The "Lord's food" (11:20, see Kremer [1996]), for Paul, was not only the blessed bread, but all the food consumed.

25. Spiritual food: 1 Cor. 10:3–4; 12:13. Possession as a Semitic notion: Kotansky (1995), 246. Coptic spell: Goodenough (1953), II:166 = Meyer *et al.* (1994), 279–80 (no. 129); similar, more Christianized versions

of this presumably Jewish spell can be found in Meyer *et al.* (1994), 244–48 (nos. 121, 122).

26. "As soon": Homer, *Odyssey* 1:150ff. Absence of respectable and presence of not-so-respectable women at banquets: Corley (1989; 1993). "Necks bare": Vergil, *Aeneid* 7:394–95. Women's loose hair in Greek ritual situations: Schüssler Fiorenza (1983), 227. India: Erndl (1993), 122. *Vaticinari*: Livy, *Roman History* 39:13.

27. Drinking: 1 Cor. 11:21. Women prophets: 1 Cor. 11:5. Musical instruments in pagan and Jewish ritual: Peterson (1933), I:228; Schmidt (1938), III:1037; Quasten (1983), 35–40. The Dionysian connection has been explored by Kroeger (1978; 1978a; 1987). On wine, see Aune (1978), 78.92.

28. For the didactic dimension of prophecy, see 1 Cor. 14:2–4.31 and Hill (1979), 110–40; for the lowly background of glossolalists, see Theissen (1982), 69–102.

29. The interpolated character of 1 Cor. 14:34–35 is discussed in Fee (1987), 699–705; a recent dissident voice is Witherington (1990), 172–77 who argues for the authenticity of the passage. No participation of women in the testing of prophecies: Witherington (1990), 172ff. On women in ecstatic rituals, see I. M. Lewis (1971); Kraemer (1979). Iconography: Torjesen (forthcoming). Nanas-inscription: Eisen (1996), 65–73.

30. Luke 1:67–79; Acts 10:44–46; 19:6. For Luke's view of the Spirit, see Menzies (1991).

31. *Didache* 10 = *SC* 248:182; Richardson (1970), 176. On the typological interpretation of Isa. 6:6–7 in the Greek and especially the Syrian church fathers, see Eschenbach (1927).

32. "After manual": Tertullian, *Apology* 39:18 = *CSEL* 1:153. "After the people": Tertullian, *De anima* 9:4 = *CCSL* 2:729–30. For North African prophecy, see Robeck (1992).

33. As sources, we have 1 and 2 Timothy (pseudo-Pauline) and Ignatius of Antioch for Ephesus, 1 Clement for Corinth, all dating from between 90 and 110 CE. Episcopal leadership: 1 Tim. 1:3; 3:1ff.; Ignatius of Antioch, *Ephesians* 1:1; 1 Clem. 42; 44. Paid staff: 1 Tim. 5:17. Teaching as bishop's task: 1 Tim. 4:13. High valuation of scriptural learning: 1 Clem. 53:1. Inspiration: 2 Tim. 3:16; 1 Clem. 45:2. For the two forms of worship among the Therapeutae, see Philo, *On the Contemplative Life* 30–31 (teaching); 83–89 (ecstasy) = Vermes *et al.* (1989), 84–85.96–99.

34. Epiphanius, *Medicine Box* 49:2 = *GCS* Epiphanius 2:243; Epiphanius (1990), 173.226.

35. Statistics: Burgess *et al.* (1989), 816; Suurmond (1990), 172.

36. Ingle (1994), 59–60. Bailey (1992), 53–54 n. 16 also comments on early Quaker worship. Bailey shows that after Fox's death in 1691, Quakers began to censure the miraculous and the bizarre when publishing Fox's papers, thus promoting the shift from enthusiasm to respectability.

37. Puritan quest for religious experience and "immediacy in relation to God": Nuttall (1992), esp. 134. "Now was heard": Andrews (1963), 144–45, who quotes from William J. Haskett, *Shakerism Unmasked* (1828).

38. "Powerful shakings": quoted in Stein (1992), 171. Stein reports extensively (165–200) on what he calls the Shakers' "spiritualistic revivals."

39. "When I was": quoted in Warner (1986), 20–21. On Methodist "falling," etc., see Taves (1993), 203–13.

40. Randolph (1855), 68.106. Methodist connection: Taves (1993).

41. Taves (1993), 209–19; Joyner (1994), 29–31.

42. On Seymour's career, see Synan (1989).

43. "Whites": Lovett (1975), 136. Bartleman, *PLA* 54. "In Los Angeles": Lovett (1975), 133.

44. Cox (1993).

45. Bartleman's writings are collected and reprinted in Bartleman (1985), with original pagination; we quote them by abbreviation of title. "Truly wonderful": Bartleman, *PLA* 50–60.

46. Pamphlets; exchange of letters: Bartleman, *PLA* 22; 18.24.33. On the Welsh revival, see Schmieder (1982), 358–67.

47. Fifteen weeks: Bartleman, *PLA* 28.

48. "Began crawling": *Los Angeles Daily Times*, April 18, 1906; reprinted in J.L. Tyson (1992), 90.

49. No hymn books: Bartleman, *PLA* 57.

50. On revivalist "altar calls," see Carwardine (1978), 13.120; Finney (1989), 115.306.

51. No sense of time: Bartleman, *PLA* 20.

52. People unaware of others: Bartleman, *PLA* 20.

53. No musical instruments: Bartleman, *PLA* 57.

54. Sarah Covington was interviewed by Christenson (1975), 27. Recent reports: Oropeza (1995), 89–90. From antiquity, the imitation of animal noises belongs to the behavior of those who are "mad" or "possessed," see Plato, *Republic* 396 B; Speyer (1989), 193–98.497.

55. Typical outlines of Pentecostal worship are discussed in Sanders (1996), 42–63.

56. For a description of communal singing, see Hustad (1992), 4. Duffield *et al.* (1983), 433.

57. Descriptions of dancing in black charismatic worship: Shopshire (1975), 180–83; Sanders (1996), 64–67.

58. "Joyful noise": Ps. 66:1 King James Version and New Revised Standard Version (1989), but not in the Revised English Bible (1989).

59. "Praying": Poloma (1989), 190.

60. "Some of our"; easily and at will: Poloma (1989),189.191.

61. Wesley (1856), XIII:443–50. An early source on Spirit-filled singing is Heinrich Müller, *Geistliche Seelenmusik* (1659), see Bunners (1966), 153.

62. Duffield *et al.* (1983), 398. On the "belts," in traditional English versions mistranslated as "aprons," see Leary (1990).

63. Anointing: Lawless (1988), 67.

64. Land (1989), 484–85.

65. Marshall (1991), 109.

66. Two types: Cartledge (1994), 90–91. "God's word": Sneck (1981), 134.

67. "Mark down": Poloma (1982), 58.

68. "God is showing; I see": Poloma (1989), 194. The designation "word of knowledge" is derived from 1 Cor. 12:8.

69. Procedure: Poloma (1982), 84 n. 6.

70. Sneck (1981), 43–51.133.148–53. Sneck relies on Yocum (1976). On the "Word of God" community and its history, see Lesegretain (1992).

71. *New Covenant* (Steubenville, OH) 21, no. 9, April 1992, p. 8. N. Keller in *Return to the Upper Room* (1992), 87.

72. Pytches (1991), 116–29; quotation, 127.

73. Recent interest: Csordas (1994), 230–59.

74. "The invisible": Csordas (1994), 235. Wesley (1984ff.), XIX: 49–51.60–61 with Taves (1993), 203–8. Woodworth-Etter: Warner (1986), P.H. Alexander (1989).

75. For the recent "prophetic" movement, see Pytches (1991).

76. "Holiness" opposition: Regmire (1990). For lack of interest in the sacraments of historical Christianity among present-day American Pentecostals, see the assessment by McDonnell (1973), 19: "The sacramental content and interest of classical Pentecostalism (typified by the Assemblies of God) in the United States is not high. Many of the American groups would hold a communion service four times a year," and consider it just a devotional exercise like others.

77. See also Luke 19:6. For the special character of Luke's view of the Spirit, see Menzies (1991). Menzies emphasizes the difference between Lucan and Pauline teaching on the Spirit. Lucan (and Pentecostal) theology takes the Spirit to be a special prophetic gift given to some Christians; according to Paul, all Christians are given the Spirit right from their conversion as the force that transforms them, thus promoting their salvation.

78. Samuel Willard, *The Child's Portion* (1684), as excerpted in: P. Miller *et al.* (1963), 369.

79. "We may": Tugwell (1976), 151. On "stages" of spiritual development in classical Pentecostal theology, see Lederle (1988), 5–32; Schmieder (1982), 205–18.313–14.352–54.

80. Melton (1988), 359–60. "A necessary": Poloma (1989), 192.

81. Markus Herrgen in a letter published in the German *Idea Spektrum* 1993, no. 39, p. 27.

82. W.J. Hattingh, in Clark *et al.* (1989), 73.

83. Justin, *First Apology* 45 = (1994), 96; Richardson (1970), 271 commenting on Ps. 110:2.

84. Chauncy (1975), 326–27.

85. Bataille (1988), 37. Paul's preference for prophecy: Smit (1994). Paul the writer: Trobisch (1994). Book-lover: 2 Tim. 4:13.

86. "The understanding": Poloma (1989), 191; Poloma's chapter 11 discusses "institutionalized" Pentecostal worship (184–206). "Africanisms": Quebedeaux (1983), 184. "Speaking in tongues": Jean Stone as quoted in Quebedeaux (1983), 184–85.

87. See above, n. 76.

Epilogue: Divine Meekness, Divine Majesty

1. "A shock; I have heard": Otto (1911), 709. "The soul; the truly": Otto (1950), 17.28.

2. Kneeling: Otto (1932), 228. On Otto's spiritualism in worship, see Dienst (1989), 82–83.

3. Campbell-Jones (1980), 97–99.

4. Rinser (1994), 200—letter of June 15, 1964 see also 40—letter of April 30, 1962.

5. "Sitting at": Vatican II: *Lumen gentium* (1964) no. 48 = *DH*, no. 4168. *A New Catechism* (1967), 490–91 (known as the "Dutch Catechism"). Greeley (1985), 199.

6. "The general": Theissen (1969), 86.

7. John Chrysostom, *PG* 58:507.

8. Cyril, *Fifth Mystagogical Lecture* 4 = *PG* 33:1112. John Chrysostom: language—*Homilies on First Corinthians* 24:3 = *PG* 61:203; *On the Priesthood* 3:4 = *SC* 272:146; *On the Incomprehensibility of God* 3:375 = *SC* 28bis:218; angels—*On the Priesthood* 6:4; *SC* 272:316/18; curtain—*Homilies on Ephesians* 3:5 = *PG* 62:29 (end) and van de Paverd (1970), 41–47.340–44; preparation—*Homilies on First Corinthians* 24:4 and 3 (end) = *PG* 61:203; *Homilies on Matthew* 82:6 = *PG* 58:746; *Exposition of the 49th Psalm 8* = *PG* 55:253.

9. Sanctus, see Spinks (1991), esp. 95–96. On the "sacralizing" of Christian worship by introducing the element of fear and awe, see Jungmann (1989), 247–55; Davies (1971/72); Gessel (1970), 101–22; Quasten (1951).

10. Recent advocate: Hoeres (1994), 23. François de Sales (1895–1902), VI:346.

11. For a critique of P. Brunner's hieratic theology of worship, see Grethlein (1989), 68–75. Dienst (1989) demonstrates Brunner's "Ottonian" connections.

12. Bernard of Clairvaux, *Sermons on the Song of Songs* 15:2 = *PL* 183:844.

13. "Approach; God": Thomas à Kempis, *Imitation of Christ* 4:5; 4:18 = (1989), 140.157.

14. Luther, *WA* 30/1:292/95. "Lie low; as a little": Edwards (1970), 35. "In a sweet": Edwards (1970), 28/32. "Is indeed": Edwards (1974), I:cxxxix—letter to Lady Pepperell, November 28, 1751. Barth (1989), 52 (god's majesty).55 (Geneva).

15. Anthropologist: Campbell-Jones (1980), 98.

16. The correct trans. of Gen. 14:19—"*owner* of the heavens, etc."—can be found as the alternative, marginal version in the New English Bible (1970) and the New International Version (1984); for philological details, see Lipinski (1993), 67–69. On God's two names, see Cassuto (1961), I:87.

17. Personal god: Isa. 44:2 (forms individual in the womb); 49:15 (loves more than a mother); see Vorländer (1975a). Renan (1953), VI:984. Pascal (1966), 309.

18. On Christ as a personal deity, see Vorländer (1975). On duotheistic theologies, see Scroggs (1993).

19. Nilsson (1948), 68–72.

20. Hinduism: Erndl (1993), 111. Lower classes: Lewis (1971).

21. Freud (1952), 770. On Freud's neglect of the mother, see Bowlby (1969), 361–65.

22. Symbiotic oral relationship: Erikson (1958). Freud (1952), 574 (lecture 20). Andreas-Salomé (1913), 465–66.

23. James (1958), 78. Pfister (1927), 22 and Erikson (1958), 98–99.257–58 move beyond Freud's merely negative view of regression as infantile behavior that avoids confronting the pressures of reality.

24. Erikson (1958), 258. On Augustine, see Brändle *et al.* (1984).

25. Tannen (1990). Freud (1952), 854 (lecture 33). Dumoulin *et al.* (1973), 131–262.

26. Hippolytus, *Apostolic Tradition* 21 = *SC* 11bis:92. Aelred of Rievaulx, *CCCM* 1:658, with commentary by Bynum (1982), 123.132.

27. The priests of the Christian Community give the blessing exclusively to communicants after communion. Some Anglican clergy and Methodist ministers invite non-communicants, both adults and children, to come forward and receive a blessing when the bread and wine are distributed. They lay hands on them in the Jesuanic gesture of blessing children (Mark 10:16). According to Colin Buchanan, this custom seems to have originated in England in the late 1940s (letter dated August 14, 1996). Csordas (1994), 55.

28. Jung (1988). God's milk: Augustine, *Confessions* 4:1[1] = *CCSL* 27:40. God as mother: Brändle *et al.* (1984), 166–67.
29. Csordas (1994), 235.
30. Playing Mass: Post (1995); a critical voice is Parsch (1930/31). Rinser (1986), 48–51. Goethe (1954), 893–94. On the idyll as a category in art history, see Bernhard (1977).
31. Lenz and Egyptian art: Siebenmorgen (1983), 82–84. Guardini (1939), 15–16. Merton (1964), 15. For the term "hieratic," see Kreitmaier (1921), 69–94. *Grand Larousse* (1973), III:2428: "qui tient sa forme d'une tradition liturgique: Gestes hiératiques du prêtre officiant."

32. *Herenbanken*, wearing hats, *voorlezer*: Haley (1972), 85.
33. Hair: Zumthor (1959), 103. *Houndenslager*: Haley (1972), 90. "A world": Sontag (1987), 130.
34. "After a biblical": Zumthor (1959), 102–3. Note-taking: Pepys (1970/83), IV:268.278. "I did entertain": Pepys (1970/83), VIII:236, entry of May 26, 1667. A century after Pepys, James Boswell (1950), 68 wrote in his London diary: "I then went to St. George's Church where I heard a good sermon. . . . I was upon honour much disposed to be a Christian. Yet I was rather cold in my devotion. The Duchess of Grafton attracted my eyes rather too much" (entry of December 5, 1762).

Illustration Credits

1a and **b** Reinhard Rohlf, Paderborn, Germany. **2** Hector Mithobius, *Psalmodia Christiana* (Jena, 1665), frontispiece. British Library, London. **3** Bildarchiv Foto Marburg, Germany, 1995. **4** Rudolf Otto, *Zur Erneuerung und Ausgestaltung des Gottesdienstes* (Giessen: Töpelmann, 1925), after p. 98. **5** Egyptian Museum, Cairo. Othmar Keel, *Die Welt der altorientalischen Bildsymbolik und das Alte Testament*. (Zurich: Benziger, 1972), 191. **6a** Martin Luther, *WA* 30/1, 143. **6b** Church of St. Maria, Wittenberg. Bildarchiv Foto Marburg, Germany. **7** Church of St. Maria zur Höhe, Soest. Ansgar Hoffmann, Paderborn, Germany. **8** The Minneapolis Institute of Art, Minneapolis, Minnesota. **9** British Museum, London. BMC 2425. **10** Paolo Segneri, *Pratica delle missioni* (Venice: Giuseppe Rosa, 1763), vol. I. Bibliothèque des Fontaines, Chantilly, France. **11** British Museum, London. BMC 13107. **12** Evangelisch-reformierte Kirchengemeinde Eiserfeld, Germany, 1991. **13** *Schönere Zukunft* (Vienna, Austria), June 16, 1929. **14** John Frederick Herrold, New York, 1996. Used with permission of The Riverside Church. The quotations are from *The Riverside Church in the City of New York: A Handbook* (New York, 1931), 10 and 37. **15** *The New Yorker*, April 7, 1986. **16** Josephus, *The Jewish War*, ed. Gaalyahu Cornfeld (Grand Rapids: Zondervan Publishing House, 1982). **17a** Othmar Keel, *Die Welt der altorientalischen Bildsymbolik und das Alte Testament* (Zurich: Benziger, 1972), 250. **17b** Heinrich Kunkel, *The Holy Sacrifice of Mass* (Fulda: Familienverlag, 1953), 24. **18** Yorkshire Carthusian Religious Miscellany. British Library, London. Additional Ms. 37049. Alms-giving after Mass, see Franz (1902), 291. **19** *Architektur des Mittelalters*, ed. Friedrich Möbius (Weimar: Böhlau, 1984), 40. **20** Heinrich Kunkel, *Der Ordenstand* (Fulda: Familienverlag, 1955), ill. 20. **21** Bayerische Staatsbibliothek, Munich, manuscript Clm. 2640. The quotation is from the *Life of Alpais of Cudot*, see Stein (1995), 155–56. **22** Charles Wheatley, *A Rational Illustration of the Book of Common Prayer* (London, 1720), frontispiece. British Library, London. **23** Charles Le Brun and Claude Mellan. Bibliothèque Nationale (Département des Estampes), Paris. **24** *Le estoire de sent Adward le rei*. Cambridge University Library, Cambridge, England. Manuscript Ee. 359, p. 37. **25** Deutsches Apotheken-Museum im Heidelberger Schloß, Heidelberg. Birgit von Ritter-Zahony, Münzenberg, Germany. **26** Maria Haesele, *Eucharistische Wunder aus aller Welt* (Zurich: Verlag Ave Maria, 1968), 241. Drawing by Francisco Garcia Estragues. **27a** Bibliothèque Nationale, Paris (manuscrit latin 10484, fol. 86). **27b** St. Martin's Chapel of the San Francesco Church, Assisi, Italy. Stefan Diller, Eisenheim, Germany. **28** Cathedral of Monreale, near Palermo, Italy. Alinari, Florence, Italy. **29** Charles W. Leadbeater, *The Science of the Sacraments* (London: St. Alban Press, 1920), 449. **30** St. Michael's Chapel, Niederolang, Tyrolia (Northern Italy). Tiroler Landesmuseum Ferdinandeum, Innsbruck, Austria. **31a** Charles Letaille & E. Boumard, Paris. Bibliothèque Nationale, Département des Estampes, Paris. **31b** *La Première Communion*, ed. Jean Delumeau (Paris: Desclée de Brouwer, 1987), after p. 160. Quotation from Thérèse de l'Enfant Jésus, *Histoire d'une âme* (Paris: Cerf, 1972), 91. **32** *Le Follet, journal des modes*, no. 1068, Paris, May 4, 1850. **33a** *Dictionnaire de la Bible*, ed. F. Vigouroux. Paris: Letouzey & Ané, 1926, vol. II, 1165. **33b** W. Corswant, *Dictionnaire d'archéologie biblique* (Neuchâtel; Delachaux & Niestlé, 1956), 106. **34** G. Peter Richardson, "Philo and Eusebius on Monasteries and

Monasticism," *Origins and Methods: Towards a New Understanding of Judaism and Christianity*, ed. Bradley H. McLean (Sheffield: Sheffield Academic Press, 1993), 334–57, fig. 7. **35** Lekythus, decorated by the Eretria painter. Staatliche Museen, Berlin. No. F 2471. *Dictionnaire des antiquités grecques et romaines*, ed. Charles Daremboug *et al.* (Paris: Hachette, 1904), vol. III/2, 1489. **36** Sarcophagus found near the Via Salaria. Arms and hands of the figure have been restored. Vatican Museums/Museo Pio Cristiano. Hirmer, Munich, Germany. **37** Museo del Arcovescovado, Rossano, Italy. Photo after *Codex Purpureus Rossanensis: editione integrale in facsimile del manoscritto* (Graz: Akademische Druck- und Verlagsanstalt, 1985), fol. 3 verso. **38** David R. Lamson, *Two Years' Experience among the Shakers* (West Boylston, MA: published by the author, 1848), 85. **39** St. Louis Post-Dispatch, summer 1890. Wayne E. Warner, *The Woman Evangelist: The Life and Times of Charismatic Evangelist Maria B. Woodworth-Etter* (Metuchen, NJ: Scarecrow Press, 1986), 144. **40** *The Pentecostal Evangel*, August 5, 1939, p. 12. Oral Roberts University Library, Tulsa, Oklahoma. **41** Author's collection. **42** Sofia Cavalletti, Rome, Italy. **43** *De Engelbewaarder* 30 (1914), 27. **44** Beuroner Kunstverlag, Beuron, Germany. **45** Rijksmuseum, Amsterdam, The Netherlands. **46** Statens Museum for Kunst, Copenhagen, Denmark.

Bibliography

Achelis, Hans and Johannes Flemming (trans.): *Die syrische Didaskalia*. Texte und Untersuchungen, new series 10/2; Leipzig: Hinrichs, 1904.

Ackerman, Susan: *Under Every Green Tree: Popular Religion in Sixth-Century Judah*. Atlanta: Scholars Press, 1992.

Adams, Doug: *Meeting House to Camp Meeting: Toward a History of American Free Church Worship*. Austin: Sharing Company, 1981.

Adey, Lionel: *Class and Idol in the English Hymn*. Vancouver: University of British Columbia Press, 1988.

Aeschylus with an English translation. Trans. Herbert W. Smyth; LCL. London: Heinemann, 1922, vol. I.

Alan of Lille: *The Art of Preaching*. Trans. Gillian R. Evans. Kalamazoo: Cistercian Publications, 1981.

Albanese, Catherine L.: *America: Religions and Religion*, 2nd edn. Belmont, CA: Wadsworth, 1992.

Albert and Thomas [Aquinas]: *Selected Writings*. Trans. Simon Tugwell; CWS. New York: Paulist Press, 1988, 361–523: "Texts on Prayer" by Thomas Aquinas.

Alexander, Bobby C.: "Pentecostal Ritual Reconsidered." *Journal of Ritual Studies* 3 (1989), 109–28.

Alexander, Patrick H.: "Slain in the Spirit." Burgess *et al.* (1989), 789–91.

Alland, Alexander: "Possession in a Revivalistic Negro Church." *Journal for the Scientific Study of Religion* 1 (1962), 204–13.

Althaus, Paul: *Die christliche Wahrheit*, 8th edn. Gütersloh: Mohn, 1972.

Amiet, Robert: "Masses, votive." *Dictionary of the Middle Ages*, ed. Joseph R. Strayer. New York: Scribner, 1987, vol. VIII:200–1.

Andreas-Salomé, Lou: "Vom frühen Gottesdienst." *Imago* 2 (1913), 457–67.

Andrews, Edward D.: *The People Called Shakers*, new edn. New York: Dover, 1963.

Angenendt, Arnold: "Missa specialis: Zugleich ein Beitrag zur Entstehung der Privatmessen." *Frühmittelalterliche Studien* 17 (1983), 153–221.

Angus, S.: *The Mystery-Religions and Christianity*, 2nd edn. London: Murray, 1925.

Aquinas: see Thomas Aquinas.

Aristides, P. Aelius: *The Complete Works*. Trans. Charles A. Behr. Leiden: Brill, 1981, vol. II.

Aristotle: *Fragmenta selecta*, ed. W.D. Ross. Oxford: Clarendon Press, 1955.

Arnold, Richard: *The English Hymn: Studies in a Genre*. New York: Lang, 1995.

Asendorf, Ulrich: *Die Theologie Martin Luthers in seinen Predigten*. Göttingen: Vandenhoeck & Ruprecht, 1988.

Assmann, Jan: "Unio liturgica." *Secrecy and Concealment*, ed. Hans G. Kippenberg *et al.* Leiden: Brill, 1995, 37–60.

Aubriot-Sévin, Danièle: *Prière et conceptions religieuses en Grèce ancienne*. Lyon: Maison de l'Orient Méditerranéen, 1992.

Auer, Alfons: *Weltoffener Christ*. 2nd edn. Düsseldorf: Patmos, 1962.

Augustine: *Sancti Augustini Sermones post Maurinos reperti*, ed. Germain Morin; Miscellanea Agostiniana 1. Rome: Tipographia Poliglotta Vaticana, 1930.

Aune, David E.: "Septem sapientium convivium." *Plutarch's Ethical Writings and Early Christian Literature*, ed. Hans Dieter Betz. Leiden: Brill, 1978, 51–105.

——: "Jesus (im Zauber)." *Reallexikon für Antike und Christentum*, ed. Ernst Dassmann *et al.* Stuttgart: Hiersemann, 1996, vol. XVII:821–37.

Avril, Joseph: "En marge du clergé paroissal: les chapelains de chapellenies (fin XII–XIIIe siècles)." *Le clerc séculier au moyen age*, ed. Société des historiens médiévistes de l'enseignement supérieur public. Paris: Publications de la Sorbonne, 1993, 121–33.

Baader, Franz von: *Sämtliche Werke*, ed. Franz Hoffmann *et al.* (1854); repr. Aalen: Scientia, 1963, vol. VII.

Baal, Jan van: "Offering, Sacrifice and Gift." *Numen* 23 (1976), 161–78.

Bailey, Richard: *New Light on George Fox and Early Quakerism*. San Francisco: Mellen Research University Press, 1992.

Baker, Charles F.: *A Dispensational Theology*. Grand Rapids: Grace Bible College, 1971.

Baker, Frank: *Methodism and the Love-Feast*. London: Epworth, 1957.

Bammel, Ernst: "Is Luke 16:16–18 of Baptist's Provenience?" *Harvard Theological Review* 51 (1958), 101–6.

——: "The Poor and the Zealots." *Jesus and the Politics of His Day*, ed. Ernst Bammel and C.F.D. Moule. Cambridge: Cambridge University Press, 1984, 109–28.

Bandmann, Günter: "Früh- und hochmittelalterliche Altaranordnung als Darstellung." *Das erste Jahrtausend*, ed. Joseph Hoster. Düsseldorf: Schwann, 1962, vol. I:371–411.

Barker, Margaret: *The Great Angel: A Study of Israel's Second God*. London: SPCK, 1992.

——: *On Earth as It Is in Heaven*. Edinburgh: Clark, 1995.

——: *The Risen Lord*. Edinburgh: Clark, 1996.

Barth, Karl: *Die kirchliche Dogmatik*. Zurich: EVZ–Verlag, 1932–67, vols. I/1–IV/4 [= *KD*]

——: *Die Kirche Jesu Christi*. Munich: Kaiser, 1933.

——: *How I Changed My Mind*, ed. John D. Godsey. Richmond: John Knox Press, 1966.

——: *Das Glaubensbekenntnis der Kirche*. Zurich: Evangelischer Verlag, 1967.

——: "Die Gemeindemäßigkeit der Predigt." *Aufgabe der Predigt*, ed. Gert Hummel. Darmstadt: Wissenschaftliche Buchgesellschaft, 1971, 165–78.

——: *Briefe 1961–1968*, ed. Jürgen Fangmeier *et al.*, 2nd edn. Zurich: Theologischer Verlag, 1979.

——: *Predigten 1954–1967*, ed. Hinrich Stoevesandt. Zurich: Theologischer Verlag, 1979a.

——: *Letters 1961–1968*. Trans. G.W. Bromiley. Grand Rapids: Eerdmans, 1981.

——: *Die christliche Dogmatik im Entwurf. Erster Band* [1927], ed. Gerhard Sauter. Zurich: Theologischer Verlag, 1982.

——: *Offene Briefe 1945–1968*, ed. Diether Koch. Zurich: Theologischer Verlag, 1984.

——: *Homiletik*, 3rd edn. Zurich: Theologischer Verlag, 1986.

——: *Karl Barth, Theologian of Freedom*, ed. Clifford Green. London: Collins, 1989.

——: *Vorträge und kleinere Arbeiten 1922–1925*, ed. Holger Finze. Zurich: Theologischer Verlag, 1990.

——: *The Göttingen Dogmatics*. Trans. G.W. Bromiley. Grand Rapids: Eerdmans, 1991, vol. I.

——: *Homiletics*. Trans. G. W. Bromiley and Donald E. Daniels. Louisville: Westminster, 1991a.

——: *Die Theologie Calvins 1922*. Zurich: Theologischer Verlag, 1993.

Bartleman, Frank: *Witness to Pentecost: The Life of Frank Bartleman*, ed. and pref. Cecil M. Robeck; The Higher Christian Life 5. New York: Garland, 1985. [Includes reprints of several of Bartleman's books, all with original pagination.]

Bataille, Georges: *Guilty*. Trans. Bruce Boone. Venice, CA: Lapis Press, 1988.

Baumann, Arnulf H.: "Fasttage in der Darstellung des Josephus." *Begegnung zwischen Christentum und Judentum in Antike und Mittelalter*, ed. Dietrich-Alex Koch *et al.* Göttingen: Vandenhoeck & Ruprecht, 1993, 41–49.

Baumgarten, Otto: "Vaterunser: II. Praktisch-theologisch." *Die Religion in Geschichte und*

Gegenwart, ed. Friedrich M. Schiele *et al.* Tübingen: Mohr, 1914, vol. V:1557–58.

Beckman, Gary: *Hittite Diplomatic Texts*. Atlanta: Scholars Press, 1996.

Behr, Charles A.: *Aelius Aristides and the Sacred Tales*. Amsterdam: Hakkert, 1968.

Benko, Stephen: *Pagan Rome and the Early Christians*. Bloomington, IN: Indiana University Press, 1984.

Bérard, Claude and Christiane Bron: "Bacchos au coeur de la cité: le thiase dionysiaque dans l'espace politique." *L'association dionysiaque dans les sociétés anciennes*. Actes de la table ronde organisée par l'École française de Rome. Rome: École française de Rome, 1986, 13–30.

Berchman, Robert M.: "Arcana Mundi between Balaam and Hecate." *Society of Biblical Literature Seminar Papers 1989*. Atlanta, GA: Scholars Press, 1989, 107–85.

Berger, Klaus: "Amen." *Neues Bibel-Lexikon*, ed. Manfred Görg *et al.* Zurich: Benziger, 1991, vol. I:86–87.

Bernand, André: *Sorciers grecs*. Paris: Fayard, 1991.

Bernhard, Klaus: *Idylle: Theorie, Geschichte, Darstellung in der Malerei, 1750–1850*. Cologne: Böhlau, 1977.

Betz, Hans D.: "Magic and Mystery in the Greek Magical Papyri." *Magika Hiera: Ancient Greek Magic and Religion*, ed. Christopher A. Faraone *et al.* New York: Oxford University Press, 1991, 244–59.

——(ed.): *The Greek Magical Papyri in Translation*, 2nd edn. Chicago: University of Chicago Press, 1992, vol. I.

Bévenot, Maurice: "*Sacerdos* as Understood by Cyprian." *Journal of Theological Studies* NS 30 (1979), 413–29.

Biblia Hebraica Stuttgartensia, ed. Karl Elliger *et al.* Stuttgart: Deutsche Bibelstiftung, 1977.

Bickerman, Elias J.: "The Civic Prayer for Jerusalem." *Harvard Theological Review* 55 (1962), 165–85.

Biel, Gabriel: *Canonis misse expositio*, ed. Heiko A. Oberman *et al.* Wiesbaden: Steiner, 1963–1976, 5 vols.

——: *Collectorium circa quattuor libros sententiarum*, ed. Wilfrid Werbeck *et al.* Tübingen: Mohr, 1979, vol. III.

Billerbeck, Paul: "Ein Tempelgottesdienst in Jesu Tagen." *Zeitschrift für die neutestamentliche Wissenschaft* 55 (1964), 1–17.

Black, Matthew: "The Doxology of the Pater Noster with a Note on Matthew 6.13B." *A Tribute to Geza Vermes*, ed. Philip R. Davies *et al.* Sheffield: Sheffield Academic Press, 1990, 327–38.

Blenkinsopp, Joseph: "The Mission of Udjahorresnet and Those of Ezra and Nehemiah." *Journal of Biblical Literature* 106 (1987), 409–21.

Bloch, Maurice: "Symbols, Song, Dance and Features of Articulation." *Archives européennes de sociologie* 15 (1974), 55–81.

Bobertz, Charles A.: "The Role of Patron in the Cena Dominica of Hippolytus' *Apostolic Tradition*." *Journal of Theological Studies* 44 (1993), 170–84.

Boehme, Jacob: *Sämtliche Schriften. Faksimile der Ausgabe von 1730*. Stuttgart: Fromann-Holzboog, 1957, vol. VI.

Boer, P.A.H. de: "Cantate Domino: An Erroneous Dative?" *Remembering All the Way*, ed. A.S. van der Woude. Leiden: Brill, 1981, 55–67.

Boisset, Jean: *Sagesse et sainteté dans la pensée de Jean Calvin*. Paris: Presses Universitaires de France, 1959.

Bonaventure: *The Soul's Journey into God—The Tree of Life—The Life of St. Francis*. Trans. Ewert Cousins; CWS. New York: Paulist Press, 1978.

Bonhoeffer, Dietrich: *Life Together*. Trans. John W. Doberstein. New York: Harper & Row, 1954.

——: *Gesammelte Schriften*, ed. Eberhard Bethge. Munich: Kaiser, 1958, vol. I.

——: *Worldly Preaching*. Trans. Clyde E. Fant, 2nd edn. New York: Crossroad, 1991.

Bonnet, Hans: *Reallexikon der ägyptischen Religionsgeschichte*. Berlin: de Gruyter, 1952, 424–

26: "Libation."

Book of Common Worship, The: approved by the General Assembly of the Presbyterian Church in the USA. Board of Christian Education of the Presbyterian Church in the USA: no place, 1946; a thoroughly revised edn. with the same title was approved by the Presbyterian Church (USA) and the Cumberland Presbyterian Church. Louisville: Westminster/John Knox Press, 1993.

Boswell, James: *Boswell's London Journal, 1762–1763*. Ed. Frederick A. Pottle. New Haven: Yale University Press, 1950.

Bowden, John: *Karl Barth, Theologian*. London: SCM Press, 1983.

Bowlby, John: *Attachment and Loss*. London: Hogarth Press, 1969, vol. 1.

Bowsma, William J.: "The Spirituality of Renaissance Humanism." *Christian Spirituality: High Middle Ages and Reformation*, ed. Jill Raitt. London: Routledge & Kegan Paul, 1987, 236–51.

Bradshaw, Paul: *Two Ways of Praying*. London: SPCK, 1995.

Brand, Carl M.: *Die Messen von Joseph Haydn*. Würzburg: Triltsch, 1941.

Brand, Dennis J. (trans.): *The Book of Causes (Liber de causis)*. Trans. Dennis J. Brand. New York: Niagara University Press, 1981.

Brändle, Rudolf and Walter Neidhart: "Lebensgeschichte und Theologie: Ein Beitrag zur psychohistorischen Interpretation Augustins." *Theologische Zeitschrift* 40 (1984), 157–80.

Brashear, William: "The Greek Magical Papyri: An Introduction and Survey." *Aufstieg und Niedergang der römischen Welt*, ed. Wolfgang Haase. Berlin: de Gruyter, 1995, vol. II.18/5, 3380–684.

Braun, Joseph: *Der christliche Altar in seiner geschichtlichen Entwicklung*. Munich: Koch, 1924, vol. II.

Bremmer, Jan N.: "Greek Maenadism Reconsidered." *Zeitschrift für Papyrologie und Epigraphik* 55 (1984), 267–86.

Bremond, Henri: *Histoire littéraire du sentiment religieux en France*. Paris: Bloud & Gay, 1928–32, vols. VII and IX.

Brent, Allen: *Hippolytus and the Roman Church in the Third Century*. Leiden: Brill, 1995.

Brightman, F. (ed.): *Liturgies Eastern and Western*. Oxford: Clarendon Press, 1896, vol. I.

Brin, Gershon: *Studies in Biblical Law*. Sheffield: Sheffield Academic Press, 1994.

Browe, Peter: *Die häufige Kommunion im Mittelalter*. Münster: Regensberg, 1938.

Brown, Colin: *Jesus in European Protestant Thought 1778–1860*. Grand Rapids: Baker Book House, 1988.

Brown, Shelby: *Late Carthaginian Child Sacrifice*. Sheffield: Sheffield Academic Press, 1991.

Bruce, Dickson D.: *And They All Sang Hallelujah: Plain-Folk Camp-Meeting Religion, 1800–1845*. Knoxville: University of Tennessee Press, 1974.

Brueggemann, Walter: *Israel's Praise*. Philadelphia: Fortress, 1988.

Brunner, Peter: "Zur Lehre vom Gottesdienst der im Namen Jesu versammelten Gemeinde." *Leiturgia: Handbuch des evangelischen Gottesdienstes*, ed. Karl F. Müller *et al.* Kassel: Stauda, 1954, vol. I:83–364.

——: *Bemühungen um die einigende Wahrheit*. Göttingen: Vandenhoeck & Ruprecht, 1977.

Buchanan, Colin: *Encountering Charismatic Worship*. Bramcote: Grove Books, 1977.

Buchrucker, Armin-Ernst: *Theologie der evangelischen Abendmahlslieder*. Erlangen: Luther-Verlag, 1987.

Bultmann, Rudolf: *Theology of the New Testament*. Trans. K. Grobel. New York: Scribner, 1951–55, 2 vols.

Bunners, Christian: *Kirchenmusik und Seelenmusik*. Göttingen: Vandenhoeck & Ruprecht, 1966.

Bunyan, John: *The Pilgrim's Progress*, ed. Roger Sharrock. Harmondsworth: Penguin Books, 1965.

Burchard, Christoph: "The Importance of Joseph and Aseneth for the Study of the New

Testament." *New Testament Studies* 33 (1987), 102–34.

Burdon, Adrian: "The Lovefeast in Methodism." *Epworth Review* 15/2 (1988), 36–43.

Burgess, Stanley M. *et al.* (eds.): *Dictionary of Pentecostal and Charismatic Movements*, 3rd edn. Grand Rapids: Zondervan, 1989.

Burke, Peter: *Die Renaissance in Italien*. Trans. R. Kaiser. Berlin: Wagenbach, 1984.

Burkert, Walter: "Glaube und Verhalten." *Le sacrifice dans l'antiquité*, ed. Jean Rudhardt *et al.* Geneva: Fondation Hardt, 1981, 91–133.

——: *Ancient Mystery Cults*. Cambridge, MA: Harvard University Press, 1987.

Busch, Eberhard: *Karl Barths Lebenslauf*, 2nd edn. Munich: Kaiser, 1975.

Butler, Cuthbert: *Benedictine Monasticism*. London: Longmans, Green & Co., 1919.

Bynum, Caroline W.: *Jesus as Mother: Studies in the Spirituality of the High Middle Ages*. Berkeley: University of California Press, 1982.

——: "Women Mystics and Eucharistic Devotion in the Thirteenth Century." *Women's Studies* 11 (1984), 179–214.

——: *Holy Feast and Holy Fast*. Berkeley: University of California Press, 1987.

Cabasilas, Nicholas: see Kabasilas.

Caesarius of Heisterbach: *Dialogus miraculorum*, ed. Joseph Strange. Cologne: Heberle, 1851, 2 vols.

Caldwell, Patricia: *The Puritan Conversion Narrative*. Cambridge: Cambridge University Press, 1983.

Calvin, John: *Institutes of the Christian Religion*. Trans. Ford L. Battles. Philadelphia: Westminster Press, 1960.

——: *Institutes of the Christian Religion* [1536 edn.]. Trans. Ford L. Battles, 2nd edn. Grand Rapids: Eerdmans, 1986.

Campbell-Jones, Susan: "Ritual in Performance and Interpretation: The Mass in a Convent Setting." *Sacrifice*, ed. M.F.C. Bourdillon *et al.* London: Academic Press, 1980, 89–106.

Campenhausen, Hans von: "Taufen auf den Namen Jesu?" *Vigiliae Christianae* 25 (1971), 1–16.

Cartledge, Mark J.: "Charismatic Prophecy: A Definition and Description." *Journal of Pentecostal Theology* 5 (1994), 79–120.

Carwardine, Richard: *Transatlantic Revivalism: Popular Evangelicalism in Britain and America, 1790–1865*. Westport: Greenwood, 1978.

Cassuto, Umberto: *A Commentary on the Book of Genesis*. Trans. Israel Abrahams. Jerusalem: Magnes Press, 1961, vol. I.

Catéchisme ou doctrine chrétienne, 2nd edn. Paris: A. Dezallier, 1679.

Catechism of the Catholic Church, pref. Pope John Paul II. London: Chapman, 1994.

Chaillot, Gilles: "L'expérience eucharistique de J.-J. Olier: Le témoignage des 'Mémoires'." *Bulletin de Saint-Sulpice* 10 (1984), 63–106.

Charlesworth, James H. (ed.): *The Old Testament Pseudepigrapha*. Garden City, NY: Doubleday, 1983–85, 2 vols.

Chateaubriand, François-René de: *Mémoires d'outre-tombe*, ed. Maurice Levaillant *et al.* Paris: Gallimard, 1951, vol. I.

——: *Génie du Christianisme* [1802], ed. Pierre Reboull. Paris: Garnier-Flammarion, 1966.

Chauncy, Charles: *Seasonable Thoughts on the State of Religion in New England* (1743); repr. Hicksville, NY: Regina Press, 1975.

Chazon, Esther G.: "Prayers from Qumran and Their Historical Implications." *Dead Sea Discoveries* 1 (1994), 265–84.

Chiffoleau, Jacques: *La comptabilité de l'au-delà*. Rome: Ecole française de Rome, 1980.

Chilton, Bruce D.: *The Temple of Jesus: His Sacrificial Program within a Cultural History of Sacrifice*. University Park: Pennsylvania State University Press, 1992.

——: *A Feast of Meanings: Eucharistic Theologies from Jesus through Johannine Circles*. Leiden: Brill, 1994.

——: *Judaic Approaches to the Gospels*. Atlanta: Scholars Press, 1994a.

Christenson, Larry: "Pentecostalism's Forgotten Forerunner." *Aspects of Pentecostal-*

Charismatic Origins, ed. Vinson Synan. Plainfield: Logos International, 1975, 15–37.

Church, Leslie F.: *More about the Early Methodist People*. London: Epworth, 1949.

Clapper, Gregory S.: *John Wesley on Religious Affections*. Metuchen: Scarecrow Press, 1989.

Clark, Alan: "The Function of the Offertory Rite in the Mass." *Ephemerides Liturgicae* 64 (1950), 309–44.

Clark, Kenneth W.: *The Gentile Bias*. Leiden: Brill, 1980.

Clark, Mathew S. and Henry I. Lederle: *What Is Distinctive about Pentecostal Theology?* Pretoria: University of South Africa Press, 1989.

Clark, Robert D.: *A History and Criticism of American Public Address*. New York: Speech Association of America, 1955.

Clerc, Jean-Benoît: *Homines Magici: Etude sur la sorcellerie et la magie dans la société romaine impériale*. Berne: Lang, 1995.

——: "Theurgica legibus prohibita: à propos de l'interdiction de la théurgie." *Revue des Etudes Augustiniennes* 42 (1996), 57–64.

Cleve, Robert L.: "Some Male Relatives of the Severan Women." *Historia* 37 (1988),196–206.

Coffin, Henry Sloane: *The Public Worship of God* (1946); repr. Freeport, NY: Books for Libraries, 1972.

Cohn, Norman: *Cosmos, Chaos and the World to Come*. New Haven: Yale University Press, 1993.

Columbus, Christopher [Colón, Cristobál]: *Textos y documentos completos*, ed. Consuelo Varela. Madrid: Alianza, 1982.

Coons, Philip M.: "Psychophysiologic Aspects of Multiple Personality Disorder." *Dissociation: The Official Journal of the International Society for the Study of Multiple Personality and Dissociation* 1 (1988), 47–53.

Cooper, Robert M.: "God as Poet and Persons at Prayer." *Religious Experience and Process Theology*, ed. Harry James Cargas *et al.* New York: Paulist Press, 1976, 411–27.

Corley, Kathleen E.: "Were the Women around Jesus Really Prostitutes? Women in the Context of Greco-Roman Meals." *Society of Biblical Literature Seminar Papers Series* 28 (1989), 487–521.

——: *Private Women, Public Meals: Social Conflict in the Synoptic Tradition*. Peabody, MA: Hendrickson, 1993.

Corpus Hermeticum: ed. A.D. Nock, trans. A.-J. Festugière. Paris: Les Belles Lettres, 1960, vol. II.

Cox, Harvey: *The Secular City: Secularization and Urbanization in Theological Perspective*. London: SCM Press, 1965.

——: "Jazz and Pentecostalism." *Archives de Sciences Sociales des Religions* 38, no. 84 (1993), 181–89.

Cranmer, Thomas: *Works*. Cambridge: Cambridge University Press, 1846, vol. I.

Crump, David M.: *Jesus the Intercessor*. Tübingen: Mohr, 1992.

Csordas, Thomas J.: *The Sacred Self: A Cultural Phenomenology of Charismatic Healing*. Berkeley: University of California Press, 1994.

Cuming, Geoffrey J.: *Hippolytus: A Text for Students*. Bramcote: Grove Books, 1976.

Cuniliati, Fulgenzio: *Il catechista in pulpito*. Venice: Bettinelli, 1768.

Cyprian of Carthage: *The Letters of St. Cyprian of Carthage*. Trans. Graeme W. Clarke. New York: Newman Press, 1984–89, 3 vols.

Dalman, Gustaf: *Arbeit und Sitte in Palästina*. Gütersloh: Bertelsmann, 1928, vol. I.

Daniel, Robert W. and Franco Maltomini (eds.): *Supplementum Magicum II*. Opladen: Westdeutscher Verlag, 1992.

Davies, Horton: *Worship and Theology in England*. Princeton: Princeton University Press, 1962–75, 5 vols.

Davies, John G.: "The Introduction of the Numinous into the Liturgy." *Studia Liturgica* 8 (1971/72), 216–23.

Davies, Stevan L.: *Jesus the Healer: Possession, Trance, and the Origins of Christianity*. London: SCM Press, 1995.

Day, Thomas: *Why Catholics Can't Sing*. New York: Crossroad, 1990.

Deferrari, Roy J. (ed.): *Early Christian Biographies*. New York: Fathers of the Church, Inc., 1952.

Deiss, Joseph J.: *Herculaneum: Italy's Buried Treasure*. New York: Crowell, 1966.

Delumeau, Jean (ed.): *La première communion*. Paris: Desclée de Brouwer, 1987.

De Nicolas, Antonio T.: *Powers of Imagining: Ignatius de Loyola*. Albany: State University of New York Press, 1986.

Derrett, J. Duncan M.: "Where two or three are convened in my name . . . : A Sad Misunderstanding." *Expository Times* 91 (1979/80), 83–86.

Diakonoff, I.M. (ed.): *Early Antiquity*. Trans. Alexander Kirjanov. Chicago: University of Chicago Press, 1991.

Dibelius, Otto: *Das Vaterunser*. Giessen: Rickert, 1903.

Dienst, Karl: "Die Religionsphilosophie Rudolf Ottos in ihrer Bedeutung für Peter Brunners Gottesdienstverständnis." *Luther* 60 (1989), 78–86.

Dillon, John: "The Magical Power of Names in Origen and Later Platonism." *Origeniana Tertia: The Third International Colloquium for Origen Studies*, ed. Richard Hanson *et al.* Rome: Edizione dell'Ateneo, 1985, 203–16.

Dingemans, Gijsbert D.J.: "Gottesdienst und Predigt als einzigartiger Raum der Begegnung zwischen Gott und Mensch." *Theologia practica* 27 (1992), 23–30.

Dionysius: see Pseudo-Dionysius.

Dockhorn, Klaus: "Rhetorica movet: protestantischer Humanismus und karolingische Renaißance." *Rhetorik: Beiträge zu ihrer Geschichte in Deutschland*, ed. Helmut Schanze. Frankfurt: Athenaion, 1974, 17–42.

Documents on the Liturgy, 1963–1979, ed. International Commission on English in the Liturgy. Collegeville: Liturgical Press, 1982.

Dolan, Jay P.: *Catholic Revivalism: The American Experience, 1830–1900*. Notre Dame: University of Notre Dame Press, 1978.

Dölger, Franz Joseph: *Ichtys*. Münster: Aschendorff, 1922, vol. II.

——: *Antike und Christentum*. Münster: Aschendorff, 1932, vol. III.

Douglas, Mary: *Natural Symbols*, 2nd edn. Harmondsworth: Penguin, 1973.

Downing, F. Gerald: "The Social Contexts of Jesus the Teacher." *New Testament Studies* 33 (1987), 439–51.

Drewermann, Eugen: *Kleriker: Psychogramm eines Ideals*. Olten: Walter, 1989.

Dschulnigg, Peter: "Überlegungen zum Hintergrund der Mahlformel in JosAs." *Zeitschrift für die neutestamentliche Wissenschaft* 80 (1989), 272–75.

Duffield, Guy P. and Nathaniel M. Van Cleave: *Foundations of Pentecostal Theology*. Los Angeles: Life Bible College, 1983.

Duffy, Eamon: *The Stripping of the Altars: Traditional Religion in England, c. 1400–c. 1580*. New Haven and London: Yale University Press, 1992.

Duling, Denis C.: "Solomon, Exorcism, and the Son of David." *Harvard Theological Review* 68 (1975), 235–52.

Dumoulin, Anne and Jean-Marie Jaspard: *Les médiations religieuses dans l'univers de l'enfant*. Leuven: Leuven University Press, 1973.

Dupuy, Michel: *Se laisser à l'Esprit: Itinéraire spirituel de J.-J. Olier*. Paris: Cerf, 1982.

Durst, Bernhard: "Inwiefern ist die Eucharistiefeier ein wahres Opfer Christi und der Gläubigen?" *Theologie und Glaube* 53 (1963), 268–87.

Dyer, Joseph: "The Singing of Psalms in the Early-Medieval Office." *Speculum* 64 (1989), 535–78.

——: "Monastic Psalmody in the Middle Ages." *Revue bénédictine* 99 (1989a), 41–74.

Easton, Burton S. (trans.): *The Apostolic Tradition of Hippolytus*. Cambridge: Cambridge University Press, 1934.

Eaton, John: *Kingship and the Psalms*. London: SCM Press, 1976.

Eddy, Mary Baker: *The First Church of Christ Scientist* (1895), 89th edn. Boston: Trustees under the Will of M. B. G. Eddy, 1960.

Edelman, Diana V.: *King Saul in the Historiography of Judah*. Sheffield: Sheffield Academic Press, 1991.

Edwards, Jonathan: *The Works*, ed. Edward Hickman (1834); repr. Edinburgh: Banner of Truth Trust, 1974, 2 vols.

——: *Religious Affections*, ed. John E. Smith. New Haven: Yale University Press, 1959.

——: *Selected Writings*, ed. Harold P. Simonson. New York: F. Ungar, 1970.

——: *The Great Awakening*, ed. C.C. Goen. New Haven and London: Yale University Press, 1972.

Eire, Carlos M.N.: *From Madrid to Purgatory*. Cambridge: Cambridge University Press, 1995.

Eisen, Ute E.: *Amtsträgerinnen im frühen Christentum*. Göttingen: Vandenhoeck & Ruprecht, 1996.

Eliade, Mircea: *Birth and Rebirth*. Trans. Willard R. Trask. London: Sheed & Ward, 1958.

Elliott, James K.: "Did the Lord's Prayer Originate with John the Baptist?" *Theologische Zeitschrift* 29 (1973), 215.

Emerson, Ralph W.: *Emerson in His Journals*, ed. Joel Porte. Cambridge, MA: Belknap Press, 1882.

——: *The Complete Works*, ed. Edward W. Emerson. Boston: Houghton, Mifflin & Co., 1903–4, vols. I and XI.

Epictetus: *The Discourses*, with trans. by W.A. Oldfather; LCL. London: Heinemann, 1925, vol. I.

Epiphanius: *The Panarion of St. Epiphanius*. Trans. Philip R. Amidon. Oxford: Oxford University Press, 1990.

Eppstein, Victor: "The Historicity of the Gospel Account of the Cleansing of the Temple." *Zeitschrift für die neutestamentliche Wissenschaft* 55 (1964), 42–58.

Erikson, Erik: *Young Man Luther: A Study in Psychoanalysis and History*. London: Faber & Faber, 1958.

Erndl, Kathleen M.: *Victory to the Mother: The Hindu Goddess of Northwest India*. New York: Oxford University Press, 1993.

Eschenbach, Johann E.: *Die glühende Kohle: Die Auffassung der Stelle Isaias, Kap. 6 Vers 6 und 7 bei den Kirchenvätern und ihre Verwendung in der Liturgie*. Würzburg: V. Bauch, 1927.

Esser, Hans Peter: *Untersuchungen zu Gebet und Gottesverehrung der Neuplatoniker*. Diss., University of Cologne. Cologne: Gouder & Hansen, 1967.

Evans-Pritchard, Edward E.: *Nuer Religion*. Oxford: Oxford University Press, 1956.

Exoo, George D. and John G. Tweed: "Peale's Secret Source." *Lutheran Quarterly* new series 9 (1995), 151–75.

Eymard, Pierre-Julien: *La divine eucharistie. Première série*, 9th edn. Paris: Bureau des œuvres eucharistiques, n.d. [1887].

Faillon, Étienne-Michel: *Vie de M. Olier*, 4th edn. Paris: Wattelier, 1873, 3 vols.

Fairbanks, Arthur: *A Study of the Greek Paean*. Ithaca: Macmillan, 1900.

Farnell, Lewis R.: *The Cults of the Greek States*. Oxford: Clarendon Press, 1909, vol. V.

——: *Greek Hero Cults*. Oxford: Clarendon Press, 1921.

Fascher, Erich: "Epoptie." *Reallexikon für Antike und Christentum* , ed. Theodor Klauser. Stuttgart: Hiersemann, 1962, vol. V:973–83.

Fee, Gordon D.: *The First Epistle to the Corinthians*. Grand Rapids: Eerdmans, 1987.

Fénelon, François de: *Oeuvres complètes*; 10 vols. Paris 1851–52; repr. Geneva: Slatkine, 1971, vol. VI.

Ferris, Paul W.: *The Genre of Communal Lament in the Bible and in the Ancient Near East*. Atlanta: Scholars Press, 1992.

Fink, Peter E.: "Eucharist, theology of." *The New Dictionary of Sacramental Worship*, ed. Peter E. Fink. Collegeville: The Liturgical Press, 1990, 431–47.

Finney, Charles G.: *Lectures on Revivals of Religion*, ed. William G. McLoughlin. Cambridge, MA: Harvard University Press, 1960.

——: *The Memoirs of Charles G. Finney*, ed. Garth M. Rosell *et al.* Grand Rapids: Zondervan, 1989.

——: *Finney's Systematic Theology*, ed. Dennis Carroll *et al.* Minneapolis: Bethany House, 1994.

Finney, Paul C.: "Early Christian Architecture: The Beginnings." *Harvard Theological Review* 81 (1988), 319–39.

FitzPatrick, P.J.: "On Eucharistic Sacrifice in the Middle Ages." *Sacrifice and Redemption*, ed. S.W. Sykes. Cambridge: Cambridge University Press, 1991, 129–56.

——: *In Breaking of Bread: The Eucharist and Ritual*. Cambridge: Cambridge University Press, 1993.

Flint, Valerie I.J.: *The Rise of Magic in Early Medieval Europe*. Princeton: Princeton University Press, 1991.

Flusser, David: *Judaism and the Origins of Christianity*. Jerusalem: Magnes Press, 1988, 126–49: "The Magnificat, the Benedictus and the War Scroll."

Fögen, Marie Theres: *Die Enteignung der Wahrsager: Studien zum kaiserlichen Wissensmonopol in der Spätantike*. Frankfurt: Suhrkamp, 1993.

Fontenrose, Joseph: *The Delphic Oracle*. Berkeley: University of California Press, 1978.

Fosdick, Harry E.: *The Modern Use of the Bible*. New York: Macmillan, 1924.

——: *On Being a Real Person*. New York: Harper, 1943.

——: *The Man from Nazareth*. New York: Harper, 1949.

——: *The Living of these Days: An Autobiography*. New York: Harper, 1956.

Foster, Kenelm: *The Life of Saint Thomas Aquinas: Biographical Documents*. Baltimore: Helicon, 1959.

Fox, Matthew: *The Coming of the Cosmic Christ*. San Francisco: Harper & Row, 1988.

Fox, Robin L.: *Pagans and Christians*. London: Penguin Books, 1986.

François [Francis] de Sales: *Œuvres. Édition complète*. Annecy: J. Niérat, 1897–1902, vols. VI, IX and XII.

——: *Introduction to the Devout Life*. Trans. John K. Ryan. Garden City: Doubleday, 1972.

Frankfurter, David: "Narrating Power: The Theory and Practice of the Magical *historiola* in Ritual Spells." M. Meyer *et al.* (1995), 457–67.

Franklin, Benjamin: *The Autobiography and Other Writings*, ed. L. Jesse Lemisch. New York: New American Library, 1961.

Franz, Adolph: *Die Messe im deutschen Mittelalter*. Freiburg: Herder, 1902.

Frazer, James G.: *The Golden Bough*. Abridged edn. London: Macmillan, 1922.

Frend, William H.C.: "The North African Cult of Martyrs." *Jahrbuch für Antike und Christentum. Ergänzungsband* 9 (1982), 154–67.

——: *The Rise of Christianity*. London: Darton, Longman & Todd, 1984.

Freud, Sigmund: *Moses and Monotheism*. Trans. Katherine Jones. New York: Vintage, n.d..

——: *The Major Works*. Chicago: Encyclopaedia Britannica, 1952, 445–636: "A General Introduction to Psychoanalysis"; 767–802: "Civilization and Its Discontents"; 803–84: "New Introductory Lectures on Psychoanalysis."

Füglister, Notker: "Die Verwendung und das Verständnis der Psalmen und des Psalters um die Zeitenwende." *Beiträge zur Psalmenforschung*, ed. Josef Schreiner. Würzburg: Echter, 1988, 319–94.

Furberg, Ingemar: *Das Pater noster in der Messe*. Lund: Gleerup, 1968.

Galy, J.: *Le sacrifice dans l'école française*. Paris: Nouvelles Éditions Latines, 1950.

Gamber, Klaus: *Das Opfer der Kirche*. Regensburg: Pustet, 1982.

Garcia Teijeiro, Manuel: "Language orgiastique et glossolalie." *Kernos* 5 (1992), 59–69.

Gatens, William J.: *Victorian Cathedral Music in Theory and Practice*. Cambridge: Cambridge University Press, 1986.

Gelineau, Joseph: "Music and Singing in the Liturgy." *The Study of Liturgy*, ed. Cheslyn Jones *et al.*, rev. edn. London: SPCK, 1992, 493–507.

George, Carol V.R.: *God's Salesman: Norman Vincent Peale and the Power of Positive Thinking.* New York: Oxford University Press, 1993.

Gerhard, Johann[es]: *Meditationes sacrae* (Jena, 1606). Published in Eng. as *Gerard's Meditations.* Trans. Ralph Winterton. Cambridge, 1635.

——: *Loci theologici.* Berlin: G. Schlawitz, 1867, vol. V.

Gerland, Manfred: *Wesentliche Vereinigung: Untersuchungen zum Abendmahlsverständnis Zinzendorfs.* Hildesheim: Olms, 1992.

Gese, Hartmut: *Essays on Biblical Theology.* Trans. Keith Crim. Minneapolis: Augsburg, 1981.

Gessel, Wilhelm: "Resakralisierungstendenzen in der christlichen Spätantike." *Probleme der Entsakralisierung,* ed. Hartmut Bartsch. Munich: Kaiser, 1970, 101–22.

Gesteira Garza, Manuel: "La eucaristia como sacrificio incruento en la tradición patrística." *Estudios eclesiasticos* 64 (1989), 401–31.

Gillespie, Thomas W.: *The First Theologians: A Study in Early Christian Prophecy.* Grand Rapids: Eerdmans, 1994.

Glendon, Lowell M.: "Jean-Jacques Olier's Shifting Attitude toward the Human." *Bulletin de Saint-Sulpice* 5 (1979), 43–49.

Glück, M.: *Priscians Partitiones.* Hildesheim: Olms, 1967.

Godsey, John D.: *Karl Barth's Table Talk.* Richmond, VA: John Knox Press, 1962.

Goering, Joseph: "The Invention of Transubstantiation." *Traditio* 46 (1991), 147–70.

Goethe, Johann Wolfgang von: "Wilhelm Tischbeins Idyllen" (1822). Goethe, *Gedenkausgabe,* ed. Ernst Beutler. Zurich: Artemis, 1954, vol. XIII:887–906.

Goodenough, Erwin R.: *By Light, Light: The Mystic Gospel of Hellenistic Judaism.* New Haven: Yale University Press, 1935.

——: *Jewish Symbols in the Greco-Roman Period.* New York: Pantheon Books, 1953, vol. II.

Goodman, Felicitas D.: *How about Demons? Possession and Exorcism in the Modern World.* Bloomington: Indiana University Press, 1988.

Göttler, Christine: "Jede Messe erlöst eine Seele aus dem Fegefeuer: Der privilegierte Altar und die Anfänge des barocken Fegefeuerbildes in Bologna." *Himmel, Hölle, Fegefeuer,* ed. Peter Jezler. Zurich: Verlag Neue Zürcher Zeitung 1994, 149–64.

——: *Die Kunst des Fegefeuers nach der Reformation.* Mainz: Zabern, 1996.

Graf, Fritz: "Prayer in Magical and Religious Ritual." *Magika Hiera: Ancient Greek Magic and Religion,* ed. Christopher A. Faraone *et al.* Oxford: Oxford University Press, 1991, 188–213.

Graff, Paul: *Geschichte der Auflösung der alten gottesdienstlichen Formen in der evangelischen Kirche Deutschlands,* 2nd edn. Göttingen: Vandenhoeck & Ruprecht, 1937–39, 2 vols.

Gramaglia, Pier Angelo: "Linguaggio sacrificiale ed eucarestia in Gregorio Magno." *Gregorio Magno e il suo tempo. XIX Incontro di studiosi dell'antichità cristiana, Roma 1990.* Rome: Institutum Patristicum "Augustinianum," 1991, vol. II:223–65.

Grand Larousse de la langue française. Paris: Librairie Larousse, 1973, vol. III.

Grasberger, Lorenz: *Erziehung und Unterricht im klassischen Altertum.* 1875; repr. Aalen: Scientia, 1971, vol. II.

Greeley, Andrew M.: *American Catholics since the Council: An Unauthorized Report.* Chicago: Thomas Moore, 1985.

Gregory the Great: *Pastoral Care.* Trans. Henry David. Westminster, MD: Newman, 1950.

Grethlein, Christian: *Abriß der Liturgik.* Gütersloh: Gütersloher Verlagshaus, 1989.

Griffith, Francis L. and Herbert Thompson (eds.): *The Demotic Magical Papyrus of London and Leiden.* London: Grevel, 1904, vol. I.

Grimal, J.: *Le sacerdoce et le sacrifice,* 2nd edn. Paris: Beauchesne, 1911.

Groll, Karin: *Das "Passional Christi und Antichristi" von Lucas Cranach d.Ä.* Frankfurt: Lang, 1990.

Grudem, Wayne: *The Gift of Prophecy in the New Testament and Today.* Eastbourne: Kingsway, 1988.

Grüneisen, Ernst: "Grundlegendes für die Bilder in Luthers Katechismen." *Luther-Jahrbuch* 20 (1938), 1–44.

Guardini, Romano: *The Spirit of the Liturgy*. Trans. Ada Lane. 2nd edn. London: Sheed & Ward, 1937.

——: *Kultbild und Andachtsbild*. Würzburg: Werkbund-Verlag, 1939.

Guéranger, Prosper: *Institutions liturgiques*, 2nd edn. Paris: Société générale de librairie catholique, 1878, vol. I.

Günthör, Anselm: *Die Predigt*. Freiburg: Herder, 1963.

Guthrie, Harvey H.: *Theology as Thanksgiving*. New York: Seabury, 1981.

Guttmann, Alexander: "The End of the Jewish Sacrificial Cult." *Hebrew Union College Annual* 38 (1967), 137–48.

Gy, Pierre-Marie: *La liturgie dans l'histoire*. Paris: Cerf, 1990.

Haarhoff, Theodore J.: *Schools of Gaul: A Study of Pagan and Christian Education in the Last Century of the Western Empire*, 2nd edn. Johannesburg: Witwatersrand University Press, 1958.

Hadewijch: *The Complete Works*. Trans. Columba Hart; CWS. New York: Paulist Press, 1980.

Haesele, Maria: *Eucharistische Wunder aus aller Zeit*. Zurich: Verlag Ave Maria, 1968.

Haley, Kenneth H.D.: *The Dutch in the Seventeenth Century*. London: Thames & Hudson, 1972.

Hallinger, Kassius: "Das Phänomen der liturgischen Steigerungen Klunys (10./11. Jh.)." *Studia historico-ecclesiastica. Festgabe L.G. Spätling*, ed. Isaac Vásquez. Rome: Pontificium Athenaeum Antonianum, 1977, 183–236.

Hambrick-Stowe, Charles E.: *The Practice of Piety: Puritan Devotional Disciplines in Seventeenth-Century New England*. Chapel Hill: University of North Carolina Press, 1982.

——: *Charles G. Finney and the Spirit of American Evangelicalism*. Grand Rapids: Eerdmans, 1996.

Hamman, Adalbert G.: *Das Gebet in der Alten Kirche*. Trans. A. Spoerri. Berne: Lang, 1989.

Hammer, Karl: *W.A. Mozart: Eine theologische Deutung*. Zurich: EVZ-Verlag, 1964.

Hammerstein, Reinhold: *Die Musik der Engel*. Berne: Francke, 1962.

Hänggi, Anton and Irmgard Pahl (eds.): *Prex eucharistica*. Fribourg: Éditions Universitaires, 1968.

Hanhart, Robert (ed.): *Esther*. Septuaginta Gottingensis. Göttingen: Vandenhoeck & Ruprecht, 1966.

Haran, Menahem: "Temple and Community in Ancient Israel." *Temple in Society*, ed. Michael V. Fox. Winona Lake: Eisenbrauns, 1988, 17–25.

Hardman, Keith J.: *Charles Grandison Finney, 1792–1875*. Syracuse: Syracuse University Press, 1987.

Harnack, Adolf von: *Das Leben Cyprians von Pontius*; Texte und Untersuchungen 39,2. Leipzig: Hinrichs, 1913.

——: *Die Mission und Ausbreitung des Christentums*, 4th edn. Leipzig: Hinrichs, 1924, vol. I.

——: *What Is Christianity?* Trans. Thomas B. Saunders. New York: Harper, 1957.

Harrington, Daniel J. and Anthony J. Saldarini (trans.): *Targum Jonathan of the Former Prophets*. Edinburgh: Clark, 1987.

Heidelberg Catechism with Commentary, The. Trans. A.O. Miller *et al.* Philadelphia: United Church Press, 1962.

Heiler, Friedrich: *Das Wesen des Katholizismus*. Munich: Reinhardt, 1920.

Hein, Wolfgang-Hagen: *Christus der Apotheker*. Frankfurt: Govi-Verlag, 1974.

Heinemann, Joseph: *Prayer in the Talmud*. Berlin: de Gruyter, 1977.

——and Jakob J. Petuchowski: *Literature of the Synagogue*. New York: Behrman House, 1975.

Heitmüller, Wilhelm: *Im Namen Jesu: Eine sprach- und religionsgeschichtliche Untersuchung*. Göttingen: Vandenhoeck & Ruprecht, 1903.

Herter, Hans: "Bacchus am Vesuv." *Rheinisches Museum für Philologie* NF 100 (1957), 101–14.

Herzog, Markwart: "Christus medicus, apothecarius, samaritanus, balneator: Motive einer medizinisch-pharmazeutischen Soteriologie." *Geist und Leben* 67 (1994), 414–34.

Hestrin, Ruth *et al.*: *Inscriptions Reveal*. Jerusalem: Israel Museum, 1973.

Hierocles: *In Aureum Pythagoreorum Carmen commentarius*, ed. Friedrich W. Koehler. Stuttgart: Teubner, 1974.

Hill, David: *New Testament Prophecy*. Atlanta: Knox, 1979.

Hippolytus of Rome: see Cuming; Easton.

Hoeres, Walter: "Die Rechtfertigung des Triumphalismus: philosophisch-theologische Reflexionen zur Verödung von Kirche und Kult." *Sinfonia sacra* 2/2 (1994), 7–32.

Hofius, Otfried: "Herrenmahl und Herrenmahlparadosis." *Zeitschrift für Theologie und Kirche* 85 (1988), 371–408.

——: "Wort Gottes und Glaube bei Paulus." *Paulus und das antike Judentum*, ed. Martin Hengel *et al.* Tübingen: Mohr, 1991, 379–408.

——: "Gemeinschaft mit den Engeln im Gottesdienst der Kirche." *Zeitschrift für Theologie und Kirche* 89 (1992), 172–96.

Hofmann, Friedrich: *Die Gemeinde lernt singen*. Kassel: Bärenreiter, 1957.

Holladay, John S.: "Assyrian Statecraft and the Prophets of Israel." *Harvard Theological Review* 63 (1970), 29–51.

Holland, DeWitte T. (ed.): *Sermons in American History*. Nashville: Abingdon, 1971.

Hollenweger, Walter J.: "Funktionen der ekstatischen Frömmigkeit der Pfingstbewegung." *Beiträge zur Ekstase*, ed. Th. Spoerri. Bibliotheca psychiatrica et neurologica 134. Basel: Karger, 1968, 53–72.

Hooker, Richard: *Of the Laws of Ecclesiastical Polity*. London: J.M. Dent, 1907, vol. II.

Horst, Pieter W. van der: "Images of Women in the Testament of Job." *Studies on the Testament of Job*, ed. Michael A. Knibb *et al.* Cambridge: Cambridge University Press, 1989, 93–116.

——: "Silent Prayer in Antiquity." *Numen* 41 (1994), 1–25.

Houtman, C.: "The Urim and Thummim: A New Suggestion." *Vetus Testamentum* 40 (1990), 229–32.

Howe, Mark A. DeW.: "Wine and Skins: On the Use and Disuse of Choral Music in the Liturgy." *Anglican Theological Review* 76 (1994), 71–83.

Humbert of Romans: "De eruditione praedicatorum." Tugwell (1982), 179–370.

Humphreys, Fisher: "Altar call (invitation)." *Encyclopedia of Religion in the South*, ed. Samuel S. Hill. Macon, GA: Mercer University Press, 1984, 24.

Hurtado, Larry W.: *One God, One Lord: Early Christian Devotion and Ancient Jewish Monotheism*. Philadelphia: Fortress, 1988.

Hustad, Donald P.: "Doxology: A Biblical Triad." *Ex Auditu* 8 (1992), 1–16.

Iamblichus: Jamblique, *Les mystères d'Egypte*. Trans. Edouard des Places. Paris: Les Belles Lettres, 1966.

Ignatius of Loyola: *Constitutiones Societatis Iesu*. Rome: Vatican Press, 1908.

Ingle, H. Larry: *First Among Friends: George Fox and the Creation of Quakerism*. New York: Oxford University Press, 1994.

Irwin, Joyce L.: *Neither Voice nor Heart Alone: German Lutheran Theology of Music in the Age of the Baroque*. New York: Lang, 1993.

Iserloh, Erwin: "Der Wert der Messe in der Diskussion der Theologen vom Mittelalter bis zum 16. Jahrhundert." *Zeitschrift für katholische Theologie* 83 (1961), 44–79.

James [Jacobus] of Voragine: *Legenda aurea*, ed. Theodor Graesse (Dresden: Libreria Arnoldiana, 1846). Published in Eng. as *The Golden Legend*. Trans. Granger Ryan *et al.* Salem: Ayer, 1987.

James, William: *The Varieties of Religious Experience* (1902). New York: New American Library, 1958.

——: *The Letters*, ed. Henry James. Boston: Atlantic Monthly, 1920, vol. II.

Jeremias, Joachim: *The Eucharistic Words of Jesus*. Trans. N. Perrin. Philadelphia: Fortress, 1977.

John Duns Scotus: *Opera omnia*, ed. L. Wadding. Paris: Vivès, 1895, vol. XXVI.

Johnston, Sarah I.: *Hekate Soteira*. Atlanta, GA: Scholars Press, 1990.

——: "Riders in the Sky: Cavalier Gods and Theurgic Salvation in the Second Century A.D." *Classical Philology* 87 (1992), 303–21.

Jone, Heribert: *Katholische Moraltheologie*, 10th edn. Paderborn: Schöningh, 1938.

Jones, F. Stanley: *An Ancient Jewish Christian Source on the History of Christianity*. Atlanta, GA: Scholars Press, 1995.

Jones, Paul H.: *Christ's Eucharistic Presence: A History of the Doctrine*. New York: Lang, 1994.

Jorissen, Hans: *Die Entfaltung der Transsubstantiationslehre bis zum Beginn der Hochscholastik*. Münster: Aschendorff, 1965.

Joyner, Charles: "Believer I Know: The Emergence of African-American Christianity." *African-American Christianity: Essays in History*, ed. Paul E. Johnson. Berkeley: University of California Press, 1994, 18–46.

Julian [the Apostate]: *The Works of the Emperor Julian*, with trans. by Wilmer C. Wright; LCL. London: Heinemann, 1923, vol. III.

Jung, Carl Gustav: *The Collected Works*. London: Routledge & Kegan Paul, 1958–80, vol. VI ("Psychological Types").

——: *Psychology and Western Religion*. Trans. R.F.C. Hull. London: Ark Paperbacks, 1988, 97–192: "Transformation Symbolism in the Mass."

Jungmann, Joseph A.: *The Mass of the Roman Rite*. Trans. Francis A. Brunner. Westminster, MD: Christian Classics, 1986, 2 vols.

——: *The Place of Christ in Liturgical Prayer*. Trans. A. Peeler, 2nd edn. London: Chapman, 1989.

Justin: *Iustini Martyris Apologie pro Christianis*, ed. Miroslav Marcovich. Patristische Texte und Studien 38. Berlin: de Gruyter, 1994.

Kabasilas, Nicholas: *A Commentary on the Divine Liturgy*. Trans. J.M. Hussey and P.A. McNulty. London: SPCK, 1960. For a bilingual edn., see *SC* 4[bis].

——: *The Life in Christ*. Trans. Carmino J. de Catanzaro. New York: St. Vladimir's Seminary Press, 1974. For a bilingual edn., see *SC* 355.

Kaczynski, Rainer: *Das Wort Gottes in Liturgie und Alltag der Gemeinden des Johanns Chrysostomus*. Freiburg: Herder, 1974.

Kant, Immanuel: *Religion within the Limits of Reason Alone*. Trans. Theodore M. Greene *et al*. New York: Harper & Row, 1960.

Kaster, Robert A.: *Guardians of Language: The Grammarian and Society in Late Antiquity*. Berkeley: University of California Press, 1988.

Kaufman, Gordon C.: *Systematic Theology: A Historicist Perspective*. New York: Scribner, 1968.

Keel, Othmar and Christoph Uehlinger: *Göttinnen, Götter und Göttersymbole*. Freiburg: Herder, 1992.

Keller, Samuel: *In der Furche*. Hagen: Rippel, 1905.

——: "Wie bringen wir Menschenseelen zu Christo?" *Auf Dein Wort* 8 (1910), 234–39.

——: *Aus meinem Leben*. Meiringen: Loepthien, 1924, vol. II.

Kendrick, Graham: *Worship*. Eastbourne: Kingsway, 1984.

Kilmartin, Edward J.: "The One Fruit or the Many Fruits of the Mass." *Proceedings of the Catholic Theological Society of North America* 21 (1966), 37–69.

Kirk, Geoffrey S.: "Some Methodological Pitfalls in the Study of Ancient Greek Sacrifice (in particular)." *Le Sacrifice dans l'antiquité*, ed. Jean Rudhardt *et al*. Geneva: Fondation Hardt, 1981, 41–90.

Klauck, Hans-Josef: *Hausgemeinde und Hauskirche im frühen Christentum*. Stuttgart: Katholisches Bibelwerk, 1983.

——: *Herrenmahl und Hellenistischer Kult*, 2nd edn. Münster: Aschendorff, 1986.

Klein, G.: "Die ursprüngliche Gestalt des Vaterunsers." *Zeitschrift für die neutestamentliche Wissenschaft* 7 (1906), 34–50.

Kleinig, John W.: *The Lord's Song: The Basis, Function and Significance of Choral Music in Chronicles*. Sheffield: Sheffield Academic Press, 1993.

Kliewer, Gerd Uwe: *Das neue Volk der Pfingstler*. Frankfurt: Lang, 1975.

Klinghardt, Matthias: *Gemeinschafismahl und Mahlgemeinschaft: Soziologie und Liturgie frühchristlicher Mahlfeiern*. Tübingen: Francke, 1996.

Knapp, Jacob: *Autobiography of Elder Jacob Knapp*. New York: Sheldon & Co., 1868.

Knohl, Israel: "Petitionary Prayer in the Qumran Writings." *Journal of Biblical Literature* 115 (1996), 29–30.

Koch, Heidemarie: "Zur Religion der Achämeniden." *Zeitschrift für die alttestamentliche Wissenschaft* 100 (1988), 393–405.

Koch, Hugo: *Cyprianische Untersuchungen*. Bonn: Marcus & Weber, 1926.

Kock, Gerard: "Between the Altar and the Choir-Loft." *Concilium* 202 (April, 1989), 11–19.

Koester, Helmut: *Introduction to the New Testament. Vol. 1: History, Culture, and Religion of the Hellenistic Age*, 2nd edn. Berlin: de Gruyter, 1995.

Kohlschein, Franz: "Die Tagzeitenliturgie als 'Gebet der Gemeinde' in der Geschichte." *Heiliger Dienst* 41 (1987), 12–40.

Konstitutionen der Regulierten Chorfrauen des hl. Augustinus der Congregatio B.M.V., Die. Essen: Fredebeul & Koenen, 1933.

Kooij, Arie van der: "Nehemiah 8:8 and the Question of the Targum-Tradition." *Tradition of the Text*, eds. Gerard J. Norton *et al*. Fribourg: Universitätsverlag, 1991, 79–90.

Kotansky, Roy: "Greek Exorcistic Amulets." M. Meyer *et al*. (1995), 243–77.

Kraemer, Ross S.: "Ecstasy and Possession: The Attraction of Women to the Cult of Dionysos." *Harvard Theological Review* 72 (1979), 55–80.

——: *Her Share of the Blessings: Women's Religions among Pagans, Jews, and Christians in the Greco-Roman World*. Oxford: Oxford University Press, 1992.

Kraus, Hans-Joachim: *Psalms 60–150. A Commentary*. Trans. H.C. Oswald. Minneapolis: Augsburg, 1989.

Kreider, Alan: *English Chantries*. Cambridge, MA: Harvard University Press, 1979.

Kreitmaier, Josef: *Beuroner Kunst*, 3rd edn. Freiburg: Herder, 1921.

Kremer, Jacob: "Herrenspeise—nicht Herrenmahl." *Schrift und Tradition*, ed. Knut Backhaus *et al*. Paderborn: Schöningh, 1996, 227–42.

Kroeger, Catherine: (with Richard Kroeger) "An Inquiry into Evidence of Maenadism in the Corinthian Congregation." *Society of Biblical Literature Seminar Papers Series* 14 (1978), 331–38.

——(with Richard Kroeger): "Pandaemonium and Silence at Corinth." *The Reformed Journal* 28 (June 1978a), 6–11.

——: "The Apostle Paul and the Greco-Roman Cults of Women." *Journal of the Evangelical Theological Society* 30 (1987), 25–38.

Kuipers, Joel C.: *Power in Performance: The Creation of Textual Authority in Weyewa Ritual Speech*. Philadelphia: University of Pennsylvania Press, 1990.

Kunkel, Heinrich: *The Holy Sacrifice of the Mass*. Trans. Donald J. Ryan. Fulda: Familienverlag, 1953.

Lackner, Bede K.: *The Eleventh-Century Background of Cîteaux*. Washington: Cistercian Publications, 1972.

Lambert, Frank: *"Pedlar in Divinity": George Whitefield and the Transatlantic Revival, 1737–1770*. Princeton: Princeton University Press, 1994.

Lampe, Peter: *Die stadtrömischen Christen in den ersten beiden Jahrhunderten*, 2nd edn. Tübingen: Mohr, 1989.

——: "Das korinthische Herrenmahl." *Zeitschrift für die neutestamentliche Wissenschaft* 82 (1991), 183–213.

——: "The Eucharist." *Interpretation* 48 (1994), 36–49.

Land, Steven J.: "Pentecostal Spirituality: Living in the Spirit." *Christian Spirituality: Post-Reformation and Modern*, ed. Louis Dupré and Don E. Saliers. New York: Crossroad, 1989, 479–99.

Landgraf, Artur M.: "Die in der Frühscholastik klassische Frage *Quid sumit mus.*" *Divus Thomas* 30 (1952), 33–50.

Landon, H.C. Robbins: *Haydn Chronicle and Works.* London: Thames & Hudson, 1977, vol. IV.

Lang, Bernhard: *Monotheism and the Prophetic Minority.* Sheffield: Almond Press, 1983.

——: "Das früheste Christentum im Konflikt mit dem jüdischen Strafrecht." *Toleranz und Repression*, ed. Johannes Neumann *et al.* Frankfurt: Campus, 1987, 155–69.

——: "Buchreligion." *Handbuch religionswissenschaftlicher Grundbegriffe*, ed. Hubert Cancik *et al.* Stuttgart: Kohlhammer, 1990, vol. II:143–65.

——: "The Eucharist: A Sacrificial Formula Preserved." *Bible Review* 10/6 (1994), 44–49.

——: "Homiletische Bibelkommentare der Kirchenväter." *Text und Kommentar*, ed. Jan Assmann *et al.* Munich: Fink, 1995, 199–218.

Latte, Kurt: *Kleine Schriften.* Munich: Beck, 1968.

Laurance, John D.: *"Priest" as a Type of Christ: The Leader of the Eucharist in Salvation History According to Cyprian of Carthage.* New York: Lang, 1984.

Law, William: *A Serious Call to a Devout and Holy Life* (1728), ed. Paul G. Stanwood; CWS. New York: Paulist Press, 1978.

Lawless, Elaine J.: *God's Peculiar People: Women's Voices and Folk Tradition in a Pentecostal Church.* Lexington: University of Kentucky Press, 1988.

Lawrence, Roy: *Christian Healing Rediscovered.* London: Coverdale House, 1976.

Lawson, John C.: *Modern Greek Folklore and Ancient Greek Religion.* Cambridge: Cambridge University Press, 1910.

Leaney, R.H.: "The Lucan Text of the Lord's Prayer." *Novum Testamentum* 1 (1956), 103–11.

Leary, T.J.: "The 'Aprons' of St Paul—Acts 19:12." *Journal of Theological Studies* 41 (1990), 527–29.

Le Brun, Jacques: *La Spiritualité de Bossuet.* Paris: Klincksieck, 1972.

Lécuyer, Joseph: "Le sacerdoce chrétien et le sacrifice eucharistique selon Théodore de Mopsueste." *Recherches de science religieuse* 36 (1949), 481–512.

——: "Le sacrifice selon saint Augustin." *Augustinus magister: Congrès international augustinien, Paris 1954.* Paris: Études Augustiniennes, 1955, 905–14.

Lederle, Henri I.: *Treasures Old and New: Interpretations of "Spirit-Baptism" in the Charismatic Renewal Movement.* Peabody, MA: Hendrickson, 1988.

Leipoldt, Johannes: *Von den Mysterien zur Kirche.* Leipzig: Koehler & Amelang, 1961.

Lesegretain, Claire: "Au commencement était Ann Arbor." *Actualité religieuse dans le monde* 102 (1992), 18–20.

Letourneux, Nicolas: *De la meilleure manière d'entendre la sainte messe.* Paris: Roulland, 1680.

Leuenberger, Samuel: *Archbishop Cranmer's Immortal Bequest: The Book of Common Prayer of the Church of England.* Grand Rapids: Eerdmans, 1990.

Levenson, Jon D.: *The Death and Resurrection of the Beloved Son: The Transformation of Child Sacrifice in Judaism and Christianity.* New Haven: Yale University Press, 1993.

Lewis, C.S.: *Reflections on the Psalms.* New York: Harcourt, Brace & World, 1958.

Lewis, Ioan M.: *Ecstatic Religion: An Anthropological Study of Spirit Possession and Shamanism.* Harmondsworth: Penguin, 1971.

Libanius: *Selected Works.* Ed. and trans. A.F. Norman; LCL. London: Heinemann, 1977, vol. II.

Lietzmann, Hans: *Mass and Lord's Supper.* Trans. and with a new study by Robert D. Richardson. Leiden: Brill, 1979.

Lightfoot, J.B. and J.R. Harmer (trans.): *The Apostolic Fathers*, rev. edn. by Michael W. Holmes. Grand Rapids: Baker Book House, 1989.

Lindemann, Andreas: "Die Versuchungsgeschichte Jesu nach der Logienquelle und das Vaterunser." *Jesu Rede von Gott und ihre Nachgeschichte im frühen Christentum*, ed. Dietrich-Alex Koch *et al.* Gütersloh: Mohn, 1989, 91–100.

Lipinski, Edward: "Qânâh." *Theologisches Wörterbuch zum Alten Testament*, ed. Heinz-Josef Fabry *et al.* Stuttgart: Kohlhammer, 1993, vol. VII, 63–71.

Loader, William R.G.: *Sohn und Hoherpriester*. Neukirchen-Vluyn: Neukirchener Verlag, 1981.

Long, A.A.: "Epicureans and Stoics." *Classical Mediterranean Spirituality*, ed. A.H. Armstrong. New York: Crossroad, 1986, 135–53.

Louth, Andrew: *The Origins of the Christian Mystical Tradition*. Oxford: Clarendon Press, 1981.

——: "Pagan Theurgy and Christian Sacramentalism in Denys the Areopagite." *Journal of Theological Studies* NS 37 (1986), 432–38.

Lovett, Leonard: "Black Origins of the Pentecostal Movement." *Aspects of Pentecostal-charismatic Origins*, ed. Vinson Synan. Plainfield: Logos International, 1975, 123–41.

Lucian: *Opera*, ed. M.D. MacLeod. Oxford: Clarendon Press, 1974, vol. II.

McAdoo, Henry R.: "A Theology of the Eucharist: Brevint and the Wesleys." *Theology* 97 (1994), 245–56.

McConnell, Dan R.: *A Different Gospel*. Rev. edn. Peabody: Hendrickson, 1995.

McDannell, Colleen and Bernhard Lang, *Heaven: A History*. New Haven and London: Yale University Press, 1988.

MacDonald, Dennis R.: "Luke's Eutychus and Homer's Elpenor." *Journal of Higher Criticism* 1 (1994), 5–24.

McDonnell, Kilian: *John Calvin, the Church, and the Eucharist*. Princeton: Princeton University Press, 1967.

——: "Eucharistic Celebrations in the Catholic Charismatic Movement." *Studia Liturgica* 9 (1973), 19–44.

McHardy, A.K.: "Ecclesiastics and Economics: Poor Priests, Prosperous Laymen and Proud Prelates in the Reign of Richard II." *The Church and Wealth*, ed. William J. Shiels *et al.* Studies in Church History 24. Oxford: Blackwell, 1987, 129–37.

McKay, Heather A.: *Sabbath and Synagogue: The Question of Sabbath Worship in Ancient Judaism*. Leiden: Brill, 1994.

McKenna, John H.: *Eucharist and Holy Spirit*. Great Wakering: Mayhew-McCrimmon, 1975.

McKinnon, James (ed.): *Music in Early Christian Literature*. Cambridge: Cambridge University Press, 1987.

McLaughlin, Megan: *Consorting with Saints: Prayer for the Dead in Early Medieval France*. Ithaca: Cornell University Press, 1994.

McLaughlin, R. Emmet: "The Word Eclipsed? Preaching in the Early Middle Ages." *Traditio* 46 (1991), 77–122.

McLean, Alexander *et al.* (eds.): *Penuel; or, Face to Face with God*. New York: Palmer, 1869.

McLean, B. Hudson: *The Cursed Christ*. Sheffield: Sheffield Academic Press, 1996.

McManus, Frederick R.: *Thirty Years of Liturgical Renewal: Statements of the Bishops' Committee on the Liturgy*. Washington: United States Catholic Conference, 1987.

MacMullen, Ramsay: *Enemies of the Roman Order*. Cambridge, MA: Harvard University Press, 1966.

MacPartlan, Paul: "Ihr werdet euch in mich verwandeln: Kirche und Eucharistie im Denken Henri de Lubacs." *Internationale katholische Zeitschrift* 22 (1993), 141–53.

Macy, Gary: *The Banquet's Wisdom*. New York: Paulist Press, 1992.

——: "The Dogma of Transubstantiation in the Middle Ages." *Journal of Ecclesiastical History* 45 (1994), 11–41.

Magne, Jean: "Carmina Christo." *Ephemerides liturgicae* 100 (1986), 3–27.113–37.386–90.

Maier, Johann: *Jesus von Nazareth in der talmudischen Überlieferung*. Darmstadt: Wissenschaftliche Buchgesellschaft, 1978.

——: "Zur Verwendung von Psalmen in der synagogalen Liturgie." *Liturgie und Dichtung*, ed. Hansjakob Becker *et al.* St. Ottilien: Eos, 1983, vol. I:55–90.

Majercik, Ruth: *The Chaldean Oracles.* Leiden: Brill, 1989.

Malherbe, Abraham J.: *Paul and the Thessalonians.* Philadelphia: Fortress, 1987.

——: *Paul and the Popular Philosophers.* Minneapolis: Fortress, 1989.

Malinowski, Bronislaw: *Magic, Science and Religion.* Garden City: Doubleday, 1954, 79–84: "Magic and Experience."

Mangenot, Eugène: "Eucharistie du XIIIe au XVe siècle." *Dictionnaire de Théologie catholique*, ed. Alfred Vacant *et al.* Paris: Letouzey & Ané, 1913, vol. V, 1302–26.

Marcus Aurelius, *The Communings with Himself*, rev. edn.; LCL. London: Heinemann, 1930.

Marinus: "Proclus or About Happiness." in: Laurence J. Rosán, *The Philosophy of Proclus.* New York: Cosmos, 1949, 13–35.

Markus, Robert A.: "Augustine on Magic." *Revue des études augustiniennes* 40 (1994), 375–88.

Marquard, Reiner: *Karl Barth und der Isenheimer Altar.* Stuttgart: Calwer, 1995.

Marrou, Henri-Irénée: "Autour de la bibliothèque du pape Agapit." *Mélanges d'archéologie et d'histoire* 48 (1931), 124–69.

——: *Saint Augustin et la fin de la culture antique*, 4th edn. Paris: E. de Boccard, 1958.

——: *Histoire de l'éducation dans l'antiquité*, 6th edn. Paris: Seuil, 1981, vol. II.

Marshall, Howard: "Preaching from the New Testament." *Scottish Bulletin of Evangelical Theology* 9 (1991), 104–17.

Martin, Ralph P.: *The Worship of God.* Grand Rapids: Eerdmans, 1982.

Marx, Alfred: *Les offrandes végétales dans l'Ancien Testament.* Leiden: Brill, 1994.

Mather, Cotton: *Magnalia Christi Americana*, ed. Thomas Robbins. Hartford: Andrus, 1853, 2 vols.

Mather, Increase: "The Day of Trouble Is Near" (1674). *Sermons for Days of Fast, Prayer, and Humiliation and Execution Sermons*, ed. Ronald A. Bosco. Delmar, NY: Scholars' Facsimiles & Reprints, 1978, 17–49.

Mayer, Günter: *Para: Die rote Kuh.* Die Mischna, ed. G. Beer *et al.* Berlin: Töpelmann, 1964.

Megivern, James J.: *Concomitance and Communion.* Fribourg: University Press, 1963.

——(ed.): *Official Catholic Teachings: Worship and Liturgy.* Wilmington: McGrath, 1978.

Mell, Ulrich: "Gehört das Vater-Unser zur authentischen Jesus-Tradition?" *Berliner theologische Zeitschrift* 11 (1994), 148–80.

Melton, J. Gordon: *The Encyclopedia of American Religions: Religious Creeds.* Detroit: Gale, 1988.

Menzies, Robert P.: *The Development of Early Christian Pneumatology.* Sheffield: JSOT Press, 1991.

Merton, Thomas: "Seven Qualities of the Sacred." *Good Work* 27 (1964), 15–20.

Merz, Aloys (ed.): *Gesammelte Schriften unserer Zeiten zur Vertheidigung der Religion und Wahrheit.* Augsburg: J.B.B. Merz, 1791, vol. VIII/1.

Messadié, Gerald: "Placebo . . . Le cerveau qui guérit." *Science & Vie* 920 (May, 1994), 64–69.

Meyendorff, John: *Byzantine Theology.* New York: Fordham University Press, 1974.

——: *Byzantine Hesychasm.* London: Variorum Reprints, 1974a.

Meyer, Donald: *The Positive Thinkers.* Rev. edn. Middletown: Wesleyan University Press, 1988.

Meyer, Marvin and Richard Smith (eds.): *Ancient Christian Magic: Coptic Texts of Ritual Power.* San Francisco: Harper, 1994.

——and Paul Mirecki (eds.): *Ancient Magic and Ritual Power.* Leiden: Brill, 1995.

Micklem, E. Romilly: "Psychological Considerations." *Christian Worship*, ed. Nathaniel Micklem. London: Oxford University Press, 1936, 189–206.

Milet, Jean: *God or Christ? A Study in Social Psychology.* Trans. John Bowden. London: SCM Press, 1981.

Milgrom, Jacob: "Israel's Sanctuary." *Revue biblique* 83 (1976), 390–99.

———: *Numbers: The JPS Torah Commentary*. Philadelphia: Jewish Publication Society, 1990.

Miller, Patrick D.: *Interpreting the Psalms*. Philadelphia: Fortress, 1986.

———: *They Cried to the Lord: The Form and Theology of Biblical Prayer*. Minneapolis: Fortress, 1994.

Miller, Perry and Thomas H. Johnson (eds.): *The Puritans: A Sourcebook of Their Writings*. New York: Harper & Row, 1963.

Miller, Robert M.: *Harry Emerson Fosdick—Preacher, Pastor, Prophet*. New York: Oxford University Press, 1985.

Mingana, A.: *Woodbrooke Studies: Christian Documents Edited and Translated*. Cambridge: Heffer, 1933, vol. VI.

Mishnah, The. Trans. Jacob Neusner. New Haven and London: Yale University Press, 1988.

Möbius, Friedrich: "Die Chorpartie der westeuropäischen Klosterkirche zwischen 8. und 11. Jahrhundert." *Architektur des Mittelalters*, ed. Friedrich Möbius *et al*. Weimar: Böhlau, 1984, 9–41.

Monier, Frédéric: *Vie de Jean-Jacques Olier*. Paris: J. de Gigord, 1914, vol. I.

Montagner, Hubert: *L'attachement, les débuts de la tendresse*. Paris: Odile Jacob, 1988.

Montefiore, C.G. *et al*.: *A Rabbinic Anthology*. New York: Schocken, 1974.

Monumenta Germaniae Historica. Epistolae, vol. 1, ed. Paul Ewald. Berlin: Weidmann, 1887.

Moos, Alois: *Das Verhältnis von Wort und Sakrament in der deutschsprachigen Theologie des 20. Jahrhunderts*. Paderborn: Bonifatius, 1993.

Morenz, Siegfried: "Entstehung und Wesen der Buchreligion." *Theologische Literaturzeitung* 75 (1950), 709–16.

Müller, Iso: "Die Altar-Tituli des Klosterplanes." *Studien zum St. Galler Klosterplan*, ed. Johannes Duft. St. Gallen: Fehr'sche Buchhandlung, 1962, 129–76.

Müller, Hans-Peter: "Die kultische Darstellung der Theophanie." *Vetus Testamentum* 14 (1964), 183–91.

Müller, Nikolaus: *Die Wittenberger Bewegung 1521 und 1522*, 2nd edn. Leipzig: Heinsius, 1911.

Murphy-O'Connor, Jerome: "John the Baptist and Jesus." *New Testament Studies* 36 (1990), 359–74.

Musurillo, Herbert (trans.): *The Acts of the Christian Martyrs*. Oxford: Clarendon Press, 1972.

Neal, Emily Gardiner: *Celebration of Healing*. Cambridge, MA: Cowley, 1992.

Neusner, Jacob: *The Wonder-Working Lawyers of Talmudic Babylonia*. Lanham, MD: University Press of America, 1987.

Nevin, John W.: *The Mystical Presence of Christ*, ed. Bard Thompson *et al*. Philadelphia: United Church Press, 1966.

New Catechism: Catholic Faith for Adults, A. Trans. Kevin Smyth. New York: Herder & Herder, 1967. [Known as the "Dutch catechism," originally published in 1966.]

Niebuhr, Reinhold: "Fosdick: Theologian and Preacher." *The Christian Century* 70 (1953), 657–58.

Nilsson, Martin P.: *Greek Piety*. Trans. Herbert J. Rose. Oxford: Clarendon Press, 1948.

Noll, Mark A.: *A History of Christianity in the United States and Canada*. Grand Rapids: Eerdmans, 1992.

Norden, Eduard: *Agnostos Theos: Untersuchungen zur Formengeschichte religiöser Rede*. Leipzig: Teubner, 1913.

Norton, David: *A History of the Bible as Literature*. Cambridge: Cambridge University Press, 1993, vol. II.

Nuttall, Geoffrey F.: *The Holy Spirit in Puritan Faith and Experience*, 2nd edn. Chicago: University of Chicago Press, 1992.

Oates, Wayne E.: "A Socio-psychological Study of Glossolalia." *Glossolalia: Tongue-*

Speaking in Biblical, Historical, and Psychological Perspective, ed. Frank Stagg *et al.* Nashville: Abingdon, 1967, 76–99.

Oegema, Gerbern S.: *Der Gesalbte und sein Volk*. Göttingen: Vandenhoeck & Ruprecht, 1994.

Olier, Jean-Jacques: *Œuvres complètes de M. Olier*, ed. Jaques-Paul Migne. Petit-Montrouge: Migne, 1856, 281–455: "Explication des cérémonies de la grand'messe de paroisse" [= *EC*].

——: *Lettres de M. Olier*. Nouvelle éd. par E. Levesque. Paris: J. de Gigord, 1935 [= *L*].

——: *Catéchisme chrétien et Journée chrétienne*, ed. François Amiot. Paris: Le Rameau, 1954, 9–92: "Catéchisme chrétien pour la vie intérieure" [= *CC*]; 93–247: "La journée chrétienne" [= *JC*].

——: *Introduction à la vie et aux vertus chrétiennes*, ed. François Amiot. Paris: Le Rameau, 1954, 7–159 [= *IVV*].

O'Meara, Dominic: "Political Life and Divinization in Neoplatonic Philosophy." *Hermathena* 157 (1994), 155–64.

Origen: *Against Celsus*. Trans. Henry Chadwick. Cambridge: Cambridge University Press, 1965.

——: *An Exhortation to Martyrdom, Prayer, First Principles*. Trans. Rowan A. Greer; CWS. New York: Paulist Press, 1979.

Oropeza, B.J.: *A Time to Laugh*. Peabody: Hendrickson, 1995.

Otto, Rudolf: "Vom Wege." *Die christliche Welt* 25 (1911), 705–10.

——: *Zur Erneuerung und Ausgestaltung des Gottesdienstes*. Giessen: Töpelmann, 1925.

——: *Sünde und Urschuld*. Munich: Beck, 1932.

——: *The Idea of the Holy*. Trans. John W. Harvey, 2nd edn. London: Oxford University Press, 1950.

Packer, J.I.: "The Spirit with the Word: The Reformational Revivalism of George Whitefield." *The Bible, the Reformation and the Church*, ed. W. Peter Stephens. Sheffield: Sheffield Academic Press, 1995, 166–89.

Parsch, Pius: "Liturgische Spielsachen." *Bibel und Liturgie* 5 (1930/31), 431.

Partee, Charles: *Calvin and Classical Philosophy*. Leiden: Brill, 1977.

Pascal, Blaise: *Pensées*. Trans. A.J. Krailsheimer. Harmondsworth: Penguin, 1966.

Paverd, Frans van de: *Zur Geschichte der Meßliturgie in Antiocheia und Konstantinopel gegen Ende des 4. Jahrhunderts*. Rome: Pontificio Istituto Orientale, 1970.

Peale, Norman Vincent: *The Power of Positive Thinking*, 15th edn. New York: Fawcett Crest, 1992.

Pepys, Samuel: *The Diary*, ed. Robert Latham and William Matthews. London: Bell, 1970–83, 11 vols.

Peterson, Erik: "Alalazô." *Theologisches Wörterbuch zum Neuen Testament*, ed. Gerhard Kittel. Stuttgart: Kohlhammer, 1933, vol. I:228.

Pettit, Norman: *The Heart Prepared: Grace and Conversion in Puritan Spiritual Life*. New Haven: Yale University Press, 1966.

Pfeiffer, Robert H. and E.A. Speiser: *One Hundred New Selected Nuzi Texts*. Annual of the American Schools of Oriental Research, 16. New Haven: American Schools of Oriental Research, 1936.

Pfister, Oskar: *Analytische Seelsorge*. Göttingen: Vandenhoeck & Ruprecht, 1927.

Pharr, Clyde *et al.* (trans.): *The Theodosian Code and Novels*. Princeton: Princeton University Press, 1952.

Pilch, John J.: "The Transfiguration of Jesus." *Modelling Early Christianity*, ed. Philip F. Esler. London: Routledge, 1995, 47–64.

Pittenger, Norman: *God's Way with Men*. London: Hodder & Stoughton, 1969.

——: *Praying Today*. Grand Rapids: Eerdmans, 1974.

Places, Edouard des: *Oracles chaldaïques*. Paris: Les Belles Lettres, 1971.

Pleket, H.W.: "Religious History as the History of Mentality." *Faith, Hope and Worship*, ed. H.S. Versnel. Leiden: Brill, 1981, 152–92.

Plüss, Jean-Daniel: *Therapeutic and Prophetic Narratives in Worship*. Frankfurt: Lang, 1988.

Plutarch: *Moralia*. Trans. Benedict Einarson *et al.*; LCL. Cambridge: Harvard University Press, 1967, vol. XIV.

Pohle, Joseph and Josef Gummersbach: *Lehrbuch der Dogmatik*, 9th edn. Paderborn: Schöningh, 1960, vol. III.

Polkinghorne, John: "Can a Scientist Pray?" *Colloquium* 26 (1994), 2–10.

Poloma, Margaret M.: *The Charismatic Movement*. Boston: Twayne, 1982.

——: *The Assemblies of God at the Crossroads*. Knoxville: University of Tennessee Press, 1989.

Popkes, Wiard: "Die letzte Bitte des Vater-Unser." *Zeitschrift für die neutestamentliche Wissenschaft* 81 (1990), 1–20.

Post, Paul: "An excellent game . . . : On Playing the Mass." *Bread of Heaven: Customs and Practices Surrounding Holy Communion*, ed. Charles Caspers *et al.* Kampen: Kok Pharos, 1995, 185–214.

Potter, David: Review of *The Chaldean Oracles*, trans. Ruth Majercik. *Journal of Roman Studies* 81 (1991), 225–27.

——: *Prophets and Emperors: Human and Divine Authority from Augustus to Theodosius*. Cambridge, MA: Harvard University Press, 1994.

Prayers We Have in Common, prepared by the International Consultation on English Texts, 2nd edn. Philadelphia: Fortress, 1975.

Praying Together: Agreed Liturgical Texts, prepared by the English Language Liturgical Consultation. Norwich: Canterbury Press, 1988.

Préaud, Maxine: *Inventaire du fonds français. Gravures du XVIIe siècle. Tome 17: Claude Mellan*, ed. Bibliothèque Nationale/Département des Estampes. Paris: Bibliothèque Nationale, 1988.

Preisendanz, Karl *et al.* (eds.), *Papyri Graecae Magicae: Die griechischen Zauberpapyri*, 2nd edn. Stuttgart: Teubner, 1973–74, 2 vols.

Price, Lucien: *Dialogues of Alfred North Whitehead*. New York: Mentor Books, 1956.

Price, Robert M.: "Punished in Paradise." *Journal for the Study of the New Testament* 7 (1980), 33–40.

Proclus: *The Elements of Theology*. Trans. E.R. Dodds. Oxford: Oxford University Press, 1963.

——: *Commentaire sur le Timée*. Trans. A.J. Festugière. Paris: Vrin, 1967, vol. II.

——: *Théologie platonicienne*. Ed. and trans. H.D. Saffrey and L.G. Westerinck. Paris: Les Belles Lettres, 1981, vol. IV.

Pseudo-Dionysius: *The Complete Works*. Trans. Colm Luibheid; CWS. New York: Paulist Press, 1987.

——: *Corpus Dionysiacum*. Vol. 2, ed. Günter Heil *et al.* Patristische Texte und Studien, vol. 36. Berlin: de Gruyter, 1991.

Puniet, Jean de: "La louange divine." *La vie spirituelle* 2 (1921), 443–52.

Punshon, John: *Testimony and Tradition: Some Aspects of Quaker Spirituality*. London: Quaker Home Service, 1990.

Pytches, David: *Some Said It Thundered: A Personal Encounter with the Kansas City Prophets*. Nashville: Oliver-Nelson, 1991.

Quasten, Johannes: "Mysterium tremendum: Eucharistische Frömmigkeitsauffassungen des 4. Jahrhunderts." *Vom christlichen Mysterium*, ed. A. Meyer *et al.* Münster: Aschendorff, 1951, 66–75.

——: *Music and Worship in Pagan and Christian Antiquity*. Trans. Boniface Ramsey. Washington, DC: National Association of Pastoral Musicians, 1983.

Quebedeaux, Richard: *The New Charismatics II*. San Francisco: Harper & Row, 1983.

Rad, Gerhard von: *Gesammelte Studien zum Alten Testament*. Munich: Kaiser, 1958.

Radl, Walter: *Der Ursprung Jesu*. Freiburg: Herder, 1996.

Raffalt, Reinhard: *Musica eterna*. Munich: Piper, 1978.

Rahner, Karl: *Theological Investigations*. Trans. Kevin Smyth. Baltimore: Helicon Press, 1966, vol. IV:287–311: "The Presence of Christ in the Sacrament of the Lord's Supper"; 312–20: "On the Duration of the Presence of Christ after Communion."

——: *Karl Rahner: Theologian of the Graced Search for Meaning*, ed. Geffrey B. Kelly. Minneapolis: Fortress, 1992.

Randhofer, Regina: *Psalmen in einstimmigen vokalen Überlieferungen: Eine vergleichende Untersuchung jüdischer und christlicher Traditionen*. Frankfurt: Lang, 1995.

Randolph, Peter: *Sketches of Slave Life*. Boston: James H. Earle, 1855.

Ratzinger, Joseph: *Liturgie und Kirchenmusik*. Hamburg: Sikorski, 1987.

Regel des heiligen Augustinus—Konstitutionen der Augustiner Chorfrauen der Congregatio Beatae Mariae. Essen: Augustiner Chorfrauen, 1986.

Regmire, R. David: *Sacraments and the Salvation Army*. Metuchen, NJ: Scarecrow Press, 1990.

Reid, Barbara E.: "Prayer and the Face of the Transfigured Jesus." *The Lord's Prayer and Other Prayer Texts from the Greco-Roman Era*, ed. James H. Charlesworth *et al.* Valley Forge: Trinity Press International, 1994, 39–53.

Reiling, J.: *Hermas and Christian Prophecy*. Leiden: Brill, 1973.

Renan, Ernest: *Œuvres complètes*, ed. Henriette Psichari. Paris: Calmann-Lévy, 1953, vol. VI.

Return to the Upper Room: 1992 National Catholic Charismatic Renewal Conference. Steubenville, OH: Franciscan University, 1992.

Reynal, Daniel de: *Théologie de la liturgie des heures*. Paris: Beauchesne, 1978.

Richards, Jeffrey: *Consul of God: The Life and Times of Gregory the Great*. London: Routledge & Kegan Paul, 1980.

Richardson, Cyril C. (trans.): *Early Christian Fathers*. New York: Macmillan, 1970.

——: review of Morton Smith's *Clement of Alexandria*, *Theological Studies* 35 (1974), 571–77.

Riché, Pierre: *Les écoles et l'enseignement dans l'occident chrétien*. Paris: Aubier Montaigne, 1979.

Riedweg, Christoph: *Mysterienterminologie bei Platon, Philon und Klemens von Alexandrien*. Berlin: de Gruyter, 1987.

Rieff, Philip: *The Triumph of the Therapeutic: Uses of Faith after Freud*. New York: Harper & Row, 1966.

Riesner, Rainer: "Synagogues in Jerusalem." *The Book of Acts in Its Palestinian Setting*, ed. Richard Bauckham. Grand Rapids: Eerdmans, 1995, 179–211.

Rinser, Luise: *Die gläsernen Ringe*. Frankfurt: S. Fischer, 1986.

——: *Gratwanderung: Briefe der Freundschaft an Karl Rahner 1962–1984*. Munich: Kösel, 1994.

——: *Saturn auf der Sonne*. Frankfurt: Fischer, 1994a.

Ritschl, Albrecht: *Unterricht in der christlichen Religion* [1875]. Gütersloh: Mohn, 1966.

Riverside Church in the City of New York. A Handbook, The. Philadelphia: Franklin Printing Company, 1931.

Robeck, Cecil M.: *Prophecy in Carthage: Perpetua, Tertullian, and Cyprian*. Cleveland: Pilgrim Press, 1992.

Rordorf, Willy: "The Lord's Prayer in the Light of Its Liturgical Use in the Early Church." *Studia Liturgica* 14 (1980/81), 1–19.

Rorem, Paul: *Pseudo-Dionysius*. New York: Oxford University Press, 1993.

Rössler, Dietrich: "Beispiel und Erfahrung: Zu Luthers Homiletik." *Reformation und Praktische Theologie*, ed. Hans Martin Müller *et al.* Göttingen: Vandenhoeck & Ruprecht, 1983, 202–15.

Rouget, Gilbert: *Music and Trance*. Trans. Brunhilde Biebuyck. Chicago: University of Chicago Press, 1985.

Rowell, Geoffrey: "The Sacramental Use of Oil in Anglicanism and the Churches of the

Reformation." *The Oil of Gladness: Anointing in the Christian Tradition*, ed. Martin Dudley *et al.* London: SPCK, 1993, 134–53.

Rudolph, Kurt: *Gnosis: The Nature and History of an Ancient Religion*, ed. Robert McL. Wilson. Edinburgh: Clark, 1983.

Ruthven, Jon: *On the Cessation of the Charismata: The Protestant Polemic on Postbiblical Miracles.* Sheffield: Sheffield Academic Press, 1993.

Ruusbroec, John: *The Spiritual Espousals and Other Works.* Trans. James A. Wiseman; CWS. New York: Paulist Press, 1985.

Sacred Congregation for Divine Worship: *General Instruction of the Liturgy of the Hours* (1971). Washington: United States Catholic Conference, 1983.

Sallustius [Saturnius Secundus Salutius]: *Concerning the Gods and the Universe.* Trans. and ed. Arthur D. Nock. London: Cambridge University Press, 1926.

Salzmann, Jorg C.: *Lehren und Ermahnen: Zur Geschichte des christlichen Wortgottesdienstes in den ersten drei Jahrhunderten.* Tübingen: Mohr, 1994.

Sanders, Cheryl J.: *Saints in Exile: The Holiness-Pentecostal Experience in African American Religion and Culture.* New York: Oxford University Press, 1996.

Sänger, Dieter: *Antikes Judentum und die Mysterien.* Tübingen: Mohr, 1980.

Santos Yanguas, Narciso: "La Dinastía de los Severos y los Cristianos." *Euphrosyne* 11 (1981/82), 149–71.

Schenkel, Albert F.: *The Rich Man and the Kingdom: John D. Rockefeller, Jr., and the Protestant Establishment.* Minneapolis: Fortress, 1995.

Schleiermacher, Friedrich: *Aus Schleiermacher's Leben. In Briefen*, 2nd edn. Berlin: Reimer, 1860, 2 vols.

——: *The Christian Faith.* Trans. H.R. Mackintosh *et al.* Edinburgh: Clark, 1928.

——: *Kleine Schriften und Predigten*, ed. Hayo Gerdes *et al.* Berlin: de Gruyter, 1970, vol. I.

——: *Friedrich Schleiermacher: Pioneer of Modern Theology*, ed. Keith W. Clements. London: Collins Liturgical Publications, 1987.

Schlink, Edmund: *Der kommende Christus und die kirchliche Traditionen.* Göttingen: Vandenhoeck & Ruprecht, 1961.

Schmaus, Michael: *Katholische Dogmatik.* Munich: Hueber, 1952, vol. IV/1.

Schmidt, Karl Ludwig: "Kymbalon." *Theologisches Wörterbuch zum Neuen Testament*, ed. Gerhard Kittel. Stuttgart: Kohlhammer, 1938, vol. III:1037–38.

Schmidt, Leigh E.: *Holy Fairs: Scottish Communions and American Revivals in the Early Modern Period.* Princeton: Princeton University Press, 1989.

Schmidt, Martin: *Wiedergeburt und neuer Mensch.* Witten: Luther-Verlag, 1969.

Schmieder, Lucida: *Geisttaufe.* Paderborn: Schöningh, 1982.

Schmitt, Jean-Claude: *La raison des gestes dans l'Occident médiéval.* Paris: Gallimard, 1990.

Schneemelcher, Wilhelm: *New Testament Apocrypha*, rev. edn. Trans. R. McL. Wilson. Cambridge: Clarke, 1991, vol. I.

Schneider, Ceslaus M.: *Die Ordensschwester.* Trans. from Père Adrien Sylvain's manual, 4th edn. Regensburg: Coppenrath, 1901.

Schoedel, William R.: *Ignatius of Antioch: A Commentary on the Letters.* Philadelphia: Fortress, 1985.

Scholten, Clemens: "Die alexandrinische Katechetenschule." *Jahrbuch für Antike und Christentum* 38 (1995), 16–37.

Schrage, Wolfgang: "Synagogê." *Theologisches Wörterbuch zum Neuen Testament*, ed. Gerhard Kittel *et al.* Stuttgart: Kohlhammer, 1964, vol. VII:798–839.

Schroeder, Hans-Werner: *Dreieinigkeit und Dreifaltigkeit.* Stuttgart: Urachhaus, 1986.

——: *Die Christengemeinschaft.* Stuttgart: Urachhaus, 1990.

Schuberth, Dietrich: *Kaiserliche Liturgie: Die Einbeziehung von Musikinstrumenten, insbesondere der Orgel, in den frühmittelalterlichen Gottesdienst.* Göttingen: Vandenhoeck & Ruprecht, 1968.

Schüssler Fiorenza, Elisabeth: *In Memory of Her: A Feminist Theological Reconstruction of Christian Origins.* London: SCM Press, 1983.

Schwier, Helmut: *Tempel und Tempelzerstörung*. Fribourg: Éditions Universitaires, 1989.

Scotford, John R.: "Can the Preacher Be Saved?" *The Christian Century* 47 (1930), 889–90.

Scroggs, Robin: "Christ the Cosmocrator and the Experience of Believers." *The Future of Christology*, ed. Abraham J. Malherbe *et al.* Minneapolis: Fortress, 1993, 160–75.

Seidel, Margot: *Novalis' Geistliche Lieder*. Frankfurt: Lang, 1983.

Seybold, Klaus: "Zur Vorgeschichte der liturgischen Formel *Amen*." *Theologische Zeitschrift* 48 (1992), 109–17.

Shaw, Gregory: "Theurgy: Rituals of Unification in the Neoplatonism of Iamblichus." *Traditio* 41 (1985), 1–28.

——: *Theurgy and the Soul: The Neoplatonism of Iamblichus*. University Park: Pennsylvania State University Press, 1995.

Shepherd, William G.: *Great Preachers as Seen by a Journalist*. New York: Revell, 1924.

Shiner, Whitney T.: *Follow Me! Disciples in Markan Rhetoric*. Atlanta: Scholars Press, 1995.

Shopshire, James M.: *A Socio-Historical Characterization of the Black Pentecostal Movement in America*. Diss., Northwestern University, 1975.

Siebenmorgen, Harald: *Die Anfänge der "Beuroner Kunstschule."* Sigmaringen: Thorbecke, 1983.

Simard, Jean: *Une iconographie du clergé français au XVIIe siècle*. Quebec: Presses de l'Université Laval, 1976.

Smallwood, E.M.: *The Jews under Roman Rule*. Leiden: Brill, 1976.

Smit, Joop F.M.: "Tongues and Prophecy: Deciphering 1 Cor 14,22." *Biblica* 75 (1994), 175–90.

Smith, Jay E.: "The Theology of Charles Finney: A System of Self-Reformation." *Trinity Journal* 13 (1992), 61–93.

Smith, Jonathan Z.: *Map Is Not Territory*. Leiden: Brill, 1978.

——: "The Domestication of Sacrifice." *Violent Origins: Ritual Killing and Cultural Formation*, ed. Robert G. Hamerton-Kelly. Stanford: Stanford University Press, 1987, 191–205.

——: *Drudgery Divine: On the Comparison of Early Christianities and the Religions of Late Antiquity*. London: School of Oriental and African Studies, 1990.

Smith, Morton: *Clement of Alexandria and a Secret Gospel of Mark*. Cambridge, MA: Harvard University Press, 1973.

——: *The Secret Gospel*. New York: Harper & Row, 1973.

——: *Jesus the Magician*. London: Gollancz, 1978.

——: "The Jewish Elements in the Magical Papyri." *Society of Biblical Literature Seminar Papers* 25 (1986), 455–62.

——: *Studies in the Cult of Yahweh*, ed. Shaye J.D. Cohen. Leiden: Brill, 1996, vol. II.

Smits, Luchesius: *Actuele vragen rondom de transsubstantiatie en de tegenwoordigheid des Heren in de Eucharistie*. Roermond: Romen & Zonen, 1965.

Sneck, William J.: *Charismatic Spiritual Gifts: A Phenomenological Analysis*. Washington: University Press of America, 1981.

Snoek, G.J.C.: *Medieval Piety from Relics to the Eucharist*. Leiden: Brill, 1995.

Söhngen, Oskar: "Theologische Grundlagen der Kirchenmusik." *Leiturgia: Handbuch des evangelischen Gottesdienstes*, ed. Karl F. Müller *et al.* Kassel: Stauda, 1961, vol. IV: 1–267.

Sontag, Susan: "The Pleasure of the Image." *Art in America* 75 (November, 1987), 122–31.

Spectator, The: ed. Donald F. Bond. Oxford: Clarendon Press, 1965, vol. III.

Speyer, Wolfgang: *Frühes Christentum im antiken Spannungsfeld*. Tübingen: Mohr, 1989.

Spinks, Bryan D.: *The Sanctus in the Eucharistic Prayer*. Cambridge: Cambridge University Press, 1991.

Spurgeon, Charles H.: *Lectures to My Students*. Grand Rapids: Zondervan, 1954.

Stackhouse, John G.: "Billy Graham and the Nature of Conversion." *Studies in Religion* 21 (1992), 337–50.

Stegemann, Wolfgang: *Zwischen Synagoge und Obrigkeit*. Göttingen: Vandenhoeck & Ruprecht, 1991.

Stein, Elisabeth: *Leben und Visionen der Alpais von Cudot*. Tübingen: Narr, 1995.

Stein, Stephen J.: *The Shaker Experience in America*. New Haven and London: Yale University Press, 1992.

Steiner, Rudolf: *The Gospel of St. John in Relation to the Three Other Gospels*. Trans. G. Metaxa. London: Humphries, 1933.

——: *Die Grundimpulse des weltgeschichtlichen Werdens der Menschheit*, 2nd edn. Dornach: Verlag der Rudolf Steiner-Nachlaßverwaltung, 1965.

——: *Von Jesus zu Christus* [1911], 6th edn. Dornach: R. Steiner Verlag, 1982.

——: *Vorträge und Kurse über christlich-religiöses Wirken II*. Dornach: R. Steiner-Verlag, 1993; with supplementary vol.

Stengel, Paul: *Die griechischen Kultusaltertümer*. Munich: Beck, 1920.

Stevenson, Kenneth: *Accept this Offering: The Eucharist as Sacrifice Today*. London: SPCK, 1989.

——: "The Unbloody Sacrifice: The Origins and Development of a Description of the Eucharist." *Fountain of Life*, ed. Gerard Austin. Washington: Pastoral Press, 1991, 103–30.

Stewart, James S.: "Our Duty of Praise." *Classic Sermons on Worship*, ed. Warren K. Wiersbe. Grand Rapids: Kregel, 1988, 84–93.

Stock, Brian: *The Implications of Literacy*. Princeton: Princeton University Press, 1983.

Stone, Lawrence: *The Familty, Sex and Marriage in England, 1500–1800*. New York: Harper & Row, 1977.

Strauss, David Friedrich: *Die christliche Glaubenslehre*. Tübingen: Osiander, 1841, vol. II.

Straw, Carole: *Gregory the Great*. Berkeley: University of California Press, 1988.

Stuiber, Alfred: "Die Diptychon-Formel für die *nomina offerentium* im römischen Meßkanon." *Ephemerides liturgicae* 68 (1954), 127–46.

——: "Amen." *Reallexikon für Antike und Christentum, Supplementband*, ed. Theodor Klauser *et al.* Stuttgart: Hiersemann, 1985, 310–23.

Suárez, Francisco de: *Opera omnia*, ed. Charles Berton. Paris: Vivès, 1866, vol. XXI.

Sundén, Hjalmar: *Religionspsychologie*. Stuttgart: Calwer Verlag, 1982.

Suurmond, Jean-Jacques: "The Meaning and Purpose of Spirit-Baptism and the Charisms." *Bijdragen* 51 (1990), 172–94.

Sweet, Leonard I.: "The View of Man Inherent in New Measures Revivalism." *Church History* 45 (1976), 206–21.

Swetnam, James H.: "Hallowed Be Thy Name." *Biblica* 52 (1972), 556–63.

Swift, Jonathan: *Irish Tracts and Sermons*, ed. Herbert Davies *et al.* Oxford: Blackwell, 1968.

Sylvain, Adrien: see Schneider, Ceslaus M.

Symonds, H.E.: "The Heavenly Sacrifice in the Greek Fathers." *Texte und Untersuchungen* 93 (1966), 280–85.

Synan, H. Vinson: "Seymour, William Joseph." Burgess *et al.* (1989), 778–81.

Taft, Robert: *The Liturgy of the Hours in East and West*. Collegeville, MN: Liturgical Press, 1986.

——: "From Logos to Spirit: On the Early History of the Epiclesis." *Gratias agamus: Studien zum eucharistischen Hochgebet*, ed. Andreas Heinz *et al.* Freiburg: Herder, 1992, 489–502.

——: "The Precommunion Elevation of the Byzantine Divine Liturgy." *Orientalia Christiana Periodica* 62 (1996), 15–52.

Talmon, Shemaryahu: "The Emergence of Institutionalized Prayer in Israel in the Light of Qumran Literature." *Qumrân—Sa piété, sa théologie et son milieu*, ed. Mathias Delcor. Paris: Duculot, 1978, 265–84.

Tannen, Deborah: *You Just Don't Understand: Women and Men in Conversation*. New York: Morrow & Co., 1990.

Tanner, Norman P. (ed.): *Decrees of the Ecumenical Councils*. London: Sheed & Ward, 1990.

Tanquerey, Adolphe: *Précis de théologie ascétique et mystique*, 4th edn. Paris: Desclée, 1924.

——: *The Spiritual Life*. Trans. Herman Branderis, 2nd edn. Tournai: Desclée, 1930.

Taves, Ann: "Knowing through the Body: Dissociative Religious Experience in the African- and British-American Methodist Traditions." *Journal of Religion* 73 (1993), 200–22.

Taylor, Jeremy: *The Rule and Exercises of Holy Living* (1650). London: Dent, 1900, vol. II.

Teilhard de Chardin, Pierre: *The Divine Milieu*. New York: Harper, 1960.

——: *Écrits du temps de la guerre, 1916–19*. Paris: Seuil, 1965.

——: *Writings in Time of War*. Trans. René Hague. New York: Harper & Row, 1968.

Theissen, Gerd: *Untersuchungen zum Hebräerbrief*. Gütersloh: Mohn, 1969.

——: *The Social Setting of Pauline Christianity*. Trans. John H. Schütz. Philadelphia: Fortress, 1982.

Thipgen, Corbett H. and Hervey M. Cleckley: *The Three Faces of Eve*. New York: McGraw-Hill, 1957.

Thomas à Kempis: *The Imitation of Christ*. Trans. William C. Creasy. Macon: Mercer University Press, 1989.

Thomas Aquinas: *Opera omnia (ut sunt in indice thomistico)*, ed. Robert Busa. Stuttgart: Fromann-Holzboog, 1980, vol. III.

——: see also Albert and Thomas [Aquinas].

Thurian, Max (ed.): *Ecumenical Perspectives on Baptism, Eucharist and Ministry*. Geneva: World Council of Churches, 1983.

Tillich, Paul: *The Courage to Be*. New Haven: Yale University Press, 1952.

——: *Perspectives on 19th and 20th-Century Protestant Theology*. London: SCM Press, 1967.

Toorn, Karel van der: "Ordeal Procedures in the Psalms and the Passover Meal." *Vetus Testamentum* 38 (1988), 427–45.

Torjesen, Karen Jo: "The Early-Christian Orans: An Artistic Representation of Women's Liturgical Prayer and Prophecy." *Women Prophets and Preachers in the Christian Tradition*, ed. Beverly Kienzle *et al*. Berkeley: University of California Press, forthcoming.

Towey, Anthony: *"Amicitia" as the Philosophical Foundation and the Principal Analogy of the Eucharistic Theology of Thomas Aquinas*. Rome: Gregorian University, 1995.

Tripp, David: *The Renewal of the Covenant in the Methodist Tradition*. London: Epworth, 1969.

Trobisch, David: *Paul's Letter Collection: Tracing the Origins*. Minneapolis: Fortress, 1994.

Trombley, Frank R.: *Hellenic Religion and Christianization, c. 370–529*. Leiden: Brill, 1993, vol. I:1–97 : "The Legal Status of Sacrifice to 529 AD."

Trouillard, Jean: "Proclus et la joie de quitter le ciel." *Diotima* 11 (1983), 183–92.

Tugwell, Simon: "The Speech-Giving Spirit." Simon Tugwell *et al*.: *New Heaven? New Earth? An Encounter with Pentecostalism*. London: Darton, Longman & Todd, 1976, 119–59.

——: "Prayer, Humpty Dumpty and Thomas Aquinas." *Language, Meaning and God*, ed. Brian Davies. London: Geoffrey Chapman, 1987, 24–50.

——: "Humbert of Romans's Material for Preachers." *De ore Domini: Preacher and Word in the Middle Ages*, ed. Thomas L. Amos *et al*. Kalamazoo: Medieval Institute Publications, 1989, 105–17.

——(ed.): *Early Dominicans: Selected Writings*; CWS. New York: Paulist Press, 1982.

Tyson, James L.: *The Early Pentecostal Revival*. Hazelwood, MO: Word Aflame, 1992.

Tyson, Ruel W.: "The Testimony of Sister Annie Mae." *Diversities of Gifts: Field Studies in Southern Religion*, ed. Ruel W. Tyson *et al*. Urbana, IL: University of Illinois Press, 1988, 105–25.

Ulanov, Ann B.: "Jung and Prayer." *Jung and the Monotheisms*, ed. Joel Ryce-Menuhin. London: Routledge, 1994, 91–110.

——and Berry Ulanov: *Primary Speech: A Psychology of Prayer*. Atlanta: John Knox Press, 1982.

Urman, Dan: "The House of Assembly and the House of Study: Are They One and the Same?" *Journal of Jewish Studies* 44 (1993), 236–57 = Urman *et al*. (1995), I: 232–55.

——and Paul V.M. Flesher (eds.): *Ancient Synagogues*. Leiden: Brill, 1995, vol. I.

Veltri, Giuseppe: "Der Aramäische Targumvortrag zur Zeit Esras." *Laurentianum* 34 (1993), 187–207.

Venard, Marc: "Le prêtre, en France, au début du XVIIe siècle." *Bulletin de Saint-Sulpice* 6 (1980), 197–213.

Verheul, Ambroise: "Les Psaumes dans la prière de heures hier et aujourd'hui." *Questions liturgiques* 71 (1990), 261–95.

Vermes, Geza: *The Dead Sea Scrolls in English*, 4th edn. Harmondsworth: Penguin, 1995.

——*et al.* (eds.): *The Essenes according to Classical Sources*. Sheffield: JSOT Press, 1989.

Versnel, H.S.: "Religious Mentality in Ancient Prayer." *Faith, Hope and Worship: Aspects of Religious Mentality in the Ancient World*, ed. H.S. Versnel. Leiden: Brill, 1981, 1–64.

Vielhauer, Philipp: "Das Benedictus des Zacharias." *Zeitschrift für Theologie und Kirche* 49 (1952), 255–72.

Virgil with an English translation. Trans. H. Rushton Fairclough, rev. edn.; LCL. London: Heinemann, 1934, vol. II.

Viva, Domenico: *Opera omnia theologico-moralia*. Ferrara: Sumptibus Remondinianis, 1757, vol. IV/1.

Vogel, Cyril: "Deux conséquences de l'eschatologie grégorienne: la multiplication des messes privées et les moines-prêtres." *Grégoire le Grand: Actes du colloque de Chantilly 1982*, ed. Jacques Fontaine *et al.* Paris: CNRS, 1986, 267–76.

Voguë, Adalbert de: "Le sens de l'office divin d'après la Règle de S. Benoît I." *Revue d'ascétique et de mystique* 42 (1966), 389–404.

Voltaire: *Oeuvres complètes*, ed. Louis Moland. Paris: Garnier, 1879, vol. XX.

——: *Philosophical Dictionary*. Trans. Theodore Besterman. Harmondsworth: Penguin, 1972.

Vorländer, Hermann: "Christus als persönlicher Gott im Neuen Testament." *Kerygma und Dogma* 21 (1975), 120–46.

——: *Mein Gott: Die Vorstellungen vom persönlichen Gott im Alten Orient und im Alten Testament*. Kevelaer: Butzon & Bercker, 1975a.

Vovelle, Michel: *La Revolution contre l'église*. Bruxelles: Éditions Complexe, 1988.

Wainwright, Geoffrey: "The Language of Worship." *The Study of Liturgy*, ed. Cheslyn Jones *et al.*, 2nd edn. London: SPCK, 1992, 519–28.

Ward, W.R. (ed.): *Early Victorian Methodism*. Oxford: Oxford University Press, 1976.

Warner, Wayne E.: *The Woman Evangelist: The Life and Times of Charismatic Evangelist Maria B. Woodworth-Etter*. Metuchen, NJ: Scarecrow Press, 1986.

Wasserschleben, Hermann: *Die Bußordnungen der abendländischen Kirche*. Halle: Craeger, 1851.

Wehr, Lothar: *Arznei der Unsterblichkeit*. Münster: Aschendorff, 1987.

Weinfeld, Moshe: *Deuteronomy and the Deuteronomic School*. Oxford: Clarendon Press, 1972.

——: "The Heavenly Praise in Unison." *Meqor Hajjim: Festschrift für Georg Molin*, ed. Irmtraut Seybold. Graz: Akademische Druck- und Verlagsanstalt, 1983, 427–37.

Weisheipl, James A.: *Friar Thomas d'Aquino*. Oxford: Blackwell, 1974.

Wengst, Klaus (ed.): *Didache, Apostellehre, Barnabasbrief, Zweiter Klemensbrief, Schrift an Diognet*. Darmstadt: Wissenschaftliche Buchgesellschaft, 1984.

Werner, Eric: *The Sacred Bridge: The Interdependence of Liturgy and Music in Synagogue and Church during the First Millennium*. New York: Columbia University Press, 1959 [= vol. I]; vol. II: New York: Ktav, 1984.

——: "The Doxology in Synagogue and Church." *Contributions to the Scientific Study of Jewish Liturgy*, ed. Jakob J. Petuchowski. New York: Ktav, 1970, 318–70.

Wesley, John: *The Journal*, ed. Nehemiah Curnock; Standard Edition. London: Kelly, n.d., vol. IV.

——: *The Works*, 11th edn. London: Mason, 1856, vol. XIII.

——: *The Works*, ed. Albert C. Outler. Nashville: Abingdon, 1984ff., vol. I: Sermons 1–33; vol. XIX: Journals and Diaries II.

West, David R.: *Some Cults of Greek Goddesses and Female Daemons of Oriental Origin*. Neukirchen-Vluyn: Neukirchener Verlag, 1995.

Westermann, Claus: *Theologie des Alten Testaments in Grundzügen*. Göttingen: Vandenhoeck & Ruprecht, 1978.
——: *Blessing in the Bible and the Life of the Church*. Trans. K. Crim. Philadelphia: Fortress, 1978a.
——: *Praise and Lament in the Psalms*. Trans. Keith R. Crim *et al*. Edinburgh: Clark, 1981.
——: *Die Geschichtsbücher des Alten Testaments*. Gütersloh: Kaiser, 1994.
Wetter, Gillis P.: *Altchristliche Liturgien II: Das christliche Opfer*. Göttingen: Vandenhoeck & Ruprecht, 1922.
Wheatley, Richard: *The Life and Letters of Mrs. Phoebe Palmer*. New York: Palmer, 1881.
White, Ellen G.: *Early Writings*. Washington, DC: Review and Herald, 1920.
——: *Testimonies for the Church*. Mountain View, CA: Pacific Press, 1948, 2 vols.
White, James F.: *Documents of Christian Worship*. Louisville: Westminster John Knox Press, 1992.
——: *Roman Catholic Worship: Trent to Today*. New York: Paulist Press, 1995.
Wigglesworth, Michael: *The Diary*, ed. Edmund S. Morgan. Gloucester: Smith, 1970.
Wilken, Robert L.: "Collegia, Philosophical Schools, and Theology." *The Catacombs and the Colloseum: The Roman Empire as the Setting of Primitive Christianity*, ed. Stephen Benko *et al*. Valley Forge, PA: Judson Press, 1971, 268–92.
Wilkinson, John: *Egeria's Travels to the Holy Land*, 2nd edn. Warminster: Aris & Phillips, 1981.
William of Ockham: *Quodlibetal Questions*. Trans. Alfred J. Feddoso *et al*. New Haven and London: Yale University Press, 1991, vol. I.
Williams, Peter: *The King of Instruments: How Churches Came to Have Organs*. London: SPCK, 1993.
Wilms, Hieronymus: *Das Beten der Mystikerinnen*, 2nd edn. Freiburg: Herder, 1923.
Wilson, Bryan R.: *Sects and Society*. London: Heinemann, 1961.
——: *Magic and the Millennium*. New York: Harper & Row, 1973.
Winter, Paul: "Magnificat and Benedictus—Maccabean Psalms?" *Bulletin of the John Rylands Library* 37 (1954), 328–47.
Wire, Antoinette C.: *The Corinthian Women Prophets*. Minneapolis: Fortress, 1990.
Witherington, Ben: *Women and the Genesis of Christianity*. Cambridge: Cambridge University Press, 1990.
——: *Conflict and Community in Corinth*. Grand Rapids: Eerdmans, 1995.
Wood-Leigh, K.L.: *Perpetual Chantries in Britain*. Cambridge: Cambridge University Press, 1965.
Yardeni, Ada: "Remarks on the Priestly Blessing on Two Ancient Amulets from Jerusalem." *Vetus Testamentum* 41 (1991), 176–85.
Yocum, Bruce: *Prophecy: Exercising the Prophetic Gifts of the Spirit in the Church Today*. Ann Arbor: Servant Books, 1976; 2nd edn. 1993.
Yungblut, John R.: *Rediscovering Prayer*. Rockport: Element, 1991.
Zahavy, Tzvee: *Studies in Jewish Prayer*. Lanham: University Press of America, 1990.
Zahn-Harnack, Agnes von: *Adolf von Harnack*, 2nd edn. Berlin: de Gruyter, 1951.
Zahrnt, Heinz: *The Question of God: Protestant Theology in the Twentieth Century*. Trans. R.A. Wilson. New York: Harcourt, Brace & World, 1969.
Zaret, David: *The Heavenly Contract*. Chicago: University of Chicago Press, 1985.
Zumthor, Paul: *La vie quotidienne en Hollande au temps de Rembrandt*. Paris: Hachette, 1959.

Index